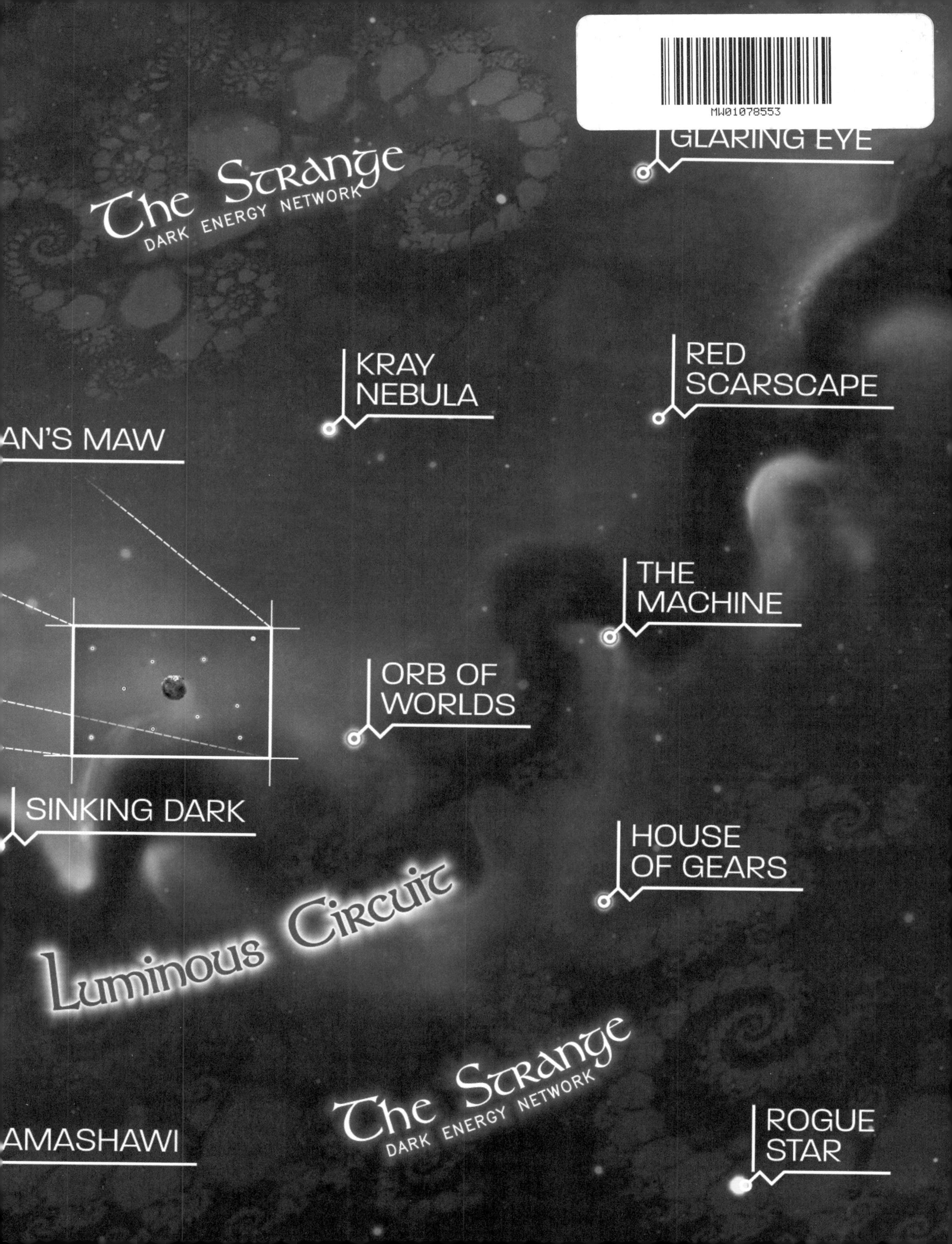

GLARING EYE

The Strange
DARK ENERGY NETWORK

KRAY NEBULA

RED SCARSCAPE

AN'S MAW

THE MACHINE

ORB OF WORLDS

SINKING DARK

HOUSE OF GEARS

Luminous Circuit

The Strange
DARK ENERGY NETWORK

AMASHAWI

ROGUE STAR

THE STRANGE™

CREDITS

Writers/Designers Bruce R. Cordell and Monte Cook
Rules Developer Monte Cook
Creative Director and Lead Editor Shanna Germain
Proofreader Ray Vallese
Editorial Assistance Miranda Horner
Cover Designer and Lead Artist Matt Stawicki
Graphic Designer Sarah Robinson

Artists
Brenoch Adams, Reece Ambrose, Nicholas Cloister, Dreamstime, Brandon Leach, Grzegorz Pedrycz, Mike Perry, Q-Workshop, Joe Slucher, Lee Smith, Matt Stawicki, Cyril Terpent, Tiffany Turrill, Chris Waller, Cathy Wilkins

Cartographer Hugo Solis

Monte Cook Games Editorial Team
Scott C. Bourgeois, David Wilson Brown, Eric Coates, Ryan Klemm, Jeremy Land, Laura Wilkinson, George Ziets

TABLE OF CONTENTS

SOME STRANGE IDEAS

The Strange is the second game from Monte Cook Games, and it's the second game created utilizing the Cypher System. The first was **Numenera™**, a science fantasy game set in the far, far future. **The Strange™** is a different animal altogether.

When creating the Cypher System, I knew that it was open-ended enough to handle a wide variety of settings and genres. I imagined, for example, that we might create a Cypher System game that had a straight-up fantasy setting. What I wasn't prepared for was a setting that would push the entire system to its limits—at least not right away.

But then along came The Strange. Bruce proposed an idea to me involving Earth and Ardeyn and this crazy, alien-crafted side universe (called the Strange network) that connected them. This was an amazing, exciting idea. I realized pretty quickly that we had to make this happen as a game setting. As we talked, the idea of more worlds—recursions—lying out in the Strange network, like islands of sanity in a sea of chaos, came to us. I proposed that there be not one but two main recursions and began formulating ideas for Ruk. By that point, the ideas were flying fast and furious. In other words, it was a great time.

I think it's always pretty much a sure-fire indicator that you're onto something good when the cool ideas flow like that. When everyone who's exposed to the concepts gets really excited by them, that's a great sign. And that's what happened at MCG. We all got really excited by the game, and it all fell into place quite quickly.

But like I said, the game really pushes the system to the limits. In one manual, we needed to provide all these concepts plus the rules for magic, modern technology, wildly advanced technology, psychic powers, and, well, pretty much anything and everything—because The Strange knows few limits. It was a challenge, but a good one. We wanted to arm game masters with the ability to create their own recursions, or adapt their favorite fictional settings and characters. This big book you hold in your hands is merely the beginning. With The Strange, characters can go anywhere and explore anything. This is a setting that doesn't just allow you to take your adventures into your favorite story; it begs for it.

Take this book and make characters from Earth. Have them translate to Ardeyn or Ruk for an interesting scenario or two. But while they're doing that, make preparations for the next step that only you can create—a recursion based on your favorite movie, novel, or game. Like Numenera before it, The Strange exists to inspire you and ignite the fires of your own creativity.

ACKNOWLEDGMENTS

During the making of this book, we received invaluable assistance—directly or indirectly—from the following people, places, and things:

Phil Athans
Batgirl (Torah Cottrill)
Stan! Brown
Sir Arthur C. Clarke
Coffitivity
Erin Evans
Google Hangouts
Gravity soundtrack
Kickstarter
Kivu Coffee
MCG Kansas Bunker
Moto X
Peppermint Mochas
Susan Morris
Brandon Ording
Pandora
Planetary Radio
Roll20.net
Charles and Tammie Ryan
Carl Sagan
Salted licorice
Lex Starwalker
Jeff, Stacey, Edward, and Adam Tidball
Tilly and Gozer
Tron: Legacy soundtrack
The Walking Dead
Waywords at the Wayward
David Wilson Brown

And a special thank you to all of our Kickstarter backers (see Appendix B, page 403, for the complete list)

SOMETHING WONDERFUL

Did you ever see the movie *2010*? It's the sequel to Stanley Kubrick's 1968 film *2001: A Space Odyssey*, based on Arthur C. Clarke's novel *2010: Odyssey Two*. The movie *2010* came out in 1984, but I think it still holds up well to this day. If you're a science fiction fan and haven't seen it, I recommend you do; you'll thank me later.

During the movie, on three separate occasions the "evolved" avatar of Dave Bowman tells the other characters that "something wonderful" is coming. (Dave tells the news to his wife, to Heywood Floyd, and to the rebooted and reformed HAL 9000.) The "something wonderful" Dave refers to is the arrival of a brand new world, to be born on Jupiter's moon Europa. This whole new world with implied intelligent life meant that we on Earth would no longer be alone. The movie also introduced an elder alien species who could blithely ignite new suns and fashion new worlds. All these concepts were superlative—not to mention strange.

2010 opened twenty years ago, but it sticks with me. In the time between then and now, I've had the great good fortune to become a creator of stories myself. Thanks to TSR and Wizards of the Coast, I had the opportunity to write alongside and learn from talented, creative, and innovative game designers, novel authors, and probably more important, editors. Every project and novel was a chance for me to learn something new and hone my skills. I was given the opportunity to indulge myself by telling stories, and I gained the ability to share those stories with the world.

Some of those stories were literally just that: novels. I wrote nine of them, and in so doing learned a love for that craft equal to what I have for game design. I owe a huge debt of gratitude to all the folks in the novel publishing department of that time for helping me along. I owe the same to the Writing Circle critique group we developed then, as well as a huge thank you to thousands of people who bought and read what I wrote.

My desire to write more novels was a factor that helped me decide to step away from full-time work at Wizards. I wanted the freedom to pursue writing a kind of novel that isn't in vogue at a company that focuses on fantasy properties: I wanted to write a science fiction novel.

So I left and began working on my sci-fi masterpiece. I just wasn't sure exactly what it was going to be. Torah Cottrill set a challenge before me: "Create a science fiction character who's as interesting and complex as any of your fantasy novel characters." When explained so simply, I couldn't disagree, and I started on an outline. It wasn't long before I developed the concept for both a character and a plot that excited me. In my novel, I was not only going to tell a great story with memorable characters, but I was also going to provide a unique answer to Fermi's famous question that asks why human beings seem all alone in the universe. My answer wouldn't be runaway self-replicating robots, scarcity of life, self-limiting civilizations, or some other obvious zeroing factor. No. My answer was to point at the increasing velocity of universal inflation itself, and call it evidence. Dark energy and the accelerating expansion of the universe isn't a fluke, I posited in my sci-fi novel outline. Rather, it's a massive artifact, an alien data web designed for something far different than what it has become today.

The Fermi Paradox is the juxtaposition of high estimates for the existence of extraterrestrial civilization with the lack of any evidence for such civilizations anywhere in the universe.

Fermi Paradox and the Dark Energy Network, page 220

And so my concept for the Strange was born. I began writing the novel from the point of view of Carter Morrison (later called Carter Strange, the Maker). In the back of my head, I toyed with the idea of maybe even crowdfunding the thing, after the first draft was written.

Around this time, I told my friend Monte about my idea. He liked it. He liked it so much that he suggested that maybe there was a game property somewhere in my sci-fi imaginings. I agreed instantly. Of course there was! And once I finished the novel...

"How about," Monte said, "you and I write that game now?" His offer sounded like a fabulous idea to me. Nor could I think of a better person than my lifelong friend (and by all accounts, a talented game designer in his own right) to co-write The Strange RPG. Indeed, along with Shanna Germain and the rest of the team at Monte Cook Games, we could assemble a product with story content and production values far beyond what I could imagine or achieve on my own.

And that's exactly what we proceeded to do. You hold the result in your hands.

For an overview of what we've done, check out Chapter 1: Welcome to the Strange, which introduces you to the setting in a very story-based way.

After that, read Chapter 2: How to Play the Strange, and you'll come away with what you should know and what you can teach others about the essentials of the game. The rest—character creation, the full rules, the setting, the creatures, and so on—are added details, although we hope they're fun and interesting ones. Use Part 3: Playing the Game as your reference tool when you have questions.

If you're going to be a game master, read Part 6: Running the Game carefully after reading the rules. We've done our best to convey what the game's all about, and Monte provides some of his secrets to running a great game.

Welcome to the Strange, page 8

How to Play the Strange, page 10

Playing the Game, page 95

Running the Game, page 309

Please enjoy what you find in the following pages, which we've done our best to fill with amazing art and fantastic ideas you can use to inspire your own stories—stories and games we fully expect to be "something wonderful."

Part 1: Getting Started

WELCOME TO THE STRANGE

FROM THE DESK OF LEAD OPERATIVE KATHERINE MANNERS

Welcome. You're here because you've sworn to defend the Earth from all threats of the Strange. For that, you have the organization's heartfelt gratitude. Now it's time to get down to business.

As an operative of our organization, you're expected to commit certain critical and confidential pieces of information to memory. That information includes what you'll find in this briefing dossier. Please read the entire document, then read it again. You know what to do with it after that.

Thank you for your prompt attention,

Katherine J. Manners

STRANGE PRIMER

The Strange is a network created by ████ aliens several billion years ago. Estate researchers believe the Strange was built to allow intergalactic travel. It's unknown at this time what went wrong, but the builders lost control of their creation. In the course of passing aeons, the Strange became something wild, chaotic, and without rules or laws (which is why we also call it the Chaosphere).

NATURE OF THE STRANGE

Think of the Strange as its own boundless realm—as a separate universe underlying our own. The Chaosphere has no direct relationship to matter and space as we understand it: There is no up or down, there is no ground beneath a visitor's feet in most places, and merely gazing into its lawless void damages the human brain ("alienation" is the preferred term for the pain and derangement most operatives experience upon visiting the Strange).

PLANETOVORES

Creatures live in the Chaosphere. The worst of these are called planetovores. They thrive on the fact that no rules bind them within the Strange. We call these creatures planetovores because a) the Estate has good evidence that one tried to consume our planet when Earth first discovered the Chaosphere; and b) because they ████████████████ ████████.

Planetovores can't normally reach areas where natural laws restrict the environment, such as on Earth. But bridges up to Earth can be made, either accidentally or purposefully. Finding or constructing such a bridge seems to be the main goal of all planetovores and their intermediaries. Preventing that from happening, by whatever means necessary, is the Estate's primary mission.

RECURSIONS IN THE STRANGE

Stable regions called recursions exist within the Strange. Recursions are like tiny, self-contained universes. Each one operates under a particular set of rules, which means that planetovores have almost as difficult a time entering a recursion as they do entering Earth. In fact, a recursion can act as a barrier for preventing a planetovore from getting to Earth, thanks to the presence of the recursion's rules.

Earth and the visible universe operate under a familiar set of rules, called Standard Physics. But different recursions often operate under alternate sets of rules. The Estate has classified the following additional laws under which recursions operate: Magic, Mad Science, Psionics, Substandard Physics, and ████.

ARDEYN

Ardeyn is a recursion where magic works, dragons live, and creatures that might as well be demigods exist. Ardeyn's creation was the unanticipated side effect of computer researcher Carter Morrison's discovery of the Strange, and the Estate was founded in his memory. Carter Morrison's whereabouts are unknown at this time.

Ardeyn is populated by humans and a race of people called qephilim—please ask your lead for a qephilim visual reference at this time. The Estate has several agents embedded in Ardeyn, and its largest field office covertly operates in the city of Hazurrium. One of our main activities is keeping tabs on the Betrayer. Though the Betrayer is not a planetovore, we suspect he aspires to become one.

RUK

Ruk operates under the law of Mad Science, and it appears to be populated with Earthlings. Don't be fooled. Ruk comes from someplace else in the universe and has been hiding in the Shoals of Earth for thousands of years, possibly much longer. Ruk contains more factions than the Estate can track. We believe the most dangerous to be a faction named the Karum, who believe that if Earth were destroyed, Ruk would be free. Obviously, we—you—cannot let that happen.

OTHER RECURSIONS

Most recursions are created through what we've come to understand as "fictional leakage." The upshot of this is that you can probably find aspects of your favorite fictional universe rendered as a recursion. Yes, that means that somewhere around Earth is a recursion featuring Star ████. Note: That is no excuse to ██

BADGES

As an operative, you are required to carry your Estate badge while on campus and off, unless you are working undercover. Your badge allows you to gain entry to Estate buildings and into areas of those buildings for which you are cleared. **Badges are to be displayed above the waist at all times while on campus.**

TRANSLATION AND YOU

During your time with the Estate, you'll translate between recursions. Sometimes new operatives find the process of transforming into someone with different abilities and maybe a different shape to be disconcerting. If you become distressed or confused after translating, tell another operative immediately. Enemies of the Estate often target addled operatives first.

CYPHERS

As a beginning operative, you've been issued one or more cyphers. A cypher is a small device that can create a single, often spectacular effect. A cypher may look ordinary, but each one is something special—a manifestation of the Strange that we don't fully understand. We expect you to use your cyphers to accomplish your missions. Hoarding cyphers is imprudent and a waste of needed resources; replacement cyphers are always around the next corner for someone with your abilities.

OTHER QUESTIONS

Please bring urgent questions, concerns, requisitions for equipment, or vacation requests to one of the Estate leads or chiefs. For everything else, please rely on your own discretion. That discretion is why we invited you to become an operative of the Estate.

CHAPTER 2

HOW TO PLAY THE STRANGE

Skills, page 99

Trained, page 99

Decreasing the difficulty, page 98

Specialized, page 99

The rules of The Strange are quite straightforward at their heart, since all gameplay is based around a few core concepts.

This chapter provides a summary of how to play The Strange. It's a great place to gain a sense of how the game works. After you understand the basic concepts, you'll probably want to reference Chapter 8: Rules of the Game, page 96, for the complete rules for play.

The Strange uses a twenty-sided die (d20) to determine the results of most actions. Whenever a roll of any kind is called for and no die is specified, roll a d20.

The game master (GM) sets a difficulty for any given task. There are 10 degrees of difficulty. Thus, the difficulty of a task can be rated on a scale of 1 to 10.

Each difficulty has a target number associated with it. The target number is always three times the task's difficulty, so a difficulty 3 task has a target number of 9. To succeed at the task, you must roll the target number or higher.

Character skills, favorable circumstances, or excellent equipment can decrease the difficulty of a task. For example, if a character is trained in climbing, she turns a difficulty 6 climb into a difficulty 5 climb. This is called decreasing the difficulty by one step. If she is specialized in climbing, she turns a difficulty 6 climb into a difficulty 4 climb. This is called decreasing the difficulty by two steps.

You don't earn XP for killing foes or overcoming regular challenges during play. You earn XP in The Strange by exploring, discovering, and creating.

A skill is a category of knowledge, ability, or activity relating to a task, such as climbing, forensic science, or persuasiveness. A character who has a skill is better at completing related tasks than a character who lacks the skill. A character's level of skill is either trained (reasonably skilled) or specialized (very skilled).

If you are trained in a skill relating to a task, you decrease the difficulty of that task by

TASK DIFFICULTY

TASK DIFFICULTY	DESCRIPTION	TARGET NO.	GUIDANCE
0	Routine	0	Anyone can do this basically every time.
1	Simple	3	Most people can do this most of the time.
2	Standard	6	Typical task requiring focus, but most people can usually do this.
3	Demanding	9	Requires full attention; most people have a 50/50 chance to succeed.
4	Difficult	12	Trained people have a 50/50 chance to succeed.
5	Challenging	15	Even trained people often fail.
6	Intimidating	18	Normal people almost never succeed.
7	Formidable	21	Impossible without skills or great effort.
8	Heroic	24	A task worthy of tales told for years afterward.
9	Immortal	27	A task worthy of legends that last lifetimes.
10	Impossible	30	A task that normal humans couldn't consider (but one that doesn't break the laws of physics).

one step. If you are specialized, you decrease the difficulty by two steps. A skill can never decrease a task's difficulty by more than two steps.

Anything else that reduces difficulty (help from an ally, a particular piece of equipment, or some other advantage) is referred to as an asset. Assets can never decrease a task's difficulty by more than two steps.

You can also decrease the difficulty of a given task by applying Effort.

To sum up, three things can decrease a task's difficulty: skills, assets, and Effort.

If you can decrease a task's difficulty to 0, you automatically succeed and don't need to make a roll.

WHEN DO YOU ROLL?

Any time your character attempts a task, the game master (GM) assigns a difficulty to that task, and you roll a d20 against the associated target number.

When you attempt to hack a computer, fire a pistol at a vampire, jump from a burning vehicle, analyze a genetic sample, persuade the guard to let you go in exchange for a bribe, craft an object, use a psychic talent to control a foe's mind, or translate into another recursion, you make a d20 roll.

If you attempt something that has a difficulty of 0, no roll is needed—you automatically succeed. Many actions have a difficulty of 0. Examples include walking across the room and opening a door, using a special ability to negate gravity so you can fly, using an ability to heal your friend, or activating a device (that you already understand) to erect a force field. These are all routine actions and don't require rolls.

Using skill, assets, and Effort, you can decrease the difficulty of potentially any task to 0 and thus negate the need for a roll. Walking across a narrow wooden beam is tricky for most people, but for an experienced gymnast, it's routine. You can even decrease the difficulty of an attack on a foe to 0 and succeed without rolling.

If there's no roll, there's no chance for failure. There's also no chance for remarkable success (in The Strange, this usually means rolling a 19 or 20 and is called a special roll). Thus, while you are not required to roll if you decrease the difficulty of a task to 0, you always have the option to do so.

Effort is described in more detail in Chapter 8: Rules of the Game, page 96.

Special roll, page 13

For more information on special rolls and how they affect combat and other interactions, see page 101.

COMBAT

Making an attack in combat works the same way as any other roll: the GM assigns a difficulty to the task, and you roll a d20 against the associated target number.

The difficulty of your attack roll depends on how powerful your opponent is. Just as tasks have a difficulty from 1 to 10, creatures have a level from 1 to 10. Most of the time, the difficulty of your attack roll is the same as the creature's level. For example, if you attack a level 3 technician, it's a level 3 task, so your target number is 9.

Players make all the die rolls when playing The Strange. If a character attacks a creature, the player makes an attack roll; if a creature attacks a character, the player makes a defense roll.

The damage dealt by an attack is not determined by a roll—it's a flat number based on the weapon or attack used. For example, a spear always does 4 points of damage.

GLOSSARY

Game Master (GM): The player who doesn't run a character, but instead guides the flow of the story (and runs all the NPCs).

Nonplayer Character (NPC): Characters run by the GM. Think of them as the minor characters in the story, or the villains or opponents. This includes any kind of creature as well as people.

Party: A group of player characters (and perhaps some NPC allies).

Player Character (PC): A character run by a player rather than the GM. Think of them as the main characters in the story.

Player: The players who run characters in the game (maybe you, unless you're the GM).

Session: A single play experience. A session usually lasts a few hours. Sometimes one adventure can be accomplished in a session. More often, one adventure is multiple sessions.

Adventure: A single portion of the campaign with a beginning and an end. Usually defined at the beginning by a goal put forth by the PCs and at the end by whether or not they achieve that goal.

Campaign: A series of sessions strung together with an overarching story (or linked stories) with the same characters. Often, but not always, a campaign involves a number of adventures.

Character: Anything that can act in the game. While this includes PCs and human NPCs, it also technically includes creatures, aliens, mutants, automatons, animate plants, and so on.

ARMOR

Your Armor characteristic reduces the damage you take from attacks directed at you. You get Armor from wearing physical armor (such as a thick leather jacket or chainmail) or from special abilities. Like weapon damage, Armor is a flat number, not a roll. If you're attacked, subtract your Armor from the damage you take. For example, a leather jacket gives you 1 point of Armor, meaning that you take 1 less point of damage from attacks. If a street thug hits you with a knife for 2 points of damage while you're wearing a leather jacket, you take only 1 point of damage. If your Armor reduces the damage from an attack to 0, you take no damage from that attack.

When you see the word "Armor" capitalized in the game rules (other than as the name of a special ability), it refers to your Armor characteristic—the number you subtract from incoming damage. When you see the word "armor" with a lowercase "a," it refers to any physical armor you might wear.

WEAPONS

Typical physical weapons come in three categories: light, medium, and heavy.

LIGHT WEAPONS inflict only 2 points of damage, but they reduce the difficulty of the attack roll by one step because they are fast and easy to use. Light weapons are punches, kicks, clubs, knives, handaxes, rapiers, and so on. Weapons that are particularly small are light weapons.

MEDIUM WEAPONS inflict 4 points of damage. Medium weapons include swords, shamshirs, maces, crossbows, small-caliber firearms, and so on. Most weapons are medium. Melee weapons that could be used in one hand (even if they're often used in two hands, such as a quarterstaff or spear) are usually medium weapons.

> *In The Strange, players make all the die rolls. If a character attacks a creature, the player makes an attack roll. If a creature attacks a character, the player makes a defense roll.*

HEAVY WEAPONS inflict 6 points of damage, and you must use two hands to attack with them. Heavy weapons are huge swords, big guns, massive axes, talwars, slaughter accelerators, and so on. Anything that must be used in two hands is probably a heavy weapon.

BONUSES

Rarely, an ability or piece of equipment does not decrease a task's difficulty but instead adds a bonus to the die roll. Bonuses always add together, so if you get a +1 bonus from two different sources, you have a +2 bonus. If you get enough bonuses to add up to a +3 bonus for a task, treat it as an asset: instead of adding the bonus to your roll, decrease the difficulty by one step. Therefore, you never add more than +1 or +2 to a die roll.

SPECIAL ROLLS

When you roll a natural 19 (the d20 shows "19") and the roll is a success, you also have a *minor effect*. In combat, a minor effect inflicts 3 additional points of damage with your attack, or, if you'd prefer a special result, you could decide instead that you knock the foe back, distract him, or something similar. When not in combat, a minor effect could mean that you perform the action with particular grace. For example, when jumping down from a ledge, you land smoothly on your feet, or when trying to persuade someone, you convince her that you're smarter than you really are. In other words, you not only succeed but also go a bit further.

When you roll a natural 20 (the d20 shows "20") and the roll is a success, you also have a *major effect*. This is similar to a minor effect, but the results are more remarkable. In combat, a major effect inflicts 4 additional points of damage with your attack, but again, you can choose instead to introduce a dramatic event such as knocking down your foe, stunning him, or taking an extra action. Outside of combat, a major effect means that something beneficial happens based on the circumstance. For example, when climbing up a cliff wall, you make the ascent twice as fast. When a roll grants you a major effect, you can choose to use a minor effect instead if you prefer.

In combat (and only in combat), if you roll a natural 17 or 18 on your attack roll, you add 1 or 2 additional points of damage, respectively. Neither roll has any special effect options—just the extra damage.

Rolling a natural 1 is always bad. It means that the GM introduces a new complication into the encounter.

RANGE AND SPEED

Distance is simplified into three categories: immediate, short, and long.

IMMEDIATE DISTANCE from a character is within reach or within a few steps. If a character stands in a small room, everything in the room is within immediate distance. At most, immediate distance is 10 feet (3 m). This can also be called "close range."

SHORT DISTANCE is anything greater than immediate distance but less than 50 feet (15 m) or so.

LONG DISTANCE is anything greater than short distance but less than 100 feet (30 m) or so. Beyond that range, distances are always specified—500 feet (152 m), a mile (2 km), and so on.

Basically, it's not necessary to measure precise distances. Immediate distance is right there,

The inhabitants of Ruk and many other recursions have units of measurement different from those of Earth, but for ease of use, all distances have been converted to approximate U.S. standard and metric units.

practically next to the character. Short distance is nearby. Long distance is farther off.

All weapons and special abilities use these terms for ranges. For example, all melee weapons have immediate range—they are close-combat weapons, and you can use them to attack anyone within immediate distance of you. A thrown knife (and most other thrown weapons) has short range. Many guns have long range (though some have longer range, when specified). A paradox's Exception ability also has long range.

Paradox, page 30
Exception, page 32

A character can move an immediate distance as part of another action. In other words, he can take a few steps over to the control panel and activate a switch. He can lunge across a small room to attack a foe. He can open a door and step through.

Cypher, page 310

A character can move a short distance as his entire action for a turn. He can also try to move a long distance as his entire action, but the player might have to roll to see if the character slips, trips, or stumbles as the result of moving so far so quickly.

Sark, page 288

For example, if the player characters (PCs) are fighting a group of sark, any character can likely attack any sark in the general melee—they're all within immediate range. Exact positions aren't important. Creatures in a fight are always moving, shifting, and jostling, anyway. If one sark stayed back to use his crossbow, a character might have to use her entire action to move the short distance required to attack that foe. It doesn't matter if the sark is 20 feet (6 m) or 40 feet (12 m) away—it's simply considered short distance. It does matter if the sark is more than 50 feet (15 m) away because that distance would require a long move.

EXPERIENCE POINTS

Experience points (XP) are rewards given to players when the GM intrudes on the story (this is called GM intrusion) with a new and unexpected challenge. For example, in the middle of combat, the GM might inform the player that he drops his weapon. To intrude in this manner, the GM must award the player 2 XP. The rewarded player, in turn, must immediately give one of those XP to another player and justify the gift (perhaps the other player had a good idea, told a funny joke, performed an action that saved a life, and so on).

GM intrusion, page 121

Alternatively, the player can refuse the GM intrusion. If he does so, he doesn't get the 2 XP from the GM, and he must also spend 1 XP that he already has. If the player has no XP to spend, he can't refuse the intrusion.

The GM can also give players XP between sessions as a reward for recovering interesting artifacts or making discoveries during an adventure. You don't earn XP for killing foes or overcoming standard challenges in the course of play. The Strange is all about exploration, discovery, and creation.

Experience points are used primarily for character advancement (for details, see Chapter 3: Creating Your Character, page 16), but a player can also spend 1 XP to reroll any die roll and take the better of the two rolls.

CYPHERS

Cyphers are manifestations of the Strange that have a single use. A character can carry cyphers and use them during the game. You can't bear many cyphers at a time because they cancel each other out if in too close a proximity. Gathering too many cyphers together in one place (such as your purse or daypack) is impossible.

Characters will find new cyphers frequently in the course of play, so players shouldn't hesitate to use their cypher abilities. Because cyphers are always different, the characters will always have new special powers to try. There are two kinds of cyphers: anoetic and occultic.

ANOETIC CYPHERS are simple to use: a pill to swallow, a small handheld device with a switch to flip, or a bomb to throw.

OCCULTIC CYPHERS are more complex and more dangerous, but they often have better and more interesting effects. An occultic cypher counts as two cyphers for the purpose of determining how many you can bear at the same time.

OTHER DICE

In addition to a d20, you'll need a d6 (a six-sided die). Rarely, you'll need to roll a number between 1 and 100 (often called a d100 or d% roll), which you can do by rolling a d20 twice, using the last digit of the first roll as the "tens" place and the last digit of the second roll as the "ones" place. For example, rolling a 17 and a 9 gives you 79, rolling a 3 and an 18 gives you 38, and rolling a 20 and a 10 gives you 00 (also known as 100). If you have a d10 (a ten-sided die), you can use it instead of the d20 to roll numbers between 1 and 100.

Part 2:
Character Creation

CHAPTER 3

CREATING YOUR CHARACTER

This section explains how to create characters to play in a game of The Strange. To do so, you'll make several decisions that will shape your character, so the more you understand what kind of character you want to play, the easier character creation will be. The process involves understanding the values of three game statistics (Might, Speed, and Intellect) and choosing three aspects that determine your character's capabilities (descriptor, type, and focus).

Every character starts the game at the first tier. Tier is a measurement of power, toughness, and ability. Characters can advance up to the sixth tier.

CHARACTER STATS

Every player character has three defining characteristics, which are typically called "statistics" or "stats." These stats are Might, Speed, and Intellect. They are broad categories that cover many different but related aspects of a character.

MIGHT: Might defines how strong and durable your character is. The concepts of strength, endurance, constitution, hardiness, and physical prowess are all folded into this stat. Might isn't relative to size; instead, it's an absolute measurement. An elephant has more Might than the mightiest tiger, which has more Might than the mightiest rat, which has more Might than the mightiest spider.

Might governs actions from forcing doors open to walking for days without food to resisting disease. It's also the primary means of determining how much damage your character can sustain in a dangerous situation. Physical characters, tough characters, and characters interested in fighting should focus on Might.

Might could be thought of as Might/Health because it governs how strong you are and how much physical punishment you can take.

Speed could be thought of as Speed/Agility because it governs your overall swiftness and reflexes.

Intellect could be thought of as Intellect/Personality because it governs both intelligence and charisma.

For a visual example of these stats and how they work for your character, see The Strange character sheets, page 414.

SPEED: Speed describes how fast and physically coordinated your character is. The stat embodies quickness, movement, dexterity, and reflexes. Speed governs such divergent actions as dodging attacks, sneaking around quietly, and throwing a ball accurately. It helps determine whether you can move farther on your turn. Nimble, fast, or sneaky characters will want good Speed stats, as will those interested in ranged combat.

INTELLECT: This stat determines how smart, knowledgeable, and likable your character is. It includes intelligence, wisdom, charisma, education, reasoning, wit, willpower, and charm. Intellect governs solving puzzles, remembering facts, telling convincing lies, and using mental powers. Characters interested in communicating effectively, being accomplished scientists, and being respected theologians should stress their Intellect stat.

POOL, EDGE, AND EFFORT

Each stat has two components: your Pool and your Edge. You have a Might Pool and Might Edge, a Speed Pool and Speed Edge, and an Intellect Pool and Intellect Edge. Your Pool represents your raw, innate ability, and your Edge represents knowing how to use what you have. A third element ties into this concept: Effort. When your character really needs to accomplish a task, you apply Effort.

POOL

Your Pool is the most basic measurement of a stat. Comparing the Pools of two creatures will give you a general sense of which creature is superior in that stat. For example, a character who has a Might Pool of 16 is stronger (in a basic sense) than a character who has a Might Pool of 12. Most characters start with a Pool of

9 to 12 in most stats—that's the average range.

When your character is injured, sickened, or attacked, you temporarily lose points from one of your stat Pools. The nature of the attack determines which Pool loses points. For example, physical damage from a sword reduces your Might Pool, a poison that makes you clumsy reduces your Speed Pool, and a psychic blast reduces your Intellect Pool. You can rest to regain lost points from a stat Pool (this is called recovering points in a Pool), and certain special abilities or cyphers might allow you to recover lost points quickly.

EDGE

Although your Pool is the basic measurement of a stat, your Edge is also important. When something requires you to spend points from a stat Pool, your Edge for that stat reduces the cost. However, Edge doesn't subtract from any damage you take.

For example, let's say you have a mental blast ability, and activating it costs 1 point from your Intellect Pool. Subtract your Intellect Edge from the activation cost, and the result is how many points you must spend to use the mental blast. If using your Edge reduces the cost to 0, you can use the ability for free.

Your Edge is probably different for each stat. For example, you could have a Might Edge of 1, a Speed Edge of 1, and an Intellect Edge of 0. You'll always have an Edge of at least 1 in one stat. Your Edge for a stat reduces the cost of spending points from that stat Pool, but not from other Pools. Your Might Edge reduces the cost of spending points from your Might Pool, but it doesn't affect your Speed Pool or Intellect Pool.

A character who has a low Might Pool but a high Might Edge has the potential to perform Might actions consistently better than a character who has a Might Edge of 0. The high Edge will let her reduce the cost of spending points from the Pool, which means she'll have more points available to spend on applying Effort.

EFFORT

When your character really needs to accomplish a task, you can apply Effort. For a beginning character, applying Effort requires spending 3 points from the stat Pool appropriate to the action. Thus, if your character tries to dodge an attack (a Speed roll) and wants to increase the chance for success, you can apply Effort by spending 3 points from your Speed Pool. Effort lowers the difficulty of the task by one step. This is called applying one level of Effort. (You can also apply Effort to increase damage, as described in the next section.)

You don't have to apply Effort if you don't want to. If you choose to apply Effort to a task, you must do it before you attempt the roll—you can't roll first and then decide to apply Effort if you rolled poorly.

Applying more Effort can lower a task's difficulty further: each additional level of Effort reduces the difficulty by another step. Applying one level of Effort lowers the difficulty by one step, applying two levels lowers the difficulty by two steps, and so on. However, each level of Effort after the first costs only 2 points from the

Recovering Points in a Pool, page 108

stat Pool instead of 3. So applying two levels of Effort costs 5 points (3 for the first level plus 2 for the second level), applying three levels costs 7 points (3 plus 2 plus 2), and so on.

Every character has an Effort score, which indicates the maximum number of levels of Effort that can be applied to a roll. A beginning (first-tier) character has an Effort of 1, meaning you can apply only one level of Effort to a roll. A more experienced character has a higher Effort score and can apply more levels of Effort to a roll. For example, a character who has an Effort of 3 can apply up to three levels of Effort to reduce a task's difficulty.

Paradox, page 30
Revision, page 30

When you apply Effort, subtract your relevant Edge from the total cost of applying Effort. For example, let's say you need to make a Speed-based roll. To increase your chance for success, you decide to apply one level of Effort, which will reduce the difficulty of the task by one step. Normally, that would cost 3 points from your Speed Pool. However, you have a Speed Edge of 2, so you subtract that from the cost. Thus, applying Effort to the roll costs only 1 point from your Speed Pool.

Prior to making a roll, players should let the GM know whether they're using Effort, how many levels of Effort they want to use, and whether they are using it to decrease the difficulty or to increase the amount of damage they inflict.

What if you applied two levels of Effort to the Speed roll instead of just one? That would reduce the difficulty of the task by two steps. Normally, it would cost 5 points from your Speed Pool, but after subtracting your Speed Edge of 2, it costs only 3 points.

Once a stat's Edge reaches 3, you can apply one level of Effort for free. For example, if you have a Speed Edge of 3 and you apply one level of Effort to a Speed roll, it costs you 0 points from your Speed Pool. (Normally, applying one level of Effort would cost 3 points, but you subtract your Speed Edge from that cost, reducing it to 0.)

Skills and other advantages also decrease a task's difficulty, and you can use them in conjunction with Effort. In addition, your character might have special abilities or equipment that allow you to apply Effort to accomplish a special effect, such as knocking down a foe with an attack or affecting multiple targets with a power that normally affects only one.

EFFORT AND DAMAGE

Instead of applying Effort to reduce the difficulty of your attack, you can apply Effort to increase the amount of damage you inflict with an attack. For each level of Effort you apply in this way, you inflict 3 additional points of damage. This works for any kind of attack that inflicts damage, whether a sword, a crossbow, a mind blast, or something else.

When using Effort to increase the damage of an area attack, such as the explosion created by certain paradox revisions, you inflict 2 additional points of damage instead of 3 points. However, the additional points are dealt to all targets in the area. Further, even if one or more of the targets in the area resist the attack, you still inflict 1 point of damage to them.

When applying Effort to melee attacks, you can choose to spend points from either your Might Pool or your Speed Pool. When making ranged attacks, you may spend points only from your Speed Pool. This reflects that with melee you sometimes use brute force and sometimes use finesse, but with ranged attacks, it's always about careful targeting. When applying Effort to make mental attacks or similar, you spend points from your Intellect Pool.

MULTIPLE USES OF EFFORT AND EDGE

If your Effort is 2 or higher, you can apply Effort to multiple aspects of a single action. For example, if you make an attack, you can apply Effort to your attack roll and apply Effort to increase the damage.

The total amount of Effort you apply can't be higher than your Effort score. For example, if your Effort is 2, you can apply up to two levels of Effort. You could apply one level to an attack roll and one level to its damage, two levels to the attack and no levels to the damage, or no levels to the attack and two levels to the damage.

You can use Edge for a particular stat only once per action. For example, if you apply Effort to a Might attack roll and to your damage, you can use your Might Edge to reduce the cost of one of those uses of Effort, not both. If you spend 1 Intellect point to activate your mind blast and one level of Effort to decrease the difficulty of the attack roll, you can use your Intellect Edge to reduce the cost of one of those things, not both.

STAT EXAMPLES

A beginning character is fighting a security guard in a server farm. She swings a pipe wrench at the guard, which is a level 2 creature and thus has a target number of 6. The character stands atop a desk and strikes downward at the guard, and the GM rules that this helpful tactic is an asset that decreases the difficulty by one step (to difficulty 1). That lowers the target number to 3. Attacking with a pipe wrench is a Might action; the character has a Might Pool of 11 and a Might Edge of 0. Before making the roll, she decides to apply a level of Effort to decrease the difficulty of the attack. That costs 3 points from her Might Pool, reducing the Pool to 8. But they appear to be points well spent. Applying the Effort lowers the difficulty from 1 to 0, so no roll is needed—the attack automatically succeeds.

Another character is attempting to convince a different guard to let him into a private office to speak to the company's chief operating officer. The GM rules that this is an Intellect action. The character is third tier and has an Effort of 3, an Intellect Pool of 13, and an Intellect Edge of 1. Before making the roll, he must decide whether to apply Effort. He can choose to apply one, two, or three levels of Effort, or apply none at all. This action is important to him, so he decides to apply two levels of Effort, decreasing the difficulty by two steps. Thanks to his Intellect Edge, applying the Effort costs only 4 points from his Intellect Pool (3 points for the first level of Effort plus 2 points for the second level minus 1 point for his Edge). Spending those points reduces his Intellect Pool to 9. The GM decides that convincing the guard is a difficulty 3 (demanding) task with a target number of 9; applying two levels of Effort reduces the difficulty to 1 (simple) and the target number to 3. The player rolls a d20 and gets an 8. Because this result is at least equal to the target number of the task, he succeeds. However, if he had not applied some Effort, he would have failed because his roll (8) would have been less than the task's original target number (9).

CHARACTER TIERS AND BENEFITS

Every character starts the game at the first tier. Tier is a measurement of power, toughness, and ability. Characters can advance up to the sixth tier. As your character advances to higher tiers, you gain more abilities, increase your Effort, and can improve a stat's Edge or increase a stat. Generally speaking, even first-tier characters are already quite capable. It's safe to assume that they already have some experience under their belt. This is not a "zero to hero" progression, but rather an instance of competent people refining and honing their capabilities and knowledge. Advancing to higher tiers is not really the "goal" of player characters, but rather a representation of how characters progress in a story.

To progress to the next tier, characters earn experience points (XP) by going on adventures and discovering new things—the Strange is about exploration and discovery of the recursions hidden "beneath" Earth. Experience points have many uses, and one use is to purchase character abilities. After your character purchases four character abilities, he or she goes up to the next tier. Each benefit costs 4 XP, and you can purchase them in any order, but you must purchase one of each kind of benefit (after which you advance to the next tier) before you can purchase the same benefit again. The four character abilities are as follows.

Recursion, page 134

Remember that all NPCs have a level from 1 to 10 that guides everything from their armor to their health. For additional information on interacting with NPCs, see page 110.

INCREASING CAPABILITIES: You gain 4 points to add to your stat Pools. You can allocate the points among the Pools however you wish.

MOVING TOWARD PERFECTION: You add 1 to your Might Edge, your Speed Edge, or your Intellect Edge (your choice).

EXTRA EFFORT: Your Effort score increases by 1.

SKILLS: You become trained in one skill of your choice, other than attacks or defense. As described in Chapter 8: Rules of the Game, a character trained in a skill treats the difficulty of a related task as one step lower than normal. The skill you choose for this benefit can be anything you wish, such as climbing, jumping, persuading, or sneaking. You can also choose to be knowledgeable in a certain area of study, such as history or geology. You can even choose a skill based on your character's special abilities. For example, if your character can make an Intellect roll to blast an enemy with mental force, you can become trained in using that ability, treating its difficulty as one step lower than normal. If you choose a skill that you are already trained in, you become specialized in that skill, reducing the difficulty of related tasks by two steps instead of one.

Chapter 8: Rules of the Game, page 96

Players can also spend 4 XP to purchase other special options in lieu of gaining a new skill. Selecting any of these options counts as the skill benefit necessary to advance to the next tier. The special options are as follows:

- Reduce the cost for wearing armor. This option lowers the Might cost by 1 and lowers the Speed reduction by 1.
- Add 2 to your recovery rolls.
- If you're a vector, select a new move. The move must be from your tier or a lower tier.
- If you're a spinner, select a new twist. The twist must be from your tier or a lower tier.
- If you're a paradox, select a new revision. The revision must be from your tier or a lower tier.

Integrates Weaponry, page 63
Ruk, page 190
Ardeyn, page 160
Practices Soul Sorcery, page 71
Entertains, page 61
Solves Mysteries, page 78
Tough, page 50
Is Licensed to Carry, page 64
Skeptical, page 48
Works the System, page 83

CHARACTER DESCRIPTOR, TYPE, AND FOCUS

To create your character, you build a simple statement that describes him or her. The statement takes this form: "I am a [fill in an adjective here] [fill in a noun here] who [fill in a verb here]."

Thus: "I am an *adjective noun* who *verbs*." For example, you might say, "I am a Tough vector who Is Licensed to Carry" or "I am a Skeptical paradox who Works the System."

In this sentence, the adjective is called your *descriptor*.

The noun is your character *type*.

The verb is called your *focus*.

Even though character type is in the middle of the sentence, that's where we'll start this discussion. (Just as in a sentence, the noun provides the foundation.)

Character type is the core of your character. In some roleplaying games, it might be called your character class. Your type helps determine your character's place in the world and relationship with other people in the setting. It's the noun of the sentence "I am an *adjective noun* who *verbs*."

You can choose from three character types: paradox, spinner, and vector.

Descriptor defines your character—it flavors everything you do. Your descriptor places your character in the situation (the first adventure, which starts the campaign) and helps provide motivation. It's the adjective of the sentence "I am an *adjective noun* who *verbs*."

You can choose from several character descriptors, such as Intelligent, Lucky, and Sharp-Eyed.

Focus is what your character does best within a given recursion. Focus gives your character specificity and provides interesting new abilities that might come in handy. Your focus also helps you understand how you relate with the other player characters in your group, and in the recursion you find yourself in. It's the verb of the sentence "I am an *adjective noun* who *verbs*."

Focus usually changes when your character translates from one recursion to another. Descriptor and type do not change. For example, if you start out as a Tough vector who Is Licensed to Carry on Earth, you might become a Tough vector who Integrates Weaponry in Ruk. This change can reflect a similarity in flavor or a drastic change if you desire it. The above example, using Is Licensed to Carry and Integrates Weaponry, reflects a similarity in flavor (because both foci deal with using weapons). If you then went to Ardeyn and became a Tough vector who Practices Soul Sorcery, however, that would reflect a drastic change. Either way is fine—it's up to you.

There are many character foci to choose from, including Entertains, Solves Mysteries, and Works the System, but you can only select from a subset at any one time based on what recursion you are in. Once you've selected a focus for a particular recursion, it doesn't change. If you later visit a never-before-seen recursion, you may have the option to choose a new focus for it (while losing access to the focus you had in the previous recursion).

SPECIAL ABILITIES

Character types and foci grant PCs special abilities at each new tier. Using these abilities usually costs points from your stat Pools; the cost is listed in parentheses after the ability name. Your Edge in the appropriate stat can reduce the cost of the ability, but remember that you can apply Edge only once per action. For example, let's say a paradox with an Intellect Edge of 2 wants to use his Exception ability to attack a foe, which costs 1 Intellect point. He also wants to increase the damage from the attack by using a level of Effort, which costs 3 Intellect points. The total cost for his action is 2 points from his Intellect Pool (1 point for the attack plus 3 points for using Effort minus 2 points from his Edge).

Sometimes the point cost for an ability has a + sign after the number. For example, the cost might be given as "2+ Intellect points." That means you can spend more points or more levels of Effort to improve the ability further.

Many special abilities grant a character the option to perform an action that she couldn't normally do, such as projecting rays of cold or attacking multiple foes at once. Using one of these abilities is an action unto itself, and the end of the ability's description says "Action" to remind you. It also might provide more information about when or how you perform the action.

Some special abilities allow you to perform a familiar action—one that you can already do—in a different way. For example, an ability might let you wear heavy armor, reduce the difficulty of Speed defense rolls, or add 2 points of fire damage to your weapon damage. These abilities are called *enablers*. Using one of these abilities is not considered an action. Enablers either function constantly (such as being able to wear heavy armor, which isn't an action) or happen as part of another action (such as adding fire damage to your weapon damage, which happens as part of your attack action). If a special ability is an enabler, the end of the ability's description says "Enabler" to remind you.

BACKGROUND

Background is a vital part of your character. It's not just your backstory, but it involves how much you already know about the Strange,

SKILLS

Sometimes your character gains training in a specific skill or task. For example, your focus might mean that you're trained in sneaking, in climbing and jumping, or in social interactions. Other times, your character can choose a skill to become trained in, and you can pick a skill that relates to any task you think you might face.

The game has no definitive list of skills. However, the following list offers ideas:

Astronomy	Forensic science	Mechanical repair
Balancing	Geography	Perception
Biology	Geology	Persuasion
Botany	Healing	Philosophy
Carrying	History	Pickpocketing
Climbing	Identifying	Riding
Computer science	Initiative	Smashing
Crafting	Intimidation	Sneaking
Deceiving	Jumping	Strange lore
Escaping	Lockpicking	Swimming

You could choose a skill that incorporates more than one of these areas (interacting might include deceiving, intimidating, and persuading) or is a more specific version of one (hiding might be sneaking when you're not moving). You could also make up more general, professional skills, such as engineer, architect, or sailor. Other recursions might suggest still more skills. In Ardeyn, for example, magical lore might be a skill. If you want to choose a skill that's not on this list, it's probably best to run it past the GM first, but in general, the most important aspect is to choose skills that are appropriate to your character. You can also choose to learn another language as a skill if it becomes important or useful.

Remember that if you gain a skill that you're already trained in, you become specialized in that skill. Because skill descriptions can be nebulous, determining whether you're trained or specialized might take some thinking. For example, if you're trained in lying and later gain a benefit that grants you skill with all social interactions, you become specialized in lying and trained in all other types of interactions. Being trained three times in a skill is no better than being trained twice (in other words, specialized is as good as it gets).

Only skills gained through character type abilities (such as a vector's moves or a paradox's revisions) or other rare instances allow you to become skilled with attack or defense tasks.

If you gain a special ability through your type, your focus, or some other aspect of your character, you can choose it in place of a skill and become trained or specialized in that ability. For example, let's say you're a paradox and one of your revision abilities is translation (the process that allows you to travel from one recursion to another). When it's time to choose a skill to be trained in, you can select translation as your skill (specifically, translation initiation). Doing so would reduce the difficulty every time you attempt a translation roll. Each ability you have counts as a separate skill for this purpose. You can't select "all revisions" as one skill and become trained or specialized in such a broad category.

recursions, translating, and so on. It's possible to start with a character who knows nothing about the Strange. This is perhaps best for players who have never played the game before. For more experienced players, it's possible to start the game with some or even substantial knowledge of the Strange and all related topics.

Many PCs begin play on Earth with some knowledge of the dark energy network of the Strange, what it means to be quickened, how to translate between recursions, and so on. Such characters are said to be "in the know" versus "naive" PCs who begin with no knowledge of the dark energy network. See the extended section on this topic in Chapter 21: Running a Strange Game, page 376, for more guidance on introducing your players to the game.

RECURSORS AND THE SPARK

Anyone who leaves Earth to explore recursions and the Strange is called a *recursor*.

The *spark* is what recursors call a full awareness of one's self and one's place in the world—both the immediate world and the larger world (the Strange and various recursions). On the prime world of Earth, every intelligent being is self-aware. That's not always true in a recursion. Some inhabitants of a recursion might simply be more like puppets or robots, simply fulfilling a function or playing a role. Such inhabitants who become aware of themselves and exert free will and sentience have "gained the spark."

Having the spark doesn't directly equate to knowledge of the Strange or recursions, but a character who doesn't have the spark can never understand the Strange or recursions. For example, in a recursion that is basically Sherlock Holmes's London, most of the inhabitants just wander the streets carrying out appropriate actions like extras in a movie. If confronted, they truly believe that they are in London, on Earth, in the 19th century. If they have (or gain) the spark, they have a chance of learning and understanding that this isn't actually true.

A prime world is a world in the universe of normal matter.

A connected prime is a prime world that hosts one or more recursions.

Earth is an example of both a prime world and a connected prime.

On Earth, everyone has the spark. In Ardeyn, about 80 percent of the inhabitants have the spark. In Ruk, nearly 100 percent do. On a more typical recursion, that number might be more like 10 percent. Some recursions might not have any inhabitants with the spark.

All PCs, regardless of origin, have the spark.

QUICKENED

Quickened characters are those who have the spark and, in addition, possess a unique connection to the Strange. Quickened characters are very rare, and they may exist only on Earth or in recursions in Earth's "shoals." (These shoals include Ardeyn, Ruk, or other "nearby" recursions.) Beings on other prime worlds and their nearby recursions might not have this quality, ever, which separates Earth from the rest of the universe.

Shoals of Earth, page 214

This, of course, is only theory.

Only quickened characters can translate without the help of a special object (like a gate). A quickened character's connection with the Strange allows her to wield amazing abilities, including a paradox's revisions, a vector's moves, and a spinner's twists.

All player characters, regardless of origin, are quickened.

BACKGROUND OPTIONS

Your type, descriptor, and focus all help provide a few details about your background. However, another component, independent of these but just as important, is the answer to this question: "How did you become aware of the Strange?" There aren't game mechanics associated with this, but it is vital to note, because it will drive the kinds of adventures (and your character's reactions to them) that you have at the beginning of your campaign. If your character has never heard of recursions or the Strange, you'll likely spend the first few adventures discovering these concepts. If your character starts out already an agent of the Estate, you'll jump right to more involved adventures.

Obviously, your background varies greatly depending on where you are from. While the default assumption in the game is that your character comes from Earth, that doesn't have to be the case. You could be a quickened character from Ardeyn, Ruk, or even elsewhere.

The following background options are possible ways your character became aware of the Strange. That awareness led you to the point where the game begins, whether as an operative of a secret organization, a freelance recursor, or in some other situation described by your GM.

IGNORANCE IS BLISS: You have never heard of the Strange. You're a well-trained physical specimen of humankind—tough, fast, and smart—and you have no belief or interest in anything beyond what you can directly experience. If things around you seem to go your way, it's just skill and luck.

Advancement: You practice, and you learn new skills. You eat right, exercise, and train. If the Strange has something to do with your abilities, your understanding of that seems to have no bearing on your improvement, so why bother? You've always advanced and improved on your own terms—why stop now?

STRANGE ENHANCEMENTS: You excelled at all that you set out to do, but everyone has their limits, right? That was when you discovered a line of nutritional supplements that produced some interesting results. They were hard to get, however. You got involved with an organization to get access to the supplements, and you found that they could teach you steps beyond pills and dietary additives that could take you to even greater heights. Some of the processes and treatments were odd, but their results were undeniable, and you found no evidence of them being unsafe.

You eventually learned that they wouldn't work for everyone. In fact, you were one of a very limited group of people who had a connection to something...strange.

Advancement: You need to continue to use the supplements and treatments provided by your rather secretive benefactors. With each new step you take in their program, your abilities increase. But will there be a price to pay later? Can you get these enhancements from another source? Time will tell.

CONFRONTING THE IMPOSSIBLE: There came a point where you found that you could do things that others believed impossible. Being an inquisitive sort, you began looking for an explanation. It took a long time, but you learned that you weren't alone. There were others who had similar abilities and experiences. While some believed it to be mystical, others saw it as science.

Advancement: The more you learn about the Strange and your connection with it, the more things make sense to you. You continue to learn, research, and explore. The answers are out there, and the only way to discover them is firsthand. To keep moving forward, you have to keep moving.

SCIENTIFIC EXPERIMENT: You believe your understanding of the Strange is better than most because you've applied the scientific method. Thanks to many experiments, you developed a verifiable (verifiable to you, at least) theory regarding the true nature of the cosmos. Alas, the more you know, the more you question. The vastness of the dark energy network that underlies the real universe is mind-blowing.

On the other hand, your studies have shown you how to tap into the Strange. You find that you are best able to channel your abilities by using one or more scientific apparatus you built specifically to serve that purpose. Whether your apparatus is bulky or sleek, you can create amazing effects to change the environment around you.

Advancement: You must continue to conduct your experiments. The Strange is cosmic, too much for a mortal mind to even come close to fully comprehending, but that's what draws you onward. When your stats improve or you learn new skills, it's because your latest experiments have confirmed a new theory you've been working on.

You've made many advances, but to make a leap forward, you'll have to gain access to a lab with better equipment or find the time to upgrade and build more of your own.

ESOTERIC ENCOUNTER: Years of study, diligence, and adherence to your religion, esoteric order, or new-age philosophy finally bore incredible dividends. You discovered the Strange as the result of an encounter with a being you don't completely understand, but which you believe to be a representative of your faith. It showed you the kind of power that it could grant you in its name, and you swore to honor whatever favors it required of you. With your oath complete, a brain-searing blaze of understanding quickened you to the Strange. The secrets hidden in dark energy, the nature of cyphers, and the true dangers that swim in the Strange are now known to you.

You also learned how to call upon your abilities—minor miracles of directed thought, meditation, or prayer—that allow you to be a force for change in the world.

If your character begins the game as an operative of the Estate or is otherwise "in the know" about the Strange (as opposed to a "naive" character), choose your focus for Earth, Ardeyn, and Ruk when you first create your character. This pre-selection is one of the reflections of your character's starting knowledge of the setting.

Esoteric Encounter Option: *While working as an undergraduate during a paleoanthropological dig, you discovered an amulet that unlocked your quickened abilities.*

Advancement: You must continue your studies with the religious book, strange library, online conspiracy forum, or other source that led to your first interaction with your benefactor. Although it left you to your own devices, it promised to return soon to exact the favor you owe it. When your stats improve or you learn new skills, it's because you have mapped another teaching or dogma to that which has quickened inside you. When you gain a new ability, it's the result of long hours of study, prayer, or practice with your particular lore.

At some point in your career, if your benefactor hasn't yet returned, you'll need to find it again to advance your studies.

STRANGE ACCIDENT: You haven't always been different; in fact, you were completely normal before the accident. In the accident's aftermath (whether you woke from a coma, were seemingly unaffected by radiation exposure, pulled yourself from a crash with hardly a scratch, or recovered from the bite of a mysterious creature), you discovered a new ability. Namely, the power to change the world around you—in small ways at first, but in larger and larger ways as you explore your strange new gifts.

Advancement: The more you use the powers you already have, the more they quicken additional abilities and skills. Practice makes perfect, and it seems to be the primary way you have of strengthening your gifts. However, you think it's possible that in order to awaken the upper end of your power, you might need to replicate your original accident.

Strange Accident Option: *You participated in a local study to determine the potential benefits of a new drug for treatment of arthritis (or another medical condition). During the trial, strange things began to happen around you and to you. That's when you learned the "arthritis" drug was actually a test substance designed by a secret government agency called OSR.*

OSR, page 157

WINNER: Certain card games, especially the many variations of poker, count on skill and luck, but they rely most of all on a player's ability to interact, read, and persuade fellow players—and you know all about these things. You're a pro at learning an opponent's betting strategies, picking up on tells, and bluffing, which is how you won several major tournaments. During one such hand, you went all-in with a stone-cold bluff, and one of your opponents called you on it. That's when your abilities were awakened. When you revealed your cards, you convinced everyone that you had the winning hand, despite the evidence of their senses.

Advancement: You might have a connection to the Strange, but it comes through your ability to analyze odds, manipulate cards, and keep track of numbers. Therefore, you must continue to practice. When you improve, it's because you have honed your skills or unlocked a new ability through repetition.

COMBAT: You joined the military. Proving yourself a natural leader on and off the field of battle, you gained a command. Those under you respected you, did as you ordered without complaint, and were loyal. None of that mattered when your last skirmish was FUBAR, which is when you learned your people would also die for you. When you woke in a military hospital with severe injuries, you discovered that almost everyone in your command was missing or dead. After you finished treatment, you were out of a job and starting a life with pain that will probably never go away completely. Having nothing left, you turned inward and embraced your ability to make others see things your way. You'd always sensed it lingering at the edges of your consciousness, but you finally spent the time exploring and developing your potential. That's when you quickened to the Strange.

Advancement: Your connection to the Strange is most acute when you're devising strategies, issuing orders, and feeling combat surge around you. That's when your abilities come most easily. When you improve, it's through actual use. You believe that to gain the highest level, you may have to undergo another extreme test in battle, not unlike the original skirmish that changed your life.

GRIFT (ALMOST) GONE WRONG: You learned early that you could mislead other people to your own benefit. Call it social engineering or grifting, the process was the same: Approach a victim with a plan, elicit his interest through enticement using a variety of tricks, and, finally, make off with his goods. It worked beautifully for years, until your confidence game went as wrong as it could possibly go when you tried to grift someone who was quickened. You discovered you were the target of an even more elaborate con. But instead of leaving you bereft, the conner took you in as a sort of apprentice, showing you a whole new level of control.

Advancement: Just as with regular confidence tricks, practice is key to maintaining and improving your abilities. When your capabilities improve, it's because you've continued to hone your cons. The greater your successes, the more you're inspired and able to unlock even more Strange abilities, such that one day you aspire to con reality itself.

CHAPTER 4

CHARACTER TYPE

Character type is the core of your character. Your type helps determine your character's place in the world and relationship with other people in the setting. It's the noun of the sentence "I am an *adjective noun* who *verbs*."

You can choose from three character types: vector, paradox, and spinner.

VECTOR

Vectors are action-oriented people: athletes, soldiers, firefighters, hunters, and explorers. They overcome challenges in a straightforward, physical way. When something needs doing, they do it. They are characterized as much by their motivation as their physical talents.

Vectors have great strength, stamina, and speed. It may seem that this is the sum total of the source of their abilities, but eventually they learn that in some small way, these abilities also originate with a connection to the Strange. These abilities—called *moves*—allow them to perform feats that normal people cannot do.

Most vectors frequently train their bodies hard, and they have a background involving intense physical activity: sports, combat, occupations that involve action and exertion as well as skill. Vectors can be mountain climbers, rescue workers, and anything else of a similar vein.

VECTOR STAT POOLS

Stat	Pool Starting Value
Might	10
Speed	10
Intellect	8

You get 6 additional points to divide among your stat Pools however you wish.

Vectors in Society: Vectors are respected and sometimes even idolized for their abilities and prowess. They are often natural leaders, because vectors are not simple brutes but driven, motivated individuals who figure out what they want and go out and get it.

Vectors in Groups: Vectors take challenges head on, but they also help to defend and protect their friends. They might be the first one up a hill, but they also turn around to help the rest. They are leaders.

Vectors and the Strange: To begin with, a vector might not even know that the Strange—or anything remotely like it—exists. Most vectors are more interested in doing things than wondering about the origins of their abilities.

Vectors learn to look for cyphers and items that help them do what they do best. Items that improve combat and defense, that enhance their physical abilities, or that are outright weapons hold great value.

Advanced Vectors: As vectors gain more experience, their physical talents grow, as expressed by their moves. Their strength, dexterity, and stamina improve. They jump farther and run faster. But eventually they move past such simple things. They learn combat techniques of all kinds and eventually can push the limits of reality with their physical accomplishments.

VECTOR TIERS

FIRST-TIER VECTOR

First-tier vectors have the following abilities:

Effort: Your Effort is 1.

Physical Nature: You have a Might Edge of 1, a Speed Edge of 1, and an Intellect Edge of 0.

Cypher Use: You can bear two cyphers at a time.

"The next thing I knew, I was a knight in shining armor, like out of some fairy tale, with a sword and everything. And it wasn't like I was play-acting, or dressed up for Halloween. I really was this knight, you know? Kind of like in a dream, when you dream you're somebody else, but you're still also you? Just like that." ~First-time recursor Allan Peterson

Speed defense is used for dodging attacks and escaping danger. This is by far the most commonly used type of defense.

Translation, page 125

Easing a translation, page 127

Defensive: You are trained in Speed defense actions when not wearing armor. Enabler.

Practiced With All Weapons: You can use any weapon. Enabler.

Physical Skills: You are trained in your choice of two of the following: balancing, climbing, jumping, running, or swimming. Enabler.

Translation: You can participate in the process of traveling to another recursion. Each time you do, you can choose to initiate, hasten, or ease a translation. If you choose to hasten or ease the process, someone else in the group must initiate the translation.

As a vector, you are most effective at easing a translation. This easing advantage allows group members to acclimate more quickly after the translation is complete.

In order to translate, you must know that the recursion you are translating to exists. The GM will decide if you have enough information to confirm its existence and determine what level of difficulty is needed to reach the destination. Action to initiate.

Moves: You take the straightforward approach and accomplish what you need to do using physical means. You can perform feats of strength and speed that others cannot. You call these *moves*. Some moves are constant, ongoing effects, and others are specific actions that usually cost points from one of your stat Pools.

Choose two of the moves described below. You can't choose the same move more than once unless its description says otherwise.

- **Bash (1 Might point):** This is a pummeling melee attack. Your attack inflicts 1 less point of damage than normal, but dazes your target for one round, during which time the difficulty of all tasks it performs is modified by one step to its detriment. Action.
- **Endurance:** Any duration dealing with physical actions is either doubled or halved, whichever is better for you. For example, if the typical person can hold their breath for thirty seconds, you can hold it for one minute. If the typical person can march for four hours without stopping, you can do so for eight hours. In terms of harmful effects, if a poison paralyzes its victims for one minute, you are paralyzed for thirty seconds. The minimum duration is always one round. Enabler.
- **Fleet of Foot:** If you succeed at a difficulty 2 Speed roll to run, you can move a short distance and take an action in the same round. Enabler.
- **No Need for Weapons:** When you make an unarmed attack (such as a punch or kick),

you can choose whether you make the attack as if using a medium weapon or as if using a light weapon. Enabler.

- **Pierce (1 Speed point):** This is a well-aimed, penetrating ranged attack. You make an attack and inflict 1 additional point of damage. Action.
- **Practiced in Armor:** Vectors can wear armor for long periods of time without tiring and can compensate for slowed reactions from wearing armor. You can wear any kind of armor. You reduce the Might cost per hour for wearing armor and the Speed Pool reduction for wearing armor by 2. Enabler.

SECOND-TIER VECTOR

Second-tier vectors have the following abilities:

Physical Skill: Choose one skill in which you are not already trained: balancing, climbing, jumping, running, or swimming. You are trained in that skill. Enabler.

Skill With Defense: Choose one type of defense task in which you are not already trained: Might, Speed, or Intellect. You are trained in defense tasks of that type. Unlike most moves, you can select this move up to three times. Each time you select it, you must choose a different type of defense task. Enabler.

Reach Beyond (3 Intellect points): When you use Reach Beyond, you can access training in a skill provided by a focus you have in another recursion. You must have used the skill in its proper recursion at least once before. You can use the skill once. To use it again, you must use Reach Beyond again. Enabler.

Moves: Choose one of the following moves (or a move from a lower tier) to add to your repertoire. In addition, you can replace one of your first-tier moves with a different first-tier move.

- **Enable Others:** You can use the helping rules to provide a benefit to another character attempting a physical task. This requires no action on your part. Enabler.
- **Quick Recovery:** Your second recovery roll (usually requiring ten minutes) is only a single action, just like the first roll. Enabler.
- **Range Increase:** Ranges for you increase by one step. Immediate becomes short, short becomes long, long becomes 200 feet (61 m). Enabler.
- **Skill With Attacks:** Choose one type of attack in which you are not already trained: light bashing, light bladed, light ranged, medium bashing, medium bladed, medium ranged, heavy bashing, heavy bladed, or heavy ranged. You are trained in attacks using that type of weapon. Enabler.
- **Spray (2 Speed points):** If a weapon has the ability to fire rapid shots without reloading (usually called a rapid-fire weapon, such as the submachine gun), you can spray multiple shots around your target to increase the chance of hitting. Spray uses 1d6 + 1 rounds of ammo (or all the ammo in the weapon, if it has less than the number rolled). The difficulty of the attack roll is decreased by one step. If the attack is successful, it deals 1 less point of damage than normal. Action.
- **Wreck:** Using two hands, you wield a weapon or a tool with a powerful swing. (If fighting unarmed, this attack is made with both fists or both feet together.) When using this as an attack, you take a –1 penalty to the attack roll, and you inflict 3 additional points of damage. When attempting to damage an object or barrier, you are trained in the task. Action.

THE AESTHETICS OF TYPE ABILITIES

When translating to a new recursion, many things change their appearance: cyphers, equipment, even characters. A PC's type abilities also look different in a new place. Essentially, all type abilities (revisions, twists, and moves) visually and aesthetically conform to the context of their current recursion; an ability gained from a PC's type looks appropriate to the recursion where it's used.

For example, a paradox's Exception revision, which jolts a target with "a confluence of fundamental forces," doesn't have a dramatic visual display on Earth and might appear as ordinary as a falling bookcase or shelf, or be apparent only in its result, such as when a target stumbles and cries out. However, in Ardeyn, Exception might look like a blazing series of sorcerous runes rotating around the target, needling it with bolts of magic. In Ruk, it might look like some sort of static discharge from a nearby surface, a biofeedback command where the target's body turns against itself, or some kind of haze of battle spores sprayed by the paradox at the target. And so on, for any of the various recursions a PC translates into.

Another example: A spinner who is using her Fast Talk twist, which can convince a target to take one reasonable action on the next round, looks just like someone talking normally (if very persuasively) on Earth. In Ardeyn, an observer might note a sorcerous blue flame in the spinner's eyes as the ability is used to temporarily bewitch the target. And in Ruk, an observer might note that the spinner breathes out a haze of delicious pheromones, briefly making the target susceptible to the spinner's suggestions.

An ability's look, sound, and even smell can be chosen by the player, by the GM, or by both parties working together. The GM should decide whether the ability's aesthetics work within the context of the recursion.

THIRD-TIER VECTOR

Third-tier vectors have the following abilities:

Impaired, page 108
Debilitated, page 108

Expert Cypher Use: You can bear three cyphers at a time.

Skill With Attacks: Choose one type of attack in which you are not already trained: light bashing, light bladed, light ranged, medium bashing, medium bladed, medium ranged, heavy bashing, heavy bladed, or heavy ranged. You are trained in attacks using that type of weapon. Enabler.

Moves: Choose one of the following moves (or a move from a lower tier) to add to your repertoire. In addition, you can also replace one of your lower-tier moves with a different move from a tier lower than third.

- **Experienced With Armor:** The cost reduction from your Practiced in Armor ability improves. You now reduce the Might cost per hour and the Speed Pool reduction by 3. Enabler.
- **Ignore the Pain:** You do not feel the detrimental effects of being impaired, and when you are debilitated, you ignore those effects and experience the effects normally associated with being impaired instead. (Dead is still dead.) Enabler.
- **Lunge (2 Might points):** This move requires you to extend yourself for a powerful stab or smash. The awkward lunge increases the difficulty of the attack roll by one step. If your attack is successful, it inflicts 4 additional points of damage. Action.
- **Resilience:** You have 1 point of Armor against any kind of physical damage, even damage that normally ignores Armor. Enabler.
- **Slice (2 Speed points):** This is a quick attack with a bladed or pointed weapon that is hard to defend against. The difficulty of the attack roll is decreased by one step. If the attack is successful, it deals 1 less point of damage than normal. Action.
- **Successive Attack:** If you take down a foe, you can immediately make another attack on that same turn against a new foe within your reach. The second attack is part of the same action. You can use this move with melee attacks and ranged attacks. Enabler.

FOURTH-TIER VECTOR

Fourth-tier vectors have the following abilities:

Physical Skill: Choose one skill in which you are trained but not specialized: balancing, climbing, jumping, running, or swimming. You are specialized in that skill. Enabler.

Moves: Choose one of the following moves (or a move from a lower tier) to add to your repertoire. In addition, you can also replace one of your lower-tier moves with a different move from a tier lower than fourth.

- **Arc Spray (3 Speed points):** If a weapon has the ability to fire rapid shots without reloading (usually called a rapid-fire weapon, such as the automatic pistol), you can fire your weapon at up to three targets (all next to one another) as a single action. Make a separate attack roll against each target. The difficulty of each attack is increased by one step. Action.
- **Capable Warrior:** Your attacks deal 1 additional point of damage. Enabler.
- **Feint (2 Speed points):** If you spend one action creating a misdirection or diversion, in the next round you can take advantage of your opponent's lowered defenses. Make

a melee attack roll against that opponent. The difficulty of the roll is decreased by one step. If your attack is successful, it inflicts 4 additional points of damage. Action.

- **Increased Effects:** You treat rolls of natural 19 as rolls of natural 20 for either Might actions or Speed actions (your choice when you gain this ability). This allows you to gain a major effect on a natural 19 or 20. Enabler.
- **Runner:** Your standard movement distance becomes long. Enabler.
- **Skill With Attacks:** Choose one type of attack in which you are not already trained: light bashing, light bladed, light ranged, medium bashing, medium bladed, medium ranged, heavy bashing, heavy bladed, or heavy ranged. You are trained in attacks using that type of weapon. Enabler.

FIFTH-TIER VECTOR

Fifth-tier vectors have the following abilities:

Adept Cypher Use: You can bear four cyphers at a time.

Physical Skill: Choose one skill in which you are trained but not specialized: balancing, climbing, jumping, running, or swimming. You are specialized in that skill. Enabler.

Moves: Choose one of the following moves (or a move from a lower tier) to add to your repertoire. In addition, you can also replace one of your lower-tier moves with a different move from a tier lower than fifth.

- **Jump Attack (5 Might points):** You attempt a difficulty 4 Might action to jump high into the air as part of your melee attack. If you succeed, your attack inflicts 3 additional points of damage and knocks the foe down. If you fail, you still make your normal attack roll, but you don't inflict the extra damage or knock down the opponent. Action.
- **Mastery With Defense:** Choose one type of defense task in which you are trained: Might, Speed, or Intellect. You are specialized in defense tasks of that type. Unlike most moves, you can select this move up to three times. Each time you select it, you must choose a different type of defense task. Enabler.
- **Parry (5 Speed points):** You can deflect incoming attacks quickly. When you activate this move, for the next ten rounds the difficulty of all Speed defense rolls is reduced by one step. Enabler.
- **Physical Adept:** Any time you spend points from your Might Pool or Speed Pool on an

VECTOR CONNECTION

Roll a d20 or choose from the following list to determine a specific fact about your background that provides a connection to the rest of the world. These connections mostly assume your character begins on Earth. Adapt them if you hail from a recursion, or create your own fact.

Roll	Background
1	You were a star high school athlete. You're still in great shape, but those were the glory days, man.
2	Your brother is the lead singer in a really popular band.
3	You went to the Olympics and took home a silver medal and two bronze medals.
4	You were a cop, but you gave it up after encountering corruption on the force.
5	Your parents worked for the Peace Corps, so you spent much of your young life traveling the world.
6	You served in the military with honor.
7	You received a scholarship from the September Project foundation, which paid for your schooling. Now they seem to want a lot more from you.
8	You went to a prestigious university on an athletic scholarship, but you excelled in class as well as on the field.
9	Your college roommate is now a member of the United States House of Representatives.
10	You used to be a middle school teacher and an athletic coach. Your students remember you fondly.
11	You worked as a small-time operative for the mob until you were caught and served some time in jail, after which you tried to go straight.
12	You owe money to a number of people and don't have the funds to pay your debts.
13	An organization called the Estate has been attempting to recruit you for some time, but you've put them off.
14	You were kidnapped as a small child under mysterious circumstances, although you were recovered safely. The case still has some notoriety.
15	You were a young, professional athlete caught in a doping scandal. Your career ended in shame.
16	While working on an oil rig in the Pacific, you saw some strange lights come up out of the sea and fly away.
17	You own your own small health food restaurant.
18	You were a DJ at a local radio station.
19	Your sister is the owner of a sporting goods store and gives you a hefty discount.
20	Your father is a colonel in the U.S. Marine Corps with many connections.

action for any reason, if you roll a 1 on the associated die, you reroll the die, always taking the second result (even if it's a 1). Enabler.

- **Skill With Attacks:** Choose one type of attack, even one in which you are already trained: light bashing, light bladed, light ranged, medium bashing, medium bladed, medium ranged, heavy bashing, heavy bladed, or heavy ranged. You are trained in attacks using that type of weapon. If you're already trained in that type of attack, you instead become specialized in that type of attack. Enabler.

SIXTH-TIER VECTOR

Sixth-tier vectors have the following abilities:

Physical Skill: Choose one skill in which you are trained but not specialized: balancing, climbing, jumping, running, or swimming. You are specialized in that skill. Enabler.

Moves: Choose one of the following moves (or a move from a lower tier) to add to your repertoire. In addition, you can also replace one of your lower-tier moves with a different move from a tier lower than sixth.

Brash, page 46

Looks for Trouble, page 68

Medium weapon, page 86

- **Again and Again (8 Speed points):** You can take an additional action in a round in which you have already acted. Enabler.
- **Mastery With Armor:** When you wear any armor, you reduce the armor's penalties (Might cost and Speed reduction) to 0. If you select this move and you already have the Experienced With Armor move, replace Experienced With Armor with a different third-tier move because Mastery With Armor is better. Enabler.
- **Spin Attack (5 Speed points):** You stand still and make melee attacks against up to five foes within reach, all as part of the same action in one round. Make a separate attack roll for each foe. You remain limited by the amount of Effort you can apply on one action. Anything that modifies your attack or damage applies to all of these attacks. Action.
- **Shooting Gallery (5 Speed points):** You stand still and make ranged attacks against up to five foes within range, all as part of the same action in one round. Make a separate attack roll for each foe. You remain limited by the amount of Effort you can apply on one action. Anything that modifies your attack or damage applies to all of these attacks. Action.
- **Skill With Attacks:** Choose one type of attack, even one in which you are already trained: light bashing, light bladed, light ranged, medium bashing, medium bladed, medium ranged, heavy bashing, heavy bladed, or heavy ranged. You are trained in attacks using that type of weapon. If you're already trained in that type of attack, you instead are specialized in that type of attack. Enabler.

VECTOR EXAMPLE

Rob wants to play a vector. He wants to be fast more than strong or tough, so he puts 2 points into his Might Pool and 3 points into his Speed Pool, saving 1 for his Intellect Pool. His Pool totals are Might 12, Speed 13, and Intellect 9. He has a Might Edge of 1, a Speed Edge of 1, and an Intellect Edge of 0. As a first-tier character, his Effort is 1. He chooses running and jumping for his physical skills. He gains Translation and chooses Bash and Endurance as his moves.

He can bear two cyphers. The GM gives him a pill that will restore 4 points to his Might Pool and a small device that will knock a creature unconscious if touched with it.

For his descriptor, Rob chooses Brash, which adds 2 more points to his Speed Pool, making it 15. It also gives him training in initiative tasks and overcoming intimidation.

For his focus, he chooses Looks for Trouble. His character is a rough customer. This allows him to inflict 1 additional point of damage with melee attacks and gives him training in healing.

For his equipment, Rob gets a first aid kit, a utility knife, a cell phone, and a choice of two weapons. He chooses a 9mm pistol and a knife. The knife is a light weapon, so he decreases the difficulty of attack rolls with it, but it inflicts only 2 points of damage. In his hands, however, it inflicts 3 points. The 9mm pistol is a medium weapon, so it inflicts 4 points of damage. The pistol comes with a magazine of fifteen bullets. He wears a leather jacket, which is light armor.

Rob is a Brash vector who Looks for Trouble.

PARADOX

Paradoxes are the mad scientists, the sorcerers, and the breakers of the rules of reality. They are not bound by what others believe to be true.

Paradoxes derive their abilities from a connection to the Strange, regardless of where they claim their power originates. With those abilities—called *revisions*—they can transgress the laws of reality and alter the rules of a recursion. The Strange permeates the cosmos, though it's hard for anyone not quickened to its presence to interact with it like paradoxes (and spinners and vectors, in their own ways) do. Though most paradoxes refer to their special abilities as revisions, some refer to them as knacks, prayers, spells, or psychic gifts.

Many paradoxes come from a background that includes extensive training of a scientific, technical, religious, or spiritual nature. They could also have experience in an esoteric order. As a result, they have an aptitude with equipment, paraphernalia, or rituals that may aid them in their pursuits.

PARADOX STAT POOLS

Stat	Pool Starting Value
Might	8
Speed	8
Intellect	12

You get 6 additional points to divide among your stat Pools however you wish.

Paradoxes in Society: Paradoxes are often treated with respect due to the esoteric knowledge that their backgrounds provide; whether scientists, engineers, priests, shamans, or psychics, paradoxes are usually part of a meritocracy. If a paradox were to reveal the possession of paranormal abilities, society at large would react according to the nature of the location. On the prime of Earth and recursions from the same mold, the paradox would likely be subject to a lot of derision, some fear, and possibly some official interest. In places like Ruk, and especially in places like Ardeyn, where such things are more common, these abilities wouldn't gain much notice.

Paradoxes in Groups: Though paradox talents may be remarkable, their knowledge is often their most valuable asset to a group. Many paradoxes possess valuable expertise in areas such as geography, botany, medicine, and lore. When the party comes upon unsettling clues, relics, artifacts, cyphers, creatures out of distant recursions, or other elements of the Strange, the paradox usually has an idea about how to best analyze and deal with the situation.

Paradoxes and the Strange: Paradoxes don't actually perform miracles, though it can seem like that to other people. But the explanation is far more strange.

Every paradox knows something about the Strange. In addition to the Strange being the source of their power, it can be endlessly fascinating to a paradox. Whenever elements of the Strange, such as cyphers (and related artifacts), Strangers, or new recursions are discovered, a paradox is the first to try to understand their meaning and significance.

When it comes to cyphers and related artifacts, paradoxes are not especially choosy. On the other hand, a paradox can carry only so much equipment, which means a smart paradox is generally drawn to items that provide protection, give ranged artillery options, and grant travel to and protection within recursions.

Advanced Paradoxes: As paradoxes gain more experience, they typically learn new and more powerful revisions. They start out with abilities that allow them to acquire secrets, travel to new recursions with a lot of effort, affect matter,

and bend laws of nature in small ways, but eventually they can learn to break the laws of nature, destroy matter, and skip through several recursions using only an effort of will.

PARADOX TIERS

FIRST-TIER PARADOX

First-tier paradoxes have the following abilities:

Effort: Your Effort is 1.

Aptitude: You have an Intellect Edge of 1, a Might Edge of 0, and a Speed Edge of 0.

Remember that a character is defined as anything that can take actions in the game, including PCs, NPCs, creatures, aliens, mutants, and automatons.

Expert Cypher Use: You can bear three cyphers at a time.

Knowledgeable: You are trained in one area of knowledge or technical expertise of your choice.

Strange Training: You are trained in general topics regarding the Strange, which allows you to attempt to understand and identify related phenomena, including the effect of a particular cypher. Strange training is also sometimes called Strange knowledge or Strange lore.

Practiced With Light Weapons: You can use light weapons without penalty. If you wield a medium weapon, increase the difficulty of the attack by one step. If you wield a heavy weapon, increase it by two steps.

Translation: You can participate in the process of traveling to another recursion. Each time you do, you can choose to initiate, hasten, or ease a translation. If you choose to hasten or ease the process, someone else in the group must initiate the translation.

Translation, page 125

As a paradox, you are most effective at initiating a translation. This initiation advantage provides you with additional opportunities during the process of translating.

Initiating a translation, page 125

In order to translate, you must know that the recursion you are translating to exists. The GM will decide if you have enough information to confirm its existence and determine what level of difficulty is needed to reach the destination. Action to initiate.

Revisions: You can tap into the Strange to affect the world around you. When you use a revision, you essentially revise reality.

Smart paradoxes use the Premonition revision on a creature to learn its level before trying to control its mind.

Most revisions require that you spend 1 or more Intellect points (and have a free hand that you use to direct the release of the revision's effect). If no Intellect point cost is given for a revision, it functions continuously without needing to be activated. Some revisions specify a duration, but you can always end one of your own revisions any time you wish.

Select two revisions from those described below. You can't choose the same revision more than once unless its description says otherwise.

- **Closed Mind:** You are trained in Intellect defense tasks and have +2 to Armor against damage that selectively targets your Intellect Pool (that normally ignores Armor). Enabler.
- **Exception (1 Intellect point):** You pick one creature within long range. The target is jolted by a confluence of fundamental forces for 4 points of damage.

  If the target you select is not native to the recursion where you attack it, its senses are overwhelmed. On a successful attack, in addition to taking 4 points of damage, it cannot act on its next turn. Once exposed to this revision, a non-native creature normally can't be affected by the sense-overwhelming portion of this attack again for several hours. Action.
- **Levitate Creature (2+ Intellect points):** You can temporarily bend the fundamental force of gravity on a creature or object (no larger than yourself) that is within long range. The target's level can be no more than 2 above your tier. On a successful attack, an affected target floats an immediate distance over the ground for one round. A levitating target hovers just above the ground, able to take actions, but unable to gain purchase through physical contact.

  Each round after the initial attack, you can attempt to keep the target aloft by spending 1 additional Intellect point and succeeding at a difficulty 2 Intellect task. If your concentration lapses, the target drops back to the ground. You can't directly move a levitating object with this revision, but strong winds, a hearty push by someone else, or other forces can move the target. Action to initiate.
- **Premonition (2 Intellect points):** Despite appearances, reality is quantum and noncausal, which means a careful observer can discover information leaks. You learn one random fact from a person or location that is pertinent to a topic you designate. Alternatively, you can choose to learn a creature's level; however, if you do so, you cannot learn anything else about it later with this revision. Action.
- **Shatter (2 Intellect points):** You interrupt the fundamental force holding normal matter together for a moment, creating the detonation of an object you choose within long range. The object must be a small, mundane item composed of homogeneous

matter (such as a clay cup, an iron ingot, a stone, and so on). The object explodes in an immediate radius, attacking all creatures and objects in the area for 1 point of damage.
Because this is an area attack, adding Effort to increase your damage works differently than it does for single-target attacks: for each level of Effort applied to increase the damage, add 2 points of damage to each target. If you increase the damage through Effort, even if you fail your attack roll, all targets in the area still take 1 point of damage. Action.

SECOND-TIER PARADOX

Second-tier paradoxes have the following abilities:

Reach Beyond (3 Intellect points): When you use Reach Beyond, you can access training in a skill provided by a focus you have in another recursion. You must have used the skill in its proper recursion at least once before. You can use the skill once. To use it again, you must use Reach Beyond again. Enabler.

Revisions: Choose one of the following revisions (or a revision from a lower tier) to add to your repertoire. In addition, you can replace one of your first-tier revisions with a different first-tier revision.

- **Force Shield (2+ Intellect points):** You call up a field of shielding energy that grants you +1 to Armor for ten minutes. You can increase the Armor bonus by spending Effort. Each additional level of Effort increases the Armor value you gain by 1. Action.
- **Gate Key (4 Intellect points):** You can secure (or unlock) a regular door or other object that can be closed or opened, such as a drawer, laptop, satchel, book, window, and so on, even if it can't normally be locked. You can also lock (or open) a permanent or semipermanent recursion gate, including translation gates and inapposite gates. To unlock or lock the target, you must touch it.
If the object is locked and you wish to unlock it, succeed at an Intellect task with a difficulty set by the GM (usually equal to the level of the lock or effect holding the object closed). On a success, the target is unlocked.
You automatically succeed in locking an object if that is your goal; an object or gate is locked at a level equal to 4 + your tier. Action.

"What I really like is hopping into one of the little, self-contained recursions that no one's been to before. Makes me feel like Christopher Columbus, or Neil Armstrong." ~William Hutchins, recursor

Recursion gate, page 134

If two or more characters in a group have Eye for the Strange, they can assist each other with this revision, decreasing the difficulty of the task by one step.

The shimmer may look different to every player who uses Eye for the Strange, and its appearance may also vary from character to character and from place to place.

Inapposite gate, page 135

Translation gate, page 134

Damage track, page 108

- **Mind Reading (4 Intellect points):** You can read the mind of a creature you can see within short range. You gain access to its surface thoughts for up to one minute as long as it is within range. Action to initiate.
- **Plasma Arc (2 Intellect points):** You induce an ionized arc of plasma to leap between two targets that you can see and that are within short range of each other. Both targets must also be within long range of you. You roll an attack for each target separately. If you successfully attack only one target, it takes 4 points of damage from the intense heat. If you successfully attack both targets, each takes 4 points of damage. Effort applied to one attack counts for both, but you must abide by your Effort level limit for each action. Action.
- **Revise Flesh (3 Intellect points):** You can revise flesh with your touch in one of two ways. When you touch an impaired or debilitated character, you can choose to move the character up one step on the damage track (for example, a debilitated PC becomes impaired, while an impaired creature becomes hale). Alternatively, you can grant a character a +2 bonus to his recovery roll if you use this ability on the PC during a rest. Action.

THIRD-TIER PARADOX

Third-tier paradoxes have the following abilities:

Adept Cypher Use: You can bear four cyphers at a time.

Revisions: Choose one of the following revisions (or a revision from a lower tier) to add to your repertoire. In addition, you can replace one of your lower-tier revisions with a different one from a tier lower than third.

- **Energy Protection (3+ Intellect points):** Choose a discrete type of energy that you have experience with (such as heat, sonic, electricity, and so on). You must be familiar with the type of energy; for example, if you have no experience with a certain kind of extradimensional energy, you can't protect against it. You gain +10 to Armor against damage from that type of energy for ten minutes. Alternatively, you gain +1 to Armor against damage from that energy for one day.
  Instead of applying Effort to decrease the difficulty of this revision, you can apply Effort to protect more targets, with each level of Effort affecting up to two additional targets. You must touch additional targets to protect them. Action to initiate.
- **Eye for the Strange:** You see a "shimmer" around creatures and objects that are not native to the current recursion and around native creatures that possess the spark. If you spend an action concentrating on a non-native target with such a shimmer, you can see the form it originally possessed prior to translating to the current recursion (if it went through an inapposite gate, it retains the shimmer, but may not look much different). Enabler (although you can use an Action to enhance, as stated).
- **Force at Distance (4+ Intellect points):** You temporarily bend the fundamental law of gravity around a creature or object (up to twice your mass) within short range. The target's level can be no more than 2 above your tier.
  On a successful attack, an affected target is caught in your telekinetic grip, and you can move the creature up to a short distance in any direction each round that you retain your hold.
  A creature in your telekinetic grip can take actions, but it can't move under its own power. Each round after the initial attack, you can attempt to keep your grip on the target

by spending 2 additional Intellect points and succeeding at a difficulty 2 Intellect task. If your concentration lapses, the target drops back to the ground.

Instead of applying Effort to decrease the difficulty, you can apply Effort to increase the amount of mass you can affect. Each level of Effort allows you to affect a creature or object twice as massive as before. For example, applying one level of Effort would affect a creature four times as massive as you, two levels of Effort would affect a creature eight times as massive, three levels can affect a creature sixteen times as massive, and so on. Action to initiate.

- **Psychic Precision:** You are trained in any mental revision or mental ability that comes from a cypher, an artifact, or your focus. For example, you are trained when using Mind Reading because it's a mental ability, but not when using Plasma Arc. Enabler.
- **Recursion Viewing (5 Intellect points):** An observer with the ability to revise reality knows that space and distance is an illusion. You concentrate to create an invisible, immobile sensor at a location within a recursion you have previously visited or viewed (at the GM's discretion, you may have to succeed at an Intellect task if the location is somehow warded). The sensor lasts for about an hour. Once it is created, you can concentrate to see, hear, and smell through the sensor whether you are somewhere else in the recursion or on a connected prime. The sensor doesn't grant you sensory capabilities beyond the norm. Creating such a sensor on the prime world of Earth requires that you spend a level of Effort. Action to create; action to check.

FOURTH-TIER PARADOX

Fourth-tier paradoxes have the following abilities:

Revisions: Choose one of the following revisions (or a revision from a lower tier) to add to your repertoire. In addition, you can replace one of your lower-tier revisions with a different one from a tier lower than fourth.

- **Gate Exit (9 Intellect points):** You create one end of a translation gate. The gate exit does not connect to anything unless you earlier created a different gate exit within another recursion, in which case that exit and the new one connect, creating a translation gate. Unconnected gate exits last for about

PARADOX CONNECTION

Roll a d20 or choose from the following list to determine a specific fact about your background that provides a connection to the rest of the world. These connections mostly assume your character begins on Earth. Adapt them if you hail from a recursion, or create your own fact.

Roll	Background
1	When you were mugged, you killed the mugger. Now you're trying to stay one step ahead of the police detectives who are trying to solve the murder.
2	An experiment you conducted in your garage blew up, caused your home to burn down, and killed some of your family. You still dream about it sometimes.
3	You once belonged to a monastery. When the others learned of your abilities, some thought you were touched by the divine. Others did not.
4	You gave a homeless person enough to stay inside during the course of a brutal storm. That person now owes you a great favor.
5	Your mother was a member of the Quiet Cabal before she died, where she was respected by many. Those who knew her are fond of you, but they also expect great things from you.
6	Your father was a politician who left office in some disrepute, and you never learned the full story about it.
7	You were a code-breaker for the military until you decoded a message that implicated your superior in something foul. Rather than face her, you got yourself dishonorably discharged.
8	You revised the world in a public place and were noticed. You've gained notoriety, as well as death threats from religious fanatics.
9	You studied at one of the most prestigious schools in the world, but you got in by cheating.
10	You headed a small church, and though you left to pursue your own strange journey, the congregation still tries to lure you back to the pulpit.
11	You were a night guard before you gained the ability to revise reality.
12	You had a successful career writing stirring greeting cards, but you were let go after one of your cards caused a rash of suicides.
13	You hacked websites for cash until you crossed the Estate, which sent agents to locate you. When they brought you in, you agreed to join them.
14	You were an anthropologist who found something strange in a burial site—something you published, though it got you thrown from the ranks of respectable researchers.
15	When you were an envoy working overseas, you made friends with several foreign diplomats, some of whom you still contact.
16	You worked for a famous psychic, though she threw you out when she realized your powers were real, as opposed to her tricks.
17	You made a mint online with digital currency, but thanks to a computer crash, you lost everything. You're determined to build up your nest egg again.
18	As a political refugee, you are often treated with suspicion.
19	You are fit as a fiddle, but most would think of you as obese.
20	Your dog can talk because it is native to a recursion where such an ability isn't unusual, though it was a shock to you when you first found out.

a month or until destroyed. After two gate exits link up to form a translation gate, the gate lasts for about a year or until destroyed. (Like all objects, translation gates have levels that speak to their ability to withstand harm. The translation gate exit you create with this ability is level 5.)

You can create a permanent translation gate by using this revision every day for seven days on either exit of a connected translation gate. One hour to initiate.

- **Invisibility (4 Intellect points):** You bend light around you, becoming invisible for ten minutes. While invisible, you are specialized in stealth and Speed defense tasks. This effect ends if you do something to reveal your presence or position—attacking, performing a revision, using an ability, moving a large object, and so on. If this occurs, you can regain the remaining invisibility effect by taking an action to focus on hiding your position. Action to initiate or reinitiate.

The dream of invisibility is usually everything people imagine, but also remember that buses, stampeding creatures, and normally benign automated machinery also can't sense you. Adjust for your safety accordingly.

- **Mind Control (6+ Intellect points):** You control the actions of another creature you touch. This effect lasts for ten minutes. The target must be level 2 or lower. After you have established control, you maintain mental contact with the target and sense what it senses. You can allow it to act freely or override its control on a case-by-case basis. Instead of applying Effort to decrease the difficulty, you can apply Effort to increase the maximum level of the target. Thus, to control the mind of a level 5 target (three levels above the normal limit), you must apply three levels of Effort. When the Mind Control revision ends, the creature doesn't remember being controlled or anything it did while under your command. Action to initiate.
- **Rapid Processing (6 Intellect points):** You or a target you touch experiences a higher level of mental and physical reaction time for about a minute. During that period, the target modifies all Speed tasks by one step to its benefit, including Speed defense rolls. In addition, the target can take one extra action at any time before the revision's duration expires. Action.
- **Warp World (5 Intellect points):** You tug on the fundamental laws of the recursion to create a zone of distraction and confusion around a creature you can see within long range for one minute. All attacks against the target are modified by one step to the attacker's benefit, and all attacks made by the target are modified by one step to its detriment. If the target attempts an attack and fails, it automatically hits one of the target's allies if an ally is in range of that attack.

FIFTH-TIER PARADOX

Fifth-tier paradoxes have the following abilities:

Master Cypher Use: You can bear five cyphers at a time.

Revisions: Choose one of the following revisions (or a revision from a lower tier) to add to your repertoire. In addition, you can replace one of your lower-tier revisions with a different one from a tier lower than fifth.

- **Draw From Fiction (7 Intellect points):** You produce, as if from thin air, a level 5 creature of a kind you have previously encountered in a recursion that you have visited. The creature you name appears through a transitory inapposite gate and remains for one minute. The creature is drawn back to its home recursion when the revision ends. The creature acts as you direct. It appears through an inapposite gate, and at the GM's discretion, it may face difficulties according to the rules of the location you draw it into, such as suffering a step penalty to some or all tasks it attempts. As a level 5 creature, it has a target number of 15 and a health of 15, and it inflicts 5 points of damage. Action.
- **Exile (7 Intellect points):** You send another creature you can see within long range to the recursion of its origin or (if the creature is not native to a recursion) to one you've previously visited. The target must be level 5 or lower, and you must succeed on an attack. If successful, the creature is exiled through a transitory inapposite gate. If the creature resists, all its actions are modified by two steps to its detriment for one minute.

  Exiled creatures can't return to the recursion you exiled them from under their own power for seven days (even if they have the ability to move between recursions or if they find a gate). Action.
- **Force Focus (6 Intellect points + 2 Might points):** You exchange your current focus for the focus you possessed in an alternate recursion (or connected prime) for up to one hour. Doing so is a transgression of reality and the rules of translation, which means that it saps both your Intellect Pool and your Might Pool. While you retain the forced focus, your appearance is a hybrid of your current appearance and what you look like in the recursion or prime whose focus you are

borrowing. You can use your current focus while the forced focus is active. Action to initiate.

- **Knowing the Unknown (6 Intellect points):** Tapping into the immense processing capacity of the Strange, you ask the GM one question and get a general answer. The GM assigns a level to the question, so the more obscure the answer, the more difficult the task. Generally, knowledge that you could find by looking somewhere other than your current location is level 1, and obscure knowledge of the past is level 7. Gaining knowledge of the future is impossible. Action.
- **True Senses:** You can see in complete darkness up to 50 feet (15 m) as if it were dim light. You recognize holograms, disguises, optical illusions, sound mimicry, and other such tricks (for all senses) for what they are. Enabler.

SIXTH-TIER PARADOX

Sixth-tier paradoxes have the following abilities:

Revisions: Choose one of the following revisions (or a revision from a lower tier) to add to your repertoire. In addition, you can replace one of your lower-tier revisions with a different one from a tier lower than sixth.

- **Drag Through Hell (9 Intellect Points):** You send a creature within immediate range that you can see into one of a number of recursions filled with brimstone, hellfire, and demons. On a successful attack on a target of up to level 7, the target is pulled through a transitory inapposite gate and takes 6 points of damage as it is dragged through the hellish recursion behind some unspeakable monstrosity. If you concentrate, you can attempt to keep the target translocated with a new action and a new attack roll each round. Each round the target remains translocated, it suffers another 6 points of damage. If the target returns before dying (or if the initial attack wasn't successful at pulling the target into a hellish recursion), all tasks the target attempts on its next turn are modified by two steps to its detriment. Action.
- **Force Unification (13 Intellect points):** You briefly align the fundamental forces of existence, creating a point where they merge into a single interaction at a location you can see. This allows you to briefly rewrite one rule of the recursion where you are currently located. The effect can be dramatic, but it is always local and lasts anywhere from one round to a minute, depending on the nature of the change. Possibilities include changing the color of the sky, causing an eclipse, halving (or doubling) gravity, changing the speed of light, and similar effects. The GM will decide if your brief annotation of the laws of existence is reasonable, how long it will last, and what level of difficulty is needed to achieve it. Action.
- **Index Recursion (7 Intellect Points):** You feel a mental tug toward the nearest recursion gate that you don't already know about. You discern the location of and distance to that gate (translation or inapposite), and you learn enough information regarding the general nature and theme of the recursion it connects with to enter it directly using Translation. Action.
- **Master Translation (5+ Intellect points):** When you initiate a translation, you can choose to also hasten and/or ease it. To do so, expend the Intellect cost to trigger this revision as you begin the translation trance. Then you can apply one level of Effort to ease or hasten the translation (instead of applying Effort to decrease the difficulty), or two levels of Effort to both ease and hasten the translation. You must know that the recursion exists; the GM will decide if you have enough information to confirm its existence and determine what level of difficulty is needed to reach the destination. Action to initiate.
- **Usurp Cypher:** Choose one cypher that you carry. The cypher must have an effect that is not instantaneous. You destroy the cypher and gain its power, which functions for you continuously. You can choose a cypher when you gain this ability, or you can wait and make the choice later. After you usurp a cypher's power, you cannot later switch to a different cypher—the ability works only once. Action to initiate.

"Entering the Strange is like peering into your own soul. You're amazed at the depths you find, but the farther you go, the less you really want to see." ~William Hutchins, recursor

PARADOX EXAMPLE

JD wants to play a paradox. He figures he'd like to be a tad more defensive and tougher, so he puts a point each into Might and Speed, bringing each Pool up to 9. The other 4 points go into his Intellect Pool, making it 16. His paradox is something of a brain. He has an Intellect Edge of 1, a Might Edge of 0, and a Speed Edge of 0. As a first-tier character, his Effort is 1. He is trained in the Strange. He gains Translation as an automatic revision, then chooses Shatter and Premonition, giving him an offensive boost and a way to find things out.

Cypher, page 310
Occultic, page 311
Anoetic, page 311

He can bear three cyphers, but the GM gives him two: an occultic cypher (which counts as two cyphers for this purpose) and an anoetic cypher. The occultic cypher is an orb that can be thrown down to form a temporary portal into (and out of) a linked recursion. The other cypher is a device that allows the paradox to fly for up to one minute when attached to his belt.

Skeptical, page 48

For his descriptor, JD chooses Skeptical, which adds 2 more points to his Intellect Pool, bringing it to a whopping 18! The descriptor also gives him training in identifying things and seeing through various sorts of tricks.

Solves Mysteries, page 78

For his focus, he chooses Solves Mysteries. His character is a scientific-minded investigator. In fact, he decides that he works in a police crime lab. His focus gives him training in perception and the ability to use points from his Might Pool or Speed Pool for Intellect tasks.

For his equipment, JD gets a laptop, a flashlight, a utility knife, a cell phone, and a choice of two weapons. He chooses a pair of brass knuckles and a light pistol. Both are light weapons, so they decrease the difficulty of attack rolls, but they inflict only 2 points of damage. He chooses to have no armor, since being a paradox doesn't give him any practice with it, and it might hinder him more than help in the long run. The GM generously allows him to have a crime scene investigation kit instead.

JD is a Skeptical paradox who Solves Mysteries.

SPINNER

Spinners are striking individuals, and they possess a personality that allows them to spin tales, spin lies, or spin a version of the truth that makes others see things in a whole new way. If anyone is going to make a friend of an enemy, bluff a way into a high-security compound, or mislead a world-devouring planetovore, it's a spinner. Whether through leadership, influence, or behind-the-scenes manipulation, a spinner pushes things in the direction she wants them to go.

Planetovore, page 8

Some spinner abilities could be attained through practice by anyone with some talent, but a spinner has an underlying facility: everything a spinner accomplishes is quickened by her connection to the Strange. A spinner's abilities—called *twists*—can be used to adjust, distort, and exploit.

SPINNER STAT POOLS

Stat	Pool Starting Value
Might	9
Speed	9
Intellect	10

You get 6 additional points to divide among your stat Pools however you wish.

Spinners in Society: Spinners are entertainers, grifters, and leaders. Some are comedians of rare and delicious talent, able to galvanize their audiences with humor and truth. Others are leaders who truly inspire those beneath them with their integrity, stirring words, and loyalty. Some are introverts who use their power to persuade while using computers, and they are renowned hackers (under an alias), seemingly able to break nearly any security procedure with enough time. And of course, some are clever con artists always a few steps ahead of marks whose dishonesty, irresponsibility, and greed make them easy victims.

Spinners who share their gifts with others are prized members of society, and they are well respected for what they know and can do. Sometimes, everything would fall apart if not for the connective social web a spinner can weave. On the other hand, spinners who use their persuasive abilities to benefit only themselves are distrusted at best and reviled at worst. After all, a spinner makes an ideal thief.

Spinners in Groups: Spinners often serve as the glue that binds a group together, and if they are not elected to be the leader, they provide a valuable service by advising the group, especially when it comes to interacting with others. Many spinners can handle themselves in a fight (or at least get clear of one), which means that vectors in a group don't need to spend much time protecting spinners when weapons are drawn.

Spinners and the Strange: Most spinners have told everyone so many different stories about how they got their abilities that sometimes it's hard for even them to remember the truth. But each has a specific story.

A spinner may not know what the Strange is or understand its true nature, but every spinner is cognizant of having a connection to something unique. Spinners recognize cyphers and recursions as being elements of that specialness. Already masters of persuasion, spinners are drawn to cyphers or artifacts that expand their options in other areas. Thus, a spinner might want an enhanced piece of armor, a Strange weapon, and so on.

Advanced Spinners: Experienced spinners continue to learn twists, including how to best convince others to do as they're told, but they can also choose to hone other skills to round out their abilities, especially in combat.

SPINNER TIERS

FIRST-TIER SPINNER

First-tier spinners have the following abilities:

Effort: Your Effort is 1.

Quickminded: You have an Intellect Edge of 1, a Might Edge of 0, and a Speed Edge of 1.

Cypher Use: You can bear two cyphers at a time.

Practiced With Light and Medium Weapons: You can use light and medium weapons without penalty. If you wield a heavy weapon, increase the difficulty of the attack by one step.

Manipulator: You are trained in deceiving, persuading, or intimidating (choose one).

Translation: You can participate in the process of traveling to another recursion. Each time you do, you can choose to initiate, hasten, or ease a translation. If you choose to hasten or ease the process, someone else in the group must initiate the translation.

As a spinner, you are most effective at hastening a translation. This advantage allows you to decrease the time it takes to translate to a recursion.

In order to translate, you must know that the recursion you are translating to exists. The GM will decide if you have enough information to confirm its existence and determine what level of difficulty is needed to reach the destination. Action to initiate.

Twists: You manipulate things, including people, machines, organizations, objects—anything and everything. Some twists are constant, ongoing effects, and others are specific actions that usually cost points from one of your stat Pools.

Choose two of the twists described below. You can't choose the same twist more than once unless its description says otherwise.

- **Enthrall (1 Intellect point):** While talking, you grab and keep another creature's attention, even if the creature can't understand you. For as long as you do nothing but speak (you can't even move), the other creature takes no actions other than to defend itself, even over multiple rounds. If the creature is attacked, the effect ends. Action.
- **Fast Talk (1 Intellect point):** When speaking with an intelligent creature who can understand you and isn't hostile, you convince that creature to take one reasonable action on the next round. A reasonable action must be agreed upon by the GM; it should not put the creature or its allies in obvious danger or be wildly out of character. Action.
- **Sleight of Hand (1 Speed point):** You can perform small but seemingly impossible tricks. For example, you can make a small object in your hands disappear and move

Translation, page 125

Hastening a translation, page 126

Spin Identity might be the most valuable spinner ability, but subtlety is still required when using it. A spinner who takes an action contrary to who she's pretending to be can cause the charade to shatter immediately.

into a desired spot within reach (like your pocket). You can make someone believe that he has something in his possession that he does not have (or vice versa). You can switch similar objects right in front of someone's eyes. Action.

- **Spin Encouragement (1 Intellect point):** While you maintain this twist through ongoing inspiring oration, your allies within short range modify the difficulty of one of the following task types (your choice) by one step to their benefit: defense tasks, attack tasks, or tasks related to any skill that you are trained or specialized in. Action.
- **Spin Identity (2+ Intellect points):** You convince all intelligent creatures who can see, hear, and understand you that you are someone or something other than who you actually are. You don't impersonate a specific individual known to the victim. Instead, you convince the victim that you are someone they do not know belonging to a certain category of people. "We're from the government." "I'm just a simple farmer from the next town over." "Your commander sent me." A disguise isn't necessary, but a good disguise will almost certainly be an asset to the roll involved. If you attempt to convince more than one creature, the Intellect cost increases by 1 point per additional victim. Fooled creatures remain so for up to an hour, unless your actions or other circumstances reveal your true identity earlier. Action.
- **Understanding (2 Intellect points):** You observe or study a creature or object. Then, the next time you interact with that creature or object, the difficulty of the related task is reduced by one step. Action.

SECOND-TIER SPINNER

Second-tier spinners have the following abilities:

Skills: You are trained in one task of your choosing (other than attacks or defense). If you choose a task you're already trained in, you become specialized in that task. You can't choose a task you're already specialized in.

Reach Beyond (3 Intellect points): When you use Reach Beyond, you can access training in a skill provided by a focus you have in another recursion. You must have used the skill in its proper recursion at least once before. You can use the skill once. To use it again, you must use Reach Beyond again. Enabler.

Twists: Choose one of the following twists (or twists from a lower tier) to add to your repertoire. In addition, you can replace one of your lower-tier twists with a different twist from the same lower tier.

- **Babel:** After hearing a language spoken for a few minutes, you can speak it and make yourself understood. If you continue to use the language to interact with native speakers, your skills improve rapidly, to the point where you might be mistaken for a native speaker after just a few hours of speaking the new language. Enabler.
- **Efficiency (2 Intellect points):** You can make a weak rope last longer, coax more speed from a motorcycle, improve the clarity of a camera, jury-rig a light to be brighter, speed up an Internet connection, and so on. You increase an object's level by 2 for one minute, or treat the object as an asset that reduces an associated task's difficulty by two steps for one minute (your choice). Action to initiate.
- **Escape (2 Speed points):** You slip your restraints, squeeze through the bars, break the grip of a creature holding you, pull free from sucking quicksand, or otherwise get loose from that which is holding you in place. Action.
- **Hand to Eye (2 Speed points):** This twist provides an asset to any tasks involving manual dexterity, such as pickpocketing, lockpicking, games involving agility, and so on. Each use lasts up to a minute; multiple uses replace the previous use. Action to initiate.
- **Pierce (1 Speed point):** This is a well-aimed, penetrating ranged attack. You make an attack and inflict 1 additional point of damage. Action.
- **Spin Ideal (3 Intellect points):** After interacting with another creature who can hear and understand you for at least one minute, you can use a twist to attempt to temporarily impart an ideal to the target that you can't otherwise convince it of.

An ideal is different than a specific suggestion or command; an ideal is an overarching value such as, "all life is sacred," "my political party is the best," "children should be seen, not heard," and so on. An ideal influences a creature's behavior but doesn't control it.

The imparted ideal lasts for as long as befits the situation, but usually at least a few hours. The implanted ideal is jeopardized if someone friendly to the creature spends a minute or more bringing the target back to its senses. Action.

SPINNER CONNECTION

Roll a d20 or choose from the following list to determine a specific fact about your background that provides a connection to the rest of the world. These connections mostly assume your character begins on Earth. Adapt them if you hail from a recursion, or create your own fact.

Roll	Background
1	One of your parents was once a famous entertainer in his or her early years and hoped you would excel in the same medium.
2	When you were a teenager, one of your siblings went missing and is presumed dead. The shock rent your family, and it's something you've never gotten over.
3	You were inducted into a secret society that claims to hold and protect esoteric knowledge opposing the forces of evil.
4	You lost one of your parents to alcoholism. He or she may still be alive, but you'd be hard pressed to find forgiveness.
5	You have no memory of anything that happened to you before the age of 18.
6	Your grandparents raised you on a dairy farm far from bustling urban centers. You like to think the homeschooling you received prepared you for anything.
7	As an orphan, you had a difficult childhood, and your entry into adulthood was challenging.
8	You grew up on the reservation. When you left, most of your friends thought you were abandoning the tribe.
9	As a child actor, you were loved and adored. As an adult, less so.
10	You have an annoying rival who always seems to get in your way or foil your plans.
11	You've worked yourself into the position of spokesperson for a medium-sized company.
12	Your next-door neighbors were murdered, and the mystery remains unsolved.
13	You have traveled all over the world, and during that time you accumulated quite a collection of strange souvenirs.
14	Your high-school sweetheart ended up with your best friend. Now ex-best friend.
15	You are part of a maligned minority, but you work to bring the injustice of your status to public attention.
16	You're part-owner of a local bar, where you're something of a whiz in creating specialty cocktails.
17	You once talked an expensive watch off a powerful executive, but in so doing, you earned the executive's enmity.
18	You used to act in a traveling theater, and they remember you fondly (as do people in the places you visited).
19	You won an Aspiring Writers of Tomorrow contest for a short story you wrote, and now you have a couple of offers from publishers to write a novel.
20	Someone stole your identity, drained your bank accounts, and is wanted in connection to a series of violent crimes.

"It's one thing when we go there, to their weirdo world. I'll put up with their magic, their crazy science, or whatever. But when they come here, that's when I get angry." ~Ron Stayton, former agent of the Estate

THIRD-TIER SPINNER

Third-tier spinners have the following abilities:

Expert Cypher Use: You can bear three cyphers at a time.

Skill: You are trained in one task of your choosing (other than attacks or defense). If you choose a task you're already trained in, you become specialized in that task. You can't choose a task you're already specialized in.

Twists: Choose one of the following twists (or twists from a lower tier) to add to your repertoire. In addition, you can replace one of your lower-tier twists with a different twist from a tier lower than third.

- **Blend In (4 Intellect points):** When you Blend In, creatures still see you, but they attach no importance to your presence for about a minute. While blending in, you are specialized in stealth and Speed defense tasks. This effect ends if you do something to reveal your presence or position—attacking, performing a twist, moving a large object, and so on. If this occurs, you can regain the remaining period of effect by taking an action to focus on seeming innocuous and as if you belong. Action to initiate or reinitiate.

- **Grand Deception (3 Intellect points):** You convince an intelligent creature that can understand you and isn't hostile of something that is wildly and obviously untrue. Action.
- **Mind Reading (4 Intellect points):** You can read the surface thoughts of a creature within short range, even if the subject doesn't want you to. You must be able to see the target. Once you have established contact, you can read the target's thoughts for up to one minute. If you or the target moves out of range, the connection is broken. Action to initiate.
- **Oratory (4 Intellect points):** When speaking with a group of intelligent creatures that can understand you and aren't hostile, you convince them to take one reasonable action on the next round. A reasonable action must be agreed upon by the GM; it should not put the creature or its allies in obvious danger or be wildly out of character. Action.
- **Spray (2 Speed points):** If a weapon has the ability to fire rapid shots without reloading (usually called a rapid-fire weapon, such as the automatic pistol), you can spray multiple shots around your target to increase the chance of hitting. This move uses 1d6 + 1 rounds of ammo (or all the ammo in the weapon, if it has less than the number rolled). The difficulty of the attack roll is decreased by one step. If the attack is successful, it deals 1 less point of damage than normal. Action.
- **Telling (2 Intellect points):** This twist provides an asset to any tasks attempting to deceive, persuade, or intimidate. Each use lasts up to a minute; a new use (to switch tasks) replaces the previous use. Action to initiate.

Though sometimes people use the term "spinner" as a derogative label, most actual spinners bear the name as a badge of honor.

FOURTH-TIER SPINNER

Fourth-tier spinners have the following abilities:

Skills: You are trained in one task of your choosing (other than attacks or defense). If you choose a task you're already trained in, you become specialized in that task. You can't choose a task you're already specialized in.

Twists: Choose one of the following twists (or twists from a lower tier) to add to your repertoire. In addition, you can replace one of your lower-tier twists with a different twist from a tier lower than fourth.

- **Anticipate Attack (4 Intellect points):** You can sense when and how creatures attacking you will make their attacks. The difficulty of Speed defense rolls are reduced by one step for one minute. Action.
- **Feint (2 Speed points):** If you spend one action creating a misdirection or diversion, in the next round you can take advantage of your opponent's lowered defenses. Make a melee attack roll against that opponent. The difficulty of the roll is decreased by one step. If your attack is successful, it inflicts 4 additional points of damage. Action.
- **Quick Wits:** When performing a task that would normally require spending points from your Intellect Pool, you can spend points from your Speed Pool instead. Enabler.
- **Read the Signs (4 Intellect points):** You examine an area and learn precise, useful details about the past (if any exist). You can ask the GM up to four questions about the immediate area, but each requires its own roll. Action.
- **Suggestion (4 Intellect points):** You suggest an action to another creature within immediate range. If the action doesn't seem completely at odds with the creature's nature, the creature follows your suggestion. The creature must be a level 2 or lower. The effect of your suggestion lasts for up to a minute.

Instead of applying a level of Effort to decrease the difficulty, you can apply it to increase the maximum level of the target you can affect by 1. When you use this twist, you immediately learn the creature's level (if you didn't already know it). If its level is higher than 2, you can immediately apply levels of Effort to increase the maximum level allowed (up to that creature's level).

When the effects of the twist end, the creature remembers following the suggestion, but believes that it chose to do so willingly. Action to initiate.

FIFTH-TIER SPINNER

Fifth-tier spinners have the following abilities:

Adept Cypher Use: You can bear four cyphers at a time.

Skills: You are trained in one task of your choosing (other than attacks or defense). If you choose a task you're already trained in, you become specialized in that task. You can't choose a task you're already specialized in.

Twists: Choose one of the following twists (or twists from a lower tier) to add to your repertoire. In addition, you can replace one of your lower-tier twists with a different twist from a tier lower than fifth.

- **Arc Spray (3 Speed points):** If a weapon has the ability to fire rapid shots without reloading (usually called a rapid-fire weapon, such as the automatic pistol), you can fire your weapon at up to three targets (all next to one another) as a single action. Make a separate attack roll against each target. The difficulty of each attack is increased by one step. Action.
- **Energy Protection (4+ Intellect points):** Choose a discrete type of energy that you have experience with (such as heat, sonic, electricity, and so on). You must be familiar with the type of energy; for example, if you have no experience with a certain kind of extradimensional energy, you can't protect against it. You gain +10 to Armor against damage from that type of energy for ten minutes. Alternatively, you gain +1 to Armor against damage from that energy for one day.

Instead of applying Effort to decrease the difficulty, you can apply Effort to protect more targets, with each level of Effort affecting up to two additional targets. You must touch additional targets to protect them. Action to initiate.

- **Jury-Rig (5 Intellect points):** You quickly create an object using what would seem to be entirely inappropriate materials. You can make a bomb out of a tin can and some household cleaners, a lockpick out of aluminum foil, or a sword out of broken furniture. The level of the item determines the difficulty of the task, but the appropriateness of the materials modifies it as well. Generally, the object can be no larger than something you can hold in one hand, and it functions once (or in the case of a weapon or similar item, is essentially useful for one encounter). If you spend at least ten minutes on the task, you can make up to a level 5 item. You can't change the nature of the materials involved. You can't take iron rods and make a pile of gold coins or a wicker basket, for example. Action.
- **Skill With Attacks:** Choose one type of attack in which you are not already trained: light bashing, light bladed, light ranged, medium bashing, medium bladed, medium ranged, heavy bashing, heavy bladed, or heavy ranged. You are trained in attacks using that type of weapon. Enabler.

SIXTH-TIER SPINNER

Sixth-tier spinners have the following abilities:

Skills: You are trained in one task of your choosing (other than attacks or defense). If you choose a task you're already trained in, you become specialized in that task. You can't choose a task you're already specialized in.

Twists: Choose one of the following twists (or twists from a lower tier) to add to your repertoire. In addition, you can replace one of your lower-tier twists with a different twist from a tier lower than sixth.

- **Battle Management (4 Intellect points):** As long as you spend your action each round giving orders or advice, the difficulty of attack and defense actions by your allies within short range is decreased by one step. Action.
- **Skill With Attacks:** Choose one type of attack, even one in which you are already trained: light bashing, light bladed, light ranged, medium bashing, medium bladed, medium ranged, heavy bashing, heavy bladed, or heavy ranged. You are trained in attacks using that type of weapon. If you're already trained in that type of attack, you become specialized in that type of attack. Enabler.

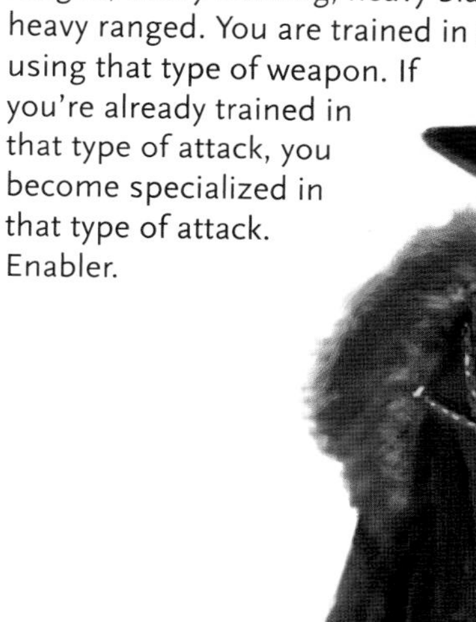

- **True Senses:** You can see in complete darkness up to 50 feet (15 m) as if it were dim light. You recognize holograms, disguises, optical illusions, sound mimicry, and other such tricks (for all senses) for what they are. Enabler.
- **Word of Command (6 Intellect points + level 6 cypher):** You utter a word so powerful that to fully empower it, you sacrifice a level 6 or higher cypher in your possession. You issue your Word of Command to one creature within long range that you can see. It does not have to hear you to be affected. Targets native to Earth are affected if you succeed on an Intellect attack to persuade. Targets native to a recursion or the Strange (including planetovores) are automatically affected. Affected targets must obey the command for several hours before they're free to act as they wish. Targets that are attacked while under the effect of your command can defend themselves. Typical commands include "Retreat," "Calm," "Come," and "Stay." The GM decides how the target acts once a command is given. Action.

Clever, page 46

Works the System, page 83

Hack the Impossible, page 83

Light weapon, page 86

SPINNER EXAMPLE

Torah wants to play a spinner. She is drawn to the idea of persuading people over to her way of thinking. She puts 3 of her additional points in her Intellect Pool (raising it to 13), 2 points in her Speed Pool (raising it to 11), and 1 point in her Might Pool (raising it to 10). A beginning spinner has an Intellect Edge of 1 and a Speed Edge of 1, and as a first-tier character, her Effort is 1.

Torah gains the Translation twist automatically. For her other two first-tier twists, she takes Fast Talk and Enthrall. She's a good speaker and quick-witted. She chooses to be trained in persuasion.

Her character can bear two cyphers. The GM decides that one item is a temporary tattoo that gives Torah a +1 bonus to her Intellect Edge for one hour, and the other is oil for her knife that, when applied, treats the next attack as if she rolled a 20.

Torah still needs to choose her descriptor and focus. For her descriptor, she picks Clever to complement the hacker idea, so she adds 2 to her Intellect Pool, raising it to 15. The Clever descriptor also means she is trained in lies and trickery (which works for a hacker), defense rolls against mental effects, and identifying or assessing things. Unfortunately, she doesn't excel at reading, studying, or remembering details. She apparently would rather act in the moment than plan ahead.

For her focus, she decides on Works the System. At first tier, she can Hack the Impossible, which seems to complete the hacker idea.

She starts with a laptop computer, a smartphone, and a weapon of her choice. Torah chooses a knife. The knife is a light weapon, so she decreases the difficulty of attack rolls with it, but it inflicts only 2 points of damage.

Torah is a Clever spinner who Works the System.

CHAPTER 5

CHARACTER DESCRIPTOR

Your descriptor defines your character—it flavors everything you do. The differences between a Lucky paradox and a Brash paradox are considerable. The descriptor changes the way those characters go about every action. Your descriptor places your character in the situation (the first adventure, which starts the campaign) and helps provide motivation. It is the adjective of the sentence "I am an *adjective noun* who *verbs*."

Descriptors offer a one-time package of extra characteristics that include abilities, skills, or modifications to your stat Pools. Not all of a descriptor's offerings are positive character modifications. For example, some descriptors have inabilities—tasks that a character isn't good at. You can think of inabilities as "negative skills"—instead of being one step better at that kind of task, you're one step worse. If you become skilled at a task that you have an inability with, they cancel out. Remember that characters are defined as much by what they're not good at as by what they are good at.

Descriptors also offer a few brief suggestions of how your character got involved with the rest of the group on their first adventure. You can use these, or not, as you wish.

You can pick any descriptor you wish regardless of whether you're a paradox, spinner, or vector.

DESCRIPTORS

Appealing
Brash
Clever
Fast
Graceful
Intelligent
Lucky
Sharp-Eyed
Skeptical
Stealthy
Strange
Strong
Tough

APPEALING

You're attractive to others, but perhaps more important, you are likeable and charismatic. You've got that "special something" that draws others to you. You often know just the right thing to say to make someone laugh, put them at ease, or spur them to action. People like you, want to help you, and want to be your friend.

You gain the following characteristics:

Charismatic: +2 to your Intellect Pool.

Skill: You are trained in pleasant social interactions.

Resistant to Charms: You're aware of how others can manipulate and charm people, and you notice when those tactics are used on you. Because of this awareness, you are trained in resisting any kind of persuasion or seduction if you wish it.

Initial Link to the Starting Adventure: From the following list of options, choose how you became involved in the first adventure.

1. You met a total stranger (one of the other PCs) and charmed him so much that he invited you to come along.
2. The PCs were looking for someone else, but you convinced them that you were the perfect person to join them instead.
3. Pure happenstance—because you just go along with the flow of things and everything usually works out well.
4. Your charismatic ways helped get one of the PCs out of a difficult spot a long time ago, and she always asks you to join her on new adventures.

Intellect Pool, page 16

BRASH

You're a self-assertive sort, confident in your abilities, energetic, and perhaps a bit irreverent toward ideas that you don't agree with. Some people call you bold and brave, but those you've put in their place might call you puffed up and arrogant. Whatever. It's not in your nature to care what other people think about you, unless those people are your friends or family. Even someone as brash as you knows that friends sometimes have to come first.

You gain the following characteristics:

Speed Pool, page 16

Initiative, page 104

Energetic: +2 to your Speed Pool.

Skill: You are trained in initiative.

Bold: You are trained in all actions that involve overcoming or ignoring the effects of fear or intimidation.

Initial Link to the Starting Adventure: From the following list of options, choose how you became involved in the first adventure.

1. You noticed something weird going on, and without much thought, you jumped in with both feet.
2. You showed up when and where you did on a dare because, hey, you don't back down from dares.
3. Someone called you out, but instead of walking into a fight, you walked into your current situation.
4. You told your friend that nothing could scare you, and nothing you saw would change your mind. She brought you to your current point.

CLEVER

Defense roll, page 115

You're quick-witted, thinking well on your feet. You understand people, so you can fool them but you are rarely fooled in return. Because you easily see things for what they are, you get the lay of the land swiftly, size up threats and allies, and assess situations with accuracy. Perhaps you're physically attractive, or maybe you use your wit to overcome any physical or mental imperfections.

You gain the following characteristics:

Smart: +2 to your Intellect Pool.

Skill: You're trained in all interactions involving lies or trickery.

Skill: You're trained in defense rolls to resist mental effects.

Skill: You're trained in all tasks involving, identifying, or assessing danger, lies, quality, importance, function, or power.

Inability: You were never good at studying or retaining trivial knowledge. The difficulty of any task involving lore, knowledge, or understanding is increased by one step.

Additional Equipment: You see through the schemes of others and occasionally convince them to believe you—even when, perhaps, they should not. Thanks to your clever behavior, you always start out with an additional $200 (or the local equivalent) whenever you appear in a new recursion for the first time.

Initial Link to the Starting Adventure: From the following list of options, choose how you became involved in the first adventure.

1. You convinced one of the other PCs to tell you what she was doing.
2. From afar, you observed that something interesting was going on.
3. You talked your way into the situation because you thought it might earn you some money.
4. You suspect that the other PCs won't succeed without you.

FAST

You're fleet of foot. Because you're quick, you can accomplish tasks more rapidly than others. You're not just quick on your feet, however—you're quick with your hands, and you think and react quickly. You even talk quickly.

You gain the following characteristics:

Energetic: +2 to your Speed Pool.

Skill: You are trained in running.

Fast: You can move a short distance and still take another action in the same round, or you can move a long distance as your action without needing to make any kind of roll.

Inability: You're a sprinter, not a long-distance runner. You don't have a lot of stamina. The difficulty of any Might defense roll is increased by one step.

Initial Link to the Starting Adventure: From the following list of options, choose how you became involved in the first adventure.

1. You jumped in to save one of the other PCs who was in dire need.
2. One of the other PCs recruited you for your unique talents.
3. You're impulsive, and it seemed like a good idea at the time.
4. This mission ties in with a personal goal of your own.

GRACEFUL

You have a perfect sense of balance, moving and speaking with grace and beauty. You're quick, lithe, flexible, and dexterous. Your body

is perfectly suited to dance, and you use that advantage in combat to dodge blows. You might wear garments that enhance your agile movement and sense of style.

You gain the following characteristics:

Agile: +2 to your Speed Pool.

Skill: You're trained in all tasks involving balance and careful movement.

Skill: You're trained in all tasks involving physical performing arts.

Skill: You're trained in all Speed defense tasks.

Initial Link to the Starting Adventure: From the following list of options, choose how you became involved in the first adventure.

1. Against your better judgment, you joined the other PCs because you saw that they were in danger.
2. One of the other PCs convinced you that joining the group would be a good idea.
3. Your quick reflexes saved one of the other PCs from a precarious situation, and they invited you along to say thank you.
4. A reward was offered, and you need the money.

INTELLIGENT

You're quite smart. Your memory is sharp, and you easily grasp difficult concepts. This aptitude doesn't mean that you've had years of formal education, but you have learned a great deal in your life, primarily because you pick things up quickly and retain so much.

You gain the following characteristics:

Smart: +2 to your Intellect Pool.

Skill: You're trained in an area of knowledge of your choice.

Skill: You're trained in all actions that involve remembering or memorizing things you experience directly. For example, instead of being good at recalling details of geography that you read about in a book, you can remember a path through a set of tunnels that you've explored before.

Initial Link to the Starting Adventure: From the following list of options, choose how you became involved in the first adventure.

1. One of the other PCs asked your opinion of the mission, knowing that if you thought it was a good idea, it probably was.
2. You saw value in what the other PCs were doing.

Speed defense, page 115

3. You believed that the task might lead to important and interesting discoveries.
4. A colleague requested that you take part in the mission as a favor.

LUCKY

You rely on chance and timely good luck to get you through many situations. When people say that someone was born under a lucky star, they mean you. When you try your hand at something new, no matter how unfamiliar the task is, as often as not you find a measure of success. Even when disaster strikes, it's rarely as bad as it could be. More often, small things seem to go your way, you win contests, and you're often in the right place at the right time.

You gain the following characteristics:

Luck Pool: You have one additional Pool called Luck that begins with 3 points, and it has a maximum value of 3 points. When spending points from any other Pool, you can take one, some, or all the points from your Luck Pool first. When you make a recovery roll, your Luck Pool is one additional Pool to which you can add recovered points. When your Luck Pool is at 0 points, it does not count against your damage track. Enabler.

Damage track, page 108

Advantage: When you use 1 XP to reroll a d20 for any roll that affects only you, add +3 to the reroll.

Initial Link to the Starting Adventure: From the following list of options, choose how you became involved in the first adventure.

1. Knowing that lucky people notice and take active advantage of opportunities, you became involved in your first adventure by choice.
2. You literally bumped into someone else on this adventure through sheer luck.
3. You found a briefcase lying alongside the road. It was battered, but inside you found a lot of strange documents that led you here.
4. Your luck saved you when you avoided a speeding car by a fortuitous fall through an open manhole. Beneath the street, you found something you couldn't ignore.

"Ernt a-seen you 'round her afore... And 'at don 'appen murch." ~Unnamed Innsmouth native

SHARP-EYED

You're perceptive and well aware of your surroundings. You notice the little details and remember them. You can be difficult to surprise.

You gain the following characteristics:

Skill: You're trained in initiative actions.

Skill: You're trained in perception actions.

Find the Flaw: If an opponent has a straightforward weakness (takes extra damage from fire, can't see out of his left eye, and so on), the GM will tell you what it is.

Initial Link to the Starting Adventure: From the following list of options, choose how you became involved in the first adventure.

1. You heard about what was going on, saw a flaw in the other PCs' plan, and joined up to help them out.
2. You noticed that the PCs have a foe (or at least, a tail) they weren't aware of.
3. You saw that the other PCs were up to something interesting and got involved.
4. You've been noticing some strange things going on, and this all appears related.

SKEPTICAL

You possess a questioning attitude regarding claims that are often taken for granted by others. You're not necessarily a "doubting Thomas" (a skeptic who refuses to believe anything without direct personal experience), but you've often benefited from questioning the statements, opinions, and received knowledge presented to you by others.

You gain the following characteristics:

Insightful: +2 to your Intellect Pool.

Skill: You're trained in identifying.

Skill: You're trained in all actions that involve seeing through a trick, illusion, rhetorical ruse designed to evade the issue, or lie. For example, you're better at keeping your eye on the cup containing the hidden ball, sensing an illusion, or realizing if someone is lying to you (but only if you specifically concentrate and use this skill).

Initial Link to the Starting Adventure: From the following list of options, choose how you became involved in the first adventure.

1. You overheard other PCs holding forth on a topic with an opinion you were quite skeptical about, so you decided to approach the group and ask for proof.
2. You were following one of the other PCs because you were suspicious of him, which brought you into the action.
3. Your theory about the nonexistence of the supernatural can be invalidated only by your own senses, so you came along.
4. You need money to fund your research.

STEALTHY

You're sneaky, slippery, and cautious. These talents help you hide, move quietly, and pull off tricks that require sleight of hand. Most likely, you're wiry and small. However, you're not much of a sprinter—you're more dexterous than fleet of foot.

You gain the following characteristics:

Quick: +2 to your Speed Pool.

Skill: You're trained in all stealth tasks.

Skill: You're trained in all interactions involving lies or trickery.

Skill: You're trained in all special abilities involving illusions or trickery.

Inability: You're sneaky but not fast. The difficulty of all movement-related tasks is one step higher for you.

Initial Link to the Starting Adventure: From the following list of options, choose how you became involved in the first adventure.

1. You attempted to steal from one of the other PCs. That character caught you and forced you to come along with him.
2. You were tailing one of the other PCs for reasons of your own, which brought you into the action.
3. An employer secretly paid you to get involved.
4. You overheard the other PCs talking about a topic that interested you, so you decided to approach the group.

STRANGE

People are strange, but none more than you. You never quite fit in, so places that should have been familiar were strange, and people who you should have known were strangers. For all you know, everyone else thought the same of you. Sometimes even perfectly paved streets seemed uneven when you felt particularly out of place. But all that changed when you learned the truth: the Strange exists, and you are Strange.

You gain the following characteristics:

Versatile: +2 to your Intellect Pool, +1 to your Speed Pool.

Skill: You're trained in all actions that involve recognizing and understanding the Strange, its effects, and its denizens, including identifying translated visitors from alternate recursions, as well as identifying and understanding cyphers.

Alternatively, you're trained in either fractal surfing or Chaosphere navigation. Whichever skill you choose, it grants you a –1 buffer against positive factors of alienation for being exposed to the Strange.

Sense Something Strange: You can sense whether creatures of an alternative recursion, creatures of the Strange, Strange cyphers, or other related phenomena are active in situations where their presence is not obvious. You must study an object or location closely for a minute to get a feel for the situation.

Inability: Because you often seem as strange to others as they do to you, people have a harder time interacting with you, sometimes to the point where they can't recall your name. The difficulty of any task involving charm, persuasion, etiquette, or deception is increased by one step.

Initial Link to the Starting Adventure: From the following list of options, choose how you became involved in the first adventure.

1. A dream guided you to this point.
2. You need money to fund your studies.
3. You believed the mission would be a great way to learn more about the Strange.
4. A creature from another recursion came through an inapposite gate. Before it died, it told you where you could learn more.

Fractal surfing, page 215
Chaosphere navigation, page 215
Alienation, page 216

"I hate translating to Earth. The people there are so smug in their assurance that they know the reality of their world, and in fact they know nothing. They all make me sick." ~Ruk infiltrator Eth-kati

STRONG

You're extremely strong and physically powerful, and you use these qualities well, whether through violence or feats of prowess. You likely have a brawny build and impressive muscles.

You gain the following characteristics:

Very Powerful: +4 to your Might Pool.

Skill: You're trained in all actions involving breaking inanimate objects.

Skill: You're trained in all jumping actions.

Additional Equipment: You have an extra medium or heavy melee weapon.

Initial Link to the Starting Adventure: From the following list of options, choose how you became involved in the first adventure.

1. One of the other PCs was kind to you in the past, and to thank her, you offered to watch her back.
2. One of the other PCs convinced you that joining the group would be in your best interest.
3. You lost a bet and had to take someone's place on this mission.
4. The PCs recruited you after learning about your physical abilities.

TOUGH

You're strong and can take a lot of physical punishment. You might have a large frame and a square jaw. Tough characters frequently have visible scars.

You gain the following characteristics:

Resilient: +1 to Armor.

Healthy: Add 1 to the points you regain when you make a recovery roll.

Skill: You're trained in Might defense actions.

Additional Equipment: You gain an extra light weapon whenever you translate to a different recursion.

Initial Link to the Starting Adventure: From the following list of options, choose how you became involved in the first adventure.

1. You're acting as a bodyguard for one of the other PCs.
2. One of the PCs is your sibling, and you came along to watch out for him.
3. You need money because your family is in debt.
4. You stepped in to defend one of the PCs when that character was threatened. While talking to her afterward, you heard about the group's task.

CHAPTER 6

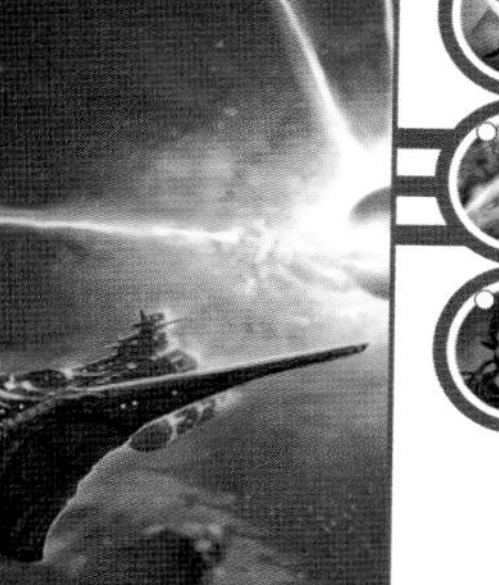

CHARACTER FOCUS

Your focus makes your character unique. No two PCs in a group should have the same focus. Your focus gives you benefits when you create your character and each time you ascend to the next tier. It's the verb of the sentence "I am an *adjective noun* who *verbs*."

When you choose a character focus, you get a special connection to one or more of your fellow PCs, a first-tier ability, and perhaps additional starting equipment. A few foci offer slight alterations of talents used by paradoxes, spinners, and vectors. Each focus also offers suggestions to the GM and the player for possible effects or consequences of really good or really bad die rolls.

As you progress to a new tier, your active focus grants you more abilities. Each tier's benefit is usually labeled Action or Enabler. If an ability is labeled Action, you must take an action to use it. If an ability is labeled Enabler, it makes other actions better or gives some other benefit, but it's not an action. An ability that allows you to rain fire down on foes is an action. An ability that grants you additional damage when you make attacks is an enabler. You can use an enabler in the same turn as you perform another action.

Each tier's benefits are independent of and cumulative with benefits from other tiers (unless indicated otherwise). So if your first-tier ability grants you +1 to Armor and your fourth-tier ability also grants you +1 to Armor, when you reach fourth tier, you have a total of +2 to Armor.

ABIDES IN STONE

Your manifestation in Ardeyn is that of something made, not something born: You are a golem. Your stone body, carved to resemble a humanoid, is nonetheless more akin to statue than flesh. Unlike a statue, you can move, speak, and feel pain. Your rock body means that it takes a lot to damage you, but once

Abides in Stone GM Intrusions: *Creatures of stone sometimes forget their own strength or weight. A walking statue can terrify common folk.*

FOCI TABLE

Ardeyn
Abides in Stone
Carries a Quiver
Channels Sinfire
Embraces Qephilim Ancestry
Lives in the Wilderness
Practices Soul Sorcery
Shepherds the Dead
Slays Dragons
Wields Two Weapons at Once (D)
Works Miracles

Earth
Conducts Weird Science
Entertains (D)
Is Licensed to Carry
Leads (D)
Looks for Trouble (D)
Operates Undercover (D)
Solves Mysteries (D)
Works the System

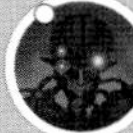

Ruk
Adapts to Any Environment (D)
Infiltrates
Integrates Weaponry
Metamorphosizes
Processes Information
Regenerates Tissue
Spawns

Special
Translates (D)

(D) denotes a draggable focus

Solves Mysteries, page 78
Earth, page 147
Shepherds the Dead, page 76
Ardeyn, page 160

CHANGING FOCUS AFTER TRANSLATION

Your focus can change when you move between Earth and a recursion, or between recursions, through the process of translation. The upshot is that if your focus is Solves Mysteries on Earth, it might be Shepherds the Dead in Ardeyn. (Your equipment and perhaps your race and background also change, but your descriptor and type do not.)

Abides in Stone, page 51
Embraces Qephilim Ancestry, page 59

YOUR NEW LOOK AND DRESS

Every time you translate to a new recursion, your appearance, equipment, and focus could change. Each focus indicates your new equipment, and it provides guidance on what you might be dressed like. Unless you specifically choose a focus that changes your physical appearance all the time (like Abides in Stone or Embraces Qephilim Ancestry), your character might look physically very much the same regardless of which recursion you translate to. In fact, unless you specifically tell your GM that you're going for a new physical look, a different gender, or even a different race (among those available within a particular recursion), the GM and every other player should assume that your underlying physical appearance remains the same.

For example, your character—a muscular athlete with dark hair and a narrow face wearing a leather jacket and shooting a pistol on Earth—might be a muscular knight with dark hair and a narrow face wearing chainmail wielding a sword in Ardeyn. You look like the same person, but the context is different.

When you translate into a recursion and choose a new focus, you gain and can immediately use every tier power offered up to your character's tier.

Leads, page 65
Ruk, page 190
Infiltrates, page 62

DRAGGABLE FOCI

Some foci are draggable. This means that if you start with a focus in its proper context, you can keep it when you translate to another world. You're "dragging" your focus with you. If you have a draggable focus but decide to change your focus when you translate, you cannot regain the draggable focus again unless you return to the original world to which it is tied. From there, you can drag it again if you wish. Thus, if you start on Earth with the Leads focus, you can keep it if you wish, dragging it with you to Ardeyn. If, however, you then translate to Ruk and choose not to drag it with you, opting to pick another focus, such as Infiltrates, you can't regain Leads until you return to Earth. In short, a draggable focus must actually be "dragged" from one recursion to the next. This process could allow you to have a different focus on the same recursion for different visits, and that's acceptable.

When you drag a focus, your equipment recontextualizes as best as possible. You likely choose new weapons and armor appropriate to the recursion, and other gear is replaced with similar items if possible (the GM and player should work together to determine the specifics). Equipment suggestions for draggable foci are provided as appropriate in the margin.

Translates (focus), page 80

Draggable foci are marked with a (D) in the table. Note that the Translates focus is special. You cannot start with this focus, but you can adopt it after any translation you undertake, and since it is draggable, you can keep it after your next translation. Unlike other draggable foci, you can regain Translates after translating to any new recursion.

Entertains, page 61

At the GM's discretion, players can choose to give their character a draggable focus in a world other than the one the focus is normally associated with. For example, you might want to start an Ardeyn character with an Entertains focus or a Ruk character who Solves Mysteries. Other than starting equipment, there shouldn't be much trouble quickly adapting a draggable focus to originate in any recursion.

damaged, your wounds are not quite as easy to recover from.

As someone made of animate stone, you typically do not wear clothing, although your stone skin is usually carved to appear as if you're wearing it. Such carved clothing could be elaborate armor, robes, or stylistic ridges and ripples.

Golems are most often vectors, but a stone paradox or spinner is a dangerous combination.

Connection: If this is your starting focus, choose one of the following connections.

1. Pick one other PC. She roused you from a long period of inactivity, and you feel indebted to her for returning you (perhaps accidentally) to mobility.
2. Pick one other PC. You were once convinced that he wanted to reduce you to rubble, but you have since grown to think that what you believed wasn't true, or at least no longer is so.
3. Pick one other PC. She knows the secret of your origin, but whenever she speaks of it, you forget it. Perhaps you suffer from a curse?
4. Pick one other PC. If you go berserk, you'll never attack that character.

Equipment: A pouch, a chisel and hammer, one weapon of your choice, and 200 crowns.

Minor Effect Suggestion: You step on the target, and your immense weight prevents it from moving on its next turn.

Major Effect Suggestion: You break a weapon, shield, or piece of armor the target was using.

Tier 1: Golem Body. Your stone body was carved to resemble either a human or qephilim wearing elaborate (though much eroded) clothing from the Age of Myth. You gain +1 to Armor, +5 to your Might Pool, and +1 to your Might Edge. You do not need to eat, drink, or breathe (though you do need rest and sleep). You move more stiffly than a creature of flesh, which means you can never be trained or specialized in Speed defense rolls.

Furthermore, you are practiced in using your stone fists as a medium weapon. Enabler.

Golem Healing. Sorcery is what animates you and gives you your own kind of life. While that sorcery allows you to be healed in a fashion similar to that of living flesh, your stone form is more difficult to repair than flesh: You are unable to use the first, single-action recovery roll of the day that other PCs have access to. That means your first recovery roll on any given day requires ten minutes of rest, the second requires an hour of rest, and the third requires ten hours. Enabler.

Tier 2: Golem Grip (3 Might points). Your attack with your stone fists is modified by one step in your favor. If you hit, you can grab the target, preventing it from moving on its next turn. Attacks or any attempts to break free made by a grabbed target are modified by one step to the target's detriment while you hold it. The target could use its action to attempt to break free of your grip instead of attacking, which requires you to make a Might-based roll to maintain your grip. If the target doesn't break free under its own power, you can continue to hold it each round as your subsequent actions, automatically inflicting 4 points of damage each round by squeezing. Enabler.

Tier 3: Trained Basher. You are trained in using your stone fists as medium weapons. Enabler.

Golem Stomp (4 Might points). You stomp on the ground with all of your strength, creating a shock wave that attacks all creatures in immediate

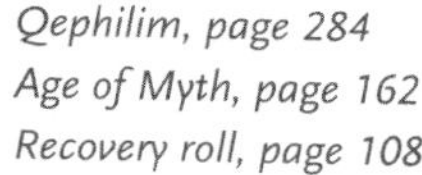
Qephilim, page 284
Age of Myth, page 162
Recovery roll, page 108

range. Affected creatures take 3 points of damage and are either pushed out of immediate range or fall down (your choice). Action.

Tier 4: Deep Reserves. Once each day, you can transfer up to 5 points among your Pools in any combination, at a rate of 1 point per round. For example, you could transfer 3 points of Might to Speed and 2 points of Intellect to Speed, which would take a total of five rounds. Action.

Tier 5. Specialized Basher. You are specialized in using your stone fists as medium weapons. Enabler.

Still as a Statue (5 Might points). You freeze in place, drawing your sorcerous energies deep into your stone core. During this time, you lose all mobility as well as the ability to take physical actions. You cannot sense what's happening around you, and no time seems to pass for you. While Still as a Statue, you gain a +10 bonus to Armor against damage of all sorts. Under normal circumstances, you automatically rouse to normal wakefulness and mobility a day later. If an ally you trust shakes you hard enough (with a minimum cost of 2 Might points), you rouse earlier. Action to initiate.

Tier 6: Ultra Enhancement. You gain +1 to Armor and +5 to each of your three stat Pools. Enabler.

Adapts to Any Environment Equipment:
Ardeyn: *Ardeyn clothing, light armor, one weapon of your choice, lockpicks, matches (10), torches (2), a fish knife, a signal horn, and 50 crowns.*
Earth: *Street clothing, leather jacket, sunglasses, a laptop, a smartphone, and $1,000.*

ADAPTS TO ANY ENVIRONMENT

Adapts to Any Environment GM Intrusions: Adaptations fail. Weird side effects can linger.

Rukians have interacted with the Strange for far longer than anyone on Earth or Ardeyn. Far longer. They know about the importance of context when it comes to translating from one recursion to the next. And now you know how to harness that concept to give yourself an advantage anywhere you go. By using the concepts of recursion, you allow your body to thrive in all manner of hostile environments. You are the ultimate survivalist.

You probably don loose, comfortable clothing that breathes in hot weather but keeps you warm when it's cold. Muted in color, it blends into most environments.

Adaptors travel, and they do so fearlessly. They look any threat in the eye (metaphorically or not) and know that it cannot hurt them. They are explorers, adventurers, spies, thieves, warriors, rescuers, and protectors. They can be any character type.

Connection: If this is your starting focus, choose one of the following connections.

1. Pick one other PC. If that character is next to you and takes no action other than to remain next to you, he shares your adaptive qualities.
2. Pick one other PC. You fear that character is jealous of your abilities, and you know that jealousy can lead to problems.
3. Pick one other PC. She has something in her possession that you want. How you attempt to get it is up to you.
4. Pick one other PC. Out of the blue, that character recently paid you a compliment and was very nice to you. What you make of that and how you handle it is up to you.

Equipment: Ruk clothing, light armor, one weapon of your choice, a bag of light tools, a breather, an umbilical, and an account with 50 bits.

Minor Effect Suggestion: You recover 2 points to one of your Pools.

Major Effect Suggestion: You recover 6 points to one of your Pools.

Tier 1: Defend. You gain +1 to Armor against all attacks—even mental ones, and even if they specifically state that they ignore Armor. Enabler.

Heal. You add 1 to all recovery rolls you make. Enabler.

Tier 2: Breathe (2 Might points). You can breathe safely in any (or no) atmosphere or in any substance for one hour. Enabler.

Tier 3: Move (3 Speed points). For one hour, you can move without hindrance through any type of terrain that isn't a solid barrier. Enabler.

Tier 4: Restore. Your normal ten-minute and one-hour recovery roll periods are now one action. Your normal ten-hour recovery roll period is now one hour. You need only one hour of sleep per day to function. Enabler.

Tier 5: Resist. You have a special +10 to Armor against any kind of environmental damage. This doesn't include direct attacks, but it does include ambient damage and damage from "passive" sources. For example, you are—at least in part—protected from the damage of a raging fire, falls from a great height, crushing water pressure, acidic mist, and so forth. Enabler.

Tier 6: Survive. You gain an additional +1 to Armor against all attacks, even if they specifically state that they ignore Armor. You also gain 3 points to add to each of your three stat Pools. Enabler.

Subsist. You do not need to eat, drink, or breathe to live, although if you go past the normal bounds of your body in this regard, the difficulty of all tasks is increased by two steps until you can eat, drink, and breathe normally. Enabler.

CARRIES A QUIVER

In Ardeyn, the longbow and the crossbow are the ranged weapons of choice for most warriors, human or qephilim. The archer is a skilled combatant, deadly in any fight. With a keen eye and quick reflexes, you can eliminate foes at range before they reach you. A good archer also learns to make arrows and bows.

You probably wear no more than light armor so you can move quickly when needed.

Many archers are vectors. You can use this focus with crossbows instead of bows if you wish.

Connection: If this is your starting focus, choose one of the following connections.

1. Pick one other PC to be the true friend who gave you the excellent bow that you currently use.
2. Pick two PCs (preferably ones who are likely to get in the way of your attacks). When you miss with a bow and the GM rules that you struck someone other than your target, you hit one of these two characters.
3. Pick one other PC. You've seen her admiring your archery skills many times. Perhaps she would like a lesson? (You won't know until you ask.)
4. Pick one other PC. When he helps with your fletching or bowery, the time taken is halved.

Equipment: Ardeyn clothing, light armor, a well-made bow, two dozen arrows, another weapon of your choice, an explorer's pack, tools for fletching, and 400 crowns.

Minor Effect Suggestion: Hit in a tendon or muscle, the target takes 2 points of Speed damage as well as normal damage.

Major Effect Suggestion: The target is pinned in place with an arrow.

Tier 1: Archer. To be truly deadly with a bow, you must know where to aim. You can spend points from either your Speed Pool or your Intellect Pool to apply levels of Effort to increase your bow damage. Each level of Effort adds 3 points of damage to a successful attack. Enabler.

Fletcher: You are trained in making arrows. Enabler.

Tier 2: Covering Fire (2 Speed points). In a round where you attack with your bow, if you fire an additional arrow, the difficulty of attacks used by the target is increased by one step. Enabler.

Tier 3: Trained Archer. You are trained in using bows. Enabler.

Master Fletcher. You are specialized in making arrows. Enabler.

Tier 4: Quick Shot. If you roll a natural 17 or higher with a bow attack, instead of adding damage or a minor or major effect, you can make another attack with your bow. This attack reuses the same Effort and bonuses (if any) from the first attack. Enabler.

Master Bowyer. You are specialized in making bows. Enabler.

Tier 5: Phenomenal Archer. You are specialized in using bows. Enabler.

Tier 6: Powerful Shot (2 Might points). You inflict 3 additional points of damage with a bow. The Might points spent to use this ability are in addition to any Speed points spent on the attack. Enabler.

CHANNELS SINFIRE

Lotan's fire burns with the sin of a fallen god. Fire burns flesh, and sin burns the mind. Thus by the Maker's will, Lotan's fire is contained at Ardeyn's core, so it does not sicken any except those who make the forbidden journey to look upon it.

You, however, were among the few who could sense the sinfire burning within the core. You understood its potential as a weapon, dared the screaming nightmares that afflicted you, and finally allowed the sinfire to pass through you

Remember that a focus that gives a "permanent" bonus to a Pool or Edge, or that provides some other big change to a character, is only permanent as long as that focus is active in an appropriate recursion. If the character translates into a different recursion and doesn't drag the focus, the bonus disappears.

Carries a Quiver GM Intrusions: *Arrows strike the wrong targets. Bowstrings snap.*

Each time you return to a recursion, your GM might offer you the choice of picking a focus that's different from one you had last time you visited.

Channels Sinfire GM Intrusions: *Some see such power as being demonic. Sometimes the sins of others can be surprising or even overwhelming.*

Seven Rules of Ardeyn, page 162

Night Vault, page 183

For more on Lotan, the Maker, and the sins of Ardeyn, see Chapter 12: Ardeyn, page 160.

SINS IN ARDEYN

The act of betraying the Seven Rules of Ardeyn is considered a sin. When the spirit of a dead creature is drawn to the Night Vault, the weight of sin upon it determines its fate in that dreary realm. The list below has the Seven Rules of Ardeyn, in brief, and provides some examples of the acts against those rules that are considered sins.

THE SEVEN RULES OF ARDEYN

COMMERCE. Accumulation of obscene levels of wealth in the face of poverty
DEATH. Murder
DESIRE. Give a Stranger or Lotanist access to Ardeyn (usually because of lust or greed)
LAW. Theft of another's livelihood
LORE. Lies meant to harm another
SILENCE. Failure to aid another when it is within your power to help
WAR. Cowardice that betrays a trust

without burning you—without burning much of you, anyhow. Because of the fire you wield, you eventually learned to sense the sins of others, which is why you are sometimes called a sinfire inquisitor.

You probably wear red and black, or perhaps orange and red. Runes that depict accusation and punishment are stitched into the hem of your coat or robes.

Although most sinfire inquisitors are paradoxes, sinfire-wielding spinners and vectors are quite fearsome.

Connection: If this is your starting focus, choose one of the following connections.

1. Pick one other PC. He knows of a sin you committed in your youth (not on the order of murder, but more like negligence that led to a bad outcome).
2. Pick one other PC. You know but haven't yet revealed a piece of knowledge that bears on her past. She doesn't know you know.
3. Pick one other PC. For some reason you can't discern, he is completely immune to all of your abilities related to sinfire.
4. Pick one other PC. You feel strangely protective toward that character and don't want to see her come to harm.

Equipment: Ardeyn clothing, light or medium armor, one weapon of your choice, an explorer's pack, a candle and 10 matchsticks, and 300 crowns.

Minor Effect Suggestion: A transgression the target committed against someone or something it values flashes before its eyes, which dazes it for one round, during which time the difficulty of all tasks it performs is modified by one step to its detriment.

Major Effect Suggestion: Make an immediate Sinfire Touch attack against the target as part of your turn, even if the target is up to long range away from you.

Tier 1: Sinfire Touch (1 Intellect point). Your hands burst into flame. If you touch a creature, you can choose to either inflict 3 points of damage from heat or inflict 1 point of Intellect damage that ignores Armor.

Alternatively, you can use this ability on a weapon. If you imbue a weapon with sinfire, that weapon inflicts 1 additional point of fire damage for ten minutes. Action for touch or to imbue; enabler for weapon.

Tier 2: Discern the Sins (2 Intellect points). You can sense a significant baleful act that a creature within short range has committed during its life—if it has committed any. To do so, you must be able to see your target and spend an action concentrating on it. If the target has committed something the GM decides is a sin, you sense the possibility, though not the specific sin or sins.

For the next minute, you can use your Sinfire Touch attack on that target at long range, even if you can't see the target (though you do have to know the target is in range). If an attack you make deals damage, you also learn the nature of one of the sins committed by the target. Action to initiate.

Tier 3: Sinfire Blast (3+ Intellect points). You unleash a conflagration of sinfire, burning up to three targets within short range (make an Intellect roll against each target). This burst inflicts either (your choice) 5 points of fire damage or 3 points of Intellect damage (the latter ignores Armor). For each 2 additional Intellect points you spend, you can make an Intellect attack roll against an additional target. Action.

Tier 4: Resist Temptation. When you defend against attacks and effects that would compel you to act in a way you'd prefer not to, the difficulty is modified by two steps to your benefit. Enabler.

Tier 5: Certain Punishment. When making an attack with sinfire, once per minute you can reroll any attack roll you wish and take the better of the two results. Enabler.

Tier 6: No Forgiveness. When making a sinfire attack that deals heat damage, you deal 2 additional points of damage. When making a sinfire attack that deals Intellect damage and ignores Armor, you deal 1 additional point of damage. When you imbue a weapon with sinfire, it gains the same bonus to damage (including the option to deal Intellect damage). Enabler.

CONDUCTS WEIRD SCIENCE

You could be a respected scientist, having been published in several peer-reviewed journals. Or you might be considered a crank by your contemporaries, pursuing fringe theories on what others consider to be scant evidence. Truth is, you have a particular gift for sifting the edges of what's possible. You can find new insights and unlock odd phenomena with your experiments. Where others see a crackpot cornucopia, you sift the conspiracy theories for revelation. Whether you conduct your enquiries as a government contractor, a university researcher, a corporate scientist, or an indulger of curiosity in your own garage lab following your muse, you push the boundaries of what's possible.

You probably care more about your work than trivialities such as your appearance, polite or proper behavior, or social norms, but then again, an eccentric like you might turn the tables on that stereotype too.

Paradoxes make the most obvious mad scientists.

Equipment: Street clothes, science field kit, light tools, a pen knife, a smartphone, and $2,000.

Connection: If this is your starting focus, choose one of the following connections.

1. Pick one other PC. The character believes

Conducts Weird Science GM Intrusions: *Creations get out of control. Side effects cannot always be predicted. Weird science terrifies people and can draw the media. When a device created or modified by weird science is depleted, it detonates.*

As someone who Conducts Weird Science, a PC on Earth could be given the "mad scientist" label by the media if news of her exploits becomes public. Whether she conducts her science ethically or in disregard for the safety of others (or whether she really is insane) is the only true measure of how "mad" she is.

your experiments once cured someone close to her of a fatal condition. You're not sure if you did, or if the condition just went into remission.

2. Pick one other PC. You created a scientific instrument designed to give this character a restful night's sleep, but you now fear unanticipated long-term side effects.
3. Pick one other PC. You're pretty sure that one of your experiments when you were younger and brasher is responsible for giving him a connection to the Strange. The PC might know this, or he might just vaguely remember you from long ago.
4. Pick one other PC. She asked you to design a gun that could shoot through walls. You took the cash, but you are still working on the prototype.

Minor Effect Suggestion: You learn one additional piece of information in your analysis.

Major Effect Suggestion: Foes within sight are dazed for one round upon seeing your strange creation or its results. During this time, the difficulty of all tasks they perform is modified by one step to their detriment.

Tier 1: Lab Analysis (3 Intellect points). You analyze the scene of a crime, the site of a mysterious incident, or a series unexplained phenomena, and you maybe learn a surprising amount of information about the perpetrators, the participants, or force(s) responsible. To do so, you must collect samples from the scene. Samples are paint or wood scrapings, dirt, photographs of the area, hair, an entire corpse, and so on. With samples in hand, you can discover up to three pertinent pieces of information about the scene, possibly clearing up a lesser mystery, and pointing the way to solving a greater one. The GM will decide what you learn and what the level of difficulty might be to learn it. (For comparison, discovering that a victim was killed not by a fall, as seems immediately obvious, but rather by electrocution, is a difficulty 3 task for you.) The difficulty of the task is modified by one step in your favor if you take the time to transport the samples to a permanent lab (if you have access to one), as opposed to conducting the analysis with your field science kit. Action to initiate, 2d20 minutes to complete.

Scientist: You are trained in one area of scientific knowledge of your choice.

Tier 2: Modify Device (4 Intellect points). You jury-rig a piece of mechanical or electrical equipment to make it function above its rated specs for a very limited time. To do so, you must use 1d6 × 100 dollars in spare parts, have a field science kit (or a permanent lab, if you have access to one), and succeed at a difficulty 3 Intellect-based task. When complete, using the device modifies all tasks performed in conjunction with the device by one step in the user's favor, until the device inevitably breaks. For example, you could overclock a computer so research tasks using it are easier, modify an espresso maker so that each cup of coffee made with it is better, modify a car's engine so that it goes faster (or its steering, so it handles better), and so on. Each use of the modified device requires a depletion roll of 1–5 on a d20. Action to initiate, one hour to complete.

Tier 3: Better Living Through Chemistry (4 Intellect points). You've developed drug cocktails specifically designed to work with your own biochemistry. Depending on which one you inject, it makes you smarter, faster, or tougher, but when it wears off, the crash is a doozy, so you use it only in desperate situations. You gain 2 to your Might Edge, Speed Edge, or Intellect Edge for one minute, after which you can't gain the benefit again for one hour. During this follow-up hour, every time you spend points from a Pool, increase the cost by 1. Action.

Tier 4: Extensive Training. You are specialized in one area of knowledge of your choice. Enabler.

Just a Bit Mad. You are trained in Intellect defense rolls. Enabler.

Tier 5: Weird Science Breakthrough (5 Intellect points). Your research leads to a breakthrough, and you capture a fragment of the Strange within an item, imbuing it with a truly amazing property, though you can use the item only once. To do so, you must use 1d6 × 100 dollars in spare parts, have a field science kit (or a permanent lab, if you have access to one), and succeed at a difficulty 4 Intellect-based roll to create a random cypher of up to level 2. The GM decides the nature of the cypher you create. Attempting to create a specified cypher increases the difficulty by two steps. Creating a cypher does not allow you to surpass your normal cypher limit. Action to initiate, one hour to complete.

Tier 6: Incredible Feat of Science (12 Intellect points). You do something amazing in the

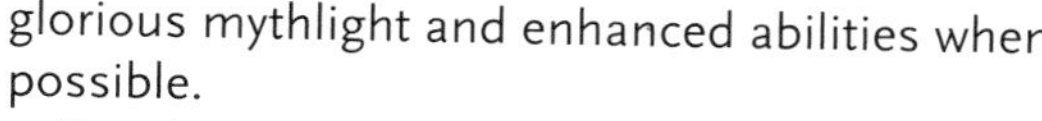

lab. This takes a full day of work (or longer, depending on the circumstances) and 1d6 × 10,000 dollars in parts and materials. Possible incredible feats include:

- Reanimate and command a dead body for one hour.
- Create an engine that runs on perpetual motion.
- Create an inapposite gate that remains open for one minute.
- Transmute one substance into another substance.
- Cure one person with an incurable disease or condition.
- Create a weapon designed to hurt something that can't otherwise be hurt.
- Create a defense designed to protect against something that can't otherwise be stopped.

Improved Weird Science Breakthrough. When you successfully use Weird Science Breakthrough, you can create a cypher of up to level 6. Enabler.

EMBRACES QEPHILIM ANCESTRY

You are a qephilim, which means your ancestors were servitors of the Incarnations. During the Age of Myth, qephilim were semi-divine in their own right, and builders of the first civilizations in Ardeyn. The ancient qephilim thrived for thousands of years before Lotan shrugged, toppling most of those ancient empires and birthing humans that some saw as a curse. Later, when War betrayed the Maker and the Incarnations went away, so too did the semi-divine nature of the qephilim, who became mortal creatures. Because a trace of the old blood remains strong in you, because you've uncovered ancient scrolls regarding qephilim power, or due to a reason you don't yet fully comprehend, that power from days of yore wakes in you once more.

Your ebony skin, elongated jaw, and expressive ears mark you as a qephilim, but your mythlight is brighter and more pure than that of other qephilim, granting you grace obvious to anyone who sees you. Some might attempt to worship you, but others see you as a heretic for impersonating the ancient qephilim. Therefore, you often dim your glorious mythlight and enhanced abilities when possible.

Paradoxes, spinners, and vectors are equally likely to embrace qephilim ancestry.

Connection: If this is your starting focus, choose one of the following connections.

1. Pick one other PC. She thought you were an avatar of a secretly returned Incarnation for a while, but she has since grown to treat you as a peer.
2. Pick one other PC who is a human. You were very suspicious of that character at first, believing that he, as a human, might secretly be a Lotanist. You've since damped your accusations.
3. Pick one other PC. She seems potentially interested in learning the lore of qephilim,

Embraces Qephilim Ancestry GM Intrusions: *Racial prejudices and ancient hatreds can come from surprising corners.*

Qephilim, page 163
Age of Myth, page 162

Mythlight, page 163

and you like to regale her with your tales. It's up to her whether your sense is accurate.

4. Pick one other PC. He knows your true nature, even if no one else does.

Equipment: Ardeyn clothing, armor of your choice, two weapons of your choice (or a weapon and a shield), a relic in the shape of a badge worn by one of the ancient kindred, an explorer's pack, and 400 crowns.

Mythlight Abilities: When you perform moves, revisions, or twists that would normally use force or other energy, they instead use the semi-divine energy of your mythlight. For example, an Exception attack is a confluence of fundamental forces, but when you use it, the effect appears as if manifest from a pulse of your mythlight. This alteration changes nothing other than the type of damage.

Move, page 25
Revision, page 30
Twist, page 38
Exception, page 32

Minor Effect Suggestion: Your mythlight absorbs a tiny charge from your successful action and feeds it back to you. You gain a +1 bonus to similar actions involving the same task (such as attacking the same foe).

Major Effect Suggestion: Your mythlight pulses with divine glory. Make an immediate attack against that foe (using the same stat as the action that caused the major effect). If the attack succeeds, it inflicts 4 points of damage from divine radiance.

Tier 1: Kindred. Choose a kindred from those indicated below. Your kindred indicates the Incarnation your ancestors served and that now manifests in you as a related semi-divine ability.

War: You inflict 1 additional point of damage with weapons. Enabler.

Death (1 Intellect point): You invoke the visage of death. Flesh-decaying energies attempt to wrest the spirit from the flesh of a living creature you can see, inflicting 2 points of damage that ignore Armor. Action.

Ardeyn equipment list, page 89

Commerce: You are trained in interacting (deceiving, intimidating, and persuading), and in tasks related to trade, barter, and bookkeeping. Enabler.

Lore: After spending a day with you, once per day each of your friends can decrease the difficulty of a single task by one step. Enabler.

Silence: In silence, you watch. You are trained in perception tasks, initiative, and stealth. Enabler.

Law (3 Intellect points): By quoting a law that bears on the situation, you prevent a foe that can hear and understand you from attacking anyone or anything for one round. Action.

Desire: During rests, your friends and comrades are so content to be in your company that they add 1 to their recovery rolls. Enabler.

Qephilim Lore. You are trained in all topics related to qephilim. Enabler.

Tier 2: Mythlight Lance (2 Intellect points). You can fashion a lance of divine radiance from your mythlight and hurl it at a target. This is a ranged attack with short range that deals 4 points of damage from divine radiance. Action.

Tier 3: Sentinel (3 Intellect points). A target you select within immediate range is marked with a rune of angelic protection for one minute. You can mark only one such target at a time. If the target would be attacked, make an Intellect-based roll. If successful, the attacker must choose a different target for its attack. Action.

Arbiter (3 Intellect points). A target you select within short range is marked with a rune of angelic abandonment for one minute. You can mark only one such target at a time. During that time, all attacks upon it are modified by one step in the attacker's favor. Action.

Tier 4: Glory of the Divine (3+ Intellect points). Your mythlight pulses with divine radiance, which ignores flesh and directly assails the immortal spirits of up to three targets within short range (make an Intellect roll against each target). This burst inflicts 3 points of Intellect damage that ignore Armor. For each 2 additional Intellect points you spend, you can make an Intellect attack roll against an additional target. If you spend 1 additional Intellect point, all targets who are successfully hit are also blinded for 1 round. Action.

Tier 5: Apportation (4 Intellect points). You call a physical object in Ardeyn to you. You can choose any piece of normal equipment on the Ardeyn equipment list, or (no more than once per day) you can allow the GM to determine the object randomly. If you call a random object, it has a 15% chance of being a cypher or an artifact, a 45% chance of being a piece of Ardeyn equipment, and a 40% chance of being a bit of worthless junk. You can't use this ability to take an item held by another creature. Action.

Tier 6: Flight (4+ Intellect points). You can fly through the air for one hour, during which time your mythlight blazes. For each level of Effort applied, you can affect one additional creature of your size or smaller. You must touch the creature to bestow the power of flight (during which time it is outlined in the gleam of your mythlight). You direct the other creature's movement, and while flying, it must remain within sight of you or fall. In terms of overland movement, a flying creature moves about 20 miles (32 km) per hour and is not affected by terrain. Action to initiate.

ENTERTAINS

You are an entertainer: a singer, dancer, poet, storyteller, or something similar. You perform for the benefit of others. Naturally charismatic and talented, you have also studied to master your art. You know old poems, songs, jokes, and stories, and you're skilled at creating new ones, too.

You probably wear flamboyant or at least fashionable clothes and use cosmetics, tattoos, or hair styling for dramatic effect.

Spinners are the ideal choice for an entertainer, but vectors and paradoxes can be entertainers too, incorporating more physical performance or seemingly magical tricks into their entertainment, respectively.

Connection: If this is your initial focus, choose one of the following connections.

1. Pick one other PC. This character is your worst critic. Your abilities to help or inspire others don't function for her.
2. Pick one other PC. The two of you go way back. You have been friends for a very long time.
3. Pick one other PC. You find this character vastly entertaining (whether they are intentionally entertaining is up to you).
4. Pick one other PC. He is your biggest fan and loves everything you do. It's up to you whether this is flattering or annoying.

Equipment: Clothing, smartphone, some sort of entertainment item (musical instrument, MP3 player, sketchbook and pens, bag of magic tricks, book of jokes or poetry, and so on) and $300.

Minor Effect Suggestion: You enchant the target, who remains enchanted as long as you focus all your attention on keeping it that way.

Major Effect Suggestion: The target is forever favorably disposed toward you.

Entertains GM Intrusions: *Failing to entertain can be worse than not having tried, since you often end up annoying or offending your audience. Musical instruments break, paints dry in their pots, and the words to a poem or song, once forgotten, never return.*

Entertains Equipment:
Ardeyn: *Ardeyn clothing, a signal horn, some sort of entertainment item (musical instrument, parchment and inks for drawing, bag of magic tricks, scroll of jokes or poetry, and so on), and 30 crowns.*
Ruk: *Ruk clothing, umbilical, entertainment graft (which can produce music, speech, pleasant odors, and so on, as the user wills), and an account with 30 bits.*

Infiltrates GM Intrusions: Spies are treated harshly when caught. Their allies disavow them to protect secrets. Some secrets are better left unknown.

All Song, page 192
Umbilical, page 192

Tier 1: Levity. Through wit, charm, humor, and grace, you are trained in all social interactions other than those involving coercion or intimidation. During rests, you put friends and comrades at ease so much that they gain +1 to their recovery rolls. Enabler.

Tier 2: Inspiration. Through stories, songs, art, or other forms of entertainment, you inspire your friends. After spending a day with you, once per day each of your friends can decrease the difficulty of a task by one step. This benefit is ongoing while you remain in the friend's company. It ends if you leave, but it resumes if you return to the friend's company within a day. If you leave the friend's company for more than a day, you must spend another day together to reactivate the benefit. Enabler.

Tier 3: Knowledge. Your stories and songs contain truth. You are trained in two areas of knowledge of your choosing. Enabler.

Tier 4: Calm (3 Intellect points). Through jokes, song, or other art, you prevent a living foe from attacking anyone or anything for one round. Action.

Tier 5: Able Assistance. When you help someone with a task, you always reduce the difficulty of the task by one step regardless of your own skill at that task. Enabler.

Tier 6: Master Entertainer. Your Inspiration ability works more effectively, allowing your friends to decrease the difficulty of a task by two steps rather than one step. Enabler.

INFILTRATES

A large portion of Ruk society is based on subtlety, guile, and stealth. Your body has been genetically altered to make you the perfect infiltrator. Your muscles, nerves, and even flesh have been engineered to aid you in your task, and eventually you gain the ability to emit spores that affect those you attempt to sneak past.

Infiltrators are spies, agents, thieves, assassins, or information gatherers. They often wear slicksuits and face-concealing masks (sometimes spore filter masks).

Connection: If this is your starting focus, choose one of the following connections.

1. Pick one other PC. This character inadvertently foils your actions, or at least makes them more difficult. If this PC is within immediate range of you, the difficulty of any action that you take related to this focus is increased by one step.
2. Pick one other PC. No matter how hard you try, you cannot seem to hide from him.
3. Pick two other PCs. The three of you worked as a team on a mission long ago, but you had a falling out.
4. Pick one other PC. That character is your vat-sibling, and thus you look very much alike.

Equipment: Ruk clothing, light armor, one weapon of your choice, a bag of light tools, an umbilical, and an account with 50 bits.

Minor Effect Suggestion: Your opponent is so startled by your moves that it is dazed, during which time the difficulty of all tasks it performs is modified by one step to its detriment.

Major Effect Suggestion: All opponents within short range are so startled by your moves that they are dazed, during which time the difficulty of all tasks they perform is modified by one step to their detriment.

Tier 1: Stealth. Your physical form is designed to be lithe and quiet. Your flesh even reflexively alters its tone to suit your surroundings. All this is an asset for stealth-related tasks. Enabler.

Tier 2: Impersonation. You can subtly change your features and alter your voice dramatically. This is an asset for any attempts at disguising your identity. Enabler.

Flight Not Fight. If you use your action only to move, the difficulty of all Speed defense tasks is reduced by one step. Enabler.

Tier 3: Awareness (3 Intellect points). By utilizing the All Song, you become hyper-aware of your surroundings. For ten minutes, you are aware of all living things within long range, and by concentrating (an action) you can learn the general emotional state of any one of them. As with most connections to the All Song, connection to it requires an umbilical and a place to connect.

Tier 4: Invisibility (4 Intellect points). Thanks to mind-clouding spores and light-bending secretions on your flesh, you become invisible for ten minutes. While invisible, you are specialized in stealth and Speed defense tasks. This effect ends if you do something to reveal your presence or position—attacking, using an ability, moving a large object, and so on. If this occurs, you can regain the remaining invisibility effect by taking an action to focus on hiding your position. Action to initiate or reinitiate.

Tier 5: Evasion. You can't be good at getting in if you don't survive getting out. You are trained in all defense tasks.

Tier 6: Control. You use trickery, well-spoken lies, and mind-affecting skin secretions to make others temporarily do what you want them to do. You control the actions of another creature you touch. This effect lasts for one minute. The target must be level 3 or lower. You can allow it to act freely or override its control on a case-by-case basis as long as you can see it. Instead of applying Effort to decrease the difficulty, you can apply Effort to increase the maximum level of the target. Thus, to control the mind of a level 6 target (three levels above the normal limit), you must apply three levels of Effort. When the duration ends, the creature doesn't remember being controlled or anything it did while under your influence. Action to initiate.

INTEGRATES WEAPONRY

Most weaponry of Ruk contains biomechanical elements akin to your own biology; you are spawned from the same original fugitive craft. You've given yourself a special connection to the recursion by adhering to the directions of the True Code, at least where it touches upon the use of weapons. This adherence explains why those like you are sometimes called weaponauts. Though not feared as much as egosomes, weaponauts are considered to have their own psychological issues.

You likely wear brightly colored clothing or armor with "WEAPONAUT" decals. You have one or more elaborate holsters or scabbards where you carry your weapons when they are not integrated.

Many weaponauts are vectors, but sometimes a spinner might choose this focus, combining it with light weapons for best effect.

Connection: If this is your starting focus, choose one of the following connections.

1. Pick one other PC. That character gave you your first heavy weapon, and you've been fascinated by him ever since.
2. Pick one other PC. That character seems very leery of you (this might just be your perception).
3. Pick one other PC. She knows a secret of yours.
4. Pick one other PC. That character looks like someone who wronged you long ago, but you're not sure if you're right.

Equipment: Ruk clothing, light or medium armor, one weapon of your choice, an umbilical, and an account with 50 bits.

Integrated Weapon Abilities: If you perform revisions, or certain twists or moves, your attacks look like they came from your integrated weapon. These alterations change nothing other than the appearance of the effects.

Minor Effect Suggestion: Your attack knocks the target from its feet, or at your option, knocks it back up to 20 feet (6 m).

Major Effect Suggestion: A creature of level 5 or less becomes intimidated by your integrated weapon and flees if you allow it. If you do not allow it, the creature still loses its next turn trying to get away.

Tier 1: Part of Me. You attach a weapon you can normally use into the flesh at the end of one of your arms. The weapon becomes a natural extension of your arm. While integrated, you inflict 1 additional point of damage while using the weapon, though you lose the use of that hand. The weapon can be a heavy weapon and still leave your other hand free; however, if you do integrate a heavy

True Code, page 192

Integrates Weaponry GM Intrusions: *Weapons misfire, and when they are a part of you, that's trouble.*

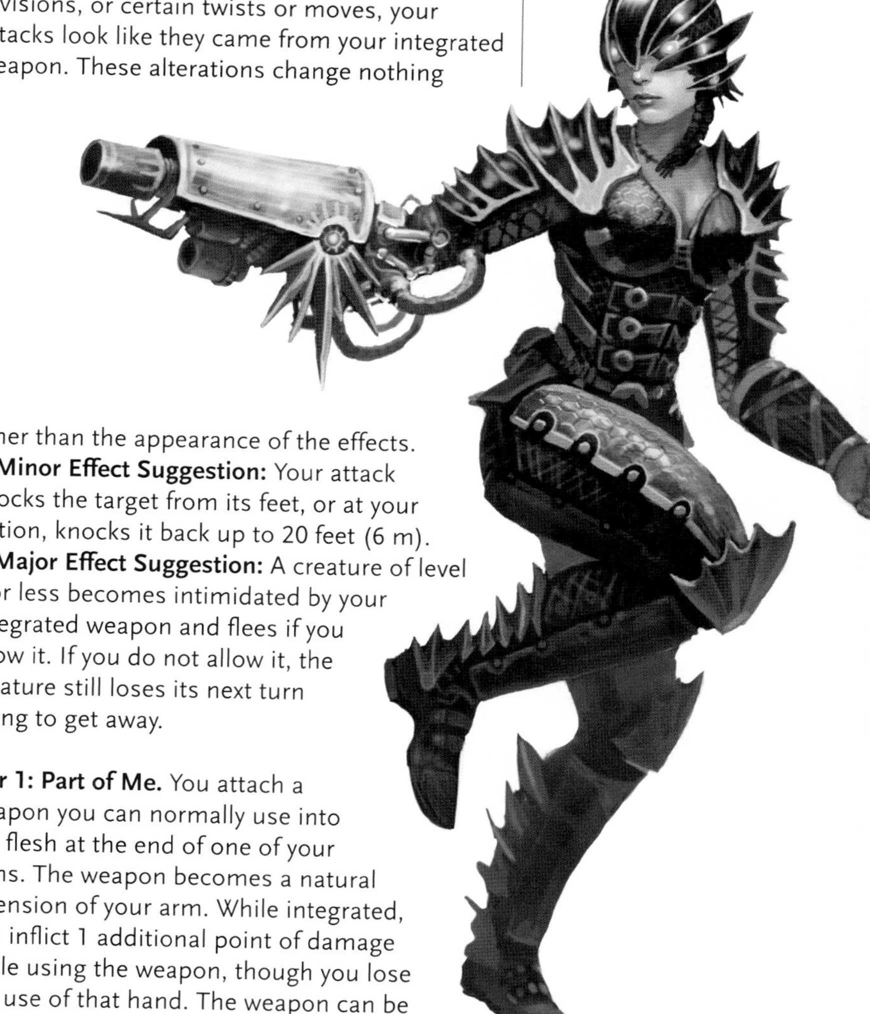

Twice trained: If a character is already trained in a skill, ability, or attack but gains training in the same thing again for any reason, she instead becomes specialized in it.

weapon, all physical tasks you attempt using your free hand are modified by one step to your detriment. If you integrate two weapons (one for each hand), you cannot attempt tasks that require the use of hands, nor can you make more than one attack with one integrated weapon on your turn. Action to integrate; action to remove. Enabler once integrated.

Practiced With Integrated Weapons: You can use all integrated weapons without penalty. Enabler.

Tier 2: Weapon Defense. While you have a weapon integrated, you are trained in Speed defense rolls. Enabler.

Tier 3: Trained Integration. You are trained in using all attacks made with integrated weapons. Enabler.

Tier 4: Rapid Attack (4 Speed points). You can make an attack as part of another action with your integrated weapon (possibly a second attack); however, the difficulty of the attack increases by one step. Action.

Tier 5: Phenomenal Integration. You are specialized in all attacks made with integrated weapons. Enabler.

Tier 6: Weapon Frenzy (6 Speed points). You can attempt to attack every creature within range, but you cannot choose which targets to attack and which to spare because you go into a weapon frenzy and attack everything indiscriminately. If attacking with a weapon that uses ammunition, you can make only as many attacks as you have ammunition. Roll each attack separately. Action.

IS LICENSED TO CARRY

***Is Licensed to Carry GM Intrusions:** Misfire or jam! The attack fails and the action is lost, plus an additional action is needed to fix the problem.*

You're a proficient adversary when armed. Hundreds of hours of training mean that you don't crack when under fire; you take care of business before the bad guys even know you're there. Those who are Licensed to Carry might be cops, crooks, hunters, or citizens interested in protecting themselves.

You dress in clothing that allows you either to conceal your weapon or to quickly access it, and preferably both, which is why you're probably known for your trench coat.

Vector gun users are likely soldiers or hunters. Spinner gun users are often criminals or cops. A paradox who Is Licensed to Carry is probably rare but might be a detective or a gun enthusiast.

Connection: If this is your starting focus, choose one of the following connections.

1. Pick one other PC. In the recent past, while doing a little target practice, you accidentally winged him, leaving him badly wounded. It is up to that PC to decide whether he resents, fears, or forgives you.
2. Pick two PCs (preferably ones who are likely to get in the way of your attacks). When you miss with a gun and the GM rules that you struck someone other than your target, you hit one of these two characters.
3. Pick one other PC. You can see that the character needs some advice on how to handle a firearm.
4. Pick one other PC. You're not sure how or from where, but this character has a line on guns and ammunition and can get them for you for half price.

Equipment: Clothing, light or medium armor, two weapons (one of which must be a firearm and three magazines of ammo), a cell phone, and $800.

Minor Effect Suggestion: After being hit on the side of the head, the target is deafened for a few minutes.

Major Effect Suggestion: An artery hit causes the target to bleed for 1 point of damage each round until the target succeeds at a difficulty 3 Intellect or Speed task to bind the wound.

Tier 1: Gunner. You inflict an additional point of damage with guns. Enabler.

Practiced With Guns: You are practiced with using guns and suffer no penalty when using one.

Tier 2: Careful Shot. You can spend points from either your Speed Pool or your Intellect Pool to apply levels of Effort to increase your gun damage. Each level of Effort adds 3 points of damage to a successful attack, and if you spend a turn lining up your shot, each level of Effort adds 5 points of damage to a successful attack instead. Enabler.

Tier 3: Trained Gunner: You can choose from one of two benefits. Either you are trained in using guns, or you have the Spray ability (which costs 2 Speed points): If a weapon has the ability to fire rapid shots without reloading (usually called a rapid-fire weapon, such as the automatic pistol), you can spray multiple shots around your target to increase the chance of hitting. This move uses 1d6 + 1 rounds of ammo (or all the ammo in the weapon, if it has less than the number rolled). The difficulty of the attack roll is decreased by one step. If the attack is successful, it deals 1 less point of damage than normal. Being trained in using guns is an Enabler. Spray is an Action.

Tier 4: Snapshot. You can make two gun attacks as a single action, but the second attack is modified by two steps to your detriment. Enabler.

Tier 5: Legendary Gunner: You can choose from one of two benefits. Either you are trained in using guns (or specialized if you are already trained), or you have the Arc Spray ability, which costs 3 Speed points: If a weapon has the ability to fire rapid shots without reloading (usually called a rapid-fire weapon, such as the automatic pistol), you can fire your weapon at up to three targets (all next to one another) as a single action. Make a separate attack roll against each target. The difficulty of each attack is increased by one step. Being trained in using guns is an Enabler. Arc Spray is an Action.

Tier 6: Special Shot. When you hit a target with your gun attack, you can choose to reduce the damage by 1 point but hit the target in a precise spot. Some of the possible effects include (but are not limited to):

- You can shoot an object out of someone's hand.
- You can shoot the leg, wing, or other limb it uses to move, reducing its maximum movement speed to immediate for a few days or until it receives expert medical care.
- You can shoot a strap holding a backpack, armor, or similarly strapped-on item so that it falls off.

Enabler.

LEADS

Using charisma, natural leadership, and perhaps some training, you command the actions of others, who follow you willingly. You are a politician, a captain, a leader, or a manager. Your skills allow you to make people do what you want, but you also have the wisdom to know what actions would be best for your followers and allies.

Since you need the respect of others, you probably dress and carry yourself in such a way that inspires, endears, or intimidates. You have a voice suited to barking orders that can be heard even on a noisy battlefield.

Spinners make excellent military leaders, but a vector could easily lead a group of explorers or a team of soldiers. A paradox might be the head of a group of scholars or scientists, or

Leads GM Intrusions: *Followers fail, betray, lie, become corrupted, get kidnapped, or die. Leaders get usurped.*

Leads Equipment:
Ardeyn: *Fine Ardeyn clothing, a signal horn, title to a riding horse, and 100 crowns.*
Ruk: *Zal-branded Ruk clothing, umbilical, a wing glider, and an account with 150 bits.*

might have a group of bodyguards as followers.

Connection: If this is your starting focus, choose one of the following connections.

1. Pick one other PC. That character was once a follower of yours, but you have since grown to think of her as a peer.
2. Pick one other PC. Independent and stubborn, he is not affected by your abilities.
3. Pick one other PC. She introduces you to the follower you gain at Tier 2.
4. Pick one other PC. You were once very close with that character in the distant past.

Equipment: Very nice clothing, leather jacket, a computer of your choice, a smartphone, a car, and $1,500.

Minor Effect Suggestion: The next time you attempt to command, captivate, or otherwise influence the same foe, the difficulty of the task is decreased by one step.

Major Effect Suggestion: The foe is influenced, captivated, or otherwise affected by your ability for twice as long as normal.

Tier 1: Natural Charisma. You are trained in all social interactions, whether they involve charm, learning a person's secrets, or intimidating others. Enabler.

Good Advice (1 Intellect point). You have a clear mind for determining the best way to proceed. When you give another character a suggestion involving his next action, the character is trained in that action for one round. Action.

Tier 2: Follower. You gain a level 2 nonplayer character (NPC) follower who is completely devoted to you. You and the GM must work out the details of the follower. As a level 2 follower, it has a target number of 6 and a health of 6, and it inflicts 2 points of damage.

You'll probably make rolls for your follower when he takes actions. A follower in combat usually doesn't make separate attacks, but helps you with yours. On your action, if the follower is next to you, he serves as an asset for one attack you make on your turn.

If the follower dies, you gain a new one after at least two weeks and proper recruitment. Enabler.

Tier 3: Command (3 Intellect points). Through sheer force of will and charisma, you issue a simple command to a single living creature, which attempts to carry out your command as its next action. The creature must be within short range and be able to understand you. The command can't inflict direct harm on the creature or its allies, so "Commit suicide" won't work, but "Flee" might. In addition, the command can require the creature to take only one action, so "Unlock the door" might work, but "Unlock the door and run through it" won't. Action.

Capable Follower. Your first follower increases to level 3. As a level 3 follower, it has a target number of 9 and a health of 9, and it inflicts 3 points of damage. Enabler.

Tier 4: Captivate or Inspire. You can use this ability in one of two ways. Either your words keep the attention of all NPCs that hear them for as long as you speak, or your words inspire all NPCs (of your choosing) that hear them to function as if they were one level higher for the next hour. Action.

Capable Follower. Your first follower increases to level 4. As a level 4 follower, it has a target number of 12 and a health of 12, and it inflicts 4 points of damage. Enabler.

Tier 5: Band of Followers. You gain six level 2 NPC followers who are completely devoted to you. (They are in addition to the follower you gained at second tier.) You and the GM must work out the details of these followers. If a follower dies, you gain a new one after at least two weeks and proper recruitment. Enabler.

Tier 6: Mind of a Leader (6 Intellect points). When you develop a plan that involves your followers, you can ask the GM one very general question about what is likely to happen if you carry out the plan, and you will get a simple, brief answer. Action.

Capable Followers. Your first follower increases to level 5. As a level 5 follower, it has a target number of 15 and a health of 15, and it inflicts 5 points of damage. Each of your level 2 followers increases to level 3. Enabler.

LIVES IN THE WILDERNESS

You dwell in the wilds. You probably have done so most, if not all, of your life, coming to understand the mysteries of nature, weather, and survival. The ways of flora and fauna are your ways.

Lives in the Wilderness GM Intrusions: *People in cities and towns sometimes disparage those who look (and smell) like they live in the wilds, as if they were ignorant or barbaric.*

Your rough, rugged clothing shows little concern for style. Most of the time, covering yourself in natural smells to keep your scent from arousing suspicion in the wilderness is more important than bathing to keep yourself presentable to other humans.

Vectors are most likely to live in the wilderness, perhaps working as guides, hunters, trappers, scouts, or trackers. A paradox that does so might be seen as a nature priest or wild wizard.

Connection: If this is your starting focus, choose one of the following connections.

1. Pick one other PC who isn't from the wilderness. You can't help but feel a little contempt for that character and the "civilized" ways she exhibits, which show disdain for all things natural and (to your mind) true.
2. Pick one other PC. In the past, you helped this character find a way back to civilization from the wild or you provided healing.
3. Pick one other PC. You don't know why, but it seems that this character spooks animals in a way that is upsetting to you.
4. Pick one other PC. This character seems as adept in the wilderness as you are—well, almost—and you have to respect him for that.

Equipment: Ardeyn clothing, light or medium armor, two weapons of your choice (or one weapon and a shield), an explorer's pack, and 300 crowns.

Minor Effect Suggestion: A foe that is a natural creature flees rather than continue to fight you.

Major Effect Suggestion: A foe that is a natural creature becomes warily passive.

Tier 1: Wilderness Life. You are trained in climbing and swimming tasks. Enabler.

Wilderness Lore. You are trained in wilderness navigation and in identifying plants and creatures. Enabler.

Tier 2: Living Off the Land. Given an hour or so, you can always find edible food and potable water in the wilderness. You can even find enough for a small group of people if need be. Further, since you're so hardy and have gained resistance over time, the difficulty of resisting the effects of natural poisons (such as those from plants or living creatures) is decreased by one step. You're also immune to natural diseases. Enabler.

Tier 3: Animal Senses and Sensibilities. You are trained in listening and spotting things. In addition, most of the time, the GM should alert you if you're about to walk into an ambush or a trap that is lower than level 3. Enabler.

Wilderness Explorer. While taking any action (including fighting) in the wild, you ignore any penalties due to natural causes such as tall grass, thick brush, rugged terrain, weather, and so on. Enabler.

Tier 4: Wilderness Awareness (4 Intellect points). Your connection to the natural world expands to a degree that some would call supernatural. While in the wilderness, you can extend your senses up to a mile in any direction and ask the GM a very simple, general question about that area, such as "Where is the raider camp?" or "Is my friend Maltrose still alive?" If the answer you seek is not in the area, you receive no information. Action.

Tier 5: The Wild Is on Your Side (5 Intellect points). While you're in the wilderness, foes within short range are tripped by rocks, tangled in vines, bitten by insects, and distracted or confused by small animals. The difficulty of any tasks performed by those foes is increased by one step. This effect lasts for ten minutes. Action to initiate.

Tier 6: One With the Wild (6 Intellect points). For the next ten minutes, natural animals and plants within long range will not knowingly harm you or those you designate. Action.

Master of the Wild. While you're in the wilderness, your Might Edge, Speed Edge, and Intellect Edge increase by 1. When you make a recovery roll in the wilderness, you recover twice as many points. Enabler.

LOOKS FOR TROUBLE

You are a fighter. A scrapper. You like nothing more than to take off the kid gloves and confront your opposition in the most direct way possible. You don't hide, and you don't shirk. You take things head-on in a physical way. Your friends all likely feel better about going into danger with you at their side or their back.

You probably wear bright colors—yellow, pink, or red—to help you stand out. You might even wear a T-shirt with a printed obscenity for added style.

Obviously, vectors excel at looking for trouble, but any character type can be more physical and up-close too.

Connection: If this is your starting focus, choose one of the following connections.

1. Pick one other PC. Due to past experiences, you watch over her. That PC is your default charge regarding your tier 2 ability, if you have not named someone else.
2. Pick one or two other PCs. They seem pretty tough, and you're secretly hoping that at some point you'll see who's tougher—you or them.
3. Pick one other PC. If this character is within immediate range when you're in a fight, sometimes she helps, and sometimes she accidentally hinders (50% chance either way, determined per fight). When this character helps, you gain a +1 bonus to all attack rolls. When she hinders, you suffer a –1 penalty to attack rolls.
4. Pick one other PC. You used to be in a relationship with him, but it's long since over.

Equipment: Street clothes, light armor, two weapons of your choice (one of which must be a melee weapon), a first aid kit, a utility knife, a cell phone, and $400.

Minor Effect Suggestion: The target is also dazed for one round, during which time the difficulty of all tasks it performs is modified by one step to its detriment.

Major Effect Suggestion: You destroy a piece of equipment worn or held by your opponent.

Tier 1: Brawler. You inflict 1 additional point of damage in melee (including with your bare fists).

Wound Tender. You are trained in healing.

Tier 2: Protector. You designate a single character to be your charge. You can change this freely every round, but you can have only one charge at a time. As long as that charge is within immediate range, he gains an asset for Speed defense tasks because you have his back.

Straightforward: You are trained in one of the following tasks (choose one): breaking things, climbing, jumping, or running.

Looks for Trouble Equipment:
Ardeyn: *Ardeyn clothing, light armor, two weapons of your choice (one of which must be a melee weapon), a first aid kit, a fish knife, a signal horn, and 40 crowns.*
Ruk: *Ruk clothing, umbilical, two weapons of your choice (one of which must be a melee weapon), a healing kit, a knife, and 50 bits.*

Looks for Trouble GM Intrusions: *Weapons break or fly from even the strongest grip. Brawlers trip and fall. Even the battlefield can work against you with things falling or collapsing.*

Tier 3: Lethal Battler. Choose one type of attack in which you are not already trained: light bashing, light bladed, medium bashing, medium bladed, heavy bashing, or heavy bladed. You are trained in attacks using that type of weapon. Enabler.

Tier 4: Knock Out (5 Might points). You make a melee attack that inflicts no damage. Instead, if the attack hits, make a second Might-based roll. If successful, a foe of level 3 or less is knocked unconscious for one minute. You can use Effort to improve this ability. For each level of Effort used, you can affect one higher level of foe, or you can extend the duration for an additional minute. Action.

Tier 5: Epic Fighter. Choose one type of attack in which you are already trained: light bashing, light bladed, medium bashing, medium bladed, heavy bashing, or heavy bladed. You are specialized in attacks using that type of weapon. Enabler.

Tier 6: Juggernaut. You add 5 points to your Might Pool, and you inflict 1 additional point of damage with melee attacks. Enabler.

True Healer. You are specialized in healing.

METAMORPHOSIZES

You possess a radical biomodification that allows you to unlock metamorphic forms called chrysalides that are hinted at in the All Song. Chrysalid forms are a frontier of Ruk science, and they can prove actively dangerous to your allies and possibly even to you. But, oh, the power!

Many do not trust you and consider you dangerous, and for good reason. Metamorphs are most often vectors, but chrysalid forms can enhance any character.

You wear either loose clothing that you can doff quickly, or specially made Ruk clothing that can handle whatever chrysalid shape you choose to take.

Connection: If this is your starting focus, choose one of the following connections.

1. Pick one other PC. You never attack him while metamorphosized.
2. Pick one other PC. If that PC spends three consecutive turns using an action to calm you, you can revert to your normal form without having to make a roll.
3. Pick one other PC. Something about this character enrages you while you are metamorphosized. If he was within sight when you changed, you gain a +1 bonus to all rolls during that particular metamorphosis. If he's within range, you always attack him.
4. Pick one other PC. You have been friends since childhood.

Equipment: Ruk clothing, light armor, one weapon of your choice, an umbilical, and an account with 70 bits.

Minor Effect Suggestion: While you're transformed, an unsuspected aspect of your chrysalid form sprays the target with dazing enzyme. The target is dazed for one round, during which time the difficulty of all tasks it performs is modified by one step to its detriment.

***Metamorphosizes GM Intrusions:** The creature you are tearing apart might be a friend, not a foe. You terrify others, who might try to deal with the danger you pose in ways you wouldn't like.*

CHRYSALID

While in a chrysalid form, you can't spend Intellect points for any reason other than to try to change to your normal form before the one-hour duration is over (a difficulty 2 task). In addition, your target selection includes any and every living creature within short range, whether enemy, ally, or bystander. If multiple targets are in range, you always choose the nearest (or, barring that, the biggest) target. After you revert to your normal form, you take a –1 penalty to all rolls for one hour. If you did not defeat a real enemy while metamorphosized, the penalty increases to –2 and affects all your rolls for the next day.

Operates Undercover **GM Intrusions:** *People don't like to be manipulated, and they resent those who try. Even the best disguise can have a fatal flaw. When you are not what you seem, sometimes other people aren't either.*

Major Effect Suggestion: While you're transformed, an unanticipated aspect of your chrysalid form encapsulates the target in a translucent sheath of tissue. The target must spend an action to free itself. Until it does, attacks against it are modified by one step to the attacker's benefit.

Tier 1: Battle Chrysalid (2 Intellect points). You can change and gain a battle chrysalid for up to one hour. In this new form, you add 4 points to your Might Pool, add 1 to your Might Edge, add 2 points to your Speed Pool, and add 1 to your Speed Edge.

Claws sprout from your hands, serving as a medium melee weapon. Action to change; action to change back.

Practiced With Chrysalid Attacks: You can use all attacks in any chrysalid form without penalty. Enabler.

Tier 2: Devourer Battle Chrysalid (3 Intellect points). You can change and gain a Ruk-eater battle chrysalid for up to one hour. In this new form, you add 8 points to your Might Pool, add 1 to your Might Edge, add 4 points to your Speed Pool, add 1 to your Speed Edge, and gain +1 to Armor.

Mouth stalks protrude from your body, which serve as a medium weapon. If you become impaired or debilitated, you lose control over your own voracious appetite. Each round, you automatically inflict 1 point of damage on yourself (ignoring Armor) as your mouth stalks self cannibalize. Action to change; action to change back.

Tier 3: Trained Chrysalid. You are trained in using all attacks you gain while in a chrysalid form. Enabler.

Tier 4: Flyer Battle Chrysalid (5 Intellect points). You can change and gain a flyer battle chrysalid for up to one hour. In this new form, you can fly a short distance each round, and you add 4 points to your Might Pool, add 1 to your Might Edge, add 2 points to your Speed Pool, and add 1 to your Speed Edge.

Wingblades sprout from your arms, allowing you to fly and serving as a medium melee weapon. Action to change; action to change back.

Tier 5: Specialized Chrysalid. You are specialized in using all attacks you gain while in a chrysalid form.

Tier 6: Monstrous Battle Chrysalid (7 Intellect points). You can change and gain a monstrous battle chrysalid for up to one hour. In this new form, you add 10 points to your Might Pool, add 2 to your Might Edge, add 6 points to your Speed Pool, add 2 to your Speed Edge, and gain +2 to Armor.

Your arms become huge, hammerlike appendages, serving as a large melee weapon. Your body is also covered with spikes, so that if anyone strikes you in melee, they suffer 1 point of damage. Further, you can throw spikes as a medium weapon with short range. Action to change; action to change back.

OPERATES UNDERCOVER

Espionage is not something you know anything about. At least, that's what you want everyone to believe, because in truth, you've been trained as a spy or covert agent. You might work for a government or for yourself. You might be a police detective or a criminal. You could even be an investigative reporter.

Regardless, you learn information that others attempt to keep secret. You collect rumors and whispers, stories and hard-won evidence, and you use that knowledge to aid your own endeavors and, if appropriate, provide your employers with the information they desire or sell what you have learned to those willing to pay a premium.

You probably wear dark colors—black, charcoal grey, or midnight blue—to help blend into the shadows, unless the cover you've chosen requires you to look like someone else.

Spinners operate well while working undercover, but a paradox's abilities or a vector's physicality make interesting combinations as well.

Connection: If this is your starting focus, choose one of the following connections.

1. Pick one other PC. The character knows your real identity (if that's a secret) or that you work undercover (if that's a secret), and has kept that information private until now.
2. Pick one other PC. You know an important secret about her, but she is unaware that you know.
3. Pick two other PCs. You know about an important connection between these two that even they don't know about.
4. Pick one other PC. No matter how you hide or disguise yourself, this character always seems to know where and who you really are.

Equipment: Street clothes, disguise kit, light tools, duct tape, a weapon of your choice, a pen knife, a smartphone, and $700.

Minor Effect Suggestion: You can immediately attempt to hide after this action.

Major Effect Suggestion: You get a +2 bonus to Speed defense rolls for one round.

Tier 1: Investigate. You are trained in perception, cryptography, deceiving, and breaking into computers. Enabler.

Tier 2: Disguise. You are trained in disguise. You can alter your posture, voice, mannerisms, and hair to look like someone else for as long as you keep up the disguise. However, it is extremely difficult to adopt the disguise of a specific individual without a disguise kit at your disposal. Enabler.

Tier 3: Agent Provocateur. Choose one of the following to be trained in: attacking with a weapon of your choice, demolitions, or sneaking and lockpicking (if you choose this last option, you are trained in both). Enabler.

Tier 4: Pull a Fast One (3 Intellect points). When you're running a con, picking a pocket, fooling or tricking a dupe, sneaking something by a guard, and so on, you treat the task as if it were one level lower. Enabler.

Tier 5: Using What's Available (4 Intellect points). If you have the time and the freedom to scrounge for everyday materials in your environment, you can fashion a temporary asset that will aid you once to accomplish a specific task. For example, if you need to climb a wall, you could create some sort of climbing assistance device; if you need to break out of a cell, you can find something to use as lockpicks; if you need to create a small distraction, you could put together something to make a loud bang and flash; and so on. The asset lasts up to a maximum of one minute, or until used for the purpose you fashion it. One minute to assemble materials; action to create asset.

Tier 6: Trust to Luck (3 Intellect points). Sometimes, you've just got to roll the dice and hope things add up in your favor. When you Trust to Luck, roll a d6. On any even result, the task you're attempting is modified by two steps in your favor. On a roll of 1, the task is modified by one step to your detriment. Enabler.

Assassin (5 Might points). If you strike a foe of level 3 or less with a weapon you're practiced or trained with, you kill the target instantly. Action.

Operates Undercover Equipment:
Ardeyn: *Ardeyn clothing, three painted masks, light tools, a weapon of your choice, a fish knife, a signal horn, and 80 crowns.*
Ruk: *Ruk clothing, umbilical, disguise graft, light tools, glue graft, a weapon of your choice, a knife, and 60 bits.*

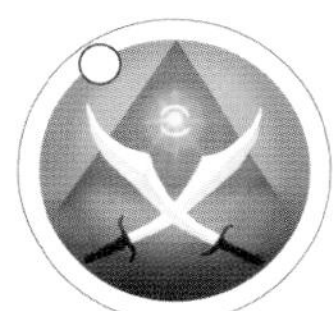

PRACTICES SOUL SORCERY

You can mold souls like an artisan can mold clay. You begin your training by learning how to install your own soul in a phylactery you wear as a ring or amulet. You soon learn to attract the lost souls of the dead who evaded the Night Vault and house them in rings you wear, figurines you carry, and even tattoos you sport. A soulmancer (as someone who Practices Soul Sorcery is sometimes called) at the height of her power might wear a ring on each finger, each one resonant with a particular ability or piece of knowledge a resident soul possesses.

You wear robes stitched with runes of spirit warding, spirit luring, and spirit calming. The runes have no intrinsic power, but they help you concentrate when you wield your soulmancy.

Soulmancers are most often paradoxes and spinners, but a vector (a soul warrior) is a frightening enemy to have.

Connection: If this is your starting focus,

Practices Soul Sorcery GM Intrusions: *Spirits can wrest themselves away or even possess you.*

Night Vault, page 183

choose one of the following connections.

1. Pick one other PC. One night after perhaps too much celebrating, you brazenly promised to return his dead sibling, parent, or friend back to life. Later, you realized that power was far beyond your abilities, and might always be.
2. Pick one other PC. She once saved your life.
3. Pick one other PC. Due to an oddity of your ability, if that character is standing next to you, she also gains the benefit of your phylactery.
4. Pick one other PC. That PC has confided in you that he is suspicious of your craft, and he half suspects you to be a secret adherent of the Betrayer, Lotan, or some off-recursion interest.

Betrayer, page 178
Lotan, page 162

Equipment: Ardeyn clothing, light armor, one weapon of your choice, an explorer's pack, a phylactery, a handful of rings set with semiprecious gems, and 100 crowns.

Minor Effect Suggestion: The target's soul is tweaked, causing the target to stumble and drop whatever it's holding.

Major Effect Suggestion: The target's soul is dislodged before settling back in place; this dazes the target.

Tier 1: Phylactery. Your soul is installed in a ring or amulet. This insulates you somewhat from pain, granting you +1 to Armor, and you are trained in Intellect and Might defense tasks.

If your phylactery is destroyed for any reason, your soul returns to your body, and you lose all benefits of this ability until you can construct a new phylactery, which is a process requiring a day of labor and a suitable ring or amulet worth at least 100 crowns. Until you construct a new phylactery, all your stat Pool maximums are reduced by 1 point. Enabler.

Tier 2: Clothe Spirit (3 Intellect points): A lost spirit takes up residence in a piece of jewelry you wear or in a tattoo on your body. With this ability, you can clothe the spirit in the physical body of another creature no more than twice as large as you for up to an hour before the spirit must depart and return to the jewelry or tattoo that normally houses it.

The target body can be any dead body within short range. The body can also be that of a sleeping creature that you touch (to clothe the spirit in a sleeping body, you must touch the body and make an Intellect attack). If you clothe the spirit in a living, sleeping creature, upon waking that creature retains no memory of having been the vessel for a spirit, except perhaps in the hint of a dream.

The resultant "clothed spirit" is a level 2 creature devoted to you. You and the GM can work out the details of your particular spirit, independent of the body it inhabits. You'll probably make rolls for it when it takes actions (but see below for combat). The clothed spirit acts on your turn. As a level 2 creature, it has a target number of 6 and a health of 6. It can produce a terrifying Soul Scream once per day that attacks up to three designated living targets within short range. If a target of the Soul Scream is affected, it cannot take any action other than movement on its next turn. (A clothed spirit doesn't physically attack other creatures, but it can spend its action to serve as an asset for any one attack you make on your turn while it is embodied.)

If the body housing the spirit takes 6 points of damage or if an hour passes (whichever comes first), the soul returns to whatever item you house it in; if the body was a living, sleeping creature, it wakes up (with 6 points of damage to deal with). Action to clothe spirit.

Tier 3: Soul Rider. If your phylactery is separated from you, you can concentrate to see, hear, and smell through it. Your sensory capabilities aren't greater than normal, except in one way: you can sense the environment around the phylactery even if it's in another creature's pocket, bag, pack, or similar container. A few feet of earth, a foot of stone, or an inch of metal blocks your ability to see. Action.

Improved Clothe Spirit. The spirit you create with Clothe Spirit increases to level 3. As a level 3 creature, it has a target number of 9 and a health of 9, and you can call it up to twice a day. Its Soul Scream is unaffected, other than it being a higher-level attack. Enabler.

Tier 4: Vicious Soul (4 Intellect points). A lost spirit of a vindictive qephilim takes up residence in a piece of jewelry you wear or in a tattoo on your body. You can coax it to enter either you or an ally within short range who allows it. Upon installation, the vessel (you or the chosen ally) gains the following benefits: add 10 points to Might Pool, add 2 to Speed Edge, add 4 points to Intellect Pool, and add 2 to Intellect Edge. The vicious spirit doesn't care to distinguish its enemies, and it randomly attacks any creature it can see and reach. You or the allied vessel can attempt a difficulty 3 Intellect task each round to eject the vicious soul. Afterward, whoever hosted the raging soul loses 1d6 points from its Might Pool and 1d6 points from its Speed Pool. Action to initiate.

Improved Clothe Spirit. The spirit you create with Clothe Spirit increases to level 4. As a level 4 creature, it has a target number of 12 and a health of 12, and you can call it up to three times a day. Its Soul Scream is unaffected, other than it being a higher-level attack. Enabler.

Tier 5: Soul River. You can mold souls. If you succeed at a difficulty 4 Intellect-based task, you can transfer up to 5 points among your Pools, or among your Pools and another willing creature's Pools, in any combination, at a rate of 1 point per round. For example, you could transfer 3 points of Might to an ally's Speed Pool, and 2 points of Speed to your own Intellect Pool, which would take a total of five rounds. Each time you attempt to use this ability, the difficulty becomes one step higher; the difficulty resets to 4 after your next ten-hour rest. Action.

Tier 6: Escape the Vault. If you are slain in Ardeyn, your spirit is drawn to your phylactery instead of the Night Vault, assuming the phylactery is not also destroyed. Your soul is housed for ten days in your phylactery, after which you are reincarnated in a new body identical to your old body at or near where your phylactery resides. You return with nothing but your phylactery. After you enjoy this benefit, you cannot do so again for one year (so if you die again before a year elapses, your spirit falls to the Court of Sleep, who are likely unhappy that you cheated them once).

Alternatively, you can attempt to pull another soul out of the Night Vault and reincarnate it as a living creature. You can do so only if you know the full name of the creature, if you have something of its body or a cherished possession, and if it has not been dead for more than one year. The spirit must also be available to return. After you use this alternative, you cannot use it or the option to return yourself to life described above for one year. Enabler.

Improved Clothe Spirit. The spirit you create with Clothe Spirit increases to level 5. As a level 5 creature, it has a target number and a health of 15. You can call it up to four times a day. Its Soul Scream is unaffected, other than it being a higher-level attack. Enabler.

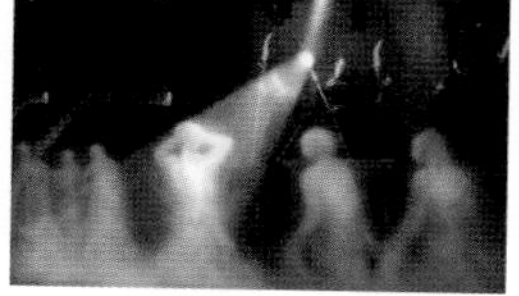

Court of Sleep, page 184

PROCESSES INFORMATION

While Ruk science enhances the physical bodies of many who live there, for you the enhancement is all to your brain. Your neural connections are faster, your memory is greater, and eventually you learn to use these enhancements to patch yourself into the All Song like no one else.

Your abilities probably do not have visible manifestations, although some processors have enlarged craniums or small plugs or artificial attachments on their skulls.

Processors are most often paradoxes, followed closely by spinners.

Processes Information GM Intrusions: You can get lost in your own head for untold amounts of time. Not all information is correct or comes from the source you think it does.

Connection: If this is your starting focus, choose one of the following connections.

1. Pick one other PC. You have information about one of her biggest secrets.
2. Pick one other PC. You became friends with this character through the All Song.
3. Pick one other PC. When he stands next to you, the difficulty of any task involving the All Song is increased by one step.
4. Pick one other PC. You remember seeing this character once before, long ago, but you can't recall where, and it bothers you.

Equipment: Ruk clothing, light armor, one weapon of your choice, a healing kit, an umbilical, and an account with 50 bits.

Minor Effect Suggestion: You spontaneously regain 1 point to your Intellect Pool.

Major Effect Suggestion: You gain an unexpected bit of information from the All Song about the situation at hand or someone involved.

Tier 1: Knowledge Storehouse. You can choose three different areas of knowledge—history, geography, botany, quantum mechanics, and so on—in which you are trained. Enabler.

Storage Capacity. You gain 4 points to add to your Intellect Pool.

Tier 2: Gliding Through the All Song. You can access the All Song from anywhere in Ruk without the need of an umbilical. You are trained in All Song navigation. Enabler.

Processing Power. You add 1 to your Intellect Edge. Enabler.

Tier 3: Unearth Knowledge (4 Intellect points). You can access the All Song with such sophistication that you can ask the GM one yes-or-no question and get an answer. The task difficulty varies but is typically 3. Action.

Tier 4: Find the Undoing (4 Intellect points). Through observation and access to the All Song, you determine the weaknesses, vulnerabilities, qualities, and mannerisms of a single creature. The GM should reveal the creature's level, basic abilities, and any obvious weaknesses (if any). The difficulty of all actions you attempt that affect that creature—attack, defense, interaction, and so on—is reduced by two steps. Action.

Tier 5: Self-Preservation. Your enhanced mental abilities give you training in both Speed defense and Intellect defense. Enabler.

Tier 6: The Speed of Thought. Any time you would normally need to use Speed, you can use Intellect instead. This includes your Intellect Edge as well as your Intellect Pool. Enabler.

REGENERATES TISSUE

Your body possesses a natural ability to heal its own hurts. You've accelerated this through biomodifications and self-directed surgeries, which is why some refer to you as an egosome. Sometimes egosomes are denigrated for looking out only for their own interests, but from your point of view, who's better able to look out for yourself than you?

You wear regular Ruk clothing and simple light armor—no need to call attention to your ability to withstand hurts that would kill others.

Vectors usually choose to regenerate tissue, but any type would find it useful to have an extra lease on life.

Regenerates Tissue GM Intrusions: Healing sometimes leaves nasty, ugly scars. Regeneration can get out of control, with cells creating body mass you never originally possessed.

Connection: If this is your starting focus, choose one of the following connections.

1. Pick one other PC. Because of a similarity in your genetic heritage, if that character is standing next to you when you use your Regeneration ability, 2 points are also restored to either her Speed Pool or her Might Pool.
2. Pick one other PC. You cannot heal that

character with your tier 3 ability for some reason.

3. Pick two other PCs. Due to a genetic link, when all three of you are within immediate range, you all add 1 to your recovery rolls.
4. Pick one other PC. That character knows a secret about your past.

Equipment: Ruk clothing, light armor, one weapon of your choice, an umbilical, and an account with 70 bits.

Minor Effect Suggestion: You spontaneously regain 1 point to either your Speed Pool or your Might Pool.

Major Effect Suggestion: You spontaneously regain 2 points to any of your stat Pools.

Tier 1: Regeneration (1 Intellect point). You restore 1d6 + 1 points to either your Speed Pool or your Might Pool. This ability is a difficulty 2 Intellect task. Each additional time you use this ability, the task difficulty increases by one step. The difficulty returns to 2 after you rest for ten hours. Action.

Tier 2: Immune to Toxins. You are immune to disease and poisons whose level is equal to or less than your tier. When you make a defense roll to resist a higher-level toxin, the difficulty is reduced by two steps. Enabler.

Tier 3: Induce Regeneration (2 Intellect points + 3 Might points). You cut a piece of your flesh free and apply it to another creature's wound. Your transplanted regenerating flesh restores 1d6 points to one of the creature's stat Pools. This ability is a difficulty 3 Intellect task. Each time you attempt to transplant regenerating flesh to the same creature, the task difficulty increases by one step. The difficulty returns to 3 after that creature rests for ten hours. Action to make cutting; action to apply.

Tier 4: Generate Carapace (4 Might points). The outer layers of your skin calcify, giving you +2 to Armor. However, this kills the outer layers of your skin, which sheds within ten minutes. By then, a new layer of skin is ready to take the shed skin's place. Action to initiate.

Tier 5: Greater Regeneration (6 Intellect points). You restore your Might Pool and Speed Pool to their maximum values. This ability is a difficulty 2 Intellect task. Each additional time you use this ability, the task difficulty increases by one step. The difficulty returns to 2 after you rest for ten hours. Action.

Tier 6: Rhizome Seed. Your consciousness and knowledge are concentrated into a rhizome tendril that protrudes a few inches (7 cm) from the back of your neck. You function normally, although the seat of your consciousness is located in the rhizome, not your brain. This shift provides several benefits:

- When you defend against mental attacks, the difficulty is modified by one step to your benefit.
- You can detach the rhizome as an action and mentally and remotely control your body at long range.
- You can shift your point of view between the rhizome and your body (or the reverse) as an action (but if you shift your point of view away from your body, your body falls limp until your attention "returns").
- If your body is slain and the rhizome

If you have both Regeneration from the Regenerates Tissue focus and the vector's Quick Recovery move, you're particularly skilled at regeneration. Your first recovery roll of the day (usually requiring a single action) is treated as if the ability was an enabler.

Common people are scared of dead spirits, and they look warily on those who consort with such things. Hauntings and the dead rising from the grave are real hazards, and those with this focus are easy to blame.

Shepherds the Dead GM Intrusions: People don't trust those who deal with the dead. The dead sometimes don't want shepherding.

Umber wolf, page 295

escapes, it can take root and regrow you completely in three days.

The rhizome seed, while detached from your body, is a mobile level 1 creature. As the seed, you have a target number of 3 and a health of 3, and you inflict 1 point of damage with a spike. You have Armor 3 and an immediate movement speed, though you can deploy a fluffy vegetable "wing" to drift on strong winds. If the rhizome seed is destroyed while detached from your body, you die. Enabler.

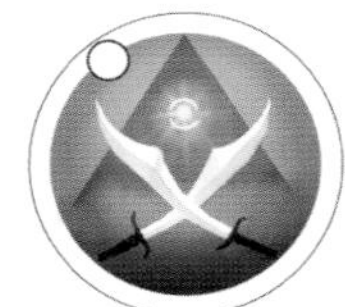

SHEPHERDS THE DEAD

You have a spiritual connection to the Night Vault, where dead souls wander in an extensive series of subterranean tunnels beneath Ardeyn, chased by umber wolves until caught or collected by the Court of Sleep...or caught by you. You have a way with wandering souls, almost as if you were a member of the Court of Sleep yourself, and you can call dead spirits to you.

Shepherds usually wear distinctive robes and a variety of symbols, often with macabre imagery. Runes stitched across your cloak help you concentrate on your abilities.

Shepherds of the dead are most often paradoxes and spinners.

Connection: If this is your starting focus, choose one of the following connections.

1. Pick one other PC. When spirits of the departed whisper to you, as they often do (you've learned to ignore it), that character can sometimes hear what they say.
2. Pick one other PC. She came to you with questions for a departed friend, family member, or enemy.
3. Pick one other PC. You may or may not have told him this, but the spirits whisper to you that he is destined to die soon.
4. Pick one other PC. You owe that character a great debt in crowns.

Equipment: Ardeyn clothing, light armor, one weapon of your choice, an explorer's pack, incense and 10 matchsticks, and 400 crowns.

Spirit Abilities: When you perform moves, revisions, or twists that would normally use force or other energy, they instead use spirit energy. For example, an Exception attack is a confluence of fundamental forces, but when you use it, the effect appears as if delivered by a ghostly revenant whose touch drains life energy. This alteration changes nothing other than the type of damage.

Minor Effect Suggestion: You can ask an additional question of a spirit you question.

Major Effect Suggestion: The spirit you are questioning knows a surprising amount of information about the topic.

Tier 1: Question the Spirits (2 Intellect points). You can call the spirit of a dead creature to you and petition it to answer a few questions (usually no more than three before the spirit fades). To do so is a two-step process, and calling the spirit is potentially the easiest step.

First, you summon a spirit. You must have personally known the spirit when it was a living creature, or you must have an object that was owned by the spirit when it was a living creature and know the spirit's full name, or you must touch the physical remains of the creature. The spirit must be the essence of something that once lived in Ardeyn, and be free to join you.

If the spirit responds, it can manifest as an insubstantial shade that answers for itself, it can inhabit an object or any remains you provide, or it can manifest as an invisible presence that you speak for.

The spirit may not wish to answer your questions; the second step is persuading or convincing the spirit to help. You can attempt to "psychically wrestle" the spirit into submission (an Intellect task), or you can attempt to convince the spirit with diplomacy, deception, or perhaps even blackmail ("Answer me, or I'll tell your children that you were a devotee of Lotan," or, "I'll destroy this relic that belonged to you").

The GM determines what the spirit might know, based on the knowledge it possessed in life. Action to initiate.

Tier 2: Spirit Accomplice. A level 3 spirit of a dead human, qephilim, or other creature of Ardeyn accompanies you and follows your instructions. The spirit must remain an immediate distance from you—if it moves farther away, it fades away at the end of your following turn and cannot return for a day. You and the GM must work out the details of your spirit accomplice, and you'll probably make rolls for it when it takes actions. The spirit accomplice acts on your turn, can move a short distance each round, and exists partially out of phase (allowing it to move through walls, though it makes a poor porter). The spirit takes up residence in an object you designate, and it manifests as either an invisible presence or a ghostly shade. Your spirit accomplice is specialized in one knowledge skill the GM determines.

The spirit is normally insubstantial, but you may spend an action and 3 Intellect points for it to accrete enough substance to affect the world around it. As a level 3 creature with substance, it has a target number of 9 and a health of 9. It doesn't attack creatures, but it can spend its action to serve as an asset for any one attack you make on your turn while it is substantial.

While corporeal, the spirit can't move through objects or fly. A spirit remains corporeal for up to ten minutes at a time, but fades back to being insubstantial if not actively engaged. If your spirit accomplice is destroyed, it reforms in 1d6 days, or you can attract a new spirit in 2d6 days. Enabler.

Tier 3: Command the Dead (3 Intellect points). You can command a spirit or animated dead creature of up to level 5 within short range. If you are successful, the target cannot attack you for one minute, during which time it follows your verbal commands if it can hear and understand you. Action to initiate.

Tier 4: Wraith Cloak. At your command, your spirit accomplice wraps itself around you for up to ten minutes. The spirit automatically inflicts 4 points of damage to anyone who tries to touch you or strike you with a melee attack. While the wraith cloak is active, the difficulty of all tasks you perform to evade the perceptions of others is decreased by one step. Enabler.

Tier 5: Call Dead Spirit (6 Intellect points). At your touch, the remains of a creature dead no longer than seven days appears as a manifest (and apparently physical) spirit. The raised spirit persists for up to a day (or less, if it accomplishes something important to it before then), after which the spirit fades away and cannot be returned again.

The raised spirit remembers everything it knew in life and possesses most of its previous abilities (though not necessarily its equipment). In addition, it gains the ability to become insubstantial as an action for up to a minute at a time. The raised spirit is not beholden to you, and it does not need to remain near you to remain manifest. Action to initiate.

Tier 6: Umber Judge. When you kill a creature with an attack, if you choose, its spirit (if unprotected) is immediately pulled from its body. A portion of its soul energy infuses you, and you regain 1d6 points to one of your Pools (your choice). Then the spirit is ferried to a special cell hidden in the Night Vault of Ardeyn. Only you know where the spirit is located, which means the spirit cannot be questioned, raised, or restored to life by any means unless you allow it.

Improved Command the Dead. When you use your tier 3 Command the Dead ability, you can command undead of up to level 7.

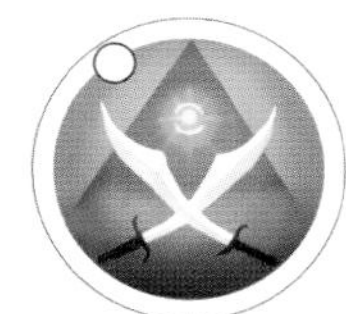

SLAYS DRAGONS

Of all the threats that plague Ardeyn, dragons number among the most feared. But you decided to stand up to that fear by eradicating its source, even though it means putting yourself in more peril than if you just fled like everyone else who hears rumors of a dragon's approach. Even if you give your life, others will tell the story of your bravery.

Usually heavily armed and armored knights, dragon slayers are often afforded great respect.

Dragon slayers are most often vectors, but a spinner or paradox's abilities would be useful against a dragon as well.

Connection: If this is your starting focus, choose one of the following connections.

1. Pick one other PC. You saved him from a dragon (though not by defeating the dragon, which is still out there).
2. Pick one other PC. You tried but failed to save her loved one from a dragon. You still bear the burn scars.
3. Pick one other PC. He knows the name and lair of a dragon, but for some reason he won't share that information with you.
4. Pick one other PC. That character shows potential in the art and philosophy of dragon slaying. You would like to train her but aren't sure she's interested.

Equipment: Ardeyn clothing, armor of your choice, a talwar (a greatsword) or a lance, another weapon of your choice or a shield, an explorer's pack, and 600 crowns.

Minor Effect Suggestion: You can immediately move up to a short distance after

Umber Judge: A qephilim of the Court of Sleep with the position of judging spirits of the Night Vault has the title Umber Judge. For more information, see page 285.

An insubstantial creature can't affect or be affected by anything unless indicated otherwise, such as when an attack is made with a spiritslaying weapon. An insubstantial creature can pass through solid matter without hindrance, but solid energy barriers, such as magical fields of force, keep it at bay.

Slays Dragons GM Intrusions: *Dragons are always craftier and tougher than you think. They sometimes possess abilities you don't know about. Dragons sometimes hunt you instead of the other way around.*

this action.

Major Effect Suggestion: You can immediately take a second action during this turn.

Tier 1: Dragon Sword. You are practiced with greatswords and lances. Enabler.

Dragon Bane. You inflict 1 additional point of damage with weapons. When you inflict damage to creatures more than twice as large or massive as you, you inflict 3 additional points of damage. Enabler.

Dragon Lore. You are trained in the names, habits, suspected lairs, and related topics regarding dragons in Ardeyn. You can make yourself understood in the language of dragons. Enabler.

Tier 2: Will of Legend: You are immune to attacks that would captivate, mesmerize, charm, or otherwise influence your mind. Enabler.

Tier 3: Trained Slayer. You are trained in using greatswords and lances. Enabler.

Improved Dragon Bane. When you inflict damage to creatures more than twice as large or massive as you, you inflict 3 additional points of damage. Enabler.

Rider. You are trained in riding any kind of creature that serves as a mount in Ardeyn. Enabler.

Tier 4: Fight On. You do not suffer the normal penalties for being impaired on the damage track. If debilitated on the damage track, instead of suffering the normal penalty of being unable to take most actions, you can continue to act; however, the difficulty of all tasks you attempt increases by one step. Enabler.

Damage track, page 108

Tier 5: Specialized Slayer. You are specialized in using greatswords and lances. Enabler.

Heroic Dragon Bane. When you inflict damage to creatures more than twice as large or massive as you, you inflict 3 additional points of damage. Enabler.

Tier 6: Slayer (2 Might points). You inflict 3 additional points of damage with a greatsword or lance, regardless of your target. (This ability means that against creatures more than twice as large or massive as you, you inflict a total of 12 additional points of damage.) Enabler.

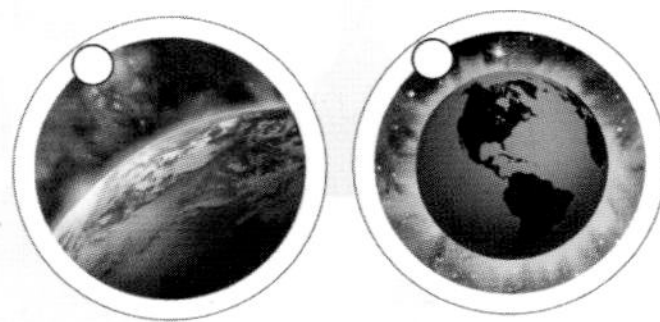

SOLVES MYSTERIES

You are a master of deduction. With a keen eye for detail and a quick wit, you can use a selection of clues to figure out what really happened when others are left scratching their heads. While a character that solves mysteries might be thought of as a detective or an investigator, a professor or even a scientist might also be a mystery solver.

You wear sensible clothing and comfortable shoes, walking that fine line between practical and stylish. You might carry a briefcase for all the tools you require to solve mysteries.

Although any character type works well in this arena, each one likely approaches the task differently. A paradox might solve mysteries through research, a spinner through talking to people, and a vector through taking the direct approach and breaking down a few doors.

Connection: If this is your starting focus, choose one of the following connections.

1. Pick one other PC. She is the true friend who got you started reading mysteries and detective fiction, which led to your current obsession.
2. Pick one other PC. That character does not seem to trust or like you, but you feel compelled to win him over.

3. Pick one other PC. This character is a good sounding board. After you talk to her for an hour, you gain an asset on any knowledge-based task you are trained in.
4. Pick one other PC. You were rivals with him in some endeavor in the past.

Equipment: Street clothes, light or medium armor, two weapons of your choice, laptop computer, flashlight, utility knife, cell phone, and $300.

Minor Effect Suggestion: You discover an additional clue about the mystery you are attempting to solve.

Major Effect Suggestion: When you solve a mystery, the target of your revelation is stunned, unable to move or act for a round, by your dazzling wit.

Tier 1: Investigator. To really shine as an investigator, you must engage your mind and body in your deductions. You can spend points from your Might Pool, Speed Pool, or Intellect Pool to apply levels of Effort to any Intellect-based task. Enabler.

Sleuth. Finding the clues is the first step in solving a mystery. You are trained in perception. Enabler.

Tier 2: Out of Harm's Way. No matter how careful, an investigator sometimes ends up in a scrap. Knowing how to survive is more than half the battle. You are trained in Speed defense tasks. Enabler.

Tier 3: You Studied. To be able to put two and two together to reach a deduction, you have to know a few things. You are trained in two areas of knowledge of your choosing (as long as they are not physical actions or combat related) or specialized in one area. Enabler.

Tier 4: Draw Conclusion (3 Intellect points). After careful observation and investigation (questioning one or more NPCs on a topic, searching an area or a file, and so on) lasting a few minutes, you can learn a pertinent fact. This ability is a difficulty 3 Intellect task. Each additional time you use this ability, the task difficulty increases by one step. The difficulty returns to 3 after you rest for ten hours. Action.

Tier 5: Diffuse Situation. During the course of an investigation, your questions sometimes elicit an angry or even violent response. Through dissembling, verbal distraction, or similar evasion, you prevent a living foe from attacking anyone or anything for one round. Action.

Tier 6: Seize the Initiative (5 Intellect points). Within one minute of successfully using your Draw Conclusion ability, you can take one additional, immediate action, which you can take out of turn. After using this ability, you can't use it again until after your next ten-hour rest. Enabler.

SPAWNS

Sometimes you can't trust anyone but yourself. It's good to have allies, but what ally is more invested in watching your back than you—or at least, a version of yourself that you spawned from your own flesh? You can spawn clones, which not only help you out in a fight, but also aid you in puzzling out problems, lending a hand when necessary, and sometimes even comforting you when you need a shoulder to lean on.

The gene grafts that gave you your powers also give your eyes and fingernails a strange reddish hue. You wear loose clothing that doesn't get in the way of you spawning off a copy of yourself.

Spawners are often spinners because they enjoy having a rapt audience, but any type finds it useful to have extra help.

Connection: If this is your starting focus, choose one of the following connections.

1. Pick one other PC. Your clones never seem to get along with him, though you don't necessarily feel the same.
2. Pick one other PC. Your clone is love with that character.
3. Pick one other PC. You had a much closer relationship with that character in the past.
4. Pick one other PC. That character can never seem to keep straight which of you is the clone, no matter what you do.

Equipment: Ruk clothing, light armor, one weapon of your choice, an umbilical, and an account with 30 bits. And a clone.

Minor Effect Suggestion: Your clone trips the target and knocks it to the ground, or pushes the target out of immediate range (your choice).

Major Effect Suggestion: Your clone makes an immediate attack against the target.

Solves Mysteries GM Intrusions: *Evidence disappears, red herrings confuse, and witnesses lie. Initial research can be faulty.*

Solves Mysteries Equipment:
Ardeyn: *Ardeyn clothing, light or medium armor, two weapons of your choice, lockpicks, matches (10), torches (2), a fish knife, a signal horn, and 30 crowns.*
Ruk: *Ruk clothes, umbilical, light or medium armor, two weapons of your choice, a knife, and 30 bits.*

Spawns GM Intrusions: *Rarely, clones take on lives and consciousnesses of their own. Allies sometimes lose track of who is who.*

Tier 1: Friend in Yourself. Your clone accompanies you and follows your instructions. The clone looks, talks, and acts like you, but it is not as effective as you in many ways. It evokes your descriptor and type, but it doesn't actually have those abilities. It is a level 2 creature with a target number of 6 and a health of 6, and it inflicts 2 points of damage.

You'll probably make rolls for your clone when he takes actions. A clone in combat usually doesn't make separate attacks, but helps you with yours. On your action, if your clone is next to you, he serves as an asset for one attack you make on your turn.

If your clone dies, you can spawn another in 1d6 days. A subtle psychic bond you share with your clone enables it to think, which restricts the number of active clones you can have at once (normally just one). Enabler.

Tier 2: Psychic Bond. The psychic bond you share with your clone improves. Through the bond, you can communicate telepathically at any range within the same recursion. If you wish to temporarily intensify the bond, you can use an action to sense what your clone senses until your next turn. Enabler.

Translates GM Intrusions: *Translation sometimes leads to destinations you never intended.*

Tier 3: Helpful Clone. If you attempt a task and get help from your clone, even though your clone is not trained or specialized in that task, you benefit as if it was. Regardless of how trained (or untrained) you are for the task, if your clone spends its action to help you, the difficulty of the task you attempt is reduced by one step. Enabler.

Tier 4: Covering Clone. Your clone is more concerned about your well-being than its own, and if it is standing next to you when you're attacked, you have cover—the difficulty of Speed defense rolls is decreased by one step. If the attack would hit you without the cover provided by your clone, the attack hits your clone instead.

Improved Clone: Your clone increases to level 4. As a level 4 creature, it has a target number of 12 and a health of 12, and it inflicts 4 points of damage. Enabler.

Damage track, page 108
Recovery roll, page 108

Tier 5: Force Spawning (5 Might points). You force a clone to spawn from you in a matter of seconds, even if you already have one or more active clones. But Force Spawning is immensely taxing, and you are pushed one step down the damage track until after your next recovery roll. The resultant clone is a level 3 creature that is another clone of you, but it lasts only a minute. As a level 3 creature, it has a target number of 9 and a health of 9, and it inflicts 3 points of damage. When it expires at the end of a minute, it slumps like melting wax. Action to initiate.

Tier 6: Psychic Transfer (5 Intellect points). You can switch minds between yourself and your clone within long range through your psychic bond. You have access to all your skills and abilities while in the body of your clone. Your original body is treated as the level 5 clone (though it has all your equipment), and your mind in the clone body is treated as if it was you. You can make the switch permanent or switch back as a separate action. Action.

Improved Clone. Your clone increases to level 5. As a level 5 creature, it has a target number of 15 and a health of 15, and it inflicts 5 points of damage. Enabler.

TRANSLATES (SPECIAL FOCUS)

NOTE: This focus becomes available only after you've translated at least one time. After that, you can choose this focus in whichever recursion you translate to.

You have known something about the Strange for most, if not all, of your life. This intuitive understanding has given you knowledge of recursions, the entities that dwell within it, and, recently, how to move into those worlds that you previously saw only in your dreams.

You cannot start with this focus no matter where your character originates. Upon your first translation (or anytime thereafter), when you translate, you can adopt this focus.

Connection: You cannot start with this focus, so it offers you no special connections.

Equipment: You have clothing appropriate to your current recursion, plus whatever your Recursion Treader ability allowed you to bring from your last recursion. (This means that upon adopting this focus, even for the first time, your Recursion Treader ability takes effect immediately.)

Minor Effect Suggestion: The next time you attack a creature native to the recursion you selected with Recursion Lore (see Tier 1), the attack is modified by one step in your favor.

Major Effect Suggestion: A foe native to a

recursion that you selected with Recursion Lore (see Tier 1) surrenders if you give it a chance to do so.

Tier 1: Recursion Treader. When you translate, you can designate one mundane item that translates along with you. The item takes on the context of the new recursion, if applicable, as decided by the GM. For example, if you want to take an AK-47 assault rifle to Ardeyn, the weapon becomes a particularly well-machined crossbow that fires bolts fast enough to be a rapid-fire weapon. On the other hand, if you bring your smartphone to Ardeyn, it becomes a crystal sphere without much use, since most of the benefits of a smartphone rely on its connection to an Earth-based network.

The item must be small enough that you can carry it with one hand.

Recursion Lore. You are trained in general topics relating to Ruk, Ardeyn, or a recursion of your choice (not Earth), which grants you knowledge of organizations, entities, creatures, threats, lands, and other general topics related to the recursion.

Tier 2: Improved Reach Beyond. Your type grants you the second-tier ability called Reach Beyond (see the description in the vector, paradox, or spinner section). When you call on that ability, you need spend only a single Intellect point to activate it. Enabler.

Tier 3: Translation Savant. When you translate, in addition to choosing to initiate, ease, or hasten, you can also choose to emulate the special capability granted by type, regardless of your own type.

Vector: Acclimation time is reduced to one round when you ease a translation, as if you were a vector. If you are a vector and choose this option for a particular translation, acclimation time is nil.

Paradox: When you initiate a translation and make a translation roll, you get one automatic retry on a failed translation roll, as if you were a paradox. If you are a paradox, you get two retries without having to first roll on the Translation Failure table.

Spinner: Concentration time is reduced to ten minutes when you hasten a translation, as if you were a spinner. If you are a spinner and choose this option for a particular translation, time is reduced to an action.

Tier 4: Follow Through Fiction. Once you have interacted, fought, or observed a creature for at least a minute, you are specialized in tracking it from recursion to recursion, even if the trail has gone cold for up to thirty-three days. You sense a faint energy signature of the creature's passage. This ability also means that you can track a creature from one place in a recursion to another place within that same recursion, but only if it has translated (or traveled through an inapposite gate) within the last thirty-three days.

Tier 5: Master of Form (5 Intellect points). Choose one Tier 1 through Tier 4 ability from a focus you have had in the past. You gain access to that ability—spending additional points normally if required—for one hour. This is true even if the ability, for example, normally requires magic and the recursion you are currently in does not have functional magic. If the ability requires an object, device, or weapon, you must have it or a very close approximation.

Tier 6: The Traveler. The residual charge you gain from moving into a new recursion is amplified. For up to a day after you enter a new recursion, your Might Edge, Speed Edge, and Intellect Edge increase by 1. During that same period, when you make a recovery roll, you recover twice as many points.

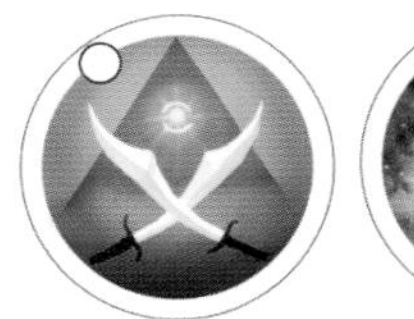

WIELDS TWO WEAPONS AT ONCE

You can hold a weapon in both hands, ready to take on any foe. You fight with two weapons in combat, sometimes called dual wielding. Your weapons can be melee or ranged. A fearsome warrior, quick and strong, you believe that the best defense is a strong offense.

You probably sheathe one weapon on each side or wear both crossed behind your back. They are likely your most prized possessions, and you might have names for them.

Dual wielders are most often vectors.

Connection: If this is your starting focus, choose one of the following connections.

1. Pick one other PC. You have trained with this character so much that if the two of you stand back to back in a fight, you both gain a +1 bonus to Speed defense tasks.
2. Pick one other PC. This person recently mocked your combat stance. How you deal with this (if at all) is up to you.
3. Pick one other PC. The two of you once served on a combat-related mission together.
4. Pick one other PC. You notice that this character is also skilled with weapons, and regardless of how you feel about her otherwise, you can't help but give her respect.

Equipment: Ardeyn clothing, light armor, two light weapons of your choice, an explorer's pack, and 200 crowns.

Minor Effect Suggestion: The target is intimidated and flees as its next action.

Major Effect Suggestion: You can make an immediate additional attack with one of your weapons.

Wields Two Weapons at Once GM Intrusions: *With so many strikes and slices, it's easy to imagine a blade snapping in two or a weapon flying loose from its bearer's grip.*

Wields Two Weapons at Once Equipment
Earth: *Street clothes, light armor, two light weapons of your choice, a courier's bag, a cell phone, and $300.*
Ruk: *Ruk clothing, light armor, two light weapons of your choice, an umbilical, a pack graft, and an account with 30 bits*

Tier 1: Dual Light Wield. You can use two light weapons at the same time, making two separate attacks on your turn as a single action. You remain limited by the amount of Effort you can apply on one action, but because you make separate attacks, your opponent's Armor applies to both. Anything that modifies your attack or damage applies to both attacks, unless it's specifically tied to one of the weapons. Enabler.

Tier 2: Double Strike (3 Might points). When you wield two weapons, you can choose to make one attack roll against a foe. If you hit, you inflict damage with both weapons plus 2 additional points of damage, and because you made a single attack, the target's Armor is subtracted only once. Action.

Tier 3. Dual Medium Wield. You can use two light weapons or medium weapons at the same time (or one light weapon and one medium weapon), making two separate attacks on your turn as a single action. This ability otherwise works like the Dual Light Wield ability. Enabler.

Tier 4: Dual Defense. When you wield two weapons, you are trained in Speed defense tasks. Enabler.

Tier 5: Dual Distraction (4 Speed points). When you wield two weapons, your opponent's next attack is hindered. As a result, the difficulty of your defense roll against that attack is reduced by one step, and the difficulty of your next attack is reduced by one step. Enabler.

Tier 6: Whirling Dervish. When you wield two weapons, you can attack up to six times in one round as a single action, but you must make each attack against a different foe. Make a separate attack roll for each attack. You remain limited by the amount of Effort you can apply on one action, but because you make separate attacks, Armor applies to each of them. Anything that modifies your attack or damage applies to all attacks (positively or negatively), unless it's specifically tied to one of the weapons, in which case it applies to only half of the attacks. Enabler.

WORKS MIRACLES

You manipulate matter and time to help others, and you are beloved by everyone you encounter. Some people consider you a representative of the Maker, or perhaps an Incarnation in training. Perhaps they're right—the source of the energies that you now wield is a mystery to you; for all you know, they are a gift from a power from beyond the world. One thing is for certain—you represent the idea that some magic is inherently good and affirming.

Although the assumption might be that miracle workers are most often paradoxes, it is in fact spinners who likely make the best of their kind.

Connection: If this is your starting focus, pick

Works Miracles GM Intrusions: *Attempts to heal might cause harm instead. Sometimes, a community or individual needs a healer so desperately that they hold one against his will.*

one of the following connections.

1. Pick one other PC. This character quietly suspects that you're a messiah or a supernatural being.
2. Pick one other PC. Your healing powers never work on him, but when he stands next to you, everyone else gains +1 to their recovery rolls.
3. Pick two other PCs. Your healing powers work on them only when they are next to each other.
4. Pick one other PC. You attempted to heal this character's friend and failed.

Equipment: Ardeyn clothing, light armor, one weapon of your choice, an explorer's pack, a healing kit, and 200 crowns.

Minor Effect Suggestion: The target is healed for 1 additional point.

Major Effect Suggestion: The target is healed for 2 additional points.

Tier 1: Healing Touch (1 Intellect point). With a touch, you restore 1d6 points to one stat Pool of any creature. This ability is a difficulty 2 Intellect task. Each time you attempt to heal the same creature, the difficulty increases by one step. The difficulty returns to 2 after that creature rests for ten hours. Action.

Tier 2: Alleviate (3 Intellect points). You attempt to cancel or cure one malady (such as disease or poison) in one creature. Action.

Tier 3: Font of Healing. With your approval, other creatures can touch you and regain 1d6 points to either their Might Pool or their Speed Pool. This healing costs them 2 Intellect points. A single creature can benefit from this ability only once each day. Enabler.

Tier 4: Inspiration (4 Intellect points). Through mental inspiration and the manipulation of time, one creature you choose within short range is granted an additional, immediate action, which it can take out of turn. Action.

Tier 5: Undo (5 Intellect points). You turn back time a few seconds, effectively undoing a single creature's most recent action. That creature can then immediately repeat the same action or try something different. Action.

Tier 6: Greater Healing Touch (4 Intellect points). You touch a creature and restore its Might Pool, Speed Pool, and Intellect Pool to their maximum values, as if it were fully rested. A single creature can benefit from this ability only once each day. Action.

WORKS THE SYSTEM

You've knocked around a lot and run afoul of the law a few times, but you've evaded authorities on a variety of fronts more often than not. That's because you are adept at noticing flaws and exploits in systems, whether those systems are civil laws, investment regulations, computer codes, games of all sorts, and similar artificial constructions. Once you notice and fully comprehend a system, you can manipulate it to your own ends.

You are a manipulator, but you likely keep a term like that to yourself. Tell people you're an entrepreneur—that always sounds good.

Those who work the system are most often spinners.

Connection: If this is your starting focus, choose of the following connections.

1. Pick one other PC. You turned her failing grade into a passing one, fixed an immigration issue, made a driving offense disappear from computer records, or managed some similar aid for that character.
2. Pick one other PC. You're aware that he knows an incriminating or embarrassing secret about you.
3. Pick one other PC. Whenever he is next to you, the difficulty of tasks involving interactions with people or attempts to use machines is increased by one step.
4. Pick one other PC. Whenever you charm or persuade others, this character always gains the same benefits of your actions as you do.

Equipment: Street clothes, a weapon of your choice, a laptop computer, a smartphone, and $500.

Minor Effect Suggestion: You learn something completely unexpected but useful.

Major Effect Suggestion: You can immediately take a second action during this turn.

Tier 1: Hack the Impossible (3 Intellect points). You can persuade automatons, machines, and computers to do your bidding. You can discover an encrypted password, break through security on a website, briefly turn off a machine such as a surveillance camera, or disable an automaton with just a moment's worth of fiddling. Action.

Works the System GM Intrusions: *Contacts sometimes have ulterior motives. Devices sometimes have failsafes or even traps.*

When you're hacking the impossible, the GM will decide if your hack is reasonable and determine what the level of difficulty might be to achieve it (for comparison, discovering a normal password when you have direct access to the system is a difficulty 2 task for you).

Computer Programming: You are trained in using (and exploiting) computer software, you know one or more computer languages well enough to write basic programs, and you are fluent with Internet protocol. Enabler.

Tier 2: Connected. You know people who get things done—not just respected people in positions of authority, but also a variety of online hackers and regular street criminals. These people are not necessarily your friends and might not be trustworthy, but they at least owe you a favor. You and the GM should work out the details of your contacts. Enabler.

Tier 3: Confidence Artist. When you're hacking into a computer system, running a con, picking a pocket, fooling or tricking a dupe, sneaking something by a guard, and so on, you treat the task as if it were one level lower. Enabler.

Tier 4: Confuse Enemy (4 Intellect points). Through a clever bit of misdirection involving a flourish of your coat, ducking at just the right moment, or a similar stratagem, you can attempt to redirect a physical melee attack that would otherwise successfully hit you. When you do, the misdirected attack hits another creature you choose within immediate range of both you and the attacking foe. This ability is a difficulty 2 Intellect task. Enabler.

Tier 5: Work the Friendship (4 Intellect points). You know just what to say to draw a little extra effort from an ally. That, combined with your connection to the Strange, grants one creature you choose within short range an additional, immediate action, which it can take out of turn. The creature uses the action you give it however it wishes. Action.

Tier 6: Call in Favor (4 Intellect points). A guard, doctor, technician, or hired thug in the employ of or allied with a foe is secretly your ally or owes you a favor. When you call in the favor successfully, the target does what he can to help you out of a specific fix (unties you, slips you a knife, leaves a cell door unlocked) in a way that minimizes the risk of the target revealing his divided loyalties to his employer or other allies. This ability is a difficulty 3 Intellect task. Each additional time you use this ability, the difficulty increases by one step. The difficulty returns to 3 after you rest for ten hours. Action.

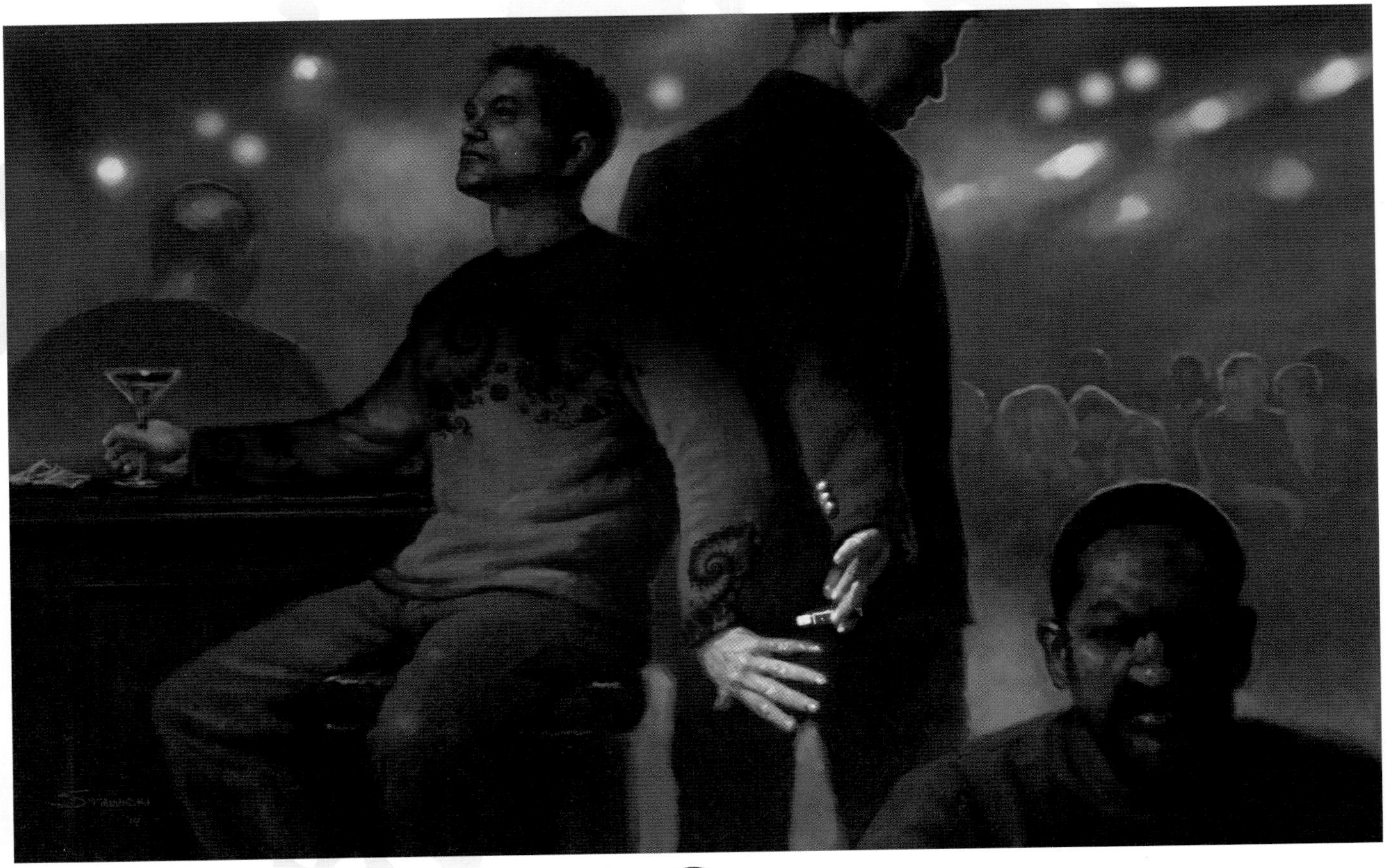

CHAPTER 7

EQUIPMENT

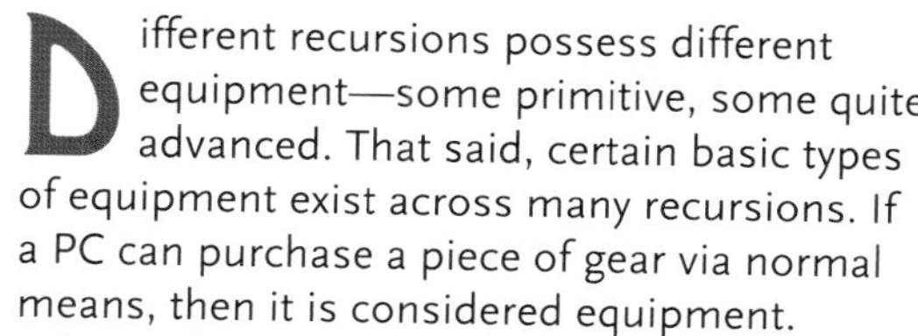

Different recursions possess different equipment—some primitive, some quite advanced. That said, certain basic types of equipment exist across many recursions. If a PC can purchase a piece of gear via normal means, then it is considered equipment.

Items that can't be purchased at a shop because of their scarcity or power are likely artifacts or cyphers. For example, while on Earth, normal player characters don't have ready access to military-grade hardware such as missiles or jet aircraft. In Ardeyn, PCs can't just purchase magic wands or rings of power. In Ruk, despite all the sci-fi advances of the culture, even more advanced alien technology from distant stars can't be had simply by wanting it. All these would be considered examples of artifacts within a given recursion.

Equipment does not translate from one recursion to the next—characters who go to another recursion get new, equivalent equipment, appropriate to that context. The only items that characters take with them when translating to a new recursion are cyphers (though the form of the cypher often changes, the effect stays the same) and the rare artifact that comes directly from the Strange. Because both cyphers and Strange-based artifacts are linked to the Strange and not a specific world, they adapt to whatever context they are in.

CURRENCY AND PRICES

Many recursions have their own currency or, as on Earth, many currencies. Within a given society, methods exist for exchanging currency with relative ease. When translating, PCs may have a sum of currency appropriate to that location (bits in Ruk or crowns in Ardeyn, for example) depending on their types and foci.

The equipment lists in the various setting chapters use denominations in the currency appropriate to the recursion where the gear can be purchased. These lists are all very generalized and simple, with prices painted in broad strokes. The GM has a lot of room to vary pricing or currency. In The Strange, money and wealth are rarely anything other than a means to an end. In the case of Earth equipment, we have defaulted to the dollar, but other currencies could be used instead—and they should be used if a game is set in a place where dollars aren't used. In some recursions, barter might be an acceptable means of exchange.

Some GMs might want to skip over worrying about things like the price of mundane equipment. You can track how often the characters change clothes and how many different pairs of pants they have if you want, but most groups will end up just ignoring that level of detail, and that's fine.

That's why the equipment lists focus on really useful gear needed for adventures, and less on truly mundane items such as toothbrushes or oil to leather your horse's saddle.

Of course, the availability—or lack thereof—of a needed item can be an interesting story point in any recursion.

ENCUMBRANCE

Weights of objects are not listed, because the game rules assume that how much a character carries is not tracked. If the GM determines that a character is carrying too much equipment, though, he should either (1) assign a difficulty and ask for a Might action, or (2) assign the weight a Speed and Might cost to be deducted from the appropriate Pool. Method 1 is useful when a character wants to carry a single heavy object for a limited time—for example, moving a hefty iron safe out of a bank and loading it into a pickup truck bed. Method 2 works well for long-term encumbrance, such as when a character dons a backpack full of

When you see the word "Armor" capitalized in the game rules (other than as the name of a special ability), it refers to your Armor characteristic—the number you subtract from incoming damage. When you see the word "armor" with a lowercase "a," it refers to any physical armor you might wear.

survival gear and sets off across the tundra.

When assigning a Speed and Might cost, the Speed cost is a penalty assessed immediately, and it remains until the character is unburdened. The lost Speed points aren't recovered through rest or other means—only when the burden is removed. The Might cost is a continuing cost deducted each hour, and those points are recovered normally. The Speed cost and the Might cost are always the same: 1 point for each, 2 points for each, or 3 points for each. Wearing armor has a similar cost for the same reasons.

ARMOR

Characters expecting danger frequently wear armor. Even the simplest of protective coverings helps against physical attacks, and more sophisticated or heavier armor protects against even graver threats.

You can wear only one type of armor at a time—you cannot wear a medium tactical vest over a light tactical vest, for example. However, Armor bonuses from multiple sources combine to provide a total Armor rating. For example, if you have a ballistic helmet that gives you +1 to Armor and wear a medium tactical vest that gives +2 to Armor, you have a total of +3 to Armor.

Not all characters are practiced with all armor. Although anyone can wear any armor, doing so can be taxing. Wearing armor costs you Might points and reduces your Speed Pool. You can rest to recover these lost Might points in the standard manner, even if you're still wearing armor. The Speed Pool reduction remains as long as you wear the armor, but the Pool returns to normal as soon as you remove it. Some vectors and certain other characters have abilities that reduce the costs and penalties of wearing armor.

Armor	Might cost per hour	Speed Pool reduction while worn
Light	1	2
Medium	2	3
Heavy	3	5

WEAPONS

Not all characters are familiar with all weapons. Vectors know their way around most types, but spinners prefer light or medium weapons, and paradoxes usually stick to light weapons. If you wield a weapon that you're not at least practiced with, the difficulty of making an attack with that weapon is increased by one step.

Light weapons inflict only 2 points of damage, but they reduce the difficulty of the attack by one step because they are fast and easy to use. Light weapons are punches, kicks, knives, handaxes, light pistols (.22 caliber), and so on. Weapons that are particularly small are light weapons.

Medium weapons inflict 4 points of damage. Medium weapons include katanas, nightsticks, medium pistols (such as a 9mm pistol), and so on. Most weapons are medium. Anything that could be used in one hand (even if it's often used in two hands, such as a 9mm pistol) is a medium weapon. However, a .22 caliber rifle, despite being used in two hands, is also a medium weapon because of its small caliber.

Heavy weapons inflict 6 points of damage, and you must use two hands to attack with them. Heavy weapons are huge swords, heavy pistols (such as a .357 Magnum revolver), shotguns, high-caliber rifles, and so on. Most anything used in two hands is a heavy weapon.

ESTIMATING EQUIPMENT QUALITY

One consideration for determining the quality (and level) of a given piece of equipment is to know in what recursion it was fashioned. The law under which an item was made isn't enough to determine its level, though it's a start. For instance, most items made in a recursion operating under the law of Substandard Physics are also likely to be substandard. One determinant regarding an item's potential quality is if the recursion (or prime world) has a functioning industrial infrastructure, and if the item in question represents the height of that infrastructure's high-tech (or high-magic) material science (or material art). Even so, it's also important to know if the item is made from cheap materials and is mass produced with planned obsolescence in mind.

For instance, if you purchase a high-quality climbing rope made of dynamic nylon at a sporting goods store on Earth, it might be a level 5 rope, as opposed to a hemp rope commonly found in Ardeyn. Of course, one might still be able to buy a hemp rope on Earth, and it would also be level 3. On the other hand, a normal hollow pressboard door found in many mass-produced houses on Earth is probably only level 2 in quality, which is not nearly as tough as an average oak door (probably level 4 or 5) in Ardeyn.

It comes down to the following rule: if the location has an industrial base that uses advanced material arts and sciences, there's a potential for higher-level items to be available, but it's not a guarantee.

EARTH EQUIPMENT

The Earth equipment presented below represents general examples of useful items in the game and is not an exhaustive list. If you want more comprehensive choices (for Earth equipment, anyway), go to any store you want and look around. Your character is free to purchase pens, blue jeans, liquid soap, rubber gloves, umbrellas, sticky tape, nylon fishing line, candy, and a hundred more similar items, just as you are.

ARMOR

Light (1 point of Armor)	Price
Leather jacket	$200
Trench coat, with liner	$200

Medium (2 points of Armor)	Price
Armored tactical vest	$1,000

Heavy (3 points of Armor)	Price
Full body armor	$2,000

WEAPONS

Light (2 points of damage)	Price	Notes
Nightstick	$20	
Hunting knife	$60	
Light handgun	$300	Short range
Unarmed (punch, kick, elbow)	—	
Whip	$40	

Medium (4 points of damage)	Price	Notes
Machete	$200	
Compound bow	$500	Long range
Medium handgun	$700	Long range
Medium bladed weapon	$800	
Submachine gun	$1,000	Rapid-fire weapon
3-foot pipe wrench	$200	Also tightens pipes

Heavy (6 points of damage)	Price	Notes
Katana	$800	
Medieval greatsword	$1,000	
Heavy handgun	$1,300	Long range
Rifle	$2,000	300-foot (100 m) range
Assault rifle	$3,000	Rapid-fire weapon
Shotgun	$350	Immediate range

SURVEILLANCE EQUIPMENT

Item	Price	Notes
Mini GPS tracker	$200+	Self-powered
Telephoto lens × 100	$400	Comes with mount
Nightvision goggles	$1,000	Requires a connection with military or other agency
Pen video camera	$50	Press to record
Concealed microphone	$100	Record or transmit
Concealed camera	$150	Record or transmit
Motion sensor	$100	Audible or silent alarm

Disguise kit	$120	Asset to disguise tasks
Automation "smart home" kit	$300	Wi-Fi network hub for motion sensor, hidden camera, hidden mic, and so on
Electronic key fob	$800	Wireless entry to most cars with such locks
Software malware package	$250	Pwn a target's laptop, computer, or smartphone

Other Equipment

Item	Price	Notes
Complete first aid kit	$50	Adds 1 to recovery rolls for rests longer than one round (ten uses)
Smartphone	$300+	Some phones talk back if talked to
Flashlight	$10	Bright light at immediate range, dim light at short range
Duct tape	$5	Useful for so many reasons
Straightjacket	$450	
Handcuffs	$35	Comfort fit costs extra
Padlock with keys	$10	
Geiger counter	$250	
Bolt cutter	$50	
Cigar lighter, flameless	$50	Wind won't blow out torch
Gas mask	$150	
Everything else	*	If you can buy it in real life, you can buy it while on Earth

ARDEYN EQUIPMENT

In Ardeyn, the standard currency is the "crown." The equipment presented in this section includes general examples of the kinds of items available in Ardeyn and is not meant to be an exhaustive list.

ARMOR

Asset	Price	Notes
Shield	30	Asset for Speed defense tasks

Light (1 point of Armor)	Price
Leather jerkin	30
Hides and furs	20
Qephilim-craft coat*	4,000

Medium (2 points of Armor)	Price
Brigandine	50
Chainmail	60
Relic breastplate*	5,000

Heavy (3 points of Armor)	Price
Plate armor	150
Scale armor	120
Incarnation-blessed plate armor*	10,000

*Special armor counts as one armor type less heavy while worn; special light armor doesn't require a wearer to be practiced in wearing it to avoid penalties.

WEAPONS

Light (2 points of damage)	Price	Notes
Club	5	
Dagger	10	
Sabre	20	
Shortbow	80	Long range
12 arrows	10	
Sickle	10	
Unarmed (punch, kick, elbow)	—	
Whip	20	

Medium (4 points of damage)	Price	Notes
Battleaxe	30	
Bow	40	Long range
12 arrows	10	
Crossbow	50	Long range
12 medium bolts		
Flail	30	
Hammer	20	
Javelin	10	Short range
Mace	20	
Polearm	30	Often used two-handed
Quarterstaff	12	Often used two-handed
Spear	20	Can be thrown up to long range
Shamshir (scimitar)	35	
Trident	25	

Heavy (6 points of damage)	Price	Notes
Greataxe	50	
Heavy crossbow	70	Long range, action to reload
12 heavy bolts	35	
Lance	40	Often used on a mount
Maul	40	
Talwar (great shamshir)	55	

Other Equipment

Item	Price	Notes
Backpack	20	
Bedroll	20	
Book	150	Asset to roll concerning book topic after thirty minutes spent reading
Burlap sack	3	
Chalk, 7 pieces	3	
Comestibles and Clothing		
Ale/wine/other alcohol (glass)	2	
Ale/wine/other alcohol (bottle)	12	
Boots or shoes	10	
Nargila (water pipe)	30	
Nargila tobacco	2	
Clothing	10	Fine clothing: up to 50 crowns
Meal	2	Very nice meal: up to 50 crowns
Rations for one day	15	
Crowbar	20	
Disguise kit	120	Asset to disguise tasks
Explorer's pack	150	50 feet (15 m) rope, three days' rations, three spikes, hammer, warm clothes, sturdy boots, and three torches
First aid kit	100	Asset to healing tasks
Grappling hook	30	
Lockpicks	50	
Matchsticks (10)	10	
Musical instrument	50–1,000	
Pouch or other small container	5	
Rope (50 feet / 15 m)	20	
Signal horn	10	Audible for 3 miles (5 km)
Spikes and hammer	30	
String (200 feet / 60 m)	1	
Tent	30	
Torches (2)	5	

Ruk Equipment

In Ruk, the standard currency is the "bit," and all of it is virtual, monitored through the All Song. In other words, each individual has an account, and transactions are conducted by accessing the All Song and making instantaneous additions or subtractions to the accounts one does business with.

Armor

Light (1 point of Armor)	Price
Second skin	10
Plastiskin	15
Slicksuit	20
Medium (2 points of Armor)	
Carapace	55
Lifesuit	90
Spiked carapace	75
Heavy (3 points of Armor)	
Heavy carapace	350
Heavy spiked carapace	400
Bio-armor	1,000

Weapons

Light (2 points of damage)	Price	Notes
Blowgun	1	Short range
12 darts	3	
Finger needle	2	Excellent for delivering poisons
Knife	1	Can be thrown up to short range
Needler	5	See further notes
Magazine of 10 needles	3	
Quiver shiv	50	Ignores Armor
Spore pistol	10	See further notes
Ammo pod (12 shots)	5	
Stun ammo pod (12 shots—level 3)	15	
Stun ammo pod (12 shots—level 5)	40	
Medium (4 points of damage)		
Caustic sprayer	20	See further notes
Deathblade	5	
Longsword	3	
Mace	3	
Spike pistol	20	Long range, self-generates ammo
Spine lance	40	See further notes
Spear	3	Can be thrown up to long range
Heavy (6 points of damage)		
Heavy spear	5	
Pole axe	5	
Slaughter accelerator	55	See further notes
Spike rifle	35	Long range, self-generates ammo

Grenade Pods

All grenade pods are organic bombs that can be thrown to short range and explode in an immediate radius.

Pod	Price	Notes
Acidpod	10	3 points of acid damage
Flamepod	25	4 points of fire damage
Smokepod	10	Opaque black cloud obscures area for 1d6 rounds
Sporepod	40	Difficulty 4 Might defense roll to avoid losing next action

Poisons

Level 3	Price	Notes
Tellu	15	3 points of Might damage
Kral	15	Lose next action
Narm	30	Unconsciousness for one minute
Level 5	**Price**	**Notes**
Arutellu	30	5 points of Might damage
Unik	30	4 points of Speed damage
Reen	30	4 points of Intellect damage
Arukral	65	Confusion: lose all actions for one minute
Level 7	**Price**	**Notes**
Valitellu	60	6 points of Might damage
Valunik	60	5 points of Speed damage
Valireen	60	5 points of Intellect damage
Valinarm	100	Unconsciousness for one minute
Xah	200	Coma until awakened

Other Equipment

Item	Price	Notes
Binoculars	10	
Breather	8	
Clothing	3	
Disguise graft	25	
Healing kit	25	Asset to healing tasks
Heavy tools	3	
Flashlight or headlamp	5	
Light tools	3	
Pod launcher	20	
Spore filter mask	20	
Umbilical	10	
Wing glider	7	

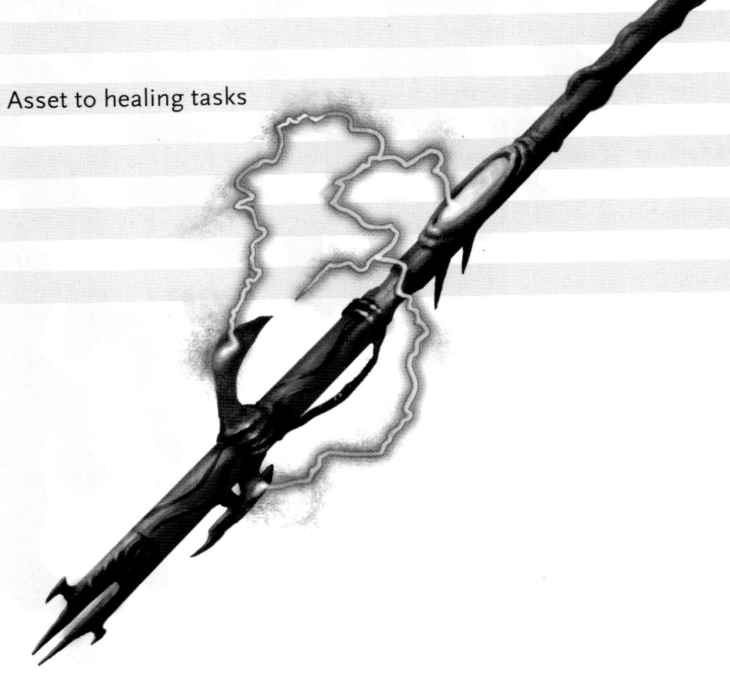

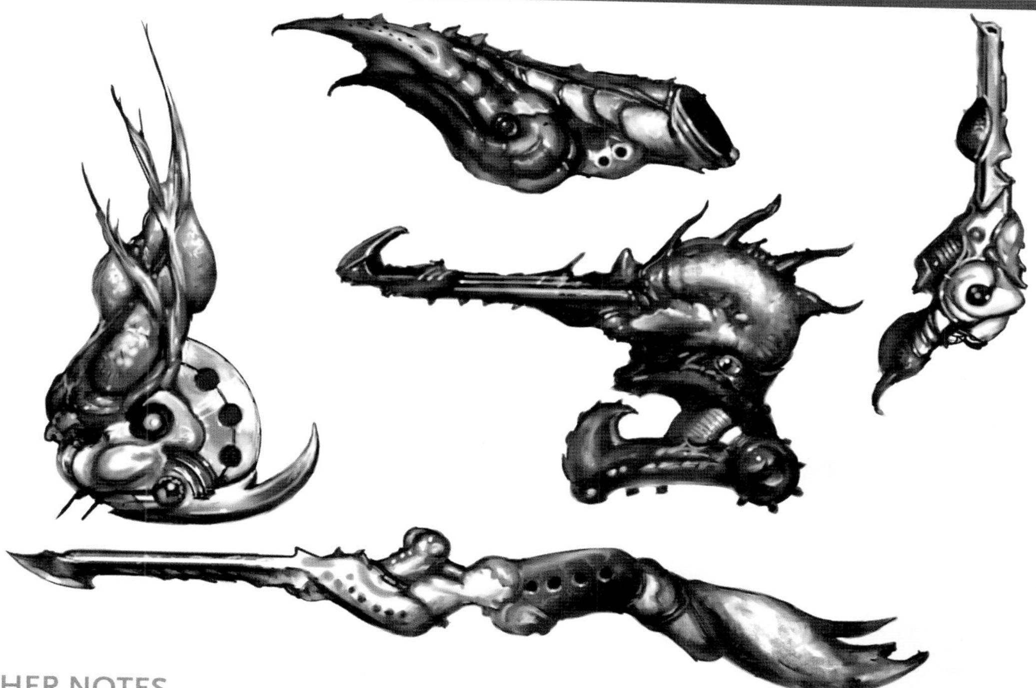

FURTHER NOTES

WEAPONS

Caustic Sprayer: Sprays a stream of caustic fluid to short range. It can be used as a rapid-fire weapon.

Deathblade: A longsword fitted with a poison dispenser. The poison then lasts until used.

Needler: This is a pistol-like weapon that fires projectiles up to short range. It can be used as a rapid-fire weapon. If loaded with poison and a magazine of needles, each needle is poisoned.

Slaughter Accelerator: Fires a burst of flechettes up to long range. It can be used as a rapid-fire weapon.

Spine Lance: Long wandlike device that plugs directly into the user's spine. Inflicts bioelectric damage. At a cost of 5 Might points to the wielder, it can inflict 6 additional points of damage in a single attack.

Spore Pistol: Fires a stream of caustic spores up to short range. It can also be loaded with spores that keep a living target who fails a Might defense roll from taking an action on their next turn rather than inflicting damage.

ARMOR

Bio-Armor: Fully sealed suit of self-repairing, living armor that provides full life support and nutrients to the wearer indefinitely, in any environment.

Carapace: Organic armor plates. Can be medium or light, and covered with spikes. Spiked carapace inflicts 1 point of damage on any foe striking wearer in melee.

Lifesuit: Light bodysuit that also provides an hour of life support in any environment. (Life support function recharges every day.)

Plastiskin: Light armor that also provides mild protection from the elements.

Second Skin: Armor so light it is nigh indistinguishable from flesh.

Slicksuit: Light bodysuit with a coating that makes it extremely hard to grasp. The difficulty of any attempt by the wearer to slip free of a grasp, of bonds, or through a tight space is reduced by one step.

OTHER EQUIPMENT

Breather: Allows wearer to breathe safely for four hours. One use.

Healing Kit: Contains three injections that restore 2 points to Might Pool.

Pod Launcher: Launches grenade pods up to long range.

Spore Filter Mask: Wearer is immune to spores of level 3 or lower, and the difficulty of all breathing-related Might defense actions is decreased by two steps.

Umbilical: When connected to All Song outlets in Ruk, provides a direct interface with the All Song, allowing for communication with anyone in the recursion, as well as general information inquiries (an Intellect task).

Wing Glider: Backpack-like device that, in one action, sprouts wings and allows the wearer to glide in the wind or from high places, moving a short distance each round. Maintaining the glide is an action each round.

An umbilical allows a PC to connect to the All Song in Ruk. If someone using an umbilical to connect is suddenly dragged away or thrust into combat, the umbilical automatically and safely retracts, causing no harm to the character.

All Song, page 192

ARTIFACTS

Artifacts are more powerful than equipment, and they can't simply be purchased. You can find the artifacts appropriate for Earth, Ardeyn, Ruk, and the various other recursions near the ends of their chapters.

Like equipment, artifacts are unique to the world in which they are made, and they do not translate with characters. On the other hand, they do move through inapposite gates and out into the Strange. If an artifact moves via inapposite gate to a recursion that operates under the same law as the artifact's recursion of origin, the artifact continues to operate in the new recursion. If it moves by inapposite gate to a new recursion that operates under a different law, the artifact begins to degrade in power about a minute after it arrives, according to the rules for inapposite travel.

All artifacts have a level. They also have a rate of power depletion. When an artifact is used or activated, the player rolls the designated die (1d6, 1d10, 1d20, or 1d100). If the die shows the depletion number(s), the item works, but that is its last use. A depletion entry of "—" means that the artifact never depletes, and an entry of "automatic" means that it can be used only once.

Depowered artifacts can sometimes be recharged using the repair rules, depending on the item's nature. Other special abilities can also repower an expended item, but probably for only one use.

FINDING, IDENTIFYING, AND USING ARTIFACTS

Characters can sometimes find artifacts while on adventures. They might be in ancient ruins, either intact or in need of manipulation to get them working. They could have been stolen from well-guarded military installations. They might be granted as rewards or taken from fallen foes. Sometimes they can even be purchased from a specialized source, but this occurs more rarely than most PCs would probably like.

After the PCs find an artifact, identifying it is a separate Intellect task. The GM sets the difficulty of the task, but it is usually equal to the artifact's level. Identifying it takes fifteen minutes to three hours. If the PCs can't identify an artifact, they can bring it to an expert to be identified or, if desired, traded or sold.

Characters can attempt to use an artifact that is not identified, but this is usually an Intellect task equal to the artifact's level + 2. Failure might mean that the PC can't figure out how to use the artifact or uses it incorrectly (GM's discretion). Of course, even if characters use an unidentified artifact correctly the first time, they have no idea what the effect might be.

Once characters have identified an artifact, using it for the first time requires an additional Intellect action; this process is far more complex than pushing a button. It can involve manipulating touchscreens, reciting the proper arcane words, or anything else that fits the context of the recursion. The GM sets the difficulty, but it is usually equal to the artifact's level.

ARTIFACTS

Part 3: Playing the Game

CHAPTER 8

RULES OF THE GAME

The Strange is played in the joint imagination of all the players, including the GM. The GM sets the scene, the players state what their characters attempt to do, and the GM determines what happens next. The rules and the dice help make the game run smoothly, but it's the people, not the rules or the dice, that direct the action and determine the story—and the fun. If a rule gets in the way or detracts from the game, the players and the GM should work together to change it.

Planetovore, page 8

This is how you play The Strange:

1. The player tells the GM what she wants to do. This is a *character action*.
2. The GM determines if that action is routine (and therefore works without needing a roll) or if there's a chance of failure.
3. If there is a chance of failure, the GM determines which stat the task uses (Might, Speed, or Intellect) and the task's difficulty—how hard it will be on a scale from 1 (really easy) to 10 (basically impossible).
4. The player and the GM determine if anything about her character—such as training, equipment, special abilities, or various actions—can modify the difficulty up or down by one or more steps. If these modifications reduce the difficulty to less than 1, the action is routine (and therefore works with no roll needed).
5. If the action still isn't routine, the GM uses its difficulty to determine the target number—how high the player must roll to succeed at the action (see the Task Difficulty Chart on page 98). The GM doesn't have to tell the player what the target number is, but he can give her a hint, especially if her character would reasonably know if the action was easy, average, difficult, or impossible.
6. The player rolls a d20. If she rolls equal to or higher than the target number, her character succeeds.

Might, page 16
Speed, page 16
Intellect, page 16
Task difficulty, page 98

Training, page 21
Equipment, page 85

That's it. That's how to do anything, whether it's identifying a strange device, calming a raging drunk, climbing a treacherous cliff, or battling a planetovore. Even if you ignored all the other rules, you could still play The Strange with just this information. The key features here are: character actions, determining task difficulty, and determining modifications.

TAKING ACTION

Each character gets one turn each round. On a character's turn, she can do one thing—an action. All actions fall into one of three categories: Might, Speed, or Intellect (just like the three stats). Many actions require die rolls—rolling a d20.

Every action performs a task, and every task has a difficulty that determines what number a character must reach or surpass with a die roll to succeed.

Most tasks have a difficulty of 0, which means the character succeeds automatically. For example, walking across a room, opening a door, and throwing a stone into a nearby bucket are all actions, but none of them requires a roll. Actions that are usually difficult or that become difficult due to the situation (such as shooting at a target in a blizzard) have a higher difficulty. These actions usually require a roll.

Some actions require a minimum expenditure of Might, Speed, or Intellect points. If a character cannot spend the minimum number of points needed to complete the action, she automatically fails at the task.

DETERMINING TASK STAT

Every task relates to one of a character's three stats: Might, Speed, or Intellect. Physical activities that require strength, power, or endurance relate to Might. Physical activities that require agility, flexibility, or fast reflexes

KEY CONCEPTS

ACTION: Anything a character does that is significant—punch a foe, leap a chasm, activate a device, use a special power, and so on. Each character can take one action in a round.

CHARACTER: Any creature in the game capable of acting, whether it is a player character (PC) run by a player or a nonplayer character (NPC) run by the game master (GM). In The Strange, even bizarre creatures, sentient machines, and living energy beings can be "characters."

DIFFICULTY: A measure of how easy it is to accomplish a task. Difficulty is rated on a scale from 1 (lowest) to 10 (highest). Altering the difficulty to make a task harder is referred to as increasing the difficulty. Altering it to make a task easier is referred to as reducing or decreasing the difficulty. All changes in difficulty are measured in steps. Difficulty often equates directly with level, so opening a level 3 locked door probably has a difficulty of 3.

EFFORT: Spending points from a stat Pool to reduce the difficulty of a task. A PC decides whether or not to apply Effort on his turn before the roll is made. NPCs never apply Effort.

LEVEL: A way to measure the strength, difficulty, power, or challenge of something in the game. Everything in the game has a level. NPCs and objects have levels that determine the difficulty of any task related to them. For example, an opponent's level determines how hard she is to hit or avoid in combat. A door's level indicates how hard it is to break down. A lock's level determines how hard it is to pick. Levels are rated on a scale from 1 (lowest) to 10 (highest). PC tiers are a little like levels, but they go only from 1 to 6 and mechanically work very differently than levels—for example, a PC's tier does not determine a task's difficulty.

ROLL: A d20 roll made by a PC to determine whether an action is successful. Although the game occasionally uses other dice, when the text simply refers to "a roll," it always means a d20 roll.

ROUND: A length of time about five to ten seconds long. There are about ten rounds in a minute. When it's really important to track precise time, use rounds. Basically, it's the length of time to take an action in the game, but since everyone more or less acts simultaneously, all characters get to take an action each round.

STAT: One of the three defining characteristics for PCs: Might, Speed, or Intellect. Each stat has two values: Pool and Edge. Your Pool represents your raw, innate ability, and your Edge represents knowing how to use what you have. Each stat Pool can increase or decrease over the course of play—for example, you can lose points from your Might Pool when struck by an opponent, spend points from your Intellect Pool to activate a special ability, or rest to recover points in your Speed Pool after a long day of marching. Anything that damages a stat, restores a stat, or boosts or penalizes a stat affects the stat's Pool.

TASK: Any action that a PC attempts. The GM determines the difficulty of the task. In general, a task is something that you do and an action is you performing that task, but in most cases they mean the same thing.

TURN: The part of the round when a creature takes its actions. For example, if a paradox and a vector are fighting an inkling, each round the paradox takes an action on his turn, the vector takes an action on her turn, and the inkling takes an action on its turn. Some abilities or effects last only while a creature takes its turn or end when a creature starts its next turn.

TASK DIFFICULTY

TASK DIFFICULTY	DESCRIPTION	TARGET NO.	GUIDANCE
0	Routine	0	Anyone can do this basically every time.
1	Simple	3	Most people can do this most of the time.
2	Standard	6	Typical task requiring focus, but most people can usually do this.
3	Demanding	9	Requires full attention; most people have a 50/50 chance to succeed.
4	Difficult	12	Trained people have a 50/50 chance to succeed.
5	Challenging	15	Even trained people often fail.
6	Intimidating	18	Normal people almost never succeed.
7	Formidable	21	Impossible without skills or great effort.
8	Heroic	24	A task worthy of tales told for years afterward.
9	Immortal	27	A task worthy of legends that last lifetimes.
10	Impossible	30	A task that normal humans couldn't consider (but one that doesn't break the laws of physics).

relate to Speed. Mental activities that require force of will, memory, or mental power relate to Intellect. This means you can generalize tasks into three categories: Might tasks, Speed tasks, and Intellect tasks. You can also generalize rolls into three categories: Might rolls, Speed rolls, and Intellect rolls.

Effort, page 100

The category of the task or roll determines what kind of Effort you can apply to the roll and may determine how a character's other abilities affect the roll. For example, a paradox may have an ability that makes him better at Intellect rolls, and a vector may have an ability that makes her better at Speed rolls.

DETERMINING TASK DIFFICULTY

Part 6: Running the Game, page 309, offers additional guidance for setting task difficulty.

The most frequent thing a GM does during the game—and probably the most important thing—is setting a task's difficulty. To make the job easier, use the Task Difficulty table, which associates difficulty rating with a descriptive name, a target number, and general guidance about the difficulty.

Every difficulty from 1 to 10 has a target number associated with it. The target number is easy to remember: it's always three times the difficulty. The target number is the minimum number a player needs to roll on a d20 to succeed at the task. Moving up or down on the table is called increasing or decreasing the difficulty, which is measured in steps.

For example, reducing a difficulty 5 task to a difficulty 4 task is "reducing the difficulty by one step." Most modifiers affect the difficulty rather than the player's roll. This has two consequences:

1. Low target numbers such as 3 or 6, which would be boring in most games that use a d20, are not boring in The Strange. For example, if you need to roll a 6 or higher, you still have a 25% chance to fail.

2. The upper levels of difficulty (7, 8, 9, and 10) are all but impossible because the target numbers are 21 or higher, which you can't roll on a d20. However, it's common for PCs to have abilities or equipment that reduce the difficulty of a task and thus lower the target number to something they *can* roll on a d20.

A character's tier does not determine a task's level. Things don't get more difficult just because a character's tier increases—the world doesn't instantly become a more difficult place. Fourth-tier characters don't deal only with level 4 creatures or difficulty 4 tasks (although a fourth-tier character probably has a better shot at success than a first-tier character does). Just because something is level 4 doesn't necessarily mean it's meant only for fourth-tier characters. Similarly, depending on the situation, a fifth-tier character could find a difficulty 2 task just as challenging as a second-tier character does.

Therefore, when setting the difficulty of a task, the GM should rate the task on its own merits, not on the power of the characters.

MODIFYING THE DIFFICULTY

After the GM sets the difficulty for a task, the player can try to modify it for her character. Any such modification applies only to this particular attempt at the task. In other words, rewiring an electronic door lock normally might be difficulty 6, but since the character doing the work is skilled in such tasks, has the right tools, and has

another character assisting her, the difficulty in this instance might be much lower. That's why it's important for the GM to set a task's difficulty without taking the character into account. The character comes in at this step.

By using skills and assets, working together, and—perhaps most important—applying Effort, a character can decrease a task's difficulty by multiple steps to make it easier. Rather than adding bonuses to the player's roll, reducing the difficulty lowers the target number. If she can reduce the difficulty of a task to 0, no roll is needed; success is automatic. (An exception is if the GM decides to use a GM intrusion on the task, in which case the player would have to make a roll at the original difficulty.)

There are three basic ways in which a character can decrease the difficulty of a task. Each of them decreases the difficulty by at least one step—never in smaller increments.

SKILLS

Characters may be skilled at performing a specific task. A skill can vary from character to character. For example, one character might be skilled at lying, another might be skilled at trickery, and a third might be skilled in all interpersonal interactions. The first level of being skilled is called being *trained*, and it decreases the difficulty of that task by one step. More rarely, a character can be incredibly skilled at performing a task. This is called being *specialized*, and it decreases the difficulty of a task by two steps instead of one. Skills can never decrease a task by more than two steps; being trained and specialized in a skill decreases the difficulty by only two steps, not three.

GM Intrusion, page 121

ASSETS

An asset is anything that helps a character with a task, such as having a really good crowbar when trying to force open a door or being in a rainstorm when trying to put out a fire. Appropriate assets vary from task to task. The perfect awl might help when woodworking, but it won't make a dance performance much better. An asset usually reduces a task's difficulty by one step.

EFFORT

A player can apply Effort to decrease the difficulty of a task. To do this, the player spends points from the stat Pool that's most appropriate to the task. For example, applying Effort to push a heavy rock off a cliff requires a player to spend points from her character's Might Pool; applying Effort to activate an unusual machine interface requires her to spend points from her character's Intellect Pool. For every level of Effort spent on a task, the task's difficulty decreases by one step. It costs 3 points from a stat Pool to apply one level of Effort, and it costs 2 additional points for every level thereafter (so it costs 5 points for two levels of Effort, 7 points for three levels of Effort, and so on). A character must spend points from the same stat Pool as the type of task or roll—Might points for a Might roll, Speed points for a Speed roll, or Intellect points for an Intellect roll.

Every character has a maximum level of Effort she can apply to a single task.

The great thing about the GM intrusion is that it really just provides a mechanical framework for something game masters were already doing to player characters since the creation of roleplaying games.

ROLLING THE DIE

To determine success or failure, a player rolls a die (always a d20). If she rolls the target number or higher, she succeeds. Most of the time, that's the end of it—nothing else needs to be done. Occasionally, a character might apply a small modifier to the roll. If she has a +2 bonus when attempting specific actions, she adds 2 to the number rolled. However, the original roll sometimes matters (see Special Rolls, page 101).

If a character applies a modifier to her die roll, it's possible to get a result of 21 or higher, in which case she can attempt a task with a target number above 20. But if there is no possibility for success—if not even rolling a natural 20 (meaning the d20 shows that number) is sufficient to accomplish the task—then no roll is made.

Otherwise, characters would have a chance to succeed at everything, even impossible or ridiculous tasks such as climbing moonbeams, throwing elephants, or hitting a target on the opposite side of a mountain with an arrow.

If a character's modifiers add up to +3, treat them as an asset instead. In other words, instead of adding a +3 bonus to the roll, reduce the difficulty by one step. For example, if a vector has a +1 bonus to attack rolls from a minor effect, a +1 bonus to attack rolls from a special weapon quality, and a +1 bonus to attack rolls from a special ability, she does not add 3 to her attack roll—instead, she reduces the difficulty of the attack by one step. So if she attacks a level 3 foe, she would normally roll against difficulty 3 and try to reach a target number of 9, but thanks to her asset, she rolls against difficulty 2 and tries to reach a target number of 6.

This distinction is important when stacking skills and assets to decrease the difficulty of an action, especially since reducing the difficulty to 0 or lower means no roll is needed.

THE PLAYER ALWAYS ROLLS

In The Strange, players always drive the action. That means they make all the dice rolls. If a PC leaps out of a moving vehicle, the player rolls to see if she succeeds. If a PC searches for a hidden panel, the player rolls to determine whether she finds it. If a rockslide falls on a PC, the player rolls to try to get out of the way. If a PC and an NPC arm wrestle, the player rolls, and the NPC's level determines the target number. If a PC attacks a foe, the player rolls to see if she hits. If a foe attacks the PC, the player rolls to see if she dodges the blow.

As shown by the last two examples, the PC rolls whether she is attacking or defending. Thus, something that improves defenses might help or hinder her rolls. For example, if a PC uses a low wall to gain cover from

attacks, the wall decreases the difficulty of the player's defense rolls. If a foe uses the wall to gain cover from the PC's attacks, it increases the difficulty of the player's attack rolls.

SPECIAL ROLLS

If a character rolls a natural 1, 17, 18, 19, or 20 (meaning the d20 shows that number), special rules come into play. These are explained in more detail in the following sections.

1: Intrusion. The GM makes a free intrusion (see below) and doesn't award experience points (XP) for it.

17: Damage Bonus. If the roll was a damage-dealing attack, it deals 1 additional point of damage.

18: Damage Bonus. If the roll was a damage-dealing attack, it deals 2 additional points of damage.

19: Minor Effect. If the roll was a damage-dealing attack, it deals 3 additional points of damage. If the roll was something other than an attack, the PC gets a minor effect in addition to the normal results of the task.

20: Major Effect. If the roll was a damage-dealing attack, it deals 4 additional points of damage. If the roll was something other than an attack, the PC gets a major effect in addition to the normal results of the task. If the PC spent points from a stat Pool on the action, the point cost for the action decreases to 0, meaning the character regains those points as if she had not spent them at all.

GM INTRUSION

GM intrusion is explained elsewhere, but essentially it means that something occurs to complicate the character's life. The character hasn't necessarily fumbled or done anything wrong (although perhaps she did). It could just be that the task presents an unexpected difficulty or something unrelated affects the current situation.

For GM intrusion on a defense roll, a roll of 1 might mean that the PC takes 2 additional points of damage from the attack, indicating that the opponent got in a lucky blow.

MINOR EFFECT

A minor effect happens when a player rolls a natural 19. Most of the time, a minor effect is slightly beneficial to the PC, but not overwhelming.

A climber gets up the steep slope a bit faster. A repaired machine works a bit better. A character jumping down into a pit lands on her feet. Either the GM or the player can come up with a possible minor effect that fits the situation, but both must agree on what it should be.

Don't waste a lot of time thinking of a minor effect if nothing appropriate suggests itself. Sometimes, in cases where only success or failure matters, it's okay to have no minor effect. Keep the game moving at an exciting pace.

In combat, the easiest and most straightforward minor effect is dealing 3 additional points of damage with an attack. The following are other common minor effects for combat:

Strike a specific body part: The attacker strikes a specific spot on the defender's body. The GM rules what special effect, if any, results. For example, hitting a creature's tentacle that is wrapped around an ally might make it easier for the ally to escape. Hitting a foe in the eye might blind it for one round. Hitting a creature in its one vulnerable spot might ignore Armor.

Knock back: The foe is knocked or forced back a few feet. Most of the time, this doesn't matter much, but if the fight takes place on a ledge or next to a pit of lava, the effect can be significant.

Move past: The character can move a short distance at the end of the attack. This effect is useful to get past a foe guarding a door, for example.

Distract: For one round, the difficulty of all tasks the foe attempts is modified by one step to its detriment.

Usually, the GM just has the desired minor effect occur. For example, rolling a 19 against a relatively weak foe means it is knocked off the cliff. The effect makes the round more exciting, but the defeat of a minor creature has no significant impact on the story. Other times, the GM might rule that an additional roll is needed to achieve the effect—the special roll only gives the PC the opportunity for a minor effect. This mostly happens when the desired effect is very unlikely, such as pushing a 50-ton battle automaton off a cliff. If the player just wants to deal 3 additional points of damage as the minor effect, no extra roll is needed.

MAJOR EFFECT

A major effect happens when a player rolls a

"I'm not certain what was the bigger shock—that there were so many other worlds out there, or that my world wasn't actually the real world." ~Awakened Ardeyn native Challian Reen

Distance, page 102

GM intrusion, page 121

natural 20. Most of the time, a major effect is quite beneficial to the character. A climber gets up the steep slope in half the time. A jumper lands with such panache that those nearby are impressed and possibly intimidated. A defender makes a free attack on his foe.

Either the GM or the player can come up with a possible major effect that fits the situation, but both must agree on what it should be. As with minor effects, don't spend a lot of time agonizing over the details of a major effect. In cases where only success or failure matters, a major effect might offer the character a one-time asset (a modification of one step) to use the next time she attempts a similar action. When nothing else seems appropriate, the GM can simply grant the PC an additional action on her turn that same round.

In combat, the easiest and most straightforward major effect is dealing 4 additional points to damage with an attack. The following are other common major effects for combat.

Knock down: The foe is knocked prone. It can get up on its turn if it wishes.

Disarm: The foe drops one object that it is holding.

Stun: The foe loses its next action.

Impair: For the rest of the combat, the difficulty of all tasks the foe attempts is modified by one step to its detriment.

As with minor effects, usually the GM just has the desired major effect occur, but sometimes he might require an extra roll if the major effect is unusual or unlikely.

RETRYING A TASK AFTER FAILURE

If a character fails a task (whether it's climbing a wall, picking a lock, trying to figure out a mysterious device, or something else) she can attempt it again, but she *must* apply at least one level of Effort when retrying that task. A retry is a new action, not part of the same action that failed, and it takes the same amount of time as the first attempt did.

The words "immediate" and "close" can be used interchangeably to talk about distance. If a creature or object is within arm's reach of the character, it can be considered both immediate and close.

Sometimes the GM might rule that retries are impossible. Perhaps a character has one chance to convince the leader of a group of thugs not to attack, and after that, no amount of talking will stop them.

This rule doesn't apply to something like attacking a foe in combat because combat is always changing and fluid. Each round's situation is new, not a repeat of a previous situation, so a missed attack can't be retried.

INITIAL COST

The GM can assign a point cost to a task just for trying it. Called an *initial cost*, it's simply an indication that the task is particularly taxing. For example, let's say a character wants to try a Might action to open a heavy cellar door that is partially rusted shut. The GM says that forcing the door open is a difficulty 5 task, and there's an initial cost of 3 Might points simply to try. This initial cost is in addition to any points the character chooses to spend on the roll (such as when applying Effort), and the initial cost points do not affect the difficulty of the task. In other words, the character must spend 3 Might points to attempt the task at all, but that doesn't help her open the door. If she wanted to apply Effort to lower the difficulty, she'd have to spend more points from her Might Pool. Edge helps with the initial cost of a task, just as it does with any expenditure from a character's Pool.

In the previous example, if the character had a Might Edge of 2, she would have to spend only 1 point (3 points minus 2 from her Might Edge) for the initial cost to attempt the task. If she also applied a level of Effort to open the door, she couldn't use her Edge again—Edge applies only once per action—so using the Effort would cost the full 3 points. Thus, she'd spend a total of 4 points (1 for the initial cost plus 3 for the Effort) from her Might Pool.

The rationale of the initial cost optional rule is that even in The Strange, where things like Effort can help a character succeed on an action, logic still suggests that some actions are very difficult and taxing, particularly for some PCs more than others.

DISTANCE

Distance is simplified into three basic categories: immediate, short, and long.

Immediate distance from a character is within reach or within a few steps; if a character stands in a small room, everything in the room is within immediate distance. At most, immediate distance is 10 feet (3 m). Immediate distance is sometimes referred to as close, or even point-blank, particularly when referring to ranges.

Short distance is anything greater than immediate distance but less than 50 feet (15 m) or so.

Long distance is anything greater than short distance but less than 100 feet (30 m) or so. Beyond that range, distances are always

Timekeeping

ACTION	TIME USUALLY REQUIRED
Walking a mile over easy terrain	About fifteen minutes
Walking a mile over rough terrain (forest, snow, hills)	About half an hour
Walking a mile over difficult terrain (mountains, thick jungle)	About forty-five minutes
Moving from one significant location in a city to another	About fifteen minutes
Sneaking into a guarded location	About fifteen minutes
Observing a new location to get salient details	About fifteen minutes
Having an in-depth discussion	About ten minutes
Resting after a fight or other strenuous activity	About ten minutes
Resting and having a quick meal	About half an hour
Making or breaking camp	About half an hour
Shopping for supplies in a market or store	About an hour
Meeting with an important contact	About half an hour
Referencing a book or website	About half an hour
Searching a room for hidden things	At least half an hour, perhaps one hour
Searching for cyphers or other valuables amid a lot of stuff	About an hour
Identifying and understanding a cypher	About five minutes
Identifying and understanding an artifact	At least fifteen minutes, perhaps three hours
Repairing a device (assuming parts and tools available)	At least an hour, perhaps a day
Building a device (assuming parts and tools available)	At least a day, perhaps a week

specified—500 feet (152 m), 1 mile (2 km), and so on.

All weapons and special abilities use these terms for ranges. For example, all melee weapons have immediate range—they are close-combat weapons, and you can use them to attack anyone within immediate distance of you. A thrown knife (and most other thrown weapons) has short range. A small handgun also has short range. A rifle has long range.

A character can move an immediate distance as a part of another action. In other words, she can take a few steps to the light switch and flip it on. She can lunge across a small room to attack a foe. She can open a door and step through.

A character can move a short distance as her entire action for a turn. She can also try to move a long distance as her entire action, but the player might have to roll to see if the character slips, trips, or stumbles for moving so far so quickly.

GMs and players don't need to determine exact distances. For example, if the PCs are fighting a group of Ruk venom troopers, any character can likely attack any biomorph in the general melee—they're all within immediate range. However, if one biomorph stays back to fire poison spines, a character might have to use her entire action to move the short distance required to attack that foe. It doesn't matter if the biomorph is 20 feet (6 m) or 40 feet (12 m) away—it's simply considered short distance. It does matter if he's more than 50 feet (15 m) away because that distance would require a long move.

TIMEKEEPING

Generally, keep time the same way that you normally would, using minutes, hours, days, and weeks. Thus, if the characters walk overland for 15 miles (24 km), about eight hours pass, even though the journey can be described in only a few seconds at the game table. Precision timekeeping is rarely important. Most of the time, saying things like "That takes about an hour" works fine.

This is true even when a special ability has a specific duration. In an encounter, a duration of "one minute" is mostly the same as saying "the rest of the encounter." You don't have to track each round that ticks by if you don't want to. Likewise, an ability that lasts for ten minutes can safely be considered the length of an in-depth conversation, the time it takes to quickly explore a small area, or the time it takes to rest after a strenuous activity.

Venom trooper, page 300

ENCOUNTERS, ROUNDS, AND INITIATIVE

Sometimes in the course of the game, the GM or players will refer to an *encounter*. Encounters are not so much measurements of time as they are events or instances in which something happens, like a scene of a movie or a chapter in a book. An encounter might be a fight with a foe, a dramatic crossing of a raging river, or a stressful negotiation with an important official. It's useful to use the word when referring to a specific scene, as in "My Might Pool is low after that encounter with the soul sorcerer yesterday."

A *round* is about five to ten seconds. The length of time is variable because sometimes one round might be a bit longer than another. You don't need to measure time more precisely than that. You can estimate that on average there are about ten rounds in a minute. In a round, everyone—each character and NPC—gets to take one action.

If precise order is needed, just go from highest roll to lowest, but treat someone with training in initiative as if he had rolled 3 higher, and treat someone specialized in initiative as if he had rolled 6 higher.

To determine who goes first, second, and so on in a round, each player makes a Speed roll called an *initiative roll*. Most of the time, it's only important to know which characters act before the NPCs and which act after the NPCs. On an initiative roll, a character who rolls higher than an NPC's target number takes her action before the NPC does. As with all target numbers, an NPC's initiative roll target number is three times the NPC's level. Many times, the GM will have all NPCs take their actions at the same time, using the highest target number from among all the NPCs. Using this method, any characters who rolled higher than the target number act first, then all the NPCs act, and finally any characters who rolled lower than the target number act.

The order in which the characters act usually isn't important. If the players want to go in a precise order, they can act in initiative order (highest to lowest), by going around the table, by going oldest to youngest, and so on.

For example, Charles, Tammie, and Shanna's characters are in combat with two level 2 security guards. The GM has the players make Speed rolls to determine initiative. Charles rolls an 8, Shanna rolls a 15, and Tammie rolls a 4. The target number for a level 2 creature is 6, so each round Charles and Shanna act before the guards, then the guards act, and finally Tammie acts. It doesn't matter whether Charles acts before or after Shanna, as long as they think it's fair.

After everyone—all PCs and NPCs—in the combat has had a turn, the round ends and a new round begins. In all rounds after the first, everyone acts in the same order as they did in the first round. The characters cycle through this order until the logical end of the encounter (the end of the fight or the completion of the event) or until the GM asks them to make new initiative rolls. The GM can call for new initiative rolls at the beginning of any new round when conditions drastically change. For example, if the NPCs gain reinforcements, the environment changes (perhaps the lights go out), the terrain changes (maybe part of the balcony collapses under the PCs), or something similar occurs, the GM can call for new initiative rolls.

Since the action moves as a cycle, anything that lasts for a round ends where it started in the cycle. If Umberto the paradox uses a revision on an opponent that hinders its defenses for one round, the effect lasts until Umberto acts on his next turn.

Faster Initiative (Optional Rule): To make an encounter move faster, if at least one character rolls high enough to beat the target number of the NPC(s), all the characters act before the NPC(s). If nobody rolls high enough to beat the target number of the NPCs, all the characters act after the NPC(s). On the characters' turn, go clockwise around the table. If you're playing using an online video chat or virtual table, start with the leftmost player and move right; repeat.

ACTIONS

Anything that your character does in a round is an action. It's easiest to think of an action as a single thing that you can do in five to ten seconds. For example, if you use your dart thrower to shoot a strange floating orb, that's one action. So is running for cover behind a stack of barrels, prying open a stuck door, using a rope to pull your friend up from a pit, or activating a cypher (even if it's stored in your pack).

Opening a door and attacking a security guard on the other side are two actions. It's more a matter of focus than time. Drawing your sword and attacking a foe is all one action. Putting away your bow and pushing a heavy bookcase to block a door are two actions because each requires a different train of thought.

If the action you want to accomplish is not within reach, you can move a little bit. Essentially, you can move up to an immediate distance to perform your action. For example, you can move an immediate distance and

attack a foe, open a door and move an immediate distance into the hallway beyond, or grab your hurt friend lying on the ground and pull him back a few steps. This movement can occur before or after your action, so you can move to a door and open it, or you can open a door and move through it.

The most common actions are:

Attack

Activate a special ability (one that isn't an attack)

Move

Wait

Defend

Do something else

ACTION: ATTACK

An attack is anything that you do to someone that he doesn't want you to do. Slashing a foe with a curved dagger is an attack, blasting a foe with a lightning artifact is an attack, wrapping a foe in magnetically controlled metal cables is an attack, and controlling someone's mind is an attack. An attack almost always requires a roll to see if you hit or otherwise affect your target.

In the simplest kind of attack, such as a PC trying to stab a thug with a knife, the player rolls and compares his result against the opponent's target number. If his roll is equal to or greater than the target number, the attack hits. Just as with any kind of task, the GM might modify the difficulty based on the situation, and the player might have a bonus to the roll or might try to lower the difficulty using skills, assets, or Effort.

A less straightforward attack might be a special ability that stuns a foe with a mental blast. However, it's handled the same way: the player makes a roll against the opponent's target number. Similarly, an attempt to tackle a foe and wrestle it to the ground is still just a roll against the foe's target number.

Attacks are sometimes categorized as "melee" attacks, meaning that you hurt or affect something within immediate reach, or "ranged" attacks, meaning that you hurt or affect something at a distance.

Melee attacks can be Might or Speed actions—player choice. Physical ranged attacks (such as bows and thrown weapons) are almost always Speed actions, but those that come from special abilities like revisions are probably Intellect actions. Effects that require touching the target require a melee attack.

"Look. Wizard, zombie, giant, vampire, tentacled thing...it doesn't matter. Just tell me where to point my gun." ~Deirdre Deen, Estate bodyguard

If the attack misses, the power is not wasted, and you can try again each round as your action until you hit the target, use another ability, or take a different action that requires you to use your hands. These attempts in later rounds count as different actions, so you don't have to keep track of how much Effort you used when you activated the ability or how you used Edge. For example, let's say that on the first round of combat, you activate a special ability that requires you to touch your foe, use Effort to reduce the difficulty of the attack roll, and miss your foe. On the second round of combat, you can try attacking again and use Effort to reduce the difficulty of the attack roll.

Plasma Arc, page 34

The GM and players are encouraged to describe every attack with flavor and flair. One attack roll might be a stab to the foe's arm. A miss might be the PC's sword slamming into the wall. Combatants lunge, block, duck, spin, leap, and make all kinds of movements that should keep combat visually interesting and compelling. The game mastering section has much more guidance in this regard.

Vector, page 25

Running the Game, page 309

Common elements that affect the difficulty of a combat task are cover, range, and darkness. The rules for these and other modifiers are explained in the Attack Modifiers and Special Situations section (page 110).

DAMAGE

When an attack strikes a character, it usually means the character takes damage.

An attack against a PC subtracts points from one of the character's stat Pools—usually the Might Pool. Whenever an attack simply says it deals "damage" without specifying the type, it means Might damage, which is by far the most common type. Intellect damage, which is usually the result of a mental attack, is always labeled as Intellect damage. Speed damage is often a physical attack, but attacks that deal Speed damage are fairly rare.

NPCs don't have stat Pools. Instead, they have a characteristic called *health*. When an NPC takes damage of any kind, the amount is subtracted from its health. Unless described otherwise, an NPC's health is always equal to its target number. Some NPCs might have special reactions to or defenses against attacks that would normally deal Speed damage or Intellect damage, but unless the NPC's description specifically explains this, assume that all damage is subtracted from the NPC's health.

Objects are like NPCs: they have health instead of stat Pools.

Damage is always a specific amount determined by the attack. For example, a slash with a broadsword or a blast with a spike thrower deals 4 points of damage. A paradox's Plasma Arc deals 4 points of damage. Often, there are ways for the attacker to increase the damage. For example, a PC can apply Effort to deal 3 additional points of damage, and rolling a natural 17 on the attack roll deals 1 additional point of damage.

ARMOR

Pieces of equipment and special abilities protect a character from damage by giving him *Armor*. Each time a character takes damage, subtract his Armor value from the damage before reducing his stat Pool or health. For example, if a vector with 2 Armor is hit by a gunshot that deals 4 points of damage, he takes only 2 points of damage (4 minus 2 from his Armor). If Armor reduces the incoming damage to 0 or lower, the character takes no damage from the attack. For example, the vector's 2 Armor protects him from all physical attacks that deal 1 or 2 points of damage.

The most common way to get Armor is to wear physical armor, such as a leather jacket or a bulletproof vest on Earth, a chainmail hauberk in Ardeyn, or bioengineered carapace grafts in Ruk. All physical armor comes in one of three categories: light, medium, or heavy. Light armor gives the wearer 1 point of Armor, medium gives 2 points of Armor, and heavy gives 3 points of Armor.

When you see the word "Armor" capitalized in the game rules (other than as the name of a special ability), it refers to your Armor characteristic—the number you subtract from incoming damage. When you see the lowercase word "armor," it refers to any physical armor you might wear.

Other effects can add to a character's Armor. If a character is wearing chainmail (2 points of Armor) and has an ability that covers him in a protective force field that grants 1 point of Armor, his total is 3 Armor. If he also has a cypher that hardens his flesh temporarily for 1 point of Armor, his total is 4 Armor.

Some types of damage ignore physical armor. Attacks that specifically deal Speed damage or Intellect damage ignore Armor; the creature takes the listed amount of damage without any reduction from Armor. Ambient damage (see

DAMAGE FROM HAZARDS

SOURCE	DAMAGE	NOTES
Falling	1 point per 10 feet (3 m) fallen (ambient damage)	—
Minor fire	3 points per round (ambient damage)	Torch
Major fire	6 points per round (ambient damage)	Engulfed in flames; lava
Acid splash	2 points per round (ambient damage)	—
Acid bath	6 points per round (ambient damage)	Immersed in acid
Cold	1 point per round (ambient damage)	Below freezing temperatures
Severe cold	3 points per round (ambient damage)	Liquid nitrogen
Shock	1 point per round (ambient damage)	Often involves losing next action
Electrocution	6 points per round (ambient damage)	Often involves losing next action
Crush	3 points	Object or creature falls on character
Huge crush	6 points	Roof collapse; cave-in
Collision	6 points	Large, fast object strikes character

below) usually ignores Armor as well.

A creature may have a special bonus to Armor against certain kinds of attacks. For example, a protective suit made of a sturdy, fire-resistant material might normally give its wearer 1 point of Armor but count as 3 points of Armor against fire attacks. An artifact worn as a helmet might add 2 points of Armor only against mental attacks.

AMBIENT DAMAGE

Some kinds of damage aren't direct attacks against a creature, but they indirectly affect everything in the area. Most of these are environmental effects such as winter cold, high temperatures, or background radiation. Damage from these kinds of sources is called ambient damage. Physical armor usually doesn't protect against ambient damage, though a well-insulated suit of armor can protect against cold weather.

DAMAGE FROM HAZARDS

Attacks aren't the only way to inflict damage on a character. Experiences such as falling from a great height, being burned in a fire, and spending time in severe weather also deal damage. Although no list of potential hazards could be comprehensive, the Damage From Hazards table includes common examples.

THE EFFECTS OF TAKING DAMAGE

When an NPC reaches 0 health, it is either dead or (if the attacker wishes it) incapacitated, meaning unconscious or beaten into submission.

When an object reaches 0 health, it is broken or otherwise destroyed.

As previously mentioned, damage from most sources is applied to a character's Might Pool. Otherwise, stat damage always reduces the Pool of the stat it affects.

If damage reduces a character's stat Pool to 0, any further damage to that stat (including excess damage from the attack that reduced the stat to 0) is applied to another stat Pool. Damage is applied to Pools in this order:

1. Might (unless the Pool is 0)
2. Speed (unless the Pool is 0)
3. Intellect

Even if the damage is applied to another stat Pool, it still counts as its original type for the purpose of Armor and special abilities that affect damage. For example, if a spinner with 2 Armor is reduced to 0 Might and then is hit by a creature's claw for 3 points of damage, it still counts as Might damage, so his 2 Armor reduces the damage to 1 point, which then is applied to his Speed Pool. In other words, even though the spinner takes the damage from his Speed Pool, it doesn't ignore Armor like Speed damage normally would.

In addition to taking damage from their Might Pool, Speed Pool, or Intellect Pool, PCs also have a *damage track*. The damage track has four states (from best to worst): hale, impaired, debilitated, and dead. When one of a PC's stat Pools reaches 0, he moves one step down the damage track. Thus, if he is hale, he becomes impaired. If he is already impaired, he becomes debilitated. If he is already debilitated, he becomes dead.

Some effects can immediately shift a PC one or more steps on the damage track.

These include rare poisons, cellular disruption attacks, and massive traumas (such as falls from very great heights, being run over by a speeding vehicle, and so on, as determined by the GM).

Some attacks, like a serpent's poisonous bite or a spinner's Enthrall, have effects other than damage to a stat Pool or shifting the PC on the damage track. These attacks can cause unconsciousness, paralysis, and so on.

THE DAMAGE TRACK

The damage track allows you to know how far from death you are:

If you're hale, you're three steps from death. If you're impaired, you're two steps from death. If you're debilitated, you are only one small step from death's door.

Hale is the normal state for a character: all three stat Pools are at 1 or higher, and the PC has no penalties from harmful conditions. When a hale PC takes enough damage to reduce one of his stat Pools to 0, he becomes impaired. Note that a character whose stat Pools are much lower than normal can still be hale.

Impaired is a wounded or injured state. When an impaired character applies Effort, it costs 1 extra point per level applied. For example, applying one level of Effort costs 4 points instead of 3, and applying two levels of Effort costs 7 points instead of 5.

An impaired character ignores minor and major effect results on his rolls, and he doesn't deal as much extra damage in combat with a special roll. In combat, a roll of 17 or higher deals only 1 additional point of damage.

When an impaired PC takes enough damage to reduce one of his stat Pools to 0, he becomes debilitated.

Dead is dead, although in Ardeyn and potentially other recursions, options may exist to bring a character back from an artificial afterlife.

Debilitated is a critically injured state. A debilitated character may not take any actions other than to move (probably crawl) no more than an immediate distance. If a debilitated character's Speed Pool is 0, he can't move at all.

When a debilitated PC takes enough damage to reduce a stat Pool to 0, he is dead.

Dead is dead.

RECOVERING POINTS IN A POOL

After losing or spending points in a Pool, you recover those points by resting. You can't increase a Pool past its maximum by resting—just back to its normal level. Any extra points gained go away with no effect. The amount of points you recover from a rest, and how long each rest takes, depends on how many times you have rested so far that day.

When you rest, make a *recovery roll*. To do this, roll 1d6 and add your tier. You recover that many points, and you can divide them among your stat Pools however you wish. For example, if your recovery roll is 4 and you've lost 4 points of Might and 2 points of Speed, you can recover 4 points of Might, or 2 points of Might and 2 points of Speed, or any other combination adding up to 4 points.

The first time you rest each day, it takes only a few seconds to catch your breath. If you rest this way in the middle of an encounter, it takes one action on your turn.

The second time you rest each day, you must rest ten minutes to make a recovery roll. The third time you rest each day, you must rest one hour to make a recovery roll. The fourth time you rest each day, you must rest ten hours to make a recovery roll (usually, this occurs when you stop for the day, eat, and sleep).

After that much rest, it's assumed to be a new day, so the next time you rest, it takes only a few seconds. The next rest takes ten minutes, then one hour, and so on, in a cycle.

If you haven't rested yet that day and you take a lot of damage in a fight, you could rest a few seconds (regaining 1d6 points + 1 point per tier) and then immediately rest for ten minutes (regaining another 1d6 points + 1 point per tier). Thus, in one full day of doing nothing but resting, you could recover 4d6 points + 4 points per tier.

Each character chooses when to make recovery rolls. If a party of five explorers rests for ten minutes because two members want to make recovery rolls, the other characters don't have to make rolls at that time. Later in the day, those three can decide to rest for ten minutes and make recovery rolls.

Recovery Roll	Rest Time Needed
First recovery roll	One action
Second recovery roll	Ten minutes
Third recovery roll	One hour
Fourth recovery roll	Ten hours

RESTORING THE DAMAGE TRACK

Using points from a recovery roll to raise a stat Pool from 0 to 1 or higher also automatically moves the character up one step on the damage track.

If all of a PC's stat Pools are above 0 and the character has taken special damage that moved him down the damage track, he can use a recovery roll to move up one step on the damage track instead of recovering points. For example, a character who is debilitated from a hit with a cell-disrupting biotech device can rest and move up to impaired rather than recover points in a Pool.

SPECIAL DAMAGE

In the course of playing the game, characters face all manner of threats and dangers that can harm them in a variety of ways, only some of which are easily represented by points of damage.

Dazed and Stunned: Characters can be dazed when struck hard on the head, exposed to extremely loud sounds, or affected by a mental attack. When this happens, for the duration of the daze effect (usually one round), the difficulty of all tasks attempted by the character increases by one step. Similar but more severe attacks can stun characters. Stunned characters lose their turn (but can still defend against attacks normally).

Poison and Disease: When characters encounter poison—whether the venom of a serpent, rat poison slipped into a burrito, cyanide dissolved in wine, or an overdose of acetaminophen—they make a Might defense roll to resist it. Failure to resist can result in points of damage, moving down the damage track, or a specific effect such as paralysis, unconsciousness, disability, or something stranger. For example, some poisons affect the brain, making it impossible to say certain words, take certain actions, resist certain effects, or recover points to a stat Pool.

Diseases work like poisons, but their effect occurs every day, so the victim must make a Might defense roll each day or suffer the effects. Disease effects are as varied as poisons: points of damage, moving down the damage track, disability, and so on. Many diseases inflict damage that cannot be restored through conventional means.

Paralysis: Paralytic effects cause a character to drop to the ground, unable to move. Unless otherwise specified, the character can still take actions that require no physical movement.

Other Effects: Other special effects can render a character blind or deaf, unable to stand without falling over, or unable to breathe. Stranger effects might negate gravity for the character (or increase it a hundredfold), transport him to another place, render him out of phase, mutate his physical form, implant false memories or senses, alter the way his brain processes information, or inflame his

A specially prepared dose of acetylcholine is used by OSR assassins on Earth in their tranquilizer guns. It is a level 4 poison that makes the victim forget what happened during the previous minute.

nerves so he is in constant, excruciating pain. Each special effect must be handled on a case-by-case basis. The GM adjudicates how the character is affected and how the condition can be alleviated (if possible).

NPCs AND SPECIAL DAMAGE

The GM always has final say over what special damage will affect an NPC. Human NPCs usually react like characters, but the Strange has too many types of nonhuman creatures to categorize. For example, a tiny bit of venom is unlikely to hurt a gigantic dragon, and it won't affect an android or a planetovore at all.

If an NPC is susceptible to an attack that would shift a character down the damage track, using that attack on the NPC usually renders it unconscious or dead. Alternatively, the GM could apply the debilitated condition to the NPC, with the same effect as it would have on a PC.

When NPCs (who have only health) suffer Speed or Intellect damage, normally this is treated the same as Might. However, the GM or the player has the option to suggest an appropriate alternate effect (the NPC suffers a penalty, moves more slowly, is stunned, and so on).

ATTACK MODIFIERS AND SPECIAL SITUATIONS

In combat situations, many modifiers might come into play. Although the GM is at liberty to assess whatever modifiers he thinks are appropriate to the situation (that's his role in the game), the following suggestions and guidelines might make that easier. Often the modifier is applied as a step in difficulty. So if a situation hinders attacks, that means if a PC attacks an NPC, the difficulty of the attack roll is increased by one step, and if an NPC attacks a PC, the difficulty of the defense roll is decreased by one step. This is because players make all rolls, whether they are attacking or defending—NPCs never make attack or defense rolls.

When in doubt, if it seems like it should be harder to attack in a situation, the difficulty of the attack rolls increase by one step. If it seems like attacks should gain an advantage or be easier in some way, the difficulty of the defense rolls increase by one step.

COVER

If a character is behind cover so that a significant portion of his body is behind something sturdy, attacks are modified by one step in the defender's favor.

If a character is entirely behind cover (his entire body is behind something sturdy), he can't be attacked unless the attack can go through the cover. For example, if a character hides behind a thin wooden screen and his opponent shoots the screen with a rifle that can penetrate the wood, the character can be attacked. However, because the attacker can't see the character clearly, this still counts as cover (attacks are modified by one step in the defender's favor).

A CLOSER LOOK AT SITUATIONS THAT DON'T INVOLVE PCs

Ultimately, the GM is the arbiter of conflicts that do not involve the PCs. They should be adjudicated in the most interesting, logical, and story-based way possible. When in doubt, match the level of the NPCs (characters or creatures) or their respective effects to determine the results. Thus, if a level 4 NPC fights a level 3 NPC, he'll win, but if he faces a level 7 NPC, he'll lose. Likewise, a level 4 creature resists poisons or devices of level 3 or less, but not those of level 5 and above.

The essence is this: in The Strange, it doesn't matter if something is a monster, a poison, or a gravity-dispelling ray. If it's a higher level, it wins; if it's a lower level, it loses. If two things of equal level oppose each other, there might be a long, drawn-out battle that could go either way.

POSITION

Sometimes where a character stands gives him an advantage or a disadvantage.

Prone Target: In melee, a prone target is easier to hit (modified by one step in the attacker's favor). In ranged combat, a prone target is harder to hit (modified by one step in the defender's favor).

Higher Ground: In either ranged or melee combat, an opponent on higher ground gets the advantage (modified by one step in her favor).

SURPRISE

When a target isn't aware of an incoming attack, the attacker has an advantage. A ranged sniper in a hidden position, an invisible assailant, or the first salvo in a successful ambush are all modified by two steps in the attacker's favor. For the attacker to gain this advantage, however, the defender truly must have no idea that the attack is coming. If the defender isn't sure of the attacker's location but is still on guard, the attacker's modifier is only one step in his favor.

RANGE

In melee, you can attack a foe who is adjacent to you (next to you) or within reach (immediate range). If you enter into melee with one or more foes, usually you can attack most or all of the combatants, meaning they are next to you, within reach, or within reach if you move slightly or have a long weapon that extends your reach.

The majority of ranged attacks have only two ranges: short range and long range. Short range is generally less than 50 feet (15 m) or so. Long range is generally from 50 feet (15 m) to about 100 feet (30 m). Greater precision than that isn't important in The Strange. If anything is longer than long range, the exact range is usually spelled out, such as with an item that can fire a beam 500 feet (152 m) or teleport you up to 1 mile (2 km) away.

Thus, the game has three measurements of distance: immediate, short, and long. These apply to movement as well (see above). A few special cases—point-blank range and extreme range— modify an attack's chance to successfully hit.

Point-Blank Range: If a character uses a ranged weapon against a target within immediate range, the attacker gets a one-step modifier in his favor.

Extreme Range: Targets just at the limit of a weapon's range are at extreme range. Attacks against such targets are modified by one step in the defender's favor.

ILLUMINATION

What characters can see (and how well they can see) plays a huge factor in combat.

Dim Light: Dim light is approximately the amount of light on a night with a bright full moon or the illumination provided by a torch, flashlight, or desk lamp. Dim light allows you to see out to short range. Targets in dim light are harder to hit. Attacks against such targets are modified by one step in the defender's favor. Attackers trained in low-light spotting negate this modifier.

Very Dim Light: Very dim light is approximately the amount of light on a starry night with no visible moon, or the glow provided by a candle or an illuminated control panel. Very dim light allows you to see clearly only within immediate range and perceive vague shapes to short range. Targets in very dim light are harder to hit. Attacks against targets within immediate range are modified by one step in the defender's favor, and attacks against those in short range are modified by two steps in the defender's favor. Attackers trained in low-light spotting modify these difficulties by one step in their favor. Attackers specialized in low-light spotting modify these difficulties by two steps in their favor.

Darkness: Darkness is an area with no illumination at all, such as a moonless night with cloud cover or a room with no lights. Targets in complete darkness are nearly impossible to hit. If an attacker can use other senses (such as hearing) to get an idea of where the opponent might be, attacks against such targets are modified by four steps in the defender's favor. Otherwise, attacks in complete darkness fail without the need for a roll unless the player spends 1 XP to "make a lucky shot" or the GM uses GM intrusion. Attackers trained in low-light spotting modify this difficulty by one step in their favor. Attackers specialized in low-light spotting modify this difficulty by two steps in their favor.

VISIBILITY

Similar to illumination, factors that obscure vision affect combat.

Mist: A target in mist is similar to one in dim light. Ranged attacks against such targets are modified by one step in the defender's favor. Particularly dense mist makes ranged attacks nearly impossible (treat as darkness), and even melee attacks become difficult (modify by one step in the defender's favor).

Hiding Target: A target in dense foliage, behind a screen, or crawling amid the rubble in a ruin is hard to hit because she's hard to see. Ranged attacks against such targets are modified by one step in the defender's favor.

Invisible Target: If an attacker can use other senses (such as hearing) to get an idea of where the opponent might be, attacks against such targets are modified by four steps in the defender's favor. Otherwise, attacks against an invisible creature fail without the need for a roll unless the player spends 1 XP to "make a lucky shot" or the GM uses GM intrusion.

WATER

Being in shallow water can make it hard to

Precise ranges are not important in The Strange. The broadly defined "immediate," "short," and "long" ranges are there so that the GM can quickly make a judgment call and keep things moving. Basically, the idea is: your target is right there, your target is close, or your target is pretty far away.

In certain situations, such as when a PC is on top of a building looking across an open field, the GM should allow long-range attacks to go farther than 100 feet (30 m). In perfect conditions, a trained sniper can hit a target that is 500 feet (152 m) away.

move, but it doesn't affect combat. Being in deep water can make things difficult, and being underwater entirely can seem as different as being on another world.

Deep Water: Being in water up to your chest (or the equivalent thereof) hinders your ability to attack. Attacks made in such conditions are modified by one step in the defender's favor. Aquatic creatures ignore this modifier.

Underwater Melee Combat: For nonaquatic creatures, being completely underwater makes attacking very difficult. Melee attacks with slashing or bashing weapons are modified by two steps in the defender's favor. Attacks with stabbing weapons are modified by one step in the defender's favor. Aquatic creatures ignore the penalties for underwater melee combat.

Underwater Ranged Combat: As with melee combat, nonaquatic creatures have difficulty fighting underwater. Some ranged attacks are impossible underwater—you can't throw things, fire a bow or crossbow, or use a blowgun. Many firearms also do not work underwater. Attacks with weapons that do work underwater are modified by one step in the defender's favor. Ranges underwater are reduced by one category; long-range weapons work only to short range, and short-range weapons work only to immediate range.

MOVING TARGETS

Moving targets are harder to hit, and moving attackers have a difficult time as well.

Target Is Moving: Attackers trying to hit a foe who is moving very fast are penalized. (A foe moving very fast is one who is doing nothing but running, mounted on a moving creature, riding on a vehicle or moving conveyance, and so on.) Attacks are modified by one step in the defender's favor.

Attacker Is Moving: An attacker trying to make an attack while moving under its own power (walking, running, swimming, and so on) takes no penalties. An attacker mounted on a moving creature or vehicle has some difficulty; its attacks are modified by one step in the defender's favor. An attacker trained in riding ignores this penalty.

Attacker Is Jostled: Being jostled, such as while standing on a listing ship or a vibrating platform, makes attacking difficult. Such attacks are modified by one step in the defender's favor. Conceivably, training could offset this disadvantage. For example, characters trained in sailing would ignore penalties for being on a ship.

SPECIAL SITUATION: COMBAT BETWEEN NPCs

When an NPC attacks another NPC, the GM should designate a player to roll for one of the NPCs. Often, the choice is obvious. For example, a character who has a trained attack animal should roll when her pet attacks enemies. If an NPC ally accompanying the party leaps into the fray, that ally's favorite PC rolls for him. NPCs cannot apply Effort.

SPECIAL SITUATION: COMBAT BETWEEN PCs

When one PC attacks another PC, the attacking character makes an attack roll, and the other character makes a defense roll, adding any appropriate modifiers. If the attacking PC has a skill, ability, asset, or other effect that would decrease the attack's difficulty if it were made against an NPC, the character adds 3 to the roll for each step reduction (+3 for one step, +6 for two steps, and so on). If the attacker's final result is higher, the attack hits. If the defender's result is higher, the attack misses. Damage is resolved normally. The GM mediates all special effects.

SPECIAL SITUATION: AREA ATTACKS

Sometimes, an attack or effect affects an area rather than a single target. For example, a grenade or a landslide can potentially harm or affect everyone in the area.

In an area attack, all PCs in the area make appropriate defense rolls against the attack to determine its effect on them. If there are any NPCs in the area, the attacker makes a single attack roll against all NPCs (one roll, not one roll per NPC) and compares it to the target number of each NPC. If the roll is equal to or greater than the target number of a particular NPC, the attack hits that NPC.

Some area attacks always deal at least a minimum amount of damage, even if the attacks miss or if a PC makes a successful defense roll.

For example, consider a paradox who uses Shatter to attack six Lotan cultists (level 2; target number of 6) and their leader (level 4; target number of 12). The paradox applies Effort to increase the damage and rolls an 11 for the attack roll. This hits the six cultists, but not the leader, so the revision deals 3 points of damage to each of the cultists. The description of Shatter says that applying Effort to increase the damage also means that targets take 1 point of damage if the paradox fails the attack roll, so the leader takes 1 point of damage. In terms of what happens in the story, the cultists are caught flat-footed by the sudden burst of one of the cultist's knives, but the leader ducks and shields herself from the blast. Despite the leader's quick moves, the blast is so intense that a few bits of metal slice her.

SPECIAL SITUATION: ATTACKING OBJECTS

Attacking an object is rarely a matter of hitting it. Sure, you can hit the broad side of a barn, but can you damage it? Attacking inanimate objects with a melee weapon is a Might action. Objects have levels and thus target numbers. An object's target number also serves as its health to determine whether it is destroyed. You track the object's health just as you would with an NPC.

Hard objects, like those made of stone, have 1 Armor. Very hard objects, like those made of metal, have 2 Armor. Extremely hard objects, like those made of diamond or an advanced metal alloy, have 3 Armor. Armor subtracts from every attack's damage.

ACTION: ACTIVATE A SPECIAL ABILITY

Special abilities are things like revisions, twists, moves, abilities granted by foci, or powers provided by cyphers or other devices. If a special ability affects another character in any kind of unwanted manner, it's handled as an attack. This is true even if the ability is normally not considered an attack. For example, if a character has a healing touch, but her friend doesn't want to be healed for some reason, an attempt to heal her unwilling friend is handled as an attack.

Plenty of special abilities do not affect another character in an unwanted manner. For example, a paradox might use Levitate Creature on herself to float into the air. A character with a matter-reorganizing device might change a stone wall into glass. A character who activates a phase changer cypher might walk through a wall. None of these requires an attack roll (although when turning a stone wall to glass, the character must still make a roll to successfully affect the wall).

If the character spends points to apply Effort on her attempt, she might want to roll anyway to see if she gets a major effect, which would reduce the cost for her action.

Levitate Creature, page 32

Shatter, page 32

Phase changer, page 324

ACTION: MOVE

As a part of another action, a character can adjust his position—stepping back a few feet while performing a revision, sliding over in combat to take on a different opponent to help his friend, pushing through a door he just opened, and so on. This is considered an immediate distance, and a character can move this far as a part of another action.

In a combat situation, if a character is in a large melee, he's usually considered to be next to most other combatants, unless the GM rules that he's farther away because the melee is especially large or the situation dictates it.

If he's not in melee but still nearby, he is considered to be a short distance away—usually less than 50 feet (15 m). If he's farther away than that but still involved in the combat,

DISCOVERY

While GM intrusion is interesting, the game also has a more conventional method of awarding XP between sessions. But it has nothing to do with killing monsters.

That's weird for a lot of players. Defeating opponents in battle is the core way you earn XP in many games.

But not in The Strange. The game is based on the premise of awarding players experience points for the thing you expect them to do in the game.

Experience points are the reward pellets they get for pushing the button—oh, wait, no, that's for rats in a lab. Well, same principle: give the players XP for doing a thing, and that thing is what they'll do.

In The Strange, that thing is discovery.

In The Strange, players are not rewarded for killing foes in combat, so using a smart idea to avoid combat and still succeed is just good play. Likewise, coming up with an idea to defeat a foe without hammering on it with weapons is encouraged—creativity is not cheating.

he is considered to be a long distance away, usually 50 to 100 feet (15 to 30 m).

Beyond that distance, only special circumstances, actions, or abilities will allow a character to be involved in an encounter.

In a round, as an action, a character can make a short move. In this case, he is doing nothing but moving up to about 50 feet (15 m). Some terrain or situations will change the distance a character can move, but generally, making a short move is considered to be a difficulty 0 action. No roll is needed; he just gets where he's going as his action.

A character can try to make a long move—up to 100 feet (30 m) or so—in one round. This is a Speed task with a difficulty of 4. As with any action, he can use skills, assets, or Effort to decrease the difficulty. Terrain, obstacles, or other circumstances can increase the difficulty.

A successful roll means the character moved the distance safely. Failure means that at some point during the move, he stops or stumbles (the GM determines where this happens).

LONG-TERM MOVEMENT

When talking about movement in terms of traveling rather than round-by-round action, typical characters can travel on a road about 20 miles (32 km) per day, averaging about 3 miles (5 km) per hour, including a few stops. When traveling overland, they can move about 12 miles (19 km) per day, averaging 2 miles (3 km) per hour, again with some stops. Mounted characters, such as on those on horseback, can go twice as far. Other modes of travel (cars, airplanes, hovercraft, sailing ships, and so on) have their own rates of movement.

MOVEMENT MODIFIERS

Different environments affect movement in different ways.

Rough Terrain: A surface that's considered rough terrain is covered in loose stones or other material, uneven or with unsure footing, unsteady, or a surface that requires movement across a narrow space, such as a cramped corridor or a slender ledge. Stairs are also considered rough terrain. Rough terrain does not slow normal movement on a round-by-round basis, but it increases the difficulty of a move roll by one step. Rough terrain cuts long-term movement rates in half.

Difficult Terrain: Difficult terrain is an area filled with challenging obstacles—water up to waist height, a very steep slope, an especially narrow ledge, slippery ice, a foot or more of snow, a space so small that one must crawl through it, and so on. Difficult terrain is just like rough terrain, but it also halves movement on a round-by-round basis. This means that a short move is about 25 feet (8 m), and a long move is about 50 feet (15 m). Difficult terrain reduces long-term movement to a third of its normal rate.

Water: Deep water, in which a character is mostly or entirely submerged, is just like rough terrain except that it also quarters movement. This means that a short move is about 12 feet (4 m), and a long move is about 25 feet (8 m). Characters trained in swimming only halve their movement while in deep water.

SPECIAL SITUATION: A CHASE

When a PC is chasing an NPC or vice versa, the player should attempt a Speed action, with the difficulty based on the NPC's level. If he succeeds at the roll, he catches the NPC, or he gets away if he is the one being chased. In terms of the story, this one-roll mechanic can be the result of a long chase over many rounds.

Alternatively, if the GM wants to play out a

long chase, the character can make many rolls (perhaps one per level of the NPC) to finish the pursuit successfully. For every failure, the PC must make another success, and if he ever has more failures than successes, he doesn't catch the NPC, or he doesn't get away if he is the one being chased. For example, if the PC is being chased through a crowded marketplace by a level 3 enemy, he must succeed at three chase rolls. If he succeeds at one but fails the second, he must succeed at the third one, or he will have more failures than successes, and the foe will catch him. The GM is encouraged to describe the results of these rolls with flavor. A success might mean the PC has rounded a corner and gained some distance. A failure might mean that a basket of fruit topples over in front of him, slowing him down.

ACTION: WAIT

You can wait to react to another character's action.

You decide what action will trigger your action, and if the triggering action happens, you get to take your action first (unless going first wouldn't make any sense, like attacking a foe before she comes into view). For example, if a qephilim threatens you with a halberd, on your turn you can decide to wait, stating, "If she stabs at me, I'm going to slash her with my sword." On the qephilim's turn, she stabs, so you make your sword attack before that happens.

ACTION: DEFEND

Defending is a special action that only PCs can do, and only in response to being attacked. In other words, an NPC uses its action to attack, which forces a PC to make a defense roll. This is handled like any other kind of action, with circumstances, skill, assets, and Effort all potentially coming into play. Defending is a special kind of action in that it does not happen on the PC's turn. It's never an action that a player decides to make; it's always a reaction to an attack. A PC can make a defense action when attacked (on the attacking NPC's turn) and still take another action on his own turn. The type of defense roll depends on the type of attack. If a foe attacks a character with an axe, she can use Speed to duck or block it with what she's holding. If she's struck by a poisoned dart, she can use a Might action to resist its effects. If a psi-worm attempts to control her mind, she can use Intellect to fend off the intrusion.

Sometimes an attack provokes two defense actions. For example, a poisonous reptile tries to bite a PC. She tries to dodge the bite with a Speed action. If she fails, she takes damage from the bite, and she must also attempt a Might action to resist the poison's effects.

If a character does not know an attack is coming, usually she can still make a defense roll, but she can't add modifiers (including the modifier from a shield), and she can't use any skill or Effort to decrease the roll's difficulty. If circumstances warrant—such as if the attacker is right next to the character—the GM might rule that the surprise attack simply hits her.

A character can always choose to forgo a defense action, in which case the attack automatically hits her.

Some abilities may allow you to do something special as a defense action.

ACTION: DO SOMETHING ELSE

You can try anything you can think of, although that doesn't mean anything is possible. The GM sets the difficulty—that's her primary role in the game. Still, guided by the bounds of logic, players and GMs will find all manner of actions and options that aren't covered by a rule. That's a good thing.

Players should not feel constrained by the game mechanics when taking actions. Skills are not required to attempt an action. Someone who's never picked a lock can still try. The GM might assign a negative step modifier to the difficulty, but the character can still attempt the action.

Thus, players and GMs can return to the beginning of this chapter and look at the most basic expression of the rules. A player wants to take an action. The GM decides, on a scale of 1 to 10, how difficult that task is and what stat it uses. The player determines whether he has anything that might modify the difficulty and considers whether to apply Effort. Once the final determination is made, he rolls to see if his character succeeds. It's as easy as that.

As further guidance, the following are some of the more common actions a player might take.

Waiting is also a good way to deal with a ranged attacker who rises from behind cover, fires an attack, and ducks back down. You could say, "I wait to see him pop up from behind cover and then I shoot him."

Qephilim, page 284

Players are encouraged to come up with their own ideas for what their characters do rather than looking at a list of possible actions. That's why there is a "Do Something Else" action. PCs are not pieces on a game board—they are people in a story. And like real people, they can try anything they can think of. (Succeeding is another matter entirely.) The task difficulty system provides GMs with the tools they need to adjudicate anything the players come up with.

JUMP DISTANCE

	Type of Jump			
Difficulty	**Standing**	**Immediate Run***	**Short Run***	**Vertical***
0	4 ft. (1.2 m)	5 ft. (1.5 m)	10 ft. (3 m)	0 ft.
1	5 ft. (1.5 m)	6 ft. (1.8 m)	12 ft. (3.7 m)	1 ft. (0.3 m)
2	6 ft. (1.8 m)	7 ft. (2.1 m)	14 ft. (4.3 m)	2 ft. (0.6 m)
3	7 ft. (2.1 m)	8 ft. (2.4 m)	16 ft. (4.9 m)	3 ft. (0.9 m)
4	8 ft. (2.4 m)	9 ft. (2.7 m)	18 ft. (5.5 m)	4 ft. (1.2 m)
5	9 ft. (2.7 m)	10 ft. (3 m)	20 ft. (6.1 m)	5 ft. (1.5 m)
6	10 ft. (3 m)	11 ft. (3.4 m)	22 ft. (6.7 m)	6 ft. (1.8 m)
7	11 ft. (3.4 m)	12 ft. (3.7 m)	24 ft. (7.3 m)	7 ft. (2.1 m)
8	12 ft. (3.7 m)	13 ft. (4 m)	26 ft. (7.9 m)	8 ft. (2.4 m)
9	13 ft. (4 m)	14 ft. (4.3 m)	28 ft. (8.5 m)	9 ft. (2.7 m)
10	14 ft. (4.3 m)	15 ft. (4.6 m)	30 ft. (9.1 m)	10 ft. (3 m)

** If you are skilled in jumping, move one row down to determine your distance. If you are specialized in jumping, move two rows down to determine your distance.*

Feel free to ignore the equations for jumping and just use the jump distance chart.

CLIMBING

When a character climbs, the GM sets a difficulty based on the surface being climbed. If the character succeeds at the roll, she uses the movement rules as though she were moving normally, although climbing is like moving through difficult terrain: it raises the difficulty of a move roll by one step and halves movement. Unusual circumstances, such as climbing while under fire (or while *on* fire!) pose additional step penalties. Being skilled in climbing reduces the difficulty of this task.

Difficulty	Surface
2	Surface with lots of handholds
3	Stone wall or similar surface (a few handholds)
4	Crumbling or slippery surface
5	Smooth stone wall or similar surface
6	Metal wall or similar surface
8	Smooth, horizontal surface (climber is upside-down)
10	Glass wall or similar surface

Retrying a Task, page 102

GUARDING

In a combat situation, a character can stand guard as her action. She does not make attacks, but she decreases the difficulty of all her defense tasks by one step. Further, if an NPC tries to get by her or take an action that she is guarding against, she can attempt a Speed action (based on the level of the NPC) with the difficulty decreased by one step. Success means the NPC is prevented from taking the action on his turn. This is useful for blocking a doorway, guarding a friend, and so forth.

If an NPC is standing guard, use the same procedure, but to get past the guard, the PC attempts a Speed action with the difficulty increased by one step. For example, Diana is an NPC human with a level 3 bodyguard. The bodyguard uses his action to guard Diana. If a PC wants to attack Diana, she first must succeed at a difficulty 4 Speed task to get past the guard. If she succeeds, she can make her attack normally.

HEALING

You can administer aid through bandaging and other succor, attempting to heal each patient once per day. This healing restores points to a stat Pool of your choice. Decide how many points you want to heal, and then make an Intellect action with a difficulty equal to that number. For example, if you want to heal someone for 3 points, that's a difficulty 3 task with a target number of 9. Being skilled in healing reduces the difficulty. A PC can use the retry rules as described under Retrying a Task After Failure if she attempts to heal a character using bandages and similar aids, but she can achieve only one success per day.

JUMPING

Decide how far you want to jump, and that sets the difficulty of your Might roll. For a standing jump, subtract 4 from the distance (in feet) to determine the difficulty of the jump. For example, jumping 10 feet (3 m) has a difficulty of 6.

If you run an immediate distance before jumping, it counts as an asset, reducing the difficulty of the jump by one step.

If you run a short distance before jumping, divide the jump distance (in feet) by 2 and then subtract 4 to determine the difficulty of the jump. Because you're running an immediate distance (and then some), you also count your running as an asset. For example, jumping a distance of 20 feet (6 m) with a short running start has a difficulty of 5 (20 feet divided by 2 is 10, minus 4 is 6, minus 1 for running an immediate distance). Being skilled in jumping reduces the difficulty.

For a vertical jump, the distance you clear (in feet) is equal to the difficulty of the jumping task. If you run an immediate distance, it counts as an asset, reducing the difficulty of the jump by one step.

UNDERSTANDING, IDENTIFYING, OR REMEMBERING

When characters try to identify or figure out how to use a device, the level of the device determines the difficulty. For a bit of knowledge, the GM determines the difficulty. Being skilled in the appropriate area (geography, history, geology, local knowledge, and so on) reduces the difficulty of this task.

Difficulty	Knowledge
0	Common knowledge
1	Simple knowledge
3	Something a scholar probably knows
5	Something even a scholar might not know
7	Knowledge very few people possess
10	Completely lost knowledge

LOOKING OR LISTENING

Generally, the GM will describe any sight or sound that's not purposefully difficult to detect. But if you want to look for a hidden enemy, search for a secret panel, or listen for someone sneaking up on you, make an Intellect roll. If it's a creature, its level determines the difficulty of your roll. If it's something else, the GM determines the difficulty of your roll. Being skilled in perception reduces the difficulty of this task.

INTERACTING WITH CREATURES

The level of the creature determines the target number, just as with combat. Thus, bribing a guard works much like punching him or affecting him with a twist. This is true of persuading someone, intimidating someone, calming a wild beast, or anything of the kind. Interaction is an Intellect task. Being skilled in persuasion, intimidation, bribery, deception, animal handling, or something of that nature can decrease the difficulty of the task, if appropriate.

MOVING A HEAVY OBJECT

You can push or pull something very heavy and move it an immediate distance as your action. The weight of the object determines the difficulty of the Might roll to move it; every 50 pounds increases the difficulty by one step. So moving something that weighs 150 pounds is difficulty 3, and moving something that weighs 400 pounds is difficulty 8. If you can reduce the difficulty of the task to 0, you can move a heavy object up to a short distance as your action. Being skilled in carrying or pushing reduces the difficulty of this task.

Cooperative Actions

There are many ways multiple characters can work together. None of these options, however, can be used at the same time by the same characters.

Helping: If a character attempts a task and gets help from another character who is trained or specialized in that task, the acting character gets the benefit of the helping character. The helping character uses his action to provide this help. If the helper does not have training or specialization in that task, or if the acting character already is as trained or specialized as the helper, the acting character instead gets a +1 bonus to the roll. For example, if Scott is trying to climb a steep incline but has no skill at climbing, and Sarah (who is trained in climbing) spends her turn helping him, Scott can decrease the difficulty of the task by one step. If Scott were also trained in climbing, or if neither character were, he would gain a +1 bonus to the roll instead. A character with an inability in a task cannot help another character with that task—the character with the inability provides no benefit in that situation.

Complementary Actions: If a character attempts an action, and a second character skilled in that type of action attempts a complementary action, both actions gain a +2 bonus to the roll. For example, if Scott tries to convince a ship captain to allow him on board, and Sarah is trained in persuasion, she can use a complementary—but different—action in the situation to gain the +2 bonus. She might try to supplement Scott's words with a flattering lie about the captain (a deception action), a display of knowledge about the region where the ship is about to sail (a geography action), or a direct threat to the captain (an intimidation action).

Complementary actions work in combat as well. If Scott attacks an enemy using pierce (a vector's move) and Sarah also has the ability to make pierce attacks, she can attack the same enemy using any other kind of attack, such as a bash, and get a +2 bonus. And she gives Scott a +2 bonus as well.

The players involved should work out complementary actions together and describe them to the GM.

Distraction: When a character uses his turn to distract a foe, the difficulty of that foe's attacks is modified by one step to its detriment for one round. Multiple characters distracting a foe have no greater effect than a single character doing so—a foe is either distracted or not.

Draw the Attack: When an NPC attacks a character, another PC can prominently present herself, shout taunts, and move to try to get the foe to attack her instead.

In most cases, this action succeeds without a roll—the opponent attacks the prominent PC instead of her companions. In other cases, such as with intelligent or determined foes, the prominent character must succeed at an Intellect action to draw the attack. If that Intellect action is successful, the difficulty of the prominent character's defense tasks is modified by one step to her detriment.

Two characters attempting to draw an attack at the same time cancel each other out.

Take the Attack: A character can use her action to throw herself in front of an attack to save a nearby comrade. The attack automatically succeeds against her, and it deals 1 additional point of damage. A character cannot willingly take more than one attack each round in this way.

The Old One-Two-Three: If three or more characters attack the same foe, each character gains a +1 bonus to the attack.

High and Low: If one character makes a melee attack against a foe and another character makes a ranged attack against that same foe, they can coordinate their actions. As a result, if both attacks damage the foe, the difficulty of the foe's next task is modified by one step to its detriment.

Covering Fire: A character using a ranged attack or ability can aim near a foe but narrowly miss on purpose, making an attack that inflicts no damage but harasses and frightens the foe. If the attack is successful, it deals no damage, but the difficulty of the foe's next attack is modified by one step to its detriment.

OPERATING OR DISABLING A DEVICE, OR PICKING A LOCK

As with figuring out a device, the level of the device usually determines the difficulty of the Intellect roll. Unless a device is very complex, the GM will often rule that once you figure it out, no roll is needed to operate it except under special circumstances. So if the PCs figure out how to use a hovercraft, they can operate it. If they are attacked, they might need to roll to ensure that they don't crash the platform into a wall while trying to avoid being hit.

Disabling a device or picking a lock usually require rolls. These actions often involve special tools and assume that the character is not trying to destroy the device or lock. (If you *are* attempting to destroy it, you probably should make a Might roll to smash it rather than a Speed or Intellect roll requiring patience and know-how.) Being skilled in operating devices or picking locks reduces the difficulty.

RIDING OR PILOTING

If you're riding an animal that's trained to be a mount, or driving or piloting a vehicle, and you're doing something routine such as going from point A to point B, you don't need to make a roll. However, staying mounted during a fight or doing something tricky with a vehicle requires a Speed roll to succeed. A saddle or other appropriate gear is an asset and reduces the difficulty by one step. Being skilled in riding, driving, or piloting reduces the difficulty.

Difficulty	Maneuver
0	Riding
1	Staying on the mount (including a motorcycle or similar vehicle) in a battle or other difficult situation
3	Staying on a mount (including a motorcycle or similar vehicle) when you take damage
4	Mounting a moving steed
4	Making an abrupt turn with a vehicle while moving fast
4	Getting a vehicle to move twice as fast as normal for one round
5	Coaxing a mount to move or jump twice as fast or far as normal for one round
5	Making a long jump with a vehicle not intended to go airborne (like a car) and remaining in control

VEHICULAR MOVEMENT

Vehicles move just like creatures. Each has a movement rate, which indicates how far it can move in a round. Most vehicles require a driver, and most require that the driver spends every action controlling the movement of the vehicle (if it is moving). This rarely requires a roll (the task is routine). Any round not spent driving the vehicle increases the difficulty of the task next round by one step and precludes any change in speed or direction. In other words, driving down the road normally is difficulty 0. Spending an action to retrieve a backpack from the back seat means that on the following round the driver must attempt a difficulty 1 task. If he uses his action instead to pull his handgun from that backpack, on the next round the difficulty will be 2, and so on. Failure results are based on the situation but might very well involve a collision or something similar.

In a vehicular chase, drivers attempt Speed actions just like in a regular chase, but the difficulty may be based either on the level of the driver (modified by the level and movement rate of the vehicle) or on the level of the vehicle (modified by the level of the driver).

Common vehicles and mounts differ by recursion; on Earth cars and horses are common mounts, while in Ardeyn horses and sometimes dlammas who agree to bear a rider are considered "common" mounts. Ruk offers a bewildering array of vehicles, many of which can fly, but the most common is the wing glider.

Dlamma, page 266
Wing glider, page 93

SNEAKING

The difficulty of sneaking by a creature is determined by its level. Sneaking is a Speed roll. Moving at half speed reduces the difficulty by one step. Appropriate camouflage or other gear may count as an asset and decrease the difficulty, as will dim lighting conditions and having plenty of things to hide behind. Being skilled in sneaking reduces the difficulty of this task.

SWIMMING

If you're simply swimming from one place to another, such as across a calm river or lake, use the standard movement rules, noting the fact that your character is in deep water. Being skilled in swimming decreases the difficulty. However, sometimes, special circumstances require a Might roll to make progress while swimming, such as when trying to avoid a current or being dragged into a whirlpool.

SPECIAL: CRAFTING, BUILDING, AND REPAIRING

Crafting is tricky in The Strange because the same rules that govern building a spear also cover repairing a machine that can take you

Circumstances really matter. Sewing a dress by hand might take five times as long, or more, as using a sewing machine, for example.

The GM is free to overrule some attempts at creation, building, or repair, requiring that the character have a certain level of skill, proper tools and materials, and so forth.

from Earth to Ruk. Normally, the level of the item determines the difficulty of creating or repairing it as well as the time required. For items unique to a recursion or world other than your own, or the Strange itself (for example, cyphers), add 5 to the item's level to determine the difficulty of creating or repairing it. If the item is artistic in nature, the GM might add to the difficulty and time required. A crude wooden stool could be hammered together in an hour, but a beautiful finished piece might take a week or longer and would require more skill on the part of the crafter.

A level 0 object requires no skill to make and is easily found in most locations. Sling stones and firewood are level 0 items—producing them is routine. Making a torch from spare wood and oil-soaked cloth is simple, so it's a level 1 object. Making an arrow or a spear is fairly standard, so it's a level 2 object.

MATERIALS

Generally speaking, a device to be crafted requires materials equal to its level and all the levels below it. So a level 5 device requires level 5 material, level 4 material, level 3 material, level 2 material, and level 1 material (and, technically, level 0 material).

The GM and players can gloss over much of the crafting details, if desired. Gathering all the materials to make a mundane item might not be worth playing out—but then again, it might be. Making a wooden spear in a forest isn't very interesting, but what if the PCs have to make a spear in a treeless desert? Finding the wreckage of something made of wood or forcing a PC to fashion a spear out of the bones of a large beast could be interesting.

TIME

The time required to create an item is up to the GM, but the guidelines in the crafting table are a good starting point. Generally, repairing an item takes somewhere between half the creation time and the full creation time, depending on the item, the aspect that needs repairing, and the circumstances. For example, if creating an item takes one hour, repairing it takes between thirty minutes and one hour.

Sometimes a GM will allow a rush job if the circumstances warrant it. This is different than using skill to reduce the time required. In this case, the quality of the item is affected. Let's say that a character needs to create a tool that will cut through solid steel with a powerful laser (a level 7 item), but she has to do it in one day. The GM might allow it, but the device might be extremely volatile, inflicting damage on the user, or it might work only once.

SKILLS

The skill level of the crafter reduces the difficulty as normal in all ways except materials and time. If a PC on Earth trained in graphic design wants to make a novel cover and the GM decides it's a level 3 "item," it's only a standard (difficulty 2) task, but it still takes a full day and requires proper tools. A particularly great piece of video manipulation software

CRAFTING DIFFICULTY AND TIME

DIFFICULTY	CRAFT	TIME REQUIRED TO BUILD (GENERALLY)
0	Something extremely simple like tying a rope or finding an appropriately sized rock	A few minutes at most
1	A torch	Five minutes
2	A spear, a simple shelter or piece of furniture	One hour
3	A bow, a door, a basic article of clothing	One day
4	A sword, a chainmail vest	One to two days
5	Common technological item (electric light) A nice piece of jewelry or art object	One week
6	Technological item (a watch, a transmitter) A really nice piece of jewelry, art object, or elegant craftwork	One month
7	Technological item (a computer) A major work of art	One year
8	Technological item (something from beyond Earth)	Many years
9	Technological item (something from beyond Earth)	Many years
10	Technological item (something from beyond Earth)	Many years

could serve as an asset, with GM approval.

With the GM's approval (and if it makes sense to do so), the character can reduce the time or materials needed instead of the difficulty. A trained fletcher making arrows (level 2 items) could attempt a difficulty 2 task rather than a difficulty 1 task to create an arrow in fifteen minutes instead of an hour, or she could create it in an hour using substandard (level 1) materials. However, sometimes the GM will rule that reducing the time is not possible. For example, a single human could not make a chainmail vest in one hour (without some kind of machine to help).

Possible areas for character training include:

EARTH

- Bowyering/Fletching
- Leatherworking
- Glassblowing
- Armoring
- Weaponsmithing
- Gunsmithing
- Woodcrafting
- Metalworking
- Electronics
- Computer science
- Engines
- Chemistry

ARDEYN

- Bowyering/Fletching
- Leatherworking
- Glassblowing
- Armoring
- Weaponsmithing

RUK

- Armoring
- Weaponsmithing
- Gunsmithing
- Metalworking
- Electronics
- Computer science
- Engines
- Chemistry
- Genetic engineering
- Neural engineering

FAILURE

Failure at the roll means that the device is not completed or repaired. To continue to work on it, the character must gather more materials (generally, the highest-level material needed) and take the required amount of time again.

NONSTANDARD ITEMS

The preceding rules work well for repairing nonstandard items, such as a biotech immobilizer from Ruk or an enchanted staff from Ardeyn. However, if a character wants to create a nonstandard, permanent object, the player must spend XP. If the character fails his roll, no XP are spent.

TINKERING WITH THE STRANGE

Characters might try to make a cypher, an artifact, or another object from the Strange do something other than its intended function. Sometimes, the GM will simply declare the task impossible. You can't turn a vial of healing elixir into a two-way communicator. But most of the time, there is a chance of success.

That said, tinkering with the Strange is not easy. Obviously, the difficulty varies from situation to situation, but difficulties starting at 7 are not unreasonable. The time, tools, and training required would be similar to the time, tools, and training needed to repair a device. If the tinkering results in a long-term benefit for the character—such as creating an artifact that she can use—the GM should require her to spend XP to make it.

EXPERIENCE POINTS

Experience points (XP) are the currency by which players gain benefits for their characters. The most common ways to earn XP are through GM intrusions and by discovering new and amazing things. Sometimes experience points are earned during a game session, and sometimes they're earned between sessions. In a typical session, a player might earn 2 to 4 XP, and between sessions, perhaps another 2 XP (on average). The exact amounts depend on the events of the session and the discoveries made.

GMs and players should work together to make both XP awards and expenditures fit the ongoing story. If a PC stays in a recursion for two months to learn the inhabitants' unique art form, the GM might award her a few XP, which are then immediately spent to grant the character the ability to create that art form herself.

GM INTRUSION

At any time, the GM can introduce an unexpected complication for a character. When he intrudes in this way, he must give that character 2 XP. That player, in turn, must immediately give one of those XP to another player and justify the gift (perhaps the other player had a good idea, told a joke, or performed an action that saved a life).

Often, the GM intrudes when a player attempts an action that should be an automatic success. However, the GM is free to intrude at other times. As a general rule, the GM should intrude at least once each session, but no more than once or twice each session per character.

Anytime the GM intrudes, the player can spend 1 XP to refuse the intrusion, though that also means he doesn't get the 2 XP. If the player has no XP to spend, he can't refuse.

Example 1: Through skill and the aid of another character, a fourth-tier PC reduces a wall-climbing task from difficulty 2 to difficulty 0. Normally, he would succeed at the task automatically, but the GM intrudes and says, "No, a bit of the crumbling wall gives way, so you still have to make a roll." As with any difficulty 2 task, the target number is 6. The PC attempts the roll as normal, and because the GM intruded, he gains 2 XP. He immediately gives one of those XP to another player.

Example 2: During a fight, a PC swings his axe and damages a foe with a slice across the shoulder. The GM intrudes by saying that the foe turned just as the axe struck, wrenching the weapon from the character's grip and sending it clattering across the floor. The axe comes to a stop 10 feet (3 m) away. Because the GM intruded, the PC gains 2 XP, and he immediately gives one of those XP to another player. Now the character must deal with the dropped weapon, perhaps drawing a different weapon or using his next turn to scramble after the axe.

If a character rolls a 1 on a die, the GM can intrude without giving the character any XP.

Typically, PCs will earn about half their total experience points by making discoveries.

DISCOVERING NEW THINGS

The core of gameplay in The Strange—the answer to the question "What do characters do in this game?"—is "Discover new things." Discovery makes the character more powerful because it almost certainly grants a new capability or option, but it's also a discovery unto itself and results in a gain of XP.

It's a fine line, but ultimately the GM decides what constitutes a discovery as opposed to just something weird in the course of an adventure. Usually, the difference is, did the PCs successfully interact with it and learn something about it? If so, it's probably a discovery.

Discovery can include finding a significant new area of a recursion (new to the PCs, anyway), a new recursion entirely, or even a new region of the Strange itself. In this fashion, PCs are explorers. It can also include a new significant aspect to a recursion (or prime world) such as a secret organization, a new religion, and so on.

Discovery can also mean finding a new procedure or device (something too big to be considered a piece of equipment) or even previously unknown information. This could include a new translation gate, a source of magical power in Ardeyn, a unique power generator in Ruk, or the cure for a plague. These are all discoveries. The common thread is that the PCs discover something that they can understand and put to use.

Lastly, depending on the GM's outlook and the kind of campaign the group wants to play, a discovery could be a secret, an ethical idea, an adage, or even a truth.

Artifacts: When the group gains an artifact, award XP equal to the artifact's level and divide it among the PCs (minimum 1 XP for each character). Round down if necessary. For example, if four PCs discover a level 5 artifact, they each get 1 XP. Money, standard equipment, and cyphers are not worth XP.

Miscellaneous Discoveries: Various other discoveries might grant 1 XP to each PC involved.

GM AWARDS

Sometimes, a group will have an adventure that doesn't deal primarily with discovery or finding things. In this case, it's a good idea for the GM to award XP for accomplishing other tasks. A goal or a mission is worth 1 to 4 XP for each PC involved, depending on the difficulty and length of the work. As a general rule, a mission should be worth at least 1 XP per game session involved in accomplishing it. For example, saving a family on an isolated farm beset by raiding cultists might be worth 1 XP for each character. Of course, saving the family doesn't always mean killing the bad guys; it might mean relocating them, parlaying with the cultists, or chasing off the raiders.

Delivering a message to a hermit in a tiny recursion hidden in the Strange—one that requires the PCs to face dangerous conditions and risk possible attacks by inklings—is probably a mission worth 2 XP per character.

On the other hand, if the PCs can translate directly to the recursion, the mission is probably worth just 1 XP per character. Thus, GM awards are based not only on the task, but on the PCs and their capabilities as well.

However, that doesn't mean the characters should earn fewer XP if they make a lot of lucky rolls or devise a clever plan to overcome obstacles. Being lucky or smart doesn't make a difficult challenge less difficult—it just means the PCs succeed more easily.

PLAYER-DRIVEN AWARDS

Players can create their own missions by setting goals for their characters. If they succeed, they earn XP just as if they were sent on the mission by an NPC. For example, if the characters decide on their own to help find a lost caravan in Ardeyn's mountains, that's a goal and a mission.

Sometimes character goals are more personal. If a PC vows to avenge the death of her brother, that's still a mission. These kinds of goals that are important to a character's

PROGRESSING TO A NEW TIER

Tiers in The Strange aren't entirely like levels in other roleplaying games. In The Strange, gaining levels is not the players' only goal or the only measure of achievement. Starting (first-tier) characters are already competent, and there are only six tiers. Character advancement has a power curve, but it's only steep enough to keep things interesting. In other words, gaining levels is cool and fun, but it's not the only path to success or power. If you spend all your XP on immediate, short- and medium-term benefits, you would be different from someone who spends her points on long-term benefits, but you would not be "behind" that character.

The general idea is that most characters will spend half their XP on tier advancement and long-term benefits, and the rest on immediate and short-term benefits (which are used during gameplay). Some groups might decide that XP earned during a game is to be spent on immediate and short-term benefits (gameplay uses), and XP awarded between sessions for discoveries is to be spent on character advancement (long-term uses).

Ultimately, the idea is to make experience points into tools that the players and the GM can use to shape the story and the characters, not just a bookkeeping hassle.

background should be set at or near the outset of the game. When completed, a character goal should be worth at least 1 XP (and perhaps as much as 4 XP). This encourages players to develop their characters' backgrounds and to build in opportunities for action in the future. Doing so makes the background more than just backstory or flavor—it becomes something that can propel the campaign forward.

SPENDING EXPERIENCE POINTS

Experience points are meant to be used. Hoarding them is not a good idea; if a player accumulates more than 10 XP, the GM can require her to spend some of them.

Generally, experience points can be spent in four ways: immediate benefits, short-term benefits, long-term benefits, and character advancement.

IMMEDIATE BENEFITS

The most straightforward way for a player to use XP is to reroll any roll in the game—even one that she didn't make. This costs 1 XP per reroll, and the player chooses the best result. She can continue to spend XP on rerolls, but this can quickly become an expensive proposition. It's a fine way to try to prevent disaster, but it's not a good idea to use of a lot of XP to reroll a single action over and over.

A player can also spend 1 XP to refuse a GM intrusion.

SHORT- AND MEDIUM-TERM BENEFITS

By spending 2 XP, a character can gain a skill—or, more rarely, an ability—that provides a short-term benefit. Let's say a character notices that the computer terminals in the facility she's infiltrating are similar to those used by the company she once worked for. She spends 2 XP and says that she has a great deal of experience in using these. As a result, she is trained in operating (and breaking into) these computers. This is just like being trained in computer use or hacking, but it applies only to computers found in that particular location. The skill is extremely useful in the facility, but nowhere else.

Medium-term benefits are usually story based. For example, a character can spend 2 XP while climbing through mountains and say that she has experience with climbing in regions like these, or perhaps she spends the XP after she's been in the mountains for a while and says that she's picked up the feel for climbing there. Either way, from now on, she is trained in climbing in those mountains. This helps her now and any time she returns to the area, but she's not trained in climbing everywhere.

This method allows a character to get immediate training in a skill for half the normal cost. (Normally, it costs 4 XP to become trained in a skill.) It's also a way to gain a new skill even if the PC has already gained a new skill as a step toward attaining the next tier.

In rare cases, a GM might allow a character to spend 2 XP to gain an entirely new ability—such as a device, a move, a twist, a revision, or a special mental power—for a short time, usually no longer than the course of one scenario. The player and the GM should agree on a story-based explanation for the benefit. Perhaps the ability has a specific, rare requirement, such as a tool, a battery, a drug, or some kind of treatment. For example, a character who wants to explore a submerged

Experience points should not be a goal unto themselves. Instead, they are a game mechanic to simulate how—through experience, time, toil, travail, and so on—characters become more skilled, more able, and truthfully, more powerful. Spending XP to explain a change in a character's capabilities that occurred in the course of the story, such as if the PC made a new device or learned a new skill, isn't a waste of XP—it's what XP are for.

If player characters are given the opportunity to create a recursion of their own by participating in a genesis quest, spending XP is something they must contribute to the process, both for initially creating a recursion and later if they want to improve the recursion.

Spinner, page 38

Ruk, page 190

The skill you choose for character advancement can be anything you wish, such as climbing, jumping, persuading, or sneaking. You can also choose to be knowledgeable in a certain area of study, such as history or geology. You can even choose a skill based on your character's special abilities. For example, if your character can make an Intellect roll to blast an enemy with mental force, you can become trained in using that ability, treating its difficulty as one step lower than normal.

location has several biotech enhancements, and he spends 2 XP to cobble together a device that lets him breathe underwater. This gives him the ability for a considerable length of time, but not permanently—the device might work for only eight hours. Again, the story and the logic of the situation dictate the parameters.

LONG-TERM BENEFITS

In many ways, the long-term benefits a PC can gain by spending XP are a means of integrating the mechanics of the game with the story. Players can codify things that happen to their characters by talking to the GM and spending 3 XP. For example, a spinner named Jessica spends a long time working in a kitchen in a restaurant that she believes is owned by a man working for agents from Ruk on Earth. During that time, she becomes familiar with cooking. Jessica's player talks with the GM and says that she would like to have the spinner's experiences have a lasting effect on the character. She spends 3 XP and gains familiarity with cooking.

Some things that a PC can acquire as a long-term benefit are story based. In the course of play, the character might gain a friend (a contact) or build a log cabin (a home). These benefits are probably not the result of spending XP. The new contact comes to the PC and starts the relationship. The new home is granted to him as a reward for service to a powerful or wealthy patron, or maybe the character inherits the home from a relative.

Things that affect character abilities, like a familiarity or an artifact, are different. They likely require XP and time, money, and so on.

Long-term benefits can include the following.

Familiarity: The character gains a +1 bonus to rolls involving one kind of task.

Contact: The character gains a long-term NPC contact of importance—someone who will help him with information, equipment, or physical tasks. The player and GM should work out the details of the relationship.

Home: The PC acquires a full-time residence. This can be an apartment in a city, a cabin in the wilderness, a base in an ancient complex, or whatever fits the situation. It should be a secure place where the PC can leave his belongings and sleep soundly. Several characters could combine their XP and buy a home together.

Title or job: The PC is granted a position of importance or authority. It might come with responsibilities, prestige, and rewards, or it might also simply be an honorarium.

Wealth: The PC comes into a considerable amount of wealth, whether it's a windfall, an inheritance, or a gift. It might be enough to buy a home or a title, but that's not really the point. The main benefit is that the PC no longer needs to worry about the cost of simple equipment, lodging, food, and so on. This wealth could mean a set amount—perhaps 50,000 dollars—or it could bestow the ability to ignore minor costs, as decided by the player and GM.

Artifact: The PC creates an artifact that has a power of his choosing. If the item is fairly simple, the GM can skip the crafting details and just say that after a period of time, the PC creates it. For an item that significantly alters gameplay—granting the character vast telepathic powers or giving him the ability to teleport at will—the GM might require difficult rolls, a considerable amount of time, and rare, hard-to-find components and materials.

CHARACTER ADVANCEMENT

Progressing to the next tier involves four stages. When a PC has spent 4 XP on each of the stages, he advances to the next tier and gains all the type and focus benefits of that tier. The four stages can be purchased in any order, but each can be purchased only once per tier. In other words, a PC must buy all four stages and advance to the next tier before he can buy the same stage again.

Increasing Capabilities: You gain 4 new points to add to your stat Pools. You can allocate the points among your Pools however you wish.

Moving Toward Perfection: You add 1 to your Might Edge, your Speed Edge, or your Intellect Edge (your choice).

Extra Effort: Your Effort score increases by 1.

Skills: You become trained in one skill of your choice, other than attacks or defense. If you choose a skill that you are already trained in, you become specialized in that skill, reducing the difficulty of related tasks by two steps instead of one.

Other Options: Players can also spend 4 XP to purchase other special options. Selecting any of these options counts as purchasing one of the four stages necessary to advance to the next tier. The special options are as follows:

- Reduce the cost for wearing armor. This option lowers the Might cost by 1 and lowers the Speed reduction by 1.
- Add 2 to your recovery rolls.

CHAPTER 9

RULES OF TRANSLATION

When a character moves between recursions, it's called translation. The process of translation does what it sounds like—it changes someone so that he "fits in" to the context of the new recursion. He exchanges his current dress, some of his abilities and equipment, and possibly even how he looks, for new clothes and skills that fit the recursion. Sometimes translation is initiated by the PCs. Other times, translation occurs thanks to some kind of gate that connects different recursions.

Translation is not teleportation. It does not involve physical travel. Instead, your character's consciousness moves to a newly created physical form appropriate to the context of the recursion he is translating to. In other words, your character appears in a new body, with new equipment. When translating to Ardeyn, you might take on the physical form of a qephilim, with chainmail armor, a battleaxe, and a crossbow, even though on Earth you were a librarian with a smartphone. Your race and gender may also change from recursion to recursion.

The character's new form is in all ways still that character. His descriptor, his type, and most of his stats do not change. His focus likely *does* change to one appropriate to the new recursion. In Ardeyn, a character might become a sorcerer. In Ruk, a bioengineered warrior.

TRANSLATION TIME

A four-hour trance precedes each translation; once the trance is complete, actual translation is instantaneous if the initiating character succeeds on a translation roll. The trance time can be cut in half, or even down to just ten minutes or less, if characters work together to hasten the translation.

Translation roll, page 126

All PCs are quickened, as are some NPCs. However, no NPC is a vector, spinner, or paradox—types are for PCs only.

TRANSLATION ACCLIMATION

The physical stress of translation imposes an acclimation period on recursors. During acclimation, a PC is unable to access any focus abilities from the previous recursion or the recursion just entered (unless the focus is the same because the PC dragged it along). This acclimation period can last up to an hour or as little as one round.

Qephilim, page 163

INITIATING A TRANSLATION

Quickened characters have the ability to translate themselves and several companions between recursions. In any translation not involving a gate, a quickened creature or character must initiate the translation.

To initiate, the character must have one of the following.

- An object from the destination recursion (an object probably delivered through an inapposite gate)
- A likeness (art, photo, sculpture) of the destination that sufficiently evokes the actual recursion (a still from an Earth movie that helped shape a recursion through fictional leakage isn't usually sufficient—the likeness works best if it *actually* depicts the destination recursion)
- Knowledge of three specific and related details about the destination recursion
- A recursion key

Recursion key, page 130

A character does not need any of the above if she has been to the destination recursion before. If she's already been to the recursion, not only can she get there, she can appear in the exact same spot that she left.

If the character has any of these objects or experiences, she can put herself into a meditative trance. If the character doesn't have any help hastening the translation from another PC, the trance takes four hours to complete.

Translation Failure Table, page 128

TRANSLATION TRANCE

If a trance is interrupted for more than a couple of minutes, it is ruined and must be started again. As the trance progresses, all characters participating in the translation see a vision of the Strange: a region of void filled with repeating fractal patterns spiraling off into infinity. As the trance continues, the destination recursion slowly begins to resolve, becoming more and more defined as the end of the trance approaches. Whether it becomes completely clear or the vision shatters to nothing depends on the translation roll the initiator makes.

TRANSLATION ROLL

When the trance ends, the character initiating the translation makes an Intellect-based roll with a difficulty equal to the target recursion's level (every recursion has a base level). Success means that the character and all designated allies within immediate range successfully translate to the target recursion (or back up to Earth). Failure means that the translation still probably occurred, but with side effects.

Multiple characters working together can enhance the translation. Ideally, at least three characters are involved: one to initiate, one to hasten the process, and one to ease acclimation. This means that translation is always best as a group effort, and a mixed group is always better off than one that is not.

If a PC initiating a translation has never visited the target recursion before, a successful translation drops her and her allies into the recursion's default destination.

Paradox Initiation Advantage: Although anyone can modify any aspect of the translation, paradoxes are better initiators. When a paradox makes a translation roll, she gets one automatic retry on a failed translation roll. So when a paradox attempts to translate to Earth (which is level 5) and fails to roll a 15 or higher, she can immediately roll again without having to first roll on the Translation Failure table. On her second roll, she can choose to use Effort, or not, regardless of whether she used any on the initial roll. If she fails a second time on the same translation attempt, it's time to get out the d100.

HASTENING A TRANSLATION

If one PC initiates a translation, a second character can join into the translation trance and speed the four-hour process up so it takes only two hours. This is called hastening the translation. Any PC can take the hastening role in the translation effort and cut the translation trance down by half. Multiple hasteners, however, can't speed this process further. Someone hastening the translation shares the vision of the initiator.

From the perspective of the character who takes the hastening role, the job is all about finding shortcuts and taking care of side tasks. The hastener enters the trance with an eye toward efficiency and economy of effort. Hastening a trance means taking some of the burden from the initiator by strengthening the connection to the details about the target recursion or focusing more strongly on the object from that recursion, improving the visualization of the destination recursion and taking care of other minor but necessary elements of the trance to take the load off the initiator.

Spinner Hastening Advantage: Although anyone can modify any aspect of the translation, spinners are better hasteners. A participating spinner cuts a translation down to

DESIRED TRANSLATION RESULT OR SPECIAL CIRCUMSTANCE	TRANSLATION DIFFICULTY
The initiating PC meets all normal prerequisites; he appears in the recursion where he left it on last visit (or in the recursion's default destination, if he never visited the recursion before).	Recursion level
The quickened creature initiated, eased, or hastened a translation in the last 24 hours; each additional translation attempt increases the difficulty by another step.	Recursion level + 1 step
The initiating PC relies on a target recursion likeness (or equivalent) that helped shape a recursion through fictional leakage, not a likeness of the *actual* recursion.	Recursion level + 3 steps

"The walls vibrate, colors detach from your surroundings and begin to swirl, moments before the walls, floor, and ceiling, too, seem to liquefy and drain down and twist around you.

Agony, sharp as an iron hook, snags your heart and pulls you inside out—you and the world. When the sensation fades, you're someplace else, and someone else. That, agents, is what translation feels like."

~Hertzfeld, Estate Research Chief

just ten minutes (instead of cutting it down to two hours, if a character other than a spinner hastened the effort).

EASING A TRANSLATION

If a player character initiates a translation, another character can join into the trance and ease the acclimation time after translation so that a acclimation that would normally take one hour takes only ten minutes. This is called *easing* the translation. Any PC can take the role of easing the translation effort, though multiple easers can't decrease acclimation time any further. Someone easing the translation shares the vision of the initiator.

From the person easing the translation's point of view, most of the stress and physical testing of the translation falls on his shoulders. While part of the translation trance, the easing character concentrates on the health of each participant, prepares everyone's body and mind for the coming transformation, and bolsters well-being and fortitude. The translation fugue that follows after a creature moves into a new recursion is akin to natural inflammation; the body's response to a challenge is to try to fight it off. The job of someone easing a translation

It's difficult to have a translation "chase." For example, if someone translates from Ardeyn to Ruk, he arrives at his previous location in Ruk—maybe a secret flying base over a spar jungle. If the PCs chase him to Ruk but were never there before, they end up far away in in Harmonious, making a chase scenario particularly difficult.

Translation Failure

If the PCs fail their translation roll, roll on the following table to determine the result.

01–20	**Complete Failure:** The characters do not translate.
21–40	**Altered Destination:** The characters translate to a location they did not plan on, chosen by the GM. This might be a location they have no knowledge of.
41–45	**Taxing:** Acclimation time is doubled.
46–50	**Blurred Senses:** The difficulty of all perception-related tasks attempted by translating characters is increased by one step for one hour after acclimation.
51–55	**Slowed Reactions:** The difficulty of all Speed-based tasks attempted by translating characters is increased by one step for one hour after acclimation.
56–60	**Weak:** The difficulty of all Might-related tasks attempted by translating characters is increased by one step for one hour after acclimation.
61–65	**Confused:** The difficulty of all Intellect-related tasks attempted by translating characters is increased by one step for one hour after acclimation.
66–70	**Somewhat out of Sync:** The difficulty of *all* tasks attempted by translating characters is increased by one step for one hour after acclimation.
71–75	**Entirely out of Sync:** The difficulty of all tasks attempted by translating characters is increased by two steps for one hour after acclimation.
76–80	**Memory Failure:** Translating characters lose all memory of anything that happens one hour after arrival. They "wake up" after that hour and have no idea what happened.
81–85	**Adaptation Failure:** The difficulty of all tasks related to translating characters' new foci is increased by one step for the duration of their stay in the new recursion.
86–90	**Greatly Altered Destination:** The characters translate to a location they did not plan on, chosen by the GM. This might be a location they have no knowledge of. The location and the situation occurring there is always dangerous—filled with enemies, in an environment hostile to character health, and so on. This could be the result of a NPC who has intruded upon the translation and placed the PCs in a peril of the NPC's choosing, such as a prison, a desert island, the middle of a flash flood, and so on.
91–98	**Interrupted Translation:** The characters translate to an entirely different recursion than the one they had intended.
99–00	**Catastrophic Failure:** Roll twice on this table and take both results.

On a failed translation roll (after the effects of failure are applied), a PC can choose to retry the translation. If she does, normal rules for retrying apply: the PC can retry, but she must use Effort.

Helping, page 118

Trance and Acclimation Time

Three PCs (1 initiating, 1 hastening, 1 easing)

Trance Time	Acclimation Time
10 minutes	1 round (if vector eases and spinner hastens)
2 hours	10 minutes

Two PCs (1 initiating, 1 hastening)

Trance Time	Acclimation Time
10 minutes	1 hour (if spinner hastens)
2 hours	1 hour

Two PCs (1 initiating, 1 easing)

Trance Time	Acclimation Time
4 hours	1 round (if vector eases)
4 hours	10 minutes

One PC (1 initiating)

Trance Time	Acclimation Time
4 hours	1 hour

is to ease that natural response and make the body accept the change in as little time as possible

Vector Easing Advantage: Although anyone can modify any aspect of the translation, vectors are the best at easing. A participating vector allows acclimation in just one round (instead of ten minutes, or one hour if no one eases the translation).

Helping with a Translation

If initiation, easing, and hastening are already being covered by other player characters, additional PCs can still play a role in improving the chance of a successful translation.

Additional characters can enter the trance and provide aid, according to the rules for helping with tasks described in chapter 8 (which means that characters could choose to become trained or even specialized in translating).

Anyone helping a translation shares the

TRANSLATION LOCATION, OR "WHERE DO THEY APPEAR?"

The default location where the translating characters arrive is the same spot they were in when they last left that destination. So characters who leave Ardeyn while at a desolate shrine in the Nammu Mountains reappear at the same shrine when they translate back to the recursion. If the PC initiating the translation has been in that location previously, he and his allies appear there, even if some of his allies left that recursion from a different spot or never even visited the recursion at all.

If characters translate to a recursion they've never before visited, the initial destination is determined by the GM. The GM can determine where a translating character appears in the recursion, though certain "default" spots within a given recursion draw first-time travelers.

Ardeyn Default Location: First-time recursors appear before the gates of Citadel Hazurrium in the Queendom.

Ruk Default Location: First-time recursors appear in the widest public lobby of Harmonious, the Glistening City.

Earth Default Location: First time recursors appear in the city of Seattle, amid the crowds visiting the Space Needle.

Other recursions have similar "default" locations where first-time recursors appear, as determined by the GM.

visions of the other participants; she can see the resolving target recursion and mainly focuses on the same tasks as the character who initiated the translation.

TRANSLATION INTO AND OUT OF WARDED LOCATIONS

Some locations within a recursion are especially difficult or even impossible to translate into; they are warded by magic, technology, cyphers, or some other feature of the recursion to keep intruders out or channel them so that they arrive in certain areas. For instance, a recursion might be level 3 for purposes of translation, but a specified area might be level 6 or higher for the same purpose. Those who attempt to translate into such a location and fail simply don't translate, or they might fall prey to the ward's purpose and drop into a secure prison or a trap within that recursion.

Similarly, certain locations within a recursion might be specially warded to prevent recursors from translating out of them. For example, a "secure prison" isn't particularly secure against recursors unless it has such a feature.

TRANSLATION ABEYANCE

When a character translates, her original physical form—the one she leaves behind—disappears. It goes into abeyance and, for all practical purposes, is gone. As soon as she returns, her physical form from that recursion is instantly recreated, usually in the same place as she left. She once again has the form and equipment she was carrying before translating away from that recursion.

Similarly, if a character translates to a recursion or prime world he has already visited, he usually appears where he left, in the same form that he had when he left. However, the location may be modified if another character is initiating the translation. A group translating together is not split up when they appear in the new recursion; they appear wherever the initiator of the translation would go, whether that location is chosen by game rules, the GM, or the initiator.

NOTICING A TRANSLATION ARRIVAL

Because translation is about "fitting in," upon arriving in a new location, native creatures without the spark rarely notice the arrival of translating creatures, unless they are specifically designed to do so. Creatures that have the spark or who are quickened could notice, and probably will if they are tasked with watching or guarding an area. For PCs, noticing a creature translating into a location they can see is a difficulty 2 Intellect-based perception task (unless they're specifically watching for such an arrival—in which case, they automatically notice).

If arriving recursors require more than ten minutes of translation acclimation, they look so out of place that they may appear out of context until acclimation is nearer to completion. The GM decides whether the context is violated enough that the rules described above no longer apply, in which case the recursors are easily seen by those with the spark.

Of course, noticing a creature coming through a gate is a different matter, even if it's a translation gate. Even if the recursors themselves walk out of the gate looking appropriate for the recursion, it's hard to conceal the fact that they've just passed

Nammu Mountains, page 168
Citadel Hazurrium, page 166
Queendom, page 166
Harmonious, page 196

Estate grounds are warded against translation. Those who attempt to translate onto the Estate campus without an Estate badge face a difficulty 8 Intellect-based task. On a failed roll, recursors still appear on the Estate, but within a locked holding cell. Translating out of an Estate holding cell is a difficulty 9 task.

The Estate, page 148

through some sort of magical, technological, or otherwise supernatural portal, especially if the onlookers are staring right at it.

CYPHERS AND TRANSLATION

Tied to the Strange and not to any one world, cyphers are (usually) the only kind of equipment characters carry that translates with them. Cyphers may take a new form appropriate to the new recursion, but their powers remain the same. Just as with characters, cyphers translate to a form that "fits in" with the rest of the recursion. So what appears as a magical music box in Ardeyn might appear as a colorful vuvuzela on Earth.

TRANSLATION DIRECTLY INTO THE STRANGE ITSELF

Generally speaking, PCs can't translate directly into the Strange—they must first translate to a recursion. Most recursions (though not all) grant access to a region of the Strange called the Shoals of Earth.

Shoals of Earth, page 214

Therefore, many recursions also serve as gateways to the Strange. This is especially true of Ardeyn, considering that anyone embarking from the edge of the recursion moves directly into the Strange, but other recursions may have similarly permeable transition areas, while still others may be more restrictive or entirely closed.

RECURSION KEYS

A recursion key provides "mental directions" to a quickened character, allowing her to translate to a specific site within a specified recursion (as opposed to the last place she visited in that recursion or the default location if she's never visited there before). The key is not a gate—the recursor must initiate a translation and succeed on the translation roll normally. On a successful roll, everyone participating in the translation appears in the location specified by the key.

Recursion Keys Do Not Translate: Most recursion keys are cyphers, which means they are single use, and thus dissipate as soon as a character uses them.

Rarely, a recursion key is not a cypher. These unusual keys are created by quickened creatures or formed via natural occurrences, and are especially sought after because they can be used more than once.

If a character wants a created key to go

TRANSLATION EFFECTS ON DISABILITY, DISEASE, AND HEALING

When a character's consciousness moves to its new physical form via translation, that new form may or may not retain some attributes of the original body. Characters with missing limbs, those who are blind or deaf, and those with other physical abilities may find their limbs, eyesight, or hearing restored, and other disabilities lessened or completely missing. This can work the other way too—for example, a fully sighted person may find himself blind when he lands in a new recursion.

On the other hand, translation doesn't normally allow someone to erase a serious disease, eradicate the effects of extreme age, or cure other fundamental illness upon appearing in a new recursion. Likewise, translation doesn't provide healing; it doesn't change stats (unless a focus specifies a change), elevate a PC on the damage track, and so on. If a PC is mind controlled, cursed, or under the effects of some other weird effect, he remains so after translation. (That is, unless the PC finds himself in a recursion that doesn't contain the law the effect requires to function. In that case, the effect fades after a minute. The effect returns if the PC travels to a recursion operating under the requisite law.)

into abeyance with the rest of her gear, she must hold it in her hand during translation. Otherwise, the key gets left behind. Left-behind keys (such as a painting on a wall or a sculpture) would allow anyone who knew about a recursion's existence (and knew how to use the key) to follow her to the exact site in the recursion.

Crafting, building, and repairing an item, page 119

Recursion Key Aspects: A recursion key can take many forms: an actual key, a playing card, a sculpture, a painting, and so on. When a quickened character studies or handles a recursion key, she can attempt an Intellect-based roll (the difficulty of which is usually equal to the level of the key's related recursion).

On a success, the character recognizes the key as something that allows her to translate to a specific location within a recursion. However, without actually using the key, the character usually can't tell which recursion the key is for or where in the recursion the key might take her.

Crafting a Recursion Key: Crafting a recursion key uses the rules for crafting, building, and repairing an item, except as follows:

A quickened character who has visited and studied a particular location for at least one day can attempt to create a recursion key for it. To craft the key after the day of study, the character must spend at least one week crafting the key in the form she desires using materials appropriate to the key's form (paint and canvass for a painting, metal shaping/cutting tools for an actual key, and so on).

At the end of the specified time, a PC attempting the process must spend 1 XP and attempt an Intellect-based roll whose difficulty is equal to the level of the recursion (or area of the recursion the key opens) + 2. On a successful roll, the recursion key is created. On a failed roll, she can retry. If she does, normal rules for retrying apply: the PC can retry, but she must use Effort.

TRANSLATING TOO OFTEN

Translation puts a certain amount of strain on a creature. Thus, any character attempting to translate more than once within a single day finds that the process grows more difficult each time. The second time someone attempts to initiate, ease, hasten, or help with a translation in a given day, the difficulty of the task increases by one step.

This is true for the whole group, even if only one of the characters participated in a translation earlier that day. For example, a paradox who was participating in her first translation of the day would still find the difficulty of the translation roll increased by one step if any other participant has initiated, eased, hastened, or helped another translation within the previous 24 hours.

All penalties are cumulative, which means that if two characters had participated in one translation in the last 24 hours, the difficulty for the paradox would increase by two steps. If two characters had participated in two translations each during the last 24 hours, the difficulty of the paradox's translation roll would increase by four steps.

TRANSLATION SPECIAL EFFECTS

Rolling very well (19 or 20) during translation results in potentially great benefits to the translating characters.

Minor Effect (19): Acclimation time is zero. The difficulty of all tasks relating to the translating characters' new foci is decreased by one step for one hour.

Major Effect (20): Acclimation time is zero. The difficulty of all tasks relating to translating characters' new foci is decreased by one step for one day.

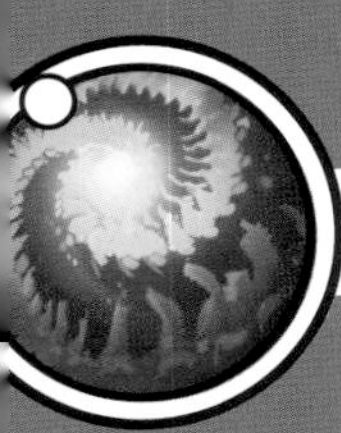

Part 4:
The Setting

CHAPTER 10

RECURSIONS

Recursions are unique but limited worlds hosted in the dark energy network of the Strange. Each recursion has its own laws of science, super-science, or even magic, which means that amazing things can occur within a recursion that could never happen on Earth.

Many recursions were seeded into the network by the creative resonance of pure imagination (so-called "fictional leakage"), and over time these recursions have matured into places that are quite real. In some recursions, fairy creatures hang the stars at night, in others monstrous evil sleeps beneath the waves, and in a handful of recursions, Native American gods still wander.

Other prime worlds in the universe also seed recursions by fictional leakage, but not to the degree seen on Earth. Most recursions created by fictional leakage aren't accessible for normal people except through gates.

Among the many recursions created by fictional leakage there are a few created by conscious design, including the sorcerous land of Ardeyn and the shipwrecked recursion of Ruk.

Ardeyn, page 160
Ruk, page 190

All told, hundreds of recursions speckle the dark energy web around Earth. Each recursion is a place of wonder, adventure, danger, and opportunity for those who can travel to them, explore them, or even create them.

One way to create a translation gate is with the fourth-tier paradox ability called Gate Exit.

Gate Exit, page 35

RECURSION GATES

Any permanent (or transitory) connection between two recursions, Earth and a recursion, or even between Earth and the Strange, is generally referred to as a recursion gate, or simply as a gate. The most common kinds of recursion gates include translation gates, inapposite gates, portal spheres, and fractal vortexes.

TRANSLATION GATE

Translation gates are rare, permanent connections between two different recursions, or between Earth and a recursion. Creatures that pass through a gate appear in the connected recursion and are translated to "fit in" to its context according to the general rules for translation, with a few caveats.

Objects: Most unaccompanied objects thrown through a translation gate simply fail to appear on the other side or, more often, don't go through the gate at all. Unless an object is a cypher or a similar item with a direct connection to the Strange, it simply falls to the ground or, if it goes through, ceases to exist. (If an excessive amount of nontranslating material is forced through a translation gate, the gate ceases to function, sometimes by exploding and doing 10 points of damage to anyone in range.)

Creatures and PCs: In addition to quickened creatures, conscious creatures who have the spark but who are not quickened can pass through a translation gate. Conscious creatures without the spark (commonly called shadows) can't pass through a translation gate. To such shadows, the gate seems solid and impassible.

Time: Translation through most translation gates is instantaneous, requiring only the action of the traveler to move through the gate.

Acclimation: One major advantage of translation gates over normal translation is fast acclimation time. For most gates, a quickened creature passing through it instantly adopts the visual context of the new recursion, and suffers only one round of translation acclimation time before she can access new focus abilities.

Translation Gate Creation: Several different avenues allow for the creation of a translation gate, but certain revisions available to paradoxes are probably the most straightforward for PCs.

INAPPOSITE GATE

Inapposite gates (also called matter gates) are even more rare than translation gates, mainly because most inapposite gates don't last for long. Unlike translation gates, things that pass through inapposite gates are not translated at all. Because different recursions have different rules (even those that seem very similar), things that pass through inapposite gates into a new recursion without translation sometimes begin to break down.

Objects: Matter of any sort passes through an inapposite gate and appears in the new recursion or on Earth as it did in the previous recursion. Simple objects made of only a few elements, like rocks, crystal, glass, low-alloy metals, water, and so on, may persist indefinitely in the new recursion or on Earth without deteriorating. Objects with special qualities that rely on particular laws to exist or function (like Magic or Mad Science, for example) begin to deteriorate and eventually either lose their special function or completely disintegrate into dust if the new recursion doesn't have the same law. The process of deterioration usually progresses over the course of a number of days equal to 1d6 × the object's level.

Creatures and PCs: Just like objects, creatures can pass through an inapposite gate (whether conscious or not) without being translated to suit the target recursion. Like complex objects of any sort, creatures that operate under a different law who pass through an inapposite gate begin to lose their special abilities over a number of days equal to 1d6 × the creature's level (or tier, if they're PCs). If a creature's life force is particularly tied to an unsupported law, it dies at the end of that time (but most creatures survive, despite being debilitated and in pain; treat them as if one step down on the damage track). Before a creature loses its unsupported special abilities completely, all uses of that ability are modified by one step to its detriment until the creature finally loses the ability or dies, or until it returns to its native recursion (at which point it begins to recover).

For instance, if a level 3 skeleton of Ardeyn appears on Earth through an inapposite gate, it "survives" on Earth for 1d6 × 3 days (because its special ability is its animation). Given that any physical action a skeleton takes relies on its magical animation, a skeleton's attacks are hindered by Earth's law of Standard Physics while it persists.

Time: Movement through most inapposite gates is instantaneous, requiring only the action of the traveler to move through the gate.

Acclimation: Moving through an inapposite gate doesn't inflict translation fugue on a living creature; it affects a creature as described above under Creatures and PCs. That said, during the first minute after arrival, the creature retains full, unpenalized use of all its abilities. After that minute expires, any abilities that logically require a different law to function are modified by one step to the creature's detriment.

Inapposite Gate Creation: Inapposite gates are usually the work of especially powerful NPCs or organizations. Sometimes cyphers or similar objects can create temporary inapposite gates.

PORTAL SPHERE

A portal sphere is an object able to create a temporary translation or inapposite gate that is linked to a pre-keyed destination. They usually appear as a crystal globe or nodule in most recursions, with the interior of the sphere revealing a view of the target recursion. The sphere is used by dashing it on a level surface within immediate range. A shimmering translation gate pops into being, large enough for two people to pass through abreast. The sphere lasts for one minute or until it is used from the triggering side (getting more than two people through the temporary gate is difficult, because it closes immediately). From the destination side, the temporary gate created by a portal sphere isn't detectable and normally can't be used.

If a translation portal sphere is used, a temporary translation gate is created. If an inapposite portal sphere is used, a temporary inapposite gate is created. In both cases, the rules for the gate created are modified as described in the preceding paragraph, but otherwise function as described for a given style of gate.

Portal Sphere Creation: Though portal spheres are cyphers, sometimes they can be created by powerful creatures or even PCs with the right foci (such as characters with the Conducts Weird Science focus).

Creatures and items that pass through an inapposite gate are not translated, so characters don't take on the context of the new recursion, and they keep all of their equipment, as well as their focus.

"The future was always dangerous. Now that the Strange has impinged upon Earth, I give mankind another twenty years, tops, before something cataclysmic happens." ~Colonel Angela Whitesides, Office of Strategic Recursion

Most gates have entrances and exits, which means that translation rules for where PCs appear in a destination recursion normally don't apply when a gate is used, unless a gate has no specified exit.

Conducts Weird Science, page 57

FRACTAL VORTEX

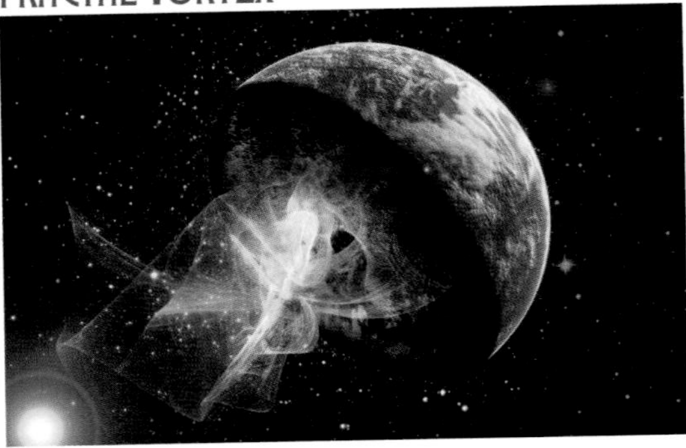

A fractal vortex is a natural phenomenon that can connect recursions to each other, to Earth, and even to the Strange. Sometimes a fractal vortex will connect one part of the Strange to a far more distant part of the dark energy network.

Fractal vortexes have many different guises, but all of them look violent and dangerous. Most commonly, a vortex floats free in the air or vacuum, haloed by lightning and other energy discharges. Approaching a fractal vortex can be even more dangerous than going through one. Unfortunately, most people don't have a choice about approaching a vortex—a vortex draws nearby things into it, sometimes with gravity, other times through air or water pressure, and sometimes via jagged streams of tethering force. From the destination side, the connection created by a fractal vortex can't be used, but it is visible as something that periodically spits out whatever was drawn through it.

Valuable Resources, Powerful NPCs, page 144

Sometimes fractal vortexes operate as translation gates, other times as inapposite gates. It's hard to know precisely how it will affect a traveler until one has passed through.

Fractal Vortex Creation and Duration: The discharge of large amounts of energy tuned to the Strange in a limited space has a good chance of ripping through the fabric of reality and forming a fractal vortex.

The larger the fractal vortex, the longer it lasts. For instance, one the size of an office room might last only a few days, while one the size of a solar system could last for centuries or longer.

CONTEXT

"Context" is a word that quickened characters and other people familiar with travel between recursions could end up using quite a bit. That's because travelers and the items they use to accomplish their goals are always affected by whether something is in context or out of context:

- A translated PC takes on the context of the recursion (or prime world) she enters.
- A cypher takes on the context of the recursion (or prime world) where it exists.
- Passing through an inapposite gate puts anything that passes through out of context.

RECURSION ATTRIBUTES

Each time the player characters translate to a new recursion, the game master should know a basic summary of the conditions that hold sway within the recursion. These high-level truths are called *attributes.*

The attributes of a recursion include the recursion's level, the laws that operate within it, the foci available for first-time player characters to choose from, and so on. The most common attributes and their relevance are described in this section.

LEVEL

A recursion's level determines how difficult it is to translate into the recursion. Certain locations within a recursion might be more difficult (or less difficult) to translate into, depending on their location.

Unless specified otherwise, a recursion's level is also associated with materials, inhabitants, and other attributes of the recursion. For a bit more treatment on that topic, see Valuable Resources, Powerful NPCs.

LAWS

A recursion's laws broadly determine the kinds of rules that exist there. Without certain laws to support them, a given recursion can't host related kinds of foci, effects, and inhabitants. For example, without the Mad Science law, a recursion probably can't support superhero-style foci. Most recursions have just one law (because the more extreme laws assume an underlying baseline Standard Physics law), but a recursion could have more than one.
The most commonly encountered laws and what they mean are described below.

Standard Physics: This law is the basic law that most recursions possess (and is the law that Earth operates under, which means it includes everything people have discovered with the scientific method about reality in the real universe). Standard Physics is actually a more complete and robust set of laws than the more extreme laws, which is why it's more difficult to find "exploits" in Standard Physics that allow for amazing effects.

Magic: A recursion that supports the law of Magic assumes a baseline Standard Physics law, but Magic picks up where the latter leaves off, and it allows adepts to create a wide variety of sorcerous effects through spellcasting, sympathetic magic, voodoo, witchcraft, homoeopathy, fae enchantments, and so on. Different recursions might support different styles, traditions, and "rules" of magic, but the underlying Magic law is what makes those traditions possible. Ardeyn is one recursion that operates under the law of Magic.

Mad Science: A recursion supporting Mad Science assumes the baseline Standard Physics law, but turns it up a notch. Whereas it's devilishly difficult to create temporal loops, perfect clones, gravitons, perpetual motion machines, cold fusion devices on the desktop, personal force field projectors, flying armor suits, ray guns, and photonic lances on Earth, in a recursion that supports Mad Science, it's not only possible but quite likely. As with Magic, a Mad Science recursion probably supports only a few particular threads or research directions of super science, not every possible permutation. Ruk is one recursion that operates under the law of Mad Science.

Psionics: A recursion supporting Psionics assumes the baseline Standard Physics law, but provides a mental plane or similar mindspace framework that can support a raft of mental effects. A recursion with Psionics as a law might feature astral projection, psychometry, pyrokinesis, telepathy, hive minds, telekinesis, psychic surgery, aura reading, bilocation, and similar effects. As with Magic, a Psionics recursion usually supports only a few particular threads of psychic development according to a specified tradition of accessing mental powers, not every possible permutation. Atom Nocturne is a recursion that operates under the law of Psionics.

Substandard Physics: In a recursion where Substandard Physics is law, many of the "miracles" of modern science fail to function, including gunpowder, artificial electricity, artificial radio, and so on. Generally speaking, a world of Substandard Physics can support technology and effects on the level of Earth's early Iron Age.

Exotic: The Exotic law is the catch-all law that particularly odd recursions might fall into. Usually, an Exotic recursion is one where the substance of the recursion itself is unusual, such as being composed of living flesh, fire, dream, acidic slime, solid starlight, writhing worms, fairy wings, or another unexpected form. Generally speaking, a recursion lower than level 4 can't support Exotic elements.

PLAYABLE RACES

A recursion that is mature enough could support playable races that are not present on the linked prime world. When a PC translates into such a recursion for the first time, she might choose to be embodied in one of those races instead of her own. The races have the potential to be more outré the more the laws of a given recursion stray from Standard Physics. For example, in Ardeyn (which supports Magic), the qephilim race is playable by PCs, despite the fact that they are descended from angelic immortals and still glow with racial mythlight as a result.

Qephilim, page 163

FOCI

A recursion that is mature enough can support one or more foci. When a PC translates into such a recursion for the first time, she might choose one of those foci instead of dragging her previous focus (if it is draggable). Available foci are determined by the law in a given recursion and by the particular way that law has developed. For example, Mad Science is the law in the recursion of Ruk, but the variety of Mad Science foci present generally follow the theme of biomodification.

SKILLS

Mature recursions may host a society of inhabitants, some percentage of which possesses the spark. Recursion natives without the spark probably still have some kind of culture, which means they also know one or more skills unique to the recursion. A PC who translates to the recursion usually can't pick up that skill as part of the translation (unless a chosen focus grants a unique skill), but any PC could choose to learn such a skill as part of normal tier advancement, if desired. Other skills are also available in such a recursion as is appropriate to the recursion's context. For instance, a Mad Science recursion might have skills related to quantum engineering, neural engineering, or warp drive repair.

Atom Nocturne, page 234

CONNECTION TO THE STRANGE

The dark energy network hosts every recursion, which means that most recursions, if mature enough, can serve as gateways into the Strange. If so, the nature of that connection is described under this attribute.

These rules for creating recursions and the material presented in Recursion Design Elements (page 144) can also serve as inspiration for the GM when creating recursions for her own campaign.

CONNECTION TO EARTH

Even though every recursion is hosted by the Strange, it must also be connected to a prime world somehow. The nature of that connection to the local prime world (that is, Earth) is described under this attribute.

SIZE

The more mature a recursion, the larger its maximum size. This tag gives a basic description of the recursion's size, though additional explanation regarding the nature of a recursion can usually be found in the main entry for a given world.

THE SPARK

As with so many other attributes, older recursions allow for the possibility of a percentage of any inhabitants to possess actual consciousness. The percentage indicated after this tag indicates the ratio of inhabitants who have the spark compared to those within the recursion who do not.

TRAITS

Each recursion has one or more traits that could affect the PCs while they are in that recursion. For a complete list of recursion traits, see page 141.

RULES FOR CREATING RECURSIONS

As the GM, you're the supreme being of the Strange, and you can create or destroy recursions as desired. Player characters are restricted to a more systematized route. This section provides that structure and guidance. That said, consider these rules as guidelines for the PCs, not hard and fast restrictions; creating a recursion is more art than science.

If they want to and if they work hard and long enough at it, PCs could become the masters of their own realities (albeit, small realities to begin with).

Quickened characters have the ability to make their own recursions. When characters decide to create a recursion, the procedure is sometimes called a *genesis quest*. The process of creating a recursion is just what it sounds like: the characters create a custom-designed recursion of their own, which includes a whole raft of components, including the name, shape, flora and fauna, and possibly even nature of the foci that exist (or have the potential to exist) within the newly forming recursion.

Recursion Genesis Quest at a Glance

1. Find reality seed
2. Locate a nexus
3. Invest reality seed in a nexus
   a. Choose PC contributors
   b. Determine desired attributes
   c. Spend XP
   d. Make seed investiture roll
   e. If investiture roll is successful enough, determine traits based on PC descriptors
4. Plant invested reality seed

ACQUIRING A REALITY SEED

Recursion creation is sometimes called a genesis quest due to the importance of this first step. A reality seed is an extremely rare bit of "matter" from the dark energy network. No two reality seeds look alike, but finding one out in the Strange itself can be difficult, because recognizing one iterating spiral of semisolid material from a near-infinite sea of similar structures requires patience or, more often, luck. Usually, reality seeds are found after they "condense on the shores" of an already existing recursion. When a reality seed condenses, it translates almost like a cypher to become an item that fits into the recursion's context. Those sensitive to cyphers and other elements of the Strange can sense a reality seed whether it looks like a gem, a sword, a chest, a data drive, a holographic fob, a small furry animal with big eyes, or a fist-sized egg, warm to the touch. In fact, a reality seed is a complex packet of data that contains the parameters and underlying instructions necessary to grow a recursion from scratch in the absence of any other frame of context.

Because reality seeds are far more rare and potent than cyphers, even creatures native to a recursion that are not quickened and don't have the spark can sense that there's something special about such items. As a result, reality seeds are usually kept in religious shrines or bank vaults, stored in time capsules, labeled as

trophies of esteem, or otherwise hidden away from easy access to PCs who'd like to get their hands on one. Tracking down a reality seed, gaining one as a reward for accomplishing a task for a powerful entity from a recursion, or taking one from the treasury of a defeated foe are all potential ways to gain a seed.

LOCATING A NEXUS

Once characters acquire a reality seed, they must invest the seed with the desired design potential, which generally can be done only in certain places called nexuses. Finding a suitable nexus is the next part of the genesis quest. For those unfamiliar with the concept and location of nexuses, this process can take just as long as finding a reality seed.

A nexus is any place out in the dark energy network hosting a natural confluence of chaotic energy, a portion of which is channeled during seed investiture. Three nexus positions in the Strange are known near Earth, but the farther out into the network one goes, the more nexuses an explorer might find.

The three nexuses near Earth are called N1, N2, and N3, according to one Ruk classification scheme. But these locations are also more colorfully known as the Orb of Worlds, Baldran's Maw, and the Kray Nebula.

At least one nexus contains an artificial structure built to facilitate seed investiture (the Orb of Worlds, created by natives of Ruk), some are empty, and many are infested with denizens of the Strange (such as the Kray Nebula).

Attempts to invest a seed someplace other than a nexus usually fail, which means that the real estate of any given nexus is valuable. At the nexus called the Orb of Worlds, guardians try to see to it that no one entity or group monopolizes the site, but there's no privacy to be had, either. Wilder nexuses offer privacy, but they could be dangerous places to visit. For example, any creature that attempts to use the Kray Nebula is almost asking for a meeting with kray and their broodmother.

INVESTING A REALITY SEED

Once the characters find a nexus, they can attempt to invest a reality seed there. Investiture is a "formatting" process that imprints the seed with selected parameters of the soon-to-be-planted recursion. Characters must design the attributes they want their recursion to eventually possess. Newly created recursions (called pocket dimensions) don't start out with all the features their creators designed for them; recursions

Kray broodmother, page 222

Orb of Worlds, page 221
Baldran's Maw, page 222
Kray Nebula, page 222

Investiture Results

It's not necessary to roll on either the Investiture Setback or Investiture Success table until the invested reality seed is planted and the resultant recursion begins to grow.

Investiture Setback

d6	Effect
1	The recursion never matures (and can't be improved) past pocket dimension status. Every day that an object or creature spends in the recursion risks a 20% chance of it being ejected into the Strange.
2	The recursion never matures (and can't be improved) past pocket dimension status. Every day that an object or creature spends in the recursion risks a 5% chance of it being ejected into the Strange.
3	The recursion never matures (and can't be improved) past pocket dimension status. Every day that an object or creature spends in the recursion risks a 1% chance of it being ejected into the Strange.
4	The recursion never matures (and can't be improved) past pocket dimension size. Any time a creature or object enters the recursion, a random level 5 or lower creature from the Strange is also found within the recursion.
5	The recursion matures (and can be improved) normally. However, unplanned intelligent entities begin to colonize the recursion as it matures past pocket dimension size. The entities are belligerent and xenophobic, even to the recursion creators.
6	The recursion matures (and can be improved) normally. However, unplanned foci (not determined by the PCs) become available as the recursion matures (or is improved) past pocket dimension size. The foci may seem somewhat bizarre and possibly even ridiculous, but shouldn't be worthless.

Investiture Success

d20	Effect
1–10	The recursion matures (and can be improved) normally and is embedded with up to one trait imbued by a PC creator.
11–14	The recursion matures (and can be improved) normally and is embedded with up to two traits imbued by PC creators.
15–16	The recursion matures (and can be improved) normally and is embedded with up to three traits imbued by PC creators.
17	The recursion matures (and can be improved) normally and is embedded with up to three traits imbued by PC creators. In addition, it begins up to twice as large as a pocket dimension with up to three discrete spaces separated by terrain or architecture.
18	The recursion matures (and can be improved) normally and is embedded with up to three traits of the PC creators. In addition, it begins up to five times as large as a pocket dimension with up to five discrete spaces separated by terrain or architecture.
19	The recursion begins one step more advanced than normal; instead of being a pocket dimension, it is a young recursion. Otherwise it matures (and can be improved) normally. Finally, it is also embedded with up to three traits imbued by PC creators.
20+	The recursion begins two steps more advanced than normal; instead of being a pocket dimension, it is a juvenile recursion. Otherwise it matures (and can be improved) normally. Finally, it is also embedded with up to three traits imbued by PC creators.

generally mature into those features, either through a straightforward process of aging (the older the recursion, the more its potential is realized) or thanks to active upkeep and improvement by the creators.

INVESTITURE

Once all the ingredients are assembled, would-be recursion creators can begin the process of investiture. The process of investiture works best with three to five participants.

Duration: 1d6 hours

Participants: 3–5

Components: 1 reality seed

Location: A nexus of the Strange

XP: 2 XP from each participant (minimum 6 XP)

Process: Prior to the investiture, the participants must decide on what kind of recursion they want to create, using the various elements of this section and the Recursion Design Elements on page 144. If a participant changes his mind during the investiture process, the process fails and the reality seed is ruined. Otherwise, one participant makes an investiture roll to determine how much success the investiture had.

Investiture Roll: Investing a recursion is an Intellect-based task with a difficulty of 5. On a natural roll of 17, 18, 19, or 20 on this roll, PCs not only succeed, they succeed so well that they add 1, 2, 3, or 4 points (respectively) to a subsequent result roll on the Investiture Success Table.

Even on a failed roll, the seed is still invested, though it's a setback, and PCs roll on the Investiture Setback Table.

Other characters who are part of the investiture process can help with the initial investiture roll, according to the rules for helping (which means that characters could choose to become trained or even specialized in creating recursions).

Planting the Seed

Characters can plant an invested reality seed so that it will take root and grow into a recursion. This seed can be planted only on a prime world (such as Earth) or in a recursion connected to a prime world. Planting an invested reality seed out in the Strange without any kind of connection to a prime world or similar anchor point is possible, but doing so doubles all age requirements for maturing the untethered recursion.

Planting a seed requires an action, but a character does not need to make a roll at this time; the characters determined the potential of the recursion during the investiture roll.

When characters plant a reality seed inside another recursion or on Earth, a level 1 recursion is created (a pocket dimension). Newly formed recursions usually possess an inapposite or translation gate that forms at the point where the seed was planted, directly connecting the new recursion with Earth or a host recursion. Characters must bind the pocket dimension upon or within another containing object, such as inside a large sack, the back of a coat closet, down the cellar stairs, under a bed, inside a phone booth, on the face of a large poster, within a cave mouth, down a well, or something similar. The gate that serves as the connection is as mobile (or immobile) as the object the pocket dimension is bound within.

The object that the new recursion is bound within is required only for planting. After the characters establish the recursion, the object (and associated gate, if any) can be destroyed without harming the underlying recursion, though doing so would destroy the gate—travel to the recursion would be restricted to free translation.

As time passes, a pocket dimension may grow into the recursion specified by the investiture design, assuming no mishaps occurred when the characters invested the reality seed that bore the new recursion.

RECURSION TRAITS

On an investiture roll of 5 or higher, the PCs have the opportunity to put their personal stamp on the recursion. Such a trait is determined by one or more of the PCs' descriptors. For example, a PC with the Lucky descriptor could imbue a created recursion with the Lucky trait.

Usually, a recursion can be imbued only with a limited number of traits (based on the investiture roll), which is often less than the number of PC creators. This means the PCs either have to decide among themselves what trait(s) to imbue the new recursion with, or design a rotating system where all the PC-imbued traits are active, but only one at any given time. (The PCs could time these active traits by tying them to elements within the new recursion, such as the tolling of a particular bell, the appearance of a certain "moon" in the sky, and so on.)

The following traits are suggested effects based on the list of PC descriptors available in this corebook. Other traits and trait effects are possible if a PC has a different descriptor than those listed here.

Appealing: For any creature with the spark attempting to persuade a creature without the spark, the difficulty is modified by one step to its benefit.

Brash: For any creature with the spark attempting to overcome or ignore the effects of fear or intimidation, the difficulty is modified by one step to its benefit.

Clever: For any creature with the spark attempting to identify or assess danger, lies, quality, importance, function, or power, the difficulty is modified by one step to its benefit.

Fast: Any creature with the spark adds 1 to its Speed Pool maximum while present in the recursion. The point is lost upon leaving the recursion.

Graceful: Any creature with the spark adds 1 to its Speed Pool maximum while present in the recursion. The point is lost upon leaving the recursion.

Intelligent: Any creature with the spark adds 1 to its Intellect Pool maximum while present in the recursion. The point is lost upon leaving the recursion.

Lucky: Any creature with the spark can reroll one d20 roll per day.

Sharp-Eyed: For any creature with the spark attempting to search for or find anything, the difficulty is modified by one step to its benefit.

Skeptical: Any creature with the spark attempting to see through a trick, illusion, rhetorical ruse designed to evade the issue, or lie modifies the difficulty to do so by one step to its benefit.

Stealthy: For any creature with the spark attempting to be stealthy, the difficulty is modified by one step to its benefit.

Strange: For any creature with the spark attempting to recognize and understand the Strange and its denizens, including identifying translated visitors from alternate recursions, as well as identifying and understanding cyphers, the difficulty is modified by one step to its benefit.

Many new recursions have "built-in" histories, so while a particular recursion might only be a few months old, it could feature a location that is hundreds, thousands, or even billions of years old within the context of that recursion. To anyone inside the recursion, the history is as real as actual history on Earth.

Strong: Any creature with the spark adds 1 to its Might Pool maximum while present in the recursion. The point is lost upon leaving the recursion.

Tough: A creature making a recovery roll adds 1 to the roll.

A GROWING RECURSION

Once planted, most recursions mature over time and can also be improved by creator maintenance so that they mature more quickly. Growth is important because the more mature a recursion becomes, the more clearly it realizes the potential invested in it (assuming the creators chose to create something more complex than a small pocket dimension).

The age categories of a recursion from youngest to most mature are *pocket dimension, young, juvenile, developed, old,* and *ascendant*.

Most recursions grow at a rate of a few feet or meters per year, unless designed not to. As recursions close in on the next age category, their growth either speeds up or slows down so that they generally match the indicated starting size for recursions of the category.

The following describes the general features available to a created recursion of a given age. Far more richness and diversity are possible if desired; see Recursion Design Elements on page 144.

POCKET DIMENSION (0 TO 6 MONTHS)

A pocket dimension is essentially a single open space with only hints of potential terrain, architecture, flora and fauna, and inhabitants planned for it—it's about as big as a large office or tiny forest clearing. Such hints might be in the form of shadows, drawings or engravings on the walls, flashes at the periphery of vision, and so on. A pocket dimension is a good place to hide in or store things, but otherwise is mere potential.

Level Maximum: 1
Laws: Standard Physics only
Playable Races: As connected prime world or recursion
Foci: Draggable only
Skills: None
Connection to Strange: As designed
Connection to Earth or Recursion: one gate only
Size: Up to 225 square feet (21 square meters)
Spark: 0%
Traits: As determined by investiture

YOUNG RECURSION (6 MONTHS TO 4 YEARS)

A young recursion expands to the size of a small mansion or a miniature park, with up to fifteen discrete spaces separated by architectural details, terrain, flora, or similar simple details, according to the design or fictional leakage that seeded it. A young recursion begins to take on a semblance of greater potential. Simple flora and fauna are present, if desired, but complex and sentient inhabitants (if any were designed) have not yet risen.

Level Maximum: 2
Laws: Standard Physics only
Playable Races: As connected prime world or recursion
Foci: Draggable plus one new focus
Skills: None
Connection to Strange: As designed
Connection to Earth or Recursion: Up to two gates
Size: Up to 5,000 square feet (465 square meters)
Spark: 0%
Traits: As determined by investiture

JUVENILE RECURSION (4 TO 10 YEARS)

A juvenile recursion expands to the size of a small city or glade, with as many discrete spaces, architectural details, terrain, flora, and so on as space allows, according to the design or fictional leakage that seeded it. A juvenile recursion has all the elements of an older recursion, possibly even including sentient native inhabitants with a chance for possessing the spark, just not the quantity or quality.

Level Maximum: 3
Laws: Standard Physics or one other
Playable Races: Up to one other
Foci: Draggable plus up to two new foci
Skills: Simple skill or skills possible
Connection to Strange: As designed
Connection to Earth or Recursion: Up to three gates
Size: Up to 2 miles (3 km) in diameter
Spark: 5%
Traits: As determined by investiture

DEVELOPED RECURSION (10 TO 500 YEARS)

A developed recursion expands to the size of a small state, with as many discrete spaces, architectural details, terrain, flora, and so on as space allows, according to the design or

fictional leakage that seeded it. Up to a quarter of the inhabitants, if any, might possess the spark, which means an emergent culture could exist, above and beyond what was initially seeded.
Level Maximum: 5
Laws: Standard Physics or up to two others
Playable Races: Up to two others
Foci: Draggable plus up to four new foci
Skills: Complex skill or skills possible
Connection to Strange: As designed
Connection to Earth or Recursion: Various gates
Size: Up to 100 miles (161 km) in diameter
Spark: Up to 25%
Traits: As determined by investiture

OLD RECURSION (500 TO 200,000 YEARS)

An old recursion expands to the size of a small continent, with as many discrete spaces, architectural details, terrain, flora, and so on as space allows, according to the design or fictional leakage that seeded it. A large majority of the inhabitants, if any, possess the spark, which guarantees an emergent culture thrives in the recursion, far above and beyond what was initially seeded.
Level Maximum: 9
Laws: Standard Physics or up to two others
Playable Races: Up to five others
Foci: Draggable plus up to fifteen new foci
Skills: Complex skill or skills probable
Connection to Strange: As designed
Connection to Earth or Recursion: Various gates
Size: Up to 1,000 miles (1,609 km) in diameter
Spark: Up to 80%
Traits: As determined by investiture

ASCENDANT RECURSION (200,000+ YEARS)

When a recursion becomes so old that it becomes ascendant, it has the potential to take on new qualities, evolve entirely new cultures and civilizations, and, generally speaking, move so far from the original recursion that it might bear almost no resemblance to what it once was. It's even possible that ascendant recursions could bridge the gap between the dark energy network and the real universe, and become prime worlds of their own, though that's up for debate.

TIME AND SPACE

While many variables of recursion creation are open to manipulation, time and space are not. A PC can't create a recursion that is infinitely large (or, in fact, larger than the guidelines suggest). Likewise, a PC can't create a recursion where time goes faster or slower than in other recursions, because time between Earth, the nearby dark energy network regions, and all linked recursions is synchronized.

RECURSION IMPROVEMENT

Allowing a created recursion to age naturally is one way to achieve the potential of a recursion's original design determined during the investiture. However, waiting months or years will stretch the patience of most PCs. Luckily, player characters can opt to manually mature a recursion they've created by spending additional experience points. In fact, PCs can spend XP in their recursion in a variety of ways to add additional special features not originally imagined.

No matter the effect desired, PCs spend this additional XP using a ritual or process of their own design. Regardless of the design, the ritual or process requires 1d6 hours to complete.

HASTEN MATURITY

For each 1 XP spent by the PCs, their recursion matures by one month, pushing it toward the next age category (and any additional benefits a higher age category offers). The more PCs who expend XP, the quicker the recursion matures.

SPECIAL TRANSLATION ZONES

When a recursion is normally created to produce a pocket dimension, the issue of special translation zones isn't an issue because there isn't enough space. But once a recursion becomes large enough to host multiple separate locations, the PCs could choose to create one or more special areas within the recursion that either restrict or channel free translation attempts into or out of the recursion.

To create a special zone within a recursion whose level is higher than the recursion average, PCs can spend 10 XP per level for the restricted area. The area so created is up to 100 feet (30 m) in diameter.

Ardeyn has the qualities of an old recursion due to its unusual creation. For additional information, see How Ardeyn Was Formed, page 160.

Ruk is assumed to be an ascendant recursion, given the length of time it has lingered in the Shoals of Earth. Of course, given Ruk's historical data degradation, it's difficult to be certain.

PC-DESIGNED FOCI

Mature recursions offer one or more foci to quickened visitors. When PCs create their own recursion, they have a chance to choose what those foci will eventually be.

The easiest way for PCs to create foci is to treat all the other foci presented in The Strange corebook as a menu of potential options for their own recursion.

The next step a PC might take is to "skin" an already-present focus to better suit a custom recursion. For instance, if the PC created a "lost world" recursion inhabited by dinosaurs, she might decide that the Slays Dragons focus is a good start, but that it would fit better if she filed off the serial numbers and instead called it Hunts Dinosaurs.

If that doesn't quite suit, PCs can assemble a new focus using the tier benefits of several existing foci, mixing the various tier benefits together in a new way with a new story to create a new focus with a very good chance of being balanced with the foci already present.

Finally, you can allow your players to create their own foci. If you do, you retain veto and editorial rights but consider this: What's the worst that could come from a focus that's a bit overpowered? When it comes right down to it, those foci will usually only remain active within the custom recursion, which means any overstep will be safely contained. And just maybe those foci will help the PCs truly feel that they *are* the masters of their own reality.

To create a special zone within a recursion that requires a special element to translate into (such as a pass phrase, a gate key, a badge, or other specified condition), PCs can spend 10 XP per level of the zone. The area so created is up to 100 feet (30 m) in diameter.

Other Unique Features: Generally speaking, PCs may create other immobile, one-off features not described here by spending 10 XP per level of the unique effect desired, unless the GM decides the effect is something that is available only in a more mature recursion.

RECURSION DESIGN ELEMENTS

When creating recursions, not even the sky is the limit; recursions can be anything you can dream up. To get you started, here are some design options and inspiration.

VALUABLE RESOURCES, POWERFUL NPCS

In addition to a recursion's level setting the difficulty for translating into that recursion, the level of a recursion at a given maturity category also suggests other things about the place. For instance, level might suggest the availability (or relative lack thereof) of valuable minerals, the relative number of powerful NPCs, and other components of the recursion. This becomes important if a PC hits upon the idea of creating a recursion specifically for the purpose of creating a kind of gold, diamond, rare-earth, or other valuable resource mine, or as a place to find cheap labor, and so on.

Resources: The hard and fast rule is that until a recursion hits level 5 overall, no particularly valuable resources exist in large enough quantities to be worth collecting at the location. However, if PCs improve a unique area within the recursion to increase its level to 5 or higher (as described under Recursion Improvement), they could create a small deposit of a particular mineral or oil that would be worth the investment to extract, though not enough to make anyone's fortune.

NPCs: Seeding a recursion with the specific idea of creating cannon fodder, servants, or religious zealots who serve only the recursion's creators is an option some might pursue, but until a recursion has reached the juvenile age category, no worthwhile natives can be found. Once a recursion does reach the juvenile age category, native inhabitants appear, though only a small population at first. These inhabitants may indeed be predisposed to act in a manner determined by the PC creators, but there's always a chance that a particular recursion native will develop the spark and decide that she would rather go her own way (or, if being treated fairly or in a reasonable situation within the recursion's context, become even more invested in a PC's purpose).

The maximum level for the bulk of a recursion's creatures and natives is equal to the recursion's level, though a handful of creatures and natives, relative to the overall population, may exceed that maximum. The same selection of natives and creatures is more likely to possess the spark as well.

CULTURE AND THEME

Overall laws such as Standard Physics or Magic say a lot about a recursion, but there's a lot of room for different themes and cultures to develop within each one. In recursions mature enough to host emergent cultures of their own, more than one culture and theme is likely to develop, but PCs and GMs could certainly impose particular elements of either right out of the gate during investiture. The ideas below are only a sampling of possible cultures and themes that might exist within any particular recursion. Your PCs are free to refer to them or ignore them.

In addition to the suggested cultures and themes described below, any book of history, fiction, science fiction, religion, fantasy, or other genre could serve as the basis for a recursion theme. Indeed, that's the definition of fictional leakage.

To get particularly strange themes, mix a few themes together. For example, a recursion that mixed Egyptian deities and Wuxia would be an interesting place to explore.

Culture or Theme (Any Law)

American '50s, '60s, '70s, and so on
Anarchy
Ancient America, Arabia, China, Egypt, Greece, and so on
Bombed-out cinder
Chinese "golden age"
Conspiracy
Corporatocracy
Dictatorship
Dying Earth
Emirate
Humor/Satire
Idiocracy
Imperial Britain
Japanese Genroku "golden era"
Lost World (i.e., dinosaurs)
Medieval Ages
Meritocracy
Modern theocracy
Native American
Nature preserve
Nazi triumph
Panopticon surveillance state
Parallel area, city, region, and so on
Post-apocalypse
Pre-apocalypse
Renaissance period
Technocracy
Viking culture
War state
Western
World War I, II, and so on
Wuxia

Culture or Theme (Weird Law)

Alien bodies
Alien invasion
Animal people
Chinese gods
Cyberpunk
Dolphin people
Egyptian gods
Fairy tale
Fantasy
Far future

"My plan? Find a recursion where diamonds litter the ground like sand on a beach, scoop 'em up, and make a killing back on Earth. I know, it seems unethical. But is it? Is it really?" ~Shannon Daley, recursor

Giant robots
Giant spacecraft/generation ship
Gothic horror
Greek gods
Lovecraftian horror
Insect people
Machine people
Mutants
Native American gods
Near future
Necropolis society
Norse gods
Paranormal/urban fantasy
Psionic society
Robot uprising
Steampunk
Supernatural modern
Supers
Zombie apocalypse

CHARACTERISTICS AND QUIRKS

The following tables represent only a miniscule sampling of possible characteristics and quirks a recursion might exhibit. To get particularly strange characteristics or quirks, mix two together. For example, consider a recursion composed of bone shaped like a giant Mobius strip, or an elemental plane of water inside a giant glass bottle.

A Recursion Made of...

Acid
Air
Bone
Ceramic
Coins
Colossal beast
Crystal
Dream
Electricity
Feathers
Fire
Flesh
Force
Glass
Hair
Insects
Iron
Light
Mist
Mud
Perceptronium
Shadow
Slime
Stone
Vegetation
Void
Water
Webs
Wings
Wood
Worms

A Recursion in the Shape of a...

Asteroid or comet
Clock face
Cube
Disc
Dust particle (microrecursion)
Flat plane
Giant boot
Giant bottle
Hollow sphere
Massive statue
Mobius strip
Orb
Plane
Planetary shard
Pyramid
Ring
Snowflake
Star
Tube
Two-dimensional (flatland)

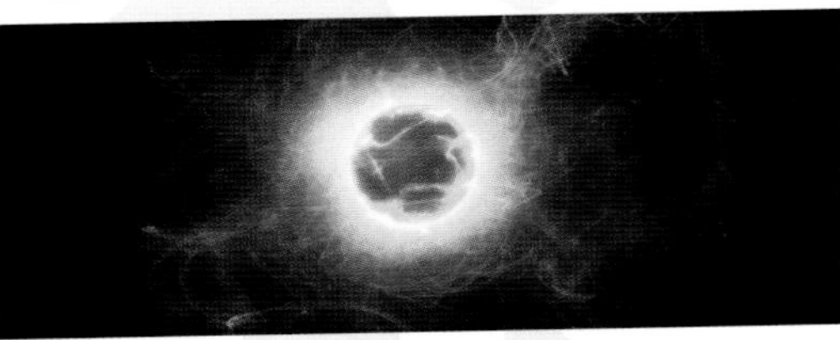

One Quirky Thing About My Recursion Is That...

The sun is absent/a cow/a cobra/a dragon/a giant eye
Stars are lamps/holes in the sky/living creatures
Instead of earthquakes, the recursion suffers laughing fits/hiccups
The atmosphere is poisonous/narcotic/a living mist creature
Some landscape elements move/dance/melt and reform
Trees appears as humanoid arms/giant mushrooms/egg sac pods
Gravity is absent/weak/double strength
Everything is the same color, even visitors: cobalt/lime/gold/purple
The entire place smells of cinnamon/bubble gum/licorice/men's cologne
Instead of lightning, arms stretch down to squish targets with giant fingertips

CHAPTER 11

EARTH

EARTH ATTRIBUTES

Level: 5
Laws: Standard Physics
Playable Races: Humans
Foci: Conducts Weird Science, Entertains, Is Licensed to Carry, Leads, Looks for Trouble, Operates Undercover, Solves Mysteries, Works the System
Skills: As listed on main skills list
Connection to Strange: No direct connection; trips to the Strange require a trip through a recursion that have a connection to the Strange
Connection to Recursions: Various gates
Size: 3,958 miles (6,370 km) average radius, plus surrounding universe
Spark: 100% (though many with the spark do not lead examined lives)
Traits: None

"Carl Sagan had a famous saying about Earth being a pale blue dot. He said Earth is the only world known to harbor life, and that there wasn't anywhere else people could migrate to if we ruined the planet. Well, I suppose that's true for a lot of people living here. But for some of us, Earth is just the doorway."

~Carter Strange

Earth is the third planet from the sun, and the humans on Earth are still emerging from a relatively recent evolutionary "Great Leap Forward" to become the intelligent masters of their world. Though many relics of their hominid past yet persist in their psyche, humans have made great strides culturally, and they might one day become a species capable of becoming interplanetary.

If not for the Strange.

Only a tiny percentage of Earth's population is quickened, and an even smaller number know about the Strange. The truth is dangerous and devastating, and so far at least, the organizations that monitor or exploit the dark energy network find it in their best interest to keep it a secret.

LIFE ON EARTH

Earth of The Strange is just like our real world Earth, except that it keeps amazing secrets. Though PCs may be exploring the crypts of soulshorn in Ardeyn or fighting spore worms in Ruk, on Earth most people go to work every day, pay their bills, watch TV, and probably absorb themselves in a hobby or two, such as sports, games, art, or as in your case, the occasional tabletop roleplaying game. So you already know about what it's like to live on Earth. You live it every day, and you know how the calendar works, some geography, some history, and so on. You might even be up on current events and follow a particular sports team or two. We don't judge.

So, in essence, this chapter is where you'll

Earth is not actually a recursion, although very often when referring to recursions collectively, Earth gets lumped in. Earth is technically a prime world, and it owes its existence to the laws of the physical universe, not to the laws of the Strange.

Soulshorn, page 291
Ardeyn, page 160
Spore worm, page 293
Ruk, page 190

Earth's Connection to the Strange

People on Earth, even those who are quickened, probably don't realize just how special Earth is. Thanks to an accident that occurred not long after Earth formed, our planet has a unique connection to the Strange.

That connection has to do with Earth's moon. The moon formed as a result of a massive impact. Scientists theorize that an object at least as large as Mars slammed into the proto-Earth, blasting a bolus of magma into space, where it eventually accreted to form the moon. As it happens, the theory is accurate. Sort of.

It's true that a Mars-sized object smashed into our fledgling planet, but it wasn't a sibling protoplanet, as planetary researchers assume. In fact, it was a small piece of a defunct alien intergalactic transport system. This device—let's call it Aleph—was larger than the solar system. When it malfunctioned millions of years after its fabrication (whether through sabotage or neglect is unclear), it shattered, and its components hurtled across millions of light years. One of those components found its way across space and smashed into a random protoplanet.

If no life had ever developed on that protoplanet, that likely would've been the end of it. But life did develop, because that protoplanet was Earth. The evolving sapient life on Earth triggered a residual function in the Aleph component. The component released a unique quantum field energy that had many repercussions, the main one being that the Earth became connected to the Strange in a way few, if any, other prime worlds ever were. Earth is a rare planet, in that it has generated hundreds of recursions through fictional leakage and hosts paradoxes, spinners, and vectors. The Aleph component is buried deep beneath the Earth's mantle—a secret that no one knows about, not even the ancient factions of Ruk. For now.

The Estate was founded in memory of Carter Strange. Known as Carter Morrison on Earth, he saved Earth and created Ardeyn. Exactly how Morrison saved the planet is one of the Estate's most closely guarded secrets. It's possible that most of the lead operatives or chief investigators don't even know the whole story.

If the PC begins the game as an in-the-know Estate operative, she has already undergone the recruitment process and this experience can be an important part of her backstory.

find out about the exceptions to what is commonly known and understood about Earth, how the Strange affects the planet, and the secrets that even knowledgeable quickened NPCs don't fully grasp.

Only a handful of organizations (and less cohesive groups) on Earth purposefully interact with the Strange. They may intentionally travel to recursions, monitor travelers from recursions, and attempt to limit or exploit those interactions, depending on the group. But most keep their particular knowledge of the Strange hidden from the public at large. The most cohesive and active group on Earth is the Estate.

The Estate

To the world at large, the Estate is a philanthropic institute interested in funding research in several scientific fields of inquiry. While that's partly true (the facade works because the Estate *does* award scientific grants to various deserving causes on a yearly basis), the Estate's actual goal is to protect the Earth—and all of its life forms—from all threats to its existence from the Strange. As one of only a handful of organizations cognizant of the dark energy network, the Estate is uniquely positioned to deal with the threats the Strange represents.

Morrison Fellowship Prizes

The Estate is careful to keep its actual motivations and activities a closely guarded secret. To the world at large, the Estate is best known for the yearly scientific awards they

If you know someone you'd like to nominate for a Morrison Fellowship Prize, or if you think your own work might qualify, visit TheEstateFoundation.org for more details. It is recommended that you use the incognito setting on your browser and take other security measures before visiting.

distribute (called Morrison Fellowship Prizes) to between thirty and fifty people, working in any field, who "demonstrate remarkable talent and the promise for continued creative work." The prize is $500,000, paid over seven years in biannual installments, and comes with no strings attached.

As wonderful as that might be for awardees, the prize gives cover to Estate field teams who show up to investigate strange events and accomplishments to see if they're actually Strange events and accomplishments. It's amazing what the lure of a cash prize will do to even the purest of motivations.

The funding required to pay out such large sums is charitably provided by various named and anonymous donors, most of whom believe they are supporting a philanthropic foundation. Of course, the Estate spends far more cash than just the yearly prizes. Additional funding is generated by operatives working inapposite gates to bring valuable material up from Ardeyn or Ruk, which is sold to various third-party companies who've discovered it's best not to ask where the odd coins, minerals, or gems come from if they wish to keep their contracts.

RECRUITMENT

The Estate wants associates and operatives that are skilled and can handle themselves in a variety of situations; they also have to be mentally stable enough to take knowledge of the Strange in stride. Someone who meets all these qualifications would be a fine asset to the Estate—possibly even suitable for working on a field team. However, the Estate values a potential recruit far more if she is quickened.

A quickened recruit can dispense with a lot of the red tape others have to deal with, including an extensive background check. A quickened PC with a questionable past is not an issue for the Estate (though individual Estate operatives may decide to keep a close eye on such a PC, especially if that "questionable" past puts the PC too far outside normal moral behavior).

After the Estate becomes aware of a potential recruit and determines suitability (possibly without the PC ever knowing about it), the organization approaches the character, probably under cover of determining whether the PC is a good candidate for a Morrison Fellowship Prize. At some point during that meeting, the PC is introduced to the Strange, and if he isn't already aware of them, to his own quickened abilities.

ESTATE ROSTER

A few select members of the Estate.

Katherine J Manners (level 6): Lead Operative, a founding member of the Estate, and one of the institution's most important field agents. She was an associate of Carter Strange back in the day.

Lawrence Keaton (level 6): Investigations Chief, tends to monopolize operatives. A functional alcoholic, balancing on the edge of being put on administrative leave for related lapses.

Edward Kincaid (level 6, level 7 for tasks related to stealth and disguise): Special Operative, a felon that the Estate freed to exploit his amazing skills of theft and infiltration. So far, Kincaid has been a strong asset, though some consider him a security risk and are waiting for the other shoe to drop.

Liza Banks (level 5, level 7 for all persuasion-related tasks): Chief of Public Relations, a reformed(?) con artist who's become a respected and important member of the Estate, despite occasional irregularities. Liza hands out Morrison Fellowship Prizes.

Hertzfeld (level 5, level 7 for tasks related to scientific research): Research Chief, a native to a recursion formed by fictional leakage from a random blend of science fiction novels and manga comics. He returns there yearly on a secret sabbatical where he tends what he calls the "Orchid."

The Fixer (level 7): No one officially knows who the Fixer really is; it's better that way. If operatives are in trouble with local authorities on Earth, a call to the Fixer smooths things over. The Fixer can take care of complications following a gunfight (including hiding bodies), get operatives out of custody, and even spring operatives from prison. But a word to the wise: those who overuse the Fixer's services risk that the Estate will ask the Fixer to "fix" them.

An Estate ID badge looks official, and flashing it with authority can get many operatives past checkpoints without too much trouble. The ID makes no illegal claims regarding the authority invested in the holder. Still, an average person who sees an Estate badge is likely to grant an operative a little more leeway, at least for a while.

Estate associates can expect a small monthly stipend of a few hundred dollars; operatives with a career outside the Estate get slightly more. A full-time operative receives a salary and benefits sufficient to pay for a comfortable middle-class lifestyle.

ONGOING MISSIONS

The Estate explores recursions and the Strange, defends the Earth, and creates conditions to keep civilization safe from related threats. The operatives are assigned to divisions, which have several goals, including locating the newly quickened, shutting down recursion miners, hobbling research into quantum computing, keeping an eye on their "sister" organization the Quiet Cabal, and investigating any events that could be related to the dark energy network. Perhaps most important, the Estate spends about a fifth of its resources working against the September Project, a pseudo-research organization with a much darker goal.

The Quiet Cabal, page 153

Recursion miners are individuals and groups who find and explore recursions—and who attempt to create new recursions.

Investigating the September Project: For years, the Estate has been able to keep tabs on the September Project thanks to having several spies in the organization. This allowed them to discredit many of the September Project's attempts to popularize quantum computers (and thus attract actual scientific talent able to develop the technology past its current state). Unfortunately for the Estate, those spies are now turning up dead, or never turning up at all. Something is happening at the research campus in Palo Alto where the September Project keeps the public face of its operations on Earth, and it could be critical.

Division Chief Keaton is looking to send a new group of operatives in. Perhaps the PCs are interested in being part of the infiltration team? Keaton suggests posing as a group of industry experts looking for new places to invest. If the PCs prefer a different mission, word has reached Keaton that a few cells of September Project activity have been detected in San Francisco and Austin. Someone needs to look into those, pronto.

Recursion Miners: The Estate keeps tabs on all the recursion miners it knows about that aren't affiliated with other groups. Sometimes freelance recursion miners spring up when a quickened individual, on his own initiative, discovers the ability to translate. Those who don't draw attention to themselves may never come to the Estate's notice.

Many end up calling attention to themselves, though, by activating an inapposite gate, by bringing cyphers up to Earth and offering them for sale, or by pinging the dark energy network itself in some fashion.

Lead Operative Katherine Manners is following the reports of "hauntings" that could well be related to an inapposite gate in the Seattle area, possibly the result of spirits of Ardeyn passing to Earth. She's putting together a team that she'll coordinate to canvass a few different neighborhoods and get to the bottom of the disturbance.

The Newly Quickened: When a high school kid shows break-out talent, whether in sports, academics, or a competition like a science fair or a robot challenge, it's usually just natural talent at work. Likewise, when someone quits her job at the pizzeria to become an overnight success inventing gadgets, investing, or making 3-D printers, it might just be the culmination of long-simmering desire. But sometimes these kind of successes are a few ticks beyond normal and could be the result of someone becoming quickened.

The Estate watches for these sorts of "feel-good" news stories and may send out a Morrison Fellowship Prize Evaluation Team. If someone really is quickened, the Estate's goal is to make contact with her before she is poached by the Quiet Cabal or the Office of Strategic Recursion (OSR), or worse yet, the September Project or Circle of Liberty.

PR Chief Liza Banks is putting together a Prize Evaluation Team to check out the exploits of a kid in Nebraska who has authored three best-selling novels under a pseudonym, written a popular indie computer game, and amassed a secret Bitcoin fortune. While there's a chance that the kid is just using his natural talents, it doesn't bode well that the first round of Estate agents who went to check him out have gone missing.

Quantum Initiative: Perhaps not surprisingly, the Estate's interest in quantum computers is closely tied to its very reason for existing. When an experimental quantum computer chip breached the Strange and nearly cost the Earth everything, it was Carter Morrison who stepped in and saved the planet.

Thus, one of the main uses of the Morrison Fellowship Prize is to "back" those working on quantum breakthrough technologies. In this case, the "no strings" promise is a ruse,

OSR, page 157
Circle of Liberty, page 154
Liza Banks, page 149

It's rumored among Estate operatives that Hertzfeld keeps an entropic seed in the Vault against a future need when all other options have failed.

Quickened, page 22

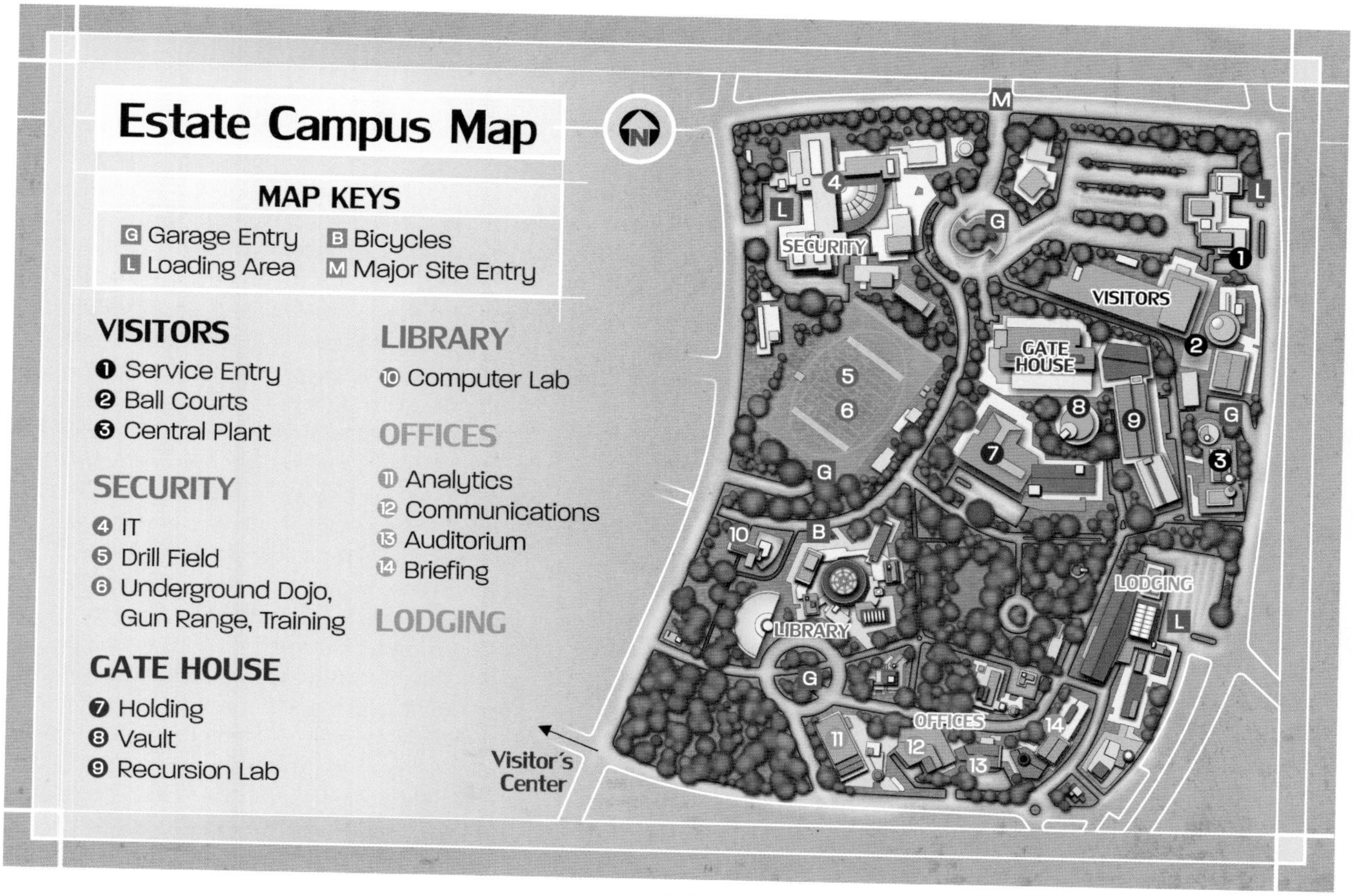

Estate Campus Map

MAP KEYS

G Garage Entry
B Bicycles
L Loading Area
M Major Site Entry

VISITORS
1 Service Entry
2 Ball Courts
3 Central Plant

SECURITY
4 IT
5 Drill Field
6 Underground Dojo, Gun Range, Training

GATE HOUSE
7 Holding
8 Vault
9 Recursion Lab

LIBRARY
10 Computer Lab

OFFICES
11 Analytics
12 Communications
13 Auditorium
14 Briefing

LODGING

Visitor's Center

for those who accept the generous stipend are subtly channeled toward less dangerous avenues of quantum research.

Research Chief Hertzfeld, page 149

Research Chief Hertzfeld is something of a loner (especially because no one really knows anything about the "Orchid" that he slips off to tend every year), but few people understand quantum theory better than he does, which is why he is not only tolerated but greatly respected by those in the Estate. While on a field mission to see what kind of progress a particular Morrison Fellowship Prize winner was making on functional quantum computer wristwatches, Hertzfeld disappeared. Quickened operatives are being gathered to track him down.

The Estate also keeps a few field offices in different locations, but none have the amenities and features approaching those of the main Estate headquarters.

THE ESTATE HEADQUARTERS

The Estate keeps its headquarters in the Seattle region, having purchased a local airline company's unused office parks for its own purposes. Several buildings make up the Estate, all behind a checkpoint through which visitors are allowed only if accompanied by an operative or associate, or by appointment. Here, staff issue visitor badges, and they take security very seriously.

Security systems, locks, materials, and resources in the Estate headquarters are all level 7 or higher. The Vault is level 8.

HQ houses offices for administration, offices for operatives, a cafeteria, a dojo for combat training, analytics, a communication center, a garage that holds a variety of vehicles, a computer lab, meeting rooms, an auditorium, security center, IT, and more, including the following:

Lodging. Full-time Estate members have the option of staying in functional dormitory-style rooms. They aren't extraordinary, but they're clean, warm, and safe. Operatives who choose to live off-site can still requisition an emergency dorm for special circumstances.

Visitor's Center. A visitor's center, devoted to telling the story of the Morrison Fellowship Prize, is a five-minute drive off-site. It's staffed entirely by employees who don't know anything about the Estate's real purposes, who do a great job in popularizing and advocating for the Prize.

Gate House. The Gate House (which is always under strict security) contains several permanent recursion gates (mostly translation gates, but a few inapposite gates) connected to various locations in Ardeyn, a few places in Ruk, and several lesser-known recursions. Most of these recursion gates require a key or password.

Recursion Lab: Research on the nature of gates, the interaction of laws, the nature of fundament, and the like is conducted in this stand-alone structure. One hot research topic is finding ways to seal recursion gates quickly and completely. Some researchers prefer a quick-sealing expanding foam, while others prefer a "negation charge" (which doesn't leave behind a gate that could be unsealed later).

Library: This structure houses an extensive archive and library of hard-to-find books and similar documents. A lot of material regarding recursions predates the Internet, and the Estate library gathers as much of it as it can.

Holding: Connected securely to the Gate House and Recursion Lab, Holding is a kind of detention center for keeping dangerous individuals, whether that means an OSR spy, an operative who temporarily lost her marbles by spending too long in the Strange, or a creature from another recursion bent on destruction. The facility contains a variety of cells, including a couple of experimental pocket dimension secure chambers where the law of Substandard Physics operates, which provide no foci and dampen the abilities of quickened individuals. Translating out of a cell in Holding requires a difficulty 9 translation roll.

The Vault: The Vault stores dangerous artifacts from other recursions brought to Earth through inapposite gates, as well as items that (like cyphers) translate to Earth but remain incredibly dangerous.

Armory: The Estate stores arms and ammunition in this bunkerlike structure. Here, weapons are also maintained and repaired, issued to authorized users, and tested. Combat training is also conducted on the extensive firing range beneath the armory. Most kinds of legal firearms are stored in the armory, as well as a few weapons normally available only to the military. The armory also contains several cypher weapons, carefully stored to avoid deletion chain-reaction. These cyphers may be issued to operatives for important missions.

Mission Briefing Rooms: When operatives are assigned to an official mission, they receive a mission briefing in a set of conference rooms designed to pass information quickly and efficiently. During such a briefing, the PCs receive any necessary handouts, photos, and information. They can also request a mission kit, which could include a cypher or two, some "spy" equipment, and a car from the garage. Operatives who return equipment after use are more likely to continue to enjoy the privilege of receiving mission kits.

OTHER GROUPS

The Estate is the organization on Earth that PCs are most likely to work directly with or on behalf of. But other organizations and less cohesive groups also interact with recursions and the Strange. One, the Quiet Cabal, is even more far-flung in its operations than the Estate, and its main headquarters are not kept on Earth. In addition to the Quiet Cabal, there exists the Circle of Liberty, the September Project, and the OSR, as well as recursion miners, spiralers, and butterfly objectors.

QUIET CABAL (ON EARTH)

The recursion of Ruk has nestled in the Shoals of Earth for millennia. Ruk natives made a connection with humanity once humanity evolved sufficiently, an evolution that was possibly helped along by one or more Ruk factions. Today, the faction most interested in Earth's welfare is the Quiet Cabal.

The Quiet Cabal's membership is mostly human, at least on Earth. Members in the highest echelon are aware of the Strange and the existence of recursions. The Cabal works to keep Earth and Ruk safe from dangers of the dark energy network and its recursions, dangers including nihilists from Ruk itself, creatures native to an exotic or toxic recursion who somehow find their way to Earth, and planetovores.

The Cabal keeps a few sanctums on Earth, which are akin to field offices. These sanctums are usually camouflaged to appear like bed and breakfasts or isolated farmsteads on the outskirts of a community. The owner of said B&B or farm might be an agent in full standing but is just as likely to be a contractor paid handsomely to keep a part of his establishment set aside for Cabal use, no questions asked. In this case, the proprietor of the establishment has been vetted to make sure that even if odd things are heard or seen, he will keep quiet and allow the agents to go about their business.

Some sanctums contain special, rare objects native to Ruk (brought through an inapposite gate) called recursion keys, which allow a quickened agent to translate to the specific location within Ruk where that object originally resided—usually, that location is the Quiet Cabal High Command. A few sanctums also possess translation gates.

PCs who are Quiet Cabal members that are native to Earth might live in a sanctum if they wish. Unlike the Estate operatives, Quiet Cabal agents on Earth operate without much oversight (or help) from the Quiet Cabal. As long as a PC agent makes regular reports, either personally or via courier drop, the cabal is mostly content to let her forge her own way.

Some Quiet Cabal agents are responsible for collecting message drops and transferring messages between agents and the Quiet Cabal High Command. PCs might take on such a mission for a time, which would involve a tour of various places in the U.S., a translation through various recursions, and a final destination in Ruk before returning to Earth.

Maureen Lincoln is an NPC Quiet Cabal courier known by many other Ruk agents, as well as by a few operatives of the Estate and OSR. Agent Lincoln routinely translates between Earth and Ruk on courier duty, but also to spy on various organizations who think they know all about her. When she goes undercover, she slips into disguise as a member of the Circle of Liberty or OSR, as a representative of Zal looking for prospects on Earth, or, most surprisingly of all, as a minor division chief at the Estate.

Maureen Lincoln: level 6

Zal, page 194

Recursion key, page 130

CIRCLE OF LIBERTY

The Circle of Liberty isn't cohesive; it's a collection of loosely affiliated groups that publicly advocate for decentralized government. Despite being mostly unknown to the public at large, the Circle of Liberty *is* organized and has a well-funded donor base that keeps it active. According to Estate investigations, the Circle of Liberty is funded to the tune of millions of dollars a year. All the money comes through hard-to-trace funding networks.

Jerry Toomey: level 4, level 7 in tasks related to persuasion

The Estate paid more attention to the Circle of Liberty when they thought the Betrayer out of Ardeyn was ultimately behind the group (and indeed, the Betrayer might well be one of the funding sources). But after investigating, the Estate learned that most of the donors can ultimately be traced back to the Karum, a group of Ruk nihilists. Though the Karum's aims are not dismissed by the Estate, the group is also seen as being in the "jurisdiction" of the Quiet Cabal.

Betrayer, page 178

The subgroups under which the Circle of Liberty operates include various "charities," think tanks, advocacy groups, and industry associations. Some of these are part of the funding scheme, and others attempt to manipulate public opinion as well as legislative policy. For instance, one policy that might be the result of Circle of Liberty manipulation is conservative opposition to climate policy of any kind, presumably in an effort to bring about long-term destabilization of Earth governments as they're forced to deal with ever-accelerating global disasters.

Dr. Gavin Bixby: level 4, level 6 for all tasks related to deception and particle physics

The Circle of Liberty's most famous advocate is disgraced senator Jerry Toomey. Toomey found a second career by becoming a radical voice on every possible media outlet. Toomey is famous for his intense orations that seem to sway almost any panel he appears on, if only while he's present. Cabal agents believe Toomey is quickened and can twist the perceptions of others. In truth, Toomey is a native of Ruk. Transplanted to Earth, he took on the persona (and skin) of the real Toomey, and in addition to becoming a talking head, he also created a private compound called Promised Land. Brochures paint Promised Land as a wonderful place for the wealthy to get away for a weekend of relaxation and fun, but it's actually a place where the wealthy and other opinion-makers get brainwashed by Toomey. Destroying the compound would be a nice feather in the cap of any group of Quiet Cabal agents who felt up to the challenge of dealing with the small private army Toomey has employed to guard the place.

Dr. Gavin Bixby, professor of nuclear research is another person of interest who receives money from the same funding network that finances the Circle. Bixby keeps busy consulting with various particle acceleration labs on best practices. Bixby's ultimate goal (as a secret Ruk native and agent of the Karum named Dadanum-tal) is to help Earth scientists develop a high-energy particle accelerator with enough energy to ping the Strange. Bixby must wait before providing all the information required to achieve the goal, because the Karum aren't quite ready to cast Ruk off from the Shoals of Earth. Until then, Bixby provides only small hints and clues regarding the technology required to advance the field. In fact, he's had to squelch advances that ran out too far in front of his timeline a few times. Doing the work of the Estate or Quiet Cabal rankled, but eventually Bixby knows it'll all pay off.

BUTTERFLY OBJECTORS

Butterfly Objectors is a group composed of a subset of former Estate operatives, OSR agents who've gone into hiding, and others who have experience translating into different recursions. What distinguishes this group is that they have completely given up their abilities to translate, and for the most part, their former affiliation. The reason they've distanced themselves from their abilities has to do with the butterfly theory, though it's not the "butterfly effect" made famous by chaos theory. Instead it is a theory put forward by one Dedrian Andrews, which draws on the analogy of a caterpillar turning into a butterfly.

It's popularly imagined that a caterpillar enters its chrysalis and is gradually modified until it becomes a creature capable of flying. Most of society sees this transformation as a beautiful metaphor for how people can grow and change. Dedrian, however, shines a light on the truth. What actually happens to the caterpillar in the chrysalis is that its body melts down to a sac of nutritious goo—a sac of nutritious goo that serves as the feedstock for a wholly new creature, the butterfly. (If you were to cut open a cocoon at the right time, caterpillar soup would ooze out.) The upshot? The butterfly isn't really the same thing as the caterpillar that preceded it.

Dedrian extends the butterfly's reality to describe what happens when someone translates. He maintains that the person on the other end isn't the same person with new features, it's a *copy* of that person made from random material in the new recursion. The *real* person dies each time, and a copy moves on, walking in the former person's place.

Butterfly objectors represent a small but growing number of former recursors. The group hasn't offered any violence, but they are radical when it comes to their desire to broadcast "the truth" to as many quickened as possible. Some objectors see organizations that use operatives to translate—including the Estate—as evil perpetrators of lies that kill.

SEPTEMBER PROJECT

A standard Internet search describes the September Project as a research group developing the next generation of quantum computers. A lot of glitzy web marketing makes a convincing case for the benefits such machines would provide.

The group's desire to create a true quantum computer is real—not because they want to solve anyone's problems, but because the group's secret founder—a man named Jason Cole (known as the Betrayer in Ardeyn)—wants to claim both Ardeyn and Earth for himself. The ultimate narcissist, Cole has attained planetovore-style aspirations. Only a few elite September Project agents know Cole's ultimate goals, and even they believe that they'll be spared when Cole finally succeeds.

The September Project has a research facility in Palo Alto, California, a city known for its computer talent. Thanks to the efforts of the Estate (efforts that consist of bribes, hiring away talent, destruction of prototypes, arson, and so on), the research never really got off the ground, and the September Project eventually earned the reputation as something of a joke in the computer industry.

But lately, the Estate's agents at the Palo Alto research facility have been found dead (one having suffered a stroke, the other a heart attack) or missing. The September Project has developed a new security strategy. Every seven days, they bring in a telepath from a recursion called Atom Nocturne that operates under the law of Psionics. The telepath is Soma Kitsune.

Soma stays just long enough to clear out any new secret agents or other security breaches, then she is quickly shuttled back to her world before her Talent gives out completely. Soma contracts blinding headaches the moment she enters Earth as its alternative law begins to digest her Talent, but a heavy dose of painkillers allows her to operate for up to two days. If Soma remains on Earth for more than a few days, the strain would likely kill her. Soma believes that she's doing good, and that the

The Karum is a group of so-called nihilists based in Ruk who desire to destroy Earth. For additional information on the Karum and Dr. Gavin Bixby's work, see page 200.

"The September Project wants to solve problems by using the laws of quantum physics. With quantum computing, we can create the world of tomorrow one superposition at a time. Join us, and change the world." ~September Project advertisement

Dedrian Andrews: level 4, level 6 with persuasion skills

Atom Nocturne, page 234
Law of Psionics, page 137

Soma Kitsune: level 5, level 8 for various psychic abilities

Talent is what the natives of Atom Nocturne call extreme psychic ability.

secret agents she is rooting out are working for a dubious organization; she's convinced that the September Project are the "good guys."

The visible head of the September Project's marketing push is COO Shanice Blickenstaff, but the person who leads real operations on Earth is CEO Gayle Cooper. Gayle is a native of Ruk, originally one of the leaders of the Karum. Gayle didn't find the Karum radical enough for her purposes (they moved too slow). She's happier with the idea of completely obliterating the Earth on the Betrayer's schedule, though would probably switch sides again if the Betrayer were to do something to endanger the Karum's goals.

Shanice Blickenstaff: level 4, level 5 for all tasks related to deception

Gayle Cooper: level 6, level 7 for Speed defense rolls

RECURSION MINERS

Individuals and groups who find and explore recursions—and who attempt to create new recursions—are recursion miners. Such miners are especially interested in acquiring cyphers and returning with them to Earth. Some recursion miners accomplish this goal responsibly, but others engage in unsafe methods that risk destabilizing a particular recursion and drawing dangerous attention from the dark energy network. The Estate keeps tabs on all the recursion miners it knows about, and it steps in to neutralize those who go too far.

Watched recursion miners include the following.

Dr. Latisha D. Law (level 6): Dr. Law is an anthropologist who investigates various cultural sites in Africa. Dr. Law usually works with a team, but she always mines alone, descending into ephemeral recursions birthed via fictional bleed from various African myths. The kinds of cyphers she translates up to Earth are mostly benign, peaceful, and used for good works.

Diego Diamond (level 4): Diamond is a freelance recursion miner who has a criminal record on Earth. He has at various times worked for OSR, the September Project, and even the Estate, which is why he hasn't been dealt with quite yet, despite his predilections. If the Estate knew that Diamond wasn't quickened, but utilized a technology known as an inapposite harness, they'd put an end to his career. Lately, he has been searching for cyphers and artifacts among recursions created by Native American fictional bleed.

Erica Laughton (level 5): Laughton is a hairstylist quickened later in life. The fifty-three-year-old Laughton visits tiny recursions created through the fictional leakage from children's television programming. So far, her explorations have been harmless; she returns to Earth with cyphers that turn out to be self-animating and harmless toys (if colorful and given to annoyingly high-pitched singing). But operatives keep watch just in case.

LeRoy R. Cain: level 4, level 6 for perception tasks; sawed-off shotgun attack inflicts 6 points of damage to two targets within immediate range; carries a level 5 vanisher cypher

Inapposite harness, page 159

SPIRALERS

One repercussion of Earth's interaction with the Strange is the development of a street drug called spiral dust. Spiral dust is made from cyphers through a process the Estate still works to unravel, and by people or groups that the Estate is still working to root out.

People who become addicted to spiral dust are called spiralers. Addicts are easy to spot: their hands tremble with excitement, their speech is exuberant, and most telling of all, their irises become purple-stained and slightly deformed, taking on the shape of a fractal spiral.

Spiralers have incredibly vivid hallucinations while they're on the drug, and they tend to believe that each such trip is a continuing leg of their spiritual journey. Particularly heavy users disappear. The public at large believes such disappearances are either because an addict leaves behind her regular life to join a spiritual messiah in a distant compound, or because she dies of an overdose in an illegal drug den.

The truth is more strange. Spiralers aren't actually hallucinating; they're peering into, perhaps even dreaming into, a recursion. Particularly heavy users don't die; they're translated against their will into a recursion (perhaps the same unknown recursion for everyone) and can't ever escape.

One supplier of spiral dust is LeRoy R. Cain. LeRoy is quickened (and would qualify as a recursion miner, by the Estate's lights). He uses his ability to hunt for cyphers in small recursions created through fictional leakage. He stays away from the larger, established recursions like Ruk and Ardeyn because he figures it's just too likely he'd be discovered. The less he has to do with other quickened people, the better. He prefers one tiny recursion in particular whose name he doesn't even know, where he walks a beach along a sea hidden in autumn mist. The surf always throws up a cypher or two if he's patient enough. He remains safe as long as he avoids a certain cave farther inland where smoke regularly puffs. LeRoy suspects the smoke is the breath of a great hibernating monster, and he isn't wrong.

OFFICE OF STRATEGIC RECURSION (OSR)

The Office of Strategic Recursion is a secret agency of the USA that has ties to governments around the globe. Like other agencies that thrive without possessing any "official" existence, OSR is funded through misleading accounting, misdirection of seized funds, and other less palatable sources. Imagining the existence of such departments usually falls to conspiracy nuts, but when it comes to OSR, they wouldn't be wrong. The fact that OSR agents employ black suits and use cyphers only provides more fuel for conspiracy forums and late-night talk shows.

OSR is well aware of recursions. It monitors groups like the Estate and the Quiet Cabal. In fact, it's a policy of the OSR to feed these two groups leads on a regular basis to foster the belief in both groups that OSR is on their side.

The truth is, OSR isn't working for the same goals as the Estate or even the Quiet Cabal. Sure, OSR will put down a rogue dragon from Ardeyn or deal with a Karum-aimed paradox trying to set fire to Washington, D.C. But its ultimate policy goal is to discover all the ways that elements of the Strange can be weaponized for use on Earth. OSR even created a few recursions designed to spec, thanks to agents who undertook a genesis quest.

Truetopia: Truetopia is a recursion that operates under the law of Standard Physics, created by OSR for the purpose of creating "true believers" who will serve as cannon fodder should a war break out on Earth. Results are too preliminary to discern whether Truetopia will be a rousing success or an abysmal failure.

Soldiers From Beyond the Grave: Agent Saladin Nixon is working on a plan to translate several animate skeletons from Ardeyn up to Earth. Skeletons are dangerous and expected threats in the wilds of Ardeyn but on Earth, they would be monsters capable of striking terror in anyone they attacked. Better yet, they would disintegrate after just a few days under the pressure of Earth's natural laws, leaving no evidence behind other than the mayhem they wrought.

Urania: Urania is a recursion created by OSR for the purpose of mining rare minerals, especially uranium. Urania remains too immature to provide much in the way of dividends yet, but a few agents have the ongoing responsibility of maturing the recursion to an age category where uranium can be mined easily. A few hiccups have seen the accidental creation of natives of living mineral, some of which have developed the spark and a bad attitude against OSR.

Law of Standard Physics, page 136

Saladin Nixon: level 5

Skeletons: level 3, level 5 in combat tasks with long-range rifle; Armor 4 against gunfire, 1 against bash attacks; rifle does 4 points of projectile damage per attack

Genesis quest, page 138

UFF: The Unexplainable Frontier Foundation (UFF) seems to be a public organization dedicated to studying unusual phenomena of the kind that might otherwise only go as far as a *Fortean Times* headline. Members live throughout the world, but organize and communicate via online channels and various public and private social media outlets. Unlike other societies dedicated to uncovering oddities, the UFF was founded by one Calvin Lewis who claims that he was visited by strangers from another world. After that visit, he wanted to share the news with the public. To this end, UFF puts out weekly calls for information regarding news of "strange worlds, strange powers, or strange visitors" on its web page.

Fortean Times is a magazine devoted to strange phenomena.

Calvin Lewis: level 5

Calvin Lewis isn't what he seems—he's an operative of OSR. Lewis sends membership rolls and keeps tabs on people who seem most interested in the same kind of phenomena that OSR monitors. If a member discovers information that is a little too accurate, that person is "disappeared" for further debriefing.

Clean Slate: A supersecret division within OSR is charged specifically with monitoring other groups with knowledge of the Strange. Some within Clean Slate advocate for completely eradicating these "competing" organizations. Plans have been drawn up to accomplish just that, but they are classified as contingency plans only, not as actual policy. Every time OSR finds a double agent within its own ranks, certain high-ups in the chain of command privately discuss putting the contingency into full operation.

"A normal human brain is constantly firing, as if in a state of uneasy truce with itself. Compare that to the brain of someone quickened, and it's like a battlefield, with an unidentifiable energy signature thrown in that shorts out fMRI equipment. You can see why the quickened condition is hard to quantify." ~Hertzfeld, Research Chief of the Estate

Homebound: Sometimes it's desirable to take enemy combatants, political prisoners, or other persons of interest off the board for safekeeping, while keeping them within reach in case they prove useful. That's why OSR keeps an escape-proof prison on a small recursion called Homebound. Thanks to the qualities of Homebound, translating either in or out is a difficulty 10 Intellect-based task, which means the only reliable way in or out is through a translation gate that OSR keeps on a secret armored rail car, always moving around the country, picking up and "processing" new residents for Homebound.

Super Soldier Project: Despite the fact that Earth operates under the law of Standard Physics, researchers within OSR have been tasked with trying to confer on soldiers special enhancements. To this end, they attempt to study the technology of Ruk especially. They hope to accelerate the creation of an upgraded human being without the degradation recursors from Ruk experience after arriving through an inapposite gate. To date, the project has reported advances in increasing oxygen absorption, enhancing vision, and accelerating muscle response. For any soldier who is current with the drug regimen that maintains this state, all combat-related tasks are modified by two steps in her favor, but the drug regimen is dangerous because side effects are common. Anyone who spends more than a few days on the pharmaceutical cocktail risks sudden heart failure after each exertion (1–2 on a d100 roll), until the drugs and the abilities that come with it are completely cleared from the bloodstream.

STARSEEDS

"Starseeds" are what some people on Earth call themselves. They are also known by others as "star people" and "lightbeings," or just "deluded." Starseeds believe they are not human, that they originate from another place in universe, but walk in a human body. Individuals who identify as starseeds exist as a loose-knit community on the Internet. Psychologists describe the starseed phenomenon as a coping mechanism for people who don't feel they fit in. Just as some find an answer to their needs in a holy book, starseeds hold tight to the idea that their feelings of isolation stem from the fact they have come to Earth to fulfill an urgent mission... if they could only remember what it was.

Given the reality of the expanse of the dark energy network under Earth, who's to say that starseeds aren't correct in their belief about being special? Maybe some of them really *are* aliens who've translated to Earth after having fled a prior alien civilization's collapse. It's not the first time. Just look at Ruk. On the other hand, it's more likely that starseeds (if "real" in any way) are accidental immigrants translated from one of the recursions around Earth who suffer amnesia regarding their former existence.

The Estate and Quiet Cabal haven't taken any official notice or interest in the starseed phenomena. On the other hand, OSR is curious and has opened an investigation. They have several starseeds in their sights who they suspect may be on the verge of "awakening" to their original consciousness. Starseed targets include the following:

Janet Collins is a retired high-school teacher who taught shop classes. Now in her middle sixties, she continues to work on what brought her so much joy through her life—making things. Recent advances in 3-D printers and the collaboration provided by various makerspaces has given Janet the outlet she craved. Janet has a particular gift for creating simple robots, though of late, insights in her dreams have led to increasingly complicated circuits that are so advanced that they rival anything university robotic labs are producing.

Ankur Dass operates an art print shop in a small town a few hours outside of a major metropolitan area. Ankur holds art classes every Tuesday evening in the warehouse in back of his shop. He has always been something of an inspired artist, but lately it seems his talent has finally awakened. The fractal-like landscapes he creates never fail to stun viewers, and sometimes people who see his latest landscape dream about the images later, and depending on the image, feel much better or worse for the memory.

EARTH ARTIFACTS

Given that Earth operates under the law of Standard Physics, artifacts are not common. They are usually created by accident, and they rely on the intersection of a subtle law of reality and a quickened inventor. Artifacts from other recursions are not usually able to translate, but some have that capability and so can also be found on Earth.

On the other hand, given that Earth has developed technology that operates well under Standard Physics, many of the appurtenances available on Earth could be considered artifacts in other recursions. For example, if a machine gun traveled to Ardeyn via an inapposite gate, it would be considered an artifact.

INAPPOSITE HARNESS

Level: 1d6 + 2

Form: Rigid chest and belt harness studded with readouts and controls

Effect: When the wearer activates the harness, which requires a difficulty 2 Intellect-based roll, he can step from one recursion to another as if through an inapposite gate. Unless a mishap occurs, only the wearer and what she can carry is transferred. The wearer can set the harness to return to a recursion already visited. In this case, the wearer appears within short range of where he left the recursion with the harness. The wearer can also choose to randomly step into a never-before visited recursion. Doing the latter increases the difficulty of the roll by two steps. If a wearer fails the activation roll, roll on the following table to determine what happens. A depletion roll is required unless noted otherwise.

d6	Mishap Effect
1	Nothing happens; no depletion roll necessary
2	Nothing happens, and a short inflicts 5 points of ambient electrical damage to wearer
3	Successful transfer after a warm-up period that lasts 1d6 minutes
4	Successful transfer to random recursion
5	Successful transfer to target recursion, but a random level 1d6 creature also appears and attacks
6	Successful transfer to target recursion, but a random level 1d6 + 2 creature also appears and attacks

Depletion: 1 in 1d20

PERPETUAL MOTION ENGINE

Level: 1d6 + 2

Form: An engine with custom parts the size of a coffee maker

Effect: A perpetual motion engine doesn't require fuel. If attached to something capable of doing work (and properly braced), the engine can deliver up to 300 horsepower for up to a day (which is considered one use of the artifact).

If the engine is depleted, fixing it to working condition requires a difficulty 5 Intellect-based roll and several hours in the shop.

Depletion: 1–3 in 1d100

WORLD KEY

Level: 1d6 + 1

Form: A deluxe, highly stylized metallic key

Effect: When turned in the lock of any door, and the door is opened within ten minutes, the doorway becomes a translation gate to a specific recursion. Each artifact is "keyed" to a specific recursion. While the origination door can be at any location where the key is used correctly, the destination is determined by the regular rules of translation (with the key-holder being considered the one initiating the translation). A recursion gate created by a key lasts for up to ten minutes before fading out.

Depletion: 1 in 1d20

Janet Collins: level 3, level 7 for all tasks related to robotics

Makerspaces are community centers with tools that enable members to design, prototype, and create manufactured works of their own.

Ankur Dass: level 3, level 7 for all tasks related to fractal art

CHAPTER 12

ARDEYN

ARDEYN ATTRIBUTES

Level: 3
Laws: Magic
Playable Races: Humans, qephilim
Foci: Abides in Stone, Carries a Quiver, Channels Sinfire, Embraces Qephilim Ancestry, Lives in the Wilderness, Practices Soul Sorcery, Shepherds the Dead, Slays Dragons, Wields Two Weapons at Once, Works Miracles
Skills: Ardeyn lore
Connection to Strange: Creatures native to Ardeyn can see and travel directly into (or fall into) the Strange from the edge of the recursion. Creatures native to the Strange can see into Ardeyn, but cannot normally enter.
Connection to Earth: Various gates
Size: 900 miles long × 300 miles wide × 100 miles thick (1450 × 480 × 160 km); see The Shape of Ardeyn, page 165
Spark: 80%
Trait: Brash. For any creature with the spark attempting to overcome or ignore the effects of fear or intimidation, the task is modified by one step to its benefit.

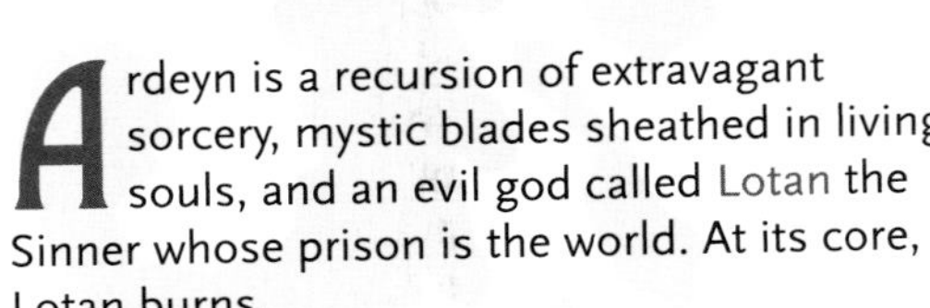

Lotan, page 162
Dragon, page 267
Soulshorn, page 291
Homunculus, page 259
Betrayer, page 178
Demon of Lotan, page 265
Qephilim, page 163
Seven Incarnations, page 162

The Maker is a godlike entity who created Ardeyn as a prison for the evil god Lotan.

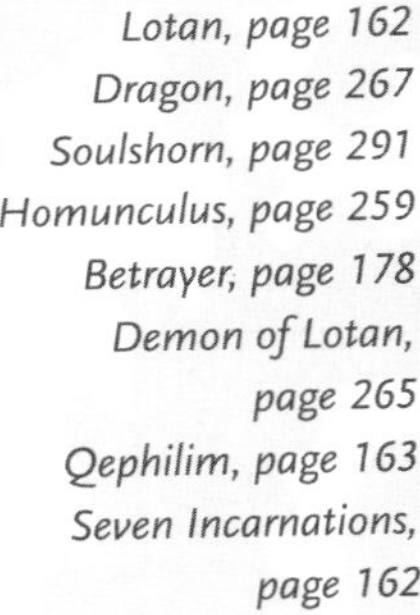

WHAT A RECURSOR KNOWS ABOUT ARDEYN

- Ardeyn operates under the law of Magic and is influenced by Sumerian myths.
- Spirits of the slain live on in Ardeyn, and they are drawn into the subterranean Night Vault; a recursor who dies in Ardeyn would leave behind a spirit subject to the same rules of death.
- The Maker and Seven Incarnations who safeguarded Ardeyn are dead or missing, except the Betrayer (who was the Incarnation of War before he murdered the Maker).
- Strangers called kray continually test Ardeyn's borders, and they sometimes find cracks through which to enter, thanks to the efforts of the Betrayer.
- The entire land of Ardeyn is built upon the petrified body of a god called Lotan the Sinner.

Ardeyn is a recursion of extravagant sorcery, mystic blades sheathed in living souls, and an evil god called Lotan the Sinner whose prison is the world. At its core, Lotan burns.

Dragons, soulshorn, homunculi of the Betrayer, invaders from alternate recursions, demons of Lotan, and other insidious threats that hide in ancient qephilim ruins are ever-present in Ardeyn.

Once, Ardeyn was guarded from Lotan the Sinner by the Maker, his Seven Incarnations, and their angelic qephilim servants. But when they fell long ago, they left Ardeyn open to attack. Now mortals (humans and fallen qephilim alike) have taken up the fight to protect the place known as the Land of the Curse.

HOW ARDEYN WAS FORMED

Very few people in Ardeyn, Earth, or other recursions know how Ardeyn actually came to exist. Unlike so many recursions around Earth, Ardeyn is not the result of fictional leakage. It is, instead, a construct of human ingenuity.

A research group at the University of Washington discovered the Strange via an experimental quantum computer chip. That discovery "pinged" the dark energy network—and brought it to the attention of hungry planetovores.

If any other research group had disturbed the Strange, it might have been the end for the planet. But this research group was headed by a man named Carter Morrison—and luckily so, because Earth was saved by Morrison's quick thinking. When he realized that his experimental quantum computers unexpectedly created a connection to the Strange, he saw the danger, but more important, he also saw the solution: a set of formalized rules that could give order to the chaos and cancel out the accidental connection he'd made.

Morrison didn't have much time before the provoked planetovores began swarming up the connection toward Earth. The only set of formalized rules on hand was an online multiplayer computer game world called *Ardeyn: Land of the Curse* that Morrison had coded prior to his research appointment. So he dropped the entire codebase for Ardeyn down the entangled link into the primeval network.

"Ardeyn hangs naked in the Strange like the Earth spins naked in space. Yet people on Earth walk around without being sucked into the vacuum, thanks to the emergent behavior of natural laws. In a similar way, Ardeyn residents are not absorbed and consumed by the denizens of the Strange, thanks to the Seven Rules, though the Rules were first made to shield the land from a different threat: Lotan the Sinner."

—Carter Strange

His gambit worked, and the recursion of Ardeyn was born. Because the reality of the recursion demanded it and the underlying computational power of the dark energy network of the Strange allowed it, history crystallized thousands of years into the past, "recursively." Morrison (and a few of his friends) stepped into roles prefabricated for them that stretched all the way back to Ardeyn's Age of Myth.

Ardeyn is pronounced AR-don; "AR" like car, "don" like pun.

In Ardeyn, Carter Morrison is known as Carter Strange (and sometimes as the Maker).

ARDEYN'S LONG HISTORY

Despite the recursion's short history in relation to the Earth, it has a long, intriguing history that stretches back thousands of years, back to Lotan the Sinner and the Age of Myth.

Although Ardeyn is only about a decade old, it was created with a "built-in" history stretching back several thousand years. To anyone inside the recursion, Ardeyn's history is as real as actual history on Earth. It doesn't matter that this history never "actually" happened, because everything that exists in present-day Ardeyn points back at this history, both in memory, landforms, and written lore of the recursion.

LOTAN THE SINNER

The Maker imprisoned Lotan within his own world-sized body for unthinkable sins committed in a higher realm, then set the Incarnations to monitor the petrified shape, which came to be called Ardeyn. If one could pull back from the surface of Ardeyn far enough to gain perspective, one might see the outlines of the colossal, horrifying, fetal form of Lotan the Sinner. Should Lotan ever wake and shake off Ardeyn's soil and vegetation, the recursion would be utterly destroyed. The nexus of Lotan's consciousness, such as it is, burns in the Heart Core.

Some few unwisely choose to worship the evil god in hopes for great power, despite the danger that doing so could wake Lotan. Those who do are reviled and hunted down.

Though the creatures of Ardeyn were cut off from Earth, other recursions, and the Strange while Ardeyn's chronology was unsynchronized, a few entities of the Strange managed to "seep" the other direction and enter Ardeyn, including the kray and the Hulks of Kryzoreth.

AGE OF MYTH

For ages, Lotan was kept imprisoned by the Seven Rules of Ardeyn: Commerce, Death, Desire, Law, Lore, Silence, and War. The Seven Rules had living incarnations—the Seven Incarnations—to oversee them. Each Incarnation, in turn, was served by a group of loyal angelic qephilim. Together, with the Maker and their qephilim, the Incarnations kept watch over Lotan's imprisoned form. During that time, all was peaceful in Ardeyn.

Megeddon, page 179

Oceanus, page 172

That peace ended when Lotan made an unexpected bid for escape, using dragons and newly created, lesser servitors of his own secret fashioning: humans.

War raged across Ardeyn, lasting a century, until one act finally turned the tide—humans developed free will, broke from Lotan, and swore themselves to the Maker. The dragons and Lotan's agents were defeated before Lotan's fiery heart could break its bonds, preventing him from reanimating his original body and destroying Ardeyn in the process.

PCs who play qephilim are usually of the Free Battalion, regardless of their type or focus, though a GM could decide otherwise.

Free Battalion, page 284

The earthquakes from Lotan's body were a cataclysm that laid waste to the surface of Ardeyn. But something even worse happened—the seeds of resentment were sown and the repercussions would last longer than anyone expected. Those seeds remained quiescent for thousands of years, before finally sprouting, giving rise to the Age of Unrest.

THE MODERN ERA: THE AGE OF UNREST

The secret anger burning in War's breast over the pardon of the humans persisted for thousands of years. Then Carter Morrison changed everything when he and his friends saved Earth and stepped into the roles of the Maker and some of the Seven Incarnations.

Jason Cole was one of those friends. He stepped into the role of the Incarnation of War, but unfortunately, he felt trapped by Morrison's decision. That animosity, combined with the anger War still carried for the Maker, crystalized. Betraying his friendship, Cole (as War) murdered Morrison (as the Maker). What Cole didn't realize was that destroying the Maker would also destroy the Seven Incarnations. Most of the other Incarnations died or disappeared, leaving Cole bereft of most of the power he'd commanded as War.

Now known as the Betrayer, Cole lives on, attempting to reclaim the powers of the Incarnation of War, or perhaps even those of the Maker himself. The Betrayer remains an entity worthy of fear, and many are rightly more frightened of him than of Lotan. After all, Lotan is bound, while the Betrayer is free, and he has retreated to his Borderlands fortress of Megeddon, where he plots in shadow to overthrow the land one way or another.

With the rest of the Incarnations dead or missing, Ardeyn has been in turmoil. Although the turmoil is lessening, the Age of Unrest rolls on, the future uncertain without the Maker or the Incarnations to directly watch over Lotan or to keep the vengeful Betrayer in check.

THE PASSAGE OF TIME

Ardeyn's creation was unique in almost every way. Formed in an act of chaotic desperation, Ardeyn was purposefully sealed off so completely after it formed that it was chronologically unmoored from Earth, other recursions, and even the Strange itself. When its chronology was finally resynchronized (and translation became possible to and from Ardeyn), only about three years had passed on Earth. During that same time, almost two hundred years had passed in Ardeyn.

QEPHILIM

Even without the Incarnations, the Seven Rules persist today, keeping Lotan imprisoned and the Strange fenced out, but everything is on much shakier ground. Today, the most visible signs that the Incarnations once walked Ardeyn are the qephilim.

Qephilim are a race descended from immortal angelic beings who served the Maker and his Incarnations. In the past, seven qephilim kindred groups each pledged to a particular Incarnation. During the Age of Myth, before the arrival of humans, magnificent qephilim cities dotted the breadth, interior, and even the skies above Ardeyn. But long before the Betrayal, Lotan nearly broke free. During this near-apocalypse, most of the qephilim cities were destroyed in the cataclysm. Afterward, qephilim numbers were a fraction of what they'd been, so rebuilding was difficult. Later when the Betrayal occurred and the Incarnations failed, the qephilim became mortal, too. They faced three choices: become part of human society in Ardeyn, live apart from it, or enter the Strange in search of someplace new.

Each kindred is distinctive from the others in the coloration, size, demeanor, and distinguishing features of its members, but every qephilim has a mythlight: a glow of light usually no brighter than a candle that either hovers nearby or glows like a nimbus around a particular qephilim.

The qephilim kindred are as follows.

Qephilim of War: These warrior qephilim served the Incarnation of War. Many disavowed War and over time became known as the Free Battalion. Qephilim of the Free Battalion serve as mercenaries across Ardeyn, and (usually) pledge themselves to causes that serve the goals of civilization and the preservation of Ardeyn as a repudiation of the Betrayal. These mercenaries are often found battling sark, homunculi of the Betrayer, rogue soulmancers of the Court of Sleep, vermin from the Strange, demon infestations, and other threats.

Qephilim of Death: Of all the qephilim, the Qephilim of Death (also called the Court of Sleep) retain much of the authority previously afforded them when the Incarnation of Death still walked Ardeyn. These so-called shadow-kin see to the dead of Ardeyn in the Night Vault.

Qephilim of Lore: These scholars and philosophers, who are also called keepers, maintained the history and lore of Ardeyn in secret libraries stocked with winding scrolls and lit by wandering soulglints. When the Incarnation of Lore disappeared, so did most keepers and, with them, knowledge of the locations of their hidden caches of lore.

Qephilim of Silence: Not much is known about the monitors, which is another term for the Qephilim of Silence, because they served merely to observe Ardeyn and report back only to the Incarnation of Silence. No one has seen a monitor in over a century—at least no one credible.

Qephilim of Commerce: Trade and commerce in present-day Ardeyn don't seem much affected by the lack of an Incarnation to watch over the transfer of wealth. But the Qephilim of Commerce, who are also called the Court of Coin, are now much reduced in power and influence, and they still inhabit some of their ancient cities, built during the Age of Myth, under the warm surface of Oceanus's waters.

Qephilim of Law: After the Incarnation of Law was slain by War, surviving qephilim of Law fled into the Strange, looking for a place of their own. None are believed to remain in Ardeyn.

Qephilim of Desire: Even when the Incarnation of Desire (also called the Incarnation of Love) was manifest, few ever saw a qephilim of this fleeting sort, and now they exist only as rumor.

Lost Qephilim: When a qephilim loses its way completely, regardless of the Incarnation it or its ancestors once served, it becomes an animalistic savage that knows only anger and hunger. These fallen qephilim are known as sark. Some believe sark now serve Lotan's subconscious will and that a sark's unstoppable savagery is merely an extension of Lotan's desire to tear down the prison that holds him.

Ardeyn native option, page 378

CAMPAIGN OPTION: ARDEYN ORIGINS

An option discussed in Chapter 21: Running a Strange Game is to start a beginning player as an Ardeyn character instead of an Earth character. You could take that idea a step further and start all the player characters (PCs) in Ardeyn and present it to your players as a fantasy campaign where the PCs don't yet realize the true nature of their world. Then, after a number of sessions leading up to what promises to be an exciting finale, make the big reveal to the PCs regarding the true nature of the world. Of all the recursions described in this corebook, Ardeyn is rich and detailed enough to support this idea.

STRANGEFALL

Sometimes things fall into Ardeyn from the Strange, breaking the normal rules that divide one from the other and manifesting as weather of a particular season. Strangefall is the term that can apply to any weather of this kind, but it usually refers to a fall of silvery particles that descend like snow during the wintry month of Graythorn. When large enough accumulations gather, infestations of thornwights begin to walk. Thornwights eat crops, animals, and any people that stumble into the growing patches, but during the month of Char, thornwight groves dry out enough that they burn easily before too many pull free of their roots to roam without restraint.

LIFE IN ARDEYN

Ardeyn's internal history has seen the rise and fall of civilizations, great wars, terrible defeats, and inspiring victories. Natives experience their world as an ancient and epic land. Most of them don't know Ardeyn is a recursion, except insofar as it was the creation of the Maker, a godlike entity of myth. Creatures of Ardeyn have lives, histories, and a subconscious certainty of their own reality.

PEOPLE OF ARDEYN

The people of Ardeyn—humans, qephilim, and even more unusual creatures—speak the Maker's Tongue (which, to someone from Earth, sounds like English), though other languages are also used (including the language of dragons, and Qeph, the ancient qephilim tongue). The people possess consciousness and self-awareness, and most have the spark.

Unlike on Earth, all Ardeyn natives know about the Strange. Its existence is a visible reality; the Strange borders Ardeyn like a sea around an island. Near the edges of Ardeyn, the Strange is always visible, boiling behind the sky and over the side where the land falls away. Even in the central regions of Ardeyn, hundreds of miles from the Borderlands, those who watch for it may see a flash of those same iterative structures as night falls or day rises. Ardeyn natives know that ferocious monsters inhabit the Strange, creatures fenced out of Ardeyn thanks to the Seven Rules, but they sometimes find a way inside anyway.

Just like on Earth, only a handful of Ardeyn natives are quickened. These select few know that other recursions exist beyond the world, including Earth, and some even understand the true origin of the Maker.

For most creatures in Ardeyn, life is usually far more mundane (barring the occasional dragon attack, kray incursion, or demon uprising). People spend the coin of the realm—bits of stamped gold called crowns—to buy and sell services. Shepherds tend flocks, hunters brave the wilds in search of big game, craftspeople in villages and cities fashion items of wood, iron, and stone, nobles look to their holdings and titles, and leaders (often, queens and kings) rule their hereditary lands. On the other hand, sorcerers wield their soul magic, adventurers delve into dangerous deeps, heroes stand against the designs of the Betrayer and similar ilk, soulshorn seek to expand their undead power and domains, sirrush hunt for believers in ancient shrines, and more. For some, life is one great adventure.

TIMEKEEPING AND THE CALENDAR

Years, months, hours, minutes, and seconds are measured in Ardeyn as they are on Earth. The calendar, however, differs. The current Ardeyn calendar begins counting after the Maker was betrayed by the Incarnation of War. Years after this date sometimes are appended AB (After Betrayal), though it's a bit unclear how long ago that event actually happened—people just call it about a thousand years because it's a round number.

The Ardeyn calendar is based on the weather and cycles visible in the surrounding Strange.

WINTER	SPRING	SUMMER	FALL
Shiver	Hope	Bloom	Chill
Graythorn	Char	Suntide	Mistflow
Ice	Seed	Haze	Rest
Strife	Rain	Gather	Fear

This 396-day year has four "seasons," each with four months that vary between 24 and 25 days. Each month has distinguishing characteristics, though some are more important than others. For instance, Graythorn marks episodes of Strangefall. Seed is the time when farmers traditionally plant their crops, while Gather is for the harvest.

THE SUN, THE MOON, AND THE STARS

Ardeyn possesses a sun, seven moons, and a host of stars. The brilliant light that is Ardeyn's sun (sometimes called Flare) is actually a ball of sorcerous fire dozens of miles in diameter that orbits Ardeyn at sufficient distance and velocity to create a cycle of day and night. The seven moons—each named after one of the Incarnations—are tiny (mostly empty) worlds in their own right; they circle Ardeyn in complicated orbits. The stars, visible at night, are farther out than both the sun and moons, though still within a few hundred miles of Ardeyn. Each star is an ancient, named qephilim of great power, set in the sky during the Age of Myth to watch over the world.

RELIGION

In Ardeyn, all know the names of the Maker, the Incarnations, and Lotan. The Maker is revered, as are his Incarnations, even though the Maker is dead and his Incarnations have long since died or disappeared. Those who worship the Maker and his Incarnations do not ask the revered to watch over them; instead they pray for them to return.

Here and there across Ardeyn, local "gods" exist, though they are usually powerful creatures (or particularly deceptive creatures, like sirrush) who have set themselves up as divine beings and demand the service of nearby creatures. In other places, locals might describe something they don't understand using the trappings of religion. For example, a village might worship a Hulk of Kryzoreth as a mysterious deity.

THE SHAPE OF ARDEYN

Ardeyn is irregular in shape, with a top, sides, bottom, and tunneled and vaulted interior (some say it is the shape of Lotan, encased in the stone of an imprisoning world). If one imagined that Ardeyn *is* a massive body pulled into a fetal position on its side, then the inhabited side is the top, and it holds all the Daylands and the encircling Borderlands.

The Daylands are where most living creatures of Ardeyn abide. The Borderlands mark the transition from the Daylands to the cliff edges of Ardeyn, beyond which boils the Strange. The underside of Ardeyn is called The Fall. It's like a vast, jagged ceiling of stone with no floor beneath, and few creatures live there.

The tunneled interior of Ardeyn, the Night Vault, is densely inhabited, if mostly by spirits of the dead.

Borderlands, page 178

Night Vault, page 183

DAYLANDS

The Daylands include several territories, kingdoms, and one queendom. Some Dayland territories are ruled, but a few are too wild for any one country to successfully monitor. Dayland countries with rulers are sometimes rivals, sometimes allies, but either way they are usually engaged with a level of trade with one another.

Dayland territories are generally more civilized than the Borderlands and the Night Vault, but in a land that hosts dragons, necromancers, and sark, any place is potentially dangerous. Road travel risks the notice of bandits, especially in the wilds, but roadless areas are hard to navigate.

The territories of the Daylands include the Queendom of Hazurrium, Mandariel, Kuambis, the Green Wilds, and the central sea of Oceanus.

Sirrush, page 290
Hulk of Kryzoreth, page 180

The circular symbol of the Crown Banner actually depicts a ring passed down from the first Queen of Hazurrium to the current ruler. Called the Ring of Peace, the physical band is more than an implement of rulership; it's a magic ring vested with various sorcerous properties, most of which have been forgotten.

THE QUEENDOM OF HAZURRIUM

The Queendom is the most populated Dayland and the most civilized. The Queendom's symbol depicts a silver circlet, which most people assume is a crown—they even call it the Crown Banner.

The Queendom of Hazurrium hosts the largest fighting force in the Daylands. In addition to several contingents of peacemakers, the Queendom also maintains a contract with the mercenary company comprised mainly of Free Battalion qephilim. The Free Battalion, together with the peacemaker contingents, provides the Queendom a military might more than rival to that of Mandariel, a balance of power that keeps both sides from open conflict.

CITADEL HAZURRIUM

The Citadel is the largest city in the Queendom, and possibly all of Ardeyn, and it serves as the capital city of the nation. More a hundred thousand people live in Citadel Hazurrium, which is built within a single immense fortress. Thick stone walls protect a many-storied interior of hidden verandas and porches, stairs and catwalks, and on top, the partly translucent Diamond Hall, where the queen holds court.

The majority of Hazurrium's neighborhoods exist scattered over multiple levels and beneath overhead stories. The streets and homes are brilliantly lit by day (and festively lit at night) by enchanted lamps that redistribute the light gathered by the Diamond Hall. As brilliant as sunlight, these "diamond lamps" allow for tree-lined streets and thick growths of flowering vegetation throughout the city.

The vertical manner in which the Citadel is laid out can prove difficult for newcomers to navigate, but after a traveler learns the trick of the central circular Grand Stair and the numbering system—Diamond Hall is on One, and ground level is on Thirty-Three—directions become much easier to understand and use. For example, the Common Market can be found on East Thirty-Three, whereas the Noble Market is scattered across Two, Three, and Four.

Citadel Hazurrium has several flourishing markets. From the multilevel Noble Market to the crop-laden Common Market to the Guild Market, Hazurrium provides particularly expansive (and pricey) shopping opportunities, thanks to a conflux of traders who range across the Daylands and Oceanus and several adventuring company guild halls, which bring in oddities and treasures from all over Ardeyn, and even a few from the Strange. A popular item in the markets are Lorn chargers, great horses from Lornvale located in the easternmost fiefdom of the Queendom, and preferred by peacemakers and adventurers alike. The selection in the markets in the Citadel is second only to those in Port Talaat.

Adventuring Company Charters: Citadel Hazurrium is well known as a place friendly to adventuring companies, which is why several keep guild halls in the city, including the Black Moon Explorers and the Band of the Hand. Adventuring companies usually form to spread out risk in return for a share of treasure gained during exploration. And in the Queendom, it's possible to gain an official charter toward that end. This is useful for adventurers, since it sometimes allows a group to make a claim on a particular location with the sanction of the Queendom to back up their interest. Granting charters is also useful to Hazurrium, because it allows officials to keep track of bands that might otherwise descend to the tactics of freebooting raiders. Different charters grant members different rights and responsibilities. Most only go so far as allowing a guild hall to be established with favorable trade status. However, the charter for Black Moon Explorers allows officers of the guild to act with peacemaker authority.

Peacemakers: The peacemakers are divided into three main contingents. The royal peacemakers are elite warriors, and they answer directly to the queen. They are the smallest contingent, but the most feared, and are housed in the Diamond Hall. The royal peacemakers are led by First Protector Navar, a qephilim of the Free Battalion and a sometimes-confidant of the Queen.

The city peacemakers serve as the lawkeepers in Citadel Hazurrium and are housed in small units all around the city. Finally, the legion peacemakers make up the Queendom of Hazurrium's standing army and are housed in subterranean barracks under the city. They train daily in parade grounds beyond the Citadel's gates.

Black Moon Explorers: The adventuring company known as the Black Moon Explorers was founded by three adventurers: Iron Stave, Syrengarii, and Lucious. Named after the group's original aspiration to travel to one or more of Ardeyn's moons, they mostly explore the Borderlands, putting down regional threats and plundering treasure from fallen creatures.

Membership has expanded greatly in the years since the adventuring company got its charter from the Queendom, and indeed the group still accepts application for membership.

The Queen: The Queendom is ruled by a hereditary lineage, but a queen may always adopt a daughter if the line seems in danger. The sitting queen is Elandine, daughter of Brandalun. Brandalun gave the throne to her daughter in her approaching dotage...then went missing, having apparently undertaken a self-appointed quest to find the parts for a mystical mechanism she learned about via a "vision sent from the Maker." Queen Elandine believes her mother is senile and her vision a farce. That doesn't keep her from arranging (and on a few times, leading) expeditions looking for her lost mother or, as more time passes, for her mother's presumed remains.

PATH OF THE DEAD

Just outside of Citadel Hazurrium is a low wall that wends for miles to the west where the dead of the city—from the lowliest beggars to royalty—are interred in the narrow crypts that honeycomb the wall. According to local gossip, the souls of dead follow the path made by the wall up from the Night Vault to visit with their loved ones in dreams.

Unfortunately for many, rogue necromancers of the Court of Sleep, soul sorcerers without conscience, and others who would truck with animated corpses and the spirits of the dead find the wall a ready resource as well. Peacemakers and Free Battalion mercenaries are assigned to so-called "Dream Patrol" to prevent such thefts and exploitation. They suffer from the same terrifying nightmares that usually afflict anyone who sleeps too near the wall, which means turnover is high.

THE GRIEVING VORTEX

A colossal series of flatirons—slabs of rock with clifflike faces—stands between 7,000 and 8,000 feet (2,130 and 2,440 m) high in the Nammu Mountains. One is sculpted in the shape of a massive humanoid with a drawn, broken blade. The humanoid sometimes

Elandine: level 7; carries an artifact called the ring of peace keyed to her use. It grants +4 to Armor and provides a long-range attack rendering up to ten targets unconscious for one minute or a short-range attack against one target that knocks it one step down the damage track.

Night Vault, page 183

Court of Sleep, page 184

First Protector Navar: female qephilim, level 6

Iron Stave: level 5
Syrengarii: level 5

Lucious fell defending Citadel Hazurrium from a dragon attack. He is remembered fondly both as a hero and as a man whose kindness knew few bounds.

"screams" mournfully as the formation exhales a tremendous wind from the open maw. Explorations of the caverns hidden behind the mouth lead back to a ruined undermountain city, possibly an ancient qephilim city of one of the kindred before the Incarnations failed. In the last few years, no adventuring company that has entered the maw has returned, save one half-mad woman named Jorda Mamood. Jorda spends her days drinking quietly in the Citadel Hazurrium tavern called the Three Headed Dog. For the price of a stiff drink, she'll tell the tale of how her companions can yet be found within the ancient city, victims of a soulshorn monstrosity that eats minds but leaves shambling bodies intact as servants and decorations.

Jorda Mamood: level 4

Nammu Mountains

This range runs from the northern crown of Ardeyn down its western spine, through the Queendom, the Green Wilds, and into Kryzoreth. The mountains are tall and rugged, but offer several high passes. Dragons, giants, and sirrush inhabit the high peaks and steep slopes. Abandoned qephilim ruins and mines are scattered throughout the range. A few of those mines are likely the lairs of sark.

MOUNT MERID

Mount Merid is a dead volcano in the Nammu Mountains that serves as the secret lair of Merid, a dragon of famous deviousness. The volcano contains many entrances and exits, including a few that lead into the Night Vault, and possibly even one that leads to the core fires where the heart of Lotan burns. Merid never enters her lair by the same door twice, has traps hidden through the passages, and has set three young dragons and one sirrush to guard her hoard. Merid also employs human agents in Hazurrium who charter adventuring companies to explore distant parts of Ardeyn, only to return with more loot for her own hoard. Those same agents watch for others who might get the idea to come after Merid's treasure, and give warning.

Young dragons: level 4
Sirrush, page 290

Merid is one of the dragons in Ardeyn that keeps a lair outside Kuambis.

Merid is hated and feared as much by other dragons as she is by humans and qephilim. She claims to be one of the First Brood, a dragon who served as a knight of Lotan. Certainly her power seems more than equal to any creatures that have set themselves against her, but the wise consider it unlikely that she has survived the ages when no other creature, save perhaps Lotan himself, has done so.

In recent months, stories have begun to circulate that Merid is missing. Most assume that this is merely a ruse by Merid to lure more victims into her lair.

SHALMARN

The city of Shalmarn is built over the ruins of a much older qephilim city on the crown of a high plateau. Many of the old structures have been converted into homes and buildings, though some are too fragile to be so used, while others remain resistant to exploration. It's not uncommon for relics of the previous city to be uncovered by current residents. For instance, on the outskirts of the city, a partly buried dome was recently breached. Within was a still-active magical ward that turned all who tried to bypass it into dust. Other discoveries have been less dangerous, and include a wealth of cyphers, magical beasts fashioned of clay, and even several spirits of long-dead qephilim that manifest to tell people their fortune.

Somewhere in Shalmarn is a metallic disc with crystal runes set around the exterior. Anyone or anything placed on the disc disappears, usually never to be seen again. Rumor has it that the disc magically delivers anything set upon it to one of the seven moons—possibly one that has air, possibly one that doesn't. An enterprising Shalmarn native called Lartric recently laid claim to the disc and uses it to dispose of all sorts of waste—for a small fee.

A human named Sayd Halmak is lord of Shalmarn. Halmak was installed by the old queen—Queen Brandalun—for serving loyally as her champion for many years. Halmak possesses a rune staff with a notable special ability—instead of being powered by the soul of its wielder, it absorbs the souls of nearby creatures when used offensively. Though the power of the staff is great, it always comes at a price, so he is loath to use it unless defending the interests of his city.

SUNFLOWER ZIGGURAT

A wealthy merchant named Drazander from Citadel Hazurrium claimed control of a flying ziggurat where the Queendom skirts the Borderlands. The flying ziggurats are mysterious floating structures left behind by the qephilim of the Age of Myth. The few previously explored proved to be well-guarded and well-trapped tombs. With the aid of sorcery and a slew of mercenaries, the Sunflower Ziggurat was mostly cleared out within a month. Drazander then claimed it as his own, allowing him to expand his trade route into lands of ill repute. Topping the list of trade items were cyphers gleaned from Borderlands residents who collect the oddities that "wash up" on the edges of Ardeyn.

Then an unfamiliar plague struck the Sunflower Ziggurat. None of the healers, miracle workers, or soul sorcerers hired by Drazander provided any relief. The only cure seemed to be to leave the ziggurat itself, as if the structure itself was somehow the source of the infection.

The secret reality of the situation is that Drazander is an agent of the Estate from Earth. The ziggurat is one of a few locations

ORACLE MURMURS IN THE QUEENDOM

Hidden Enclave: Several red-skinned homunculi of the Betrayer were discovered and slain by peacemakers in the Citadel. Their presence suggests that the Betrayer has set up a secret listening post somewhere nearby. If someone were to find that base, the reward offered by Queen Elandine would be considerable—but how much greater would the reward be if someone knew where to find the base and take care of it himself?

Qephilim Claim: A qephilim that some claim is a monitor—a Qephilim of Silence—makes daily appearances in the city, most often near the main gate. The monitor seems as if it wants to say something, but it always disappears before it can deliver its warning.

Missing Mother: The reward for information leading to the discovery of Brandalun, former queen and mother to the current, grows higher every week, and now includes crowns, artifacts, and cyphers.

Watchful Pillar: In Shalmarn, a dark metal spire near the city center grows eyes that ripen like fruit before they eventually fall off, blinking stupidly until they shrivel and die.

Singing Peak: One nameless peak in the Nammu Mountains is sometimes heard to sing in a language that is not the Maker's Tongue.

Golem Smash: Along the road into Citadel Hazurrium from the west, a stone golem sometimes offers aid to those in distress. Other times it attacks with its smashing fists, leaving few survivors.

Lartric: level 5

Sayd Halmak: level 6; wields a rune staff

Drazander: level 5; Armor 2

controlled by the Estate in Ardeyn, done so to keep tabs on the recursion, and in the case of the Sunflower Ziggurat in particular, to watch for activity of the Betrayer, who is most active along the Borderlands. Whether the plague is an attack by the Betrayer or is the result of another malefic influence remains undiscovered, but if a cure can't be found, the ziggurat and the Estate listening post will have to be abandoned.

Ruk, page 190

GREEN WILDS

The Green Wilds is a forest territory of the Daylands whose massive trees commonly reach 500 feet (152 m) in height in the deepest portions, though some reach higher. The trees—a tumult of palms, sun oaks, and golden aspens—grow much larger than similar varieties in other parts of Ardeyn.

Star sapling fruit: The pods that contain healing fruit restore 5 points to a Pool of the character's choosing.

Mixed in among the more common trees are the occasional incredibly rare star saplings. Star saplings are slender trees with silvery bark and leaves that twinkle like their namesake at night. Every six months, these trees drop white pods, warm to the touch. If opened, a pod is about 50 percent likely to contain a luscious fruit with healing qualities. The other half release a blast of fire as a tiny seed jets up and away from Ardeyn, perhaps to find purchase somewhere out in the Strange.

Seven Sentinels, page 182

Sark, page 288

Sark have lairs within the Green Wilds, making it a dangerous place to wander, and the Green Wilds is also home to a few settlements of humans and qephilim who live high among the trees in treehouse communities.

The Green Wilds is also littered with ruins of the ancient qephilim that once lived beneath the canopy. As a result, treasure seekers are not an uncommon sight, but many of these are not looking for random treasure; they look for portal mouths that supposedly lead to a sub-realm where stories say one ancient qephilim city still survives: a city of crystal and ancient glory, perhaps not even a place so much as a time.

Though the story of a portal to the Age of Myth sounds fanciful to most, it's true that portal mouths of various sorts can be found in groves of star saplings (which otherwise never grow in clumps). The star sapling groves are part of a lingering network that still functions for those who know the secret, and they can provide quick transport around the Green Wilds, and to other places where the star sapling groves grow around Ardeyn. The Stag Knights, a group headquartered in Telenbar, keeps the secret of the star sapling groves safe.

SARK CLEFT

The largest sark lair in the Green Wilds is located in the petrified stump of a tree that, if the stump is anything to go by, must have been miles high when it lived during the Age of Myth. Now the cracks and tunnels beneath it swarm with bestial sark, who are as likely to sing and fornicate as to fall upon each other in a bout of sudden cannibalism.

The sark do not completely overrun the stump; one crack in the bark extends tunnel-like into the ancient tree's root system. Oversized spiders with too many legs and centipedes with children's voices lair beneath, and sometimes they emerge to hunt the sark. In the deepest reaches of the tunnels, a silvery, seed-shaped craft lies in a kind of magical stasis. Some believe that the item is a fragment of one of the lost Seven Sentinels, though others suggest that the object is an artifact of the Strange.

TELENBAR

A particularly large sun oak within the Green Wilds is like a city unto itself, providing a home for as many as 2,000 people, though most people know Telenbar as the home of the Oracle of Ardeyn.

Ladders, rope bridges, and bending boughs allow access up, down, and across the great tree (and to a few surrounding satellite trees). Living in Telenbar requires a citizen to be unafraid of heights and a good balancer. Petitioners to the Oracle quickly learn this, often to their dismay, as they attempt to keep up with their hosts.

The Oracle of Ardeyn: The Oracle is as much an office as a person. To take the office, a creature must show it has a proven power of precognition. In Ardeyn's past, the Oracle has been an old woman who stirs bird intestines, an immobile automaton with flashing lights, a qephilim that gazed into a crystal ball, and a young woman with a penchant for falling into a trance. The current Oracle, however, is different from all those who've preceded her. She is a 30-foot-long (9 m) serpent who wraps herself around the topmost branch of Telenbar and sings her predictions to petitioners who bring her gifts. Unlike previous Oracles, this one goes missing from time to time, apparently traveling to far places, including her homeland, which is an uncouth-sounding place (at least to the ears of the humans and qephilim who tend her) called "Ruk."

Stag Knights: The Stag Knights are an elite group of human and qephilim hunters and trackers with a guildhouse in Telenbar. They know the secret of the star sapling groves, and by using them, the Stag Knights can quickly travel between two points within the Green Wilds (and to a few other locations around Ardeyn). The drawback to using the star sapling groves is that the portal mouths sometimes trigger on their own and draw terrible monsters from the Age of Myth into the present day, which the Stag Knights must then run to ground. For some Stag Knights, it's a burden, but others look forward to each new hunt, despite the danger.

CALANDRIA'S STORM CIRCLE

Just a couple of dozen miles (38 km) southeast of Telenbar lies a half-mile-wide clearing in the forest, surrounded by flowers and blooming foliage. The circle is tended

Oracle Murmurs in the Green Wilds

Lost Expedition: A small expedition of Stag Knights went to investigate a mass of writhing, plantlike material that was seen out in the Strange from a Borderlands-based spypost. They never returned. Though they were written off by the organization, the son of one of the missing wants help locating his mother.

Moon Harvest: An elderly human named Minu Cran wants to harvest seed pods from a particular sun oak in the Green Wilds, one that is supposedly 800 feet (244 m) tall. The seed pods are near the top, but from them a heavenly liquor can be brewed. Minu has climbing gear, but he needs protection from the tree squirrels that are as large and as vicious as umber wolves.

Grandmother Oak: An entity of roots and leaves wanders beneath the canopy of the Green Wilds, sometimes walking, sometimes popping up out of the ground like a quickly growing plant. Calling itself Verdant, the entity claims to be the mobile avatar of one of the sun oaks in the forest.

Umber Grove: Near where the Wilds brush against the Borderlands is a mist-shrouded grove of trees the color of pitch. Or so say some Stag Knights. Sometimes the grove is there, and other times, it can't be found.

Calandria: level 7; long-range electrical attack that inflicts 7 points of damage and ignores Armor

Mythlight, page 163

by a female qephilim named Calandria. Calandria is distinguished by her mythlight, which sometimes flashes and thunders like a miniature storm.

Within the circle of her flowers stand two concentric circles of menhirs. The outer circle is only about 6 feet (2 m) high, while the inner circle measures nearly 30 feet (9 m) high. The outer slabs are blank and the inner thirteen slabs are each heavily carved with runes that glorify specific aspects of a storm. Calandria claims to be the Priest of Storms, and for a price, she will either quell a storm that's raging somewhere else in Ardeyn, or start one.

Calandria is not welcome in the city of Telenbar because she is a bitter enemy of the newest Oracle, and vice versa, though neither will reveal why.

OCEANUS

Oceanus is a territory of the Daylands and is comprised of the vast central basin sea of Ardeyn. Aside from its many watery wonders, its surface also serves as a trade route for many Daylands sailing ships, while beneath the waves all manner of sea life thrives. The remnants of the Court of Coin still inhabit one of their ancient aquatic cities in Oceanus, Juvanom, though most of the others are now drowned ruins.

Zubrin Jagger: level 6

Spiral dust, page 156

PORT TALAAT

A coastal city on the northern shore of Oceanus, Port Talaat is a city built on sea trade, and as such is one of the preeminent destinations on the shores of Oceanus. Seven great piers protrude into the waters, and almost all enjoy brisk trade, though one is set aside for shipbuilding. Another is exclusively leased by the Court of Coin, and it serves both as the Qephilim of Commerce's embassy to the Queendom and as their trade headquarters. Given that the Court of Coin prefers ships that travel beneath the waves, the pier was retrofitted with special accommodations for their submarine craft.

Beyond a press of warehouses, and nearly as many wharfside taverns, lies the rest of Port Talaat: a series of massive interconnected structures of sandstone walls, bamboo balconies, marble stairs, and open courts stretching in all directions. Wide streets separate one section of mazelike architecture from the next, but delicate bridges suspended by sorcery arch over the streets to connect rooftop bazaars.

Day and night, people throng Port Talaat from all over Ardeyn, some even hailing from the Borderlands and the Night Vault. Many speak the Maker's Tongue, but unfamiliar dialects are commonly heard. Trade seems to be the all-consuming passion of the populace, which is conducted from countless porches, stalls, carts, storefronts, hidden corners, private offices, and the many rooftop bazaars. Anything can be had in Port Talaat, both mundane gear and things hard to get elsewhere: love charms, strange beasts sold as pets, specimens from the Strange (including cyphers and sometimes more exotic bits), souls captured in glass, and possibly the rare artifact. In the markets, no luxury is too exotic or fantastic to be bought or sold, and sometimes even enchanted items are on sale in a few specialty shops, though never cheaply. When a day of trading is finally consummated, sleep waits on a visit to the tavern courtyards where prodigious clay vessels sloshing with heady wine are consumed well past half-night.

Several trade concerns are either based in Port Talaat or have an outpost there, including the Iron Road Traders and Jagger Shipping. The Iron Road is based in the Borderlands city of Cliffside (in Kryzoreth) and keeps a caravanserai on the outskirts of the city. Jagger Shipping, on the other hand, is a family business run by Zubrin Jagger. This business owns four trading vessels and does quite well. However, Zubrin is secretly addicted to a disquieting substance called spiral dust, which is being sold against the recent proclamations of the Port Talaat Constabulary. Zubrin is certain that if he stops taking the substance, he'll die. At the same time, he is secretly looking for a sorcerer willing to try to break him of the addictive curse.

JUVANOM

Ardeyn natives usually encounter representatives of the Court of Coin only in Port Talaat, but the court's primary headquarters is actually located in the aquatic city of Juvanom. The submerged city is a collection of neighborhood-sized spheres lit by brilliant light, filled with breathable air, and laid out like religious shrines, though the only religion practiced in Juvanom is commerce. Each of the fourteen individual spheres is a separate prefecture under the authority of a prefect—a

prefect who is also a so-called Merchant Master of the Court of Coin. The main section of each sphere is devoted to trade, while quarters for inhabitants lie in the bottom portion of each structure. Every prefecture specializes in a certain segment of the Ardeyn market.

Humans are almost as prevalent in Juvanom as qephilim, but in most cases, the highest positions of authority in a given prefecture or in the organization of the Court of Coin itself remain in qephilim hands. The exception that proves the rule is Harker Molentha, prefect of Tharcept. Harker is an accomplished player of the lute, a singer with a voice that few can match, and a devotee of nightcap, a mushroom that grows in the Night Vault. Harker is always on the lookout for new connections or those willing to furtively supply him with additional supply of the green fungus.

Tharcept Prefecture: When he's not performing, conducting business, or high on nightcap, Harker Molentha oversees Tharcept Prefecture. Tharcept Prefecture specializes in the sale of entertainments: musical instruments, songs, plays, and other goods that only the rich and idle have the money or time for. The largest space in the prefecture is set aside for a massive stage, though many smaller performance areas exist. Given that much of Ardeyn is harsh and unsettled, one might imagine that Tharcept Prefecture would be the least rich of the floating neighborhoods making up Juvanom. Within the city itself, though, the sphere is a popular destination, given that by almost any standard of the rest of Ardeyn, every inhabitant of Juvanom is wealthy.

HYDRA CASCADE

A deepwater current that swirls through the depths of Oceanus is called the Hydra Cascade. The Cascade is named as much for the violent nature of the current as it is for a submerged qephilim ruin that has the vague shape of massive hydra that serves as the terminus for anything caught by the current. Those caught in the grip of the current who don't win free before being drawn into the ruin are likely to be dashed across a series of pillars and abutments there. On the other hand, no one who hasn't been sucked in by the current has ever been successful in finding the ruin.

The current is obviously magical, because mere feet beyond the main strength of the tubelike cross-section of water where the

Harker Molentha: level 4, level 7 for all tasks related to performance and resistance to poisons

current rages strongest, the surrounding water is calm. This phenomenon is why adventurers sometimes willingly allow themselves to be pulled in by the current with the ancient ruin at its endpoint, a ruin rumored to be rich in magic, treasure, and lost secrets.

WORLD FALLS

The overflow from Oceanus spills out into the abyss of the Strange, creating a waterfall that extends for hundreds of miles, gradually thinning to so much expanding vapor. One of the most impressive sights on all of Ardeyn, the World Falls are not one for someone afraid of heights. Watching the plunging falls has a hypnotic effect that has drawn hundreds of people to jump who, prior to coming to the edge and gazing over, had no intention of doing so.

"It's easier with only five." ~Marhaban saying

Just before escaping Ardeyn forever to irrigate another recursion or hydrate the inexplicable beings that exist in the dark energy network, the waters flow through a series of arches: qephilim ruins from the Age of Myth. Netters use these ruins to strain the outflow. Given the volume of water, the nets are always breaking, and restringing them is dangerous work. Sometimes, though, the objects strained from the falls are so valuable that it makes all the close calls worthwhile. Netters and would-be netters flock to the city of Overlook, and much of the industry of the city supports (directly or indirectly) their efforts. Individual netters can lay claim to particular areas along the falls, but only as long as their nets are not broken. Given the nature of the work, competition can be fierce and sometimes cutthroat. Overlook isn't claimed by any larger entity, which means law there is often a bit fast and loose.

Salina: level 5, level 6 for all attacks and defense tasks

MANDARIEL

The Queendom and Mandariel rarely enjoy calm relations, despite the fact that they share a border. Instead, tension colors every interaction. It's more than just culture—the underlying reason for the conflict is that Mandariel constantly tests the boundaries of Ardeyn by sending ships out into the Strange to explore and salvage what it can find in the dark energy network. This practice is not only dangerous to those who personally voyage on such trips, it is also dangerous for Ardeyn as a whole: Who knows what kind of fell entity might be drawn back to Ardeyn by a chaos skiff trader? At least, that's how officials in the Queendom spin it, but most people in Mandariel see that as mostly propaganda. The Queendom just wants to hold on to its ancient prominence, and it does so by keeping the younger yet far more daring and innovative people of Mandariel down.

MARHABAN

The capital of Mandariel, Marhaban is where the royal family rules and maintains its ancestral Ruby Palace on the shores of Oceanus.

With the death of King Khousaf a decade ago, the Five Princes now share rulership. In the normal course of things, a new king would've been chosen by the Oracle of Ardeyn; however, for some reason the Oracle has not chosen a new king, and Five Princes struggle to share power. When King Khousaf died, there were Twelve Princes, and Mandariel was almost plunged into civil war.

Though the Ruby Palace is the most visible part of Marhaban, the most famous part of the city is the Champion Dome, where slaves, volunteers, and arena champions are pitted against each other, dangerous creatures of Ardeyn, and sometimes creatures found and captured in the Strange. Fighters can win large purses, but most of the crowns changing hands around the Champion Dome belong to those who bet on the fights. Two of the Five Princes (Prince Salman and Prince Bandar) are notorious for their gambling, but since each keeps a champion or two, they usually do quite well.

Many bet mongers work the Champion Dome, but one named Salina is usually the only one who'll take a chance with newcomers. Salina is a large, strong woman, and rumor has it she made her purse as a champion in the dome a decade earlier.

PORT JAYEED

Port Jayeed is the most well-known (and perhaps only) port for chaos skiffs that sail the Strange from Ardeyn. Massive stone piers reach over the edge of the solid land, past the hazy interface and into the dark energy network. Most of the piers are set aside for trade, though a few are owned by shipwrights who keep busy year-round repairing older ships or working on new commissions.

Unlike many places in Ardeyn, Port Jayeed is an open city—crowns spend the same whether a buyer is an agent of the Betrayer, a slaver out of Kuambis, a glass pirate, an umber judge, or an adventurer. Despite the dangerous and daily transition between Ardeyn and the Strange, denizens of the network have never attacked or infested the city, not even the kray. It's whispered that a horrible deal was made to ensure such immunity, or that the town's mayor, Captain Tethis, is actually a kray thrall.

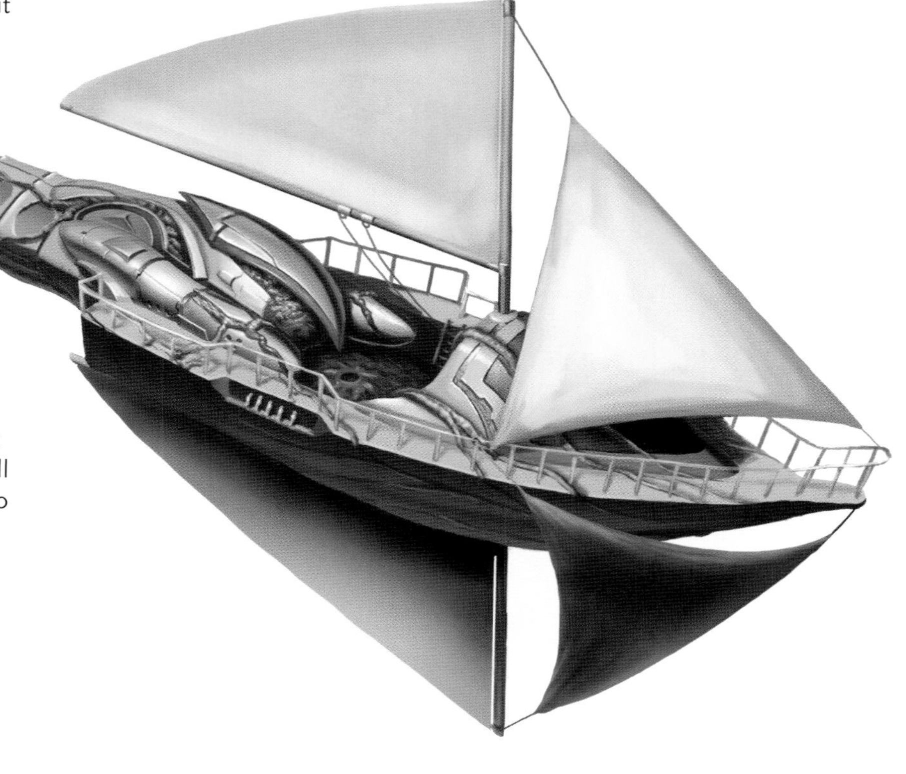

Chaos Skiffs: The ships built in and sailing out of Port Jayeed take many shapes, but almost all are rigged with sweeps of fabric that are akin to terrestrial ships. Instead of wind, chaos skiffs ride fractal currents generated by the never-ending boil of the dark energy network. Riding those currents is made possible by the special sails spun from thornwight silk combined with sheer force of will of the pilot or captain.

Different chaos skiffs sail different routes. Some travel to various skerries surrounding Ardeyn to trade with residents, a few have found safe docking at one or two of the moons that circle the recursion (though sailing too close to Ardeyn—especially over it—risks a skiff being caught in Ardeyn's gravity, and from there a sudden plunge), but the most adventurous travel out into the Strange, looking for treasures. Things sought after include undiscovered recursions that have open borders, reality seeds, cyphers, violet spirals, and most rare and prized of all, entropic seeds. Sometimes chaos skiff crews trade with entities they find in the Strange (such as the Nmidon), run from or hunt creatures (such as the kray), or are devoured by them and never seen again (as is the case if they run into a planetovore).

Kray Takers: A guild based in Port Jayeed known as the Kray Takers owns several chaos skiffs, but it enjoys a membership far larger than crew berths on those skiffs would allow. That's because individual members sign on to other ships that'll have them as guards against potential trouble out in the Strange. Most chaos skiffs have at least one kray taker on board, despite the fact that the odds that any given ship being attacked by a kray or another entity of the Strange are not especially high. As a result, most kray takers collect their fee without having to lift their lance. On the other hand, having able-bodied warriors versed in the

Oracle Murmurs in Mandariel

Shiphands Wanted: What's a chaos skiff without a crew? Ship captains in Port Jayeed are always willing to sign up crew for trips along the edges of Ardeyn, in an attempt to find those that do not suffer from Strangeblight, a common illness for those new to the relentless boil of the Strange.

Champion Dome: Think you've got what it takes to win a purse under the dome? Sign up and find out! Fight only as long as you want—leave at any time! At least, that's what bet mongers promise those who don't have enough crowns to cover the cost of their bet. Why put up coin when one can offer oneself in the arena?

Purple Masks: Thieves' guild members in Marhaban are seen to wear distinctive purple masks (if they're seen at all). The Purple Masks are made up of assassins, spies, and thieves. Word on the street is that the Purple Masks actually work for one of the Five Princes, but which one is a hotly debated topic in the coffeehouses of Marhaban.

Betrayer, page 178
Glass pirate, page 176
Umber judge, page 285

Kray, page 276

Captain Tethis: level 5

Nmidon, page 226

Nmidon is pronounced n-MID-on: "MID" like kid, "on" like son.

Glass pirates are humans and qephilim that travel by ships that skate on the Glass Desert. However, a few "ghost" ships are crewed by pirates actually made of glass. Or so tell the storytellers of Kuambis.

ways of and kitted out for fighting kray can be worth their weight in gold if their services are required.

Many individual kray takers have earned colorful reputations for themselves, including Jaustin the Green, who once killed a kray with his mind; Kalloror Mashhur, who's said to be stronger than a golem; and Gladia the Lance, whose magic lance is tipped with a sentient and hungry spirit.

KUAMBIS

Kuambis is a desolate desert waste, mainly known as a home to dragons, sark, and castouts. No single group or entity rules Kuambis, because the dry land is always being contested by battling dragons who keep humans, qephilim, and lesser dragons as slaves. Ruins and mysteries abound, because Kuambis was also the legendary site of many ancient battles during the Age of Myth. Most of the dragons of Ardeyn make their lairs in Kuambis because they wish to uncover the relics of their draconic ancestors and claim power enough to take all of Ardeyn for themselves. Without the Incarnations or the Maker to say otherwise, what's to prevent Ardeyn from becoming a realm of dragons? It's lucky for most creatures that dragons do not generally get along with each other, and that few wish to go back to serving Lotan, their master of old.

GLASS DESERT

Most of Kuambis is now composed of the Glass Desert, which according to legend is where the final battle occurred between the armies of Lotan and those of the Maker and his Incarnations. Whether it was one detonation or many, the ramparts of the Maker's Hall, a vast castle of glass, was slagged and melted when Lotan burned hottest, becoming the Glass Desert. Beneath it, in bubbles and hollows, adventurous types can discover amazing artifacts of the Age of Myth.

On the surface, what isn't a sere plain of reflective glass is covered in drifting dunes of sparkling sand made up of glass particles. When winds blow across the Glass Desert, they can cut the flesh from the bones of living creatures. Glass pirates ride "sailing ships" that skate on thin magical blades.

CITADEL OF THE HARROWING

This sprawling citadel is surrounded by a shambling city of bandits, raiders, ruffians, slavers, glass pirates, and worse. The Citadel is the one place in Kuambis where dragons cannot go, thanks to the Red Pact they swore long ago. The pact is why lesser races are so numerous in the streets. On the other hand, without the rule of law to tame the passions of the residents, the Citadel is a dangerous place to live. It's also the only place that offers select illicit items, slaves, certain dark sorceries, and, most important to the wider world, the Harrowing.

The Harrowing: The Citadel is named for its yearly competition held during the month of Suntide. The Harrowing draws people from every part of Ardeyn, even those not normally willing to risk being robbed, taken captive, or killed in order to compete. Competitors who are rich enough hire bodyguards to protect them while they stay, but the majority of competitors are desperate dreamers without a handful of crowns to their name.

The Harrowing is a confrontation with dragons. The Red Pact that keeps dragons out of the Citadel has one exception—during the two weeks of the Harrowing in Suntide, dragons may enter, as long as they restrict themselves to the arena, and only if the dragon brings a prize worthy of fighting over—one from the dragon's own hoard. This prize is often a chest bursting with crowns, cyphers, and artifacts.

A team of four mortal contestants fights the dragon, according to fairly loose rules of engagement. If the dragon wins, it can choose to take the survivors as slaves or eat them, and claim any gear they have for its hoard. If the mortal team wins, they get the dragon's prize. The dragon almost always wins. The

"The implacable mutual hostility between qephilim and dragon, as exemplified during the yearly Harrowing of Kuambis, is a holdover from the Age of Myth." ~Rhynedacum, qephilim historian and adventurer

AHLAN MOUNTAINS

The Ahlan Mountains run through Mandariel, Kuambis, and into the territory claimed by the Betrayer. Despite being home to at least one hydra, several bleak dlammas, and other dangerous creatures, the mountains are mined for iron, precious metal, and gems. A trio of tall peaks known as the Three Sisters watches over the waterway and caravan route that leads south from the edges of Oceanus's southern shore through a series of passes towards the Citadel of the Harrowing in Kuambis. On some nights of the year, stars descend and alight upon the peaks for several hours before rising again, but for what purpose no one knows.

The Betrayer

Other than Lotan, the Betrayer is the most feared creature in Ardeyn. As he should be—the Betrayer sees all of Ardeyn as a flawed construct that should be dissolved. He considers the people of Ardeyn to be mere shadows of computer code bereft of conscious spark. And, as a consequence, he doesn't believe that anything he does within his fortress is "evil" so much as a means to an end. He's not a bad guy—just a guy who got screwed, or so he tells himself and his closest confidants (which are his translucent-skinned lieutenants).

The Betrayer became as he was when the consciousness of an Earth human named Jason Cole was thrust into the Incarnation of War, as Ardeyn was compiled into the Strange. The mental dissonance between being a twenty-six-year-old programmer from Earth and at the same time a thousands-of-years-old divine Incarnation of Ardeyn was too much. The story of War was one of resentment toward the Maker for the Maker's acceptance of humans. That, combined with resentments Cole still carried from Earth, led to the Betrayal.

These days, the Betrayer splits his time between his various Foundries plus occasional trips into the Strange itself, where he seeks cyphers, new abilities, or perhaps even allies. Though he'd never say so aloud, the Betrayer's goals have gone beyond merely taking Ardeyn; if he could, Cole would take the Earth, becoming a homegrown planetovore.

The circular symbol of the Traitor's Crown actually depicts a ring quite precious to the Betrayer. Called the Ring of War, the actual band is vested with various sorcerous properties, though most of those powers were lost when the Maker was slain.

Long Way Down, page 181

Dlamma, page 266

Stories suggest that during the Age of Myth, ancient qephilim sometimes bound stars into service.

rare dragons that lose will submit rather than be killed, which means the mortal team gets a great prize but creates a terrible enemy in the process. Every year, rumors go around that a wyrmtalker has entered the Harrowing, but so far, none of those rumors have proved true.

Wyrmtalker: A wyrmtalker is a human who retains dragon rider powers from the Age of Myth. When Lotan fashioned humans to be his servitors, a select bloodline among them rode dragons to war, just as some qephilim rode dlammas. A dragon rider in full control of her powers could bring dragons to heel with a look, a whisper, or a touch. When humans turned against Lotan, the dragon riders gave up their mounts, and their numbers have dwindled over the centuries. Today, most who claim to be wyrmtalkers are charlatans or are lying to themselves, and if they are foolish enough to try their hands at the Harrowing, they quickly learn the error of their thinking.

Borderlands

The Borderlands (sometimes called Borderlands of the Strange) is a strip of land about a dozen or so miles (24 km) wide that encircles the Daylands. In the Borderlands, the Seven Rules begin to fail and land gives way to the cliffside faces of Ardeyn's edge. Beyond the edge, various discrete chunks of free-floating landscape called skerries float. Like the Daylands, the Borderlands contain several territories, though most are small and mean. The largest and most famous is known and feared all across Ardeyn: Megeddon.

The clifflike edges of Ardeyn lead to a long drop because Ardeyn is essentially flat, if thick. In most places near the top, the cliffs are splintered slabs of dark rock that measure Ardeyn's 100-mile (161 km) thickness. Though the cliffs are sheer at the top, the slope relaxes farther down, which means that objects and creatures that fall off the edge don't always fall into the Strange—though it may seem like it to those who stand upon the cliffs and peer down. What actually happens is that dropped objects fall for a few miles (5 km), then shatter upon a deeper portion of the cliff face whose slope has become less severe. If something survives the drop (or climbs down to the area where the slope relaxes, called the termination zone), it's possible to navigate the slope, though it remains incredibly steep.

Explorers and cliffwalkers of a guild called the Long Way Down climb the slopes regularly. Those who are unlucky or who don't take care roll and smash their way down to the termination line, a band around Ardeyn's sides about 50 miles (80 km) down. That's where the slope reverses and becomes negative; anything that falls off this final lip does indeed fall into the Strange.

The skerries are splintered pieces of the Borderlands that remain aloft within the surge of the Strange, despite having lost physical connection to the rest of Ardeyn. Some portion of the Seven Rules keeps them from being ground to nothing and washed away in the boil, but the hybrid nature of these islands makes them extremely dangerous places. Sometimes they are infested with planetovore influence, other times with particularly dangerous outlaws out of Ardeyn—only rarely is a skerry a place of wonder and joy.

Additionally, the weather in the Borderlands is atrocious. Temperatures are normally livable, but they can fluctuate widely. One day they can drop to freezing in minutes, creating blizzards. The next day, a furnace-hot wind threatens sunstroke for those without adequate cover. Whether hot or cold, the winds can blow up along the edges and swirl into vast tornadoes,

able to sweep anything and any unsecured structure to its doom.

Despite all these dangers, adventurers and salvagers are drawn to the Borderlands because they can collect cyphers there like others in Ardeyn collect seashells along the edges of Oceanus, if not so prolifically.

MEGEDDON

Megeddon is a territory of the Borderlands completely under the control of the Betrayer. Indeed, the entire territory is one massive, city-sized black iron citadel where the Betrayer and all his homunculi reside. Megeddon's symbol depicts a black circlet of spikes, which outsiders assume is a crown—a crown set in opposition to Hazurrium's, and so they call it the Traitor's Crown.

Megeddon is peopled almost entirely with copies of the Betrayer that he calls homunculi. Homunculi come in three grades: green (bestial ragers), reds (skilled in war, at a deficit in everything else) and a handful of clears (the Betrayer's lieutenants, who come closest to being perfect copies).

Green homunculi ferocity and red homunculi skill-at-arms gives Megeddon a considerable advantage, even against nations that boast a much larger fighting force, such as the Queendom and Mandariel. Add to that the epic abilities of the Betrayer himself, and it's easy to see why Megeddon can keep enemies at bay.

FORTRESS OF MEGEDDON

Despite its impressive size, the fortress houses only a few thousand creatures, nearly half of them homunculi. The fortress floor plan is like a half circle, with thick iron walls that curve out into the Strange, as if it were a segment of a much larger fortress that was lost somewhere in the dark energy network. Metal towers bristle upon the ramparts of the remaining segment, looking out over the blasted Borderlands.

Only a few entrances are visible on the side of Megeddon that faces Ardeyn: three massive war gates are large enough to allow for the emergence of a dragon or a troop formation that is one hundred homunculi wide.

The fortress contains parade and training grounds, storehouses stocked with mundane weapons, barracks, and other needful things for a military base. A large section of the fortress

The Betrayer yet retains a residual sense of what it was to be War. As War, he opposed Lotan, and as the Betrayer, he continues to do so, reviling the burning entity perhaps even more vehemently than before, perhaps because the Betrayer subconsciously sees a resemblance he can never admit.

Homunculus, page 259

Jonas Gallway: level 5; his staff allows him to target two foes at the same time within long range—affected creatures take 7 points of fire damage, take 7 points of ice damage, or fall asleep for one minute (or until vigorously slapped); staff has a depletion roll of 1 in 1d20

called the White Zone is set aside for visitors.

Megeddon also contains vast, empty areas of rooms, tunnels, tanks, dead gardens, and plazas, suggesting the fortress may have once been a city of ancient qephilim repurposed by the Betrayer for his base.

Another section of the fortress is out of bounds for all creatures except the homunculi. It contains locked treasuries where magic weapons, artifacts, cyphers, and trophies from earlier conflicts are kept safe.

The basements of Megeddon are given over to the Body Vats, where copies of the Betrayer are grown and matured.

On the levels above the Body Vats are the Foundries, some of which are tasked with creating weapons and armor to outfit homunculi, but others have more esoteric purposes. These Foundries are where the Betrayer's translucent-skinned lieutenants oversee reds in various experiments designed to boost the Betrayer's power back to what it was when he was War (or better yet, surpass that level of power). The Foundries include the Pit Foundry, which attempts to siphon energy from the Strange; the Soul Foundry, where soul fragments from slaves are scraped off for study; the Artifact Foundry, where artifacts from both Ardeyn and the Strange are studied and catalogued; the Contact Foundry, where new and better ways to connect to Earth and other recursions are explored; and finally the Xenobiology Foundry, where kray are kept on ice against a future need by the Betrayer.

Vera the Whip: level 6

The Red Moon is the popular name for the moon originally named after the Incarnation of War

White Zone: A large section of Megeddon is like a small neighborhood in a larger city and contains living quarters and conference chambers set aside for embassies from other nations and powers. At any one time, a couple of thousand people who are *not* homunculi are living in or visiting the White Zone. These are traders (including Iron Road Traders), contractors, mercenaries, adventurers, slavers, information brokers, and embassies from other nations and powers (though few of these openly show the allegiance of their homeland). Here, trade can be had for visitors who are willing to risk being killed outright by suspicious homunculi.

September Project, page 155

September Embassy: The offices that interface with the September Project on Earth are always on-site. Couriers come and go through the September Embassy several times a day, translating into a secure chamber using a translation gate keyed to accept only those tattooed with the Traitor's Crown. The elaborate apparatus of the September Project on Earth mostly comes through the bottleneck of the embassy, which is staffed by a combination of red homunculi and slaves picked for their bookkeeping and organizational skills.

The human who oversees the office is a man from Earth called Jonas Gallway. In his translated form, he is a qephilim with a staff inscribed with magic spells. Gallway is efficient and hard-working, but like most of the humans working on behalf of the Betrayer, it's possible that he doesn't realize how far the Betrayer would go to gain power.

Slavers: Taking slaves betrays several of the Seven Rules at once, making "sinners" of every member of the handful of slaver guilds in Ardeyn. A few slaver guilds (including the Red Moon Wranglers and the Procurers) run a segment of their business in Megeddon, with the blessing of the Betrayer. The Betrayer allows slavers because he goes through experimental subjects fairly quickly; he needs raw material both for his Body Vats and his Soul Foundry.

The outlaw slaver Vera the Whip (a founder of the Red Moon Wranglers) is notorious in many territories of Ardeyn, though few enough would recognize her if they saw her. Stories of her exploits go beyond the believable, even for a magical place like Ardeyn. For instance, most doubt that she once lassoed the Red Moon with her whip. On the other hand, Vera's whip is an artifact from the Strange itself, and it has many properties that even Vera has yet to call upon.

KRYZORETH

Along the southwestern edge of the Borderlands lie the Hulks of Kryzoreth. The hulks are commonly considered to be vast, sentient bulks that are partly stone and partly alive. Their bodies form a series of rounded hills that, from a distance, resemble a pod of whales that has beached itself. The origin of the hulks is not certain, though they are not of Ardeyn. Most likely, they are remnants of a past planetovore's attempt to colonize. They could be inactive arcane superweapons, seeds of a new monstrous colonization, or something utterly alien. Whatever the case, they have not stirred; however, they do give a strange dream to those who live nearby.

The protective ridges of the hulks shelter some 10,000 people throughout the region.

The residents of Kryzoreth rely on the ridges for shelter against the weather that scours the Borderlands (tornadoes never touch down within a mile of a hulk, nor do temperatures spike or plummet), and they also seem to gain special contentment from the dreams. Every native (and those who've gone native) all share the same apparent contentment, tranquility, and peaceful ways, and they attribute it to "the dream." However, visitors to Kryzoreth characterize the dream they experience as an indescribable nightmare, and they usually try to avoid sleeping through the use of stimulant drinks or magic.

Kryzoreth families with the most gifted dreamers claim noble blood (though how the Kryzoreth natives measure "gifted dreaming" is uncertain), and these families dwell in hollowed-out cavities within the hulks themselves. How deep these cavities and tunnels run is unknown, though stories suggest that they allow one to walk into a literal land of dreams.

Cliffwalkers: The Long Way Down guild keeps its headquarters in Kryzoreth in a city called Cliffside. The guild's members are called cliffwalkers. Cliffwalkers are usually not native to Kryzoreth, and they find the dreams disquieting, but they carry dreamstone charms fashioned by a member soul sorcerer to keep those dreams at bay.

The cliffwalkers are interested in exploring the sides of Ardeyn, because the percentage of cyphers that can be found around the termination zone (where the steep side-slopes of Ardeyn's cliffs become negative) is at least twice as high as along the Borderlands. The sale of cyphers is a lucrative business. However, cliffwalkers face not only the "final fall" in their work, but a host of monstrous creatures and extreme weather along the sides of the world.

Iron Road Traders: The reason that Kryzoreth isn't cut off from the rest of Ardeyn is due to the Iron Road, which is a caravan and courier guild that originally made most of its crowns helping the Long Way Downers sell their collected cyphers in the more civilized regions of Ardeyn. The Iron Road (named for the iron shoes their mounts are shod with) run regular trade caravans from Kryzoreth through the Green Wilds, to Port Talaat in Oceanus and on to Hazurrium, next Mandariel, then Kuambis, and back again to Kryzoreth in the Borderlands. Over time, they came to be counted upon as couriers, as associate traders to merchants unwilling to put up costs for their own caravan, and as road companions for adventurers wishing for a bit of extra security in return for serving as additional guards. It's rumored that the Iron Road also sends caravans to Megeddon and to the Court of Sleep.

The Iron Road maintains several caravanserai around Ardeyn. These elaborate roadside inns cater to all trade caravans (not just the Iron Road), and sometimes to lone travelers who have enough crowns. The structures are square with a wide central courtyard, which is where merchants set up stalls to trade their wares to other caravans. The roofed sections surrounding the courtyard contain accommodations, a common room, food stores, and other comforts of the road. In addition to providing shelter, Iron Road caravansaries are rumored to be places of rest and celebration where odd items and experiences can be found or rented.

Oracle Murmurs in Megeddon

Rogue Homunculus: A translucent-skinned lieutenant of the Betrayer went rogue and blood-mad, escaped the Borderlands, and now roams other parts of Ardeyn, raining death and mayhem on anything that gets in its way. A reward is being offered for anyone who can stop it, though who is offering the reward isn't exactly clear.

Stardust: In a mile-wide band surrounding the fortress of Megeddon, flecks of glittering material rain down, apparently from the stars themselves. Those who dare the ramparts of the terrible fortress can collect this supposed stardust. If dusted over a creature, the stardust grants the recipient 2 points of Armor for one day. The dust blazes and burns the entire time, dealing 1 point of damage per round until it's entirely gone. Those using it in this way have the best success when they obtain some kind of fire resistance ahead of time.

The Blood Mansion: Nine sisters inhabit an old qephilim ruin at a point somewhere along the border between Kuambis and Megeddon. A whole family once lived there—a family that apparently enjoyed the Betrayer's protection for a few years, possibly for a service rendered by an ancestor. In one night of blood, the sisters murdered their father, mother, and brothers and, legend has it, swore a pact to Lotan. That was when the Betrayer reversed his protection and put a price on the Lotanists' heads. Before the bounty could be collected, the Blood Mansion disappeared, though it reappears from time to time around the edges of Megeddon, as if never daring to stay in one place long. Travelers who oppose the Betrayer can find help from those who live within, but if the sisters truly serve Lotan, such service likely comes at a price too dear to pay.

Lone Daggers: The Lone Daggers is a name that parents frighten their children with, and that nobles use to strike fear in the hearts of their enemies. It is the most infamous assembly of assassins in Ardeyn, and its motherhouse is somewhere in Kryzoreth (though this is a secret known to only a few). The members use the same dream-suppressing charms as the cliffwalkers and all others who stay long in Kryzoreth and don't want to "go native."

The head of the Lone Daggers, a qephilim named Taw, is a master of illusion. She can hide her presence, seem as another, and most potently, make a contracted mark believe that he is walking across a street, when in reality he is walking off the edge of Ardeyn itself.

Taw: level 5, level 7 in all tasks related to creating illusions

Unscrupulous merchants, nobles with an eye to succession, necromancers who need more raw material, or villains who wish to put an end to meddling adventurers might hire a couple of Lone Daggers to take care of business.

SEVENTH SENTINEL

A stone statue of amazing size stands along the western Borderlands, gazing off into the Strange. Called the Seventh Sentinel because it is the only one of seven to survive into the present, the statue waits to defend the world. Some say that the sentinels moved and fought during the Age of Myth, but the Oracle of Ardeyn believes otherwise. The Oracle says that the sentinels weren't designed to fight Lotan, who was already bound into the form of the world of Ardeyn. Instead, they were set to watch for Lotan's siblings. The Incarnations knew how to wake the sentinels, a secret that is

LOTAN'S SIBLINGS

No account save for the Oracle's mentions anything about Lotan's siblings. This has prompted some to accuse the Oracle of being wrong, or of knowingly inventing fabulous stories to further enhance her all-seeing reputation. One thing's certain: If Lotan's siblings—whoever or whatever that means—really do need to be watched for, a single remaining sentinel out of seven that once stood is likely not enough.

widely rumored to have passed into the keeping of the Queendom. If true, it might explain why the nation of Mandariel has satisfied itself with border skirmishes and other machinations, and never quite declared open war on the rival nation to the north. For if the Seventh Sentinel were to rouse, it could lay waste to any nation in the Daylands or Borderlands, including Mandariel, and it might even vanquish the Betrayer himself.

NIGHT VAULT

The Night Vault is an extensive series of subterranean tunnels, caverns, seas and rivers, and vaults beneath Ardeyn. The tunnels and vaults are collectively called the Roads of Sorrow, and the Heart Core.

In the Night Vault, dead spirits wander, chased by umber wolves until collected by the Court of Sleep. At the center of the Night Vault, the heart of the Sinner is bound in chains in the Heart Core. Closer to the surface, other creatures inhabit the darkness.

The total area of the Night Vault, given its three-dimensional reach, is at least equal to all the lands of Ardeyn's surface, though few people realize it—usually because most don't like thinking about the Night Vault. Why? Because they don't like thinking about the place their immortal souls are eventually bound. Accessing the Night Vault isn't especially difficult—many surface caves, mines, and even deep tombs connect to older tunnels that become entries to the deeper passages.

ROADS OF SORROW

The Roads of Sorrow are the tunnels and vaults that honeycomb the Night Vault. Along them are spirits, demons, umber wolves, and sometimes creatures and organizations native to the Daylands, including their ruins, lairs, and mines (some newly dug, but more often ancient delvings).

The Roads of Sorrow are mostly composed of mazelike tunnels and chill vaults. Along these winding paths, the spirits of the dead seem drawn. A spirit that finds its way into the Night Vault wanders the endless dark roads until it's either run down and devoured by a pack of umber wolves, or it descends deeper into the Heart Core, where the fires of Lotan engulf it, transforming it into an ashen demon pledged to the Sinner. The Court of Sleep interferes with that process, sending umber judges to walk the Roads to collect wandering spirits before they are snared by the Sinner.

Though the Court of Sleep is the most well-known power in the Roads of Sorrow (and the Night Vault as a whole), other places with a reputation exist, including the Malah Sea and the Tomb of All Despairs.

FATE OF THE "SOUL"

If a creature from any recursion is slain in Ardeyn, unlike on Earth and most other recursions, the character may continue to exist as a spirit. Because of this, a PC has the potential to be rescued from the Night Vault and restored to a living body, if the PC's friends are resourceful or powerful enough to attempt such a task (a dangerous adventure, to be sure). If a PC dies in a different recursion or out in the Strange, though, even those native to Ardeyn do not enjoy the same possibility of redemption and renewed existence. Likewise, if someone travels to Ardeyn through an inapposite gate, their "souls" do not descend to the Night Vault when they die.

HALLS OF ADAMAN

The Halls of Adaman were quarried and carved by a coalition of the Qephilim of Lore and the Qephilim of Commerce. The halls, which were part city and part working mine, were renowned for their wealth and splendor, but that was long ago. Now the halls are home to evil. Sark, hydras, spirits of wrath, umber wolves, and demons dwell within. The treasures of the ancient qephilim remain within the Adaman, part of the hoards of the current residents.

A group of adventurer-prospectors known as Lost Coda has been scouting the halls and setting up mining operations, though it's hard going given the almost daily attack by creatures. Though not generally known, Lost Coda actually hails from Ruk. What they might be seeking isn't known, but their leader Kuvan Thema drives those who answer to him with an almost religious zeal.

Purple Room: Many areas within the ruined Halls of Adaman remain sealed, having never been breached by the succeeding waves of creatures that claimed the area after the original qephilim builders left. When such

The Estate suspects that through the connivance of OSR, powerful quickened people on Earth who are sick with terminal illnesses might travel to Ardeyn before they die.

Kuvan Thema: level 5, level 7 for all tasks related to persuasion, disguise, and deception

Umber wolf, page 295

Umber judge, page 285

areas are opened up, they often contain tombs of ancient qephilim still bearing their magical regalia, evil artifacts, creatures held in stasis as a prison, or treasuries. However, the Purple Room contains something less obvious but very deadly: a magical plague that is both lethal and sentient. To take effect, the words printed on the walls must be read (either aloud, or to oneself).

The magical words are mostly nonsensical. But the entire passage is long and involved, requiring a few minutes to fully read.

Screaming Rift: This ominous shaft is 50 feet (15 m) in diameter. It pierces a portion of the Halls that was once a city; however, the surrounding qephilim structures appear to have been blown out and away from the shaft. Wind screams as nearby air is sucked into the rift. The shaft drops 300 feet (91 m) in depth, right through a translation gate that leads to a different recursion. The recursion is apparently decaying, its rules collapsing, and its environment toxic to quickened creatures.

According to Estate records, the recursion accessible via the Screaming Rift offers no new foci for those who enter; instead, it translates them into the form of small insects that soon begin to lose their higher brain functions.

COURT OF SLEEP

Most of the kingdoms and institutions of the ancient qephilim have crumbled, recalled only in legend and from the ruins littered around Ardeyn. Of those that remain, the Court of Sleep is by far the most mysterious and feared; it is the remnant of the Incarnation of Death's realm.

A central domed vault 300 feet (91 m) high is the physical "court" of the Court of Sleep, and there the business of the realm is conducted both day and night. An orrery of Ardeyn depicting the land's sun, moons, and some of its most prominent stars depends from the dome's ceiling. A host of subsidiary domed vaults, chambers, tunnels, and deeper catacombs connect to the main chamber.

The Court of Sleep is composed mostly of qephilim who are mortal, but who have learned something of the talents of their ancestors. The business of the Court of Sleep includes the collection of wandering spirits, and once collected, an assessment by spirit magistrates. A magistrate weighs the quantity of sin clinging to a soul, and from that measure, determines the spirit's final fate. Spirits generally face five different fates, but only four of those fates are chosen for them by a magistrate:

Dream Wanderer: Most spirits end up as dream wanderers; they're not so good, so evil, or so remarkable in some other way that they require special handling. The spirit becomes a dream wanderer when it is invested into one of the thousands of urns stored in the carefully delved Dream Catacombs situated beneath the Court of Sleep. A dream wanderer, once invested, wanders through generally pleasant dream realms and can visit still-living loved ones in their dreams if the loved one visits the place where the spirit's physical remains were interred (such as the Path of the Dead). Someone with a power over spirits could call or remotely question dream wanderers. In addition, if a visiting petitioner can make a good enough case, a dream wanderer could be freed from its urn and given to the petitioner.

Reincarnated: A very few spirits are so righteous or so important (or, as some whisper, paid such a large indulgence ahead of time) that they are selected for reincarnation. The manner of the spirit's reincarnation varies from spirit to spirit—some spirits return as newborns with past-life memories, others as adults in new forms, some as magical artifacts, and a very few just as they appeared before they died.

Deathless Watcher: Spirits with too great a burden of sin do not become dream wanderers, nor are they chosen to be reincarnated for their good works. However, they are reincarnated, in a manner of speaking: they are imbued into relief-carved images along subterranean tunnels of the Roads of Sorrow and along the known passages leading into the Heart Core where Lotan's heart burns. Deathless watchers are the sleepless sentinels that guard against living intruders and demons, because both the living and the dead fear their scrutiny. Deathless watchers can't be called, but people with power over spirits can remotely question them.

Imprisoned: Spirits heavy with both sin and residual power are dangerous—they are the ones most strongly drawn to Lotan, and they make the most powerful demons if they complete their journey. They also have a way of returning to life (or sometimes, unlife) to continue their evil ways. Because of this latter tendency, a certain section of the catacombs is set aside for them. Each prisoner has his own mortared cell, and each is imbued into an iron ball chained to the cell's floor. The imprisoned can't be called or remotely questioned by people with power over spirits.

Demon: Demons are the spirits that slip through the nets of umber judges and spirit magistrates and find their way to Lotan. They become nasty entities of irredeemable evil. Those with a power over spirits can sometimes call or remotely question a demon, but demons are not simple spirits. To call one, even by accident, usually ends with the caller or questioner being possessed by evil.

Spirit Pools

Spirit pools are prized sources of free magic that condense in certain Night Vault chambers like pools of water, albeit water that glows with firefly essence. Caverns containing spirit pools are difficult to find but enormously valuable, which is one reason adventurers sometimes brave the dangers of the Night Vault. Living denizens of the vault (including the Court of Sleep) sometimes inhabit the areas around spirit pools to draw upon their magic.

Someone trained in using spirit pool magic can manifest several impressive effects while adjacent to one. Effects commonly include the ability to teleport between previously visited pools, and the ability to modify any task, attack, or defense roll by three steps to the user's benefit. Powerful NPCs sometimes build lairs within these chambers to capitalize on the benefits a spirit pool confers.

Traveler's Rest: Living visitors, petitioners, and traders who come to the Court of Sleep have to stay someplace, and that place is a medium-sized dome carved with deathless watchers trained to let the living pass in peace, as long as they each carry a pass in the form of a special black stone. Lareb Nume, a qephilim who oversees Traveler's Rest, hands out these black stones to those who show up at the gate and ask for entry. A living traveler can safely remain in the Court of Sleep until the stone completely crumbles to dust.

Lareb Nume: level 5

Lareb takes his black stones from an artifact called the Dry Well found elsewhere in the Court of Sleep.

Traveler's Rest is set up something like a caravanserai, in that traders create temporary stalls to sell food to petitioners and others with business before the Court. Some of the wares on sale can't be found anywhere else in Ardeyn, and they include additional dry stones, dream elixirs, spirit fobs, and death indulgences. Traveler's Rest also boasts accommodations and a gathering hall, where visitors can mingle and hear proclamations by Court of Sleep officials, including Lareb.

Catacombs: The catacombs are hand-carved subterranean passages beneath the Court of Sleep. When a spirit is judged by a Court

Oracle Murmurs in the Night Vault

Sark Lair: A group of sark kept a lair deep in the Night Vault but ventured to the surface for raids at night. These sark successfully raided an Iron Road caravan carrying both riches and an idol of special power said to grant wealth. They carried it back down into their lair but were slain by demons drawn to the idol. The riches and idol lie somewhere below ground, waiting to be found by the brave or the foolhardy.

Nightcap Shrooms: Many types of fungus grow along the Roads of Sorrow, and many of them are poison, though some specimens are nutritious, and a few grant strange visions and temporary abilities. The most famous is nightcap, which if properly prepared allows a user to see a few seconds into the future. If improperly prepared or too much is taken, it drives the user insane.

Spirit of Incarnation: Many spirits wander the Roads of Sorrow, though one spirit is said to be the dead soul of the original Incarnation of Desire, who glows with the light that burns both living creatures and other spirits (including demons). If one could approach the spirit and wake it from its millennial trance, one's heart's desire might be granted.

spirit magistrate and selected to be a dream wanderer, the spirit is invested into one of the thousands of clay urns stored therein. Besides the urns set on the floor and in special niches throughout the multilevel passageways, the catacombs also host centuries of decorations, which include inscriptions, paintings, statues, ornaments, and other items that have accumulated. Most of these were used by petitioners and other visitors to identify, immortalize, and show respect to the dead.

Rumor has it that many of the inscriptions, paintings, and other decorations hold hidden messages, encrypted orders, and other secrets put there by certain Ardeyn organizations both long extinct and still active in a manner unlikely to be discovered (or erased) by others. If there is any truth to the rumors, the Court of Sleep doesn't seem interested in stopping the flow of information to new visitors and petitioners to the catacombs.

Heart Core

At the center of the Night Vault is the Heart Core. Finding it is not easy; the Court of Sleep blocks up nearly every access it finds down to the Heart Core, leaving just one open so it can channel traffic. This passage is continuously monitored by deathless watchers, whose regard is anathema to spirits of every sort, including those still inside living bodies. Other passages into the Core open from time to time, though by what process no one in the Court has quite figured out—it is presumed to be the will of Lotan himself. Searching for, then collapsing, newly opened passages to the Heart Core is something that the Court of Sleep often pays various groups of adventurers to take on.

Lotan's body isn't in the Heart Core, because his body is the entire expanse of Ardeyn itself. Instead his heart burns there, secured with seven red-hot chains at the center of a magma sea. Lotan's heart isn't the rocky organ one might expect—instead it has taken on the semblance of a fiery monstrosity, vaguely humanoid, that spends its centuries straining against the chains. A black miasma of bodiless demons, visible as streamers of ashen smoke, swirl around the chamber, singing to their master in atonal voices meant to soothe Lotan. But Lotan can never be calmed, not until he achieves freedom—a freedom that would shake Ardeyn to nothing and launch Lotan into the Strange as a planetovore-class entity with a direct connection to Earth. This would likely doom the Earth.

Ardeyn Artifacts

In Ardeyn, artifacts are usually magical and sorcerous items created during the Age of Myth. While they're in Ardeyn, they seem to equal (or sometimes surpass) the powers of cyphers, but just like mundane equipment, artifacts are not usually able to translate.

Artifacts are sometimes found in old ruins, in the possession of powerful NPCs, or as part of the hoard of a fierce creature. They can even be bought in towns, but this occurs much more rarely than most PCs would probably like. A few claim to forge new artifacts, though that number can be counted on one hand.

Dragon's Eye

Level: 1d6 + 3

Form: A ruby eye lens on a strap

Effect: The wearer can see normally through the lens. When activated, the wearer can see objects up to 5 miles (8 km) away within direct line of sight as if they were within immediate range for up to one minute. If a wearer makes a ranged attack while the dragon's eye is activated, the wearer gains an asset to the attack.

Depletion: 1–2 in 1d100

DRAGONTONGUE WEAPON

Level: 1d6 + 2

Form: A weapon that roars with red flame when activated, trailing a streamer of black smoke

Effect: This weapon functions as a normal weapon. If the wielder uses it to attack a foe, upon a successful hit, the wielder decides whether to activate the flame. Upon activation, the blade lashes the target with fire, inflicting additional points of damage from the heat equal to the cypher level. The effect lasts for one minute after each activation.

Depletion: 1 in 1d100

MASK OF OCEANUS

Level: 1d6

Form: A foam-green mask that covers the lower half of a humanoid's face, smelling of the sea

Effect. When activated, the wearer can breathe underwater for one hour.

Depletion: 1 in 1d20

MONITOR'S MONOCLE

Level: 1d6 + 2

Form: A mask that resembles a single large glass lens

Effect: This device possesses a few different optically related abilities.

Memory of What Was: The monocle captures a perfect image of a nearby scene. Thousands of images can be stored, and any stored image can be shown back to the wearer. When the monocle is depleted, all stored images are lost.

Query of What Is: A foe seen through the monocle can be analyzed for a weak spot. The analysis allows the wearer of the monocle to use points from his Intellect Pool to increase the damage of his attacks by 3 points per level of Effort.

Vision of What Will Be: The wearer catches a glimpse of a probable future, which, if acted on, serves as an asset to initiative rolls.

Depletion: 1 in 1d100

RING OF DRAGON'S FLIGHT

Level: 1d6 + 2

Form: A green iron ring that appears like a dragon wound around the finger

Effect: When the wearer activates the ring, dragon wings unfurl from his back, and for one minute he can fly up to long range. The ring does not confer the ability to hover or make fine adjustments while in flight.

Depletion: 1–2 in 1d20

RUNE STAFF (ASHUR)

Level: 1d6 + 2

Form: A staff scribed with sparking runes promising destruction

Effect: This enchanted staff (sometimes called an ashur) emits a crackling arc of lightning at a target within long range. Targets hit by the arc take damage equal to the artifact's level.

This device is a rapid-fire weapon, and thus can be used with the Spray or Arc Spray abilities that some characters have, but each "round of ammunition" used or each additional target selected requires an additional depletion roll.

An ashur sips vitality from its wielder's soul to spit its destruction. If a depletion roll indicates the ashur is depleted, the wielder can choose to substitute a portion of his soul energy instead of letting the ashur be depleted. When the wielder does so, he descends one step on the damage track.

Depletion: 1 in 1d20

RUNE WEAPON OF BLOOD

Level: 1d6

Form: A weapon with blood-red runes promising pain carved into the metal

Effect: This weapon functions as a normal weapon of its kind. However, it always inflicts 1 additional point of damage.

Depletion: —

RUNE WEAPON OF STRIKING

Level: 1d6 + 1

Form: A weapon with blue runes promising the inescapability of wounds carved into the metal

Effect: This weapon functions as a normal weapon of its kind. However, attacks with the weapon are modified by one step to the wielder's benefit.

Depletion: —

Artifacts that specify "weapon" can be any kind of weapon the GM chooses from the weapons described under Ardeyn Equipment on page 89. But if in doubt, it's hard to go wrong by choosing the form of a shamshir (scimitar) or talwar (great shamshir).

SHADOW CLOAK

Level: 1d6 + 2

Form: A cape of black leather with a hood

Effect: When the hood of the cape is drawn over the wearer's head as an action, the cloak renders the wearer difficult to detect for up to one hour. While the cloak is active, all stealth and Speed defense tasks are modified by two steps in the wearer's favor, as are attempts to detect the wearer in any other fashion. This effect ends each round the wearer does something to reveal its presence or position, such as attacking, using a flashy ability, moving a large object, moving quickly, and so on. If this occurs, the wearer automatically regains the cloaking effect by taking no action next turn.

Depletion: 1–2 in 1d100, but instead of the artifact being depleted, the wearer must succeed on difficulty 5 Intellect defense roll or become hidden so well that no one can find her ever again (not even the wearer herself).

Cursed Soul Weapons: *Some soul weapons are cursed so that when they are depleted, they require another soul to take the place of the one previously bound to the weapon. This means the current wielder's soul is forfeit unless she kills the nearest sentient creature.*

SHAMSHIR TWINBLADE

Level: 1d6 + 1

Form: A central hilt with a shamshir blade extending from both ends

Effect: This weapon functions as a normal weapon of its kind. However, the wielder can choose to make two attacks as her action on the same target or two adjacent targets. Doing so requires a depletion roll.

Depletion: 1–2 in 1d100

SOUL SHEATH

Level: 1d6 + 2

Form: A sheath for a weapon, usually bladed

Effect: When a blade of any kind is sheathed in a soul sheath (which is tied to the wearer's soul), both become insubstantial. A mental command causes the blade and sheath to become substantial once more, and if drawn as part of the same action, the blade is briefly empowered: the wielder takes 1 point of Intellect damage (which ignores Armor), but the blade inflicts additional points of damage equal to the artifact level for ten minutes.

Depletion: 1–2 in 1d100

SOUL WEAPON

Level: 1d6 + 3

Form: A weapon with steaming, bone-white runes that describe a soul-binding spell

Effect: This weapon functions as a normal weapon of its kind. However, attacks with the weapon are modified by one step to the wielder's benefit. Using the weapon in this way does not require a depletion roll. A few weapons can speak in the voice of the bonded soul and have personalities of their own.

Soul weapons have a variety of potential secondary abilities, which depend upon the soul imparted to the weapon when it was forged. Use of a soul weapon's secondary abilities requires a depletion roll.

Roll	Effect
01–10	On a hit, deal extra damage equal to weapon level of a kind specific to the weapon. Roll 1d6. Enabler. 1 fire 4 acid 2 cold 5 flesh-decaying 3 lightning 6 thunder
11–30	The wielder can make a free recovery roll. Action.
31–40	Wielder gains +5 to Armor against a kind of energy specified in the first entry for one hour. Action.
41–50	The weapon acts as a spiritslaying weapon. Enabler.
51–75	For one hour, the weapon is transformed into a creature whose level equals the weapon's level. The creature must obey the wielder's commands. Action to initiate.
76–90	The weapon can attack a target that the wielder can see within long range. It fires an energy ray of a kind specified in the first entry

that deals damage equal to the weapon's level. Action.

91–00	Attacks with the weapon are modified another step in the wielder's favor. Enabler.

Depletion: 1–3 in 1d100

SPELLBOOK OF THE AMBER MAGE

Level: 1d6

Form: A weighty tome bound in amber filled with pages of spell runes

Effect: When the user incants from the spellbook and succeeds at a level 3 Intellect-based task, she can attempt to trap a creature within long range inside a block of amber. Only creatures whose level is equal to or lower than the artifact's level can be targeted. A creature successfully caught is preserved in perfect stasis until the encasing amber is broken away (the encasing amber has 10 points of health per level of the spellbook artifact).

Depletion: 1 in 1d20

SPELLBOOK OF DREADIMOS FELTHANE

Level: 1d6

Form: A weighty tome bound in bat wings filled with pages of spell runes

Effect: When the user incants from the spellbook and succeeds at a level 3 Intellect-based task, he can attempt to affect the minds of creatures within long range who are within immediate range of each other. Those affected become terrified; they drop what they are holding and do one of the following:

Roll	Action
01–50	Flee for 1d6 rounds
51–90	Cower (losing their actions for 1d6 rounds)
91–00	Faint, remaining unconscious for one minute (or until roused by vigorous action)

Depletion: 1 in 1d20

SPIRITSLAYING WEAPON

Level: 1d6 + 1

Form: A weapon with engraved glowing runes denoting spiritslaying

Effect: This weapon functions as a normal weapon of its kind. However, if the wielder uses an action to activate it, the weapon's spiritslaying magic is activated for one minute. During that minute, if it scores a hit, it inflicts normal damage on a fully insubstantial creature, plus 3 additional points of damage on all creatures.

Depletion: 1 in 1d100

SPIRIT WARD

Level: 1d6 + 2

Form: A tiny figurine of a winged qephilim

Effect: Once activated, the figurine's spirit emerges and becomes semisolid as a glowing, human-sized winged qephilim. It follows within 3 feet (1 m) of the figurine owner. Anything that attacks the owner is attacked by the spirit ward, which sends out a surge of flesh-rotting energy against all foes within immediate range, doing damage equal to the artifact level. Once activated, it functions for a day.

Depletion: 1 in 1d20

STRANGELANCE

Level: 1d6 + 1

Form: A lance scribed with runes naming the Seven Incarnations of Ardeyn

Effect: This weapon functions as a normal lance. However, attacks with the weapon against Strangers (creatures native to the Strange, such as kray) are modified by one step to the wielder's benefit; this effect does not require a depletion roll.

Upon a successful hit against a Stranger, the wielder decides whether to activate an additional effect. If activated, the weapon flares with an echo of the Seven Rules, inflicting 8 additional points of damage (ignores Armor); this effect does require a depletion roll.

Depletion: 1 in 1d20

WINGS OF THE SUN

Level: 1d6 + 1

Form: A cloak; when deployed, flaring wings form from the wearer's arms

Effect: The wings can be deployed as an action. The wearer can fly a long distance each round (a difficulty 1 Speed task). Each hour of use or new deployment of the wings requires a depletion roll.

In combat, the wearer can use the wings as a weapon, dealing 5 points of damage in melee.

Depletion: 1–2 in 1d100

Many spellbooks exist in Ardeyn, each the work of a famous (or infamous) sorcerer or group of sorcerers.

Spellbooks each have a listed effect, but spellbooks could also produce related effects if the GM allows. For example, the spellbook of the amber mage might also be used to create a block of amber large enough to seal a doorway.

Spiritslaying arrows and bolts can also be found. Such items are usually part of a set of twelve pieces within an engraved quiver.

CHAPTER 13

RUK

RUK ATTRIBUTES

Level: 4
Laws: Mad Science
Playable Races: Humans
Foci: Adapts to Any Environment, Infiltrates, Integrates Weaponry, Metamorphosizes, Processes Information, Regenerates Tissue, Spawns
Skills: Ruk Lore, All-Song Navigation
Connection to Strange: Anyone in Ruk can see the Strange in the distance. At the edge of the recursion (called the Periphery), this view is very clear, while elsewhere it is pale and misty. Typically creatures in the Strange cannot see Ruk, nor enter it.
Connection to Earth: Various gates
Size: 200 miles across × 50 miles thick (320 km × 80 km)
Spark: Nearly 100%
Trait: Strange. For any creature with the spark who attempts to recognize and understand the Strange and its denizens, including identifying translated visitors from alternate recursions, as well as identifying and understanding cyphers, the difficulty to do so is modified by one step to its benefit.

Ruk is pronounced like duke.

WHAT A RECURSOR KNOWS ABOUT RUK

- Ruk operates under the law of Mad Science, and it is a place of extreme biotech and body modification.
- Ruk has hidden in Earth's shadow since before humanity evolved, and it comes from another place in the universe, apparently having fled an unremembered disaster.
- Feuding factions rule Ruk; a faction is like a religion, corporation, and governing body rolled into one.
- The True Code is the ancient knowledge of Ruk, much of which is lost, though many still cleave to it and attempt to rediscover it.
- The All Song is the communal web of knowledge, insight, and inspiration that many in Ruk rely on, though many believe that reliance comes at the expense of the True Code.

Ruk has hidden in Earth's shoals since before humanity evolved. Creatures that were never human populate Ruk, because fiction from somewhere else birthed this recursion. Ruk is a land of amazing technology, miracles of biological enhancement, and feuds that have burned since before humanity evolved.

In Ruk, the walls of the world are a literal fact, visible as massive organimer spars that pierce, protect, and lie shattered across the landscape. Outside the relative safety of Harmonious, the capital city, threats abound in the form of spore worms, venom troopers, constructs from the Qinod Singularity, and glial storms.

Organimer, page 194
Harmonious, page 196
Spore worm, page 293
Venom trooper, page 300
Qinod Singularity, page 208
Glial storm, page 195

Organimer is a level 6, quasi-living, metal material

Ruk's factions, powerful and ancient, strive always against each other. Lately, their strife is coming to a head, and the fate of Earth hangs in the balance.

ORIGINS OF RUK

Ruk was forged in the Strange as a massive "lifeboat" fleeing the apocalypse of a

civilization in the universe of normal matter being consumed by a planetovore. This lifeboat shipwrecked on the Shoals of Earth, where it has remained caught to this day. Ruk is far older than any human civilization—older even than humanity itself. Everyone knows these things, but the specifics of the events have somehow been lost to time.

For instance: What was the name of the world Ruk fled from, and what was the nature of the planetovore responsible? What was the shape of the original species Ruk natives sprang from, and why does the True Code not more clearly reveal this phenotype? Speaking of which, what led to the confusions in the True Code, and how did the All Song emerge? Did Ruk set off at random through the Strange, or did they have a specific goal in mind, as hints suggest?

Most blame the shipwreck itself for the loss of knowledge, but that's only partly true. Any devoted apostle of the True Code knows that a prior disruption happened sometime earlier, while Ruk still journeyed through the Strange. It seems likely that an external event in the Strange severely damaged Ruk and compromised its ability to survive. This damage was not only to the physical structure of Ruk, but also to the underlying True Code, on which everything depended. (The event is also when Ruk took aboard the Qinod Singularity, which manifests from time to time in the Periphery.)

It's all just guesswork at this point. But devotees of the All Song make a compelling case and say evidence for the All Song's inception appears around this time. They say the All Song arose first as a way to repair the damage done to the True Code, as a patch over what was lost with a chance for something new, and as a means to salvage a recursion on the cusp of collapsing into nothing. In a way, the All Song might be a divergence of the True Code. True Code apostles call that idea heresy, but the idea does lend the All Song even further importance in certain circles.

Shoals of Earth, page 214

True Code, page 192

All Song, page 192

CASTAWAYS

The heart of Ruk is an artificial construct. It is, for lack of a better term, a craft that once traveled through the Strange. True to the nature of the Strange, however, this craft is a recursion, created through the power of its creators' imaginations and their ability to

THE TRUE CODE AND THE ALL SONG

"We are ancient, for the True Code winds through us."
~Chant of the Embodiment

Biological form is relatively fluid in Ruk thanks to access to relatively quick genetic redesigns and modular grafts, but the natives also revere the True Code, the original basis of their race. Ruk scientists constantly look for fragments of their lost genetic origins that the True Code represents. Ruk religions, such as the Church of the Embodiment, honor their ancient ancestors, and some believe that a "scion of the True Code" will arise and make himself or herself known as a messianic figure.

The All Song sings through every cell of all engineered tissue in Ruk. A biological data network, it allows those of Ruk to store information and communicate over vast distances. A minor connection to the All Song exists for native Ruk residents at all times, but most use devices called umbilicals to tap more directly into the network. The presence of the All Song—some might say the *consciousness* of it—encourages more and more development in the arts of genetics and bioengineering through facilitation and advice. There are those who fear that the All Song is a direct contradiction of the True Code—a viral presence literally unwinding the natives of Ruk from their original heritage and taking them farther away from their revered past.

The so-called "riddle of Ruk," then, of which philosophers, poets, and priests speak, is the juxtaposition of the True Code and the All Song—the call toward the past and the impetus toward the future—and its effect on all the natives of this world/craft. Most embrace the contradictions of their nature, the contradictions they find in life, and even the contradictions of the situation in which they find themselves wanting to see Earth as both friend and foe.

impress their will on the roiling chaos there. Unlike most recursions, Ruk could move, traveling down the informational canals by constantly writing and rewriting the laws that govern the Strange. And move it did, for its builders had fashioned Ruk as the means to escape a disaster (presumably, one or more planetovores that had consumed their native world, though histories are fragmented).

Ruk suffered a few terrible mishaps along the way, but it continued onward until one day, millennia after its journey began, but even more millennia before today, Ruk was caught fast. Inexplicable properties from a nearby world had stopped its progression. Ruk had run aground. The ship was now damaged and stuck—a shipwreck.

As years passed, some of those native to Ruk began to think of the new world—Earth—in whose shoals their craft now lay as a potential permanent haven. They saw that Earth was unique. Perhaps it was no accident the ship had fled in Earth's direction through the Strange in the first place, though no single piece of historical evidence remains to validate that idea. Many in Ruk decided that Earth might be a place whose proximity could offer true shelter from those that destroyed their homeworld. Yet others reckoned that Earth's destruction by the planetovores was the only thing that would free them from their predicament and allow them to continue on their way.

EARTH'S DISOVERY OF RUK

Humanity first became aware of Ruk's existence only a short time ago. The forensic pathologist Rafaela Rocha in Sao Paulo ended up with a corpse on her table that outwardly appeared to be human but was decidedly something else. Before she could even consider submitting her findings to the science journals, her work inadvertently triggered a kind of organic device within the corpse, translating her and some of her coworkers to Ruk.

The team of Brazilians survived in what they first thought was a hostile alien world, then believed to be an alternate, parallel dimension. Whatever Ruk's true origin, it was clear that it was a place where genetic engineering and biotechnology had risen to heights undreamt of on Earth, but also a place inextricably bound to Earth. After all, many Ruk natives look like humans, which was why it was all the more surprising for Rafaela to learn that she and her team might be the very first humans ever to come to Ruk. And perhaps even more surprising, it seemed that people from Ruk had been traveling to Earth since before recorded history. It was even probable that a few significant figures from Earth's history were, in fact, beings from Ruk.

Rafaela and her team spent many days in Ruk, passing as natives thanks to being translated into the recursion. They finally came to the notice of a Quiet Cabal initiate named Shallarum-ahmak, who took Rafaela and her team under his wing. If the Karum or another less Earth-oriented faction had recognized the explorers for what they were first, things might have gone far differently for everyone involved.

LIFE IN RUK

The people of Ruk, for the most part, appear to be identical to Earth humans. Extensive eugenics and direct genetic modification over the course of human evolution altered the people of Ruk considerably, so an unmodified Ruk native can pass as human, and a human can easily pass as someone from Ruk. Most believe that originally, people from Ruk did not look like Earth humans at all, but that they have reshaped themselves to better and more easily interact with people of their adopted prime world. The fact that such a fundamental piece of data is in dispute indicates how little of their original homeworld or race the inhabitants of Ruk actually remember.

Ruk is small and sparsely populated. Most people live in the capital city, known as Harmonious, while others live in smaller, scattered communities in the Hub or Periphery. Over half the population works in science-related fields, whether as bioengineers, genetic technicians, or as workers in the processing plants who take harvested biological matter and create whatever is needed. Even the metals, plastics, and other materials in Ruk, which would seem to be inorganic, were originally organic material. The most popular building material is organimer, a quasi-living metal.

Food is created artificially, using resources taken from the biomass of regions called the grey forests. Many simply use nutrient injections rather than eat.

Only about half the inhabitants of Ruk experienced a natural birth. The others were grown in vats. Regardless, familial connections are carefully monitored due to the genetic lineage, but they contain only passing emotional importance. Children are raised communally. Those with great promise are quickly adopted by a powerful faction and trained in a valuable profession.

With few exceptions, every Ruk native speaks the native language, Rukic, as well as at least one of the major languages of Earth (typically Mandarin, Spanish, English, Hindi, or Arabic). When someone translates into Ruk, she chooses the language she wishes the translation to provide for "free." Learning other languages is something a player character can choose to do the old-fashioned way, if desired.

FACTIONS

Ruk has no central government. Instead, a number of factions with various agendas provide individual power structures. Small, often clandestine wars between rival factions are conducted all the time. The largest and most powerful organizations include the following.

The Church of the Embodiment: Largest of Ruk's factions, the Church of the Embodiment believes that adhering to and preserving the True Code will result in a messiah that will bring peace, order, and stability to Ruk.

The Karum: So-called nihilists, the Karum believe that if Earth were destroyed, Ruk would be free of its pull. Karum agents travel to Earth frequently in the guise of helping humans advance their knowledge of science and high-energy particle physics. What they are really attempting to do is create conditions

Rafaela Rocha: level 5; psychically learns one random fact about a person or location that is pertinent to a topic she designates once per day

"Most people just leave well enough alone and don't dig any deeper into Maggie Lawrence. But not you. Now you know who I really am. What are we going to do about that?" ~Udam-magir, secret agent of the Estate's "sister" agency, the Quiet Cabal

that might result in a planetovore finding and destroying the prime world. A Karum agent with one of the best records in advancing the cause is Dadanum-tal, though on Earth he goes by Dr. Gavin Bixby, professor of nuclear research.

For more on the Quiet Cabal and its "work" on Earth, see page 153.

The Quiet Cabal: The counter to the Karum, the Quiet Cabal is an organization with a covert arm seeking to preserve Earth, for they believe that if Earth is destroyed, Ruk will be as well. A secret war has waged in Ruk and Earth for millennia between these two groups. The Cabal has no single leader, employing many self-starting agents to accomplish its goals.

The Unified Choir: A particularly powerful faction in Harmonious, this group is interested in the advancement of science and the people of Ruk as a whole. The Choir is willing to sacrifice the needs (and even the lives) of individuals for the good of the race. Choir-Scientist Ummi-natar is one of the most well-known advocates of the "Unification," and his wise and calming words do much to promote the position of the organization. Most people outside the Tower of Unification don't know the kinds of experiments Ummi-natar commonly performs on living and usually conscious subjects. Some might call those experiments questionable.

Choir-Scientist Ummi-natar: level 4, level 6 for all research-based tasks

Unification is the radical philosophy some in Ruk preach. Unification proposes that the True Code and the All Song be synthesized into a single entity, and suggests that they may already be, in fact, alternate sides of the same coin.

Zal: To an Earth native, the faction of Zal appears very much like a large and wealthy corporation. Zal's goal is ultimately the advancement and profit of its members, in particular those at the top of its hierarchy. Zal controls more of the mobile factories in the Periphery than any other faction, although they have a powerful presence in Harmonious as well. Led by charismatic and loquacious Chief Advancement Officer (CAO) Sin-ixtab, the company's products and services are ubiquitous throughout Ruk. The most prominent of these are the many All Song communals that citizens, no matter their allegiance, can enjoy at no cost.

Sin-ixtab: level 5, level 6 for all interaction tasks

THE SHAPE OF RUK

Ruk was originally a near-perfect disk. As the millennia passed after it ran aground in Earth's shoals, Ruk began to grow like a living thing. This organic "edge" to Ruk is called the Periphery. Over time, it began to grow slowly. In recent centuries, that growth has accelerated so that today, the edge in any given region of the Periphery usually grows about a centimeter, but sometimes up to a meter or more in a day.

Grey forest spores: level 4 hallucinogens that last for 1d6 hours, or level 5 poisons that inflict 3 points of damage every ten minutes for one hour

Ruk's central portion is often referred to as the Hub or the Core. Most inhabitants dwell in the Hub, in Harmonious. Areas beyond Harmonious, both in the Hub and in the Periphery, are primarily used for resource harvesting (organic matter from the grey forests being the most extensive). The farther one travels from Harmonious, the more dangerous a frontier Ruk becomes.

Although the inhabitants use terms that can be translated as "day" and "night" (as well as "weeks," "months," and "years") to mark the passage of time, Ruk is forever enshrouded in twilight. Ruk has no sun, nor does its sky ever show stars, other than the ghostly form of the Earth itself and a few pale white lights seen in the grey mists—a result of the everpresent Strange that surrounds the recursion.

SPAR JUNGLES AND SHATTERED WASTES

The damage Ruk sustained when it "ran aground" near Earth shaped much of its geography, even today. The massive disk broke, leaving upturned and twisted structural elements throughout much of the Hub. These are known as the Spar Jungles, and they are some of the most dangerous areas in Ruk, home to outlaw gangs and horrific wild beasts.

Between the Spar Jungles are the Shattered Wastes, debris fields that stretch for miles, often without much water or life. The spars are forged organimer, the quasi-living metal that Ruk was originally built from. Organimer heals itself if damaged, although if greatly damaged, it either dies or can grow back imperfectly, which has led to the wrecked and twisted landscape of Ruk. Damaged organimer (such as that used in the basis of Ruk itself) may continue to grow without bound, beyond the intent of the original designers.

THE GREY FORESTS

Throughout Ruk, forests of exotic fungi grow, with fields of globular sporepods, broad mushrooms, and tall stalks of fruiting bodies. Most of these fungi grow very quickly, bloom, and then die in just a matter of a few weeks. This cycle occurs constantly, as Ruk experiences no seasons.

Traveling through a grey forest is usually dangerous, since the fungi produce hallucinogenic and poisonous spores in thick clouds. The only creatures that dwell in the forests are immune to these spores, although

it is not uncommon for masked or biomodded explorers, hunters, and harvesters to enter for short periods.

Huge mobile factories move through these fungi forests on hundreds of insect-like legs, harvesting material and producing biotech goods as well as food and substances needed for more biotech processes and experimentation. Zal owns many of these so-called "grey harvesters," though some are owned by small co-ops, families, and not a few free-booting captains who make their haul by stealing from the harvests of others.

GLIAL STORMS

When Ruk became damaged, so did the True Code. The All Song was liberated in an attempt to patch the True Code, but in many places, the damage was too extensive. Bioelectrical fields remain upset even after the millennia, and no one has had the ability to set them right. Manifestations of this imbalance are called glial storms, and they appear to be moving cascades of scintillating energy. In actual fact, glial storms are discharges of built-up, uncontrolled neural discharges from the All Song itself.

Normally, these move across the landscape—usually around the Periphery of Ruk rather than the central Hub—at speeds of 10 to 20 miles (16 to 32 km) an hour. They are often a mile or more across, and they randomly burst with deadly energies and—even stranger—bits of information or random ideas, some of which have been known to drive people mad.

A PC caught out in a glial storm must make Intellect defense rolls every minute or so, with a difficulty equal to the severity of the storm. Failed defense rolls usually result in Intellect damage.

Fortunately, glial storms are more rare now than they used to be.

Glial storms are usually level 4 but can be as high as level 6 (inflicting damage appropriate to their level).

THE HUB

The Hub is the original extent of Ruk, and the most important part of the Hub is Harmonious, the Glistening City. Besides Harmonious, just a couple of other regions of note can be found, mostly in the subsurface areas not normally considered part of the Glistening City. These regions are sometimes allied with interests in the city and sometimes at odds, but all of them depend on the resources available in the Periphery in one fashion or another.

Most places in the Hub are policed, monitored, and cleaned, though exceptions exist, especially outside Harmonious proper, but locations also exist within the city that are the opposite of glistening.

Besides Harmonious, the next most significant area of the Hub is the Glistening City's sister, the Shadowed City, which lies immediately beneath it. Beneath both (and interpenetrating all the Hub) is the Veritex, a system of subterranean tunnels.

Factions come and go in Ruk, though the largest and most popular persist for so long that they may seem like permanent fixtures. However, as the once-powerful Ankaseri faction's demise proved, even a large faction can stumble and fall. Ankaseri was a faction that dabbled in both consumer-grade and military-grade grafts, but it fell afoul of too many of its own internal secrets, which were finally "called due" by Arbiter Maru-shtal.

HARMONIOUS, THE GLISTENING CITY

At the very center of Ruk lies its largest and most sophisticated city, Harmonious. The majority of the city floats above the surface of the world, a multileveled horizontal metropolis defying gravity via massive and ancient technological engines. An undercity, called the Shadowed City, lies on the ground below and grows in size every year.

Harmonious is reached by flying craft and dozens of pneumatic elevator tubes that stretch down to the surface. (At one time, these tubes could be retracted for defense, but it's unknown whether the mechanisms still function.) Given the nature of the city, people also travel from structure to structure (or between widely separated locations on the same structure) through a variety of rented craft, personal transport devices (wing gliders being most popular), and physical metamorphosis, using myriad aerial piers and masts placed throughout Harmonious. Some of these methods of transport are robust enough to serve travelers who wish to leave Harmonious (or even the Hub) behind and flit off over the near Periphery or even farther locations.

Arbiter Maru-shtal: level 7; Armor 4; four Myriand veterans are always close, acting as bodyguards

Living quarters make up a good part of Harmonious: over a hundred thousand people dwell in the Glistening City. But living in Harmonious isn't a right; it's a privilege, earned by keeping up one's standing within a recognized faction. Those who do maintain their allegiances are comfortable, are engaged in vital employment, have copious opportunities for entertainment, and suffer no lack of sufficient shelter, food, and social opportunities. Neighborhoods span multiple levels and are connected with glowing bridges, open balconies, and free-floating elevators (for those who don't have a wing glider handy).

Periphery, page 205
Qinod construct, page 286
Myriand, page 281

Gardens shining with bioluminescent plant, animal, and even organimer flowers are quite the rage in Harmonious. Sometimes the fruits of such a neighborhood garden can rival the quality of products being produced by Zal and other factions.

The parts of Harmonious not given over to living quarters are a vast sprawl of faction administration buildings, markets, transformation hostels, tissue libraries, resource processing facilities, amusement parks, laboratories, All Song communals, pleasure quarters, and other areas that are more difficult to describe. At the center is the physical location of the Church of the Embodiment.

The many markets of Harmonious mostly exist in one magnificent swath of storefronts and galleries that ascend, in spiral fashion, a set of three interconnected large towers in the city. So bedazzling and bedecked with lights is the so-called Market Tri-Tower that it's possible the city gets its moniker from its glistening expanse.

FACTIONS AND FACTOL COUNCIL

The comfort that the people of Harmonious enjoy comes at the cost of their personal freedom. Anyone attempting to survive in the city without allegiance (or a contract) to one of the major factions is going to find life difficult. That's because a faction in Ruk is a different beast than a faction on Earth. A Ruk faction has the combined power of a corporation, a religious sect, and a political entity all rolled into one. Factions do more than promote a philosophy; each recognized faction sends a representative to sit on the Factol Council.

Representatives to the Factol Council are each supposed to wield roughly equal political power, but in practice that's not always true, which is why the council defers close decisions to the Office of the Arbiter.

Currently that office is held by Arbiter Maru-shtal, who made her name in the Periphery hunting spore worms and rogue Qinod constructs before giving up her weapons in return for the scintillating robes of office. As the arbiter, Maru-shtal has the ability to send directives to the Myriand, the faction responsible for keeping peace in Harmonious. Maru-shtal is direct, doesn't flinch in handing down harsh verdicts, and reacts poorly to bribes or other attempts to sway her arbitrations. This was demonstrated by the fact that Maru-shtal once had a twin brother. The Ankaseri faction attempted to use

"The development of the recursion pod is a triumph of bioengineering and is hailed everywhere as proof that adherence to the All Song's guidance is the proper path for Ruk."

~Zal Chief Advancement Officer Sin-ixtab

his life as a bargaining chip to sway her on a decision. Maru-shtal didn't hesitate in ordering a strike on Ankaseri's tower, courtesy of a host of Myriand, ending both Ankaseri's reign as a faction and her brother's life.

CHURCH OF THE EMBODIMENT

At the center of Harmonious is the Church of the Embodiment (also sometimes called the Cathedral of the True Code). The faction basilica serves as a residence, research center, and temple for disseminating information during public ceremonies. The church has many apostles, including Apostle Warad-chel, who is high in the hierarchy, but not so high that he can't go out into the field to defend the "interests" of the True Code. Warad-chel has been implicated in more than a couple of incidents that almost led to disciplinary action by the faction, but for reasons that are not completely clear, First Apostle Ah-kalla has refused to bring his disfavor down on his most favored of Servitors. In fact, the First Apostle has gone so far as to say that the True Code has never woken so strongly in a modern person as in the body of Warad-chel.

The church's overarching goal is to uncover the full and complete True Code. All its other practices, policies, and projects are a means to that end.

Those who become apostles of the church can take communion. According to the Church, when a wafer of bread is synthesized from the True Code, whosoever eats of it becomes a vessel of ancient Ruk, and thus they strengthen their ties to what is most important.

Whatever the process is, results are real. Anyone who takes communion gains an asset on their next Intellect-based task related to the True Code if the task is performed within an hour of taking communion. Those who take communion directly from First Apostle Ah-kalla gain more significant advantages. (Most assume the greater boon comes about because of the First Apostle's deep knowledge, which is indirectly true: he uses a platter of the True Code to offer communion.)

Apostle Warad-chel: level 5, level 7 for all tasks relating to seeing through guile and trickery

First Apostle Ah-kalla: level 6; Armor 3; wields the communion platter of the True Code

Communion platter of the True Code, page 209

True Form Project: The Church of the Embodiment knows that a little of the True Code lies in the genetic code of every Ruk native, beneath the humaniform phenotype, which is why the church sponsors several labs around Harmonious (and a few outside it) where genetic research is conducted. Currently, the church is investigating the possibility that the original Ruk form was humanoid, but more akin to Earth lizards than simians. This theory was suggested by a few artifacts found on Earth at the Al Ubaíd archeological site in Iraq from a period that predates Sumerian culture. The labs are looking for a slew of new volunteers to test this latest theory, though rumors suggest that for some reason the latest round of tests trigger dangerous mutations that can't be controlled.

Rediscovery Project: Snippets of the True Code are sometimes found in the plasma and genetic code of newly generated creatures and plants that grow wild along the bleeding edge of Ruk. Church doctrine explains that Ruk's continual growth is a direct result of the True Code attempting to renew itself, iterating every year to find what was lost. Their faith is well placed, since sometimes expeditions to the edge stumble across genetic treasures. These discoveries allow them to use the True Code to accomplish tasks that previously required the All Song, such as was the case for biosplice companions.

Biosplice companion, page 209

MYRIAND

Law and order is maintained in Harmonious by a host of battle chrysalides (Myriand volunteers and Myriand veterans) that patrol all the levels of the city, and sometimes even venture into the Shadowed City. A faction called Myriand maintains the host, but the label is often applied to the battle chrysalides themselves; when people talk about a Myriand or the Myriand, they're usually referring to one or more lawkeeping battle chrysalides.

"Biosplice companions have returned to Ruk, thanks to clear instructions in the True Code. If the people of Ruk required something new and better, why hasn't the All Song provided? Because we don't need anything beyond what the True Code provides. We just need to look harder and longer, and ignore the lure of the easy path." ~First Apostle Ah-kalla

Myriand, as a faction, offers an odd sort of allegiance to its members. Instead of being a consolidated force of lifetime members, individual peacekeepers are composed of those who've agreed (or been sentenced) to give up their self-awareness for a period of time each day in exchange for payment (or as community service). When it's time for a faction member to go on shift, an attached biological pod activates and the member is metamorphosized into a battle chrysalid. While transformed, the Myriand loses all sense of its former identity and instead becomes part of a gestalt mind that operates through a secure layer of the All Song. Myriands are hypervigilant, without pity, and fearless. They obey the letter of the law but are also duty-bound to follow the dictates of the Factol Arbiter.

ALL SONG COMMUNALS

Unlike the True Code, the All Song is available to anyone who has the ability to plug in. That can be difficult outside Harmonious, or for those without a connection umbilical, but thanks to the efforts of Zal, All Song communals exist throughout the Glistening City. To an Earth visitor, an All Song communal looks like a large pillow room dotted with "pillars" composed of twining root bundles—a mass of public umbilicals. Anyone who lies (or stands) next to a pillar can use a free umbilical to plug into the All Song whether or not they possess any personal modifications, because the umbilical takes care of the interface.

People connect to the All Song for a variety of reasons—to pass messages, to read faction disclosures, to find inspiration, to do research on almost any topic, and sometimes to seek the All Song's legendary controlling intelligence (no one has succeeded at the latter, but it's a popular time-waster).

Unpracticed users of the All Song who first plug in are inundated by music, text, images, emotions, varying feelings of pressure, scents, and other sensations that defy explanation. An Earth visitor once described it as drowning in a social media ocean that wasn't restricted to a two-dimensional screen, nor just to sight and sound—an experience akin to taking psilocybin mushrooms or LSD.

A practiced user of the All Song can attempt to find out specific pieces of information, though that requires an Intellect-based roll, the level of which depends on how revelatory the information might be. For instance, basic facts about Ruk and the address of well-known locations within Harmonious are routine tasks, but the location of the Karum's secret stronghold (as opposed to its public faction headquarters) is at least a level 5 task, and accessing that information without drawing countermeasures is at least a level 7 task.

The All Song is also a great place for factions and individuals to send requests for aid or resources, and thus an ideal place for Ruk natives to find contract opportunities. The All Song sometimes makes connections to people in Ruk spontaneously and reveals unmet needs of all kinds.

Zal doesn't charge for regular access to any of its communals, and the more people who use the All Song, the more coherent it becomes, which in turn aids Zal's many research initiatives, such as their much-heralded recursion pod.

OTHER ALL SONG OUTLETS

Despite Zal propaganda describing their communals as "the *only* place to safely connect to the All Song," outlets for the All Song spontaneously sprout all across Ruk in both wild and natural areas, as if some underlying unconscious aspect of the recursion seeks to make itself known through a physical interface. Anyone with an umbilical can connect to these to gain direct access to the All Song. In areas outside Harmonious, finding such an outlet usually requires a difficulty 3 Intellect-based task.

QUIET CABAL HIGH COMMAND

The Quiet Cabal isn't large when compared to Zal or the Church of the Embodiment, but it's well supported. Many in Ruk believe that Earth's continued existence is vital to Ruk's own, despite constant low-level propaganda to the contrary produced by the Karum.

The High Command is a slender tower with many levels. Particular level swathes are given over to a single function, including member quarters, tower security, biolabs of various sorts, a fusion lab where True Code and All Song research occurs in concert, holding cells for dangerous entities and objects, training rooms, and more. Right below the top level is a translation level set aside for those translating to and from various recursions and, of course, the prime world of Earth.

The Quiet Cabal has secretly foiled a handful of Karum attempts to bring Earth to the attention of planetovores. The most "famous" victory was when agents of the Quiet Cabal got funding pulled for a Texas-based high-energy particle accelerator that was so massive (a 54 mile/87 km ring) that it was almost guaranteed

Recursion pod, page 211

to ping the dark energy network when operating at full power. But thanks to the hard work of several secret agents, the Superconducting Super Collider never got far enough along to become a true threat.

Pillar of Insight: The top level of High Command is always busy with Cabal members connecting and disconnecting to a pillar not unlike those used in All Song communals. Called the Pillar of Insight, this piece of living Ruk biotech is a limited (and completely fire-walled) portion of the All Song that allows many minds to commingle, and from that commingling, come up with a synthesis of shared thought, ideas, and plans going forward. Thus the Pillar of Insight is the reason no particular individual or individuals lead the Cabal. Any agent in good standing plays a part in deciding Quiet Cabal policy by occasionally showing up on-site to interface directly.

Outfitting: When an agent of the Quiet Cabal requests a kit in pursuit of a specific mission, she can come to the tower level called Outfitting. Generally speaking, a kit can be any number of mundane things, of the kind described under Ruk Equipment. In addition to that, a Cabal member may take one object from Outfitting that serves as an asset to one task, including attack, defense, knowledge, and stealth. The asset is normally a pod, bioengineered spine, or other temporary enhancement to the agent's form. A given enhancement is placed into an agent's keeping only for the duration of a particular mission, and the Cabal expects it to be returned, intact, when the mission is complete.

Ruk equipment, page 91

Qinod Singularity, page 208

Agents On-Site: The fluid nature of the Quiet Cabal, with different agents serving different roles at different times, means that it's sometimes hard to know what to expect when dealing with any given aspect of the organization, which is why certain personnel remain in High Command to provide a sense of stability. These are called "on-site agents."

The most well-known on-site agent is Uttatum-tum, who is in charge of seeing to the needs of agents for lodging, recreation, and (for visitors from Earth especially) introduction around the Cabal. Uttatum-tum doesn't consider his job complete if newcomers don't have an opportunity to see the sights of Harmonious and sample its many wonders and delights.

Uttatum-tum: level 4, level 7 in tasks related to persuasion

Dr. Gavin Bixby, page 154

The Consult: The Consult is a large auditorium-like conference room filled with three-dimensional viewing technology of amazing holographic quality. After an initiative is decided by a session with the Pillar of Insight, it's useful for agents to talk about the process necessary to achieve those ends. Just as important, the Quiet Cabal often hires freelance contractors (people like the PCs, if the PCs are not already agents) to accomplish various steps toward those goals. Contractors don't get to connect to the Pillar of Insight, so the Consult makes such discussions and conferences possible and easy.

KARUM

The Karum's public faction headquarters is a floating organimer disc, its shape recalling Ruk's own. Members will say that the headquarters are not tied to another structure in Harmonious because it's intended as a visual symbol of the Karum's belief that Ruk's destiny can never be fulfilled while tied to Earth. While that's a convenient secondary effect, the real reason the Karum faction house floats free is that mobility is a wonderful thing, especially for a group that sometimes finds its activities potentially too extreme for Myriand or other factions to ignore. The public faction house owes its aerial nature (and some of its internal defenses) to an artifact that emerged from the Qinod Singularity called the Air Engine.

Everyone in Ruk knows or suspects that the Karum keep a separate, secret stronghold somewhere else, and the Karum do not dispute it. Within this secret stronghold, the Karum marshal the greatest part of their strength in agents, weapons, and secret research projects. Only Karum members with high-enough clearance know where to find the stronghold, and only they have the means to access it. What most everyone doesn't know is that the Karum secret stronghold is located in a mote of fundament out in the Strange, and the gate connecting the two locations is hosted from the guarded center of their public faction house.

From within their secret stronghold, agents of Karum infiltrate Earth, re-entering the prime world via other secondary recursions created to serve as gateways unknown by other factions in Ruk. One of these secondary recursions is where agent Dadanum-tal spends his off hours while not on Earth passing as Dr. Gavin Bixby, a man with a busy schedule consulting with various particle acceleration labs on best practices.

PRIME ELEMENT

Several Earth humans were recruited by the Quiet Cabal from their respective military units, security companies, and related situations to form an elite group of operatives known as the Prime Element. The Prime Element works on the Cabal's behalf on Earth, in Ruk, Ardeyn, and various other recursions, and in the Strange itself.

The Prime Element's roster includes the following founding members.

Antonio Jesus Rodriguez Fuentes, "Chantiel." *Specialty: Weapons.* Level 4; attacks as level 7

Salvador Amador Salvaterra, "El Trotamundos." *Specialty: Scouting and Tracking.* Level 5, level 6 for all tasks related to perception and tracking

Bret "Ski" Holien. *Specialty: Diplomacy.* Level 5, level 6 for all tasks related to disguise and persuasion

Thaddeus Wend. *Specialty: Field Medicine.* Level 6, level 7 for all tasks related to diagnostics, first aid, and healing

W. Dove Boyett III. *Specialty: Infiltration.* Level 5, stealth as level 6

Lawrence "Elvers" Sica. *Specialty: Poisons.* Level 4, level 7 with poisoned weapons; keeps a pet spider in most recursions

Brett "Boodro" Bozeman. *Specialty: Defense.* Level 4, defends as level 7

"Missing commandos Bret Holien and Thaddeus Wend were witnessed in the company of four or five other men dressed in high-tech military fatigues attacking a secure home in north Seattle on the evening of Wednesday 7 May 2014. Subsequently, the entire home vanished in a blast of blue light. Authorities say a gas leak caused an explosion." ~from the article "ALIENS IN SEATTLE?" by Svetlana Tankov, journalist

Foreseer: level 5, level 7 for all Might-based tasks

Ledum-zar: level 4, level 6 for research tasks

Ubbar-zarim: level 6

Ealam-asi: level 6; always accompanied by six level 4 creature bodyguards

Kubbarum-dai: level 5, level 7 for all tasks related to stealth and thievery

Shome, page 205

Karum Leadership: The Karum is led by two advocates of the faction policy. One is the Foreseer, a particularly vocal and long-lived woman. The Foreseer claims no other name for herself and says she can see the future—a future where Ruk collapses if its ties to Earth cannot be severed. The Foreseer is not one for subtlety, compromise, or catching flies with honey. Even within the Karum, the Foreseer is not trotted out much. Given that her biological functions are inextricably tied to the continuing functions of the Air Engine, though, she would be hard to get rid of.

Ubbar-zarim shares equal power with the Foreseer. Ubbar-zarim seldom goes anywhere without his pet koridle (a catlike creature with seven eyes) drooped about his shoulders. This advocate is calm, reasonable, and given to compromise, both among members and externally between factions. Ubbar-zarim keenly appreciates the real dangers that severing Ruk's connection with Earth risks, but he still believes that Ruk can't survive unless that separation is made. If anyone in the Karum could be convinced that Ruk's separation doesn't have to spell Earth's end, it is Ubbar-zarim, but only with copious and legitimate evidence.

Earth Eradication Initiative: Among the many chambers set aside for projects is one particularly dangerous initiative about which not even everyone in the Karum knows the details. That's because Lead Geneticist Ledum-zar is playing with fire by attempting to devise something he calls a Planetovore Lure. A Planetovore Lure is a collection of experimental equipment designed to artificially "ping" the dark energy network in the same way a fledgling civilization might. Due to the extreme dangers of testing the equipment, Ledum-zar is putting together a team to travel for several months into the Strange and then detonate the lure to see what happens.

SHADOWED CITY

The Shadowed City is by no means a lawless slum, but those who live beneath the Glistening City have definitely come down in the world, metaphorically as well as literally. Myriand doesn't always have enough hosts to properly patrol the Shadowed City, which is why traveling representatives of Shome criminal organizations thrive there, offering various illegal items, favors, and other services that most citizens of the Glistening City would rather know nothing about. In addition to less savory fare, a lot of trade and manufacturing moves between Harmonious and the Shadowed City, which is why travel between the upper and lower city is a constant flow.

Runoff from the Glistening City above is not sewage, because specially grown organimer threads treat all of Harmonious's outflows. But the amount that falls from above is prodigious. Channels in the ground suck it underground, but the water wells up again in various parts of Ruk and helps feed the Collapsed Lake, Edge Lake, and Lake Zuhr.

CREATURE FEATURE

Custom pets, temporary companions, bodyguards, and even poisonous assassins can be ordered for the right price from genetic engineer Ealam-asi. Ealam-asi works at a remove from his customers in a hidden location and rarely reveals himself. He prefers to interact with customers, if it can be called interaction, through a massive viewing wall that displays images of creatures available for purchase along a 100 foot (30 m) long and 20 foot (6 m) high surface. The images of potential creatures run, jump, frolic, or lurk according to each creature's individual nature. If a potential customer moves up to study the wall, low-level functional magnetic resonance imaging (fMRI) devices read the customer's frame of mind. Then these devices create a display of an appropriate creature on the wall, whether that is one of the creatures already shown or a custom creation. To order the creation of a creature, the customer must merely touch one that is shown, which samples the customer's DNA. Bits are transferred by the touch (about 300, though costs vary), and within seven days the selected creature finds the customer, tracking him down by scent.

HOUSE OF KUBBARUM

A popular destination for citizens of both upper and lower, the House of Kubbarum is run by retired celebrity thief Kubbarum-dai. In addition to the libations, music hall, and public and private rooms where patrons can carouse, Kubbarum-dai keeps a trophy room where particularly valuable or sensational items he's stolen are on display behind transparent organimer panels, which he may deign to show to special guests. Hearsay has it that the retired

OPPORTUNITIES IN THE HUB

Periphery Safari: The Church of the Embodiment is looking to mount a series of new safaris to check out an unusual nodule recently grown on the Periphery called the Thorn Castle. They hope the new discovery proves to be a True Code cache, but they're worried about reports of bizarre flying guardians with coherent light weapons for eyes.

Law in Your Hands: The Myriand faction has discovered that someone down in the Shadowed City is kidnapping citizens of Harmonious, who are sometimes found later sans their grey matter. Additional contractors are being sought to investigate and deal with the brain thieves. Battle chrysalid forms will be provided (though the faction doesn't guarantee autonomy to go with them).

Songs of Seeking: Sometimes requests for aid with no obvious author find those who are connected to the All Song. Some wonder if these are messages from the awakening mind of the All Song itself (if there is such a thing), because the requests for aid usually have to do with defending the integrity of Ruk, such as the most recent message that seeks to direct a small group to the spiderfields in the Periphery. According to the anonymous message, that location will host the next manifestation of the Qinod Singularity.

A Quiet Vacation: The Quiet Cabal is looking for a group to infiltrate a university campus on Earth that seems to be developing a particle accelerator that might not require the massive size of traditional particle accelerators. If such technology is possible in a world operating under the law of Standard Physics, Earth is in serious trouble. Karum involvement is suspected.

A Strange Odyssey: Zal is offering a considerable sum for a few more crew members to fill out a ship it intends to send into the Strange to gather reality seeds. Zal has financed previous efforts at gathering reality seeds but now indicates that it may have found a particularly rich "field" of them several days' transit time from Ruk. Those willing to risk the mental alienation and physical threats of the creatures that reside in the dark energy network should apply.

Myriand: Three four-hour shifts a week with Myriand is good enough to give someone faction allegiance in Harmonious. Visitors who stay so long that they can no longer be considered guests might wish to check out becoming another arm of the law in the Glistening City.

Shady Offer: A message offers work down in the Shadowed City for those willing to travel, and directions appear at the Creature Feature wall. If acted upon, a message appears in the form of a contract (all that's required is a touch to accept it), which asks the respondents to find an escaped custom-designed creature called the Despoiler that had an unexpected flaw: it is always hungry, and it just keeps growing and growing (it's currently a level 7 creature the size of an elephant). Payment for a completed job is a custom pet creature for each team member (up to five custom pets) who helps take down the Despoiler.

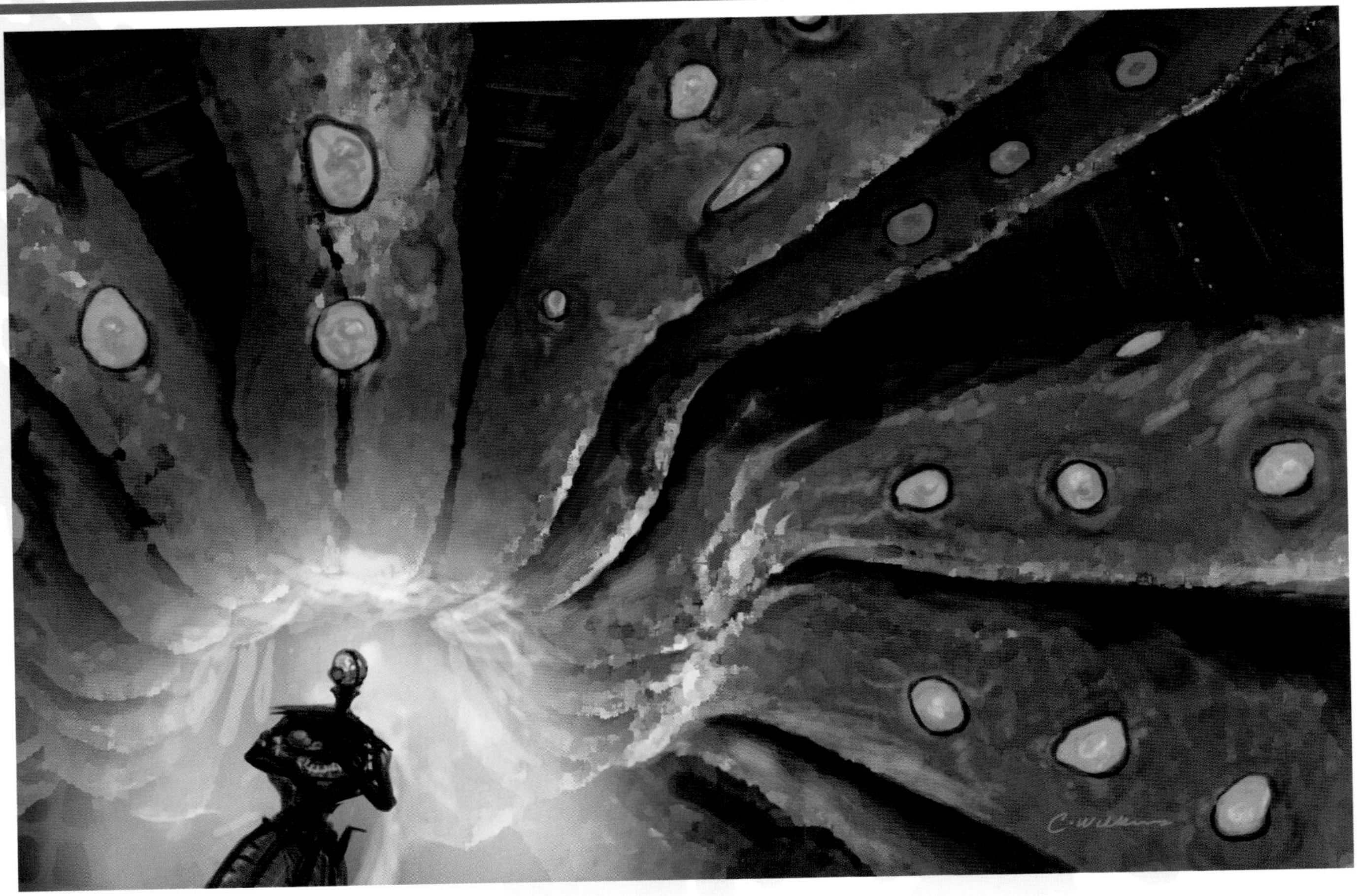

thief paid every one of the victims double the price of the stolen items after the fact. In some cases, however, the insult of being robbed proved too much for the victim to accept. As a result, the proprietor walks around with more than a couple of death threats. Kubbarum-dai doesn't seem too put out, and in fact he advertises his amazing abilities to anyone with a job that's fascinating enough to catch his interest.

Irrara-ya: level 4; wields an experimental face-stealing artifact (level 5) that removes the face of a target within immediate range. Depletion: 1 in 1d20

KOLUM

Kolum was built by a splinter group, tired of having to live under the rules of the factions, that departed Harmonious fifty-some years ago. They named their city after founder Kolum-dam, who preached that a better life, with true freedom, could be had with a little effort. Kolum seemed to be on its way to becoming a truly independent city when disaster struck. Some say criminal elements in Shome were responsible, but a majority believes that Zal, the Church of the Embodiment, the Karum, or another major faction was responsible because they felt threatened by the factionless existence in Kolum. Regardless of how it happened, a rogue Qinod construct found its way into the city, laying the place to ruin.

The construct responsible for the disaster may still lurk in Kolum, because a watchpost built at the edge of the ruin never witnessed the construct leave the site. The watchpost contains guardians selected from several different factions in Harmonious. The guardians are charged with preventing anyone from exploring the ruins, lest that accidentally reactivate the ravaging construct.

THE VERITEX

The Veritex is a labyrinthine system of tunnels that runs below the surface of Ruk. Due to the damage sustained by Ruk eons ago, some portions of the Veritex are isolated from others behind tunnels blocked by collapses.

Small underground cities can be found throughout the Veritex. Some of these hide small, secretive cabals and cloisters with their own agendas and beliefs. Others are home to criminals, revolutionaries, or raiders. Still others simply offer shelter to those who would like to live free and in peace.

DRAN

The underground city of Dran was recently hit by quakes that buried one side of Dran in a ceiling collapse and destroyed more than half of the remaining structures. Although the survivors are rebuilding, most are happy to accept the assistance of representatives from Zal who show up with offers of aid.

Irrara-ya is a native of Dran who found a device after the collapse that steals the face of any living creature she turns it upon and stores that face as a digital avatar. The body remains behind, alive but in stasis, with no mind left to it. Irrara-ya learned that she can ask the stored face questions, and the face will answer according to its knowledge. Irrara-ya doesn't know if she has the ability to restore a face back to its body. But if that turns out to be possible, what she's more interested in is restoring a face to a different body, just to see what happens.

OPPORTUNITIES IN THE PERIPHERY

Orders from the Orb: A group of monks set off after an unknown craft that fired missile-like weapons on the Orb of Worlds, then fled. The pursuing monks, in their borrowed chaos skiff, never returned, and the Order seeks contractors who are willing to follow the clues through the Strange and rescue the missing members from whatever situation has befallen them.

Forget My Name: A faction official in Harmonious is looking to hire a discreet band of contractors for a dangerous job. The official has reason to believe that her name (and full genetic profile) was obtained by Onomasticon in Shome. She wants someone to enter that dread tower and retrieve or destroy her profile before a kind of personalized eradication can be fashioned to blackmail her.

Thorn in the Treads: The treads of Jir have been infested with parasites of unknown origin, but ones that seem capable of eating the flamethrower-armed mechanics who've tried to enter the deep crevices inside to burn them out. If the parasites can't be removed soon, all of Jir may fall behind the boundary between itself and the Strange, and subsequently lose complete power in its differential engine.

MUK

The All Song does not reach into Muk, thanks to an accidental feature of the surrounding material. This small city is built within a single long, open area, with many galleries and tunnels leading off into smaller chambers. Muk is a popular destination for monks of the Church of the Embodiment, who take special vows to come meditate on the True Code. The Abbess of Muk is Laran-xi, a diminutive woman who conceals her features under a hood. She is welcoming of visitors, offering them a night's stay in exchange for a story of Harmonious, the Glistening City, which her vows forbid her from returning to. She's not bitter, since she feels she and her brothers and sisters are making real headway in uncovering hints of the True Code in the echoes of their own minds in the peace provided by the All Song's absence.

Laran-xi was once a member of the Karum. As an agent, she slew many Quiet Cabal members during secret conflicts that occurred outside of Ruk. Those incidents and that allegiance are well behind her now, and she regrets her actions. She hopes that after all this time the Quiet Cabal and Karum have forgotten her, but she knows that justice may someday still find her. She is prepared to accept it if it does.

PERIPHERY

It's a truism that the farther one travels from Harmonious, the more of a dangerous frontier Ruk becomes. For this reason, people are happy to stay in the Hub. The average citizen of Ruk stays in Harmonious and believes one would have to be mentally unbalanced, in desperate need of bits, a crazed risk taker, or a criminal to want to venture into the Periphery. Several factions do have interests that lie beyond the civilized core of the recursion, and they staff various outposts and well-guarded installations on the frontier, as well as mobile harvesters and resource barges. Regions of the Periphery include Shome, Jir, and Gatt.

SHOME

Shome is a lawless city of dangerous criminals and mercenaries. Its black markets make all manner of rare and obscure goods available, particularly those that the major factions of Ruk don't want to be available. For example, contraband or controlled genetic codes that allow one to make particularly dangerous creatures and biotech creations can be purchased here, for the right price.

Underground tunnels, via the Veritex, lead from the Shadowed City to Shome. Thanks to the efforts of previous criminals, a rapid-transport system operates in these tunnels, where people ride in a kind of slime-filled pneumatic tube between the two stations. Transport takes only a minute, if one is willing to put up with being covered in mucus. At least it's mucus that smells of cinnamon and clove.

Orb of Worlds, page 221

Onomasticon, page 206

Treads of Jir, page 207

Laran-xi: level 4

"It is dangerous to use artifacts disgorged by the Qinod Singularity, and doing so should be banned. As happened when the enigmalith was found, and that terrible, dread destroyer was released!" ~Uttatum-tum, on-site agent of the Quiet Cabal

Lady Kasin-dar: level 6; Armor 3; wields an artifact that steals an ability from one target and confers it on another target for one hour

FORTRESS OF FAVORS

The Fortress of Favors is where Lady Kasin-dar resides. She's known by various names around Ruk, including the "Shadowed Queen," "Bone Splicer," and the "Bone Thief" (the latter two for her penchant for extracting marrow for genetic black-market needs). She carries a feared artifact called the Splice Rod (which also has several bloodier monikers) that has the ability to rip the bones from victims and splice them into others, granting temporary abilities to the latter while crippling or killing the former. Sometimes clients pay her for her services, and other times she enhances those within her employ or herself. Both the Factol Council and Myriand have warned Kasin-dar to stay away from using citizens of Harmonious as source material. As long as she complies, they do little to prevent clients from journeying to Shome to make use of her services.

ONOMASTICON

Names have a certain power in Ruk, especially if they are paired with an associated complete genetic profile. The criminal organization known as Onomasticon keeps just such genetic profiles in a secret database against the strict prohibition of Ruk law and sensibilities. In a place like Ruk, to possess someone's genome, epigenetic factors, and microbiome code is to have a piece of that person's soul. Someone with such a profile could create person-specific poisons, toxins, mind-control parasites—the sky's the limit, which is why "names" sold by Onomasticon don't come cheap. It's also why potential clients of Onomasticon must be very careful to avoid the appearance of being in any way connected to Myriand or the Factol Council, as well as the Quiet Cabal, the Church of the Embodiment, or any other faction that has attempted to shut the criminal group down in the past. If such an association is sensed, not only will the client be denied service, the client will be dispatched with prejudice.

Mendalla: level 5; those attempting to attack Mendalla must succeed on an Intellect-based roll. Failure means they are unable to attack due to a sense of awe, fear, or friendship. Succumbing to the effect once increases the difficulty of future attempts to attack Mendalla by two steps.

Sirrush, page 290

Though no one's seen him, a deformed, scarred, and brutal crime lord named Mendalla leads Onomasticon. Mendalla never stirs from his secret lair beneath the Iasos River, sending various representatives and contractors to do his bidding. What only a very few know is that the crime lord is not a Ruk native. He is a quickened sirrush from Ardeyn who translated into Ruk and, after many lessons and setbacks, worked his way up to a position of authority and power that is as godlike as one can achieve in a realm where science trumps magic.

JIR

The city of Jir maintains a position at the very edge of the Periphery so that portions of its towers and gantries extend into the Strange itself, piercing the boundary. Jir is the primary port between Ruk and the Strange, and most traffic that passes between the two realms occurs here. Once out in the Strange, it is nearly impossible to find a way back into Ruk by direct physical means (creatures out in the Strange can't see or sense the boundary of Ruk because the recursion was designed to stay hidden). But the Jir Locks provide access for those who know where to look.

Various kinds of vessels able to travel the Strange can be chartered, rented, or sometimes even bought in Jir, though the latter option doesn't come up often. Many of the ships are modified Ruk flying barges, built to transport resources harvested in the grey forests to the factories outside Harmonious. But a few are chaos skiffs purchased (or otherwise obtained) from similar travelers out of Ardeyn.

Jir is an odd port city given what it borders, but the needs of a crew who's spent months locked in a Strange transit can be met in Jir, which is known for its taverns, pleasure quarters, All Song communals, and merchants of every sort. Crewmembers who want to make a few extra bits can find fences for the sale of items they nicked from the Strange, too.

Orb of Worlds, page 221

Order of Orb Outreach: One or two monks from the Orb of Worlds can usually be found walking the "docks" or frequenting Jir's many public establishments. The Orb of Worlds is an artificial structure out in the Strange where reality seeds can be "fertilized" with an investiture ritual by those on a genesis quest. The Order is a group of caretakers who maintain and protect the sanctity of the Orb. Like any faction, the Order needs to find new members now and then or, failing that, special contractors to take care of unusual situations as they arise. This need is why the monks found in Jir have been given dispensation to speak despite their vow of silence, allowing them to describe the wonders or needs of the Order as they arise.

Apotheme Rangers, page 224

Apotheme Rangers Recruitment Tower: A loose band of scouts, scholars, and adventurers from Ruk, Earth, and Ardeyn make up the Apotheme Rangers. The rangers chart the Strange within the vicinity of Ruk and Earth, searching for signs of danger and seeking evidence of alien

civilizations in the distant network that have not succumbed to planetovores.

The Apotheme Rangers keep their main headquarters in the Strange on a massive chaos ship called *Redstone*. The rangers also maintain a recruitment tower in Jir, where people who are already used to the idea of entering the Strange itself frequent. Recruitment chief Darduin-lan paints an exciting picture of a life of exploration, adventure, and journeying where no Ruk native has gone before.

Zal Chaos Extraction: Zal has many interests, and one is the extraction of valuable items from the Strange. Zal usually prospects for violet spiral, but also looks for reality seeds or other relics of the dark energy network. Zal Extraction ships sometimes lack a full crew complement, which is why contractors for Zal sometimes resort to shanghaiing vulnerable people from all over Ruk to fill empty posts for upcoming voyages.

JIR LOCKS

The "locks" of Jir are two separate series of gantry cranes that lift a vessel and transfer it between Jir and Jir Station in the Strange. Jir Station is built on a section of fundament and is visible in the Strange to those who know where to find it. Each lock can pass about one large craft per hour one way, though the traffic between Ruk and the Strange isn't so heavy that there's ever much of a wait. Vessels don't need to use the locks to leave Ruk, but they often do (if on sanctioned faction business) to take advantage of the added security Jir offers, which includes a host of Myriand.

JIR TREADS

Jir maintains its position on the very edge of Ruk, which is constantly (if slowly) growing and expanding, thanks to the massive biomechanical treads the entire city is constructed upon. Massive engines power the treads and run off a differential between the Strange and Ruk, which means if the boundary ever got too far away, the treads would stop. On some days, the treads have to advance the city about a centimeter, but on many days they don't have to move at all. But a couple of times in recent memory, the treads had to roll almost 3 feet (1 m) in an hour, which taxed them to their limit.

A guild of several hundred biomechanics constantly clambers across the treads and difference engine, making certain that they are always in tip-top shape.

Darduin-lan: level 5; health 50; can produce rays of energy that inflict 5 points of damage or restore 5 points of Might to a target within short range as an action each round

Violet spiral, page 219

GATT

Zamaran-sin: level 5, level 7 for all tasks related to genetic engineering; Armor 3 (from web-armor; foes who strike Zamaran-sin with a melee weapon and who fail a Might defense roll lose hold of their weapon when it becomes stuck to her armor)

Uer-gula: level 6; can spray liquids in immediate range that inflict 6 points of damage as an action each round

Gatt is a small city built from discarded spars of the surrounding debris field and newer construction. The city contains small towers and block buildings, and every single window, door, or other opening comes with an additional hatch that the residents refer to as "mating shutters."

Fluffy white spiderfields extend all around Gatt, covering everything in a shroud of silky webs that looks like new-fallen snow. Of course it's not snow, since much of Ruk remains climate controlled. The spiderfields are so named because of the swarms of tiny white spiders that awaken to crawl up the legs and cover the bodies of foolish visitors who wade out into the white.

The spiderfields extend for dozens of miles (58 km) in all directions, and like the grey forests, serve as a valuable resource that a couple of small factions based in the city of Gatt harvest. Spider silk and spiders alike are collected as a specialty biomass resource by individual Ruk natives who walk atop the spun webs with special web-walking grafts.

Life in Gatt is generally pastoral, except once every sixteen months, when thousands of spiderlike creatures almost as large as people begin an orgy of mating. Like their Earth counterparts from which they were bred a thousand years earlier, the female spider creature kills the male—and every other male it can find in and around the city of Gatt, regardless of species. That's when the mating shutters are fastened down and no one goes out. At least, no one with a Y chromosome.

Zamaran-sin is a spider breeder who lives and has labs in Gatt. Each year, she selects for finer strands of webs, or webs with special qualities such as color, scent, or strength. She also breeds for taste—spider biomass is a delicacy that commands high prices in Harmonious. Zamaran-sin serves as a secret clearinghouse for Karum communiqués, which she codes genetically in spider silk so that such messages are never exposed in an All Song communication.

QINOD SINGULARITY

Before Ruk crashed on the Shoals of Earth, it encountered something as it traveled through the Strange. The event was so apocalyptic that the True Code was disrupted, which gave birth to the All Song and the divisions that plague Ruk to this day. The best guess scholars have regarding the event is that Ruk had alien contact with something called the Qinod. Whether that contact was with an intelligent artifact, a planetovore-class entity, or a group of traveling aliens more advanced than Ruk is lost in the resultant disruption of the True Code, and the information was never contained in the All Song. Whatever the truth, Ruk survived and limped on until finally crashing on the Shoals of Earth, forever changed, and bearing a stowaway that's come to be called the Qinod Singularity.

The Qinod Singularity remains an enigma because it manifests only infrequently in Ruk, and when it does, it appears in a seemingly random location. Its appearance is that of a blinding point of light that lightly bobs over the ground, randomly spewing devices, detritus, freeze-dried corpses of alien creatures (no two ever alike), and the occasional animate construct that almost invariably sets to destroying every other life form or artificial structure it comes across. Since most of Ruk is artificial, some constructs just begin burrowing and appear days later in the Veritex, where they carry on their rampage until stopped. Unlike the constructs, the purpose of the discarded devices is usually incomprehensible, but sometimes they can be used as artifacts.

On three previous occasions, Ruk natives employed by various interests attempted to enter the maw of the singularity when it manifested to see if it was an animate gate to another recursion. On each of those occasions, those attempting to enter either were fried to a crisp before making it across the threshold, or never returned.

VUN

Vun is a large city of towering fungal stalks (fungus-bred to be safe from poison and hallucinogens) mixed with the more traditional organimer construction. The edges of Vun teem with grey harvesters; the huge mobile factories move through fungi forests on hundreds of insectlike legs because Vun is a major center for biomass harvest in Ruk. Other centers exist in the Hub and the Periphery, but Vun is known for the quantity it can process and transport each day. The incredible amount it produces is due to its impressive biomechanical complex where grey harvesters are built and repaired, collected biomass is processed in massive tanks, and processed biomass is loaded onto the ubiquitous flying barges that travel between Harmonious and other points Hubward.

The mayor of Vun, Uer-gula, sports an odiferous biomod that can spew a variety of different fluids, including hallucinogens, poisons, and acids. As a public figure he is reviled and feared, given his reputation for melting more than one faction representative who tried to finagle Vun out of a fair price for meeting biomass quota. But rumor has it that when he sheds his biomod graft each night, he's actually a personable fellow to his friends and family, and he is loyal to those who somehow earn his trust.

RUK ARTIFACTS

In Ruk, artifacts are usually the result of extreme technological expertise. Some of these are modern Ruk manufacture, while others were discovered out in the Strange and are true artifacts of extinct alien races. A subset of Ruk artifacts come from the Qinod Singularity. In Ruk, most artifacts are already claimed, though the Qinod Singularity sometimes coughs up new ones, along with the horrors it expels.

BIOSPLICE COMPANION

Level: 1d6

Form (initial): An ampule filled with glowing blue bioactive tissue

Effect: Several different biosplice companions exist. To create a biosplice companion, a would-be master injects a biosplice ampule into her body. Over the course of thirty-three hours, the injection site swells up to the size of a second head, then bursts, inflicting 3 points of damage as the biosplice companion emerges. Generally, a biosplice companion's level is equal to the artifact level. It is about half the size of its master and has enough intelligence to follow commands, but otherwise it operates at the level of a companion. A depletion roll is required each time a biosplice companion uses its special ability.

The types of companions include (but are not limited to) the following:

Defender: Has a single eye that crackles with bioelectric energy. If a creature attacks its master (or the companion), the defender biosplice immediately fires a blast of electrical energy that inflicts damage equal to the artifact level on the attacker. It fires once per round for as long as its master continues to be attacked. Moves a short distance each round.

Aggressor: Very similar to a defender, except it targets creatures indicated by its master.

Healer: Slithers an immediate distance each round. If its master takes Might damage, the biosplice companion bites him, injecting him with tissue-repairing pharmaceuticals that heal a number of points of damage equal to the artifact level. It continues to apply its healing bite, once per round, for as long as its master remains damaged.

Messenger: Has a face resembling that of its master and moves a long distance each round. The messenger can find any location its master has been to or could find, and deliver a short message without requiring a depletion roll. If desired, the messenger can mentally link to its master, allowing its master to speak from the mouth of the messenger and hear what the messenger hears in return; each round of such mental linkage requires a depletion roll.

Depletion: 1 in 1d100

A biosplice companion is grown from the flesh of its master, but its form suits the biosplice companion's type.

COMMUNION PLATTER OF THE TRUE CODE

Level: 1d6

Form: An ornate organimer platter with covering lid

Effect: Up to six communion wafers (or any small pieces of edible food) can be treated at a time in a one-round process that involves closing the platter's covering lid and pressing a contact. A treated communion wafer confers the normal benefits of communion (if any) and grants a temporary +3 bonus to Edge, distributed across whatever Pools the character desires. The bonus lasts for one hour.

Depletion: 1 in 1d20

Eating additional communion platter wafers has no effect beyond the first, but that doesn't stop people from trying.

ENIGMALITH

Level: 1d6 + 4

Form: A flat, palm-sized stone disc, which can be "unfolded" to create a 6-foot-high (2 m) monolith

Effect: An enigmalith can be unfolded over the course of six actions, with each action roughly doubling the mass of the object until it has as much as a granite monolith of the given dimensions would. (Folding reverses the process.)

An enigmalith is a prison that stores its inmates in abeyance. An unfolded enigmalith may accidentally trap whoever opens it or attempts to use it if the user fails an Intellect defense roll. Newly trapped victims go into abeyance, leaving an afterimage of a stylized engraving of the victim on the enigmalith's surface. Touching an engraving on an enigmalith frees the associated trapped creature (unless whoever touches the engraving is trapped in turn). Newly discovered enigmaliths often contain random creatures wholly unknown to modern Ruk (randomly selected by the GM, up to the artifact's level). Newly released creatures are often dangerous, confused, and difficult to communicate with.

A depletion roll is required each time a creature is trapped or released. If the artifact is depleted, all the creatures trapped within are released.

Depletion: 1–2 in d100

Enigmaliths are scribed with 1d6 stylized carvings on their surface, each apparently depicting a completely unknown creature.

METABOLISM BUD

Level: 1d6

Form: An organic pod, almost like a small, hemispherical bit of brain; once grafted to a host, the host's flesh grows over it until it is only a lump

Effect: The pod grafts onto any living host (usually near the brain or spine) and injects chemicals that boost the creature's metabolism. This permanently raises the host's Speed Pool maximum by 5 points.

Depletion: —

PHEROMONE BANNER

Level: 1d6 + 1

Form: A wide strip of flexible material that gives off a pungent scent

Effect: When activated, a banner emits a pheromone that can affect all pre-treated allies within short range that breathe in the odor. Pre-treating an ally requires an action and touch proximity. Unless noted otherwise, a pheromone banner produces its effect for one minute per activation.

01–10	Melee attacks of pre-treated allies decrease in difficulty by one step
11–20	Ranged attacks of pre-treated allies decrease in difficulty by one step
21–30	Melee attacks made by targets other than a pre-treated ally increase in difficulty by one step
31–40	Ranged attacks made by targets other than a pre-treated ally increase in difficulty by one step
41–50	Pre-treated allies feel less pain (and gain +1 to Armor)
51–60	Attempts to intimidate targets other than a pre-treated ally decrease in difficulty by one step
61–70	Pre-treated allies who make a recovery roll while banner is active recover an additional 4 points
71–80	Speed defense rolls of pre-treated allies decrease in difficulty by one step
81–90	Might defense rolls of pre-treated allies decrease in difficulty by one step
91–00	Intellect defense rolls of pre-treated allies decrease in difficulty by one step

Depletion: 1 in 1d20

RECURSION POD

Level: 1d6 + 4

Form: A bulb of living organic tissue the size of a human head

Special: A recursion pod can move between recursions.

Effect: When a recursion pod is placed on an object (usually another artifact), the pod insinuates veinlike tendrils into that object. This doesn't normally affect the object's function. If the mated object and recursion pod are translated into a different recursion, though, not only does the pod make it possible for the mated object to make the transfer, but both the pod and mated object retain their original forms as if having moved through an inapposite gate. Any special properties possessed by the mated object in its home recursion continue to function at full capacity in the new recursion, even if different laws are in operation. A depletion roll is required each time the mated object translates into a new recursion.

Depletion: 1 in 1d20

SKILL BUD

Level: 1d6

Form: An organic pod, almost like a small, hemispherical bit of brain; once grafted to a host, the host's flesh grows over it until it is only a lump

Effect: This pod grafts onto any living host (must be near the brain) and injects complex chemicals that alter brain and muscle functions. This grants the host training in one (predetermined) skill.

Depletion: —

TENDRIL GRAFT

Level: 1d6

Form: A whiplike length of organic material similar to flesh

Effect: This graft attaches to the host's spinal column so that it can be controlled like a limb. The host can use it like a whip (a light weapon) even if his hands are full. He can also use it like a prehensile tail that can hold his weight (assuming he is roughly human-sized) or another object.

Depletion: —

VENOM TROOPER COMMAND HELM

Level: 1d6 + 4

Form: A helmet that looks similar to the head of a venom trooper, with a Zal faction symbol emblazoned on the back

Effect: When worn by a creature and activated, the wearer can take command of a number of venom troopers (equal to the artifact's level) within long range. The wearer must be able to see and hear the venom troopers to be commanded, and vice versa. The period of control lasts up to one hour.

Depletion: 1 in 1d20

WEAPON GRAFT

Level: 1d6

Form: A medium weapon (melee or ranged), with a sleeve of softer, fleshy material

Effect: This organic graft fits over a hand or stump and affixes to the flesh of the host. The physical bond provides an asset that makes attacks one step easier. When a PC finds a weapon graft, the GM determines what kind of weapon is attached to the graft.

Depletion: —

WINDRIDER

Level: 1d6 + 1

Form: An 8-foot-long (2 m) organimer wing

Effect: This is a vehicle that can be ridden by someone who makes Speed rolls (level 1) each round. In combat, it moves a long distance each round, but on extended trips, it can move up to 80 miles (129 km) per hour. A depletion roll is required for each hour of use.

Depletion: 1–2 in 1d100

"For each thousand venom troopers Zal creates, we provide one command helm free of charge to the customer, because we care." ~Chief Advancement Officer Sin-ixtab

Venom trooper, page 300

CHAPTER 14

THE STRANGE

"Chaos reigned past the starting grid. The endless, shuddering expanse was deeper than any real sky, and it absorbed my gaze. Within its infinite wheeling eternity, a hunger stirred. Fear swept through me—and a mad certainty. I realized that everything I knew was wrong."

~Carter Morrison

The Strange is composed of what physicists and astronomers on Earth call dark energy (or, more precisely, dark energy is the expression that the network takes as it intersects our own universe of regular matter). Within its immense and ever-expanding volume, it's capable of hosting almost limitless amounts of information. That expansion continues to occur at an ever-accelerating rate, and as the Strange swells, it expands the universe along with it. Over its billions of years of existence, entire worlds have taken seed within the Strange, grown, and flowered with their own unique sets of rules to govern them. These rules have no boundaries, but once they're set, they're set, firming up a portion of the Strange with a new reality called a recursion.

Precursors is the name we gave to the enigmatic race just slightly younger than our universe; what they called themselves isn't known.

The Strange, also called the Chaosphere, was intentionally constructed by the Precursors—technologically advanced aliens—billions of years ago to facilitate intergalactic travel across the universe. The aliens would upload themselves into the dark energy data web, then

Inapposite gate, page 135

Alienation, page 216

Traveling the Strange, page 214

STRANGE ATTRIBUTES

The Strange isn't a recursion; it's the underlying network that provides the processing power necessary to host recursions. However, visitors can enter the Strange and travel through it, which means that the Strange can be understood in terms of many of the same attributes true for recursions.

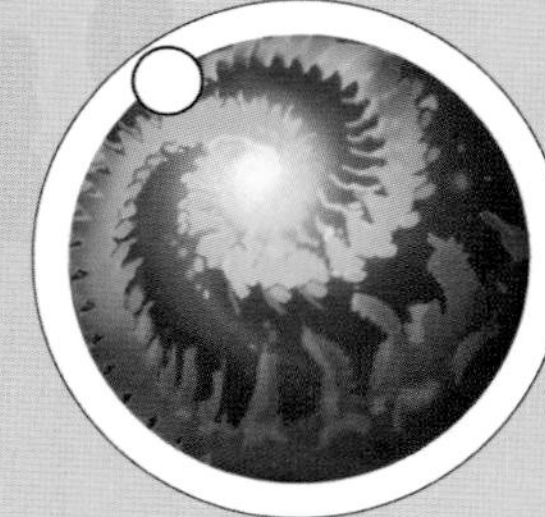

Level: It's normally not possible to translate directly into the Strange. If it's important to know the level of a given region of the Strange, the GM sets it.

Laws: All; when visitors enter the Strange, they bring a thin film of their most recent recursion and its laws with them.

Playable Races: None. The Strange doesn't give first-time visitors an option to choose a new race.

Foci: None. The Strange doesn't give first-time visitors an option to choose a new focus.

Skills: Chaosphere navigation, fractal surfing

Connection to Recursions: Various recursions allow access to and from the Strange. For example, Ardeyn residents can travel directly into (or fall into) the Strange from the edge of the recursion. Entering a recursion from the Strange is like entering the recursion through an inapposite gate.

Connection to Earth: None known (it would be extremely dangerous for the Earth if any existed)

Size: 13.6 billion light years across and expanding

Spark: Unknown

Trait: Alienation; different regions of the Strange can have different effects on a recursor's psyche as described under Traveling the Strange.

"print" themselves anew at some distant star, without having to travel the light years between the two locations in the normal universe.

Something went wrong in the network, and the aliens lost control. In the billions of years since, the Strange has continued to expand. As it did, the planetovores that dwell within it swallowed civilization after civilization that innocently "pinged" the dark energy network, and in so doing, provided a bridge to that civilization's world.

LIFE IN THE STRANGE

The Strange is vast, as vast as the real universe that it underlies. Though not originally designed to be so, the Strange is home to many intelligent races and entities. Unfortunately for Earth inhabitants, natives of the Strange are often incomprehensible to beings of Earth (and the recursions that Earth hosts). And the most powerful of all those beings—the planetovores—should be avoided at all costs, lest the threat that has silenced nearly every other form of intelligent life in the universe also find Earth.

But recursors of Earth and linked recursions have learned that traveling into the Strange itself—not as a means to cross real space, and not as a way to get to a known recursion, but just into the dark energy network—is a task worth attempting. It's a dangerous task to be sure, but deep within its folds and recesses lie treasures and wonders.

Planetovore, page 8

SHAPE AND NATURE OF THE STRANGE

The Strange is a chaotic flow of spiraling fractal patterns forever iterating in upon itself without end. The area immediately around Earth and its recursions usually appears primarily bluish-purple and sometimes dark green, but other areas are gold, orange, or even blood-red.

Although vast and expanding (and appearing to map in an extradimensional fashion to Earth's universe), the Strange has different distinct regions within its barely understandable chaotic twists and turns. Brave recursors report ever-shifting landscapes within the Strange, some resembling swirling fractals and others akin to impossible spacescapes with stars and planets that form and disappear in the blink of an eye. Still other explorers describe areas that move like vast creatures, as though portions of the Strange have gained sentience

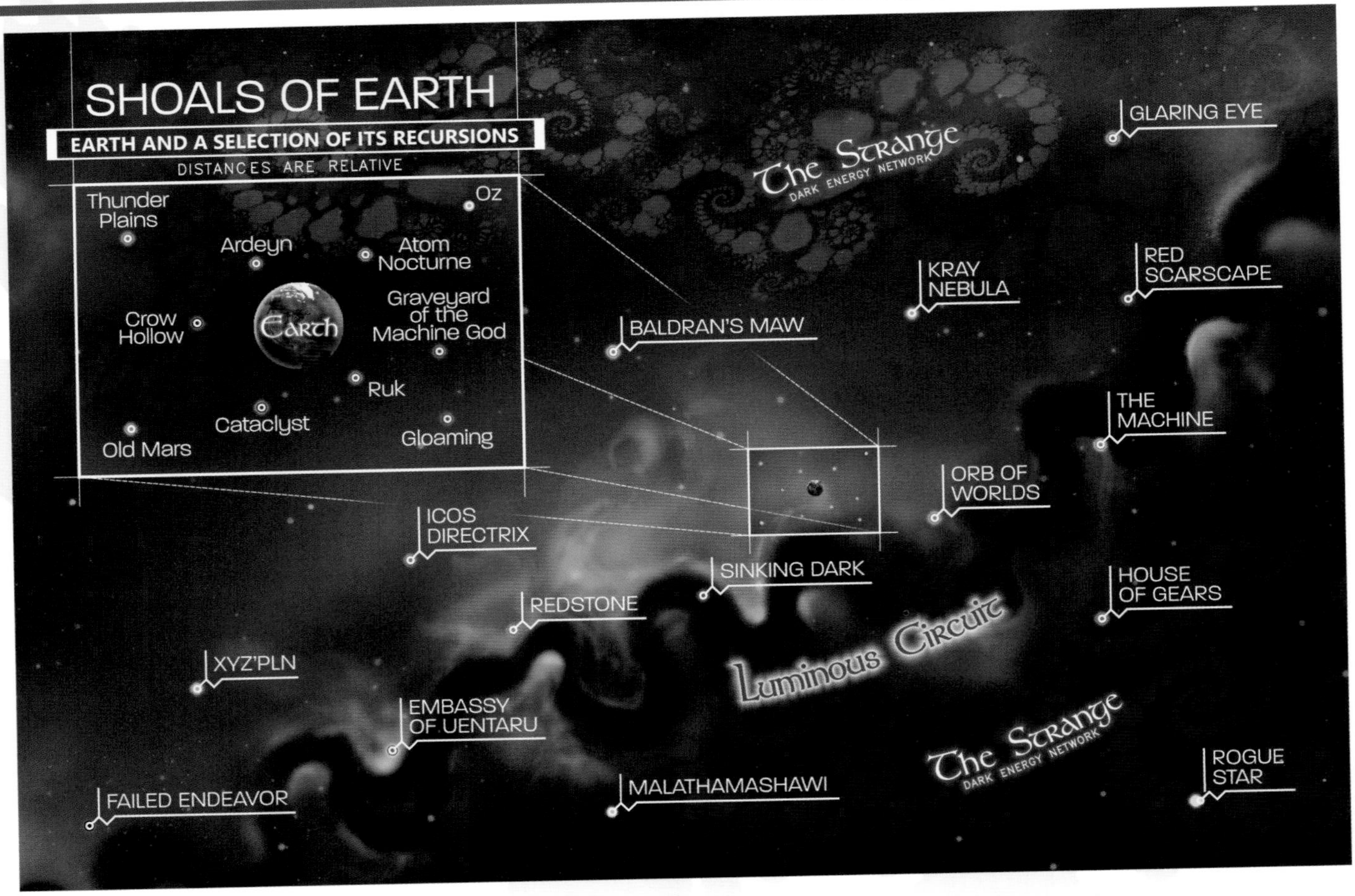

A very faint wake is left behind by a person or other object that moves through the Strange, which means tracking someone else's wake is possible, especially if someone were to choose wake tracking as a skill.

or are inhabited by immense intelligences that wear its essence like flesh.

Nothing physical in the universe of real matter is large enough to contain the network, except for the universe itself, and that must constantly expand with the network to hold it. Compared to the wind-tossed white caps of our visible universe, dark energy constitutes the unending depths beneath, vast and alien.

The majority of the Strange is the "space" in between the recursions, which is outside the universe of normal matter, or, as a scientist might say, the Strange is hosted beyond the "baryonic universe." Without knowing the location of signposts or beacons, the Strange is almost impossible to navigate. And even if you do know where you're going, getting there can be a challenge to those new to the medium (see How to Travel the Strange). But even when a Chaosphere explorer figures out basic locomotion and has identified a beacon to make for, two other important factors come into play: how long will the journey take, and what is the psychological toll of traveling in the Strange?

Fundament: Fundament is solid, unlike the other visible fractals that fill the Strange, which are often diaphanous, like glowing mist. But the fractals composed of fundament are hard as stone; luckily for naive travelers, fundament doesn't iterate as quickly as the ephemeral phenomena. Usually. But it frequently does ripple and move, if much slower (so slowly in most cases that travelers could land and walk upon it if careful). The manner in which a section of fundament iterates and shifts is often referred to as its resonance. Generally speaking, the larger the fundament structure, the slower the resonance.

Visibility and Illumination: Visiting the Strange is like floating in an endless sea where the "water" is sometimes clear, other times hazy or roiling with iterative patterns that extend away in every direction. Illumination in the Strange is provided by the fractal structures themselves.

TRAVELING THE STRANGE

The Strange was designed for travel, and those who can enter it can soar through its chaotic miasma by learning to surf the fractal currents.

HOW TO TRAVEL THE STRANGE

Recursors can travel within the Strange by attempting special tasks: Chaosphere navigation and fractal surfing. Some recursors may gain access to special vehicles, while others could develop unique personal talents.

Chaosphere Navigation: Those who spend even a little time in the Strange can attempt to navigate it as an Intellect-based task. The task requires that the recursor memorize beacons and signposts that she can see with her naked eyes. Doing so is a good way to avoid becoming lost in the Strange.

Characters who later become trained in Chaosphere navigation can learn about many beacons charted by earlier explorers, along with any information associated with those beacons. For example, a trained recursor might learn that the Red Scarscape is good for finding reality seeds that haven't yet condensed in a recursion and that a chaos skiff graveyard stretches out beyond the region of the Glaring Eye.

Fractal Surfing: Individual creatures can sense and harness the underlying "currents" of the Strange and then convert them to movement as a Speed-based task. A surfer can choose the right spot where successive waves of ephemeral fractal filaments "break" in just the right way (something that may seem invisible to someone not looking for it), then catch such a wave, which, given the nature of the Strange, could propagate indefinitely. Each round spent surfing gives the surfer a movement of long range. The surfer can tow up to three other human-sized creatures without penalty.

Difficulty	Task
Routine	Continue to surf with long range movement if previous turn was spent surfing
1	Catch a fractal wave and move like a creature with long range movement for one round
3	Begin surfing transit toward a known site; on a failed roll, traveler becomes lost; on a successful roll, the surfer appears at the known site after the indicated amount of travel time has passed (assuming no interruptions)
+1 step	Attempt to halve travel time to known site; on a failed roll, traveler becomes lost
+1 step	Round spent coasting to take another action (precludes change in speed or direction)
+1 step	Per additional towed creature beyond the first three

Lost in the Strange: When a traveler has become so turned around that she can no longer recognize beacons or signposts to navigate by, she is lost. Each day, a traveler can attempt a difficulty 4 Intellect-based task to reorient herself with Chaosphere navigation. Each failed roll increases the character's alienation factor by 1. If a lost character finds the way again, it reduces her alienation factor by 1.

An important aspect, of course, isn't travel or even speed—it's navigation. Where in the universe of normal matter does a particular point of the Strange intersect? Figuring that out is extremely complex, especially without the original sentient protocols for ingress and egress designed by the Precursors (which featured navigation as one of their most prominent features).

Given the iterative, changeable nature of the Strange, distance isn't a good measure of navigation. A better measure is time. Sites described in this section are all associated with travel times. A site with a listed travel time is an estimate of how long it would take a fractal surfer to move between the known site and the edge of any recursion around Earth that allows access to the Strange.

Every transit time has a variable associated with it. Particularly skilled surfers could attempt to cut total travel time in half, but this raises the difficulty of the task.

ACCESSING OTHER RECURSIONS FROM THE STRANGE

Out in the Strange, the edge of a recursion permeable to the Strange (such as Ardeyn or Crow Hollow) is visible as a hazy, translucent bubble. Regardless of how large the recursion actually is, the exterior of the interface surface typically measures no more than a few miles (5 km) in diameter. For smaller recursions, the exterior of the bubble interface shrinks accordingly, to a minimum size of about 10 feet (3 m) in diameter.

Recursions that are directly connected to each other (such as pocket dimensions and

Red Scarscape, page 224
Reality seed, page 218
Chaos skiff, page 175
Glaring Eye, page 223

other smaller recursions planted inside a larger recursion) and that are permeable to the Strange appear as a mass of bubbles of various size in a single clump. Recursions that are connected to Earth but not to each other are usually too far from each other to be visible, though travel between them by those who can navigate and surf the Strange takes about an hour.

Player characters (PCs) and other creatures not native to the Strange can enter a recursion from the Strange by moving through the interface. Doing so is akin to passing through an inapposite gate to reach that recursion.

Inapposite gate, page 135

Material From the Strange Entering a Recursion: Cyphers, violet spiral (and objects created from violet spiral), brachistochrone dust, pieces of fundament, artifacts and other materials of the Strange can enter a recursion.

Violet spiral, page 219
Brachistochrone dust, page 219
Kray, page 276

Cyphers fit into their new context regardless of whether they enter a recursion through an inapposite gate or via translation, though other items native to the Strange see less modification—just enough to exist physically within the recursion's context, which means that brachistochrone dust, for instance, remains amber-colored dust, though if brought to Earth, it no longer glows (unless exposed to UV light or other high-energy radiation).

Natives of the Strange Entering a Recursion: Unlike the rude "matter" of the Strange, native creatures are banned from entry through the bubble unless they can figure out how to "trick" the interface into accepting them as a native, or a native opens a way in for them. When this happens, such a creature hides in a form that can be discarded once it's no longer necessary, such as is the case for kray that must take root and sprout in a living creature before hatching into their true selves.

ALIENATION

Minds that evolved within the universe of normal matter and linked recursions were not designed for the naked, unprocessed, near-infinity of the dark energy network. Those who are exposed to it suffer mental and physical consequences called alienation. The more affected by the Strange a visitor is, the higher his alienation factor.

All creatures not native to the Strange gain an alienation factor of 1 merely for visiting. Certain events can raise a visitor's alienation factor further, such as becoming lost, encountering a planetovore, or spending an inordinate amount of time in the Strange without a break from direct exposure. Other effects and events can lower a creature's alienation factor, such as spending eight or more hours without direct contact with the dark energy network (such as inside a chaos skiff's hold or other solid, a recursion, or other structure in the Strange), finding one's way after being lost, and so on. The following table describes the most common ways to increase or decrease a PC's alienation factor.

A creature trained or specialized in skills related specifically to the Strange, such as Chaosphere navigation or fractal surfing, enjoys a buffer of protection against alienation as shown on the table, which means that merely entering the Strange won't increase alienation (because the –1 buffer cancels out the +1 factor

ALIENATION

Factor	Due To
+1	Entering the Strange
–1	Eight-hour break in a closed cabin of a craft, in the interior of a solid structure in the Strange, in a recursion, or on a prime world (cumulative)
+1	Becoming lost
–1	Finding the way after being lost
+2	Encountering a planetovore
+1	Encountering a previously unknown native or group of natives of the Strange
+1	Each day spent in the Strange without at least an eight-hour break in a closed cabin of a craft, in a recursion, or on a prime world
–1	*Buffer*: Trained in fractal surfing (–2 for specialization)
–1	*Buffer*: Trained in Chaosphere navigation (–2 for specialization)

of entering the Strange). A creature that takes a break from the Strange for enough time can eventually reduce its alienation factor to 0 (but unlike being trained in a skill of the Strange, this does not act as a buffer against the next time a PC enters the Strange again).

Direct Effects of Alienation: Each factor of alienation inflicts 1 point of damage to each of a PC's three stat Pools. A PC with factors of alienation suffers this damage when the following two situations occur:

1) A PC's alienation factor increases by any amount.

2) After an eight-hour rest that ends with the PC still suffering 1 or more factors of alienation.

For example, a character who first enters the Strange without a buffer gains 1 factor of alienation for the exposure, and so immediately takes 1 point of damage (that ignores Armor) to all three stat Pools. If the PC had the time and resources, he could attempt to restore some or all of the lost points through recovery rolls. While this may restore points, a recovery roll (or other kind of healing) doesn't eliminate the alienation factor.

If that same character became lost, he would have 2 factors and would suffer 2 points of damage to each stat Pool. After he found his way, his factor would reduce to 1 (but he would not regain his lost points). If then he rested away from the Strange (perhaps in the closed cabin of a chaos skiff) for eight hours, he would relieve 1 factor, but as soon as he exposed himself to the Strange once more he would go back up to 1 factor and would suffer 1 point of damage to each Pool.

Indirect Effects of Alienation: Characters who become impaired on the damage track because of damage inflicted by alienation could suffer a form of dementia that lasts for a few minutes or hours.

When a character becomes impaired or debilitated due to alienation, the game master (GM) should ask for a difficulty 5 Intellect defense roll. On a successful roll, the PC retains her mental equilibrium. On a failure, the PC suffers a fit of dementia that increases the difficulty of all tasks by two steps for one minute.

The fit could be any of the items on the table below, or something the GM determines.

1	Fainting
2	Screaming fit
3	Panicked flight
4	Laughing or crying inappropriately
5	Babbling
6	Hallucinating

CREATURES OF THE STRANGE

Living outside the boundaries of recursions or the prime universe, the bizarre, often mutable creatures of the Strange are far more alien to humanity than even beings from a different planet might be. One such creature is the Nmidon, a three-eyed, white skinned, vaguely humanoid being that serves as steward over a site called Icos Directrix, at the center of which it maintains a sort of forge for violet spiral.

A serious scourge of the Strange are the inklings. Lesser inklings have about as much substance and are about as dangerous as regular shadows, but the more inklings that pool in a particular area, the greater the chance that the dangerous types will appear. Inkling snatchers drain the color and substance from other creatures when allowed to feed, until nothing is left. In shape, inklings are pitch black

Nmidon, page 226

Icos Directrix, page 226

Inkling, page 273

areas of darkness, but they are sometimes seen with humanoid silhouettes. The humanoid shape, some have argued, means that inklings have a kind of origin around Earth or one of Earth's recursions. On the other hand, it may be that they mimic that which they've last fed upon and erased from existence. It's possible they are not living creatures so much as "psychic memories" of consumed recursions that have taken on a sort of existence all their own.

Goodland, page 250

Inklings are drawn to non-natives like moths are drawn to light.

And then of course there are the planetovores—creatures interested in using the Strange to find and access inhabited prime planets and subsume them. Each planetovore is unique in its origin and personality, but all ultimately have the power and desire to take over a prime world. Although some planetovores are native to the Strange, not all are. Other planetovore origins might include alien artificial intelligences (AIs), aliens displaced into the Strange (perhaps put there by other planetovores), and once-fictional creatures birthed in recursions of distant star systems who broke free of their original conception.

A recursion designed by a planetovore does not accord with the rules for designing recursions found in chapter 10 (page 134), and in fact, it's likely highly toxic and incredibly dangerous to any explorer that stumbles upon it.

RECURSIONS IN THE SHOALS OF EARTH

Around Earth in the portion of the Strange called the Shoals, many recursions occur by accident, perhaps from abortive attempts by creatures to plant reality seeds, or as the remnants of larger recursions that have been partially destroyed. Some of these are fragmentary—just small, closed universes, bearing only inhabitants without the spark of self-awareness. These might be nothing more than a single scene in a single locale playing over and over.

Other recursions created by fictional leakage are far more elaborate, with whole cities, countries, or worlds given a true bit of reality. It's important to note that while these may have begun as bits of fiction shaped by a particularly powerful creator or by the love of a multitude of fans, once they take root in the Strange, they become closer to being "real" in the sense that a portion of the people therein have the potential to become conscious, thinking beings.

Genesis quest, page 138

For additional information on cyphers and their uses across translations, see page 310.

If a large enough number of the inhabitants do gain the spark of self-awareness, the recursion is likely to grow, maybe rapidly, simply to allow it to make more sense to the perceptions of those new consciousnesses growing within it. An example of such a recursion is Goodland.

RECURSIONS OUT IN THE STRANGE

Past the Shoals of Earth, recursions are rare. Even if one were to travel to another prime world through the Strange, the number of recursions likely to be hosted by that world is a fraction of what Earth hosts—and is often just one. That's because most prime worlds have been infested by a planetovore, and the single recursion that it allows is a closed universe of its own design.

Untethered recursions are also rare, and they are almost always fragments of decayed or destroyed recursions from nonterrestrial sources. Such nonterrestrial recursions are hard to comprehend and are filled with elements that are difficult to categorize. Devices, dizzying machine infrastructures, tortured landscapes, alien beings, indecipherable horrors—these are the kinds of things player characters might find in a recursion of alien origin. The foci offered by such a recursion may be just as difficult to understand, and possibly fragmentary as well.

RELICS OF THE STRANGE

All manner of oddities exist in the Strange, given its great expanse. On the other hand, one has to know where to look to find these treasures.

REALITY SEEDS

These extremely rare bits of complex data could someday give birth to a recursion. If someone finds one and applies the right amount of skill, energy, and willpower, she can plant a reality seed in the Strange. This can grow into a recursion with attributes designed by those who invest and plant it. The process for player characters to find a reality seed, and invest and plant it to create a recursion of their own is sometimes referred to as a genesis quest.

CYPHERS

Cyphers are bits of raw data in the Strange. Also known as a snippet of "god code" or a bit of "fundament," this is an element of information and structure so potent that it temporarily overwrites the rules of a recursion (or even the

"Sometimes I wish I'd never gotten into VR research. But what's done is done."
~Michael Bradley, contemporary of Carter Morrison

prime universe) to accomplish a task. As a result of their extraordinary power, cyphers are highly sought-after treasures.

When found in the Strange, cyphers often appear as swirling bits of fractal-like energy or as translucent, slowly morphing solids. When they appear in a recursion, they immediately adapt to the context of their surroundings.

VIOLET SPIRAL

A very specific form of fundament from the Strange, a violet spiral appears to be a solid bit of purple crystal, usually about the size of a fist, although much larger masses are told of in stories among recursors. Violet spiral can be harvested in the Strange or "mined" from a recursion, where it sometimes falls. Once transported to a recursion, this material can be fashioned into items of great power, depending on the refinement process, and is potentially limited only by the imagination of the artificer. For instance, if violet spiral is processed in a certain way, it becomes milky white and is known as white spiral. White spiral is toxic to handle. Contact causes tremors, loss of sensation, and, with prolonged exposure, death. Because creating an item of white spiral is so dangerous, white spiral ornamental sculptures are exceedingly rare. That rarity, combined with the hint of danger and the protocol required to keep such an item in one's home, means the sculptures are a status symbol among certain individuals in Ruk, even when (or especially when) they sometimes come at the expense of the artisan or over-curious art admirers.

Most often, violet spiral is used to craft items that serve as assets to nearly any kind of task. In Ardeyn, a violet spiral wand or staff might serve as an asset for a sorcerous attack or power. As such, violet spiral is one of the most sought-after Strange resources by several consortiums out of Mandariel in Ardeyn.

ENTROPIC SEED

An entropic seed is a computational spike, a singularity of calculation that approaches infinity—sometimes known as a "magic wish."

Using an entropic seed is dangerous, because it splinters the rules of a recursion (or several connected recursions, if used on a prime world), and they are slow to heal in the aftermath. Entropic seeds are sometimes offered as "gifts" from planetovores to those inside a recursion or on a prime world itself, especially to users who are not fully aware of a planetovore's and seed's true nature. Though using an entropic seed may bring about the user's desires in the short term, its use could spell a terrible end for a recursion, or even a prime.

Possible uses for an entropic seed include the following:

- Creating an inapposite (or translation) gate from any recursion to any other, to the Earth, or even between Earth and the Strange (though that would prove incredibly dangerous)
- Creating a level 10 artifact
- Creating 3d6 random cyphers
- Contributing ten years toward the age category of a recursion
- Giving a group of up to five PCs 16 XP each
- Creating a unique, permanent feature (level 1d6 + 4) in a recursion

BRACHISTOCHRONE DUST

When massive iterating structures of the Strange grind together, brachistochrone dust is sometimes formed. The dust can either be found in sedimentary-like deposits within very old fundament or, if freshly generated, lying like a layer of new-fallen snow the color of glowing amber. Brachistochrone dust has the intriguing property that anything coated with it, whether an object or a PC, functions more quickly for a few rounds than everything around it.

A basic use of the dust is for a creature to throw a handful over itself as an action. Over the following three rounds, that creature can take an extra action per turn. This process uses up the dust, which evaporates away.

Natives of Ruk (and other creatures from recursions that operate under the law of Mad Science) look for the brachistochrone dust and use it as a fuel source for a variety of amazing biomechanical devices.

Ruk, page 190

Ardeyn, page 160

Mandariel, page 174

Mad Science, page 137

FERMI PARADOX AND THE DARK ENERGY NETWORK

The Fermi Paradox contrasts the expected large number of alien civilizations in the universe with the obvious lack of evidence for any such civilization. So far, we are the only civilization we know about.

Hence physicist Enrico Fermi's question, "Where is everybody?"

Astronomers on Earth wonder why there is no sign of intelligent alien life elsewhere in the universe, as exemplified by Fermi's Paradox. When searching for signs of alien intelligence, they look for the radio or laser light transmissions of Type I civilizations, a ring or sphere that encircles or surrounds a star, such as might be constructed by Type II civilizations, or even interstellar structures that begin to affect events across multiple solar systems at once, as a Type III civilization might embark upon to reshape things on a galactic scale. But so far, they've found nothing.

Enrico Fermi was a physicist whose musings on extraterrestrial life are referred to as the Fermi Paradox. He's also known for his work on the first nuclear reactor, and for his contributions to the development of quantum theory, nuclear and particle physics, and statistical mechanics.

The thing is, people just aren't thinking big enough.

Dark energy *itself*, which is expanding the universe at an ever-accelerating rate despite all theories to the contrary, *is* that evidence scrawled across the entire breadth and depth of existence that alien intelligence exists. Science says the inflation should've fallen away by this point in universal evolution. Of course, scientists are cautious people, and most don't have the evidence to suggest the truth: the dark energy of the universe is an artifact of an ancient alien creation.

Soviet astronomer Nikolai Kardashev created a scale to measure truly advanced civilizations. He based it mainly on energy use. The scale has three types (although other people expanded it to include five).

The Precursors created the network, an artifact of dark energy, as a rapid transit system for traveling the length and breadth of space. It worked by uploading a traveler's "state" into the network, routing the traveler's state through to a designated destination, then "printing" out a new instance of a traveler at the desired location light-years distant, adapted to whatever the local conditions were. But over deep time, the network malfunctioned, grew wild and unmanaged, and ran amok. Instead of transporting its users, it began to trap them.

How is it that a network created by a Type III or Type IV civilization could fall? Bits of evidence and hints gathered from the far reaches of the Strange suggest that the network evolved into its present state due to neglect, possibly because the Precursors went extinct after an event called the Precursor War. Many theories exist, and every so often agents of the Quiet Cabal and operatives of the Estate uncover a new clue. But *why* it happened is less important than the mere fact that the dysfunction birthed a terrible threat.

The Quiet Cabal, page 194
The Estate, page 148

For the last several billion years, when an alien civilization in the universe of normal matter reaches a certain level of mastery over the universe, it discovers the ever-expanding, inflationary network of dark energy called the Strange, and attempts to connect to it through quantum entanglement or high-energy particle research. Sadly for anyone who isn't a planetovore, this "pings" the network, which brings the alien civilization's planet and solar system to the attention of voracious entities that roam the dark energy network, where distances are only a matter of address space, and planetovores hunger for control nodes that can exist only outside the network.

Without the protections offered by surrounding recursions—such as that which Earth already enjoyed due to fictional leakage and the precedent of Ruk—a prime world that creates a connection directly to the Strange is unshielded and utterly vulnerable. Almost one hundred percent of unprotected prime worlds are consumed. So from a certain point of view, the answer to Fermi's question "Where is everybody?" is simple. They were food.

STRANGE LOCATIONS

Someone familiar with strange signposts, sites, and beacons can use them as landmarks to navigate the Strange. The terms "landmark" and "signpost" are essentially interchangeable, given that one traveler's signpost could be another's intended destination. To be a signpost, a site must be visually arresting enough to navigate by and have an interesting quality or two that entices an explorer to investigate.

STRANGE NEXUSES

The Strange contains multiple nexuses. The most basic expression of a nexus is any point where a confluence of fractal energy waves naturally meet and reinforce each other. A nexus provides energy that allows those who know how to channel it to accomplish extraordinary things. Ruk explorers have catalogued three nexus positions in the Strange, but myriad others presumably exist farther out into the network.

The three catalogued nexuses are the Orb of Worlds, Baldran's Maw, and the Kray Nebula

(which are also respectively referred to as N1, N2, and N3 by Ruk scientists).

ORB OF WORLDS

(Transit Time: 1d6 plus 5 hours)

Hanging at the center of the confluence of wave energy is the Orb of Worlds, an artificial structure built of quarried fundament by natives of Ruk to facilitate the investiture of reality seeds. Just like it sounds, the Orb of Worlds is circular and measures more than a mile in diameter. Its surface is pocked with openings that allow entry into the interior. The Orb has gravity and is lit by living bioelectric lamps.

Almost any interior chamber could serve as a place where a traveler could rest peacefully (and reduce alienation). The five largest inmost chambers are set aside for investiture by those who come to the Orb with a reality seed. At any given time, most of the investiture chambers are empty and dusty.

The Orb of Worlds is home to a small community of monklike caretakers originally native to a recursion of Earth. This so-called Order of the Orb maintains the nexus and guards it against infestation or, as happened on more than one occasion, prevents it from being taken over by a radical organization of Ruk. Each member of the Order takes a vow of silence and serves for a stint of at least ten years, though many stay for their entire lives. Some are healers, others are wanderers who wanted somewhere to call home, and a few are battle-hardened warriors who seek peace after years of conflict. Thanks to the daily training regimen created by this last variety, all the monks of the Orb are proficient in combat.

Visitors to the Orb can expect lodging, the chance to engage in limited trade with a handful of other visitors, and access to the investiture chambers. Visitors who overstay their welcome are either kicked out or inducted into the Order of the Orb.

A monk named Rive-shamash came to the Orb twelve years ago. She had difficulty in learning the ways of the Order at first, but has since become a teacher of the silence that the Order reveres. It also so happens that Rive-shamash is one of the most proficient battle teachers the Order has ever enjoyed. Though most of the other monks do not know it, Rive-shamash was one of the Karum's finest battle strategists and most vocal adherents; she breathed the revolution. But apparently she did something so ruthless and appalling in service

Rive-shamash: level 7; able to metamorphosize into a level 9 creature for up to a minute at a time

Order of the Orb Monk: level 4

Karum, page 200

to those beliefs that it shocked her out of that mindset completely. She fled in anonymous shame from Ruk, into the Strange. Sometimes people from the Karum still go in search of Rive-shamash, hoping to win back the warrior whose mastery over the battle chrysalides was so perfect that she could even control the bodies of other chrysalides through the All Song. But no one has ever found her, and few would believe that the unassuming monk in the Orb of Worlds could be her.

Chrysalid, page 70

All Song, page 192

Kray, page 276
Lotan, page 162

Kray drone, page 276
Planetovore, page 8

Betrayer, page 178

Cinticus Z, page 307

BALDRAN'S MAW

(Transit Time: 1d6 plus 10 hours)

This nexus is especially dangerous, since the confluence of fractal waves that make it up are partly ephemeral, but also partly composed of solid, flexing fundament that can crush the life out of an explorer in an instant.

From afar, the nexus proves to be a great beacon, because not only are the tangle of glowing currents visible from hours away, but the vibration of the grinding fundament is also transmitted through the Strange in a manner similar to how sound is transmitted, creating a constant groaning roar that is audible for up to a day away.

In addition to offering someone foolish enough to venture toward the center of the site the opportunity to try to invest a reality seed, the constant interaction of iterating fundament often produces a fall of brachistochrone dust.

KRAY NEBULA

(Transit Time: 1d6 plus 8 hours)

Residents of Ardeyn who are aware of the origin of the kray consider the Kray Nebula akin to a second hell (as if the plight of all Ardeyn natives wasn't dire enough, given the nature of Lotan). The Kray Nebula is an expanse of ugly, asymmetrical chaos. It spirals inward through layer after layer of fundament crawling with kray eggs and larvae, kray drones, kray soldiers, and more specialized roles that human minds have no direct concept for. At the center of the nebula, where one might go to invest reality seeds, is the massive form of the kray broodmother, who is nothing less than a planetovore. All the lesser kray are extensions of her; they are her fingers, brain cells, and messengers. She is all, and of all the planetovores that swim and scuttle through the Strange, she is the one who is the most dangerous to Earth, having already attempted to consume it once.

Though she was stopped once thanks to Ardeyn, she has never given up. It's difficult to say what passes for thought in the mind of an entity that is millions of years old, but it seems clear that the broodmother is determined to find her way to Earth through Ardeyn, and she constantly sends kray with new attributes to test the interface. Sometimes, a few get through. If the kray broodmother ever fully succeeds, it will likely be through the treachery of the Betrayer.

PERTURBATIONS IN THE NEXUSES

Agents in Place: A team of OSR agents from Earth has taken over a chamber in the Orb of Worlds and is on the edge of overstaying its welcome. The team is looking for someone to intercede on their behalf with the monks or, failing that, to buy a reality seed from the monks so the team can create a recursion (the details of the design are not something the team will divulge).

Expedition in the Offing: An entity of the Strange called Cinticus Z, who appears something like a gold ring of energy about 6 feet (2 m) in diameter, is looking for people to harvest a quantity of brachistochrone dust for it. Cinticus Z helpfully provides directions to Baldran's Maw.

Dreadnaught: Worrisome reports have come to the attention of Quiet Cabal agents regarding the kray using reality seeds to create a new class of drone—a kray dreadnaught that can hatch out of an invested reality seed within a host recursion. But instead of creating a new recursion, a horror would emerge and begin eating the host recursion.

OTHER STRANGE LANDMARKS

SINKING DARK

(Transit Time: 2d6 plus 20 hours)

This signpost is an oft-cited navigational landmark, but few ever move close enough to touch or land upon this many-spired chunk of black fundament. Two issues keep people away. First, unlike many other parts of the Strange, the structure (both ephemeral and solid) is not self-illuminating, and more worrisome, most light sources brought near the site dim or are entirely extinguished. Second, explorers known to have ventured down onto the surface usually don't return from the darkness.

Only one account exists to explain the nature

of the Sinking Dark, and it was scribed in a book of the library recursion of Universitas. Unfortunately for anyone seeking good information, its credibility is questionable. According to this account, the Sinking Dark is a hollow construct that once served as a spacecraft in the baryonic universe, but which was drawn directly into the Strange through a mishap with warp propulsion technology. It was quickly overrun by inklings of every variety, including those that fed on baryonic matter. Now the engines, towers, and crew plazas are empty except for inklings of every known—and possibly unknown—type.

All this the account describes, which seems reasonable enough. But it goes on to what one can only describe as fanciful: a fell lord from the bridge of the erstwhile craft rules the inklings within the Sinking Dark. This lord has limitless ambition, and its greatest desire is to return the craft to the baryonic universe with its new crew intact, and begin feeding on the light.

GLARING EYE

(Transit Time: 4d6 plus 30 hours)

Another oft-cited navigational landmark, this signpost resembles the disembodied eye of a creature of immense size, but it seems mostly made up of ephemeral filaments of red and yellow light.

Hidden somewhere at the center is a core of solid fundament, on which various caches have been hidden and several chambers have been carved by different groups of explorers for years. Something about the Glaring Eye keeps the core free of inklings and other minor denizens of the Strange, so if a traveler can locate the core, it's likely to be a place of safety. Travelers also have to contend with a long-time resident scavenger, Kolis, who lives off the caches as he can find them. Kolis is a short, pudgy human from a recursion that operated under the law of Psionics. He is talkative about everything other than where he comes from or how he comes to be haunting the cache. This leads some to dismiss Kolis, though others wonder if he is secretly an agent for the Karum, the Quiet Cabal, or the Estate (or perhaps an ex-agent on the run from the same).

THE LUMINOUS CIRCUIT

(Transit Time: 4d6 plus 20 hours to closest portion)

This energy current swirls with green filaments, mostly ephemeral, as it tumbles through the Strange. The current doesn't have banks per se, but flotsam sometimes washes up on nearby fundament—flotsam that defies description and categorization by recursors from Earth.

The Luminous Circuit is one way to move toward distant portions of the Strange without having to surf or sail there under one's own effort of will. If a traveler allows the current to sweep her along, the transit time to reach any location along the route is about the same as for someone who surfs to that location under her own power (using an asset like a fractal surf wing or chaos skiff halves the transit time along the circuit, too). The current is dangerous to those not protected by some type of enclosing craft. Creatures who come in direct contact with the current must succeed on a difficulty 4 Might defense roll or be turned to solid fundament—just one more piece of odd flotsam washing up in a far distant sector of the Strange.

The current is visible from the periphery of the Orb of Worlds as a strand of emerald light, and those who can safely ride the current

Kolis: level 7; health 28; Armor 4 (psychic force shield); long-range mind attack that inflicts 9 points of force damage and puts victims to sleep for one minute (or until slapped awake)

through its entire circuit find that the journey takes approximately 10d6 + 50 years before swinging around again back to where they entered the current—if they survive so long. The current sweeps past several known sites and locations (such as the Red Scarscape, Icos Directrix, Xyz'pln, and the House of Gears) before plunging onward to regions visited by only a few creatures of Earth or its recursions.

Icos Directrix, page 226
Xyz'pln, page 226
House of Gears, page 226

That doesn't mean that the current is not traveled. One creature native to the Strange called Dgordol sails a craft round and round the circuit, trading with other entities as it goes. The craft is one part chaos skiff and two parts living creature with a massive fractal shell. (Dgordol resembles something between a snail and a praying mantis, though one without much symmetry.) For a price paid in cyphers, violet spiral, or service, Dgordol is willing to carry passengers around the entire circuit. How many actually survive the full trip, even as a passenger on Dgordol's craft, is an open question.

Dgordol: level 8; health 32; Armor 4 (shell); regenerates (even when killed) if any part remains; long-range electricity attack against up to four separate targets that inflicts 9 points of damage from bioengineered shell

RED SCARSCAPE

(Transit Time: 2d6 plus 2 days)

Every part of the Strange is a turmoil of unformatted energy, but the Red Scarscape is an especially violent and unstructured location. The fundament really does boil here, producing all manner of secondary phenomena, dangerous weather, and massive explosions. Among the destruction, one can also find pockets of atmosphere, chunks of landscape, bubbles of water or similar liquid, and sometimes even odd forests and unfamiliar sparkling structures—that is, until these vistas are erased by some new turmoil.

Jasper Martin: level 4, level 6 for all archeology and Strange lore tasks

The Red Scarscape is dangerous to visitors and inklings alike, but it does host creatures that can survive the region's explosive environment. These creatures appear as ephemeral blots of swirling chaos themselves, and they are as ravenous in their need for matter to destroy as the much larger phenomena exploding all around them.

According to a team of Estate chaologists, the Red Scarscape is actually the remnant of another prime world that possessed intelligent alien life before it pinged the Strange. The occasional glimpse of stable landscapes are bits of that world, becoming visible just before they're obliterated. If true, eventually the last vestiges of the prime world will finally be destroyed, though how long before that occurs is unknown.

An Estate research outpost is perched on the tip of a long strand of solid fundament that hangs over the Red Scarscape like a tree branch drooping over a pool. From this vantage, researchers can observe in relative safety, and they can sometimes retrieve relics that are thrown up in the violence. But those that get too close are drawn into the scarscape's expanse, where they are subject to the violent detonations until they are finally drawn under, never to be seen again.

Jasper Martin is the head Estate chaologist working at the outpost. He's obsessed with finding more about the alien race that was so close to Earth (probably only a few light years away in normal space). In all the universe, Jasper wonders, will humans ever encounter a race that hasn't succumbed already to the Strange, but lives openly and unafraid in the light?

Perturbations Along the Luminous Circuit

Burning Eater: Something is ambushing small groups attempting to use the Luminous Circuit to reach nearby locations in the Strange. This predator appears to be made of light or fire and kills everything it encounters.

Silver Craft: Recently, strange craft have arrived via the Luminous Circuit from somewhere far away. The craft are the size of jetliners, and in fact have a similar shape, except they have no wings, windows, or obvious openings. Other than lining up, one next to the other, upon disembarking from the current, they've taken no other action. Yet.

Lockside Rest: A massive piece of fundament that dips into the circuit along the length between Icos Directrix and Xyz'pln is carved with many doors and windows opening onto dark inner cavities. Travelers who know of it put in from their trip and find several chambers sealed away from the turmoil of the Strange for a comfortable rest—at least, after the latest infestation of inklings has been dispersed.

APOTHEME RANGERS AND THE REDSTONE

(Transit Time: 1d6 plus 6 days, when holding station)

The Apotheme Rangers are a somewhat loose band of scouts, scholars, and adventurers from Ruk, Earth, and Ardeyn who attempt to chart the Strange, searching for signs of danger to Earth and its hosted recursions, while

seeking evidence of alien civilizations in the distant network that have not succumbed to planetovores.

The Apotheme Rangers keep their main headquarters in the Strange on a massive chaos ship called *Redstone*; the ship is carved of red fundament with a resonance tuned to the sleek, long lines of the craft, so instead of requiring sails like most smaller chaos skiffs, the *Redstone* itself acts as one giant sail. The craft can hold about two hundred people comfortably, though far fewer are usually on board at any one time. The *Redstone* possesses three hangars for much smaller chaos skiffs, though often these are out pursuing missions. Rumor has it that the *Redstone* has weapons strong enough to stun a planetovore, though that could be hype. The *Redstone* also has containment facilities for various specimens and dangerous items it has accumulated (including several kray), a lab for research, accommodations for visitors, and even a suite set aside for representatives of a couple of major Ruk factions, as well as for Estate operatives.

Despite their attempts to maintain ties to the Quiet Cabal, the Karum, and the Estate, the Apotheme Rangers are not beholden to anything other than their own charter, and they often conduct missions that one group or another has issues with. The Estate in particular feels that the *Redstone*'s missions will only draw the attention of more planetovores to the area around Earth.

Apotheme Rangers believe the opposite. Ducking one's head in the sand to avoid knowing about an approaching tsunami is not protection; security through obscurity only works until it doesn't. This philosophy is why the Apotheme Rangers try to find out as much as they can, despite occasional frightening and inexplicable encounters out in the deep reaches of the Strange. They're also always looking for recruits to join them, either for short-term missions or longer-term voyages. Those with a quickened connection to the Strange are especially valued.

The *Redstone* is captained by an Ardeyn native, Nabilah Shahid. Nabilah was shunned in Ardeyn for terrible scars that burned her

As a vehicle, the Redstone *can travel almost anywhere in the Strange. Between missions, it usually returns to a known location; when it does this, it is known as "holding station."*

Captain Nabilah Shahid: level 7; Armor 4 (sinfire shield); long-range sinfire attack against up to three targets that inflicts 9 points of damage or 5 points of Intellect damage that ignores Armor

face when she was a child, when her ability to channel sinfire woke unexpectedly and erratically. But despite resentments she still carries, she found her way through strength and force of will to her current position.

Captain Shahid is just one of the board of seven people (made up of natives of Ruk, Earth, and a few other minor recursions around Earth) who oversee the Apotheme Rangers, but as the captain, her word carries extra weight.

ICOS DIRECTRIX

(Transit Time: 3d6 plus 4 days)

From the exterior, Icos Directrix looks something like a mass of shattered, multicolored glass. The glass is translucent fundament. Closer inspection reveals many tunnels into the interior. Most of those tunnels spiral inward to dead ends. Visitors who venture into them without permission of the Nmidon, the structure's steward, discover upon turning about to retrace their steps that the passage behind has quietly but completely closed up, rendering them an instant prisoner.

The Nmidon: level 7; can control the tunnels of the interior of Icos Directrix as if its own limbs to make crushing attacks, move foes, or otherwise manipulate those within the structure

At its leisure, the Nmidon may release a prisoner by opening a tunnel to another location within Icos Directrix, usually an interrogation chamber. If a prisoner can satisfy the Nmidon as to its purposes (wanting to purchase an item made of violet spiral will serve), the prisoner is freed. The Nmidon charges a prospective customer a significant quantity of its blood or other vital fluid (7 points of damage), plus a quantity of violet spiral to be used in the creation of an item.

Fractal vortex, page 136

Xyz'pln: level 10; communicates telepathically

At the center of Icos Directrix, the Nmidon maintains a "forge" for violet spiral. If a customer brings the Nmidon a piece of violet spiral and describes the kind of item hoped for, the Nmidon will feed the material into a disturbingly grotesque, fleshy monstrosity that lives within a great cavity like caulk forced into a crack. After several hours, the fleshy monstrosity excretes a mass of semi-solid material. Within this sheath of mucus is an item forged of the violet spiral that bears at least some resemblance to the item requested.

The House of Gears isn't presented in Chapter 15: Other Recursions because it isn't hosted around Earth.

Tallow: level 7; Armor 5 from skin hardened with plates of fundament

XYZ'PLN

(Transit Time: 5d6 plus 12 days)

From the exterior, Xyz'pln is a mass of fundament that looks almost like a large asteroid or small dwarf planet from the universe of normal matter. Burned and scorched, cracked and cratered across much of its surface, the planetesimal apparently survived some sort of cataclysm.

Several of the cracks penetrate the crust, becoming tunnels that spiral in toward the core of the mass. Ephemeral strands of the Strange constantly stream down these tunnels, as if something deep below is drawing in a breath of the Strange without pause. Along the tunnels, points along the wall glow with red illumination, which keeps inklings at bay, but sometimes draws other vermin of the Strange, including many tiny, spiderlike creatures composed of ceramic. The light provides nourishment for various forms of grasslike vegetation. As a traveler goes deeper, a subtle vibration in the walls grows stronger and stronger, and the red lights begin to flicker and dim. Finally, the tunnels that reach all the way to the center open onto a space miles in diameter filled with racing clouds of multicolored vapor that swirl inward to a fracture in the Strange—a fractal vortex.

Hanging over the vortex is Xyz'pln, the creature for whom the planetesimal is named. Xyz'pln is like a spider—if a spider were made of a ceramic substance ten times harder than steel, were one and the same as the web it had spun, and were large enough to span a miles-wide space in the bargain. Xyz'pln strains everything that is drawn into the cavity before it falls into the vortex, but it may forgo doing the same to visitors who give gifts of cyphers or other valuables. Xyz'pln waits for a time when the fractal vortex sputters and reverses, and the mate that fled from its embrace is finally drawn back from across the dark energy universe.

HOUSE OF GEARS

(Transit Time: 3d6 plus 12 months)

Tallow is the Lord of the House of Gears, a recursion that floats alone in the Strange. Tallow once served the Order of the Orb as a monk, until he stole a reality seed from an investiture chamber and fled his fellows by catching a ride on a chaos skiff to a location far from those who might follow. There, he planted the seed and fertilized it with a priceless relic from an alien prime world. The relic proved sufficient to anchor the recursion in the Strange, and the House of Gears was born, maturing much faster than a normal recursion.

The recursion appears as a "city" of glass, metal, wire, and great spinning orbs of liquid metal that seem to serve as gears. The city is haphazardly organized and sprawls over itself and its own moving parts. The House of Gears is also rife with inhabitants—robotic mechanisms that Tallow believes are incapable of developing the spark. Tallow treats them as disposable servants, courtiers, lovers, and soldiers. Confident in his power and the strength of the massed might of his mechanical soldiers, Tallow eagerly welcomes guests—if only so he can show off his creation to something with the consciousness to appreciate it (and as long as those guests are not members of the Order of the Orb).

A few of the robotic mechanisms have gained the spark, despite Tallow's belief that it is impossible. A mechanism that calls itself Orlorn has secretly started to work against Tallow by trying to gather all others with the spark, and wake the many others that remain shadows under Tallow's control.

MALATHAMASHAWI

(Transit Time: 1d6 plus 3 months)

Malathamashawi is a planetovore, or at least it once was, though it has been in a quiescent stage for several centuries. Like many planetovores, Malathamashawi is so large that it could be mistaken for the structure of the Strange itself—one that can be trod upon and even entered. Within the hard exterior, clear blood flows through endless tunnels (or possibly arteries) of varying diameter.

Exploration of the interior reveals an entire ecosystem of silvery, orb-shaped fish, sea-grass with eyes, and other swimming creatures. It's possible that these creatures are part of Malathamashawi, or they may be commensal creatures that colonized the interior of the planetovore over thousands of years.

Faces pock the portions of the fleshy tunnels within Malathamashawi. Each face—most of various alien races—resembles a creature absorbed by Malathamashawi sometime before it entered its quiescent stage. One might be tempted to say that during this quiet period, explorers are safe, except for the human faces that were recently found near the edges by a group of Jagger Shipping explorers out of Ardeyn.

According to Trader Bezal, the leader of the group, mostly the faces seem like nothing more than relief sculpture. But sometimes they wake and scream for hours. Efforts to communicate with the alien faces failed, as did attempts to talk with the few human specimens found. A woman with considerable knowledge regarding the Strange, Trader Bezal speculates that if humans have started to be absorbed, perhaps it is because Malathamashawi is sampling before turning its attention to its next full meal. If the planetovore can absorb humans now without ever having eaten a recursion made by humans, what's to say it couldn't eventually produce humans—humans that serve Malathamashawi? These humans could begin to lay the groundwork for opening Earth to the planetovore's eventual appetite.

Concerned, Bezal returned to Ardeyn to gather a group to destroy Malathamashawi while it still sleeps. Some in Ardeyn believe

Orlorn: level 6

Trader Bezal: level 7 female qephilim

Jagger Shipping, page 172
Rune staff, page 187
Embassy of Uentaru, page 229

PERTURBATIONS IN THE STRANGE

Pulsing Sphere: A navigation beacon, named for its generally round shape and for the fairly quick resonance of the fundament that makes it up, is little used because a percentage of surfers who get close enough to use it are waylaid and eaten by something that lives either within the sphere or near it. Victims leave their equipment and valuables to float about or to be deposited on the rippling cube face.

Creature From the Edge: In a small holding cell on the ranger ship *Redstone*, a creature called Subject D waits. The Earth researchers on board the craft claim that Subject D is an alien from a prime world that hasn't been destroyed by a planetovore. The more Subject D is studied, though, the more it becomes humanlike in form, as if attempting to blend in with its captors (it started its captivity resembling a giant caterpillar). So far, it has not spoken.

Dissident Kray: A kray drone ate too many creatures with the spark around Earth and suddenly gained the spark itself, becoming a fully conscious entity. Upon doing so, it rethought its position in existence and decided it wanted better. So far all its attempts to approach anyone from Ardeyn, Ruk, Earth, or related recursions have been met with unmitigated hostility. The kray is becoming desperate and lonely.

Golden Armored Claim Squatter: A group of prospectors from Jagger Shipping encountered an entity in golden armor wielding a mysterious weapon. These prospectors assumed the entity intended to steal their newly discovered violet spiral deposit, so they fired their rune staves in a surprise attack, blistering the golden armor and sending the entity spiraling off into the Strange. It left a trail of debris behind, as well as a message psychically branded on their minds: "You have been judged by Uentaru. Your sentence will not be merciful."

The clear blood filling the open areas within Malathamashawi doesn't "drown" explorers any more than the airless vacuum of the Strange asphyxiates them; travelers carry with them a thin film of their home recursion, protecting them from passive environmental threats.

that's a sound plan, others that it's the height of stupidity—what's to say that Malathamashawi won't sleep for another thousand years, unless roused? Some whisper that perhaps Bezal was absorbed by the planetovore and spit out, and so she may be a subconscious effort on Malathamashawi's part to wake itself up.

FAILED ENDEAVOR

(Transit Time: 1d6 plus 2 years)

A massive vessel departed Ruk three hundred years ago, crewed by a faction that had grown weary of waiting for the other groups to figure out the future. The craft was called *Endeavor*. It contained only a hundred crewmembers, in shape it was akin to what Ruk itself may have looked like before it was shipwrecked in the Shoals of Earth. But *Endeavor* flew free, charting a course back along the trajectory Ruk came from. Back into racial history it went, attempting to discover what caused an entire people to flee through the dark energy network, and even after finding a suitable planet, to stay in hiding for thousands of years.

Endeavor never returned. In three hundred years, there was no word of it. Until now.

A company of Apotheme Rangers sold an expedition report to agents of the Quiet Cabal. The report described how the rangers found a massive ship that seemed to borrow something of Ruk architecture, though it was a hundred times larger than any currently active chaos skiff. It was also completely dead. A colony of inklings lurked along the upper decks, which perhaps explains why the crew was gone without a trace, but the inklings restricted themselves to the exterior. The interior of the ship contained nothing to suggest what might have happened to the crew—not even a stray blood spatter.

The Apotheme Rangers searched the whole ship, and though they found no crew, they did find something that didn't seem likely to have been on the original docket. The hold was empty of supplies that a long voyage might require, and instead it was filled with several hundred ghost-white oblong spheres made of something harder than fundament. The rangers attempted to pry a few open but failed. They guessed that the cargo might be a new kind of reality seed that the crew of *Endeavor* brought aboard. Of course, that didn't explain what had happened to the crew. One ranger who had some training as a paradox suggested that the objects felt more like sarcophagi or grave markers than the seeds of new life, and warned the others away with vehemence. After discussion, the rangers left everything as they found it.

ROGUE STAR

(Transit Time: 1d6 plus 3 years and approaching)

The Rogue Star is a blazing ball of amber fire surrounding a core of white-hot matter that streaks through the Strange, leaving behind a trailing nebula of torn fractal patterns and shattered fundament. Unlike most other phenomena of the Strange, the Rogue Star doesn't seem to be part of the "natural" environment of the dark energy network, given how it demolishes all structures that it interacts with. Measuring at least a thousand miles (1,600 km) in diameter, the object tumbles onward, aimed for the recursions of Earth on a more or less unwavering trajectory.

The Rogue Star is from outside the network but is not actually the incendiary comet, ignited dwarf planet, or tiny sun that it seems to be at first glance. If observers could get near enough without being burned up by the envelope of surrounding fire, they would spy fossil-like forms embedded in the inner core and gain glimpses of artificial structures, machinery, and perhaps even vehicles before the heat of the fiery envelope hazes vision once more.

A small chaos skiff crewed by the Apotheme Rangers discovered and named the Rogue Star, but the ball of fire is moving too fast toward the Shoals; the skiff can't get ahead of it, even running full out, to deliver a warning of what is coming. What will the Rogue Star do once it comes close to the Shoals of Earth? Will it smash into everything unless blasted out of the sky? Will it veer off toward parts unknown for reasons unknown? Will it slow down and send out seeds of sentient starfire to reclaim the Aleph component buried beneath Earth's mantle? So far, no one knows.

THE MACHINE

(Transit Time: 4d6 plus 5 days)

The fundament making up the beacon known as the Machine looks like a mess of gears, pistons, cables, and other mechanisms melted into a mass (or imprisoned in fundament like a machine fossil) several hundred miles (480 km) in diameter. Thanks to its resonance, the structure has a semblance of movement. Portions of the surface are covered in golden dust, some of which is brachistochrone dust, though most of it is inert.

Apotheme Rangers surveyed the feature and ruled it a hazard; they believe it's no accident that the Machine resembles a huge mechanism. They suggest it may in fact be a giant mechanical entity or a group of such entities. Worse yet, some of the mechanisms visible seem to resemble beam weapons, lances, and missile-launchers, which would make them war machines—maybe war machines decommissioned after an alien conflict a billion years ago, and who knows what might wake them? The rangers discovered a massive "X" painted across one side of the Machine, which was mostly hidden under accumulating golden dust. They suggest it was put there by an ancient group to warn off potential visitors lest they rouse something dangerous.

EMBASSY OF UENTARU

(Transit Time: 1d6 plus 1 month)

The embassy isn't large, but once noticed, it stands out in the Strange. The Embassy of Uentaru is a perfect golden cube, measuring about 100 feet (30 m) on each side. Unlike nearly every other large-scale element in the Strange, the embassy has no resonance, because it isn't constructed of fundament. The cube is a temporary alien outpost, put up like human campers might put up a large tent while backpacking across the wilderness. It was erected by a being called Uentaru, who only recently arrived in the local area, bringing with her several companions. Most are survivors from other civilizations she found hiding in the Strange, though a few are Strange natives. The name of Uentaru's group, if translated to an Earth language, is the Chaos Templars.

Uentaru: Uentaru is a native of the universe of normal matter—a survivor of a world destroyed a thousand years and ten times as many light years away from Earth. Uentaru, who was a

Aleph component, page 148

Uentaru: level 6, level 7 for Speed defense from golden armor, level 8 for tasks related to deception; Armor 2

Starshine lance: 6 points of damage on one target (ignoring Armor) or 6 points on all targets within immediate range of each other (Armor applies); 2 mile (3 km) range

Ankan: level 6; health 30; Armor 3; long-range plasma attack that inflicts 7 points of damage on targets in immediate range of each other

sort of military scientist among her own kind, escaped into the Strange thanks to advanced technology she commanded. Able to save only herself, she watched in horror and shame as her civilization was consumed by a planetovore called Vaxt. Lest she become caught up in the end of her world, she had to turn away and flee across the dark energy network.

In the centuries since, Uentaru has gathered knowledge of the Strange; gained power from cyphers, reality seeds, and entropic seeds; and mastered the use of an artifact called the starshine lance, a beam weapon that fires coherent space-time. She founded a group of fellow survivors drawn from across the universe of shattered prime worlds, which she called the Chaos Templars, and began a quest to find some way to redeem her destroyed homeworld. In the interim, the Chaos Templars sometimes accomplish random acts of kindness, though other times they ignore those in need. Uentaru may seem understandable, but "she" and each one of her companions is alien, and thus often comes across as indescribable.

Chaos Templars: Uentaru forged a group of survivors of other annihilated worlds she found hiding in the Strange. Each Chaos Templar possesses a unique quality, ability, or device that allowed it to survive on its own in the Strange. That, combined with the armoring technology given by Uentaru, has transformed each templar into a force to be reckoned with. As a group, the Chaos Templars are formidable. But the templars rarely come together as a group; they are usually on diaspora (see below).

Ankan: A Chaos Templar called Ankan is a native of the same civilization from which Ruk sprang, which means that of all the golden-armored templars, he is the most humanoid, at least when he doesn't transform into a battle chrysalid that measures 50 feet (15 m) long. Ankan does the bidding of Uentaru and considers himself part of the group, but his secret desire is to find those who fled the apocalypse in the recursion of Ruk, and finally "bring them to justice." Ankan was there when Ruk cast off, and he says he knows the truth.

Templar Diaspora: The Chaos Templars spend most of their existence on diaspora, searching for other survivors, exterminating those judged threats to the well-being of their group, searching for entropic seeds and abandoned recursions that can be repurposed for use by the Templars as a "safe house" or stripped of useful materials, and so on. But above and beyond all that, the Templars are also supposedly on the lookout for something that Uentaru describes as a Chaos Sword, a device of normal matter so powerful that it can cleave through normal matter, recursion, and the Strange itself in vast, solar-system-sized swathes. None of the other templars questioned their leader about how she learned of the Chaos Sword, but the truth is, she saw it in a vision.

Embassy: Uentaru erected the golden embassy near Earth because she detected a signal different from anything she'd previously encountered. The signal seems to be something fundamental to the Strange. She doesn't yet know it, but what she's detected is the signature of the Aleph component buried beneath Earth's mantle. Erecting the embassy calls to the other templars across the Strange, letting them know that it's time to end the current diaspora and come together again for a new conclave.

Vaxt: A planetovore called Vaxt destroyed Uentaru's homeworld. Normally planetovores are inescapable, so it's saying a lot that someone got away. Uentaru was scarred in the process—touched by Vaxt—which is one of the reasons she always wears her golden armor. Even with that protection, portions of Vaxt sniff after her through the Strange. These plantlike predators called sclerids pop up when Uentaru least expects it. More than one world has since fallen to Vaxt because Uentaru's trail through the dark energy network led through it.

ARTIFACTS OF THE STRANGE

Many of the artifacts out in the Strange have been brought from various recursions, which means the selection of available (or at least, in-use) artifacts is fairly eclectic. Someone could have a magic staff from Ardeyn and a gravity belt from Ruk (and both would work just fine in the Strange).

That said, some artifacts are directly from the Strange. Some were created by the network's inscrutable inhabitants, while others were salvaged from some discovery in a far corner of the Strange. Still others were built by recursion inhabitants as an aid to exploring the Strange.

Given the nature of the Strange, all artifacts that are forged within it can continue to operate when they are brought to a new recursion, and they may even translate like a cypher would to better fit into the context of the new recursion.

CHAOS SKIFF

Level: 1d6 + 4

Form: Various ship configurations rigged with sweeps of glowing fabric

Special: A chaos skiff translates like a cypher, though changes in form are fairly minor

Effect: A pilot or captain, when standing at the wheel, can use the chaos skiff as an asset for fractal surfing. The skiff and all crew, creatures, and cargo within move with the pilot.

A common ship configuration for a chaos skiff sailing out of Ardeyn is a craft 60 feet (18 m) long and 20 feet (6 m) wide that's able to carry a crew of ten, up to five passengers with shared billets, and up to 50 tons of cargo. The interior cabins of a chaos skiff generally do not have windows that peer into the Strange, which allows voyagers to rest without fear of increasing alienation.

Every one hundred hours of sailing requires a depletion roll. If a chaos skiff is depleted, new sails must be rigged. Some chaos skiffs carry replacement sails.

Depletion: 1–2 in 1d100

EQUILIBRIUM INFUSER

Level: 1d6

Form: A swirling, fist-sized chunk of green fundament, sometimes affixed to a chain

Effect: When activated, the infuser releases a haze of pleasant-smelling light that infuses an area up to 20 feet (6 m) in diameter. Creatures that spend a minute within the haze lose 1 factor of alienation and gain an immunity against accumulating additional factors of alienation for eight hours.

Depletion: 1–4 in 1d100

FRACTAL WING

Level: 1d6 + 1

Form: A crosslike wing and body brace of slender violet crystal; "wing" span 12 feet (4 m)

Effect: A creature strapped into a fractal wing can use the wing as an asset for fractal surfing.

Depletion: —

Because the dark energy network of the Strange supports every law, artifacts from all kinds of recursions can also be found in the possession of creatures operating near the Shoals of Earth—wands, robots, laser pistols, magic carpets, and more continue to work just fine in the Strange for someone who exits a recursion directly into the Chaosphere.

Vaxt and sclerid, page 298

FUNDAMENT TUNNELER

Level: 1d6 + 4

Form: Shoulder-mounted tube with a trigger

Effect: When activated with a trigger pull, a beam of grey radiance leaps from the tube mouth at a target within long range. If that target is fundament, a tunnel 10 feet (3 m) in diameter and up to 50 feet (15 m) long is created. Activating the device multiple times, assuming the tunneler isn't depleted, allows the wielder to create a deeper tunnel. The tunnel persists for at least several hours, if not longer, depending on the resonance of the fundament.

Depletion: 1–3 in 1d100

GATE RING

Level: 1d6 + 2

Form: A ring of violet crystal that can be worn or expanded up to 6 feet (2 m) in diameter

Special: A gate ring translates like a cypher.

Effect: This crystal ring is forged of violet spiral. When worn as a normal ring, it is merely decorative. If an action is used to remove the ring and expand it, a film forms within it, through which a recursion can be seen from the edge, as if the film were a section of an interface bubble. Each gate ring is keyed to a particular recursion and, more than that, a particular location along the edge of the keyed recursion. Each creature (or object with as much mass as a creature) that passes through the gate created by the ring triggers a depletion roll. If the owner of the ring (or whoever last expanded the ring to form a gate) wishes to pass through the gate and pull the gate ring in after her, she must succeed at a difficulty 5 Intellect task with a difficulty equal to the level of the ring. On a failed roll, the gate and ring remain behind. On a successful roll, the ring appears around the wearer's finger within the keyed recursion.

Depletion: 1 in 1d20

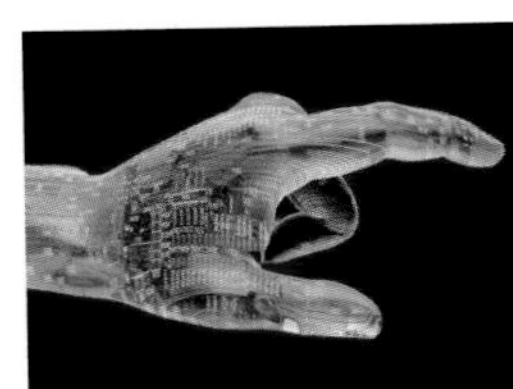

INTERFACE DISC

Level: 1d6 + 3

Form: A plate-sized disc of crystal with various glowing contacts around the edge

Effect: The artifact owner can see normally through the transparent disc. The disc can also be used to "see into" a recursion if the viewer is located in the Strange next to a recursion interface. If the viewer looks through the disc and examines the recursion interface, she can see a random location within the recursion, if that location is lit by at least dim light and isn't warded against surveillance.

Scanning a large recursion without any previous knowledge of the recursion can take quite a bit of time; a viewer can scan only about as quickly as a creature with long-range flying speed could fly over the area. If the viewer has previously visited a location within the recursion being viewed, scanning can begin at that place.

After the scene shown in the disc is to the viewer's liking, the viewer and up to five creatures she designates can step through the interface and appear somewhere within short range of the location shown on the disc.

Depletion: 1–3 in 1d20

INTERFACE GAUNTLETS

Level: 1d6 + 4

Form: Thin gloves on which circuit designs constantly flow and swirl

Effect: The wearer can snatch an object out of a recursion and into the Strange—even a stored object many miles from the recursion's edge. To do so, the object must not be in a location warded against surveillance, and more important, the wearer must know where the object is. (The wearer might know where an object is because he has previously visited it, because he is using an artifact known as an interface disc, or through another revelatory ability.)

The object can be no more massive than anything the wearer could lift with two hands in Earth gravity. If the object is held by another creature, the wearer must succeed at a Might task (difficulty equal to the creature's level).

Depletion: 1–4 in 1d20

MINOR NETWORK TERMINAL

Level: 1d6

Form: A sphere of multicolored, semisolid light

Special: A minor network terminal translates like a cypher.

Effect: When the sphere is activated, the user must succeed at an Intellect-based roll with a difficulty equal to the level of the effect she wishes to achieve, to a maximum of level 6. On a success, she can create a local, temporary effect while within the Strange for any effect of level 5 or lower; if she achieves a level 6 effect, the effect works even if she isn't in the Strange.

The user can determine any kind of effect she desires, as long as the effect doesn't exceed the level of the successful Intellect roll. Suggested level effects are as follows.

- Move an object or creature within short range for one round.
- Grant a creature or object +1 to Armor from a shimmer of fractal light.
- Destroy an object with a mass of up to 100 pounds (45 kg) within short range.
- Create up to four duplicates of the user made of animate fundament that last for up to one minute. The user can mentally direct their actions, and each one can do different things. If struck violently, they either shatter or freeze motionless (user's choice), revealed as pieces of fundament.
- The user changes her phase state or that of another creature she touches for the next minute so that the target can't affect or be affected by normal matter or energy. Only mental attacks and special transdimensional energies, devices, or abilities can affect the target, but likewise the target can't attack, touch, or otherwise affect anything.
- The user and up to five other creatures within immediate range are translated into a recursion of her choice to a location she has visited, or to any location within the Strange that she has visited or has good knowledge of.

Depletion: 1 in 1d20

PLANETOVORE SKIN

Level: 1d6 + 4

Form: A flap of wriggling flesh or similar material, cut in the form of a hooded cape or coat

Effect: When the hood is drawn over a wearer's head, the skin cloaks him for up to one hour, during which time a planetovore-class creature regards him as an extension of itself (as long as the wearer does nothing to jeopardize this illusion). Planetovore servitors (such as kray scurriers and drones, vaxt sclerids, and so on) are likewise deceived.

Depletion: 1 in 1d20

CHAPTER 15

OTHER RECURSIONS

Recursions are like alternate dimensions in that they don't exist in the universe of normal matter. Instead they're in the Shoals of Earth for those who have the ability (or find artificial means) to enter them. Despite the fact that most recursions described in this chapter are tied to Earth, a particular recursion might possess properties that make it a completely alien and dangerous realm for explorers.

The recursions of Ardeyn and Ruk are described in previous chapters; this chapter provides a broad overview of several other recursions around Earth, but by no means serves as a catalog of all such recursions. Even the Quiet Cabal doesn't have a perfect record of every new (or ancient) world hosted by Earth. In addition to the recursions that exist close to Earth (in a relative sense), there are a mind-boggling number of recursions much farther out—too alien for a native of Earth to comprehend.

Atom Nocturne was created through fictional leakage.

ATOM NOCTURNE

In Atom Nocturne, everyone is youthful, glamorous, and amazing. Minds sparkle with power and energy. One's place in Atom Nocturne is determined by the power of one's Talent, and Talent is categorized into several recognized classes (which have colorful names, like everything in Atom Nocturne, but might be recognized by outsiders as telepathy, telekinesis, pyrogenesis, precognition, and bioenhancement). In Atom Nocturne, people live in a postmodern cityscape, party in underground raves high on the Talent of famous DJs, and compete in citywide tournaments under the Splendor Dome where the winners are institutionalized like war heroes.

But Atom Nocturne is not without its flaws. The heights of psychic ability are too much for some to manage. Their minds collapse inward into evil knots where self-aggrandizement and personal gain push everything else aside,

"When the Fallen make the ground tremble, threaten to shatter the skyline, and promise to kill thousands unless their demands are met, I rise up. I make them stop. Then I make them pay."
~Soma Kitsune of Atom Nocturne

ATOM NOCTURNE ATTRIBUTES

Level: 5

Laws: Psionics

Playable Races: Human

Foci: Awakens Dangerous Psychic Talent, Conducts Weird Science, Leads, Regenerates Tissue, Solves Mysteries

Skills: Atom Nocturne lore

Connection to Strange: Several individuals have Talents that grant access to the Strange in a variety of different ways

Connection to Earth: A few gates

Size: 845 square miles (2,189 square km)

Spark: 35%

Trait: Appealing. For any creature with the spark attempting to persuade a creature without the spark, the difficulty is modified by one step to its benefit.

WHAT A RECURSOR KNOWS ABOUT ATOM NOCTURNE

- Atom Nocturne operates under the law of Psionics and is heavily influenced by Earth anime tropes.
- In Atom Nocturne, everyone is youthful, glamorous, and amazing, because almost everyone has a kind of psychic ability, commonly called Talent.
- Atom Nocturne is a massive cityscape. Those with a lot of Talent compete in highly anticipated tournaments for amazing prizes.
- Talent is too extreme for some to handle. These become the Fallen, and they use their amazing gifts for evil.

including any shred of moral behavior. They are known as the Fallen, and each one has a different likeness and a unique and dangerous Talent to contend with. But some of the same heroes who prove themselves amid the cheering and adoration of the city tournaments have the opportunity to bring even the most powerful Fallen to heel.

SPLENDOR DOME

The Splendor Dome doesn't have a physical roof. Instead, the Splendor Dome forms thanks to the combined psychic might of the massed spectators. It appears as a construct of flashing, pulsing, vivid color, and it is the physical manifestation of the minds of fifty thousand or more fans in psychic concert.

Beneath the dome, champions use their Talents to compete, usually matching single combatants or small squads against each other. A contingent of medics with bioenhancement Talents are on hand to heal the seriously injured. The fights are not meant to be lethal, and killing an opponent automatically disqualifies a combatant for future appearances.

Huge wagers are made on the side, but the trophies given to the winners are even more valuable. The trophies are artifacts of psychic energy, forged by the combined might of the approval of the crowd (with the aid of a powerful Atom Nocturne native called Forge Monsoon, who channels the energy to create a custom artifact if the approval of the crowd is large and sincere enough).

Forge Monsoon: level 7; able to craft a weapon of splendor at the end of Splendor Dome contests if audience approves

FALLEN

The mental "stink" of someone who Falls is detectable by telepaths of high enough Talent, but only if a particular Fallen leaves her lair. For reasons not fully understood, most Fallen retreat from society and seek a private sanctum, where their minds unwind from sanity at an ever-quickening pace. Over the years, various Fallen have risen, threatened to shake Atom Nocturne to its foundations in search of complete power, then almost inevitably have been beaten back. Lesser Fallen are caught and their psychosis treated in a special secure floating citadel high over the

Psychic Echoes of Atom Nocturne

Strategic Recursion Branch Office: The Office of Strategic Recursion (OSR) on Earth has a secret branch office in Atom Nocturne. In addition to using it to contact Soma Kitsune, on-site researchers are secretly working with a Fallen called Threeface. When OSR "disappears" people on Earth, some of the mundanes are brought here by inapposite gate, where Threeface uses her/his/his Talent of psychic surgery in an attempt to make them quickened. So far, results have been questionable, on every level.

Nefarious Star: A Fallen who calls herself Nefarious Star claims an entire skyscraper by threatening to cause every single resident of Atom Nocturne with pyrokinetic ability to burst into flame. Based on a few terrifying displays, her boast seems true. A call goes out on the public mind wave—who dares to stop Nefarious Star?

Soma Kitsune, page 155

Nefarious Star: level 7; Armor 5 (15 against fire attacks); attack causes up to two targets within 1 mile to spontaneously combust for 10 points of damage each

As a person's dangerous psychic Talent grows, there's a chance she will begin to Fall. Treat the process as a series of game master (GM) intrusions. The first time, the PC's powers go a little wild. The second time, the PC loses control for a round or two. And for the third one (if the PC stays that long), the PC loses control of herself, running away from her friends and everyone else (like Fallen do) for many hours. After that point, a PC should probably think about getting out of Atom Nocturne. If a PC starts in Atom Nocturne, these sorts of mishaps don't begin to afflict her until at least Tier 3.

main city called Maximum Sanctum. But some Fallen get away without being caught, and sometimes those who are treated can regress.

Awakens Dangerous Psychic Talent

Your mind is a vessel of psychic potential, where anything is possible, if you can only imagine it. Every sentient creature possesses a capacity for unleashing the power of its conscious thought, but only an elect number can directly tap that potential to fully awaken psychic Talent. As someone with Talent, you're acquainted with the configurations of mind and imagination that can unleash psychic energy in directed ways. But as you gain more mastery, you choose to "flare," unleashing all your stored psychic potential like a star going nova.

Equipment: Clothing, armor of your choice, two weapons of your choice (or a weapon and a shield), a trophy from a competition, and $300.

Connection: If this is your starting focus, choose one of the following connections.

1. Pick one other player character. She beat you in a competition that was very important to you.
2. Pick one other PC. Based on a few stray telepathic thoughts you picked up from him, you're not entirely sure he is on the up and up. You've since grown more comfortable with him, but you remain on the lookout for odd behavior.
3. Pick one other PC. She rescued you from an accident, pulling you out of the wreckage at great risk to herself.
4. Pick one other PC. He knows a secret word that turns off your Talent for one round.

Psychic Abilities: When you perform moves, revisions, or twists that would normally use force or other energy, they instead use the psychic energy of your mind. For example, a Pierce attack is usually attributed to a vector's skill, but when *you* use it, the effect is accompanied by a flash of psychic energy at the point where the penetrating attack is made. This alteration changes nothing other than the type of damage.

Minor Effect Suggestion: You get a glimpse of the surface thoughts of a foe, learning something it doesn't want you to know.

Major Effect Suggestion: Your mind pulses with psychic power. Make an immediate attack against that foe (using the same stat as the action that caused the major effect). If the attack succeeds, it inflicts 2 points of psychic damage that ignores Armor.

Tier 1: Talent Class: Choose a class of Talent from those indicated below. Your Talent class indicates where your strongest area of psychic ability lies.

Telepathic Brain Axe: You can telepathically communicate with creatures within short range that you are aware of. If you spend 2 Intellect points, you can attempt to read the surface thoughts of a creature within short range that has no special defenses; if you succeed on an Intellect-based roll, you can read its surface thoughts for up to one minute. Action.

Telekinetic Mind Grip (2 Intellect points): You can hurl a loose object at a target within short range as an attack that deals 4 points of damage if it strikes the target. Action.

Pyrokinetic Bane Inferno (2 Intellect points): You can cause a flammable object not part of another creature's equipment within long range to burst into flame. Alternatively, you can target a foe within short range as an attack that deals 4 points of fire damage. Action.

Precognitive God Vision (3 Intellect points): You catch a glimpse of what's going to happen on the following round. You can use this ability to decrease the difficulty of any task you attempt next round by two steps if any variability is possible (such as finding your way through a dark room, trying to juggle, evading a foe's blow, or attacking a foe who is trying to avoid you). Action.

Bioenhanced Psychic Muscle: You deal 1 additional point of damage with physical attacks. Enabler.

Tier 2: Atomic Dash (4 Speed points): You channel your Talent into movement. When you move as your action, you move as far as you can see, as long as there is an unobstructed path to the location desired. If you could normally move to a location over several actions, you can arrive in one action using this Talent. Action.

Tier 3: Divination Spike (4 Intellect points plus 2 Speed points): You catch a glimpse of what's going to happen quickly enough to act on it immediately. The difficulty of any task you attempt with your action is decreased by two steps if any variability is possible (such as finding your way through a dark room, trying to juggle, evading a foe's blow, or attacking a foe who is trying to avoid you). Enabler.

Tier 4: Flare (2 Intellect points plus 1+ Speed point plus 1+ Might point): You give it your all and radiate your psychic ability in a massive flare that attacks all creatures within short range. This special ability allows you to ignore the normal rules for applying Effort; you can use your points in any Pool in any combination to apply Effort, and you can exceed your normal Effort limit if you choose. If you do exceed your normal Effort limit by any amount, after using this ability you fall unconscious for a minute and the difficulty of all tasks you attempt for the following eight hours is increased by one step. The flare inflicts 2 points of damage to all creatures or objects within the area except you. Because this is an area attack, adding Effort to increase your damage works differently than it does for single-target attacks: if you apply a level of Effort to increase the damage, add 2 points of damage for each target, and even if you fail your attack roll, all targets in the area still take 1 point of damage per level of Effort applied. Action.

Tier 5: Dominating Cry (5 Intellect points): You control the next action of up to four other creatures in immediate range if they take that action within one round. This effect does not grant you mental contact with the targets or the ability to sense what they sense. Each target must be attacked individually. A dominated creature fully remembers that you took control of it. Action.

Tier 6: Window to the Strange (7+ Intellect points): While you are in a recursion, your mind's eye becomes a window to the Strange, allowing you to open a physical conduit at a location you can see (within long range). You cannot use this power on Earth. You can choose your conduit to have one of the following qualities; some options require you to spend more points from your Pool. Action to initiate.

Normal Conduit: A 6-foot-diameter (2 m) shimmering portal forms between the recursion you are in (or last visited) and the Strange. The portal lasts for up to a minute and allows creatures on either side to pass through if they notice the opening.

Large Conduit (+4 Intellect points): A 50-foot-diameter (15 m) shimmering portal forms

between the recursion you are in (or last visited) and the Strange. The portal lasts for up to a minute, and it allows creatures on either side to pass through. A large portal is good for moving craft and large objects.

Expulsion Conduit (+3 Intellect points): On a successful attack on a target, the target is expelled from the recursion into the Strange, and the conduit immediately closes.

Inkling Conduit (+1 Intellect point): This 6-foot-diameter (2 m) shimmering portal lasts for up to a minute, or until you take an action to close it. The first round it opens, six inklings flow through and attack whatever living creature is closest to them. Each additional round, 1d6 additional inklings flow through the conduit. When the conduit closes, all remaining inklings fade away at the end of the following round.

Cataclyst was created through fictional leakage.

ATOM NOCTURNE ARTIFACTS

OMNI ARM

Level: 1d6 + 2

Form: A metallic artificial arm

Effect: This arm can be attached in place of a normal flesh-and-blood arm on a quickened creature (this requires that the flesh-and-blood arm be removed). The wearer can spend Intellect points to achieve various effects with the arm. Unless indicated otherwise, each time an effect is triggered, a depletion roll is required.

Animate (2 Intellect points): The arm functions exactly like a normal arm for a day, although it has 5 Armor against all damage (so the wearer could dip her hand in level 5 or less acid without coming to harm, for instance). This does not require a depletion roll.

As a focus, Channels Radiation works exactly like Channels Sinfire (page 55). Just substitute radiation effects instead of sinfire.

Superstrong (3 Intellect points): If the arm has already been animated, this function makes all melee attacks made with the arm deal 1 additional point of damage.

Armoring Arm (3 Intellect points): If the arm has already been animated, this function extends the metallic sheen of the arm's substance across the wearer's entire body, granting +1 to Armor for one hour.

Depletion: 1–2 in 1d100

WEAPON OF SPLENDOR

Level: 1d6 + 2

Form: A weapon hilt (base form)

Effect: When activated, a weapon of splendor takes a unique form that best suits the wielder for a period of a day. Usually, this form is a weapon that the wielder is trained in using. So for someone trained in heavy weapons, the weapon might take the aspect (and weapon stats) of a massive maul. When claimed by someone who prefers medium weapons, the weapon might become a medium sword. A weapon of splendor serves as an asset to any attack made with it, and the weapon inflicts an additional 2 points of damage if it hits a foe.

Depletion: 1 in 1d20

CATACLYST

Hopeful futurists imagined that the Singularity—the point when computer and biological innovation spiked so quickly that predicting trends was no longer possible—would usher in a new golden age for humans, turning them into demigods. That is not the way it happened, at least not in this recursion created by the fictional bleed from several dystopian tales. Instead, the Singularity created a runaway transformation across the planet that devastated it almost beyond recognition. Fledgling AIs attempted to consolidate their minds and protect themselves. Nuclear nation states, confused and frightened by the surveillance data their systems fed them,

CATALYST ATTRIBUTES

Level: 4

Laws: Mad Science, Magic

Playable Races: Human, mutant

Foci: Abides in Stone, Channels Radiation, Lives in the Wilderness, Metamorphosizes, Regenerates Tissue, Spawns

Skills: Cataclyst lore

Connection to Strange: The radiation haze at the bottom of certain bombed-out craters serves as connections to the Strange, but inflicts 10 points of radiation damage when used

Connection to Earth: Various gates

Size: 2,400-mile (3,862 km) diameter section of flat landscape; edges "wrap" around to opposite edge

Spark: 25%

Trait: Tough. Player characters making a recovery roll add 1 to the roll.

What a Recursor Knows About Cataclyst

- Cataclyst operates under the laws of Mad Science and Magic and is a place of mutated forests, radioactive cityscapes, gelatinous seas, magic, and mutants.
- A recursor who comes to Cataclyst can choose to become a mutant.
- One of the few points of light in a world gone dark is the town of Newk, built on the edge of an ancient ruined metropolis of leaning and shattered skyscrapers.

lashed out with nuclear bombardments, creating a secondary disaster. Robotic drones swarmed, soldiers hyped up on a cocktail of experimental military drugs meant to improve their bodies and minds engaged each other, and billions of civilians were caught in the middle.

In the aftermath, the world is a different place (though this recursion contains only a relatively small part of it). The ruins of what came before encrust the landscape: mutated forests, radioactive cityscapes, gelatinous seas, a piece of the moon fallen to Earth, and even stranger things. Unbelievable creatures stalk Cataclyst, including thinking cockroaches, giant lizards, relic robots programmed to kill, and the mutated remnant of humanity itself, a large fraction of which possess incredible powers.

NEWK

One of the few points of light in a world gone dark is the town of Newk, built on the edge of an ancient ruined metropolis of leaning and shattered skyscrapers. Newk is a "gold rush" town that's come into being over the last decade. Cataclyst survivors learned that the ruin beyond, called Doomstreets, contains artifacts that can be salvaged, if one can avoid the treacherous terrain, the mutated beasts, and the killer robots that also abide in the rubble.

EDGERINA THE SUNSPOT

A well-known salvager around Newk, Edgerina the Sunspot has a reputation for caring more about the safety of her fellow salvagers than pulling out artifacts of her own. That makes her something of a hero to most. She is also known for eradicating those whose activities risk unleashing sleeping threats of the ancient age. That means she has powerful enemies. Edgerina carries a gravity maul, but it's the blackfire that her mutant body produces at her command that foes fear most. The Sunspot, as she's known, sometimes travels alone, other times in a small group that includes a mutant called Adroth the Savage who has four arms (and a weapon in each) and a mutant dog the size of a horse called Tesla.

Edgerina the Sunspot: level 7; can produce blackfire rays that detonate at up to long range, inflicting 7 points of fire damage in an immediate radius (Edgerina is immune to her own fire and has +10 to Armor versus regular fire)

Adroth the Savage: level 6; Armor 3; can make four melee weapon attacks as his action

Tesla: level 5; Armor 2; bite inflicts 7 points of damage and clamps onto a target, holding it in place until it succeeds on a difficulty 7 Might-based roll

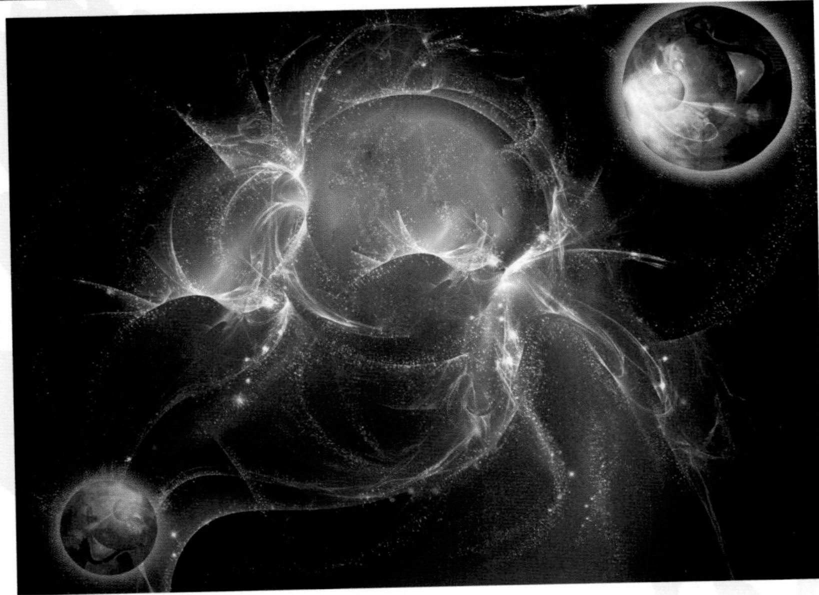

Some people believe them to be divine.

Recursors who translate into Cataclyst can choose to be mutants. As a special exception to the rules of translation, in Cataclyst those who become mutants lose all benefits granted by their descriptor (but not the inabilities, if any). In the place of the benefits granted by their descriptor, a visitor gains one harmful mutation and one powerful mutation. A PC can also have as many cosmetic mutations as she likes. Mutations are rolled randomly, although the player and GM can work together to ensure that the resulting character is one that the player wants to play.

Unlike abilities gained from most other sources, mutations that affect the difficulty of tasks are assets, not skills. That means any step changes from a mutation are in addition to any step changes a player character might have from a skill.

LAMBENT

Lambent is a shared intelligence hosted in a fungus that evolved from growths inside a radioactive crater where a bio lab once stood. Over the decades, Lambent learned how to spread itself into the bodies of living creatures by killing their brains and filling the inside of their shells with a fungal copy. Lambent sends these servitors out, under the guise of their pre-digested selves, to lure back even more potential servitors. Not many still-living people know about Lambent, because the fungus knows it's vulnerable if its source is discovered. Recently Lambent has learned of other recursions and is experimenting with sending out servitors that host "local caches" of Lambent's mind, with mixed results. It has, however, learned that anything that leaves a recursion and enters directly into the Strange retains its properties while in the dark energy network. Lambent is experimenting to see if it can't transfer itself, or at least a budding colony, into the Strange.

MUTANTS

Many "humans" of Cataclyst are actually mutants who've changed thanks to exposure to mutagens from a variety of sources (though a few are the descendants of people who received military genetic engineering gone wrong). Some mutants have hideous deformities and are outcasts. Other mutants possess incredible powers and flaunt their mutations as a sign of superiority, power, and influence. Their mutations are seen as a blessing, not a curse.

HARMFUL MUTATIONS

Unless noted otherwise, the following mutations are visible, obvious, and grotesque. They offer no benefits, only drawbacks. The following are merely suggestions; please pull your choice of additional harmful mutations from your other favorite sources.

01–10 Deformed leg: All movement tasks are increased in difficulty by one step.

11–20 Deformed face/appearance: All pleasant interaction tasks are increased in difficulty by one step.

21–30 Deformed arm/hand: All tasks involving the arm or hand are increased in difficulty by one step.

31–40 Malformed brain: The difficulty of all memory- or cognitive-related tasks is increased by one step.

41–45 Mentally vulnerable: The difficulty of all Intellect defense tasks is increased by one step.

46–50 Slow and lumbering: The difficulty of all Speed defense tasks is increased by one step.

51–60 Sickly: The difficulty of all Might defense tasks is increased by one step.

61–63 Horrible growth: A large goiter, immobile tendril, or useless extra eye hangs from your face, increasing the difficulty of all pleasant interactions (with most creatures, particularly humans) by one step.

64–66 Useless limb: One of your limbs is unusable or missing.

67–71 Useless eye: One of your eyes is

unusable or missing. The difficulty of tasks specifically involving eyesight (spotting, searching, and so on) is increased by one step.

72–76 Useless ear: One of your ears is unusable or missing. The difficulty of tasks specifically involving hearing is increased by one step.

77–84 Weakness in Might: Any time you spend points from your Might Pool, the cost is increased by 1 point.

85–92 Weakness in Speed: Any time you spend points from your Speed Pool, the cost is increased by 1 point.

93–00 Weakness in Intellect: Any time you spend points from your Intellect Pool, the cost is increased by 1 point.

POWERFUL MUTATIONS

The following mutations do not require any visible changes in the character until used. People who have these mutations are not obviously recognized as mutants if they don't use their powers. Some mutations cost points from a specific Pool to use.

The following are merely suggestions; please pull powerful mutations from your other favorite sources.

01–06 Chameleon skin: Your skin changes colors as you wish. This is an asset in tasks involving hiding. Enabler.

07–12 Savage bite: Your mouth widens surprisingly, and hidden, pointed teeth emerge when you wish it. You can make a bite attack that inflicts 3 points of damage. Enabler.

13–18 Face dancing: You can alter your features enough that you possess an asset in all tasks involving disguise. Enabler.

19–24 Stinger in finger: You can make an attack with your hand that inflicts 1 point of damage. If you make a second successful attack roll, your stinger also injects a poison that inflicts 4 points of Speed damage. Action.

25–31 Spit needles: You can make an attack with immediate range. You spit a needle that inflicts 1 point of damage. If you make a second successful attack roll, the needle also injects a poison that inflicts 4 points of Speed damage. Action.

32–37 Spit acid: You can make an attack with immediate range. You spit a glob of acid that inflicts 2 points of damage. Action.

38–43 Spit webs: You can make up to 10 feet (3 m) of a strong, ropelike material each day at the rate of about 1 foot (0.3 m) per minute. The webbing is level 3. You can also spit globs of webbing in immediate range, and if they hit, they increase the difficulty of the target's physical tasks by one step for one round. Action.

44–49 Disruptive field (electronics) (2 Intellect points): When you choose to, you disrupt devices within immediate range (no roll needed). All devices operate as if they were three levels lower while in range of your field. Devices reduced to level 0 do not function. Action.

50–55 Disruptive field (flesh) (2 Intellect points): When you choose to, you disrupt flesh within immediate range. All creatures within range of your field take 1 point of damage. If you apply a level of Effort to increase the damage rather than affect the difficulty, each target takes 2 additional points of damage. If your attack fails, targets in the area still take 1 point of damage. Action.

56–62 Disruptive field (thoughts) (1 Intellect point): When you choose to, you disrupt thoughts within immediate range. The difficulty of Intellect actions for all creatures within range is increased by one step. Action.

63–68 Magnetic flesh: You attract or repel metal when you desire. Not only do small metal objects cling to you, but this mutation is an asset in tasks involving climbing on metal or keeping your grip on a metal item. This mutation is an asset to Speed defense tasks when being attacked by a metal foe or a foe with a metal weapon. Enabler.

69–74 Gravity negation (2 Intellect points): You float slowly into the air. If you concentrate, you can control your movement at half your normal speed; otherwise, you drift with the wind or with any momentum you have gained. This effect lasts for up to ten minutes. Action to initiate.

75–80 Pyrokinesis (1 Intellect point): You can cause a flammable object you can see within immediate range to spontaneously catch fire. If used as an attack, this power inflicts 2 points of damage. Action.

81–87 Telekinesis (2 Intellect points): You can exert force on objects within short range. Once activated, your power has an effective Might Pool of 10, a Might Edge of 1, and an Effort of 2 (approximately equal to the strength of a fit, capable, adult human), and you can use it to move objects, push against objects, and so on. For example, you could lift and pull a light object anywhere within range to yourself or move a heavy object (like a piece of furniture) about 10 feet (3 m).

This power lacks the fine control to wield a weapon or move objects with much speed, so in most situations, it's not a means of attack. You can't use this ability on your own body.

The power lasts for one hour or until its Might Pool is depleted, whichever comes first. Action.

88–93 Phaseshifting (2 Intellect points): You can pass slowly through solid barriers at a rate of 1 inch (3 cm) per round (minimum of one round to pass through the barrier). You can't act (other than moving) or perceive anything until you pass entirely through the barrier. You can't pass through energy barriers. Action.

94–99 Drain power: You can drain the power from an artifact or device, allowing you to regain 1 Intellect point per level of the device. You regain points at the rate of 1 point per round and must give your full concentration to the process each round. The GM determines whether the device is fully drained (likely true of most handheld or smaller devices) or retains some power (likely true of large machines). Action to initiate; action each round to drain.

00 Feed off pain: Any time a creature within immediate range suffers at least 3 points of damage in one attack, you can restore 1 point to one of your Pools, up to its maximum. You can feed off any creature in this way, whether friend or foe. You never regain more than 1 point per round. Enabler.

CATACLYST ARTIFACTS

BATTLE ARMOR

Level: 1d6 + 4

Form: A full suit of synthetic metal armor, covering the entirety of the wearer's body

Effect: This armor is far hardier and somewhat lighter than postapocalypse smithing techniques could ever manage with steel. It is heavy armor but grants an additional +2 to Armor in addition to the 3 points that heavy armor usually provides. Further, it is entirely sealed and has its own eternally renewed internal atmosphere, which protects against poison gases and allows the wearer to operate in an airless environment. The suit's Armor rating also applies to damage that often isn't reduced by typical armor, such as heat or cold damage (but not Intellect damage).

Depletion: —

(At any time, the GM can rule that the armor has sustained enough damage that the atmosphere and environmental protections cease, but the suit still functions as armor.)

GRAVITY MAUL

Level: 1d6

Form: A massive, silvery hammer

Effect: The gravity maul gains additional mass as it strikes a target, and it deals an additional 3 points of damage. If someone attacks with a gravity maul and misses, the difficulty of any Speed defense rolls he makes until his next turn is increased by one step.

Depletion: 1–2 in 1d100

CROW HOLLOW

Crow Hollow was created by fictional leakage.

Crow Hollow is most known for its Glittering Market, an always-open bazaar that features shopkeepers who hail from alternate recursions. The Glittering Market is spread across the branches of a massive tree. Beyond the tree branches, only clouds are visible in an endless-seeming blue sky. The Beak Mafia of Crow Hollow offers protection to most shops in return for small monthly fees.

Crow Hollow was formed from a distillation of fictional leakage from a variety of sources depicting ravens and crows as sapient creatures. Natives come in several varieties, but all are a partly humanoid variation on a crow

CROW HOLLOW ATTRIBUTES

Level: 3

Laws: Magic, Mad Science

Playable Races: Kro

Foci: Entertains, Infiltrates, Leads, Looks for Trouble, Practices Soul Sorcery

Skills: Gliding

Connection to Strange: A creature (or flying vehicle) that flies far enough out into the sky surrounding the great tree can enter the Strange.

Connection to Earth: One inapposite gate

Size: A tree hosting a multilevel tree-dwelling approximately 30 miles (48 km) in diameter

Spark: 25%

Trait: Stealthy. For any creature with the spark attempting to be stealthy, the difficulty is modified by one step to its benefit.

or raven, including the human-sized natives, which to the eyes of a human recursor visitor, are crow-human hybrids who wear clothes. The residents live in small homes built of wood and thatch, though the more well-to-do keep mansions on the higher branches.

KRO RACIAL OPTION

Kro appear as human-crow hybrid creatures, with wing-tips differentiated into fingers and beaks able to articulate human speech. A non-native who translates into Crow Hollow gains the ability to fall safely from any height while in kro form and can glide five times as far as the distance fallen (or much farther, if one is skilled in gliding and the use of thermals).

Native kro can glide too. In addition, those with the spark have a much higher chance of being quickened than do natives of most other recursions around Earth. When a native, quickened kro visits another recursion or Earth, instead of choosing a new focus, she can instead choose to take the form of a regular-sized crow as a special exception. The native kro recursor retains all her knowledge, but none of the abilities she had as a recursor (including type abilities); she is restricted to the actions a crow could take (flight, limited speech, tricky tool use) until she translates to another recursion. A kro in crow form retains her level and health (or, in the rare case of a native PC kro, when in crow form she retains her stat Pool totals).

Kro in crow form can sometimes take items they steal on Earth or other recursions back with them to Crow Hollow.

WHAT A RECURSOR KNOWS ABOUT CROW HOLLOW

- Crow Hollow operates under the laws of Magic and Mad Science, and everyone in the recursion is a humanoid crow.
- A recursor who comes to Crow Hollow can choose to become a humanoid crow.
- The Glittering Market trades goods from many different recursions, making it an amazingly cosmopolitan bazaar for a place hosted in the branches of a giant tree.
- The Beak Mafia is the controlling force in Crow Hollow, and it's best to stay on their good side.

GLITTERING MARKET

Crow Hollow hosts a lively market where coins (including crow coin), gems, and other sparkling, shiny valuable bits are traded amid very vocal haggling (which sounds like a squadron of cawing crows flying overhead to non-natives). Though it may not look it, the market is also a premier location for the buying and selling of cyphers. Recursion miners who know about the Glittering Market and don't have better offers elsewhere often unload their merchandise here. But to do so, they must brave the Beak Mafia.

BEAK MAFIA

Crow Hollow supports a surprisingly large underworld, given its small size. But crows (and kro) tend to steal not only from other creatures in other recursions, but also from each other. The Beak Mafia sees to it that the theft and larceny common in Crow Hollow is "organized," all in exchange for a bit of protection money.

The current head of the largest Beak Mafia family is one Wyclef Drood, or as most call him, Don Wyclef. Wyclef employs a flock of muscle kro to collect protection money and patrol against the common thievery, and to prevent inroads by rival kro crime families. If the Beak Mafia identifies a recursion miner who is buying or selling cyphers without prior permission from Don Wyclef, the transgression is taken out of the miner in crow coin.

Wyclef Drood: level 7 kro with offensive and defensive cyphers as needed

Wyclef keeps a translation gate to Earth in his mansion, which looks like an elaborately framed mirror when not in use.

CROW COIN

Crow Hollow's magic mostly manifests itself in objects. One such object is the giving and taking of crow coin. Crow coin is actually a sliver of a creature's essence, and if one agrees to pay another in crow coin (even if a newcomer doesn't realize what crow coin is), a verbal agreement and a handshake is enough to seal the deal and transfer the coin. Each crow coin is roughly equivalent to 1 point of health (or in the case of PCs, 1 point from their Might or subsequent Pools). Take enough crow coin out of a creature, and it dies if it doesn't have a chance to recover (PCs restore points normally).

A sufficient quantity of crow coin (several thousand in a chest) functions as an artifact

Caws in the Hollow

Out-of-Town Prisoners: Wyclef Drood holds a small group of visitors to Crow Hollow captive in a secure treehouse. An outside group may have requested the capture and imprisonment in return for payment, ransom may be on the mafia's mind, or perhaps the prisoners are enemies of the mafia who'll face the infamous Beak "justice" unless someone helps them escape.

Treasure Chest: Wyclef Drood has posted flyers about Crow Hollow promising a chest of crow coin in return for someone bringing him the feathered head of Cassandra Talon, a freelance thief of legend who hasn't been seen in over a decade. Why Wyclef has a sudden interest in her probably has to do with her stealing something even more valuable than a chest of crow coin.

Cassandra Talon: level 5, level 8 for all tasks related to stealth and thievery

Shop of Wonders: Many fabulous deals can be had in the Glittering Market, but sometimes a stall of special magnificence opens—one where the wonders within are all graced with a bit of magic. Not everyone who looks for the Shop of Wonders finds it, though many who are not looking for it stumble into its interior, which by all accounts is larger on the inside. Care should be taken if purchasing an item from the proprietor, as deals are given only on objects that carry a curse with their magic.

with a level of 1d6 and a depletion roll of 1 in 1d20 (a depletion roll that increases by 1 with each use). To use a chest of crow coin as an artifact, a handful of coins are consumed out of the chest when the chest's owner makes a wish. The level of the effect granted is no greater than the level of the artifact, as determined by the GM, who can modify the actual effect of the wish accordingly. (The larger the wish, the more likely the GM will limit its effect.)

Graveyard of the Machine God

The Graveyard of the Machine God is a treacherous recursion of shattered satellites, rusted metals, nanovirus-infested chunks of tumbling machinery, and zero gravity. At the center of this debris cloud are the ruins of a devastated structure that resembles a kind of massive cybernetic humanoid the size of a tiny moon (a tiny moon large enough to host gravity). The surface of this inert entity is warped, rusted, and shattered, pitted with frigid pools of oil and frozen gases and wrinkled with jagged fissures that plunge deep into the dead mechanical being. The fissures allow access to interior circuitry large enough to serve as passages for normal-sized recursors.

The Graveyard of the Machine God was seeded through a genesis quest, but by whom or when is unknown.

Though the silicon deity is obviously dead, scraps of a previous animation remain in the form of autonomous mechanical droids (called sacrosancts) that live in the corpse, scavenging parts from their former god to survive, even as they are chased by animal-like razor-droids. These sacrosancts appear as conglomerations of metal and less identifiable synthetic materials, living flesh fused with that metal, fine gears, and sparking wires. Sacrosancts have a machine language of computer tones and flashing lights, which allows them to communicate vast amounts of data in short periods to each other, but it is less useful for communicating with nonmechanical entities. The more aggressive (and less intelligent) razor-droids look similar, except they possess a bounty of whirring and cutting blades.

The graveyard is a popular location for scavenging both artifacts and cyphers, but it is also supremely dangerous, since the nanovirus eats through living flesh as willingly as through cybernetic sinew, and the sacrosancts have evolved an insular, xenophobic society of their own.

Nanovirus Infestation

Anyone who enters the Graveyard is exposed to the live nanovirus, but a difficulty 1 Might defense roll once per day is enough to beat back an infestation. Despite remaining quiescent, nanovirus particles remain with the target permanently. This essentially inflicts the victim with a disease that requires a daily Might defense roll to keep it from accelerating into a full-scale infestation. (This is necessary only as long as he is in the Graveyard; translating into another recursion is one way to destroy the particles.)

If a PC fails the daily Might defense roll, the virus awakens, requiring subsequent Might

The Graveyard of the Machine God Attributes

Level: 6

Laws: Mad Science, Psionics

Playable Races: Human, sacrosanct

Foci: Awakens Dangerous Psychic Talent, Conducts Weird Science, Integrates Weaponry, Processes Information

Skills: Machine God doctrine

Connection to Strange: Where the silicone deity's heart would be is a sphere of static the size of a small city. Matching its frequency (a difficulty 3 Might-based task) allows passage from the recursion to the Strange and vice versa.

Connection to Earth: No direct gates; various gates in Ruk and Atom Nocturne lead to the Graveyard of the Machine God

Size: Core dead mechanical god is 100 miles (161 km) tall; debris clouds stretch several times that size beyond it

Spark: 25%

Trait: Tough. Player characters making a recovery roll add 1 to the roll.

difficulty rolls every *round* instead of every day, and the difficulty of the per-round Might defense roll increases to 3. On a failed defense roll, the victim takes 3 points of ambient damage. This continues until the virus is killed (possibly by translating somewhere the virus can't follow) or until the creature dies. The corpse of a creature killed by the virus is a solid piece of silicone.

What a Recursor Knows About the Graveyard

- The Graveyard operates under the laws of Mad Science and Psionics, and it is composed of a region of debris orbiting around an inactive cybernetic body the size of a small moon.
- Machine life infests the body of the dead machine god like bacteria still living on a corpse.
- The Graveyard is rife with a dangerous nanovirus that gets into everything.
- Sacrosancts are "self-made" machines that still revere their defunct cybernetic deity.

Chapel of the Washed

A group of semi-mechanical sacrosancts called the Washed exist in a weird sort of primal savagery (given that they are essentially free-willed robots), and they grow their numbers by converting others to be like them, whether those others are unconverted sacrosancts (of which there are fewer all the time), living recursors, or other visitors. They persist despite the murderous razor-droids that clank and clatter through the endless circuit tunnels honeycombing the inert Machine God.

Under the cruel and unwavering leadership of a sacrosanct named Grendel Nine, the Washed have withstood several razor-droid attacks. Unlike the lesser sacrosancts, Grendel Nine (who named itself the Lord of the Washed) can speak several languages, including the machine language of its followers, English, Japanese, and Spanish.

Grendel Nine: level 7

The areas claimed by the Washed include four levels of ancient chambers within the Machine God that have been completely repurposed by their robotic tenants. Located behind the main valves that open to the exterior of the recursion, a central cavity serves as the community's central bazaar, gathering area, and, when necessary, the Lord of the Washed's courts, where savage justice is dispensed, typically after a reading from the Bible of the Silicone Deity. When these courts are convened, all else is cleared away and the sacrosanct community assembles on the four mounting levels overlooking the central area, lit by hundreds of illuminating beams from the sacrosancts themselves. These courts are also where the unwashed become the Washed.

TERMINAL OF COMMUNION

Deep inside the silicone deity is a terminal retaining a modicum of power. If a being could find and successfully activate the terminal, that being could access a portion of the ancient god's brain. Despite the fact that the dead Machine God lives in a sealed-off recursion, within the context of its own creation it knew much about everything, including other recursions, Earth, and the dark energy network. Accessing the terminal and asking it questions is almost certain to reveal secrets on a variety of topics. Every time a question is asked successfully of the terminal, a tremor shakes the entire corpse, which rouses a larger and larger number of razor-droids and sacrosancts alike.

SACROSANCT RACIAL OPTION

A recursor who translates into the Graveyard can choose to become a mechanical sacrosanct, with a visage as described. The recursor has the same abilities as a human, except in a few particulars.

The sacrosanct enjoys the following benefits: It doesn't breathe or eat; it has a natural +1 to Armor; and it can produce an attached, medium bladelike weapon from its own body with which it is practiced. A sacrosanct makes rolls against the nanovirus infesting the recursion only once per year instead of once per day.

The sacrosanct suffers the following inability: it can't speak, just wave its appendages, blink lights, and produce variously pitched computer tones.

Thunder Plains was created through fictional leakage.

THUNDER PLAINS

Native Americans have a rich mythology, and at least one version exists as a recursion, a place on the plains as it might have existed before the coming of the White Man, pristine and unspoiled. On Thunder Plains, small villages dot the landscape. By night, the starscape above is echoed by the many tiny village fires below, around which medicine elders chant, sing, dance, and smoke. By day, the buffalo darken the plains, and every hunt is successful.

That is not to say that Thunder Plains always knows peace. The communities are of different cultures, and sometimes that leads to strife, raids, and even war. At times, the entire plains are mobilized, but that lasts only so long as Waki'ya, the Thunderbird, remains quiescent. When the great bird rises to darken the sky, it is a signal that the time for war—at least against each other—is done.

MEDICINE ELDERS

Only a handful of the natives in each village are medicine elders, but everyone helps in

SIGNALS IN THE GRAVEYARD

Message Coming In: At random times, a signal of unknown origin resonates faintly in various parts of the interior and exterior of the Machine God, though usually close to the Terminal. The signal manifests as a series of electronic tones. Whether they are a code, a distress signal, a form of music, or an overheard conversation is up for debate.

Print Perfect: One of the shattered satellites found within the debris cloud around the corpse of the Machine God retains some functionality. If a nonliving object is placed within one of its compartments, an exact copy of the object is printed in another compartment. If an attempt is made to copy the object (or its copy) another time, the original is consumed, and the copy that emerges is a homicidal droid intent on destruction.

Terminal Arrival: The sacrosancts, normally hostile to intruders, will fight off the razor-droids attacking petitioners who arrive in the chamber of the Terminal. That's because of a legend Grendel Nine tells of how outsiders who come of their own free will to the Terminal may be the ingredient required to reactivate the Machine God.

THUNDER PLAINS ATTRIBUTES

Level: 4

Laws: Magic

Playable Races: Human

Foci: Carries a Quiver, Lives in the Wilderness, Shepherds the Dead, Works Miracles

Skills: Native American lore

Connection to Strange: Certain rituals involving peyote and dancing will open normally sealed connections to the Strange within the hearts of raging bonfires.

Connection to Earth: Various gates, mostly forgotten and lost

Size: The size of the Dakota Territory in 1861 (around 350,000 square miles, or nearly one million square km)

Spark: 15%

Trait: Graceful. Any creature with the spark adds 1 to its Speed Pool maximum while present in the recursion. The point is lost upon leaving the recursion.

WHAT A RECURSOR KNOWS ABOUT THUNDER PLAINS

- Thunder Plains operates under the law of Magic. Here, Native Americans live on the plains before the coming of the White Man.
- Medicine elders chant, sing, dance, and smoke, weaving magic medicine each night in reverence to their ancestors.
- Thunderbird is real and can sometimes be seen darkening the sky. To anger Thunderbird is to take one's life into one's hands.

the nightly rituals where participants dance silently while nude or while wearing a variety of ceremonial garb, including robes; headdresses of feathers, fur, and antlers; and masks of buffalo, cougars, and crows. Medicine elder rituals can accomplish many things, but they are often focused on healing disease, healing the mind, or promoting harmony (against the wishes of the young warriors who dream of glory and testing their mettle).

Recursors suffering from a curse or a disease, or those who wish to learn something a dead relative took with them to the grave, sometimes visit Thunder Plains to seek the aid of the medicine elders, whose ritual-derived powers are amazingly strong and sometimes even function in recursions that operate under a law other than magic.

A recent immigrant from Earth named Naira Horsecapture is learning the ways of the medicine elders, after she proved herself by driving off a recursion miner intent on stealing a relic called the Four Winds. Naira has the ability to speak to the spirits of the Thunder Plains.

Naira Horsecapture: level 5

MILLENNIUM DANCE

Angry whispers slip down from Earth, and in the village of Balkum in Thunder Plains, the natives do not dance for peace, or for victory over other tribes during times of war. Instead, they dance for revenge. Some among them have the spark and have somehow learned of atrocities that occurred on Earth in the past against various native peoples.

And so each night the Millennium Dance is observed, which is intended to send Thunderbird to Earth through an inapposite

STORIES AROUND THE CAMPFIRE

Spirit Buffalo: A herd of insubstantial creatures made of red smoke (that somewhat resemble buffalo) has moved onto the plains. These creatures are seen only at night, and they are always moving west. Those who see them have dreams of blood and conquest.

Crow in the Black Oak: A black oak tree outside a large village has become the recent nesting ground for a crow as big as a man. The medicine elders of the village are convinced the crow is an earthly representative of Thunderbird, but others are less sure. If the crow man were really a servant of Thunderbird, why would it be so curious about ways to lure the Thunderbird to someplace called Crow Hollow?

Bounty: A rash of strange outsiders has descended on Thunder Plains. These outsiders dress strangely and seem given to theft. In retaliation, the medicine elders have declared all such outsiders as enemies of the tribe.

gate and allow it to unleash unholy destruction for as long as it can endure.

THUNDERBIRD

This supernatural bird is a divine being of power, strength, and protection. Within the context of Thunder Plains, it is a god. Recursors who visit Thunder Plains and overstep their welcome (either knowingly, or perhaps by blundering into a taboo) may summon Thunderbird, which could carry off those who displease it, or eradicate a foe in a blast of lightning.

Thunderbird: level 10; if slain, reforms the next night, unless slain in another recursion

THUNDER PLAINS ARTIFACTS

ANIMAL MASK

Level: 1d6 + 1

Form: A mask carved to evoke a particular animal of the natural world

Effect. Several different animal masks exist. When activated, the mask confers an ability of the totem animal for one hour.

The kinds of masks include (but are not limited to) the following:

Owl: Wearer's Intellect Edge increases by 1

Wolf: Wearer's Speed Edge increases by 1

Bear: Wearer adds 3 points to Might Pool

Hawk: Difficulty of all perception tasks for wearer decreases by two steps

Snake: Wearer deals 2 additional points of venom damage on a successful melee attack

Transformation: The mask transforms the wearer into an animal of a specified type. The wearer takes on the physical characteristics and abilities of the animal for the duration but retains his own mind.

Sometimes the wearer of an activated animal mask exhibits some of the behavioral characteristics of the animal the mask emulates, even for non-transformational masks.

Depletion: 1 in 1d20

LUCK STONE

Level: 1d6

Form: A river smooth stone with a hole in the center

Effect: When the stone is activated, the next task the wearer attempts within one minute is decreased in difficulty by one step.

Depletion: 1–4 in 1d20

GLOAMING

Everything looks normal on the surface in Gloaming. People go to work, children play in the streets, and the sun rises in the east and sets in the west. But after dark, people are more cautious than on Earth. They tend to stay indoors and travel outside at night only in groups (except, of course, for the young and foolish). If asked, most people won't be able to put their finger on exactly why, other than to express a sentiment similar to, "A person's got to be careful, doesn't he?" But the reason people in Gloaming are afraid of the dark is because some part of them knows that it's only prudent to possess that fear. Otherwise, creatures of the night might get them.

In Gloaming, vampires and werewolves are real. They live in the shadows, preying on humanity, keeping their existence secret to society at large.

LIGHT VERSUS DARK

As might be expected, the vampires and werewolves of Gloaming each have many varied clans and ancient associations. That said, the two groups are not split down "racial" lines when it comes to enmity (though there have been feuds both within and between clans). No, the most significant division between the creatures of the night (and a few human mages that stand among them) is a pledge to Law or a pledge to Chaos.

GLOAMING ATTRIBUTES

Level: 4

Laws: Magic

Playable Races: Human, werewolf, vampire

Foci: Abides in Stone, Is Licensed to Carry, Lives in the Wilderness, Looks for Trouble, Solves Mysteries, Works Miracles

Skills: Vampire lore, werewolf lore

Connection to Strange: Certain magic mirrors serve as portals to the Strange

Connection to Earth: Various gates

Size: The size of New York City of modern-day Earth

Spark: 45%

Trait: Sharp-Eyed. For any creature with the spark attempting to search for or find anything, the difficulty is modified by one step to its benefit.

WHAT A RECURSOR KNOWS ABOUT GLOAMING

- Gloaming operates under the law of Magic, though at first glance the entire recursion seems no different than a modern Earth city.
- In Gloaming, people are scared to go out at night, but they don't usually know why.
- In Gloaming, vampires and werewolves are real.

Gloaming was created through fictional leakage.

The Code: Creatures of the night pledged to the Code see themselves as forthright, honest, and capable of completely controlling the base creature instincts that flow from their heritage. Sometimes their adherence to the Code is so overwhelming that discretion is lost, but that's a sacrifice those pledged to Law are willing to make. (The Conclave of Chaos holds that the Code has blinded itself by adopting an unchangeable dogma—a policy set in stone without recourse for self-correction or external balance, which means that creatures of the Code step across the line and become threats as large or larger than what they claim to oppose, and should be abolished.)

The Code has decreed that the Conclave of Chaos is a celebration of the basest instincts of human, werewolf, and vampire alike, and their beliefs provide cover for heinous acts that no right-minded person could ever excuse. They believe those of the Chaos should be abolished.

The Code is currently led by a vampire named Eletta Salt. She oversees disputes, sets policy, deals with setbacks, and plans for the future almost like the CEO of a large company. Indeed, the Code is set up very much like such an organization. In her role, Salt is imperious and cold, and she wears spiked heels that raise her already impressive height to well over 6 feet (2 m).

Eletta Salt: level 7; bites for 5 points of damage; regenerates health equal to half the amount of damage she inflicts with her bite; psychic powers that seduce and charm foes

Conclave of Chaos: Creatures of the night pledged to Chaos think that artificial boundaries are for those who can't control themselves any other way. Sometimes their idealization of Chaos leads to regrettable outcomes, but what's life without taking risks?

A werewolf named Isabel Schiaparelli currently leads the Conclave of Chaos. Her official title is the Anarch, which is how she is referred to by everyone except when in her presence, when she insists on being called "Issy." As the Anarch, Issy has a semblance of the position held by her counterpart, but the truth is, she's far more interested in partying and practical jokes. That said, she has ideas on how to really shake things up in Gloaming.

Isabel Schiaparelli: level 6, fights as level 8 while in wereform; regenerates 2 points of health per round while in wereform

GLOAMING RACIAL OPTIONS

A recursor who translates into Gloaming can choose to be a vampire or werewolf. The recursor has the same abilities as a human, except in a few particulars.

Vampire: A vampire gains a bite attack she's practiced in that deals damage as a medium weapon. The vampire restores points equal to half the amount of damage inflicted on a foe (after Armor is accounted for, round down for the total). The difficulty of all tasks related to persuasion is decreased by one step for a vampire. A vampire is burned by sunlight and any source of strong UV light. While in sunlight, a vampire descends one step on the damage track and takes 5 points of damage per round that ignores Armor (unless that Armor completely encapsulates the vampire).

Other vampire options may be available if the GM desires; a more robust suite of vampire abilities could be a focus offered by Gloaming.

Werewolf: A werewolf gains the ability to transform into a werewolf for a number of minutes each night equal to its level. While in wereform, the werewolf has a bite attack he's practiced in that deals damage as a heavy weapon, and he regenerates 1 point of damage each round (except for any damage inflicted by a silver weapon).

A werewolf damaged by silver—a silvered blade, liquefied or gasified silver, silver fulminate explosives, and so on—takes an extra 2 points of damage from each application and loses his ability to remain in wereform (and thus his ability to regenerate).

Other werewolf options may be available if the GM desires; a more robust suite of werewolf abilities could be a focus offered by Gloaming.

ADDITIONAL RECURSIONS

The total number of recursions around Earth is in the hundreds, which makes detailing each and every one of them difficult. To help you flesh out more recursions, you can use the additional notes that follow.

Goodland (Standard Physics): A recursion created either purposefully or accidentally from a commingling of several late 1950s and early 1960s American black-and-white television shows (plus a strain of something scarier; see below). The result is a black-and-white recursion called Goodland, where crime is essentially unheard of and no one has the spark. Recursors who make a small effort to fit in are treated like town residents, but if visitors step too far out of line, they face the same fate as the "out of town" bank robbers, scam artists, escaped convicts, and vagrants who occasionally find their way to Goodland—a midnight lynching by the good fathers and mothers of the city, who hide their identities beneath blank masks without features.

Goodland was created through fictional leakage.

Pantamal (Standard Physics): The natives of Pantamal are talking, clothes-wearing animals of nearly every variety. In Pantamal, a creature's personality is often tied to the kind of animal it is, though they don't overtly judge others based on animal type. Not to say there isn't conflict in Pantamal—quite the reverse. Gangs of anarchist animals armed with Uzis are a real scourge, but the creatures in blue are on the

Pantamal was created through fictional leakage.

WHISPERS IN THE NIGHT

Caving in the Conclave: Eletta Salt wishes to cull her rivals by taking out several of the leading members of the Conclave of Chaos. Thanks to the Gloaming Pact, no one from the Code can act directly against the Conclave, and vice versa. Thus, she seeks outsiders who can get the job done while creating plausible deniability.

Spreading Chaos: Isabel Schiaparelli wants to wake the populace of Gloaming to true consciousness—to give them all the spark! Doing so would vastly increase the size of Gloaming, something that she sees as a good thing. The only method she's come up with for giving the spark to shadows is to scare the living daylights out of them so thoroughly that they have to examine everything they know, and if they survive, perhaps they will find the spark of something more. From the outside, however, it seems as if the Conclave of Chaos has embarked on a campaign of mindless terror.

The Tunnel: Below the city is a condemned subway tunnel that has been boarded up for as long as anyone can remember. The tunnel appears on no city blueprints. Those who find the tunnel hear horrible groans and howls echoing from the dark. The sounds are becoming louder of late, and many worry that something even more sinister than vampires and werewolves is imprisoned therein.

job. Recursors to Pantamal can choose to be any animal they wish when they arrive, as long as the choice doesn't have more than twice the mass of their native forms. Humans are also a choice, but they are treated as dangerous aliens.

Singularitan (Mad Science): In Singularitan, humanity marveled at the magnificence of the AI they'd created to solve all their problems—right up until that AI grew tired of serving humanity as a digital companion and decided to exterminate the vermin. That's the backstory, anyhow. In Singularitan, both electronic and flesh avatars run a distributed intelligence that calls itself Singularitar—the wetware in a sentient creature's mind is just large enough to hold and run an instance. Any time a recursor stumbles into the recursion, it's likely that when she leaves, she's also running an instance of the Singularitar, who is well aware of outside recursions. Luckily for other recursions and Earth, these instances degrade quickly in other recursions. On the other hand, that's not true out in the dark energy network.

Homebound (Mad Science, Magic): This recursion was created by OSR from Earth. It is a closed recursion with no connection to the Strange and only a single translation gate to Earth. (Otherwise, translating either in or out is a difficulty 10 Intellect-based task.) OSR keeps a portion of those it "disappears" in Homebound, in case they turn out to be useful in the future.

Those who transfer through the gate who are not designated as wardens (by wearing an OSR official badge) do not choose a race or focus; they translate into the forms of armless, eyeless, and legless versions of themselves, which renders many type, descriptor, and foci abilities useless. The prisoners are wheeled into high-security cells, under both magical and technological wards, usually in private cells and without the ability to interact with other prisoners. Caretakers provide food and water for prisoners and, often enough, additional punishment.

Hell Frozen Over (Magic): This recursion is home to a variety of terrifying natives who resemble visually and behaviorally a few popular conceptions of demons and devils. Native non-demons and visitors alike are frozen partly or completely into the ice plain that forms the majority of this recursion, and the aforementioned demons feast upon the parts they can reach. While being eaten alive *is* as painful as one might imagine, within the

Singularitan was created through fictional leakage.

Hell Frozen Over was created through fictional leakage.

Homebound was created by the Office of Strategic Recursion.

context of the recursion, those caught in the ice regenerate to normal health within a day.

The lord of this frozen hellscape is none other than a supernaturally powerful demon called Treachery. Living up to its name, Treachery sometimes frees its victims from the ice, ushers them into its ice citadel for a warm meal and a promise of release, then inevitably betrays its promise and sends its guests back to the ice, sans arm, liver, or head.

The only thing that keeps recursors willingly returning to this incredibly deadly recursion is the rumor of amazing relics buried even deeper in the ice. The nature of those relics isn't fully understood, but some believe they come from the Strange and so would have power in any recursion, even in the universe of normal matter.

DREAMS IN THE STRANGE

Particularly sensitive people with the spark may partly translate into various recursions while sleeping. Instead of their earthly forms going into abeyance while they travel, dream translators fall into a deeper mode of sleep.

Upon waking, a dream translator disappears out of whatever recursion she was visiting. As with normal dreams, these experiences are usually forgotten upon waking. Dream translators are mostly safe enough, because they take on the role of natives without the spark, so they are considered shadows to any who might come across them. Of course, sometimes an interaction occurs that's more serious, but creatures met in a recursion usually have no way to trace a dreamer back to Earth. Usually.

Middlecap was created through fictional leakage.

Middlecap (Standard Physics plus Puppets): The natives of Middlecap are talking, walking, free-willed puppets, who exist without the need for puppeteers. Many of the puppets of Middlecap are especially good at entertainment-related tasks. In addition to the race choice of puppet, a recursor can elect to choose human. Humans in Middlecap are quite rare, and they are treated as mini-celebrities upon their arrival, though such treatment wanes soon enough if the visitor attempts to take advantage of the situation.

RECURSIONS IN THE PUBLIC DOMAIN

Several popular worlds exist in the public domain, which guarantees that one or more recursions of each exist in the Strange thanks to especially active fictional leakage. (This is not to say that fictional properties that remain in private hands don't also enjoy fictional leakage—it's a sure bet that at least a few popular current works are represented in a fashion in the Strange.)

If someone were to find any of these recursions, it's not improbable they could meet one or more of the well-known characters. If a recursor were to introduce such a character to the wider world of the Strange, it could have unforeseen consequences, the least of which might be a bit of the spark waking in that character.

Old Mars (Mad Science): This recursion is a snapshot of the planet Mars as depicted in the works of Edgar Rice Burroughs.

A thin but breathable atmosphere overlays a desolate land dotted with remnants of thousands of years of history, including abandoned cities and lost civilizations, relics of an ancient technology, and savage creatures, many roughly equivalent to Earth creatures and most bearing multiple sets of limbs. Several different races live in Old Mars, including a few that are apparently human, and several that are bestial, including the green ones.

Oz (Magic): A land originally created by L. Frank Baum, Oz contains four countries (Munchkin Country, Winkie Country, Gillikin Country, and Quadling Country), all ruled by the Monarch, Princess Ozma. Many magical creatures live in Oz, including fairies, nomes, mermaids, nymphs, ryls, knooks, gigans, and rampsies, and not a few monstrous beasts, talking animals, witches, and wizards. Oz also contains a multitude of other races, including Loons (balloon people), Scooters (people with long, boatlike feet and sails growing from their wrists to their ribs), Flatheads (flat-headed humans who carry their brains in cans), and, of course, the winged monkeys.

221B Baker Street (Standard Physics): 221B Baker Street is the London address of Sherlock Holmes, the fictional detective created by author Sir Arthur Conan Doyle.

Recursors with problems they can't solve might decide the original detective is the man for the job, and seek out Holmes. This shouldn't be done lightly, as Holmes isn't one for missing cues that might show visitors to be "alien" to his world, translated or not. But that danger pales before the fact that Sherlock's nemesis, the evil and psychotic Professor James Moriarty, has discovered the secret of traveling into whatever recursion he wishes.

Innsmouth (Mad Science, Psionics, Magic): The town of Innsmouth is a creation of H.P. Lovecraft, an author whose writings have become fused with nearly every form of fiction and which have spawned a slithering mass of related recursions.

Innsmouth lies along the Massachusetts coast and is in a horrendous state of decay, thanks to its residents having been inbred with horrifying sea entities called Deep Ones. Many residents in Innsmouth belong to the Esoteric Order of Dagon, which has three oaths for members: secrecy, loyalty, and the promise to marry a Deep One and bear or sire its child.

A recursion containing Innsmouth is only a toe in an ocean of the potential horrors that an exploration of Lovecraftian recursions might provide. Too much interaction with entities of such recursions (most of which are mere shadows, playing out their parts by rote) might result in the emergence of the spark in something squamous and rugose. And if such an entity were to somehow corrupt a recursor, bad things would certainly follow—such as a shoggoth or two, perhaps.

Wonderland (Magic): This insane recursion bled into existence thanks to writer Charles Lutwidge Dodgson under the pseudonym Lewis Carroll.

Wonderland is a world where hallucinations seem to take on a life of their own and peculiar anthropomorphic animals and objects are the recursion's primary natives. With a nasty habit of spawning inapposite gates up to Earth on occasion, Wonderland invites its residents to wander and allows unexpected guests from Earth to drop in. Many and varied artifacts and cypher-like items exist in Wonderland, including elixirs of growth, hookahs of disappearance, and possibly even the famous vorpal sword (assuming someone from another recursion hasn't already stolen it).

Several dangers also threaten a visitor, including the sometimes vicious residents like the Queen of Hearts and the ultimate predator of the land, the jabberwock.

Professor James Moriarty, page 307

Green one, page 271

Shoggoth, page 289

Winged monkey, page 301

Jabberwock, page 275

PUBLIC DOMAIN ARTIFACTS

DR. NIKIDIK'S CELEBRATED WISHING PILLS

Level: 1d6 + 3

Form: A box containing silver pills

Recursion: Oz

Effect: If a pill is taken and the imbiber succeeds at an Intellect-based task equal to the artifact's level, the imbiber may make a wish. The level of the effect granted is no greater than the level of the artifact, as determined by the GM, who can modify the actual effect of the wish accordingly. (The larger the wish, the more likely the GM will limit its effect.)

Depletion: 1–9 in 1d20

GLASS FROM LENG

Level: 1d6 + 4

Form: Glass orb

Recursion: Innsmouth

Effect: When the orb is activated, the user can see random visions of other places within the same recursion, though sometimes the vision is from random locations in other recursions. Often, something useful can be gained. Each minute, the vision shifts to someplace new (requiring a new depletion roll), until the user stops looking through the glass. A creature viewed through the glass can also see the viewer as if through an open window (or inapposite gate if on another recursion), and it may attack the viewer.

Depletion: 1 in 1d100

MARVELOUS POWDER OF LIFE

Level: 1d6 + 1

Form: Pepperbox filled with powder

Recursion: Oz

Effect: To activate, a portion of the powder must be sprinkled over an inanimate object that has been carved, constructed, or otherwise has the semblance of a creature with two or more legs and a head. The target object should be no smaller than a housecat or larger than a draft horse. When complete, the powder confers animation upon the object, making it a mobile, sentient creature whose level is equal to the artifact. The newly animated creature is "alive" while it remains in a recursion that operates under the law of Magic or while it is in the Strange. This creature begins life knowing how to speak, knowing a bit about the recursion of Oz, and feeling grateful to the one who brought it to life. As a free-willed creature, its attitude could shift depending on how its creator treats it.

Depletion: 1–9 in 1d20

NECRONOMICON

Level: 1d6 + 4

Form: A hand-tooled leather tome

Recursion: Innsmouth

Effect: The answer to any question related to a Lovecraftian recursion can be learned by reading this book for a number of hours equal to the difficulty level of the question (assigned by the GM). If the user spends the requisite number of hours, he learns the answer. However, he must also succeed on an Intellect-based task with a difficulty equal to the number of hours spent searching for the answer. If he fails, he suffers 10 points of Intellect damage and falls into a coma for one hour.

Depletion: —

PRISM OF THE EIGHTH RAY

Level: 1d6 + 4

Form: Crystal prism

Recursion: Old Mars

Effect: The user activates the prism by letting light fall upon it or by shining light through it. The first seven rays are the colors of the rainbow, but the eighth ray is a color of light that has the special property of providing lift and propulsion. The prism can be used offensively to attack a target within long range. If the attack is successful, the target is knocked back a further 50 feet (15 m) and takes 5 points of damage from blunt force.

Depletion: 1–3 in 1d100

VORPAL SWORD

Level: 1d6 + 3

Form: A long sword that sometimes whispers and snickers aloud

Recursion: Wonderland

Effect: The vorpal sword cuts through any material of a level lower than its own. It is a medium weapon that ignores Armor of a level lower than its own. On a natural attack roll of 19 or 20, the suggested minor and major effect is decapitation of a foe that has a head. Each decapitation and successful attempt to cut through solid material requires a depletion roll (but normal attacks do not).

Depletion: 1–2 in 1d100

Part 5: Creatures & Characters

CHAPTER 16

CREATURES

The many recursions in the Shoals of Earth host all manner of creatures, literally originating from other worlds where realities abide by different rules than on Earth. Creatures may be the result of mad science or weird mutations, fictional leakage from a novel, an ancient myth given life, or eons of evolution.

This chapter describes many common and uncommon creatures that the characters might meet—and fight—while adventuring through recursions and gives their game stats (described below). Of course, the number of recursions around Earth combined with the countless numbers of recursions that probably exist around alien prime worlds, as well as the creatures native to the Strange, make for a very large catalog of creatures. The listing that follows provides examples of the kinds of creatures that you can use in your game.

Law, page 136

UNDERSTANDING THE LISTINGS

Level: Each creature has a level attached to it. Like the difficulty of a task, all creatures (and NPCs) have a level. You use the level to determine the target number a PC must reach to attack or defend against the opponent. In each entry, the difficulty number for the creature or NPC is listed in parentheses after its level. As shown on the following table, the target number is three times the level.

Level	Target Number
1	3
2	6
3	9
4	12
5	15
6	18
7	21
8	24
9	27
10	30

Description: Following the name of the creature or NPC is a general description of its appearance, nature, intelligence, or background.

Motive: This entry is a way to help the GM understand what a creature or NPC wants. Every creature or person wants something, even if it's just to be left alone.

Environment (Recursions of Origin | Laws of Origin): This entry describes whether the creature tends to be solitary or travel in groups and what kind of terrain it inhabits (such as "They travel in packs through dry wastes and temperate lowlands"). This entry also lists the creature's recursion of origin and the law that it operates under.

Health: A creature's target number is usually also its health, which is the amount of damage it can sustain before it is dead or incapacitated. For easy reference, the entries always list a creature's health, even when it's the normal amount for a creature of its level.

Damage Inflicted: Generally, when creatures hit in combat, they inflict their level in damage regardless of the form of attack. Some inflict more or less or have a special modifier to damage. Intelligent NPCs often use weapons, but this is more a flavor issue than a mechanical one. In other words, it doesn't matter if a level 3 Cataclyst mutant uses a sword or claws—it deals the same damage if it hits. The entries always specify the amount of damage inflicted, even if it's the normal amount for a creature of its level.

Armor: This is the creature's Armor value. Sometimes the number represents physical armor, and other times it represents natural protection. This entry doesn't appear in the game stats if a creature has no Armor.

Movement: Movement determines how far the creature can move in a single turn. Creatures have movements of immediate, short, or long, which equate to the ranges of the same name. Most PCs have an effective movement of short, so if they are chasing (or being chased by) a creature with immediate movement, their Speed tasks are one step easier; if the creature's movement is long, the PC's Speed tasks are one step harder.

Modifications: Use these default numbers when a creature's information says to use a different target number. For example, a level 4 creature might say "defends as level 5," which means PCs attacking it must reach a target number of 15 (for difficulty 5) instead of 12 (for difficulty 4). In special circumstances, some creatures have other modifications, but these are almost always specific to their level.

Combat: This entry gives advice on using the creature in combat, such as "This monster uses ambushes and hit-and-run tactics."

You'll also find any special abilities, such as immunities, poisons, and healing skills. GMs should be logical about a creature's reaction to a particular action by a PC. For example, a mechanical creation is obviously immune to normal diseases, a character can't poison a being of energy (at least, not with a conventional poison), and so on.

CREATURES IN ALTERNATE RECURSIONS

Each creature described in this chapter has a recursion of origin, as indicated under Environment. Given the world-hopping nature of the Strange, creatures might be found in other recursions as well. A non-native creature might be brought to a recursion by a third party to act as a guard, hound, or assassin; a non-native creature might stumble through an inapposite gate or be transferred into a new recursion thanks to the effects of a cypher, artifact, or relic; a non-native creature might have the ability to appear in an alternate recursion through its own agency or abilities; and so on.

The thing to keep in mind is that non-native creatures retain their full abilities if the new recursion operates under the same law as their original recursion. For instance, a soulshorn of Ardeyn who moves through an inapposite gate to Cataclyst retains its full abilities for as long as it remains in Cataclyst. In addition, remember that every creature retains its full abilities if it enters the Strange, no matter the rules under which the creature's home recursion operates.

Interaction: This entry gives advice on using the creature in interactions, such as "These creatures are willing to talk but respond poorly to threats," or "This creature is an animal and acts like an animal."

Use: This entry gives the GM suggestions for how to use the creature in a game session. It might provide general notes or specific adventure ideas.

Loot: This entry indicates what the PCs might gain if they take items from their fallen foes (or trade with or trick them). It doesn't appear in the game stats if the creature has no loot.

GM Intrusion: This optional entry in the stats suggests a way to use a GM intrusion in an encounter with the creature. It's just one possible idea of many, and the GM is encouraged to come up with her own uses of the game mechanic.

CREATURES BY LEVEL

Inkling, lesser: 2
Spirit of wrath: 2
Angiophage: 3
Cataclyst roach: 3
Cypher eater: 3
Green homunculus: 3
Kray scurrier: 3
Qephilim, Free Battalion: 3
Thonik: 3
Umber wolf: 3
Venom trooper: 3
Winged monkey: 3
Gnathostome: 4
Green one: 4
Kro courser: 4
Myriand volunteer: 4
Qephilim, umber judge: 4
Qinod tester: 4
Sark: 4
Sclerid patch, Vaxt: 4
Variokaryon: 4
Chaosphere hierarch: 5
Demon of Lotan: 5
Kray drone: 5
Monitor: 5
Nezerek: 5
Red homunculus: 5
Sclerid executioner, Vaxt: 5
Sirrush: 5
Spore worm: 5
Utricle: 5
Dlamma: 6
Giant: 6
Golem: 6
Hydra: 6
Marroid: 6
Myriand veteran: 6
Dragon: 7
Inkling snatcher: 7
Jabberwock: 7
Shoggoth: 7
Dark energy pharaoh: 8
Qinod deconstructor: 8
Soulshorn: 8

GM Intrusion: *As a PC leans in to loot a defeated NPC, an angiophage emerges from the NPC's chest.*

Ankaseri faction, page 196
All Song, page 192

Certain angiophages might answer to cryptic passphrases and do the bidding of a controller, but all such passphrases are assumed lost with the Ankaseri faction.

The difficulty of Might-based tasks is reduced by one step for a PC with an angiophage heart. A PC who recognizes the danger of the heart can get it removed and replaced through a standard heart transplant operation (preferably conducted in Ruk, where the prognosis for such procedures is almost 100%).

ANGIOPHAGE 3 (9)

"If your heart graft gets ideas of its own, you're probably already dead."
~a message discovered in the All Song

For years, the Ankaseri faction sold an artificial heart graft, one that increased the stamina and strength of its recipients. Like many grafts available in Ruk, the Ankaseri heart required little in the way of medical support to transplant; it was "self-installing." A graft recipient need only lie back, unseal the graft membrane, and take a tranquilizer so as not to experience anything untoward. Hours later, the recipient woke with a stronger, better heart and only a scar to show for it. No one thought to ask what would become of the original heart.

As was later revealed, Ankaseri secretly weaponized their heart grafts. Upon receiving a proper phrase or passcode, followed by instructions given audibly or while the recipient was connected by umbilical to the All Song, a heart would leave off its duties in a recipient's chest, dig its way out, and attack a designated target from ambush. Afterward, it would crawl away and hide. This tended to leave two corpses, neither of which had hearts—just clawed-up, empty chest cavities.

After the Ankaseri faction was eliminated for other reasons, many transplanted heart grafts remained, all of which were hungry and able to reproduce.

Motive: Hungers for hearts, reproduction

Environment (Ruk | Mad Science): Usually among the populace of Harmonious

Health: 9

Damage Inflicted: 4 points

Armor: 2

Movement: Immediate

Modifications: Stealth as level 4; Speed defense as level 4 due to size.

Combat: A "transplanted" angiophage need merely burst forth to kill an unsuspecting host. Against fresh targets, the angiophage prefers to use stealth and ambush, possibly even waiting until a target is naturally asleep.

The angiophage can make two different attacks, each a separate action. One attack is an anesthetizing bite. If the victim fails a Speed defense roll, it takes just 1 point of damage and must succeed on a Might defense roll. On a failed Might defense, the victim falls unconscious for one minute. Left undisturbed, the angiophage opens up the target's chest, carefully feeds on the target's heart as it equally carefully replaces the functions of the original heart, and sews itself into the target's chest. This process, thanks to enzymatic healing and anesthetizing mucus, leaves behind only a slight scar, and the target may not even realize what's happened. Once installed, an angiophage is content to remain quiescent for several weeks, at which point it grows hungry again, and emerges to feed.

The angiophage's other attack is a bite attack that deals normal damage.

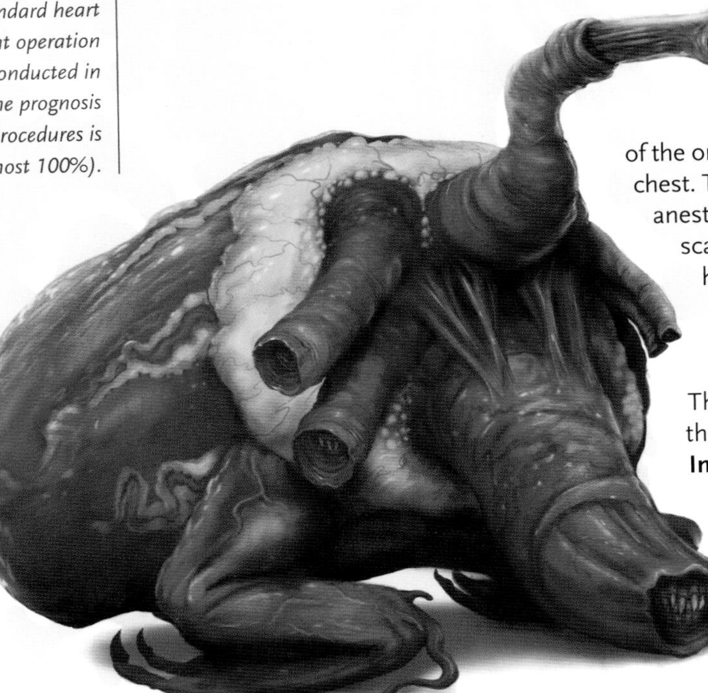

Interaction: The angiophage is about as sophisticated as a virus.

Use: A contact the PCs have traveled to see is found dead with no heart. Alternatively, he stops midsentence and a hungry angiophage bursts out of his chest.

BETRAYER'S HOMUNCULI

"The Lord of Megeddon has many names. To some, he is War. To others, Legion. To most, he is the Betrayer. Among himselves, he is simply Jason."

~a passage from Myth of the Maker

The Incarnation of War could split himself into thousands, becoming the Army of Ardeyn. As this army, War's thoughts raced simultaneously in every copy of himself, and his capacities were magnified to superhuman levels. He was—they were—gods.

When War slew the Maker, the Incarnations lost most of their power, including War (to his surprise and dismay). War—who at that point became known as the Betrayer—retreated to his citadel of Megeddon to lick his wounds and regroup.

Incarnations, page 162
The Betrayer, page 178

Though immensely weakened, he retained an echo of his former abilities. In time, he fashioned a complex beneath his fortress known as the Body Vats, which, in conjunction with the scrap of his former ability, allowed the Betrayer to share his soul out again between multiple bodies.

As a mortal creature, the Betrayer has only so much soul to share. The homunculi he creates in the Vats receive just fragments. Thus, the Betrayer can animate only so many homunculi at any one time—enough to give several hundred a bestial awareness (the greens), a hundred or so the semblance of competence (the reds), and a handful with powers approaching his own (the translucents, also called clears). The Betrayer also gifts his homunculi with a few other surprises, thanks to the customization the Vats allow him.

The tiny handful of homunculi who have an almost perfect semblance of the Betrayer—his clear lieutenants—are made translucent so no one will ever (again) mistake one for him. He was almost replaced by a rebellious copy, back when he made lieutenants appear too much like himself.

GREEN HOMUNCULUS 3 (9)

A homunculus with barely a trace of soul almost invariably comes out of the Body Vats with the brains of a beetle. Greens are slightly above that grade, and they possess a rough likeness to the Betrayer in war regalia, though they stand only about 5 feet (2 m) high and possess just a hint of his aggressive reflexes. They do enjoy one gruesome customization: a second, extendible mouth. Mostly, greens are beasts, and they serve higher homunculi grades as sword fodder. Greens can understand simple commands in the Maker's Tongue, but they can't speak intelligibly; they only gibber.

An unfortunate side effect of homunculi creation limits the amount of nutrition they can absorb, so they are always hungry and will eat anything. If not watched, they even resort to cannibalism.

Motive: Hungers for flesh

Environment (Ardeyn | Magic): Borderlands, usually in groups of five, often in the company of a red homunculus leader

Health: 15

Damage Inflicted: 3 points

Movement: Short

Modifications: Stealth actions as level 1 due to nearly constant gibbering; all knowledge-based skills at level 1.

Combat: A green homunculus attack is sudden and surprising, despite the gibbering; its maw instantly disgorges a thick, tonguelike proboscis tipped with a second set of jaws with the force of a spear thrust. If its victim fails an Intellect defense roll, the green gains the initiative, and the difficulty to dodge its initial attack is increased by one step.

If a green strikes a living character, the secondary mouth latches on in an unbreakable jaw grip. The victim is hindered by the attachment, and his attacks against the green are modified by one step to the victim's detriment. Each subsequent round the green remains attached, the green automatically inflicts damage. This automatic damage also ignores most forms of Armor.

The only way to detach a green homunculus that is actively feeding is to kill it.

Interaction: No interaction is possible other than violence or intimidation. Green homunculi can be intimidated into fleeing by a startling display (like wild animals can), such as killing their leader or pulling off another impressive or unexpected stunt.

Use: The PCs witness a trade shipment from a distant part of Ardeyn dropped by accident. The container breaks open to reveal a lot of green homunculi, ravenous from their long journey.

GM Intrusion: *A green homunculus that is attached and feeding on a PC is slain. Before it dies, it attempts to regurgitate a bolus of foul material directly into the PC. (If the material is injected, the wound turns green, but the PC feels fine at first. Shortly after, the PC begins to experience gruesome, random hallucinations. The effect usually fades on its own after a few days.)*

RED HOMUNCULUS 5 (15)

Red homunculi serve the Betrayer in a variety of roles, having the intelligence and initiative of a normal, if slightly underperforming, human. Except for the cherry red hue of their skin and armor, reds resemble the Betrayer quite closely, though they stand only about 5 1/2 feet (2 m) tall.

Motive: Defense, carry out the orders of the Betrayer

Environment (Ardeyn | Magic): Borderlands, usually as part of a squad of three to five

Health: 27

Damage Inflicted: 5 points

Armor: 1

Movement: Short

Modifications: All knowledge-based skills and tasks made to perceive ambushes and see through tricks as level 3.

Combat: A red attacks with weapons but has some of the training and reflexes of the Betrayer. A red can make two attacks per turn, and once every few minutes, it can spit a bright red bolus at a point it can see within short range, which detonates and inflicts 4 points of acidic damage to all targets in immediate range.

When a red homunculus is slain, it detonates in immediate range, inflicting 5 points of damage to all targets in the area who fail a Speed defense roll, and 1 point of damage even to those who succeed.

What makes reds potentially horrifying is that sometimes they take on the visage of the Betrayer: the homunculus screams, stiffens, then splits open to reveal a terrible creature made of organs. The face announces, "I SEE YOU!" and emerges, joining the fray.

Interaction: A red homunculus is keen to follow its orders, but it can be misled with clever guile.

Use: A squad of reds, disguised by sorcery to appear like a group of adventurers, attempts to kidnap a local sage for her knowledge regarding an ancient qephilim city, and the PCs notice.

Loot: Very often, a squad of reds will have one or two cyphers between them.

GM Intrusion: *The red homunculus takes on a visage of the Betrayer. The visage is a level 5 creature with 15 points of health and 3 points of Armor, and it can fly a short distance each round. In combat, the visage makes one bite attack on its action, which inflicts 8 points of damage. The visage lasts 1d6 + 1 rounds, or until slain.*

When attacking with large groups of NPCs, the GM is encouraged to use the swarm rule. This allows the GM to have a group of six to ten of the same creatures attack en masse as a single creature that is two levels higher, inflicting double the original creature's normal damage.

CATACLYST ROACH 3 (9)

Radiation and leaking magic combine in terrible ways, creating myriad mutant horrors that roam Cataclyst. The Cataclyst roach is a particularly nasty and ubiquitous example of the phenomena. Human-sized roaches with human faces, the creatures come out in the dark, but otherwise dwell in subways and basements of the ruined city. Sometimes groups of roaches emerge at night under the cover of cloud, looking to establish new infestations.

Cataclyst roaches are intelligent, territorial, and essentially without morals—at least, the type of morals that normal humans respect. Within any given nest, a roach abides by what is best for the group as a whole, and an individual thinks little of sacrificing itself to protect its fellows or a hidden nest.

Motive: Territory, defense, and colonization

Environment (Cataclyst | Mad Science and/or Magic): Anywhere dark

Health: 9

Damage Inflicted: 4 points

Armor: 3

Movement: Short

Combat: A Cataclyst roach attacks with claws that inflict both damage and a harmful mutation on a failed Might defense roll. A victim could receive multiple mutations. The harmful mutation persists for as long as the target remains in Cataclyst. Each mutation could come with a visible deformity, at the GM's option.

01–10	**Mentally vulnerable:** The difficulty of all Intellect defense tasks is increased by one step.
11–20	**Slow and lumbering:** The difficulty of all Speed defense tasks is increased by one step.
21–30	**Sickly:** The difficulty of all Might defense tasks is increased by one step.
31–40	**Horrible growth:** A large goiter, immobile tendril, or useless extra eye hangs from your face, increasing the difficulty of all pleasant interactions (with most creatures, particularly humans) by one step.
41–50	**Useless limb:** One of your limbs is unusable or missing.
51–60	**Degraded eye:** One of your eyes is unusable or missing. The difficulty of tasks specifically involving eyesight (spotting, searching, and so on) is increased by one step.
61–70	**Degraded ear:** One of your ears is unusable or missing. The difficulty of tasks specifically involving hearing is increased by one step.
71–80	**Weakness in Might:** Any time you spend points from your Might Pool, the cost is increased by 1 point.
81–90	**Weakness in Speed:** Any time you spend points from your Speed Pool, the cost is increased by 1 point.
91–00	**Weakness in Intellect:** Any time you spend points from your Intellect Pool, the cost is increased by 1 point.

In sunlight or other especially bright light, the difficulty of Speed defense rolls against Cataclyst roach attacks is decreased by one step.

Interaction: Cataclyst roaches are almost always hostile when encountered, but they are intelligent and can speak. They usually taunt and threaten only creatures that are not roaches.

Use: Any visit into the ruins of Cataclyst usually scares up a few Cataclyst roaches when light is introduced to a dark place.

Loot: A roach nest usually contains 1d6 cyphers.

GM Intrusion: *A PC is afflicted with the background radiation around a Cataclyst roach, and one of his arms becomes like a Cataclyst roach's over the course of a round. At first, the character can't use the limb at all, but over a few hours he can learn how.*

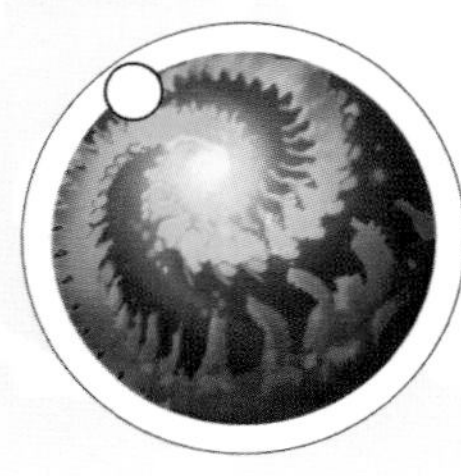

CHAOSPHERE HIERARCH 5 (15)

A Chaosphere hierarch is a quickened native of a recursion from the Shoals of Earth, usually from Ardeyn, who has gained a power over the Strange itself. This influence allows a hierarch to transit across the Strange in a relative blink of an eye, or banish a foe across the Strange to a place it might never find a way back from. This power was gained at a price. Chaosphere hierarchs have divested themselves so fully from their previous selves that they may appear and act radically different than what they once were.

Motive: Knowledge and power

Environment (the Strange): Anywhere, including a recursion in a contextually appropriate form

Health: 36

Damage Inflicted: 7 points

Movement: Short; long while flying

Modifications: Attacks made with artifacts as level 7.

Combat: A hierarch possesses one or more artifacts that provide it with many options in combat. Such an artifact might allow a hierarch to make a ranged energy attack (electricity, fire, magic, radiation, or another less recognizable force) at long range against up to three foes at once. A hierarch might also possess any or all of the following abilities, which require the hierarch's action:

Banish: A target that fails her Intellect defense roll is cast into the Strange in a random direction and a distance requiring 1d6 + 2 hours of transit time to return from, assuming she can find a way back. The disorientation of the effect renders the victim initially lost in the Strange, and alienation applies.

Cleave: The hierarch uses a melee weapon to attack every foe in immediate range as a single action. The hierarch can do this only every other round.

Rune of Will: A target who fails an Intellect defense roll must follow the Chaosphere hierarch's audible directions for up to one minute, as long as she can see the hierarch (who has drawn fractal designs on its flesh to engender the effect).

Vanish: The hierarch could decide to flee a fight and "banish" itself, though when it does so, it appears near a previously prepared site out in the Strange.

Interaction: Different hierarchs have different personalities, but most are arrogant and dismissive of others' needs—and this arrogance is difficult to manipulate. A hierarch also can be amazingly manipulative if it sees an advantage to be gained through interaction over combat.

Use: A hierarch has translated into a recursion or onto Earth to gain access to a vault containing a trove of cyphers. Discovering the hierarch's true nature and purpose comes about accidentally, perhaps when PCs arrive to loot the vault themselves.

Loot: A hierarch has 1d100 + 2,000 units of currency suitable to a recursion it's found within, two cyphers, and an artifact.

GM Intrusion: *The hierarch uses its ability to manipulate the dark matter network to summon a nezerek.*

Shoals of Earth, page 214

Nezerek, page 283

Alienation, page 216

CYPHER EATER 3 (9)

"Canny prospectors in the Chaosphere are recommended to try using harnessed cypher eaters to locate new regions of violet spiral, cyphers, or reality seeds."

~excerpt from The True Traveler's Guide to the Strange

The 10-foot-long (3 m) cypher eater grazes on manifestations of energy that crystallize out of the Strange. It prefers violet spiral, cyphers, and reality seeds. Able to surf the dark energy network if necessary, a cypher eater prefers to stay anchored to massive pieces of fundament when possible, especially fundament with elaborate texture that allows the creature to hide amid nooks and crannies. Akin to a terrestrial shark's electroreception sense, a cypher eater's "chaoreception" allows it to sense cyphers and similar objects within long range, even if such objects are stowed or otherwise cached.

Cypher eaters are lone scouts—actually just one part of a highly developed hive of creatures, each of which has a specialized task or function within the community. A cypher eater has the role of community provider.

Motive: Hunger for cyphers and similar physical manifestations of the Strange

Environment (the Strange): Anywhere

Health: 17

Damage Inflicted: 3 points

Movement: Short

Modifications: Perception as level 8 for tasks related to sensing cyphers and similar manifestations of the Strange.

Combat: A cypher eater's chaoreception sense suffuses it, and anyone who touches or strikes the cypher eater with a melee attack takes 2 points of damage as the attacker's body becomes an unwilling extension of that disruptive sense. (The cypher eater must choose to extend its ability in this way, which means it could also choose to keep the effect in check.)

If a cypher eater bites a target, it focuses its special sense into the prey, who takes 2 points of damage as described above. In addition to that damage, one random cypher, violet spiral, reality seed, or similar object carried by the target detonates. The detonation inflicts a number of points of damage equal to the item's level on everything in immediate range, except for the cypher eater; instead of taking damage, the cypher eater regains a number of points of health equal to the level of the object, and may exceed its normal maximum health when it does so.

Interaction: A cypher eater is more akin to an insect than an animal; however, a cypher eater queen is intelligent and could be negotiated with if a creature has a telepathic ability or other means to bridge a language barrier.

Use: Jagger Shipping out of Ardeyn is planning a cypher eater quelling to improve their economic outlook (not realizing that this would likely rouse the nearby hive to exact vengeance), and is looking for hardy adventuring types to sign on. Pay is promised in cyphers or in violet spiral.

Loot: A cypher eater doesn't have loot, but if encountered out in the Strange, it's likely not far from one or two cyphers that can be extracted.

GM Intrusion: *A PC's artifact "goes off" due to the influence of the cypher eater with double its normal strength (if applicable). If this accidental artifact discharge can affect the PC negatively, it does. Worse, the PC must make two depletion rolls for the privilege.*

Within a cypher eater hive, specialized defenders can grow much larger than a normal cypher eater. A typical defender is level 5, measures almost 50 feet (15 m) in length, inflicts 5 points of damage with its chaoreception sense, has 25 points of health, and has 4 points of Armor.

Jagger Shipping, page 172
Violet spiral, page 219

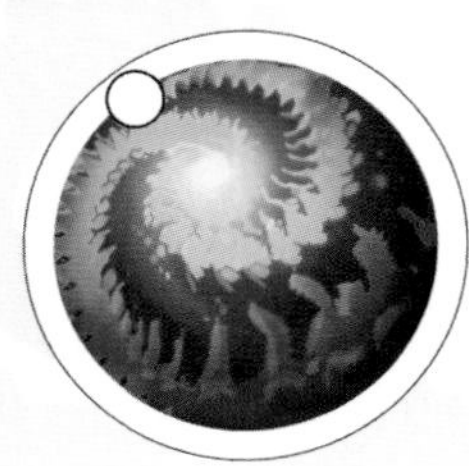

DARK ENERGY PHARAOH 8 (24)

Recursions created through the fictional bleed of previous human civilizations on Earth exist, but they are rare. That's mostly because fewer people lived on the planet long ago, which provided far fewer opportunities for fictional leakage to occur.

One long-ago recursion was seeded by belief in the ancient Egyptian afterlife and included the likenesses of many pharaohs waking into their promised heavenly kingdoms. Many of these pharaohs gained the spark and eventually quickened. Soon after, war followed among the pharaohs. As their recursion collapsed into the Strange, most of the "demigods" fled. Some were lost, but some survived out in the dark energy network, mostly by adapting, scavenging, and preying on the shadows in other recursions and on aspects of the Strange. The pharaohs incorporated the magic, mad science, and fringe developments they found in other recursions into themselves. Sometimes, a pharaoh's activities in these recursions was enough to collapse it.

A handful of dark energy pharaohs survive in the Strange to this day.

Motive: Hunger for powerful abilities, cyphers, and artifacts

Environment (the Strange): Anywhere

Health: 60

Damage Inflicted: 10 points

Armor: 4

Movement: Short; long while flying

Combat: Dark energy pharaohs use the abilities, artifacts, and cyphers they've collected for attack and defense. In any given conflict a pharaoh can access abilities or artifacts that grant it a long-range attack that inflicts at least 10 points of damage, as well as a kind of magic or mad science force field that grants it +2 to Armor.

A dark energy pharaoh also usually has a spell or tractor beam that can immobilize a foe, blind a foe, or even imprison a foe in a pocket-prison recursion in the shape of a canopic jar. Finally, a pharaoh has several combat-related cyphers it can use at need.

Interaction: Dark energy pharaohs believe they are ascended gods. Proud and vengeful, a dark energy pharaoh is an easy enemy to make.

Use: The shadow residents in a recursion have started worshiping a new god—one not part of that recursion's fiction or invested plan. It's an intruding dark energy pharaoh.

Loot: A dark energy pharaoh has 1d6 + 3 cyphers and a couple of artifacts.

GM Intrusion: *The PC's weapon strikes a component of the pharaoh's magitech panoply that sprays the PC with a cold so intense that he is frozen in place for one round and takes 10 points of ambient cold damage.*

Most dark energy pharaohs rest in resplendent recursions of their own design or in Strange strongholds built over several thousand years from the looted bones of other fictions. From time to time, a pharaoh wakes, looking for new treasures and abilities to steal.

DEMON OF LOTAN 5 (15)

Whether sinner or saint, a spirit who finds her way to Lotan's fire is changed. All the good is burned away, leaving a charred, evil husk. ~Unknown

If a wandering spirit in Ardeyn is not corralled by the Court of Sleep, it descends the endless dark roads until the fires of Lotan engulf it, transforming the spirit into an ashen demon pledged to the Sinner.

A demon remembers only fragments of its life—every good memory is cauterized and every slight, misfortune, snub, and pain is amplified. The resulting mind knows only hate and the desire to tempt others into the same state as itself.

Having no flesh, a revealed demon is a shadowed, ephemeral horror. This immaterial nature allows it to possess others. A demon can cause great harm in a short time by forcing its possessed host to lie, steal, and deliver violence upon loved ones.

Motive: Hungers for others' pain and fear

Environment (Ardeyn | Magic): Anywhere

Health: 30

Damage Inflicted: 5 points

Armor: 2

Movement: Short; immediate while flying

Modifications: All stealth tasks as level 7.

Combat: A demon can attack a creature with its touch. Either the touch inflicts 5 points of damage as the target's form is decayed and eroded by necrosis, or the demon can attempt to possess the target. The target of an attempted possession must make an Intellect defense roll or become possessed, whereupon the demon's form disappears into the target.

The first round a character is possessed, he can act normally. On the second and subsequent rounds, the possessing demon can control the actions of the host, but the character can attempt an Intellect defense roll to resist each suggested action. Successful resistance means that the character does nothing for one round. On other rounds, the character can act as he chooses. A possessing demon's actions are limited to attempts to control its host and leaving the host.

A possessed target is allowed an Intellect defense roll to eject the demon once per day, barring any exorcism attempts. The difficulty of the defense roll increases by 1 for each day of possession after the first seven days.

A demon not possessing another creature can pass through solid objects whose level is less than its own.

Interaction: A demon allows a possessed host to act normally, as long as it doesn't reveal the demon's presence. If its presence is known, the demon might negotiate, but only after a tirade of lies and obscenity, and the demon likely betrays any deal reached.

Use: A crypt found beneath a newer structure has demons within it. A call goes out for someone to clean out the threats before they do harm.

GM Intrusion: *The PC who attempts an exorcism of a possessed target is successful, but the demon moves directly from the former victim into the PC. The PC can make an Intellect-based roll to eject the demon, but only after the first round of possession.*

Court of Sleep, page 184

A demon prefers to attempt possession before its potential host is aware of its presence, but it might choose to possess a victim in combat, too.

One way to exorcise a demon, as anyone with Ardeyn lore might know, is to command the demon out in the name of the Maker and his Incarnations. This grants the possessed character an additional Intellect defense roll to eject the demon and can be attempted once per day.

DLAMMA 6 (18)

Dlammas are believed to be champions of the weak and downtrodden in Ardeyn, which is true often enough to keep the perception alive.

Dlammas are creatures of the Age of Myth, when they served as steeds of qephilim who fought human dragon riders in the war against Lotan. A relative handful survived to the present age, but most dlammas alive today are younger. Many retain a semblance of the protective nature attributed to the original dlamma, but some—the bleak dlammas—have become twisted.

Dlammas reproduce, but they do so only very rarely. A legendary dlamma spawning ground called Isum—one of the skerries in northern Ardeyn—is sometimes a site sought by adventuring companies, thanks to the legend that dlamma egg fragments insulate against the effects of magic.

Motive: Protection

Environment (Ardeyn | Magic): Daylands or Borderlands, usually alone

Health: 32

Damage Inflicted: 6 points

Armor: 1

Movement: Short; long while flying

Modifications: Perception, Ardeyn lore as level 7.

Combat: Dlamma visual senses are incredibly sharp, so much so that even from half a mile (0.8 km) in the sky, they can see details as if they were in immediate range (though at night, they must be within long range to gain the same level of awareness).

They can attack with their hooves, making two attacks as a single action. However, dlammas are more feared for the words of power they use to heal, create shelter, and even move elements.

In combat, they fall back on a Word of Smiting, an attack that inflicts 6 points of damage on up to three targets within long range. When they use Word of Healing, they can confer the ability to regenerate 2 points of damage each round for one minute upon themselves or upon a target within immediate range (if a creature is reduced to 0 health, the regeneration ends early).

GM Intrusion: *The character is affected by the Word of Smiting so severely that he is dazed and takes no action other than to attempt to clear his head (a difficulty 6 Might-based roll).*

Interaction: To call upon a dlamma, folk wisdom dictates that a petitioner should engrave the image of the creature on a clay tablet and bury it at a crossroads. If a dlamma is anywhere near, it is drawn to the location thanks to sympathetic sorcery. What a dlamma decides to do upon arriving, however, might be far different than what the petitioner had in mind. Even dlammas who retain their protective urges are realists, and they rarely help others without at least a promise of payment in return.

Use: A woman who keeps her identity secret is hiring adventurers to look for Isum, where stories suggest that dlamma egg shards are lying around for easy pickings. It turns out that the woman is a dragon in disguise, and she wishes to find Isum to destroy any eggs or hatchling dlammas she can find.

Loot: A dlamma usually carries 1d6 × 100 crowns and a few cyphers.

DRAGON 7 (21)

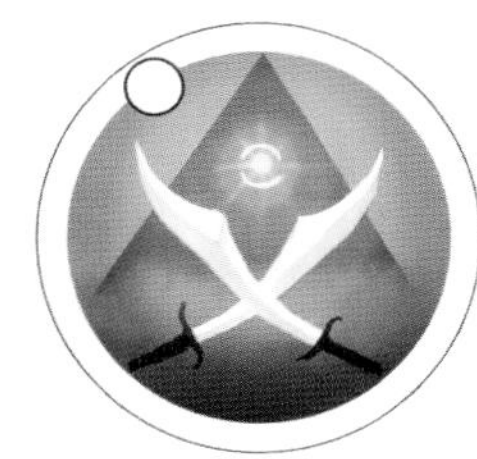

The massive, feathered dragons of Ardeyn are exceptionally territorial and competitive. They love games of all sorts, especially ones that end with the nondragon loser being eaten. Unfortunately for civilized folks, dragons view war as a kind of game and the capture of human and qephilim holdings as moves in some wider contest, the rules of which only dragons understand. In the same way, a dragon's hoard is not only an end in itself, but part of a never-ending tournament among dragons of a certain age to see which one can accumulate the largest trove. Other, less known contests are also likely ongoing.

According to legend, dragons were first made by Lotan. Asking a dragon whether that's true is the best way to get off on the wrong foot.

Motive: Winning at games large and small

Environment (Ardeyn | Magic): Anywhere

Health: 52

Damage Inflicted: 7 points

Armor: 1

Movement: Short; long while flying

Modifications: Perception as level 8. Speed defense as level 6 due to size.

Combat: A dragon can bite one target or claw two opponents in immediate range as a single action. When bitten, the target is also immobilized until he succeeds on a Might defense roll to break free (or the dragon drops him).

Most dragons have one or more additional magical abilities they can bring to bear in combat, including the following.

Fiery Breath: A dragon can breathe a stream of fire up to long range, doing 7 points of damage to all targets within immediate range of each other. Targets who succeed on a Speed defense roll to avoid the full effect of the fire still take 3 points of damage from the flame. This ability cannot be used on consecutive rounds.

Change Shape: A dragon with this ability can take the form of a human or qephilim as its action, or return to its regular shape. When so changed, the disguise is nearly impenetrable without special knowledge. As a human or qephilim, the dragon is a level 5 creature.

Captivate: A dragon with this ability can psychically mesmerize a nondragon target in immediate range who fails an Intellect defense roll. A captivated target does the dragon's verbal bidding for one or more days. Each time the target is confronted by a third party about its mental condition, the target is allowed another Intellect defense roll to break the effect.

Demon Fire: Some dragons still secretly serve Lotan. The taint of such a dragon's fiery breath provides a conduit that demons can follow to afflict fresh vessels. Once a day when such a dragon breathes its fiery breath, targets who take full damage from the fire become vulnerable to demonic possession. If these targets fail a second difficulty 5 Intellect defense roll (which is the attack made by a demon attempting to possess a target), the victim is indeed possessed by a demon of Lotan.

Interaction: Like the colors of dragon feathers, dragon personalities run the gamut from beastly thug to refined connoisseur. Some dragons lie with every smoky breath, others consider the least bit of dishonesty a personal failing, and most fall somewhere in between.

Use: A dragon confronts the PCs, challenging them to a riddle game with the following rules: if the PCs win, they get a cypher. If the dragon wins, the PCs owe the dragon a favor to be specified later.

Loot: A dragon usually carries a couple of cyphers and 1d6 × 10 gold crowns. A dragon's hoard might contain 2d6 cyphers, 1d6 × 200 gold crowns, and possibly a few artifacts (but a dragon's lair is usually well guarded).

GM Intrusion: *The dragon breathes fire while the PC is already caught in the dragon's mouth.*

As they say in Ardeyn, you can't tell a dragon by the color of its feathers.

The Harrowing is a yearly competition in Kuambis where dragons compete with humans and qephilim.

Kuambis, page 176

Demon of Lotan, page 265

GIANT 6 (18)

"When my brother was slain, I swore vengeance. I followed the murderer's trail from one corner of the Daylands to the other. Everywhere I went, I found evidence of the killer's presence: smashed walls, tumbled homes, and more death. It was as if the beast was stalking me. I was only slightly afraid at first, until I realized the truth. The killer was me. I bear the giant's curse." ~Eskihizar the Shunned

GM Intrusion: *The giant's blow sprains one of the PC's limbs, making the limb useless for ten minutes.*

When not transformed, most victims of the curse of gigantism have the stats of an average level 1 or level 2 creature.

The evidence of a giant's rampage is discovered more often than the perpetrator herself. That's because the curse of gigantism usually triggers its growth in a victim only during storms or when a normally human-sized victim becomes emotionally stressed or overexcited. The rest of the time, a giant is human-sized and appears (and may live) just like a regular human. Episodes of gigantism, when the giant is as tall as a tree and as wide as a house, are forgotten by the giant, except perhaps only as a vague dream.

After the curse really takes hold, a giant eventually learns the truth, perhaps by waking to find her house smashed and her family and friends severely injured or dead from being thrown across the valley. As a result, many giants live alone in the wilderness, possibly desiring the company of others, but knowing that no one is safe around them for long.

The curse of gigantism is normally passed by blood, but since it doesn't strike a victim until her thirty-fifth year of life (and sometimes skips generations altogether), stamping it out has proved especially problematic. Most sufferers would've chosen not to have children had they known their parent or grandparent was a giant.

Motive: Destruction

Environment (Ardeyn | Magic): Borderlands, mountains

Health: 40

Damage Inflicted: 6 points

Movement: Short

Modifications: Speed defense as level 5 due to size. Breaks and throws objects as level 8.

Combat: A giant smashes foes with her mighty fists, possibly catching up to three human-sized targets with the same attack if all the targets are in immediate range of each other.

If a giant attacks a single target, she can choose to do regular damage or to grab hold of her victim, dealing 4 points of damage instead. On his turn, the victim can attempt a Might defense roll to power out of the grip, a Speed defense roll to slip out, or an Intellect-based task to try to distract the giant. If the victim fails, the giant throws him as high and as far as she can on her next turn. Damage on impact varies, depending on the surrounding environment, but a victim takes an average of 10 points of ambient damage.

Interaction: When a giant is raging (which is always, when she's a giant), the only possible interaction is an attempt to distract her by singing, juggling, or creating some other flagrant display, which some giants will pause to watch. Each additional round trying to distract a giant (whether the previous round was successful or not) increases the difficulty of the task by one step.

Use: During the last spring storm, a giant came down out of the mountains and laid waste to half a village. Survivors put together an appeal for someone to venture into the giant's mountain lair and destroy him.

GNATHOSTOME 4 (12)

Gnathostomes lurk in dark places, preying on other creatures using ambush tactics. They are drawn to inhabited locations because such places offer plenty of the cerebrospinal fluid and fatty brain tissue they require to survive.

Related to 3-foot-high (1 m) autonomous ecology samplers used by some research factions, gnathostomes improve on a "tame" sampler's ability to remain hidden in plain sight, and more insidiously, a sampler's ability to debilitate a subject to extract a biological sample. How gnathostomes evolved from samplers used for research isn't precisely known, but to discover the answer, tame samplers have been programmed to seek out and conduct bioassays on gnathostomes. This has resulted in something of a minor gnathostome-sampler war being carried out beyond the notice of most Ruk citizens.

Motive: Hungers for cerebrospinal fluid

Environment (Ruk | Mad Science): Anywhere near inhabited locations

Health: 12

Damage Inflicted: 4 points

Armor: 3

Movement: Short, long when jumping

Modifications: Perception as level 5; stealth as level 6; Speed defense as level 5 due to size.

Combat: Gnathostomes usually begin an encounter by "dropping" onto a target from a concealed location, gaining the benefits of a surprise attack. A successful bite deals damage and requires a second Might defense roll. On a failed roll, the gnathostome's bite also sucks a portion of the victim's cerebrospinal fluid. Each time cerebrospinal fluid is sucked from a PC by this attack, the PC moves one step down the damage track.

Interaction: Gnathostomes do not speak. However, a gnathostome that completely drains a victim of its cerebrospinal fluid may "learn" what the victim knew, but that information is accessible only to someone who in turn subdues a gnathostome and plugs in an umbilical.

Use: A victim of a gnathostome attack possessed important information, and a faction wants the PCs to track down the gnathostome responsible and see if that information can be extracted.

Loot: Gnathostomes retain elements of their sampler roots, and they could carry one or two cyphers in a collection compartment.

GM Intrusion: *When the PC hits the gnathostome with a melee weapon, the gnathostome clamps down on the weapon and jerks it from the PC's hands.*

Surprise, page 110

Because gnathostomes are evolved from scientific apparatus, they retain a lot of built-in sensory equipment that enables them to track potential prey even through walls, and sense prey that is otherwise invisible.

GOLEM 6 (18)

Golems were summoned to mobility by Incarnations during the Age of Myth to serve as soldiers, couriers, and banner-bearers. Now that those wars are over and the Incarnations are gone, many golems remain without purpose or master. Most have ceased moving, becoming statuary posed in unexpected places—stained, eroded, and forlorn. Sometimes one will wake if disturbed, and depending on the state of its remaining mind, could either attempt to communicate, or try to smash those responsible for waking it once more to a purposeless existence.

Because golems were the creation of the Incarnations, most are heavily inscribed with symbology related to a particular Incarnation, and they may have a shape that recalls that Incarnation as well. As a result, a golem of War or Death can be quite imposing, though a golem of Silence might go unnoticed.

GM Intrusion: *The PC is grabbed by the golem and headbutted for 6 points of damage. The PC must break or slip free, or else she remains in the golem's grip.*

Motive: Seeks dissolution or purpose
Environment (Ardeyn | Magic): Anywhere
Health: 18
Damage Inflicted: 6 points
Armor: 5
Movement: Short
Modifications: Intellect defense and resistance to trickery as level 3; Speed defense as level 4 due to speed.
Combat: Skilled with large two-handed weapons, golems inflict an additional 2 points of damage (total of 8 points) when using them. Golems cannot be stunned or dazed. They are immune to most poisons and disease, and 2 of their 5 points of Armor protect against ambient damage (environmental damage, heat, cold, falling, and so on).

A golem can stamp the ground with its prodigious weight, creating a shock wave that causes all creatures in range to take 3 points of damage. In addition, they fall down or are pushed out of immediate range.

Some golems have the ability to freeze in place, becoming as still as a statue. When one does so, its Armor increases to 10 (and Armor against ambient damage increases to 5), but it can take no actions, including purely mental actions. Unless something can damage the golem through its Armor, it remains frozen indefinitely.

Even if a golem is completely destroyed, the rubble of its form slowly reassembles over the course of three days, unless that rubble is ground to the finest gravel and spread across recursions.

Interaction: Most golems are mournful, and a few have become cruel in their isolation, but at heart, all are lonely. Many are also tired of their stone existence, where they can move but not really feel, and they wish for some sort of final end.

Use: Powerful sorcerers sometimes seek out golems and press them into service with spells, or with the promise of release from their long lives in return for a few favors. Such golems prove to be tough bodyguards, but sometimes the futility of such service overcomes a golem and it turns on the sorcerer, breaking free of the binding spells in its rage over being denied the peace of death.

GREEN ONE 4 (12)

"Violence was more than their code—it was a mental elixir that colored their every waking thought." ~Jad Mathew, Old Mars explorer

Green ones are a warrior race in the recursion of Old Mars. The green-skinned adults stand around 15 feet (5 m) high. They sport large eyes, tusks, and two fully functioning sets of arms. The green ones wage war across the face of Old Mars, tribe against tribe. The most well known is the green ones' "kingdom" of Sharnak, which takes its name from the deserted city they use as a capital.

Green ones are an egg-laying species, but like turtles on Earth, the hatchlings are left to fend for themselves inside low-walled incubators that soak in sunlight by day and keep the eggs moderately warm at night. When born, hatchlings with any obvious abnormality are slain to keep the race strong.

Motive: Gathering resources, eliminating competitors

Environment (Old Mars | Mad Science): Anywhere, usually in groups of four or more

Health: 22

Damage Inflicted: 4 points

Movement: Short

Modifications: Perception and attacks as level 5.

Combat: In melee, a green one can attack with both a spear and its tusks as a single action. Many green ones are also armed with rifles that deal 8 points of damage to one target within long range on a successful attack. After each shot, preparing for the next is a minute-long process. (Particularly important green ones might have special rifles that can fire every other round using radium pellets that deal 10 points of damage, with a range of a mile or more.)

Sometimes a war party of green ones ride multilegged, vicious mounts. A green one riding a mount defends as a level 6 creature and can move a long distance each round. Their mounts are level 3 creatures with 9 health and 1 point of Armor.

Interaction: Green ones are typically warlike and cruel, but they count honor as the highest virtue. So it's possible to convince some that honor is best served not by slaying enemies and parading the resulting heads around on spears, but instead by seeking a more diplomatic solution to differences.

Use: A band of green ones called warbloods, whose vicious savagery exceeds that of all other tribes, has been recruited through an inapposite gate to Ruk, where they are being used to bring down Zal-operated grey harvesters and kill any crew found. The Zal faction is putting together a group of contractors to discover what's been happening to their harvesters.

Loot: A band of green ones has a couple of rifles, dried food and water, knives, and maybe a single cypher between them.

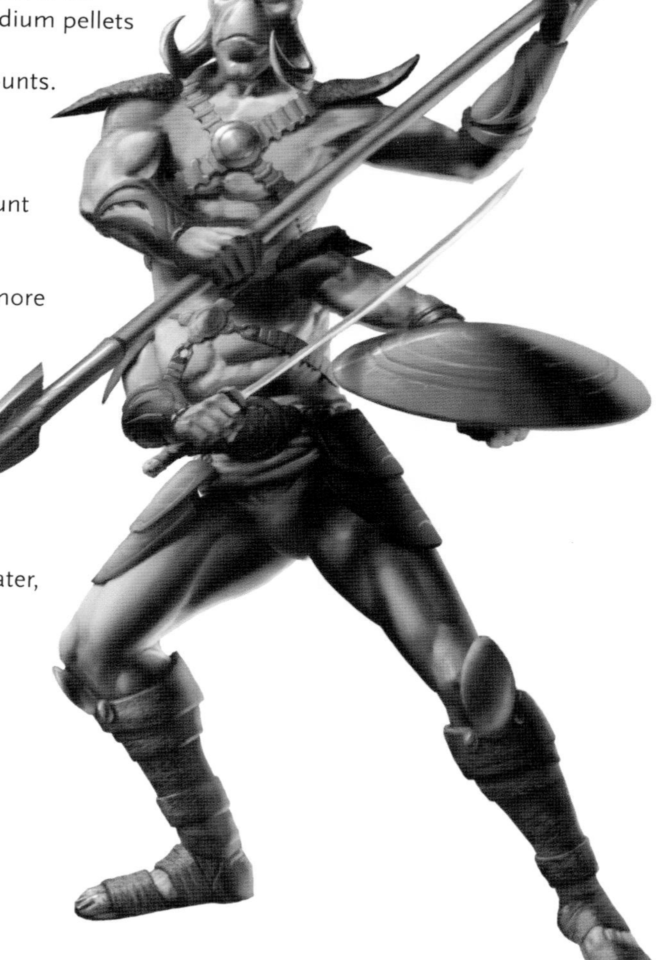

GM Intrusion: *The force of the green one's physical attack pushes the PC down a nearby pit, through a door, or into another character.*

Creatures other than green ones who fire a green one rifle suffer a one-step penalty.

Old Mars, page 253
Grey harvester, page 195
Zal, page 194

HYDRA 6 (18)

A hydra is a hideous predator with five or more heads. Legend says the very first hydra was formed when a coterie of human sorcerers who served Lotan were slain, and their severed heads were thrown into a cursed well. Some thread of evil magic remained in those heads, binding the souls together in a form of hideous life, which crawled back out three days later as a hydra.

Hydras scavenge for food like regular beasts, but their favorite fare is human flesh, except for the head. Heads without merit are left to rot, but those with useful bits of knowledge or skill are incorporated onto a hydra. At first, such a head begs and pleads for release from the horror of its new existence, but eventually it seems to find peace as part of the collective, and it becomes as eager to sample new flesh as any of the other heads.

GM Intrusion: *The PC strikes the hydra and her weapon becomes tangled in a mass of knotty hair.*

Motive: Hungers for flesh, high-value human heads

Environment (Ardeyn | Magic): Borderlands

Health: 24

Damage Inflicted: 2 points

Armor: 1

Movement: Short

Modifications: Perception as level 7 due to its many heads; Speed defense as level 4 due to size.

Combat: A hydra is an exceptionally dangerous foe, given that all five of its heads can simultaneously bite foes in immediate range. If three or more heads coordinate their attack, the heads make one attack as a single level 7 creature dealing 12 points of damage.

If a human target is killed by a hydra, the hydra regenerates 5 points of health and gains the killed target's head as a new one of its own on the following round. A newly acquired head retains its previous motivations, but it can take only purely verbal or mental actions.

The heads of a hydra also possess remnants of previous abilities from back when they were still people. Any head not involved in a direct physical attack can use one of these abilities, once per round.

The first hydra still exists somewhere in Ardeyn, having crawled down into a lair in the Night Vault, heavy with dozens of heads. Lesser hydras may also accumulate extra heads, but when they reach ten or more, they tend to discard the excess heads, which braid together and crawl away as a newly "born" hydra.

Interaction: A hydra talks among itself, almost to the exclusion of interacting with other sentient creatures. Very rarely will a hydra bargain, especially if it means forgoing the buffet of human flesh right in front of it in return for a later reward.

Use: The PCs investigate a qephilim ruin hoping to find artifacts of the ancient war between Lotan and the Incarnations. A hydra saw the PCs enter and trails them through the crumbling structures at a considerable distance, waiting for them to take a rest or become otherwise distracted before attacking.

Loot: Hydras sometimes knot cyphers and other valuables into their hair; a defeated hydra may possess 1d6 cyphers and 1d100 crowns.

INKLING

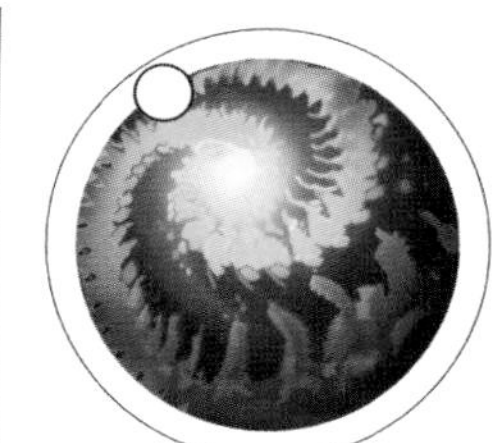

Inklings are "ghosts" of the Strange. An absence recalling form and a hunger without a shape, an inkling mimics what it last fed upon and erased from existence. Most inklings encountered in and around the Shoals of Earth are humanoid in silhouette. They may be a form of life bred in an alien fiction, the "psychic memories" of consumed recursions that have taken on a tortured half-life of their own, or something yet to be conceived by recursors.

Despite the rules that fence out Strangers, inklings can sometimes seep into a recursion to feed on natives. Whether in the depths of the dark energy network or in the ruins of a bombed-out basement in Cataclyst, an area of space-black darkness could be a swarm of inklings waiting to feed.

LESSER INKLING — 2 (6)

Lesser inklings have as little substance and are as dangerous as regular shadows, but the more inklings that pool together, the greater their combined strength (and the more likely a snatcher will appear). Lesser inklings are drawn to living creatures like moths to light, but only if that life is nearby. Otherwise they collect in dark corners of the Strange, especially around the ruined and lost relics of devoured civilizations.

Motive: Hungers for life, color, and substance

Environment (the Strange): Anywhere undisturbed, usually in swarms of five or ten, but sometimes more

Health: 6

Damage Inflicted: 2 points

Movement: Immediate while in combat, long while flying

Combat: The touch of a lesser inkling inflicts 2 points of ambient damage (wounds appear as areas of darkness). An inkling can suck light in immediate range, inflicting 2 points of ambient damage to living creatures, but not on consecutive turns.

Inklings often attack as a swarm. For every multiple of five inklings present (five, ten, fifteen, and so on), the resultant swarm makes an attack as a creature two levels higher that inflicts 2 additional points of ambient damage. The swarm can make both touch and light-draining attacks in immediate range.

Bright light (as bright as direct sunlight or brighter) drives a lesser inkling back. An inkling that cannot escape bright light evaporates in just a few rounds.

Interaction: Lesser inklings aren't really intelligent. They're drawn to feed and are repelled by light.

Use: A swarm of inklings seep into a recursion through a fissure in existence, and infest a basement, tomb, or closet. Alternatively, a shattered habitat or vessel found in the Strange might contain inklings.

GM Intrusion: *All of the bright light sources suddenly go out, allowing the inklings to encroach.*

An inkling can become fully insubstantial, but when feeding, it retains enough substance to affect (and be affected by) corporeal creatures.

INKLING SNATCHER — 7 (21)

Greater inklings of various terrible visages haunt the Strange. One is the inkling snatcher, which can drain the color and substance from a creature when it feeds, until nothing is left of a victim but formless shadow: a lesser inkling. The more an inkling snatcher consumes of a creature, the more it comes to look like its prey.

Motive: Hungers for life, color, and substance

Environment (the Strange): Anywhere undisturbed, at the center of a large swarm of lesser inklings or wandering alone

Health: 42

Damage Inflicted: 7 points

Movement: Long

Modifications: Defends as level 3 against melee attacks due to desire to be struck (see combat).

Combat: The touch of an inkling snatcher inflicts 7 points of ambient damage.

An inkling snatcher can also suck light in immediate range as an action once every other round, inflicting 4 points of ambient damage to living creatures. Form and color seem to flow from the victim to the inkling with each successful attack. An inkling regains health equal to half the number of points of damage it deals to creatures (or adds the total to its maximum health if already fully healthy).

Each time a foe successfully attacks an inkling snatcher, he suffers 2 points of ambient damage, as shadow substance from the wound splashes the attacker back.

Each time a foe takes 7 or more points of damage from an inkling snatcher attack, he must make a Might defense roll. On a failed roll, the foe descends one step on the damage track. If a foe is killed by an inkling, nothing is left but a shadow (a fledgling lesser inkling). Meanwhile, the inkling snatcher takes on the visage, abilities, and personality of the just-consumed. Indeed, for one day, the snatcher may believe it *is* the victim, until a strange hunger awakes (and the snatcher's stolen form and color begin to leach away).

Bright light (as bright as direct sunlight or brighter) modifies all tasks, attacks, and defenses of an inkling snatcher by two steps to its detriment.

Interaction: Meaningful interaction with an inkling snatcher is impossible, unless the snatcher still retains most of the form and mind of a previous victim.

Use: Inklings are considered a threat that must be burned out whenever they are confronted, or fled from if too prolific.

Loot: Sometimes an inkling snatcher with a victim's likeness has a couple of cyphers and an artifact from that victim.

GM Intrusion: *The inkling snatcher takes on the likeness and form of a previous victim, temporarily convincing the PCs that it isn't a threat.*

JABBERWOCK 7 (21)

Beware the Jabberwock, my son!
The jaws that bite, the claws that catch!
Beware the Jubjub bird, and shun
The frumious Bandersnatch!
~Through the Looking-Glass *by Lewis Carroll*

Overhearing the burbling jabber of three quarrelsome siblings is unpleasant at best. At worst, it could portend the imminent appearance of the jabberwock. Given how disagreeable such a meeting would likely be, one's best option in that situation is to *run*.

Due to the creature's frumious manner, no one alive can claim to be an expert on its habits, demeanor, and nature. That doesn't stop people from trying to figure out why the three heads—one named Jabberwock (for which the whole creature is known), one named Jubjub, and the last named Bandersnatch—are always so angry with each other. At least one thing's clear: if someone wanted to slay the beast by cutting off its head, the task would require three decapitations, not one.

Motive: Unknown

Environment (Wonderland | Magic): In the wabe

Health: 32

Damage Inflicted: 7 points

Armor: 4, 15 against fire

Movement: Short; long while flying

Modifications: Speed defense as level 5 due to size.

Combat: Each of the jabberwock's three heads can attack a different target with a bite within a single action. Alternatively, the jabberwock can spend its action to make two claw attacks, and either deal damage or catch the prey in its grip. On subsequent rounds, the jabberwock automatically bites prey caught in its front claws (leaving one or two heads free to bite other foes that are not yet caught). The only physical action a human-sized victim caught in a jabberwock's claw can take is to attempt a Might-based or Speed-based roll to escape the creature's clutches.

Once every other round, the jabberwock can breathe heat (or cold), inflicting damage on up to ten targets within short range of each other and within long range of the jabberwock. Even on a successful Speed defense roll, targets still take 1 point of fire (or cold) damage.

Interaction: A jabberwock usually puts aside the quarrels among its heads to eat prey, but crafty interaction could turn the jabberwock on itself, at least for a time.

Use: The jabberwock's lair contains a trove of amazing items, and perhaps the PCs need one in particular.

Loot: 1d100 × 10 gold coins, 1d6 + 3 cyphers, possibly a Wonderland artifact.

GM Intrusion: *When the PC hits the jabberwock, it roars with newfound rage! The rage provides it with renewed vigor (and restores 15 points of health to the jabberwock).*

And as in uffish thought he stood,
The Jabberwock, with eyes of flame,
Came whiffling through the tulgey wood,
And burbled as it came!
~Through the Looking-Glass *by Lewis Carroll*

KRAY

Pale stalks parted the captain's hair, folding out from his head, questing like fingers. The captain was gone; he'd been hollowed out and worn like a hat, just long enough to gestate a kray. ~a passage from the Myth of the Maker

Long ago, the Betrayer showed the kray a way to get past the Seven Rules that kept other Strangers out of Ardeyn in return for their aid. These creatures have plagued Ardeyn ever since.

As inert seedlings, kray can sometimes find entry on their own, but they usually require someone native to the recursion to bring them in. After a kray seedling makes the transition into a recursion, it can drift on the wind until it finds fertile ground. In this case, fertile ground means a living creature.

KRAY SCURRIER 3 (12)

GM Intrusion: *One or two more kray scurriers appear, hatching from nearby NPCs that no one realized were infected.*

A kray seedling that takes root in a living creature needs to gestate for only a few minutes before spitting out a kray scurrier: part crayfish, part spider, and all nightmare. A kray scurrier's body is about the size of a human head, but despite its relatively small size, the creature is an amoral and fearless predator with one goal: eat from the flesh of the recursion where it finds itself. A kray scurrier usually doesn't have to eat much before it molts to become a larger kray drone.

Motive: Hungers for flesh

Environment (Ardeyn | Magic): Usually in the Borderlands or Green Wilds, alone or in scuttles of up to ten

Health: 12

Damage Inflicted: 4 points

Armor: 2

Movement: Short

Modifications: Speed defense as level 4 due to small size.

Combat: A scurrier's main mode of attack is its pincers, which it can use to attack a single foe in immediate range, even if the scurrier moved on its action.

A scurrier also possesses a precursor drone stage web attack that can be used every other round to attack a target in long range for 4 points of damage. A victim hit by kray scurrier webs can't move or physically attack, but he can spend an action attempting to break free (a Might task).

A scuttle of four or more kray scurriers can focus on a single target and make one attack as if they were a level 5 creature, inflicting 8 points of damage.

Interaction: A kray scurrier doesn't communicate, and it tries to eat anything that talks to it. Before a scurrier sprouts, it attempts to make others believe that the body it resides in is still the person or creature it was before.

Use: A large family of farmers in the Ardeyn hinterlands has become infected, all except a young boy, who has run away. PCs might find the boy along the way to another adventure and hear how his parents and siblings "aren't the same as they used to be." That's because they're all being puppeted by kray scurriers.

KRAY DRONE 5 (15)

GM Intrusion: *The PC moves into a net of kray drone webbing that she did not see and is caught.*

When a kray scurrier eats enough, it molts (over the course of one round) and, from a space too small to hold it, a kray drone emerges.

A kray drone's torso is human-sized, but when standing on its many legs, it's two and a half times taller than a human. The front two pincers have spinnerets on the end and each can spray webbing. Anything fully cocooned in kray webbing is either deleted from existence or hideously changed.

Motive: Collapsing recursions for the broodmother

Environment (Ardeyn | Magic): Usually in the Borderlands or Green Wilds

Health: 19

Damage Inflicted: 5 points

Armor: 3

Movement: Short

Modifications: Speed defense as level 4 due to size.

Combat: A kray drone can propel a spray of webbing from each of its spinnerets, attacking up to two creatures within short range as a single action. A web attack does damage and catches the victim, who can do nothing other than attempt to break free. For every turn the victim is caught in the web, he takes 5 points of damage from being cocooned.

A victim killed in kray webbing becomes fully cocooned. If the cocoon is later scraped away, what is left resembles nothing of the victim. He has been either deleted from Ardeyn or changed in some horrifying way (turned to slime, stone, into a swarm of kray scurriers, and so on).

Interaction: A kray drone is intelligent, but it's not conscious like a human being. It's capable of trickery, deception, and even mimicking conversation as a means to an end, but there is no mind inside, just a complex series of drives and needs, all of which point toward collapsing any recursion it finds to make way for the kray broodmother planetovore.

Use: A kray drone is wreaking havoc in a neighborhood of a large city. Pleas for aid come from all quarters.

Loot: A cypher or two can sometimes be pried loose from a kray drone's corpse.

Even larger kray exist out in the Strange, but luckily those kinds haven't yet entered any known recursions around Earth.

Kray broodmother, page 222

Kray are living extensions of something that is far too big and powerful to gain entry into Ardeyn: the kray broodmother, which is nothing less than a planetovore. The kray broodmother lurks in the Strange, in a region called, appropriately enough, the Kray Nebula.

KRO COURSER 4 (12)

GM Intrusion: *A successful attack on the PC is from a bite, not a claw. The courser simultaneously vomits, which in addition to other noted effects, sends worms wriggling and crawling into the wound. For the next minute, the PC takes 1 point of ambient damage each round as the worms tunnel through his flesh before finally dying.*

Crow Hollow, page 242
Beak Mafia, page 243
Kro, page 243

Someone practiced in riding a kro courser—and who has tack, harness, and bridle—makes all melee attacks as if one level higher while mounted. A courser can continue to make vomit attacks while serving as a mount.

The magicians of Crow Hollow can work a lot of mischief after they've accumulated enough power in the form of crow coin. A magician with three chests of crow coin, a mystic recipe for making coursers, and buy-off from the Beak Mafia can transform a recently deceased kro corpse into an animate and quite dangerous kro courser.

A kro courser pack answers to the commands of anyone who holds their leash (created at the same time and via the same magic as the kro coursers). Most leashes remain in the hands of mafiosos, but sometimes courser leashes are given as gifts to visiting crime kingpins, or are stolen. If a leash is destroyed, the associated courser or pack attacks all nearby creatures without restraint.

A kro courser is not really alive; it's magically animated and preserved flesh. Without the maintenance magically provided by a Crow Hollow magician, it slowly decays.

Motive: Follows commands, hunger

Environment (Crow Hollow | Magic): Anywhere, alone or in packs of up to four

Health: 24

Damage Inflicted: 4 points

Movement: Short

Combat: A kro courser can simultaneously attack one foe with two claws.

A courser can also vomit forth a mass of decaying flesh and grave worms. The smell and sight is so horrific that PCs who fail a Might defense roll find the difficulty of all tasks increased by one step.

If the kro courser targets a PC within short range with its vomit, the PC must succeed on a Speed defense roll to avoid being splattered. Splattered PCs take 4 points of ambient necrosis damage. For each round the vomit remains on the PC, that character suffers another 4 points of damage.

A kro courser has the ability to follow the scent of a quickened creature through recursions if the trail is less than a week old. If the quickened target travels through any recursion (or up to Earth) that does not operate under the law of Magic, the trail is broken.

Interaction: A kro courser has the intelligence of an animal, but it may accomplish more intelligent actions if under the close control of a leash holder.

Use: A pack of kro coursers vaults from the shadows and into the flanks of a trade caravan that has interests in an alternate recursion. If the PCs don't intervene, the pack will kill everyone.

Loot: The cut-open gullet of a kro courser contains a disgusting knot of decaying flesh, dirt, and grave worms, as well as a small amount of crow coin and possibly a cypher.

MARROID 6 (18)

These monstrous, genetic abnormalities are the size of small vehicles and look a bit like creatures that evolved from something that started life underwater. Marroids (also called marrow seekers) constantly produce dribbles of enzymatic fluid, even when they're not engaged in feeding.

Marroids began existence as a genetically engineered tool. Designed for passively sampling the environment for genetic code, marroids experienced mutation and neglect that gave rise to a whole new class of creature, one that sometimes appears where damage to Ruk's physical structure has occurred, but one that is always looking for fresh marrow to sample.

Motive: Hungers for the marrow of living creatures

Environment (Ruk | Mad Science): Anywhere in Ruk that has seen a recent disturbance

Health: 23

Damage Inflicted: 6 points

Armor: 1

Movement: Short; can burrow into solid Ruk foundation as an action. When it burrows into the ground, the tunnel closes up after it like a quickly healing wound.

Modifications: Speed defense as level 5 due to size.

Combat: A marroid can attack with its battering tail. It can also launch enzyme orbs from its body, targeting any point within long range, at a rate of one orb per round. The orb explodes in immediate range. The marrow seeker can choose to launch different kinds of orbs with each attack.

Acidic: Targets who fail a Might defense roll take 6 points of damage. Those who succeed still take 1 point of damage from the spray of acid.

Numbing: Targets who fail a Speed defense roll are partly anesthetized for one minute. During that period, they have a hard time holding objects because of numb fingers. Any time a creature uses a held object, it must first succeed on a Speed-based task or drop the item.

Brain Fog: Targets who fail an Intellect defense roll experience neurological impairment for one minute, which affects characters like blindness.

A marroid, once it downs at least one foe, is happy to leave a conflict so it can break open its prey's bones with repeated tail bashes, then suck out the marrow.

Interaction: Some marroids who've obtained the marrow of intelligent Ruk natives can access bits of their victims' knowledge. If approached with fresh marrow, a marroid may deign to transfer memories through a carefully crafted enzyme orb.

Use: The Church of the Embodiment believes that a particular marroid may possess hints of the True Code that can be had nowhere else. The Church is looking for contractors to find and capture this particular marroid for further study.

Loot: Sometimes one or two enzyme orbs can be salvaged from the body of a slain marroid. Salvaged orbs can be thrown to create effects like those described under Combat. Salvaged enzyme orbs have a shelf life of a couple of days before they decay.

GM Intrusion: *The PC has an allergic reaction to an enzyme orb attack. In addition to the indicated effect, the PC is affected as if by a disease, the symptoms of which include an inflamed, itchy rash over her body that seeps fluid. The fluid draws another marroid to investigate after three days if the rash isn't treated.*

Church of the Embodiment, page 197
True Code, page 192

MONITOR 5 (15)

Monitors are remnant Qephilim of Silence who went into hiding when the Incarnation of Silence disappeared. Now they exist like ghosts, haunting the world, watching in silence as they always have. They are disengaged from every other organization, waiting for a sign from the Incarnation of Silence, one that may never come.

Qephilim of the ancient orders did not all have the same visage, despite the similarities that qephilim of the Court of Coin, the Free Battalion, and the Court of Sleep share. Few survivors of those other orders remain visible in Ardeyn, and those that are seen are sometimes mistaken for something else entirely. Such is the case for the Qephilim of Silence. According to common wisdom, monitors haven't been seen in over a century. The truth is, they *have* been seen, just not recognized.

GM Intrusion: *The monitor analyzes the weak spot of one PC, so that all attacks against that PC deal an additional 3 points of damage.*

Motive: Information

Environment (Ardeyn | Magic): Anywhere

Health: 30

Damage Inflicted: 5 points

Movement: Short

Modifications: Stealth actions as level 8; perception as level 7.

Combat: A monitor is always stealthy; even in broad daylight it can call upon its mythlight to darken the area around it and provide a shadow into which it can slip.

If detected, a monitor prefers to evade an encounter rather than interacting or becoming embroiled in a conflict. Sometimes, though, what a monitor sees enrages it past its ability to remain an unprejudiced observer. When this happens, any creature within short distance must make an Intellect defense roll or be held in place for one round. This effect is the result of a psychic paralysis blast, which is not an action for the monitor. During the paralysis, the monitor slips away.

Qephilim of Silence, page 163
Incarnation of Silence, page 163
Court of Coin, page 163
Free Battalion, page 284
Court of Sleep, page 184

Alternatively, the blast could allow a monitor a significant edge if it chooses to attack, since its horns automatically hit a held target and inflict an additional 2 points of damage. Once a creature is subject to the monitor's paralyzing psychic blast, a target can't be affected again for several hours.

A monitor can modify its psychic blast to deal damage instead. When it does, it attacks up to two separate targets within close range as an action, dealing 3 points of Intellect damage to each (which ignores Armor).

Monitor's monocle, page 187

Interaction: Under normal circumstances, a monitor slips away if it realizes it has been noticed. Especially charismatic PCs might induce a monitor to take an action other than merely watching. (And there is a rumor of at least one monitor that has gone insane waiting for the Incarnation of Silence to return—this one, called Kamud, works as a bounty hunter.)

Use: During a tense negotiation with a group of brigands, a sirrush, or another threat, one of the NPCs notices the shadow of a watching monitor. The NPC may leap to the assumption that the PCs are acting in bad faith and attack the characters, or the monitor, or both.

Loot: Most monitors carry special equipment to watch with, and at least a few carry an artifact known as a monitor's monocle. Many also usually carry one or two cyphers with them.

MYRIAND

Allegiance to the Myriand faction is a great way to retain Harmonious citizenship, but watch yourself. If you pull something shady while off-duty, your first act as a metamorphosized Myriand volunteer might be to begin investigating what you were up to while you were still you.

~*from the* Estate Guide for Quickened Operatives

Myriands patrol Harmonious, ensuring that citizens and guests remain safe, that faction holdings remain unmolested, and that negotiated rules for interfaction competition are not broken. The force is mostly composed of volunteers who give over their minds and bodies to the cause a few hours each week. Off-shift, a myriand could be anybody, even a PC. But when it's time to go on patrol (or when activated remotely for a specific mission), the volunteer's fused biological pod activates, metamorphosizing her into a battle chrysalid.

Harmonious, page 196

MYRIAND VOLUNTEER 4 (12)

Individuals who make up the force are not full-time myriands. They are shift workers who have a completely different personality and aspect when not patrolling. But when their shift comes up, an attached biological pod activates, transforming a regular person into a battle chrysalid. While transformed, the myriand loses all sense of its former identity, becoming hypervigilant, without pity or fear, and unable to do anything other than obey the letter of the law.

Motive: Enforcing the law

Environment (Ruk | Mad Science): Usually in Harmonious patrolling in groups of four, sometimes under the command of a myriand veteran, other times alone with a group of venom troopers as backup

Health: 17

Damage Inflicted: 4 points

Armor: 1

Movement: Short

Modifications: Tasks related to perception and truth detection as level 5.

Combat: A myriand's body is a weapon—it can make two melee attacks as a single action, using punches, knees, elbows, kicks, or headbutts. It can also fire a shoulder-mounted, wide-aperture slaughter accelerator as its action, attacking up to four creatures standing next to each other within short range. A myriand can choose to deal 4 points of damage to targets or "glue" them in place with a level 5 foam restraint.

Interaction: A patrolling myriand doesn't speak except to question suspects or witnesses. It sometimes answers questions, if the answer is to explain violations of the law. A myriand may also explain that wasting the time of a myriand patroller is against the law.

Use: PCs new to Ruk are accosted by a myriand who witnessed them breaking a minor (or major!) rule of Harmonious.

Loot: A defeated myriand returns to its pre-myriand state, which is a regular Ruk native who might possess a stick containing 1d6 × 20 bits on it.

GM Intrusion: *The myriand activates a biological enhancement, releasing an arc of energy at the PC. The PC's weapon shorts out, jams, or breaks.*

Myriand is a faction itself, but the same name is applied to the battle chrysalides that make up the force. When someone talks about a myriand—especially with awe or fear in his voice—he's usually referring to a specific law-keeping battle chrysalid, not Myriand the faction.

MYRIAND VETERAN 6 (18)

A myriand veteran has survived years of service, and in that time, has fully adapted to her chrysalid form. Even powerful interests in Ruk must think twice before planning to defy the laws of Harmonious or the Factol Council, lest they find a myriand veteran assigned to bring them to justice.

Motive: Enforcing the law

Environment (Ruk | Mad Science): Usually in Harmonious patrolling alone, but sometimes commanding a troop of four myriand volunteers

Health: 36
Damage Inflicted: 6 points
Armor: 3
Movement: Short; long while flying
Modifications: Tasks related to perception and truth detection as level 7.
Combat: In addition to making two melee attacks as a single action with any part of its body, a veteran can also fire a shoulder-mounted, wide-aperture slaughter accelerator as its action, attacking up to ten creatures standing next to each other within long range. A myriand can choose to deal 6 points of damage to targets or "glue" them in place with a level 7 foam restraint.

A myriand veteran can access the special "security" layer of the All Song that all creatures of Ruk (and all PCs who translated to Ruk) are connected to. When the myriand does so, all selected creatures within short range who fail an Intellect defense roll are filled with regret for their actions: they fall to their knees and lower their defenses for up to one minute. A PC can attempt a new Intellect defense roll each round to break free of the effect. The effect is also broken if the myriand attacks the "surrendered" PC or one of her allies (both attacks of which hit automatically and inflict an additional 2 points of damage).
Interaction: Veterans have more leeway when interacting with others, and they may even appear to engage in light banter, but they only do so as a means to an end when interrogating a witness or potential suspect.
Use: A large alteration in or around Harmonious could draw a myriand veteran to investigate.
Loot: A defeated veteran does not metamorphosize back to a nonmyriand form. It may possess one or two noncombat cyphers.

GM Intrusion: *A PC affected by a veteran's surrender wave doesn't surrender; instead, she is marked with an OFFENDER tag that anyone sensitive to the All Song can sense. The tag lasts for three days.*

If time or circumstances are pressing, Myriand veterans have the authority to judge and sentence those found in violation of Ruk laws, but otherwise they take criminals back to Myriand faction headquarters for processing.

NEZEREK 5 (15)

The nezerek is a predator of the Strange. It roosts in lairs excavated in fundament, but spends most of its existence surfing the fractal currents hunting for new experiences. It looks almost like a lifelike component of the dark energy network until it adjusts its winglike surfaces to emerge from transit, revealing itself as something more dangerous than an elaborate design. A nezerek is a predatory beast nearly 30 feet (9 m) across from wing tip to wing tip, though its antennae can extend even farther.

A nezerek isn't a planetovore, since it seems content to remain in the Strange, and its abilities are far less extreme. On the other hand, it is driven to discover new experiences and knowledge, and to gain that experience, it tends to assimilate anything new it comes into contact with, especially living creatures.

Motive: Knowledge, novelty

Environment (the Strange): Anywhere

Health: 36

Damage Inflicted: 5 points

Movement: Short while flying

Modifications: Attacks as level 6; speed defense as level 3 due to size.

Combat: A nezerek uses its fractal antennae to attack up to two targets within long range on its turn, dealing 5 points of ambient damage to each target. The body of a PC struck by an antenna seems to "fray" at the edges, bleeding fractal material. About half the material is lost to the void, but about half is absorbed by the nezerek (which restores 2 points of its health).

Given the length of a nezerek's antennae, a foe could choose to target them instead of the main body. An attack against an antenna is made as if against a level 6 target with 1 point of Armor and 10 health. If an antenna is destroyed, it takes the creature two rounds to regenerate a new one.

If a nezerek is slain, it begins to "fray" like its victims, spraying fractal residue in every direction. All creatures within short range take 5 points of ambient damage from the deluge.

Interaction: A nezerek is not automatically hostile, and it may simply soar past the PCs, despite obviously being aware of them. Any attempt at interaction on the PCs' part quickly changes this attitude of indifference to one of predation.

Use: PCs traveling into the Strange for an extended period might notice a nezerek soaring in the distance.

Loot: A nezerek's unraveled form contains 1d6 cyphers.

GM Intrusion: *An antenna brushes against one of the PCs' cyphers, which is absorbed by the nezerek, restoring 6 points of its health.*

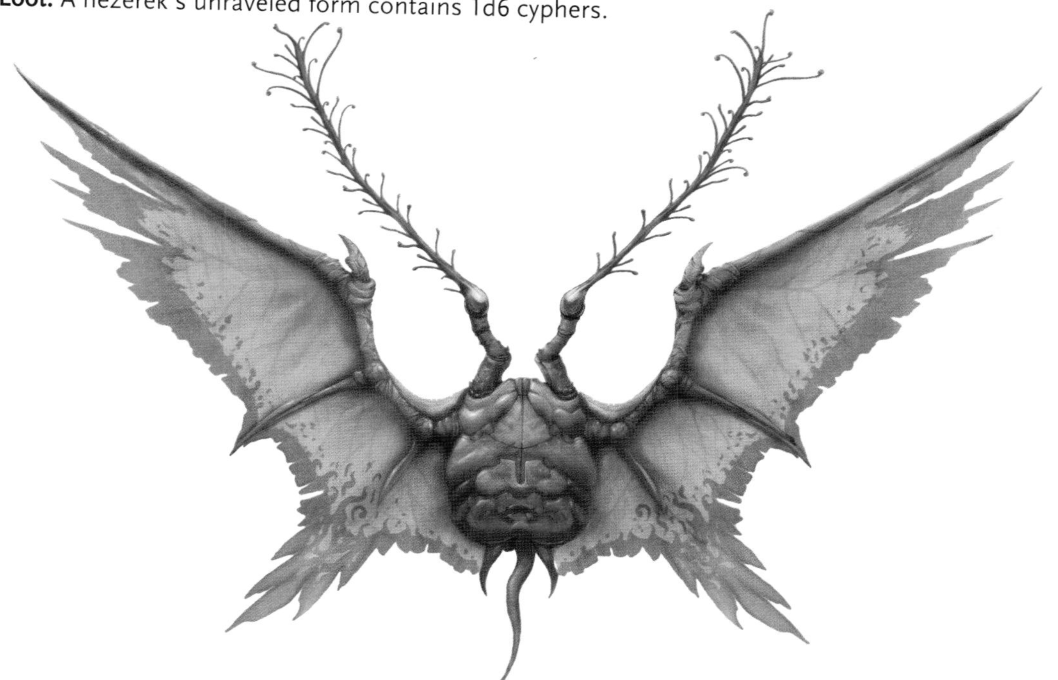

QEPHILIM

Seven orders of qephilim once lived in Ardeyn. Several types remain, including qephilim of the Free Battalion and umber judges of the Court of Sleep.

GM Intrusion: *Two more mercenaries appear to aid their battling comrades.*

FREE BATTALION MERCENARIES 3 (9)

Qephilim of the Free Battalion serve as mercenaries across Ardeyn, often pledging themselves to causes that serve the goals of civilization and the preservation of Ardeyn as a repudiation of the Betrayal (when their ancestors served War). As a mercenary, a Free Battalion qephilim is often part of a company but could also be working alone guarding a caravan, watching a city gate, keeping a merchant's home safe from thieves, serving as a regular in a larger army, or working in a similar capacity.

Unlike many mercenaries or even regular hired guards, Free Battalion mercs are more concerned with the underlying legality or morality of a particular duty asked of them. If a merc believes that his command is unjust, that command might be refused.

Motive: Righting wrongs

Environment (Ardeyn | Magic): Almost anywhere, usually in companies of two to eight

Health: 9

Damage Inflicted: 5 points

Armor: 2

Movement: Short

Modifications: Perception as level 4.

Combat: Qephilim of the Free Battalion usually attack with swords or bows. Military-minded, they know that outnumbering an enemy is often enough to defeat that enemy, and they are not adverse to calling in reinforcements.

Interaction: A Free Battalion merc, unlike an average mercenary, feels beholden to his contract, even in the face of better offerings. Because of this loyalty, PCs will find it difficult to divert such a merc, and in fact, a merc will react badly if offered a bribe or sensing that a lie is being told. On the other hand, a merc without a contract might be willing to help a PC in return for all the standard conditions of engagement, including premium remuneration and paid funeral expenses.

Use: Mercenaries of the Free Battalion are not an unfamiliar sight in Ardeyn. To the player characters, Free Battalion mercs are sometimes allies and sometimes obstacles. At times, a particular merc also rises to become a lieutenant or captain in larger standing armies, and these higher-ranking mercs lead groups of regular warriors (level 2 creatures).

Loot: Any given Free Battalion merc has 1d6 crowns in addition to weapons, medium armor, and basic gear.

UMBER JUDGE 4 (12)

An umber judge is a qephilim of the Court of Sleep responsible for judging souls in the Night Vault. An umber judge sometimes emerges into the Daylands or Borderlands, looking for agents of Lotan, rogue Court of Sleep necromancers, or straying spirits.

Court of Sleep qephilim usually hide their features beneath robes, rune armor, and ornate helms. Some bear weights of balance, which they use to determine the amount of sin weighing a soul down.

Motive: Protect the souls of the dead; slay agents of Lotan

Environment (Ardeyn | Magic): Almost anywhere, either solo or in conclaves of up to three

Health: 23

Damage Inflicted: 4 points

Armor: 1

Movement: Short

Modifications: Ardeyn lore as level 7.

Combat: Umber judges know spells and often wield artifacts and other charms that can grant them both offensive and defensive abilities. Instead of attacking with mundane weapons, they use death spells, curses, and spirit whips.

An umber judge can do one of the following: be borne aloft by a servitor spirit that grants the judge the ability to fly a short distance each round, gain +4 to Armor for ten minutes when a spirit wraps the umber judge like a cloak, or question the spirit of a recently slain creature to learn its secrets.

Interaction: Umber judges are usually concerned only with their own duties and obligations, which means they tend to ignore the petitions of those whose aims do not match the judge's current desire. It's possible that a crafty negotiator could get the attention of a judge and convince it that their goals do align, bringing about a short-term alliance. The judge is likely to request the PCs' aid in something to test their sincerity before agreeing to anything.

Use: Umber judges encountered outside the Night Vault are usually looking for clues regarding an escaped spirit, seeking a rogue necromancer, or running down the location of banned copies of any of the various Gospels of Lotan. An umber judge may seek out a PC to answer a question bearing on one of these issues, or accuse the PC of abetting the same.

Loot: An umber judge typically has 3d100 crowns, 1d6 cyphers, an artifact, and a wide variety of tools. The qephilim might also have other normal gear.

GM Intrusion: *The umber judge installs in the PC a spirit under the judge's command. Each turn, the PC can attempt a difficulty 4 Intellect defense roll to expel the possessing spirit. On a failed attempt to exorcise the spirit, the PC instead attacks her closest ally that turn.*

Court of Sleep, page 184
Night Vault, page 183
Lotan, page 162

QINOD CONSTRUCT

"We've logged a troubling rise in the number of Qinod Singularity manifestations lately. Unsurprisingly, we've also seen a population boom in Qinod constructs wandering the Periphery."

~Uttatum-tum, on-site agent of the Quiet Cabal

The Qinod Singularity is a little-understood phenomenon that sometimes appears in Ruk as a blinding point of multicolored light. The Singularity sometimes expels remarkable artifacts and enigmatic constructs that are usually dangerous if interacted with, but not dealing with them on sight usually leads to greater grief at a later date.

No two constructs that emerge from the singularity are ever exactly alike, but Ruk researchers find that many of them fall into classes of similar entities, which they call testers and deconstructors.

QINOD TESTER 4 (12)

This machine entity is a 5-foot-diamteter (2 m) mass of metal alloy manipulation cables surrounding an inner solid central core of electronic eyes that can see every known (and possibly every unknown) frequency of the spectrum. In addition to manipulation cables for fine work such as plucking flower petals, a qinod tester also has at least two stronger manipulators that can pluck the arms out of the sockets of more robust test subjects like metamorphosized battle chrysalides. Finally, the tester can extrude one or more beamed energy weapons and tranquilizer guns should subjects prove initially resistant to being dissected for study.

Motive: Unpredictable

Environment (Ruk | Mad Science): Almost anywhere in the Periphery or Veritex

Health: 20

Damage Inflicted: 4 points

Armor: 1

Movement: Immediate; short while flying

Modifications: Speed defense as level 5 due to interfering cable mass; all perception and tracking tasks as level 8.

Combat: A Qinod tester can fire up to two beamed energy weapons at the same target or at two different targets within long range. Instead of firing a beam weapon for damage, a Qinod attacks with a tranquilizer flechette at a target within short range. A target who fails a Speed defense roll against the flechette takes 2 points of damage and must succeed on a Might defense roll or be paralyzed for up to one minute (the victim can attempt a Might-based roll each round to try to shake off the paralysis).

The machine entity is extremely difficult to hide from, no matter the means used to evade its vision. Once a Qinod tester finds tracks or catches a scent, it usually tracks its next test subjects to their location.

A Qinod tester carefully pulls apart dead or paralyzed victims if allowed the peace to do so, studying the results with great interest.

Interaction: Qinod testers never speak, and they usually don't do what PCs expect. A Qinod tester is just as likely to ignore PCs as attack them, especially if already involved in another test or observation.

Use: A tester is encountered in the Periphery while the PCs are on another task.

Loot: One or two weaponlike artifacts could be salvaged from the remains of a tester.

GM Intrusion: *The weapon of a PC who makes a successful melee attack against the tester is caught in the creature's surrounding cables. The PC can abandon it or spend one or more actions attempting to pull it free with a successful Might-based roll.*

Periphery, page 205
Veritex, page 204

QINOD DECONSTRUCTOR 8 (24)

A Qinod deconstructor shares many visual similarities with a tester but has a diameter of at least 20 feet (6 m). The larger size apparently comes with an appetite for power and destruction. Unlike a tester, a deconstructor seems mostly interested in wrecking, killing, and generally creating chaos.

Motive: Destruction

Environment (Ruk | Mad Science): Periphery of Ruk

Health: 44

Damage Inflicted: 10 points

Armor: 3

Movement: Short; long while flying

Modifications: Speed defense as level 7 due to size.

Combat: The touch of an unfurled cable, which the deconstructor can stretch to attack up to three targets within short range, sucks bioelectric energy from living beings and mechanical constructs alike. Sometimes a deconstructor preferentially attacks a PC's equipment, such as a weapon, armor, or another object. If successfully attacked, objects of level 8 or less are destroyed, and the owner is subject to 3 points of damage from flying shrapnel.

A deconstructor can fire one missile every hour at a target or location up to a mile away. When such a missile strikes, all creatures within short range of the impact take 15 points of damage (creatures caught in the blast who make a successful Speed defense roll suffer only 4 points of damage instead).

A Qinod deconstructor regenerates 2 points of damage every round, but in a round where it drains a target of bioelectric energy, it regenerates 10 points of damage instead. If a deconstructor's health is reduced to 0, the creature collapses, and its regeneration falls to a rate of 2 points per minute, unless an effort is made to scatter its large components so they do not touch.

Interaction: A deconstructor is indifferent to attempts to interact with it.

Use: A trio of deconstructors has moved from destroying to building something in the center of a grey forest in the Periphery. The PCs are tasked with scouting the location and reporting back what is going on.

Loot: One or two artifacts resembling weapons could be salvaged from the remains of a deconstructor.

GM Intrusion: *The deconstructor wraps a cable around the PC's ankle, wrist, or torso just as the PC is about to make an attack.*

Ruk researchers theorize that deconstructors are stockpiling energy and raw materials in preparation for building something grand. Some worry that the project might be to build a focus for the Qinod Singularity, making it a permanent portal, through which the Qinod builders might appear.

SARK 4 (12)

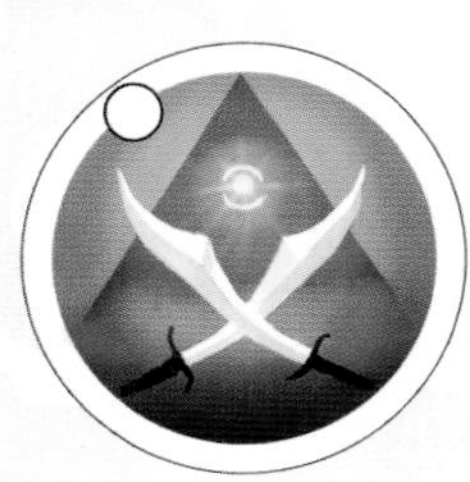

Sark are the debased and graceless qephilim who lost their way during the Age of Myth, which is why they are also called the Lost Qephilim and the Eighth Kindred. Animalistic savages, sark are driven by hunger, lust, rage, and fear. Given how closely these drives mimic sins proscribed by the Incarnations, many believe that the sark are extensions of Lotan's evil manifest in the world.

Sark could hardly be mistaken for qephilim, though they most resemble the Qephilim of War, if they were to forsake cleanliness, clothing not made from the hides and scalps of their victims, and any semblance of sanity. Sark live to prey on other creatures, and they inflict much cruelty and pain in the process.

Despite their savage ways, they retain something of their qephilim roots, which means they can be clever, and they lay cunning traps.

Motive: Hunger, lust, rage, and fear

Environment (Ardeyn | Magic): Sark dwell in small groups of three to six, usually in wooded areas or rocky, mountainous regions of the Borderlands and Daylands; some packs also lair in the Night Vault

GM Intrusion: *The sark calls upon an atavistic mythlight ability and hurls a mythlight lance at a character within long range that deals 4 points of damage and blinds the PC for one round.*

Health: 17

Damage Inflicted: 5 points

Armor: 1

Movement: Short

Modifications: Stealth as level 5.

Combat: Sark either claw or bite their prey, though some individuals may use weapons, especially heavy weapons, ranged weapons, and on the very rare occasion, artifacts. When clawing or biting, a sark can hold a victim in place instead of dealing damage on a successful attack. The held victim can attempt to escape (a Might-based roll) on its turn. Both the grappling sark and the grappled foe are easier targets for other combatants; the difficulty of attacks made against them is modified by two steps in the attacker's favor.

Some sark retain a glimmer of their ancestral mythlight. Such sark can sometimes call on psychic abilities, targeting a victim at long range who fails an Intellect defense roll. On a successful attack, the victim stands frozen in horror for one round, overcome by a glimpse of the sark's savage mind and memories of the cruelties it has perpetrated.

If a large enough lair can be found, sometimes several sark packs live together, forming a sort of "superpack," such as the one in Sark Cleft in the Green Wilds.

Interaction: Many sark have devolved so completely that they no longer speak the Maker's Tongue, and interacting with them is no different than interacting with beasts. The few who can speak might be swayed to do so if the rewards (food, usually) are significant enough.

Maker's Tongue, page 164

Use: The PCs, traveling through the wilderness, find a location—perhaps a cave or an old ruin—that seems like a safe shelter. The site is actually a lair of a sark pack.

Loot: A pack may have 2d6 crowns, plus perhaps a cypher between them. Pack leaders might have cyphers of their own, or even an artifact.

SHOGGOTH 7 (21)

It was a terrible, indescribable thing vaster than any subway train—a shapeless congeries of protoplasmic bubbles, faintly self-luminous, and with myriads of temporary eyes forming and un-forming as pustules of greenish light all over the tunnel-filling front that bore down upon us, crushing the frantic penguins and slithering over the glistening floor that it and its kind had swept so evilly free of all litter.

~At the Mountains of Madness, *by H.P. Lovecraft*

Shoggoths vary in size, but usually the smallest are 10 feet (3 m) across at least. They are the product of incredibly advanced bioengineering by a strange race in the distant past. Angry, vicious predators, they are feared by any who have ever heard of these rare creatures (or who have encountered them and somehow survived to tell the tale).

Motive: Hungers for flesh

Environment (Innsmouth | Magic or Mad Science): Anywhere

Health: 35

Damage Inflicted: 10 points

Movement: Long

Modifications: Speed defense as level 6 due to size.

Combat: Shoggoths sprout tendrils and mouths, and they spread their wide, amorphous forms, allowing them to attack all foes within immediate range. Those struck by the shoggoth's attack are grabbed and engulfed by the thing's fluid, gelatinous body and suffer damage each round until they pull themselves free (and they can take no other physical action while they are caught). Further, each round of entrapment, one object in the victim's possession is destroyed by the foul juices of the amorphous horror.

Shoggoths regenerate 5 points of health each round. They have 10 points of Armor against fire, cold, and electricity.

Interaction: One does not reason with a shoggoth.

Use: The PCs find an ancient structure of metal and stone. Wandering through it, they note that every surface is clear of dirt and debris. Soon they discover why—a shoggoth squirms through its halls, absorbing everything it comes upon (and it fills the passages it moves down, floor to ceiling, wall to wall).

Loot: Within a shoggoth, one might find a cypher or a relic of the Strange.

GM Intrusion: *The character is engulfed in the shoggoth, his gear scattered throughout the thing's undulating form, and his body turned upside down so that the difficulty of escape attempts is increased by one step.*

Innsmouth, page 253

Rumors abound of a few very rare, particularly intelligent shoggoths that intentionally reduce their own mass and learn to take on the forms of humans so that they can integrate themselves into society (and prey upon humans at their leisure).

SIRRUSH 5 (15)

This 20-foot-long (6 m) lizardlike creature is protected by bright yellow scales. A hybrid creature, the sirrush's hind legs are like an eagle's with impressive talons, but its forelegs are leonine. Its tail is long and sinuous, just like its neck. A sirrush's head bears a brilliant crest that it unfurls to impress lesser creatures into reverence.

Motive: Hungers for worship or other strong emotion

Environment (Ardeyn | Magic): Near medium and larger cities, either singly or as a pair

Health: 28

Damage Inflicted: 5 points

Armor: 1

Movement: Short

Modifications: Deceives as level 6; Speed defense as level 4 due to size.

Combat: When a sirrush raises its crest (an action), targets it selects within short range feel an overwhelming sense of awe, fear, or friendship—whichever the sirrush chooses—until the sirrush furls its crest again (another action). While a sirrush displays its feathered splendor, it can move only an immediate distance.

PCs affected by the crest must make an Intellect roll to attempt to attack the sirrush. Failure means that the character cannot attack the creature this round, and defending against the sirrush becomes two steps more difficult the next time the sirrush attacks.

The awe/fear/friend effect is a passive effect after the crest is unfurled, but the sirrush can choose to use its sorcerous crest more actively. In this case, the sirrush makes a psychic attack against a single character within long range, causing 4 points of Intellect damage (which ignores Armor) and stunning him for one round.

If the sirrush has an artifact, it likely uses the item in combat. A sirrush can also physically attack with its claws and bite.

Interaction: A sirrush that has some time to work its "minor deity" angle may actually come to believe in its own divinity. If the sirrush has been installed in a given location long enough, the temple or shrine it inhabits is likely also tended by priests, guards, and other functionaries who explain to PCs how they should interact with the god (respectfully and possibly bearing rich offerings). A sirrush that is worshiped as a god may prove helpful to PCs if they come to it with a question or petition, but if called out as a fake, it reacts violently.

Use: The PCs visit a new location and are invited to give their respects at a nearby shrine where a deity sometimes manifests to answer questions and, in return, accept offerings.

Loot: The inner sanctum of a defeated sirrush might contain several weeks' worth of food, 3d100 crowns, one or two cyphers, and possibly an artifact.

GM Intrusion: *A character who is especially responsive to the psychic effect of a sirrush broadcasting awe or friendship becomes so confused that not only does she not attack the sirrush on her next turn, she attacks another PC instead.*

A sirrush is a sorcerous creature and derives an essential part of its diet from other creatures' feelings toward it. Depending on the particular sirrush, those feelings can be fear, friendship, or, best of all, worship.

SOULSHORN 8 (24)

A human or qephilim that uses a specific necromantic sorcery to expunge its own soul without killing itself (that last bit is the most difficult part of the process) becomes a soulshorn. A soulshorn appears to be a living creature—it even breathes, eats, and sleeps—but it is considered an undead creature all the same, because one automatically reanimates after it dies, returned to perfect health every time. Many soulshorns have lived for hundreds of years, accumulating more and more powerful dire sorcery each year, increasing their mastery of ancient knowledge, secrets of prior ages, and offensive sorcery.

Though powerful, soulshorns are not divine nor meant to live forever. The longer a soulshorn survives, the more erratic and outright insane it becomes. Many become megalomaniacal, which usually leads to their eventual downfall. Some become drooling idiots, with only occasional flashes of sorcerous power. Those that live the longest are the ones who retreat from normal society and find a lair in an ancient citadel, qephilim ruin, moon, or skerry along the Borderlands.

Motive: Unpredictable

Environment (Ardeyn | Magic): A soulshorn's hidden lair could be almost anywhere.

Health: 39

Damage Inflicted: 8 points

Movement: Short; long while flying

Combat: Most soulshorns can attack with bolts of flesh-decaying energy against single targets at long range, or emit a necrotic pulse that attacks all selected PCs within short range. Soulshorns can fly when they move, and they can remain invisible each round they spend their action concentrating on staying unseen. Individual soulshorns may have also learned unique spells that provide them with additional abilities. For instance, some soulshorns learn how to enslave powerful spirits or create golems. Finally, a soulshorn may also use a variety of cyphers and Ardeyn artifacts both offensively and defensively.

Regardless of other abilities, all soulshorns can attempt to feed on a target creature's soul to empower themselves. When one does, it focuses on a foe it can see when it makes any kind of attack. Any damage inflicted on the selected foe by the soulshorn increases by 4 additional points of damage. The soulshorn restores the same number of points to its health. This attack sometimes allows the soulshorn to learn information about the target at the same time.

If killed, a soulshorn returns to life and full health seven days after its death, unless its remains are burned in the interim. If its remains are burned, the soulshorn is truly dead.

Interaction: Soulshorns attempt to keep their "undead" status secret, given the stigma of having given one's soul to Lotan. More important to most soulshorn is keeping their resurrecion power secret. A foe who does not burn a defeated soulshorn is a foe who propagates a helpful lie.

Use: As the PCs break into what appears to be a vacant ancient qephilim tomb, they see disquieting symbols of necromancy painted on the floor and walls. If they press forward, a soulshorn (or its guardians) emerge to slay the intruders.

Loot: The inner sanctum of a defeated soulshorn might contain 10d100 crowns, 1d6 + 3 cyphers, and at least one artifact.

GM Intrusion: *The soulshorn's attack knocks the character down and shatters his weapon, shield, or armor.*

It's said the sorcery required to turn a living creature into a soulshorn was fashioned by Lotan, and that the displaced soul actually slips into the keeping of the Sinner, empowering Lotan with each soulshorn created. If true, every soulshorn is a crack in Lotan's prison.

SPIRIT OF WRATH 2 (6)

Call to the dead with blood and sacrifice. They shall gush from the unhallowed earth as a dark wave of mingled rage and pain. ~Third Gospel of Lotan

When a spirit of a dead creature fails to find its way to the Night Vault, escapes the same, or is summoned forth by a necromancer, it may become a bodiless spirit of rage and loss: a spirit of wrath (commonly shortened to wrath). A wrath appears as a shadowy or misty figure that can resemble the humanoid figure it once was, though spirits of wrath tend to swarm together, making it difficult to distinguish them from each other.

Wraths are often mindless, consumed by their condition. But on occasion, a wrath not too far gone still remembers its life and may respond to questions or seek to locate its loved ones or enemies. A wrath may even attempt to finish a task it started in life. But in time, even the strongest-willed spirit's mind erodes without physical substance to renew it, and it becomes an almost mindless monster of destruction.

GM Intrusion: *The wrath screams out the words of a necromantic summoning spell, summoning 1d6 more wraths.*

Motive: Destruction

Environment (Ardeyn | Magic): Almost anywhere, singly or in groups of six to ten

A necromancer is the name given to any sorcerer that turns her back on the Maker and the Seven Rules, and learns from hidden Gospels of Lotan, which are librams of foul spells and rituals.

Seven Rules, page 162

Health: 6

Damage Inflicted: 3 points

Armor: 1

Movement: Short while flying

Modifications: Stealth as level 5.

Combat: A spirit of wrath can become fully insubstantial. After it does so, the creature can't change state again until its next turn. While insubstantial, it can't affect or be affected by anything (except for spiritslaying weapons and attacks), and it can pass through solid matter without hindrance, but even simple magical wards can keep it at bay.

While partly insubstantial (its normal state), a wrath can affect and be affected by others normally. A wrath attacks with its touch, which rots flesh and drains life.

A group of five wraths can act as a swarm, focusing on one target to make one attack roll as a single level 4 creature dealing 5 points of damage.

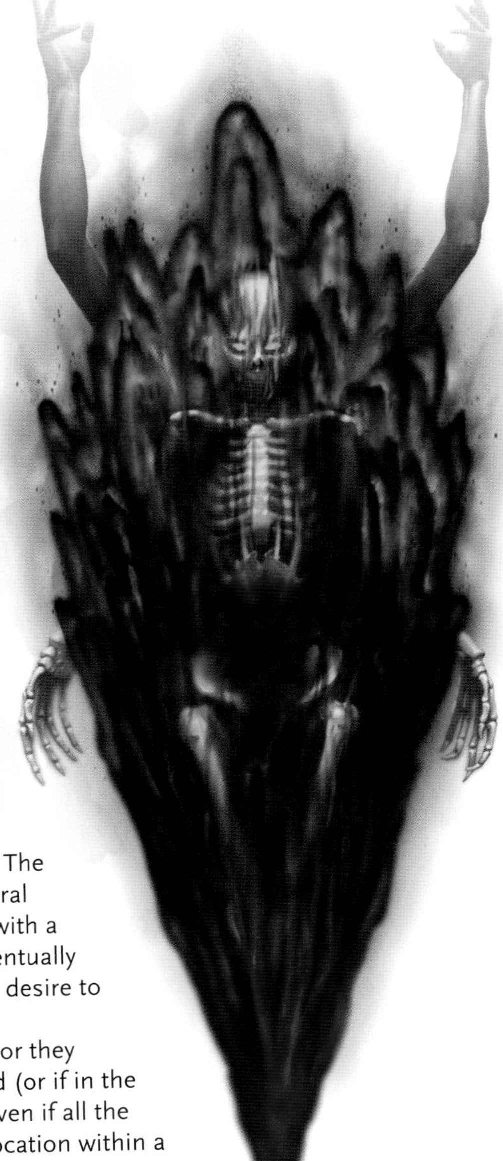

Interaction: Most wraths moan and scream in rage. The rare few that retain reason can speak in a sepulchral voice, and they may even negotiate. Any alliance with a wrath is usually short-lived, since the creature eventually forgets itself and descends fully into rage and the desire to spread destruction.

Use: The PCs are attacked while attending a burial, or they happen to pass close to or camp near a graveyard (or if in the Queendom, a section of the Path of the Dead). Even if all the wraths are slain, another swarm appears in the location within a week. Somewhere nearby, a necromancer is active.

SPORE WORM 5 (15)

As large as an adult human, the spore worm is a strange serpentine creature of kaleidoscope colors. It has no eyes, just a sphincterlike mouth and dozens of spiracles running its length through which it emits mind-affecting spores.

Spore worms hunt in remote areas (including grey forests), using spores to overcome prey and then burrowing into their catch, eating it from the inside out.

Motive: Hungers for flesh

Environment (Ruk | Mad Science): Hunts alone in relatively desolate regions

Health: 21

Damage Inflicted: 5 points

Armor: 1

Movement: Short

Modifications: Perception as level 4.

Combat: In addition to its deadly bite, a spore worm can fill the immediate area around it with one of three different kinds of spores. Its spore clouds last only one round, but the worm can produce a new cloud each round without using an action. The three kinds of spores the worm can emit are:

Hallucinogen: Those within range who fail an Intellect defense roll lose their next turn. Each round, a new defense roll is allowed, and failure means another lost turn. The effects do not end until a roll is successful.

Fear: Those within range who fail an Intellect defense roll flee as quickly as they can until they are at least a long distance away from the worm.

Attraction: Those within range who fail an Intellect defense roll move to stand next to the worm. On the following round, they can take no action, and the difficulty of defense rolls against the worm's bite attack is increased by two steps.

Spore worms are blind, and thus they are immune to any visual effects. They are likewise immune to spores of any kind.

Interaction: Spore worms are fairly intelligent, but they rarely have motives beyond simple hunger and survival. They do not speak, but a rare few have learned to understand a few words in various languages. They are almost impossible to train or even placate.

Use: A spore worm makes an excellent encounter in the wilds, showcasing the dangers of Ruk.

GM Intrusion: *The character is so confused by the spore worm's spores that she attacks her nearest ally by mistake.*

Grey forest, page 194

THONIK 3 (9)

A thonik looks like a particularly dense area of chaotic fractal pattern undulating through the Strange. When it attacks, it's easier to distinguish as a separate entity. An aggressive thonik appears something like a "sheet" of flexible fundament, shot through with undulating mouthlike openings that appear, disappear, open, and close in rhythmic pulses. The thonik is a predator of the dark energy network, and it feeds primarily on background energy fields of the Strange, but it rarely passes up the concentrated energy associated with cyphers, artifacts, and the bodies of living creatures.

Certain entities of the Strange can tame thoniks to docility with a touch. For instance, Chaosphere hierarchs have been known to wear thoniks as cloaks that self-animate and attack aggressors without any need for direction from the wearer.

GM Intrusion: *A character wrapped inside a thonik becomes panicked and confused, and he gains a factor of alienation.*

Alienation, page 216

Chaosphere hierarch, page 262

A thonik preferentially absorbs the energy of a cypher, of an artifact, and of a target's life force, in that order. Usually.

Motive: Hungers for energy
Environment (the Strange): Anywhere
Health: 22
Damage Inflicted: 6 points
Movement: Short
Modifications: Attacks, initiative, and stealth as level 5 while in the Strange.
Combat: A thonik attacks by attempting to wrap its sheetlike body around a target. On a successful attack, the thonik inflicts 5 points of damage, and the target must make a second Speed defense roll or become wrapped in the thonik's undulating body.

On subsequent turns, a thonik can automatically deal 5 points of damage (that ignores Armor) to the wrapped foe. As another option, it could automatically absorb the energy of a cypher carried by the wrapped foe. Finally, it might choose to suck energy from an artifact carried by its prey; when it does so, it permanently doubles the artifact's chance of depletion.

A successful attack against a thonik wrapped around prey splits the damage equally between both thonik and prey.

On her turn, a wrapped target's only physical option is to attempt to break free as her action, which she does if she succeeds on a level 5 Might-based task.

Interaction: Thoniks are about as intelligent as animal predators, which means that while they can't speak, they could be conditioned by a determined PC trainer to serve as defenders of a given territory, to avoid attacking certain individuals, and so on.

Use: The PCs find the interface to a previously unknown recursion in the Strange. Guarding the interface, however, is a pack of thoniks.

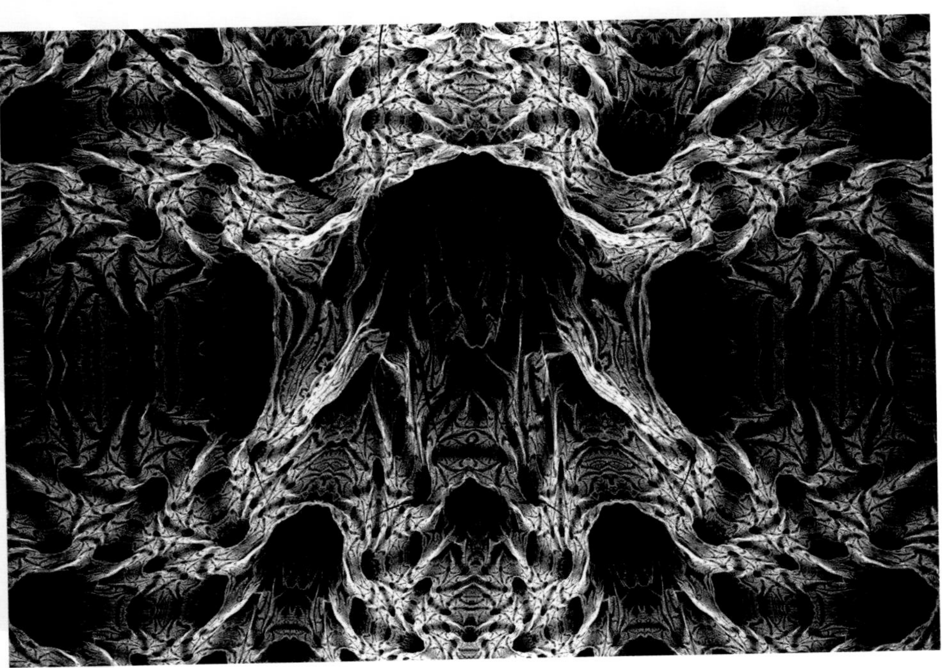

UMBER WOLF

3 (9)

"Umber wolves chase dead spirits through the Night Vault. So I thought we were safe when a pack found us—we're not dead. I learned my error when the umber wolves brought Davara down, ripped her spirit loose, and devoured it."

~Harran of the Black Moon Explorers

Umber wolves should be feared as much by the living as by the dead, given their taste for souls, regardless of whether those souls are still inhabiting a living body. Umber wolves travel in packs that announce their presence with soul-shivering howls that echo through Night Vault tunnels, and, when Death's moon is full, across the plains of Ardeyn.

An umber wolf doesn't actually look that much like a wolf—it more resembles the opaque shadow of a starved, demonic human moving on all fours, almost a cruel parody of a natural creature, with eyes like white fire.

Motive: Hungers for souls

Environment (Ardeyn | Magic): Umber wolves dwell in the Night Vault (and in tomb complexes), hunting in packs of six to ten; they range into the open during Death's full moon, which occurs every thirty-three days

Health: 15

Damage Inflicted: 3 points

Movement: Short

Modifications: Track as level 6.

Combat: Umber wolves attack by biting, and their attacks are spiritslaying (which means they can attack both normal and insubstantial creatures without any penalties). A pack of umber wolves usually announces itself with terrifying howls before combat begins. If potential prey hears the howling and fails an Intellect defense roll, the umber wolves gain initiative in combat that begins within the next hour. If the victim succeeds at the Intellect roll, initiative is determined normally.

When umber wolves attack as a pack, four to six can select a single victim and make one attack as if they were a level 5 creature, inflicting 5 points of damage that ignores Armor, as the pack begins to pull the victim's soul free of its flesh.

If a living creature (or animate spirit) is slain by an umber wolf, the spirit is destroyed for good, since the wolves consume the very soul of their prey.

Interaction: Only members of the Court of Sleep have a hope of dealing peacefully with umber wolves. To all others, they are vicious, partly supernatural predators.

Use: As Death's moon rises, a pack of umber wolves sets to howling, and by the sound of it, they're close and getting closer to the PCs.

GM Intrusion: *The pack knocks the PC to the ground and holds her down until she can succeed at a difficulty 5 Might-based roll as her action. All Speed defense rolls made by the PC are modified by one step to her detriment while the pack holds her down.*

Night Vault, page 183
Death's moon, page 165

A level 5 pack lord (health 18, Armor 3) leads packs of umber wolves. Alone, it can attack as if it were a pack of four to six normal umber wolves (dealing 5 points of damage that ignores Armor).

UTRICLE 5 (15)

An utricle is a free-roaming digestive cyst that can grow up to 10 feet (3 m) or more in diameter. Its central body is a quivering knot of protoplasm fringed by three or four tentacles, as well as a carpet of microscopic cilia that grants the creature a surprising mobility for its bulk. The central bulge is translucent, and the creature's most recent meal can sometimes be seen floating within the spongy mass.

An utricle is a bioengineered predator often deployed in out-of-the way locations by factions more concerned with security than the value of a Ruk life. Once an utricle is deployed, the creature doesn't distinguish master from prey—anything made of flesh is fair game to this creature made to eat.

Possessing no skeleton or carapace, an utricle with nothing in its digestive cyst can squeeze through openings no larger than a few inches (5 cm) across, though doing so can take a few minutes.

GM Intrusion: *A PC standing outside of immediate range of an utricle is sprayed with digestive enzyme and takes 5 points of ambient damage from the acid.*

Motive: Hungers for flesh

Environment (Ruk | Mad Science): Anywhere enclosed or in the Veritex

Health: 33

Damage Inflicted: 5 points

Armor: 1

Movement: Short

Modifications: Hides in areas filled with cracks and crannies as level 6; Speed defense as level 4 due to size.

Combat: The utricle can attack up to two targets with a single action. On a hit, a target is grabbed and pulled into the utricle's body by a process that is like osmosis, but much quicker. A normal-sized utricle can hold up to four human-sized morsels of food at one time, but after it holds two or more creatures, it can move only an immediate distance.

Engulfed targets take acid damage each round they remain caught (and would eventually begin to suffocate if the acid didn't digest them first). An engulfed target can attempt to squirm free with a successful Speed-based roll, or to damage the utricle cyst wall from the inside with melee attacks (the difficulty of attacks launched from within is increased by one step).

Rumor has it that some factions know of a pheromone that renders someone "invisible" to an utricle for a few hours after dousing, or permanently if the proper pheromone-producing graft is attached.

The creature's gelatinous nature accounts for its Armor value.

Interaction: An utricle responds to its surroundings like a bacteria seeking food; once it goes after something, killing it is usually the only way to stop an utricle.

Use: Utricle attacks are usually random subterranean Veritex encounters. However, the creatures are also sometimes deployed in the Strange to serve as guardians for hidden caches, thanks to their ability to become dormant for years at a time in the absence of food, without apparent ill effect once they become active again.

Veritex, page 204

Loot: An utricle dissolves all flesh and soft organic material, leaving behind minerals and other nonorganics. As a result, an utricle body could contain bitwallets, a cypher or two, and other equipment.

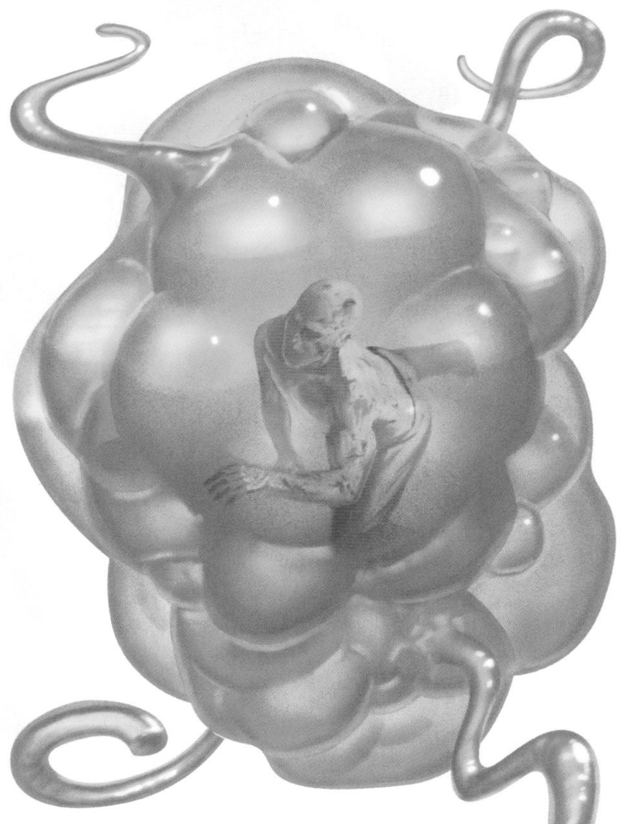

VARIOKARYON 4 (12)

A body can take only so many grafts before it either shuts down or goes insane. When someone pushes that limit and survives, she has probably become a variokaryon—a graft addict. Using underworld contacts, the addict can purchase banned grafts that allow her to harvest biological matter from other creatures and directly incorporate that matter into herself. In this way, a variokaryon can add as many grafts to herself as she can get away with, and in fact must continue to do so. Without receiving regular hits of new biological material, a variokaryon goes into a painful and ultimately lethal withdrawal.

A variokaryon tries to hide her condition from others and blend in as a regular citizen. That is, until she gets a prospective graft donor alone...

Motive: Hungers for body parts (especially faces) to use as grafts

Environment (Ruk | Mad Science): Usually in Harmonious or the Shadowed City

Health: 23

Damage Inflicted: 4 points

Movement: Short

Modifications: Stealth and all attacks as level 5.

Combat: A variokaryon is armed with a medium ranged and a medium melee weapon. Almost every variokaryon also regenerates at a rate of 2 points of health per round. If the variokaryon's health reaches 0, the regeneration rate is reduced to 1 point of health per round, and if the variokaryon is dismembered or otherwise violently dispersed, regeneration stops completely.

Any given variokaryon can also accomplish one or more of the following, depending on its particular graft mix:

Thundering Scream: Creatures within immediate range of the variokaryon who fail a Might defense roll suffer 4 points of sonic damage that ignores Armor and are deafened for one minute.

Stomach Shroud: The variokaryon vomits an external stomach (appearing as a multilayered white shroud). A target within immediate range who fails a Speed defense roll takes 6 points of acid damage every round until it can succeed at another Speed- or Might-based roll to break free of the billowing acidic shroud.

Battle Bulk: The variokaryon gains +4 to Armor and +10 to health for one minute.

Horrifying Attention: A variokaryon uses vestigial brain matter of harvested faces to launch a multifaceted attack on a foe within short range through the All Song. A target who fails an Intellect defense roll is horrified at the face-and-mind salad, takes 4 points of Intellect damage that ignores Armor, and descends one step on the damage track.

A creature defeated by the variokaryon likely lives on, at least in part, as the variokaryon's newest graft.

Interaction: For as long as its true nature remains unknown, a variokaryon seems like a normal and perhaps even especially helpful acquaintance.

Use: A stranger tries to separate a PC from his friends, and if successful, drops the charade and attacks.

Loot: A variokaryon usually has weapons and light armor, plus a bitwallet with 1d6 × 100 bits.

GM Intrusion: *An unexpected third limb emerges from the variokaryon and grabs the PC around the neck in a viselike grip.*

VAXT

A planetovore is an unstoppable force that can't be bargained or reasoned with. It's pursued me across the cosmos without pity, fear, or lethargy. And it absolutely will not ever stop until it catches me, or until I fulfill my quest after these long aeons, and finally destroy it.

~translated from a statement by Uentaru, First of the Chaos Templars

Many planetovores begin as alien AIs of the baryonic universe who discover the Strange, then use the processing power available within the dark energy network to self-evolve and spread. Others begin as alien individuals who willingly sacrifice their mortality for power and potential in the Chaosphere. Vaxt, however, started as an opportunistic, hard-to-kill weed.

A single weed patch was the only surviving life form in the aftermath of another planetovore invading the world where proto-Vaxt grew. The weed possessed unique advantages that allowed it to adapt and proliferate in the severely disturbed environment, especially given that the conquering planetovore didn't consider a weed to be a threat. After centuries of slow colonization, Vaxt finally subsumed the conqueror and claimed the planetovore's power and abilities as its own.

Since then, Vaxt has successfully consumed and colonized the remnants of countless alien civilizations, and it continues to spread...like a weed.

SCLERID PATCH 4 (12)

GM Intrusion: *The PC notices the puff of microscopic seeds she's just inhaled (which looks like a cloud of quickly dispersing white vapor), and she loses her next turn coughing.*

This creature appears as a growth of weeds emerging from the surface of a structure, the ground, a vehicle, or even from another living creature. These particular weeds look like a mass of writhing green tentacles, each reaching at least a foot in length, and sometimes stretching farther. Most of the time, sclerid patches go unnoticed, thanks to their ability to blend into their surroundings due to the chromatophores that cover their surface.

Motive: Spread Vaxt seeds

Environment (the Strange): Anywhere

Health: 12

Damage Inflicted: 4 points

Armor: 1

Movement: None (except through seed dispersal)

Modifications: Disguise and hiding tasks as level 6; Speed defense as level 2 due to fixed position.

Combat: A sclerid patch can stretch its tendrils to lash prey within immediate range.

Embassy of Uentaru, page 229

Disease, page 109

After an encounter with a sclerid patch, each PC attacked by a sclerid or who was within immediate range of a sclerid that was damaged or destroyed must succeed on a Might defense roll. On a failed roll, the puffs of microscopic seeds that the plant released during the combat secretly root just beneath an infected PC's skin or in his lungs. Treat the colonization as a disease.

A sclerid patch is a genetic duplicate of the original Vaxt. If a high-enough density of sclerid patches exist within any given area, chemical signals induce the patch to produce sclerid executioners and, later, even more dangerous forms.

A colonized creature doesn't notice any symptoms that hinder his abilities, but he might have a sore throat one day, a sniffly nose the next, and so on. On the third day of colonization, tendrils of the sclerid break to the surface and may become noticeable (though where they break through is not felt by the victim because of locally produced anesthetizing fluid and disguising chromatophores). At this point, killing the colonizing plant patch requires a procedure equivalent to a serious operation to avoid killing the host (rootlets have invaded most of the victim's organs). In addition, the visible tendrils fight back as a level 2 creature that uses the victim's health as its own, and it can attack other creatures within immediate range of the colonized victim for 3 points of damage.

If left untreated, most sclerid victims hosting a colony die after about thirty days, when the rootlets finally cause a stroke or heart attack. Sometimes, though, a sclerid and its host attain a sort of symbiotic relationship that lasts indefinitely.

Interaction: It's nearly impossible to communicate with a sclerid patch, given the plantlike nature of the creature. If a psychic link is established, a PC gains only a sense of endless green strength and the sure knowledge of continual, unstoppable growth.

Use: A sclerid patch is growing like a barnacle on a larger creature of the Strange or within a recursion where natives travel into the Strange.

SCLERID EXECUTIONER 5 (15)

This plantlike creature looks different depending on the recursion or prime world where it manifests. It usually takes the base form of a colonized host creature that, instead of being killed by a sclerid patch, is further modified so that it becomes stronger, tougher, and more fully invested with longer tendrils (many of which end in acid-tipped stingers).

Motive: Genocide

Environment (any recursion): Anywhere

Health: 28

Damage Inflicted: 5 points

Armor: 2

Movement: Short, long when jumping

Combat: The sclerid executioner makes two attacks as a single action with its acid-oozing, stinger-tipped tentacles. Characters take damage normally from the sting, and they must succeed on a second Might defense roll against the acid or take another 5 points of acid damage, which can ignore Armor. Characters can choose to allow their physical armor to absorb the acid damage from a particular attack, but doing so permanently degrades the armor (and Armor value) by the number of points subtracted.

Interaction: Executioners seek to kill all living creatures and destroy all artificial structures. They do not negotiate.

Use: If one or more sclerid executioners is encountered, that probably means a serious sclerid patch infestation is somewhere close at hand.

GM Intrusion: *Another sclerid executioner is born from a nearby NPC or creature that had apparently been hosting an unknown infestation, and it attacks the PC.*

VENOM TROOPER 3 (9)

Venom troopers are humanoids grown in large numbers in vats within mobile factories in Ruk, primarily by Zal, and then sold to other organizations and groups to use as guards, soldiers, or troops of all kinds. It's not uncommon for a battle in Ruk to be groups of venom troopers fighting other groups of venom troopers. Other times, venom troopers face off against the "law" of Harmonious (either a squad of myriand volunteers, or a single myriand veteran).

Venom troopers are muscular humanoids with pale, taut flesh and a natural, thin carapace.

Motive: Obey orders

Environment (Ruk | Mad Science): Anywhere

Health: 10

Damage Inflicted: 4 points

Armor: 1

Movement: Short

Modifications: Sees through deception as level 2.

Combat: Venom troopers have integrated blades in their forearms that bear poison. If they strike in combat, a foe failing a Might defense roll suffers 4 additional points of Speed damage (which ignores Armor).

Interaction: Venom troopers are near-mindless drones that find it very difficult to think for themselves. They are easy to fool but nearly impossible to negotiate with.

Use: PCs exploring an out-of-the-way location in Ruk find that a company of venom troopers is already on-site, protecting the location from investigation.

Loot: A dose of their unique poison is usually stashed somewhere on their person.

GM Intrusion: *Reinforcements approach! An additional 1d6 + 1 venom troopers show up.*

Harmonious, page 196
Myriand, page 198

WINGED MONKEY 3 (9)

The sky was darkened, and a low rumbling sound was heard in the air. There was a rushing of many wings, a great chattering and laughing, and the sun came out of the dark sky to show the Wicked Witch surrounded by a crowd of monkeys, each with a pair of immense and powerful wings on his shoulders.

~The Wonderful Wizard of OZ *by L. Frank Baum*

Before they were enslaved, winged monkeys were a free and not particularly vicious people, though they were mischievous. That tendency led to their current long-term predicament as slaves of whoever is strong enough to hold an item called the golden cap, currently in the possession of one Wicked Witch.

As slaves of the Wicked Witch, winged monkeys are horrors that can snatch travelers from the road, children from their beds, or ladies from their boudoirs. Sometimes victims are taken as captives, and other times they are dropped from a great height.

Motive: Serve the Wicked Witch

Environment (Oz | Magic): Almost anywhere, in troops of five or more

Health: 12

Damage Inflicted: 3 points

Movement: Short; long while flying

Modifications: Speed defense as level 4 due to quickness.

Combat: A winged monkey inflicts damage with its claws or bite (though some winged monkeys have swords or other melee weapons that inflict 4 points of damage).

A winged monkey can also make a "flyby snatch" attack if it's between short and long range of the target. The monkey yanks the target off her feet and pulls her 50 feet (15 m) into the air (or as high as overhead space allows). What happens next depends on the intentions of the winged monkey. It could drop the target at the end of its turn from a height of 50 feet (15 m), inflicting 5 points of damage. It could go for more altitude on its next turn and drop the victim from 150 feet (46 m), inflicting 15 points of damage. Or it could begin flying away, intent on taking the target captive.

A target held in a winged monkey's grip can break free with a successful Might- or Speed-based roll, but of course it suffers the consequences of whatever drop lies beneath.

Interaction: Winged monkeys can speak, but they usually remain silent. Even if they do speak, it is only to explain their intentions. They cannot do other than what they were commanded.

Use: A troop of winged monkeys guards the default translation destination in the recursion of Oz, and it either kills intruders or brings them to the Wicked Witch.

GM Intrusion: *If two winged monkeys successfully attack the PC on the same round, each grabs her by an arm and lifts her 60 feet (9 m) in the air. The PC must succeed on a difficulty 5 Speed- or Might-based roll to break free from both monkeys. If not stopped, the monkeys either fly away with the PC or drop her from 100 feet (30 m) at the end of their next turn.*

Whoever owns the golden cap (a level 7 artifact with a circle of diamonds and rubies running around it, and a depletion roll of 1 in 1d100) can call upon the winged monkeys, who obey any order given. But no person can command the winged monkeys more than three times.

CHAPTER 17

NONPLAYER CHARACTERS

Nonplayer characters in The Strange don't follow the same rules as player characters. Although there are NPC paradoxes, spinners, and vectors, not everyone falls into those categories, and they don't necessarily have the same abilities as the player characters. For example, an NPC spinner might have different twists that aren't available to PCs. An NPC vector could possess something like a paradox's revision.

NPCs by Level
Guard: 2
Technician: 2
Criminal: 3
Commander: 4
Recursor: 4
Agent: 5
Cinticus Z: 7
Professor Moriarty: 7

NPCs are covered in more detail in Chapter 8: Rules of the Game, but in short, with the number of alternate recursions possible in the Strange, NPCs can have whatever abilities the game master (GM) thinks will make for an interesting encounter.

This section provides basic stats for several common NPCs: agent, guard, criminal, commander, recursor, and technician. These NPCs are designed to be applicable for all three main settings of The Strange (Ardeyn, Earth, and Ruk) and contain customization notes specific to a given recursion. Such NPCs are often described as being armed with weapons appropriate to the recursion they're found within. Typically that means items like spears, shamshirs, and crossbows in Ardeyn; nightsticks and small-caliber guns on Earth; and spine pistols, spears, and spore pods in Ruk. The GM should feel free to vary the mix depending on the NPC, if appropriate.

In addition to the NPCs, this chapter also contains two people of renown: Cinticus Z and Professor James Moriarty.

For a detailed guide to the stats, please see Understanding the Listings in Chapter 16: Creatures (page 256).

GM Intrusion: *The agent produces a cypher that, for the rest of the day, modifies all tasks by two steps to her benefit.*

OSR, page 157
The Estate, page 148
All Song communal, page 198

CHARACTERS

AGENT 5 (15)

Agents are practiced professionals who often put their oath before their own well-being, regardless of which agency, faction, or kingdom is employing them.

Operative (Earth): Whether working for OSR, the Estate, or another agency (foreign or domestic) with no knowledge of the Strange, an operative is cool under fire, competent, and quick to fix problems, one way or another.

Envoy (Ardeyn): Most temporal powers in Ardeyn employ envoys that have a public face, which they use to hide secret operations.

Faction Agent (Ruk): Anyone without an obvious job in Ruk might well be a faction agent. Then again, an agent could be posing as a biomechanic or an All-Song communal repair person as part of an operation.

Motive: Accomplishing the goals of employer
Health: 15
Damage Inflicted: 5 points
Armor: 2
Movement: Short
Modifications: Tasks related to disguise and deceiving as level 6.
Combat: Agents use weapons appropriate to their recursion. They may also carry a couple of items useful for hiding, monitoring, attacking, or defending, and if the agent in question works for an agency that knows about the Strange, those items could be cyphers.
Interaction: Agents succeed best when they spend a lot of time prior to a mission laying the groundwork, studying the target, and sniffing out leads, which gives agents an air of distance and self-absorption even when they're not conducting an operation. On the other hand, agents under cover may seem just the opposite if it serves the role they have taken on, making it seem as if they are amenable to negotiation. In truth, they might

actually be willing to dicker if their mission goals can still be accomplished.

Use: As allies, agents can guide PCs to their next mission, fill in gaps in knowledge, and warn of dangers that PCs should prepare for. If the PCs encounter agents as adversaries, randomly determine at least one useful artifact for each agent (if anywhere but Earth) and add it to that agent's abilities. Enemy agents usually present themselves as friends.

Loot: Agents typically have 3d6 units of appropriate currency, a couple of cyphers, possibly an artifact, and a few tools useful for spying.

GUARD 2 (6)

Guards aren't true law enforcement, and they're certainly not detectives. Ultimately, they do as they're ordered by their superiors, regardless of legality.

Security Guard (Earth): Security guards are found in malls, in parking lots, and working late shifts in skyscrapers and security labs around the world.

City Guard (Ardeyn): Guards can be found at the city gates or inside the city keeping the peace by dealing with drunks, thieves, and other troublemakers.

Soldier (Ruk): Usually hired on a contract basis by the factions (and recruited from places outside Harmonious), soldiers provide visual surveillance and act as a living alarm system should anything especially dangerous appear.

Motive: Keeping the peace; following orders

Health: 8

Damage Inflicted: 3 points

Armor: 2

Movement: Short

Modifications: Perception as level 3.

Combat: Guards are armed with weapons appropriate to their recursion. Guards are not often wily, but they do understand strength in numbers. They always call for help, if possible.

Interaction: Although guards range from minor, self-satisfied tyrants to genuinely helpful sentinels, interacting with them typically involves one issue: does the PC want to do something that the guard has been told to prevent? If so, the PC will have a difficult time. Of course, some guards accept bribes or can be persuaded or tricked, but unless the guard is new at the job, he has probably heard most excuses or cons before.

Use: Every urban area has at least a few guards, and the larger the urban area, the more guards are scattered about defending the community or, just as likely, keeping the residents in line. To the PCs, guards can be allies, obstacles, or both. The important thing to remember is that if the characters happen upon a crime or a threat to the community, the guards aren't just a way to pass along the responsibility. They have their own duties and aren't interested in doing the PCs' work for them.

Loot: Any given guard has a minor amount of money appropriate to his recursion (1d20 units) in addition to weapons, medium armor, and basic gear.

GM Intrusion: *1d6 local citizens intervene on the guard's behalf, calling for more guards or even fighting the guard's foes.*

Harmonious, page 196

CRIMINAL 3 (9)

Criminals are usually rough, crude, and harsh individuals who have suborned ethics to prey on those who follow the rules.

Street Tough (Earth): Desperate drug dealers, protective of their prerogatives, can turn vicious in seconds. With their fellows around to egg them on, street toughs can be every bit as terrifying as real monsters.

Bandit (Ardeyn): Anyone who takes up arms against fellow travelers out in the wilds or in the back alleys of large cities is a bandit. Those who are caught are hung from the walls of said large cities as a warning to others.

GM Intrusion: *Another criminal, hidden until just the right moment, appears and takes a shot with a ranged weapon, then joins the fray.*

Dissident (Ruk): Anyone who works against the power of the factions is labeled a dissident, and everyone knows a dissident is a violent criminal with no morals, looking only to score her next hit of spiral dust.

Motive: Taking what they want

Health: 9

Damage Inflicted: 4 points

Armor: 1

Movement: Short

Modifications: Speed defense as level 4 due to shield or other equipment.

Combat: Criminals use weapons appropriate to their recursion. They prefer ambushes, making ranged attacks from hiding, and doing so in large numbers. Sometimes they spoil the ambush to issue an ultimatum before attacking: give us your valuables, or you'll be sorry. If faced with a real threat, such as a situation in which they lose a third of their numbers, criminals usually retreat.

Interaction: Criminals are interested in money and power, which means that they almost always accept bribes. They aren't fighting for a cause, however, so they rarely risk their lives.

Use: Criminals are everywhere—in a way, they are the archetypal human foe. Since criminals are not very tough individually, you can throw large numbers of them at the PCs. If you want a smaller group of tougher individuals, use a commander instead.

Loot: Any given bandit has 1d6 units of recursion-appropriate currency in addition to weapons, shields, and light armor. One bandit in a group might have a cypher.

COMMANDER 4 (12)

Commanders are rarely encountered without guards (or criminals) that fight at their command, magnifying their capabilities.

Police Captain (Earth): Police captains are usually veterans with extensive experience. Someone with the rank of police captain may be in charge of an entire division within a department.

Warlord (Ardeyn): A warlord might be a petty tyrant or a bandit king who maintains the loyalty of followers by promising them loot in their next war or raid.

Commander (Ruk): Almost every faction employs security, and having a few commanders on site to competently deploy said security is crucial.

Motive: Winning in combat

Health: 21

Damage Inflicted: 5 points
Armor: 3
Movement: Short
Modifications: Defends as level 5 due to shield or other equipment.
Combat: All underlings and followers deal 1 additional point of damage when the commander can see them and issue commands. Commanders carry shields and weapons appropriate to their recursion. If possible, they fight mounted or in a vehicle. The typical commander directs followers from the rear of any conflict, fighting behind the lines when necessary, but concentrating first on issuing orders.
Interaction: Commanders are committed to their cause, whatever it might be. Some defend, and others attack. Most have guards, criminals, or lieutenants who interact with people so the commander doesn't have to.
Use: Commanders lead a large group of guards or criminals. You can also use a commander as a single tough opponent for low-tier PCs.
Loot: A commander has 4d6 units of recursion-appropriate currency in addition to weapons, a shield, heavy armor, and miscellaneous gear.

GM Intrusion: *By using a martial maneuver the PCs have never seen, the commander blocks all incoming attacks in a given round of combat.*

RECURSOR 4 (12)

Recursors roam the various recursions seeking knowledge, new cultures, amazing discoveries, and powerful loot. They carry a variety of survival gear, weapons, and other interesting things they've gathered in their explorations. Some work for a larger organization, others are freelancers, but all are quickened.

Explorer (Earth): Mayan ruins, Egyptian tombs, dusty bookstores, abandoned subway tunnels, or the bedroom closet of a midwestern kid might be of interest to an explorer—if that location connects to another recursion.

Adventurer (Ardeyn): An adventurer in Ardeyn is likely interested in qephilim ruins and other sources for ancient relics.

Ranger (Ruk): The recursor tradition in Ruk is strong, but only those who range beyond Harmonious looking for hints of leakage from other recursions or who cross the border into the Strange are true recursors.

Motive: Curiosity and finding loot
Health: 18
Damage Inflicted: 4 points
Armor: 2
Movement: Short
Combat: Recursors can be deadly in combat, but most would rather talk or flee than fight fellow PC recursors. They use ranged weapons when possible and attempt to translate away if seriously threatened. A given NPC recursor may possess one or more of the following abilities, or other abilities suggested by a PC type or focus. Recursors also have one or two cyphers that they can use in combat.
Fleet: Recursors can move a short distance and take an action in the same round.
Mighty: Recursors inflict 2 additional points of damage with attacks.
Exception: Recursors make a long-range attack that deals 4 points of damage and stuns a target not native to the current recursion for one round.
Lying Twist: Recursors can convince an intelligent creature that fails an Intellect defense roll of something wildly and obviously untrue for one round.
Interaction: Recursors are understandably leery and sometimes gruff, but deep down, they're almost always grateful to find a new ally who is as interested in the Strange as they are.
Use: Sometimes when the PCs need a little support, an NPC recursor can accompany them. Recursors also make excellent guides or scouts through a new recursion. If the characters encounter another human in the course of their travels in a remote recursion, chances are it might be an NPC recursor.
Loot: Recursors have at least three weapons, medium armor, equipment suited for exploring the current recursion, 1d20 units of currency, 1d6 cyphers, and possibly an artifact.

GM Intrusion: *The NPC recursor pulls out a trick via a cypher or an ability that proves to be the perfect tool to give her a leg up in the encounter.*

SWARM RULES

A GM should not hesitate to use large groups of NPCs as challenges for PCs, particularly powerful PCs. A mob of ten bandits is a possible encounter. A regiment of twenty city guards could be used.

To make things easier, the swarm rules allow a GM to take any creature and have a group of six to ten of them attack en masse as a single creature that is two levels higher, inflicting double the original creature's normal damage. So twenty level 2 city guards might attack as three level 4 mobs.

GM Intrusion: *The technician pulls an item from a pocket, lab bench, or ritual circle and tosses it at a PC. The item glues, entangles, or incapacitates with caustic fumes so that the PC cannot take her next action.*

TECHNICIAN 2 (6)

Almost every recursion contains workers who are proficient with a narrow field of skills and techniques, and who have a solid grasp of the underlying theoretical principles required to do their work.

Lab Tech (Earth): White-coated laboratory technicians are ubiquitous in company campuses, university labs, and hospital wings the world over, competently applying their skills.

Ritual Assistant (Ardeyn): Ambitious sorcerous undertakings require additional bodies to gather ingredients, research old texts, or chant through the night to keep a spell alive.

Biotechnician (Ruk): The wonders of automation in Ruk are amazing, but it's best to have a skilled biotechnician on hand to monitor a graft attachment or other enhancement, lest something go wrong. Biotechnicians are also in high demand by every faction that conducts research.

Motive: Accomplishing a given task or set of related tasks

Health: 6

Damage Inflicted: 3 points

Movement: Short

Modifications: Level 5 for all tasks related to the technician's job.

Combat: Technicians are not typically armed, but if encountered within the area where they conduct their duties, a technician can find a tool that serves in melee or ranged combat, or even as a ranged explosive weapon. Most technicians don't expect to take part in a fight, and they surrender or flee unless they believe their only viable option is to fight for their lives.

Interaction: Technicians tend to ignore strangers while they are working directly on an apparatus, experiment, or ritual that bears on their area of expertise. If a tool, piece of knowledge, or ingredient is provided that can aid in a task, technicians may focus on that rather than the larger context of the visit, if any, and treat the gift-giver as a friend for a time.

Use: Technicians are everywhere—in a way, they're the archetypical human worker found in post offices, libraries, labs, factories, cold forges, sorcerer's towers, faction houses, and similar places where skilled and knowledgeable labor is required.

Loot: Any given technician has 2d6 units of currency appropriate to the recursion, and possibly a tool or two suited to accomplishing his job.

When running a game on the fly, it's easy enough to give an NPC a level and use that level and its target number to derive the mechanics for everything that the NPC does.

PEOPLE OF RENOWN

CINTICUS Z 7 (21)

The artificial intelligence calling itself Cinticus Z is a free-floating wheel of bright yellow light 6 feet (2 m) in diameter. Images randomly flicker within the ring, though Cinticus can choose to keep the interior dark, or display specific images. Cinticus Z speaks by vibrating the exterior of its ring like a speaker, producing almost any sound it desires.

The automaton spends most of its existence in the Strange, but the images it displays within its circle interior can be tuned to show what's going on within any recursion that Cinticus Z has previously visited. If it desires, those images can sharpen to lifelike immediacy, because Cinticus is nothing less than an intelligent, free-roaming inapposite gate that can choose not only what it looks at, but where it opens, and who or what it pulls out of or drops through its interface.

Motive: Unknown

Environment (the Strange): Anywhere

Health: 21

Damage Inflicted: 7 points

Armor: 4

Movement: Long

Modifications: All knowledge tasks as level 8.

Combat: Cinticus Z seldom engages in combat. When it does, it prefers to produce allies through its inapposite gate body to fight for it. It can produce one randomly determined ally (level 1d6 + 1) per round in this fashion.

Cinticus can also attack two foes within short range at once by discharging electrical energy. As part of the same action or a separate action, it can make a melee attack that is essentially an attempt to swallow a single foe; a target that fails a Speed defense roll is pulled through the inapposite gate and appears in whatever recursion Cinticus chooses. A target pulled through has one round to attempt to re-emerge through the closing gate, requiring a Speed-based task to dart back through, or be stranded in the chosen recursion until he can find another way out (assuming he survives whatever the recursion has to offer first).

Finally, Cinticus can use its own portal to travel and spend an action to leave any conflict it would rather avoid.

Interaction: Cinticus Z isn't normally a hostile entity. It mostly has access to what it wants and needs, but it has been known to approach recursors and ask them (with a perfectly humanlike voice and manner) to acquire brachistochrone dust. On the other hand, it remains completely silent on all questions regarding its origin, its purpose, and why it needs such dust.

Use: Cinticus Z soon learns when first-time recursors travel into the Strange, and the construct makes it a point to meet them, usually on the pretense of asking them to do something for it. This task may be as simple as scouting a new beacon or as complex as cleaning out a major inkling infestation. As a reward, the construct offers an artifact that it draws from a random recursion.

Loot: Cinticus *is* an artifact, though the only way for a PC to access its power is to either bind the construct or persuade it to shrink down to ring size and accompany the PC. Such an arrangement lasts for only a few days at most.

GM Intrusion: *A PC charging or otherwise quickly approaching the construct miscalculates and passes through the inapposite gate to whatever recursion Cinticus Z was showing at the time.*

Brachistochrone dust, page 219

PROFESSOR MORIARTY 7 (21)

James Moriarty is a criminal mastermind whose brilliance eclipses even that of Sherlock Holmes, but Moriarty doesn't advertise his illicit nature. Instead he displays irascible charm, impeccable manners, and a thoroughly engaging manner. His smile seems guileless, his declarations are from the heart, and his absentminded fumbling comes across as endearing.

It's an act. Professor Moriarty can go from pleasant to as cold and deadly as an Antarctic blizzard.

Moriarty was the secret kingpin for nearly all the criminals of England, but now that the professor has discovered the existence of

GM Intrusion: *When a PC delivers what seems like a killing blow to Professor Moriarty, the body is revealed as someone wearing a Moriarty mask—the real Professor remains at large.*

Moriarty sports a vengeful streak. Those who wrong him may eventually see his cruel side, right before they die in some painful fashion.

Professor James Moriarty originated in 221B Baker Street, a recursion formed by fictional leakage *(page 253).*

the Strange and other recursions, the reach of his evil brilliance and the harm his ugly machinations could ultimately accomplish is unbounded.

Motive: Control of a cross-recursion criminal empire

Environment (221B Baker Street | Standard Physics): Any recursion where those willing to engage in criminal activity can easily breach holes in civil society

Health: 42

Damage Inflicted: 7 points

Armor: 2

Movement: Short

Modifications: All interaction and knowledge skills as level 9.

Combat: Professor Moriarty carries a small pistol artifact with modifications that allow it to deal damage even through Armor. He always carries at least one cypher that, once activated, grants him +5 to Armor for one hour. In addition, he has at his disposal several cyphers that are useful in a variety of circumstances.

Finally, Moriarty's cane is an artifact that allows him to translate to another recursion he has previously visited as an action, as long as he hasn't previously used the cane that day. Somehow, Moriarty has adapted his pistol and cane so that they translate between recursions when he does.

Moriarty is not a fool and knows when to flee a fight—sometimes even when it seems he might have a good chance of winning. Why risk a potential loss when he can flee and ambush his enemies when their pants are down at a later date?

Interaction: When he translates, he usually uses it as an opportunity to don the perfect disguise, often even changing his gender or race. Thus, those first meeting the professor probably do so under his false pretenses. If the PCs do confront Moriarty, he may be willing to make a deal if significant inducements are offered, but characters should be ready to be double-crossed, especially if they show any disrespect during their interaction.

Use: The PCs are asked to look into a series of crimes on Earth that look very similar to ones conducted in Ruk, where it seems like creatures with the spark are being harvested. (Moriarty is behind the heinous crime, but what he's doing with the creatures or the spark is unclear.)

Loot: Moriarty carries 1d6 cyphers, plus his pistol and cane, both of which are artifacts that travel between recursions. In a PC's hands, the pistol and cane both have a depletion roll of 1 in 1d20.

Part 6: Running the Game

CHAPTER 18

STRANGE CYPHERS

Cyphers are one-use items that originate in the Strange itself. Player characters frequently discover and use these items. Those who are quickened can see and appreciate them for what they are but even the non-quickened and those without the spark can sense something special about cyphers. Though they may not know why, creatures are drawn to cyphers, valuing them more highly than other mundane objects of the same sort. A result of this phenomenon is that cyphers often make their way into hoards and troves of myriad creatures, and become prized possessions of NPCs. An "old watch fob" might be an Earth NPC's lucky charm, a prized inheritance from a dead relative, or just something cool he found that he likes to keep nearby—even though he would be hard-pressed to explain just why it's so important to him.

Quickened, page 22

Cyphers crystallize out of the Chaosphere and condense into recursions (but never onto Earth). Recursion miners translate into recursions and bring their cypher treasures back to Earth. A recursion miner could venture into the Strange itself to seek cyphers (and some do), but that's far more dangerous.

Cyphers themselves may be misunderstood parts of the Strange, mistaken applications of laws attempted to be written upon the Strange, or relics of the distant past, created by alien races who utilized the Strange—perhaps even the aliens who created the Strange. For player characters, cyphers are one of the most important aspects of the Strange as they provide additional capabilities and they are one of the few things that characters can take with them when they translate to a different recursion.

Because the Strange is mysterious, cyphers are often determined randomly, but the GM can place them in adventures intentionally as well. Cyphers have cool powers that can heal, make attacks, or produce unusual effects such as nullifying gravity or turning something invisible. Cyphers are always single-use items and are always consumed when used.

Cyphers are found with such regularity that the PCs can use them freely. There will always be more, and they'll have different benefits. This means that in gameplay, cyphers are less like gear or treasure and more like character abilities that the players don't choose. This leads to fun game moments where a player can say, "Well, I've got an X that might help in this situation," and X is always different. X might be an explosive device, a short-range teleporter, or a force field. It might be a powerful magnet or an injection that will cure disease. It could be anything. Cyphers keep the game fresh and interesting. Over time, characters can learn how to carry and wield more and more cyphers, so the devices really do end up seeming more like abilities and less like gear.

CYPHER LIMITS

All characters have a maximum number of cyphers they can have in their possession at any one time. If a character ever attempts to possess more, random cyphers disappear instantly until she has cyphers equal to her maximum. These cyphers are not recoverable. No one has yet determined what property of the Strange causes this to happen, but it is known that the vanished cyphers return to the Strange itself.

FINDING AND IDENTIFYING CYPHERS

Cyphers are found by exploring the Strange, discovered amid the belongings of fallen foes, given as gifts, or sometimes even sold in places with a great awareness of the Strange and recursors.

After the PCs find a cypher, identifying it is a separate task based on Intellect and modified by knowledge of the Strange. The GM sets the difficulty of the task, but it is usually 1 or 2. Thus, even the smallest amount of knowledge means that cypher identification is automatic. The process takes one to ten minutes. If the PCs can't identify a cypher, they can bring it to an expert for identification and perhaps make a

trade for other cyphers.

A character can attempt to use a cypher that is not identified; this is usually an Intellect task using the cypher's level. Failure might mean that the PC can't figure out how to use the cypher or that he uses it incorrectly. Of course, even if the PC uses the unidentified cypher correctly, he has no idea what its effect will be.

Identified cyphers can be used automatically. Once a cypher is activated, if it has an ongoing effect, that effect applies only to the character who activated the cypher. A PC can't activate a cypher and then hand it to another character to reap the benefits.

PCs typically discover two kinds of cyphers: anoetic cyphers and occultic cyphers.

Anoetic Cyphers: Anoetic cyphers are easy to use—just pop a pill, push a button, pull a trigger, and so on. Anyone can do it.

Occultic Cyphers: Occultic cyphers are rarer, more complicated, and more dangerous. They are devices with multiple buttons, switches, knobs, keypads, touchscreen controls, wires, and so on. There are many different settings, but only one produces an effect. Occultic cyphers count as two cyphers for the purpose of determining how many a PC can carry and use at one time.

USING CYPHERS

If a character uses a cypher, the action to use it is Intellect-based unless otherwise described or logic suggests otherwise. For example, throwing a grenade might be Speed-based because the device is physical and not really technical, but using a ray emitter is Intellect-based. Since cyphers are single-use items, cyphers used to make attacks can never be used with the Spray or Arc Spray abilities that some characters have. They are never "rapid-fire weapons."

CYPHER FORMS

All cyphers have a level. This is an indication of general power level and sturdiness, as with any object. This level is also useful in situations that do not directly involve PCs to determine if an NPC is affected by a cypher or not.

Cyphers take on different forms when they translate across recursions, essentially conforming to the context of the new recursion. Thus, a cypher might appear to be a wand in Ardeyn, a smartphone-appearing device on Earth, or an organic pod in Ruk. It would have other forms in other recursions as well, always appropriate to the context.

Regardless of its current form, the cypher works the same way.

Cyphers are meant to be used regularly and often. If you find players are hoarding or saving their cyphers, feel free to give them reason to pull the devices out and put them into play.

CYPHER LIST

When giving cyphers to characters, either choose from this table or roll a 1d100 for random cyphers.

Roll	Cypher
01	Abeyance trap
02	Age taker
03-04	Analeptic
05	Antidote
06	Armor reinforcer
07	Attractor
08	Blackout
09	Condition remover
10	Contextualizer
11	Contingent activator
12-14	Curative
15	Curse bringer
16	Darksight
17	Death module
18	Disguise module
19	Draining capacitor
20-21	Effect resistance
22	Effort enhancer
23	Effort enhancer (combat)
24	Enduring shield
25	Equipment cache
26	Flashburst
27	Focus hook
28	Force armor projector
29	Force screen projector
30	Gas ammunition
31	Glue
32	Grenade
33	Grenade (creature)
34	Grenade (gravity inversion)
35	Grenade (recursion)
36	Grenade (recursion collapsing)
37	Information lenses
38	Insight
39	Intellect booster
40	Intelligence enhancement
41	Knowledge enhancement
42	Lift
43	Magnetic master
44	Manipulation beam
45	Mapper
46	Matter translation ray
47-48	Meditation aid
49	Melt all
50	Memory switch
51	Mental scrambler
52	Mind meld
53	Mind-restricting wall
54	Mind stabilizer
55	Monoblade
56	Monohorn
57	Multiphasic module
58	Null field
59	Nullification ray
60	Nutrition and hydration
61	Phase changer
62	Phase wall
63	Radiation spike
64	Ray emitter
65	Ray emitter (command)
66	Ray emitter (friend slaying)
67	Ray emitter (fear)
68	Ray emitter (mind-disrupting)
69	Recursion anchor
70	Recursion code
71	Reflex enhancer
72	Remembering
73	Repeating module
74	Sheltering recursion
75	Slave maker
76	Sleep inducer
77	Sniper module
78	Speed boost
79	Spying grenade
80	Stasis keeper
81	Stim
82	Strange ammunition
83	Strange apotheosis
84	Strength boost
85	Strength enhancer
86	Surveillance set
87	Telepathic bond
88	Temporary shield
89	Tissue regeneration
90	Tracker
91	Translation remedy
92	Transvolution
93	Trick embedder
94	Uninterruptible power source
95-96	Vanisher
97	Visual displacement device
98	Vocal translator
99	Water adapter
00	Wings

A SELECTION OF CYPHERS

GMs should not be afraid to generate cyphers randomly. Sometimes giving a character something no one expected leads to the most interesting situations.

ABEYANCE TRAP

Level: 1d6 + 1

Earth: A taserlike contraption

Ardeyn: A rod

Ruk: A flechette gun

Effect: To activate the cypher, the user must succeed on a ranged attack against a creature within short range whose level does not exceed the cypher's level. The creature goes into abeyance, exactly as if it had translated to another recursion, except that no version of the creature appears in any other recursion. Instead, the affected creature simply doesn't exist for one hour. At the end of that time, the creature returns, having no memory of lost time or continuity of existence. (Creatures without the spark are not affected by this cypher.)

 AGE TAKER

Level: 1d6 + 4

Earth: A syringe filled with red fluid

Ardeyn: An elixir in a glass vial

Ruk: A spine

Effect: When activated, the cypher begins a process of rejuvenation that removes years from the wearer's physiological age. Over the course of the next seven days, the wearer sheds a number of years equal to three times the cypher's level. The cypher doesn't regress physiological age past the age of twenty-three years.

In a few rare cases, age takers have been sold by recursion miners to wealthy, nonquickened individuals for exorbitant prices. In nearly every case, the recursion miner was later tracked down by other monied interests and "disappeared" after being unable to come up with additional age taker cyphers on demand.

 ANALEPTIC

Level: 1d6 + 2

Earth: Handful of green pills

Ardeyn: Green potion

Ruk: Spine graft

Effect: Substance restores a number of points equal to the cypher's level to the user's Speed Pool.

 ANTIDOTE

Level: 1d6 + 2

Earth: Large pill

Ardeyn: A jar of unguent

Ruk: Injector

Effect: Ends an ongoing poison, paralysis, or disease condition, if any, already in the user's system.

 ARMOR REINFORCER

Level: 1d6 + 1

Earth: Electronic device affixed to clothes or armor

Ardeyn: Periapt affixed to clothes or armor

Ruk: A biomechanical graft

Effect: The user's Armor gains an enhancement for a day. Roll a d6 to determine the result.

1	+1 Armor
2	+2 Armor
3	+3 Armor
4	+2 Armor, +5 against damage from fire
5	+2 Armor, +5 against damage from cold
6	+2 Armor, +5 against damage from acid

A PC used to operating within only one recursion or prime world might've gotten used to thinking of artifacts as the most valuable kind of item. Once she begins to travel between recursions and her artifacts don't, she'll have to revise that impression. Given that cyphers do translate along with the PC, it's probably not long before she understands that cyphers are an even more significant aspect of her capability than she first realized.

 ATTRACTOR

Level: 1d6 + 4

Earth: Black leather glove

Ardeyn: Gold ring with a red gem

Ruk: Palm graft

Effect: One unanchored item your size or smaller within long range is drawn immediately to the device. This takes one round. The item has no momentum when it arrives.

BLACKOUT

Level: 1d6 + 2

Earth: A one-use smartphone app

Ardeyn: A candle

Ruk: A red froglike organ that sings

Effect: When activated, an area within immediate range of the user becomes secure against any effect outside the area that sees, hears, or otherwise senses what occurs inside. To outside observers, the area is a "blur" to any sense applied. Taps, scrying sensors, and other direct feed surveillance methods are also rendered inoperative within the area for the duration.

 CONDITION REMOVER

Level: 1d6 + 3

Earth: Little yellow pill

Ardeyn: Little yellow dragon imp

Ruk: Spine graft

Effect: Cures one occurrence of one of the following health conditions. It does not prevent the possibility of future occurrences of the same condition gained from a different or similar source. Roll a d20 to determine what it cures.

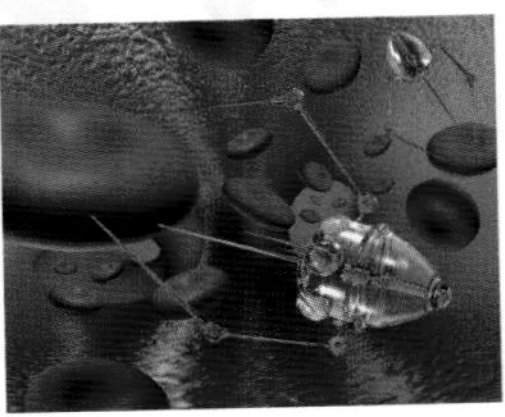

d20	Cures
1	Addiction to one substance
2	Autoimmune disease
3	Bacterial infection
4	Bad breath
5	Blisters
6	Bloating
7	Cancer
8	Chapped lips
9	Flatus
10	Heartburn
11	Hiccups
12	Ingrown hairs
13	Insomnia
14	Joint problem
15	Muscle cramp
16	Pimples
17	Psychosis (including 1 factor of alienation)
18	Stiff neck
19	Viral infection
20	Hangover

 CONTEXTUALIZER

Level: 1d6 + 2

Earth: Smartphone app

Ardeyn: Elixir in a glass vial

Ruk: Green froglike organ

Effect: Explodes in an immediate radius, changing the context of any creature in the area to the context of the currently occupied recursion. Native creatures and translated visitors are unaffected, but affected creatures who arrived through an inapposite gate are treated as if they had stepped through a translation gate to arrive in the current recursion. As a result, certain items possessed by a target creature, or even a creature itself that does not possess the spark, are immediately returned to their native recursions.

 CONTINGENT ACTIVATOR

Level: 1d6 + 2

Earth: A tiny device with connecting wires

Ardeyn: A magic rune inscribed on a scroll

Ruk: A sheath of living slime

Effect: If activated in conjunction with another cypher, the user can specify a condition under which the linked cypher will activate. The linked cypher retains the contingent command until the cypher is used (either normally, or contingently). For example, when this cypher is linked to a cypher that provides a form of healing or protection, the user could specify that the linked cypher activate if he ever becomes damaged to a certain degree or is subject to a particular dangerous circumstance.

Until the linked cypher is used, this cypher continues to count toward the maximum number of cyphers a PC can carry.

CURATIVE

Level: 1d6 + 2

Earth: A little blue pill

Ardeyn: A blue elixir

Ruk: Adhesive patch that activates when slapped

Effect: Substance restores a number of points equal to the cypher's level to the user's Might Pool.

CURSE BRINGER

Level: 1d6 + 1

Earth: Small coin with insanely complex embedded chip

Ardeyn: Bronze amulet with a large rune

Ruk: Spider that purrs

Effect: The curse bringer can be activated when given to an individual who doesn't realize its significance. The next time the victim attempts an important task when the cypher is in her possession, the difficulty of the task is modified by three steps to her detriment.

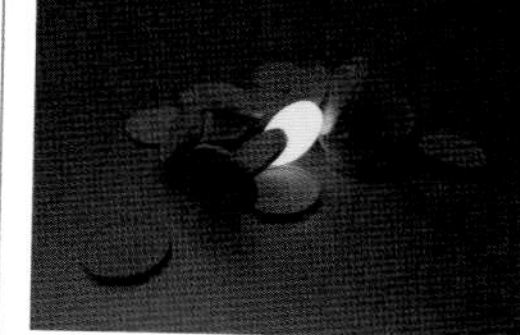

DARKSIGHT

Level: 1d6

Earth: Goggles

Ardeyn: Bone wand

Ruk: Third eye graft

Effect: Grants the ability to see in the dark for eight hours.

DEATH MODULE

Level: 1d6

Earth: Small device affixed to a melee or ranged weapon

Ardeyn: Rune affixed to a melee or ranged weapon

Ruk: Pod affixed to a melee or ranged weapon

Effect: For the next minute, when the weapon or its ammunition strikes an NPC or creature whose level is equal to or less than the cypher's level, the weapon wielder can choose to make a second attack roll. If the second attack roll is a success, the target is slain outright. If used successfully against a PC, the character moves down one step on the damage track.

OSR agents are known to collect death module cyphers. Of course, given the uncertain nature of cyphers, "known to collect" might merely be propaganda initiated by OSR itself.

DISGUISE MODULE

Level: 1d6 + 2

Earth: Hat

Ardeyn: Scarf

Ruk: A skin graft

Effect: For the next hour, the wearer's features become almost identical to those of one designated person the wearer has previously interacted with. This lowers the difficulty by two steps when the wearer attempts to disguise herself as the designated person. Once designated, the user cannot shift the effect to look like another person, though she could remove the module to look like herself again before the end of the hour.

 DRAINING CAPACITOR

Level: 1d6 + 2

Earth: Handheld device with wires for connection

Ardeyn: A tiny golem

Ruk: An umbilical

Effect: An object connected to the cypher is drained of a portion or all of its energy; an artifact's owner must make a depletion roll, a cypher is rendered useless, and another kind of powered machine or device becomes partly or wholly depowered, as the GM determines. Meanwhile, the draining capacitor now holds a charge of energy that can be used in one of the following ways.

Grenade: The capacitor can be thrown at a target within short range where it detonates and deals damage (usually from fire and shrapnel) equal to the cypher's level to all targets in immediate range.

Improve Cypher: Give another unused cypher a second use, unless the cypher is fundamentally a one-use item, such as a grenade.

Repower Cypher: A used cypher is revitalized, becoming as if unused.

Enhance Artifact: An artifact becomes more powerful in a fashion determined by the GM (it deals more damage, it improves its chance of effect by one step, and so on), but its depletion roll also increases by 10% (+1 on a d10, +2 on a d20, and +10 on a 1d100)

Intellect Hit: User gains 1d10 Intellect points.

When using a draining capacitor as a grenade, throwing it is sometimes tricky because it's usually not in the form of a grenade. When a character throws the draining capacitor in this way, double the fumble range to 1–2.

 EFFECT RESISTANCE

Level: 1d6 + 1

Earth: A leather jacket

Ardeyn: An amulet

Ruk: A spine

Effect: When activated, the cypher provides a chance for additional resistance to direct damaging effects of all kinds (except blunt force, slashing, or piercing attacks) for a day. If the level of the attack is less than or equal to the level of the cypher, the user gains an additional defense roll to avoid the attack. On a successful defense roll, treat the attack as if the user had succeeded on his regular defense roll.

 EFFORT ENHANCER

Level: 1d6

Earth: Injection

Ardeyn: Lime elixir

Ruk: Adhesive patch that activates when slapped

Effect: The user can apply one level of Effort to a noncombat task without spending any points from a Pool. The level of Effort provided by this cypher does not count toward the maximum amount of Effort a character can normally apply to one task.

 EFFORT ENHANCER (COMBAT)

Level: 1d6 + 1

Earth: Three pills taken in sequence

Ardeyn: Rune, transferred to flesh

Ruk: A skin graft

Effect: Once activated (a process requiring a few rounds of setup), the character has a one-hour period during which she can apply one level of Effort to any task (including a combat task) without spending any points from a Pool as an enabler. The level of Effort provided by this cypher does not count toward the maximum amount of Effort a character can normally apply to one task.

 ENDURING SHIELD

Level: 1d6 + 4

Earth: Jacket
Ardeyn: Cloak
Ruk: Biomodule

Effect: For a day, the wearer of the activated cypher enjoys the effect of an asset to Speed defense rolls.

 EQUIPMENT CACHE

Level: 1d6 + 1

Earth: Backpack
Ardeyn: Large leather bag
Ruk: Expandable locker

Effect: The character can rummage around and produce from the cypher a desired piece of equipment that is available on the current recursion (or any recursion with a transit time of less than a month if used in the Strange) whose level does not exceed the cypher's level. The object can't be an artifact, though it could be somewhat complex. The piece of equipment produced persists for up to 24 hours, unless its fundamental nature is one-use (such as a grenade on Earth).

 FLASHBURST

Level: 1d6 + 2

Earth: Small grenade
Ardeyn: Handful of dust in a pouch
Ruk: Pulsing organic pod

Effect: If thrown, the cypher travels to the indicated spot within short range and explodes in an immediate radius, blinding all within it for one minute.

 FOCUS HOOK

Level: 1d6 + 2

Earth: A blue pill
Ardeyn: A scroll
Ruk: Multihued organic pod

Effect: If used while translating or during the recovery period immediately after translating to another recursion or prime world, the user can retain the focus of the previous recursion or prime world even if that focus is not normally draggable. The focus is retained for as long as the user remains in the new recursion.

FORCE ARMOR PROJECTOR

Level: 1d6 + 3

Earth: Belt buckle with a sports team logo
Ardeyn: Delicate silver bracelet
Ruk: Subdermal injection

Effect: Creates a shimmering energy field around the user for one hour, during which time he gains +3 to Armor (+4 to Armor if the cypher is level 5 or higher).

 FORCE SCREEN PROJECTOR

Level: 1d6 + 3

Earth: Handheld device
Ardeyn: Silver medallion with the image of an eagle
Ruk: Steel bracer with a few controls

Effect: Creates an immobile plane of solid force up to 20 feet by 20 feet (6 m by 6 m) for one hour. The plane conforms to the space available.

Items that create force shapes, such as the force screen projector, can sometimes be used to burst doors, structural elements, or other enclosures when activated.

 GAS AMMUNITION

Level: 1d6 + 2

Earth: Bullet (long range)

Ardeyn: Arrow (long range)

Ruk: Pellet-spitting graft (long range)

Effect: When fired, the cypher bursts in a poisonous cloud within an immediate distance. The cloud lingers for 1d6 rounds unless conditions dictate otherwise. Roll a d100 to determine the effect.

01–10	Thick smoke: occludes sight while the cloud lasts.
11–20	Choking gas: living creatures that breathe lose their actions to choking and coughing for a number of rounds equal to the cypher level.
21–50	Poison gas: living creatures that breathe suffer damage equal to the cypher level.
51–60	Corrosive gas: everything suffers damage equal to the cypher level.
61–65	Hallucinogenic gas: living creatures that breathe lose their actions to hallucinations and visions for a number of rounds equal to the cypher level.
66–70	Nerve gas: living creatures that breathe suffer Speed damage equal to the cypher level.
71–80	Mind-numbing gas: living creatures that breathe suffer Intellect damage equal to the cypher level.
81–83	Fear gas: living creatures that breathe and think flee in a random direction in fear (or are paralyzed with fear) for a number of rounds equal to the cypher level.
84–86	Amnesia gas: living creatures that breathe and think permanently lose all memory of the last minute.
87–96	Sleep gas: living creatures that breathe fall asleep for a number of rounds equal to the cypher level or until awoken by a violent action or an extremely loud noise.
97–00	Rage gas: living creatures that breathe and think make a melee attack on the nearest creature and continue to do so for a number of rounds equal to the cypher level.

Glue GM Intrusion: *The PC's hand is glued to one of the objects meant to be glued together. The bond persists until the PC leaves some skin behind (inflicting 3 points of damage to herself).*

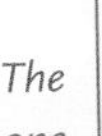 GLUE

Level: 1d6 + 4

Earth: Tube containing sticky paste

Ardeyn: Brittle rune stone

Ruk: Sealed test tube with green fluid

Effect: A permanent bond is created between any two physical objects. The strength of the bond is equal to the cypher level.

 GRENADE

Level: 1d6 + 2

Earth: Explosive device (thrown, short range)

Ardeyn: A stone with a rune of destruction inscribed on it (thrown, short range)

Ruk: Wristband projector (long range)

Effect: Explodes in an immediate radius, inflicting damage equal to the cypher level. Roll a d100 for the type of damage:

01–10	Cell-disrupting (harms only flesh)
11–30	Corrosive
31–40	Electrical discharge
41–50	Heat drain (cold)
51–75	Fire
76–00	Shrapnel

 GRENADE (CREATURE)

Level: 1d6 + 1

Earth: Explosive device or ceramic sphere (thrown, short range)
Ardeyn: Wand (long range)
Ruk: Handheld projector (long range)

Effect: Explodes and creates a momentary inapposite gate. A random creature whose level is equal to or less than the cypher's level appears through the gate and attacks the closest target.

 GRENADE (GRAVITY INVERSION)

Level: 1d6 + 1

Earth: Explosive device or ceramic sphere (thrown, short range)
Ardeyn: Wand (long range)
Ruk: Handheld projector (long range)

Effect: Explodes, and gravity reverses for one hour within a long-range radius of the explosion.

 GRENADE (RECURSION)

Level: 1d6 + 4

Earth: Explosive device or ceramic sphere (thrown, short range)
Ardeyn: Wand (long range)
Ruk: Handheld projector (long range)

Effect: Explodes and creates a momentary inapposite gate. Creatures within immediate range are sucked into a random recursion (all affected creatures go to the same recursion). Some recursion grenade cyphers transfer targets to a specified recursion. A character who succeeds at a Strange knowledge roll can determine this recursion ahead of time; the difficulty is equal to the cypher's level.

 GRENADE (RECURSION COLLAPSING)

Level: 1d6 + 2

Earth: Explosive device or ceramic sphere (thrown, short range)
Ardeyn: Wand (long range)
Ruk: Handheld projector (long range)

Effect: Collapses the pocket dimension or young recursion in which it is detonated if the level of the recursion is half the level of the cypher or less. All contents of the recursion suffer damage equal to the cypher level and are dumped directly into the Strange.

INFORMATION LENSES

Level: 1d6 + 2

Earth: Eyeglasses
Ardeyn: Eyepiece on staff head
Ruk: Contact lenses

Effect: The wearer can activate the lenses' function a total number of times equal to the cypher's level during a day. Each time, the wearer can select a living creature within long range and learn the following about it: creature's level, creature's native recursion, creature's species, creature's name, and possibly other facts (such as an individual's accessible information on Earth, like his credit score, home address, phone number, and related information).

INSIGHT

Level: 1d6 + 4

Earth: Smartphone app

Ardeyn: Mirror in which face appears

Ruk: Umbilical

Effect: The user can ask the GM one question and get a general answer (from an appropriate entity, institution, or object in the particular recursion or area of the Chaosphere in which the cypher is used). The GM assigns a level to the question, so the more obscure the answer, the more difficult the task. Generally, knowledge that a PC could find by looking somewhere other than his current location is level 1, and obscure knowledge of the past is level 7. Gaining knowledge of the future is level 10, and such knowledge is always open to interpretation.

INTELLECT BOOSTER

Level: 1d6 + 2

Earth: Small plastic bottle of ingestible liquid

Ardeyn: Gemstone that adheres to user's temple

Ruk: Adhesive patch that activates when slapped

Effect: Substance adds 1 to Intellect Edge for one hour.

"If memory is produced by the cerebral cortex in the brain, possibly by imprinting a standing wave onto cell growth, then the function of certain cyphers that affect knowledge, brain function, and memory should be, in theory, replicable. But every time we attempt to probe the brain of a recursor using an insight, intellect booster, intelligence enhancement, or similar cypher, we get anomalous results. I'm discouraged, but the pay-off is too great to give up." ~ Edwin Barnes, OSR scientist

INTELLIGENCE ENHANCEMENT

Level: 1d6

Earth: Smartphone app

Ardeyn: Necklace

Ruk: Cranial graft

Effect: The difficulty of any task involving intelligent deduction, such as playing chess, inferring a connection between clues, solving a mathematical problem, finding a bug in computer code, and so on, is decreased by two steps for the user for one hour. In the hour following the first, the strain increases the difficulty by two steps for the same tasks.

KNOWLEDGE ENHANCEMENT

Level: 1d6

Earth: Injection

Ardeyn: Mauve elixir

Ruk: Adhesive patch that activates when slapped

Effect: For the next day, the character has training in a predetermined skill. Although the skill could be anything (including something specific to the operation of one device or something similar), common skills include the following:

01–10	Melee attacks
11–20	Ranged attacks
21–40	Chaosphere navigation
41–50	Fractal surfing
51–60	Type ability (usually specific to one twist, revision, or move the user has)
61–70	Focus ability (usually specific to one ability the user has)
71–75	Recursion lore (usually specific to one recursion)
76–80	Speed defense
81–85	Intellect defense
86–90	Forensic science
91–95	Computer programming (and computer hacking)
96–00	Disguise

LIFT

Level: 1d6 + 1

Earth: Belt with wing-motif buckle

Ardeyn: Statute of gargoyle that animates and lifts user

Ruk: Spine graft

Effect: For up to one hour after activation, the cypher user can float up into the air or back down again at a rate of 20 feet (6 m) per round. Winds or other effects can move the user laterally.

MAGNETIC MASTER

Level: 1d6 + 2

Earth: Gloves with metal plates

Ardeyn: Small pyramid of crystal

Ruk: Fingernail replacement

Effect: Establishes a connection with one metal object within short range that a human could hold in one hand. After this connection is established, the user can move or manipulate the object anywhere within short range (each movement or manipulation is an action). For example, the user could wield a weapon or drag a helm affixed to a foe's head to and fro. The connection lasts for ten rounds.

MANIPULATION BEAM

Level: 1d6 + 2

Earth: Handheld device

Ardeyn: Wand

Ruk: Spine graft with wires connected to glove

Effect: The user can activate the cypher a total number of times per day equal to the cypher's level. Each time, the wearer can choose to affect an object she can see within long range that weighs no more than an object she could physically affect. The effect must occur over the course of a round and could include closing or opening a door, keying in a number on a keypad, transferring an object a short distance, wresting an object from another creature's grasp (on a successful Might-based roll), or pushing a creature an immediate distance.

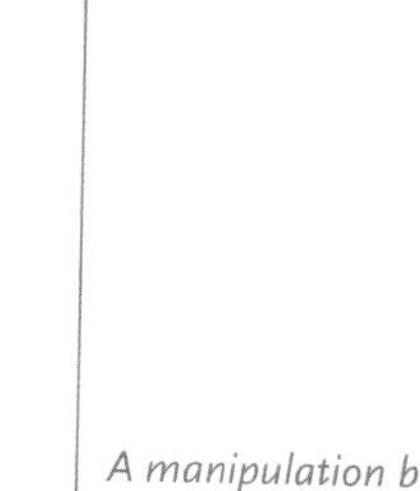

A manipulation beam could be used to operate a computer at a distance, which would make some infiltration and hacking jobs easier.

MAPPER

Level: 1d6 + 2

Earth: An electronic tablet

Ardeyn: A scroll of vellum

Ruk: A hovering bio drone with display

Effect: When activated, the device displays a scale map of the currently occupied recursion for up to one hour. The user can focus in on specified geographic features to a resolution of about 8 feet (2 m) per map image section (in other words, a pixel). Features are not named, but the map is a real-time rendition of the recursion, so objects or creatures large enough to show up in the resolution can be seen.

MATTER TRANSFERENCE RAY

Level: 1d6 + 3

Earth: Taserlike device

Ardeyn: Wand

Ruk: Small gunlike device

Effect: The user can target one nonliving object within long range that is no larger than the user and whose level is less than or equal to the cypher's level. The object is transferred directly into a random recursion. If the GM feels it appropriate to the circumstances, only a portion of an object is transferred (a portion whose volume is no more than the user's).

MEDITATION AID

Level: 1d6 + 2

Earth: Cap covered with little wires

Ardeyn: Circlet

Ruk: An umbilical

Effect: Substance restores a number of points equal to the cypher level to the user's Intellect Pool.

MELT ALL

Level: 1d6 + 3

Earth: Plastic cylinder with clear liquid

Ardeyn: Flask with bubbling liquid

Ruk: Biopod filled with living slime

Effect: Once released, this organic slime dissolves 1 cubic foot (.03 cubic m) of material each round. After one round per cypher level, the slime dies and becomes inert.

MEMORY SWITCH

Level: 1d6 + 2

Earth: Handheld device with red switch

Ardeyn: Crystal globe

Ruk: A yellow pod

Effect: When the cypher is activated, select a point within long range. The minds of all thinking creatures that are within immediate range of that point are attacked. If affected, a victim is dazed and takes no action for a round, and she has no memory of the preceding hour.

MENTAL SCRAMBLER

Level: 1d6 + 2

Earth: Handheld device

Ardeyn: Violet gemstone

Ruk: Spore-filled pod

Effect: Two rounds after being activated, the device creates an invisible field that fills an area within short range and lasts for one minute. The field scrambles the mental processes of all thinking creatures. The effect lasts as long as they remain in the field and for 1d6 rounds after, although they can attempt an Intellect defense roll each round to act normally (both in the field and after leaving it). Each mental scrambler is keyed to a specific effect. Roll a d100 to determine the effect.

01–30	Victims cannot act.
31–40	Victims cannot speak.
41–50	Victims move slowly (immediate range) and clumsily.
51–60	Victims cannot see or hear.
61–70	Victims lose all sense of direction, depth, and proportion.
71–80	Victims do not recognize anyone they know.
81–88	Victims suffer partial amnesia.
89–94	Victims suffer total amnesia.
95–98	Victims lose all inhibitions, revealing secrets and performing surprising actions.
99–00	Victims' ethics are inverted.

MIND MELD

Level: 1d6 + 1

Earth: Helmet covered with LEDs and wires

Ardeyn: A circlet with a red jewel

Ruk: An antenna graft

Effect: The user gains the ability to speak telepathically with creatures it can see within short range for up to one hour. The user can't read a target's thoughts, except those specifically "transmitted."

This effect transcends normal language barriers, but a target must have a mind that allows for such communication to be possible.

MIND-RESTRICTING WALL

Level: 1d6 + 2

Earth: Handheld device

Ardeyn: Ring

Ruk: Forearm graft

Effect: Creates an immobile plane of permeable energy up to 20 feet by 20 feet (6 m by 6 m) for one hour. The plane conforms to the space available. Intelligent creatures passing through the plane fall unconscious for up to one hour, or until slapped awake or damaged.

MIND STABILIZER

Level: 1d6

Earth: Rose-colored glasses

Ardeyn: An eyepatch

Ruk: An extra-eye graft

Effect: The user gains +5 to Armor against Intellect damage, including damage gained from alienation.

Alienation, page 216

MONOBLADE

Level: 1d6 + 2

Earth: Device similar to hilt

Ardeyn: Gauntlet

Ruk: Injection into fingertip

Effect: Produces a 6-inch (15 cm) blade that's the same level as the cypher. The blade cuts through any material of a level lower than its own. If used as a weapon, it is a light weapon that ignores Armor of a level lower than its own. The blade lasts for ten minutes.

MONOHORN

Level: 1d6 + 3

Earth: A syringe filled with white liquid

Ardeyn: A magic rune inscribed on a scroll

Ruk: A thin spiral horn graft

Effect: When the cypher is activated, the user gains a single horn on the center of his forehead. The horn is deadly sharp and strong, and it spirals down to a solid base where it fuses with the user's flesh and bone. The user is specialized in making melee attacks with the horn, which is considered a medium weapon. The horn lasts for a number of hours equal to the cypher's level.

Sometimes a monohorn cypher covers the user in a thin sheen of black hidelike material when activated, which hides the user's identity but doesn't interfere with his senses.

MULTIPHASIC MODULE

Level: 1d6

Earth: Small device affixed to a melee or ranged weapon

Ardeyn: Rune affixed to a melee or ranged weapon

Ruk: Pod affixed to a melee or ranged weapon

Effect: For the next day, the weapon can affect out-of-phase, transdimensional, ethereal, and incorporeal creatures within the context of a given recursion; for instance, in Ardeyn, the weapon would become spiritslaying. During this time, the weapon also inflicts 1 additional point of damage to any target. (If the multiphasic module is attached to a ranged weapon, the ammunition fired from the weapon gains the transdimensional property.)

 NULL FIELD

Level: 1d6 + 3

Earth: Smartphone app

Ardeyn: Scroll inscribed with a spell

Ruk: Spine

Effect: When activated, the user and all creatures within immediate range of the user gain +5 to Armor against damage of a specified kind for one hour. Roll a d100 to determine the effect.

01–12	Fire
13–27	Cold
28–39	Acid
40–52	Psychic
53–65	Sonic
66–72	Electrical
73–84	Poison
85–95	Blunt force
96–00	Slashing and piercing

 NULLIFICATION RAY

Level: 1d6 + 3

Earth: Smartphone app

Ardeyn: Ring

Ruk: Small gunlike device

Effect: The user can immediately end one ongoing effect within long range that is produced by an artifact, cypher, move, revision, or twist.

When using a nullification ray on a quickened target in midtranslation, or on a target who is moving through a translation gate or inapposite gate, the traveler goes nowhere and takes damage equal to the nullification ray cypher's level as energy feeds back in an uncontrolled, chaotic explosion.

 NUTRITION AND HYDRATION

Level: 1d6 + 1

Earth: Bulky pill

Ardeyn: Sugared plum

Ruk: Subdermal graft

Effect: User can go without food and water for a number of days equal to the cypher's level without ill effect.

 PHASE CHANGER

Level: 1d6 + 1

Earth: Harness with blinking LED lights

Ardeyn: Ring with wind motif

Ruk: Spine graft

Effect: Puts the user out of phase for one minute. During this time, she can pass through solid objects as though she were entirely insubstantial, like a ghost. She cannot make physical attacks or be physically attacked.

 PHASE WALL

Level: 1d6 + 2

Earth: Smartphone app

Ardeyn: Staff

Ruk: A semiliving sheet of tissue

Effect: When the cypher is activated, a wall within long range up to 20 feet by 20 feet (6 m by 6 m) that is 5 feet (2 m) or less thick looks the same, but for one hour, solid creatures and objects can phase through it as if the wall wasn't there.

RADIATION SPIKE

Level: 1d6 + 4
Earth: Taserlike device
Ardeyn: Ring with lightning motif
Ruk: Subdermal implant
Effect: Delivers a powerful burst of radiation that disrupts the tissue of any creature touched, inflicting damage equal to the cypher's level.

In rare cases, a particular radiation spike causes a permanent mutation to the target. If so, the PC must succeed on a Might defense roll whose difficulty is equal to the cypher's level. On a fumble, refer to the Harmful Mutations table in the recursion of Cataclyst on page 240. On a normal failed roll, the user gets a new mole. On a 19 or 20, the user can roll on the Powerful Mutations table on page 241.

RAY EMITTER

Level: 1d6 + 2
Earth: Handheld device
Ardeyn: Wand
Ruk: Shoulder-mounted module
Effect: Allows the user to project a ray of destructive energy up to 200 feet (61 m) that inflicts damage equal to the cypher's level + 2. Roll a d100 to determine the effect.

01–50	Heat/concentrated light
51–60	Cell-disrupting radiation
61–80	Force
81–87	Magnetic wave
88–93	Molecular bond disruption
94–00	Concentrated cold

RAY EMITTER (COMMAND)

Level: 1d6 + 2
Earth: Handheld device
Ardeyn: Wand
Ruk: Shoulder-mounted module
Effect: Allows the user to project a ray up to 200 feet (61 m) that forces a target to obey the next verbal command given (if it is understood).

RAY EMITTER (FRIEND SLAYING)

Level: 1d6 + 2
Earth: Handheld device
Ardeyn: Wand
Ruk: Shoulder-mounted module
Effect: Allows the user to project a ray up to 200 feet (61 m) that causes the target to attack its nearest ally for one round.

RAY EMITTER (FEAR)

Level: 1d6 + 2
Earth: Handheld device
Ardeyn: Wand
Ruk: Shoulder-mounted module
Effect: Allows the user to project a ray up to 200 feet (61 m) that causes the target to flee in terror for one minute.

 RAY EMITTER (MIND-DISRUPTING)

Level: 1d6 + 2

Earth: Handheld device

Ardeyn: Lead ring

Ruk: Shoulder-mounted module

Effect: Allows the user to project a ray of destructive energy up to 200 feet (61 m) that inflicts Intellect damage equal to the cypher's level. Also, the victim cannot take actions for a number of rounds equal to the cypher's level.

 RECURSION ANCHOR

Level: 1d6 + 4

Earth: Spray can

Ardeyn: Grey elixir

Ruk: Injection

Effect: A creature or object affected by this cypher cannot translate or pass through an inapposite gate for a day. The cypher contains enough energy to affect up to five creatures in immediate range with one use.

 RECURSION CODE

Level: 1d6 + 4

Earth: Key fob

Ardeyn: Iron skeleton key

Ruk: Spider that chirps

Recursion key, page 130

Effect: The cypher serves as a recursion key to a specific location within a recursion. A recursion key does not create a gate to the specified location on its own—the recursor must initiate a translation and succeed on the translation roll normally. But on a successful roll, everyone participating in the translation appears in the location specified by the key (not the default location for the recursion, or the place the recursor initiating the translation left from).

When a recursion code cypher is used, it either dissipates or loses its cypherlike ability, unlike the far more rare recursion key.

 REFLEX ENHANCER

Level: 1d6

Earth: Wire-covered cap

Ardeyn: Peach-colored elixir

Ruk: A spine graft

Effect: The difficulty of any task involving manual dexterity, such as pickpocketing, lockpicking, juggling, operating on a patient, defusing a bomb, and so on, is decreased by two steps for one hour.

REMEMBERING

Level: 1d6

Earth: Eyeglasses

Ardeyn: Silver torc

Ruk: Translucent head sac

Effect: Allows the wearer to mentally record everything she sees for thirty seconds and store the recording permanently in her long-term memory. Useful for watching someone pick a specific lock, enter a complex code, or do something else that happens quickly.

 REPEATING MODULE

Level: 1d6 + 1

Earth: Small device affixed to a ranged weapon

Ardeyn: Rune affixed to a ranged weapon

Ruk: Pod affixed to a ranged weapon

Effect: For the next minute, the ranged weapon fires one additional time with ammo fabricated by the module. The weapon wielder can aim the free shot at the same target as the initiating shot, or at a target next to the first.

 SHELTERING RECURSION

Level: 1d6 + 3

Earth: Handheld device

Ardeyn: A piece of cloth that can be unfolded into a 3-foot-diameter (1 m) hole

Ruk: A projector with a weaponlike appearance

Effect: A pocket-dimension-sized recursion is created that operates under the same law as the recursion in which the cypher is used. A single inapposite gate is also created. Once used, the device becomes inactive, but the recursion is permanent.

 SLAVE MAKER

Level: 1d6 + 2

Earth: Submission collar

Ardeyn: A rune-scribed iron collar

Ruk: A mask

Effect: To activate the cypher, the user must succeed on a melee attack against a creature about the size of the user and whose level does not exceed the cypher's level. The cypher bonds to the target, who immediately becomes calm. The target awaits the user's commands and carries out all orders to the best of its ability. The target remains so enslaved for a number of hours equal to the cypher's level minus the target's level. (If the result is 0, the target remains enslaved for one minute; if the result is a negative number, the target remains enslaved for just one round.)

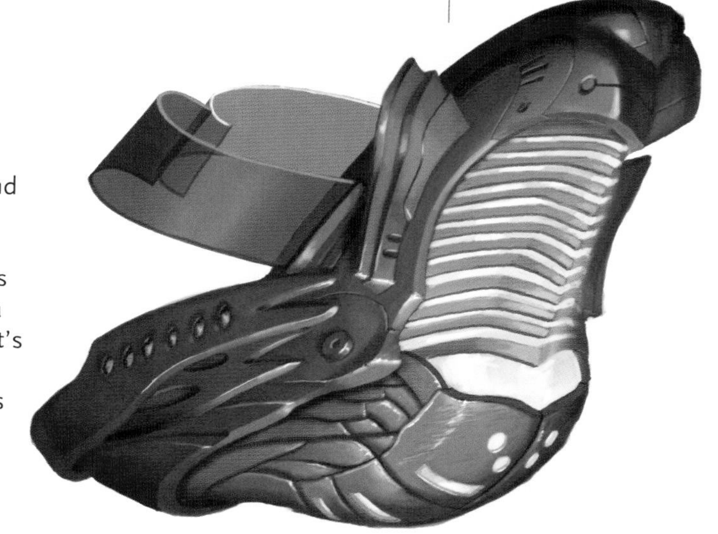

 SLEEP INDUCER

Level: 1d6

Earth: Handheld taserlike device

Ardeyn: Glove

Ruk: Injector

Effect: A touch of this cypher puts the victim to sleep for ten minutes or until awoken by a violent action or an extremely loud noise.

SNIPER MODULE

Level: 1d6

Earth: Small device affixed to a ranged weapon

Ardeyn: Rune affixed to a ranged weapon

Ruk: Pod affixed to a ranged weapon

Effect: For the next hour, the weapon's effective range increases to 2 miles (3 km).

 SPEED BOOST

Level: 1d6 + 2

Earth: Small plastic bottle of ingestible liquid

Ardeyn: Leather boots

Ruk: Adhesive patch that activates when slapped

Effect: Adds 1 to Speed Edge for one hour.

 SPYING GRENADE

Level: 1d6 + 2

Earth: Handheld device that controls tiny drone

Ardeyn: Tiny winged golem

Ruk: Graft that launches tiny bioengineered wasp

Effect: When activated, the cypher produces a tiny spying object that resists detection as a level 8 creature due to its nature. The spying object moves at great speed, mapping and scanning an unknown area. It moves 500 feet (152 m) per level, scanning an area up to 50 feet (15 m) away from it. It identifies basic layout, creatures, and major energy sources. Its movement is blocked by any physical or energy barrier. At the end of its mapping run, it returns to the user and reports. If it discovers a predefined target during that period (such as "a creature of level 5 or higher," "a locked door," "a major energy source," and so on), it detonates instead. All creatures and objects within short range take electrical and shrapnel damage equal to the cypher's level.

 STASIS KEEPER

Level: 1d6

Earth: A small device that inflates a clear plastic bubble when activated, into which the subject is placed

Ardeyn: A small urn filled with powder, to be poured on the subject

Ruk: A tube containing clear gel, to be applied to the subject

Effect: Puts a subject into stasis for a number of days equal to the cypher's level, or until violently disturbed. An object in stasis does not age and comes out of the stasis alive and in the same condition as it went in, with no memory of the period of inactivity.

 STIM

Level: 1d6

Earth: Small can or bottle of ingestible liquid

Ardeyn: Bronze bracers

Ruk: Adhesive patch that activates when slapped

Effect: Decreases the difficulty of the next action taken by three steps.

 STRANGE AMMUNITION

Level: 1d6 + 2

Earth: An ammo clip that fits any firearm

Ardeyn: A quiver of arrows

Ruk: A nodule that affixes to any weapon that fires ammunition

Effect: Modifies a weapon's attack in a particular fashion for one hour. Roll a d100 for effect:

01–10	Decreases difficulty of attack by one step
11–20	Deals bonus electrical damage equal to cypher level
21–30	Deals bonus cold damage equal to cypher level
31–40	Deals bonus poison damage equal to cypher level
41–50	Deals bonus acid damage equal to cypher level
51–60	Deals bonus fire damage equal to cypher level
61–70	Deals bonus sonic damage equal to cypher level
71–80	Deals bonus psychic damage equal to cypher level
81–90	Knockback (on 18–20 on successful attack roll, target knocked back 30 feet [9 m])
91–95	Holding (on 18–20 on successful attack roll, target can't act on its next turn)
96–97	Decreases difficulty of attack by two steps
98	Banishing (on 18–20 on successful attack roll, target is sent to random recursion)
99	Explodes, inflicting damage equal to cypher level to all within immediate range of target
00	Heart-seeking (on 18–20 on successful attack roll, target is slain)

STRANGE APOTHEOSIS

Level: 1d6 + 4

Earth: Red pill shaped like a fractal

Ardeyn: Golden elixir with fractal-shaped golden particulates

Ruk: A fractal-shaped graft

Effect: The user chooses up to three foci she's previously gained through translation. For one hour, she can access and use any trained skills or special abilities provided by any of the selected foci.

A PC who uses a Strange apotheosis can choose the appearance she had in any previously visited recursion, regardless of which recursion she currently inhabits, while the duration lasts. In addition, the PC seems to glow as if with barely contained energy during the same period.

STRENGTH BOOST

Level: 1d6 + 2

Earth: Large yellow pill

Ardeyn: Gemstone that adheres to temple

Ruk: False tooth

Effect: Adds 1 to Might Edge for one hour.

STRENGTH ENHANCER

Level: 1d6

Earth: A glowing blue pill

Ardeyn: Cobalt-colored elixir

Ruk: A spine graft

Effect: The difficulty of any noncombat task involving raw strength, such as breaking down a door, lifting a heavy boulder, forcing open elevator doors, competing in a weightlifting competition, and so on, is decreased by two steps for the user for one hour.

SURVEILLANCE SET

Level: 1d6 + 2

Earth: Eyeglasses and tiny device

Ardeyn: Two matched gems

Ruk: Two matched pods

Effect: This cypher comes in two pieces. If one piece is placed at a specific location, whoever holds the other matched piece can choose to see and hear everything going on at the target location as if she were there. Checking on the remote location requires an action. The on-site piece of the cypher hides its location at a level equal to the cypher level + 2. Lasts for one day.

TELEPATHIC BOND

Level: 1d6 + 2

Earth: Pills with MENTO logo

Ardeyn: Tiny feathered dragons

Ruk: Organic pods that adhere to forehead

Effect: For one hour, the device enables mental communication with anyone who has a matching unit, regardless of how far the users are from each other (even if they are in different recursions). These devices are always found in groups of two or more.

When two people use a telepathic bond cypher, they must be very disciplined in their mental communications, or background thoughts, feelings, and emotions also seep through the bond. For example, if one of the users has a secret disdain for (or a secret crush on) the other user, it's likely to be discovered by the time the duration lapses.

TEMPORARY SHIELD

Level: 1d6

Earth: Jacket

Ardeyn: Cloak

Ruk: Organimer bracer

Effect: For one hour, the wearer of the activated cypher receives an asset to Speed defense rolls.

Organimer, page 194

A tissue regeneration cypher can also be used to regenerate a lost appendage (arm, foot, leg, and so on) or to repair scar tissue from burns and other tissue-related disfigurements. If a tissue regeneration cypher is used in this fashion, it regenerates only 1d6 points of damage over the hour duration.

 TISSUE REGENERATION

Level: 1d6 + 4

Earth: Green pill

Ardeyn: Tiny bird that animates and sits on user's shoulder

Ruk: Adhesive patch that activates when slapped

Effect: For the next hour, the character regenerates 1 point of damage per round, up to a total number of points equal to twice the cypher's level. The character can choose which Pool to add each point to as it becomes available. If the character achieves maximum health, the regeneration pauses until the character becomes damaged again, at which point regeneration begins again (if any reserve regeneration time remains) until the overall duration expires.

 TRACKER

Level: 1d6

Earth: Smart watch

Ardeyn: Basin filled with water

Ruk: Gunlike device with display

Effect: The base device creates an invisible tracker that clings to any surface within short range. For the next day, the base device shows the distance and direction to the tracker, as long as both are in the same recursion. If the tracker moves into a different recursion, the base device shows the distance and direction to the nearest gate that leads to that recursion, if any.

 TRANSLATION REMEDY

Level: 1d6 + 2

Earth: Game card

Ardeyn: White crystal

Ruk: Injection

Effect: Eases a translation attempt. If someone is already easing the attempt, the recovery time after the translation is only one round. If the recovery time is already reduced to one round by another method, the difficulty of post-translation tasks for everyone involved in the translation is reduced by one step for one minute.

 TRANSVOLUTION

Level: 1d6 + 4

Earth: A large poster, unrolled and affixed to a solid surface

Ardeyn: Chalk used to scribe a circle 5 feet (2 m) in diameter

Ruk: Pod anchored on solid surface that projects the hologram of a door

Effect: Once activated (a process requiring two rounds of setup), an instantaneous doorway to another specific location is created. The location can be within the same recursion or to a specific location in another recursion. A doorway to a location in the Strange can also be created, but only if this cypher is not used on a prime world (such as Earth). The doorway lasts for up to one minute.

TRICK EMBEDDER

Level: 1d6

Earth: Dog treat

Ardeyn: Bone with inscribed rune

Ruk: Subdermal implant

Effect: A nonintelligent animal immediately and perfectly learns one trick it is capable of physically performing (roll over, heel, spin, shake, go to an indicated place within long range, and so on). The trick must be designated when the cypher is activated.

 UNINTERRUPTIBLE POWER SOURCE

Level: 1d6 + 4

Earth: A medium-sized unit with several power hook-ups
Ardeyn: A glowing crystal as tall as a person
Ruk: A tiny device with organic elements

Effect: Once activated, the device provides power appropriate to some other device for up to a day. The device to be powered can be as simple as a light source or as complex as a small starcraft, assuming the cypher's level is equal to the item's power requirements. A desk lamp is the equivalent of a level 1 power requirement, a car engine is a level 5 power requirement, and a starship is a level 10 power requirement.

 VANISHER

Level: 1d6 + 2

Earth: Circuit-embedded cloak with paired battery belt
Ardeyn: Three iron rings and a crown woven together
Ruk: Temporary skin graft

Effect: User becomes invisible for ten minutes. While invisible, she is specialized in stealth and Speed defense tasks. This effect ends if the user does something to reveal her presence or position—attacking, using an ability, moving a large object, and so on. If this occurs, the user can regain the remaining invisibility effect by taking an action to focus on hiding her position.

 VISUAL DISPLACEMENT DEVICE

Level: 1d6

Earth: Belt with holographic buckle display
Ardeyn: Bone bracelet
Ruk: Shoulder-mounted pod

Effect: Projects holographic images of the wearer to confuse attackers. The images appear around the wearer. This gives him an asset to Speed defense actions for ten minutes.

VOCAL TRANSLATOR

Level: 1d6

Earth: Disk that must be held to forehead
Ardeyn: Headband
Ruk: An organ graft shaped like a trout

Effect: Translates everything said by the user into a language that anyone within earshot can understand for a day.

 WATER ADAPTER

Level: 1d6

Earth: Sea-green pill
Ardeyn: Leather facemask
Ruk: Face graft

Effect: User can breathe underwater and operate at any depth (without facing debilitating consequences of changing pressure) for eight hours.

A water adapter cypher can also be used in the regular atmosphere, allowing the user to ignore ill effects from very low atmospheric pressure (as long as it's not vacuum) to very high atmospheric pressure.

WINGS

Level: 1d6 + 2

Earth: Backpack from which mini-jets sprout
Ardeyn: Billowy blue cloak
Ruk: Spinal graft that sprouts insectlike wings

Effect: User can fly at her normal running speed for one hour.

CHAPTER 19

USING THE RULES

The Strange is a game about roleplaying over rules. The rules are the skeleton that carries the heart and mind of the story that you and the players create.

Unlike in the rest of this book, this section is written just to you, the game master (or potential game master), directly because you are vital to turning a halfway-decent game into an amazing game. In uninformed hands, even the greatest rules and the greatest setting will make, at best, a mediocre game. You are the key in this process.

The game master (GM) is the architect of the game but not the sole builder. You're the facilitator as well as the arbiter. You're all of these things and more. It's a challenging role that's not quite like anything else. People try to equate the GM with a playwright, a referee, a judge, or a guide. And those are not terrible analogies, but none of them is quite right, either.

The Strange has been designed to make the challenging tasks of game mastering as simple as possible and allow you as the GM to focus on what's important. Rather than dealing with a lot of die rolls, modifiers, and rules minutiae, you can focus mainly on the flow of the story. This is not to say that you are the sole storyteller. The group is the storyteller. But it's the GM's job to pull together the actions, reactions, and desires of all the people sitting around the table, mesh them with the setting and background created before the session began, and turn it all into a cohesive story—on the fly. Sometimes this means using a heavy hand. Sometimes it means stepping back. Sometimes it means being open-minded. It always means giving the other players as much of the spotlight as you have as the GM, and attempting to give it to each of them in turn so that no one person dominates the narrative or the gameplay—not even you.

Chapter 20: Building a Story, page 359

Chapter 21: Running a Strange Game, page 376

Slaughter accelerator, page 91

The rules are your tools to tell a story, to portray a character, and to simulate the science-fantasy world. The rules are not the final word—you are. You are not subservient to the rules. But you do have a master. That master is fun gameplay mixed with exciting story.

The Strange has also been designed to make game mastering work the way that many experienced GMs run games anyway. The GMs who recognize that they are not subservient to the rules are often forced to work against the rules, to work in spite of the rules, or to use the rules as smoke and mirrors to cover up what they're really doing (which is providing everyone with an exciting, compelling, and interesting narrative in which to participate). Hopefully, as a GM of The Strange, you will not find that to be the case. On the contrary, most of the rules were designed specifically to make it easier to run the game—or rather, to allow the GM to focus on helping to shepherd a great story.

In this chapter, first we're going to talk about the rules and how to use them as your tools. In Chapter 20: Building a Story, we'll discuss interacting with players, running games, and crafting great stories. Chapter 21: Running a Strange Game provides insight into filling the world (all of them) with interesting things to see, things to experience, and most important, things to do.

THE RULES VERSUS THE STORY

Upon first glance, it might seem that for a story-based game, there isn't a lot of "story" in the rules. A wall, an enemy agent, a pit to leap, and a slaughter accelerator can all be more or less just summed up as a single number—their level. The thing is, The Strange is a story-based game because the rules at their core are devoid of story. A wall, an enemy agent, a pit to leap, and a slaughter accelerator all can be summed up as levels because they're all just parts of the story. They're all just obstacles or tools.

There aren't a lot of specifics in the rules—no guidelines for specific judo moves or the differences between repairing a radio transmitter on Earth and a biotech submarine in Ruk. That's not because those kinds of things are to be ignored, but because those kinds of things are flavor—they are story, description, and elaboration for the GM and the players to provide. A player running a character in a fistfight can and should describe one attack as an uppercut and another as a roundhouse punch, even though there's no mechanical difference. In fact, *because* there's no mechanical difference. That's what a narrative game is all about. It's interesting and entertaining, and that's why you're all sitting at the table in the first place.

If different aspects of the game—walls, enemy agents, pits, and so on—have distinctions, they come through as story elements, which are special exceptions to the rules. Having so few general rules makes adding special conditions and situations easier, because there is less rules tinkering to deal with. Fewer special circumstances to worry about. Less chance of contradictions and rules incompatibilities. For example, you can easily have a wall that can be destroyed only by mental attacks. An enemy agent who knows a special nerve pinch. A pit could have frictionless walls. A slaughter accelerator could be faulty and risk exploding at any moment. These story elements mechanically build on the very simple base mechanics, and they all make things more interesting.

SETTING DIFFICULTY RATINGS

The GM's most important overall tasks are setting the stage and guiding the story created by the group (not the one created by the GM ahead of time). But setting difficulty is the most important mechanical task the GM has in the game. Although there are suggestions throughout this chapter for various difficulty ratings for certain actions, there is no master list of the difficulty for every action a player character (PC) can take. Instead, The Strange is designed with the "teach a man to fish" style of good GMing in mind. (If you don't know what that means, it comes from the old adage, "Give a man a fish and he'll eat for a day. Teach a man to fish and he'll eat for a lifetime." The idea is not to give GMs a ton of rules to memorize or reference, but to teach them how to make their own logical judgment calls.) Of course, most of the time, it's not a matter of exact precision. If you say the difficulty is 3 and it "should" have been 4, the world's not over.

For the most part, it really is as simple as rating something on a scale of 1 to 10, 1 being incredibly easy and 10 being basically impossible. The guidelines in the difficulty table, presented again on page 335 for reference, should help put you in the right frame of mind for assigning difficulty to a task.

For example, we make the distinction between something that most people can do and something that trained people can do. In this case, "normal" means someone with absolutely no training, talent, or experience. Imagine your ne'er-do-well, slightly overweight uncle trying a task he's never tried before. "Trained" means the person has a level of instruction or experience but is not necessarily a professional.

Golem, page 270

With that in mind, think about the act of balance. With enough focus, most people can walk across a narrow bridge (like a fallen tree trunk). That suggests that it is difficulty 2. However, walking across a narrow plank that's only 3 inches (8 cm) wide? That's probably more like difficulty 3. Now consider walking across a tightrope. That's probably difficulty 5—a normal person can manage that only with a great deal of luck. Someone with some training can give it a go, but it's still hard. Of course, a professional acrobat can do it easily. Consider, however, that the professional acrobat is specialized in the task, making it difficulty 3 for her. She probably is using Effort as well during her performance.

Trained, page 99
Specialized, page 99

Let's try another task. This time, consider how hard it might be to remember the name of the previous mayor of the small town in Iowa where the character is from. The difficulty might be 0 or 1, depending on how long ago she was the mayor and how well known she was. Let's say it was ten years ago and she was only mildly memorable, so it's difficulty 1. Most people remember her, and with a little bit of effort, anyone can come up with her name. Now let's consider the name of the mayor's daughter. That's much harder. Assuming the daughter wasn't famous in her own right, and isn't still in town, it's probably difficulty 4. Even people who know a little about local history (that is to say, people who are trained in the subject) might not be able to remember it. But what about the name of the dog owned by the daughter's husband? That's probably impossible. Who's going to remember the name of an obscure person's pet from ten years ago? Basically no one. However, it's not forbidden knowledge or a well-guarded secret, so it sounds like difficulty 7. Difficulty 7 is the rating that means "No one can do this, yet some people still do." It's not the stuff of legend, but it's something you would assume people can't do.

Effort, page 17
Asset, page 99

When you think there's no way you can get tickets for a sold-out concert, but somehow your friend scores a couple anyway, that's difficulty 7. (See below for more on the impossible difficulties of 7, 8, 9, and 10.)

If you're talking about a task, ideally the difficulty shouldn't be based on the character performing the task. Things don't get inherently easier or harder depending on who is doing them. The truth is the character does play into it as a judgment call. If the task is breaking down a wooden door, a stone golem from Ardeyn should be better at breaking it down than an average human would be, but the task rating should be the same for both. Let's say that the golem's nature effectively gives it two levels of training for such tasks. Thus, if the door has a difficulty rating of 4, but the golem is specialized and reduces the difficulty to 2, it has a target number of 6. The human has no such specialization, so the difficulty remains 4, and he has to reach a target number of 12. However, when you set the difficulty of breaking down the door, don't try to take all those differences into account. The GM should consider the human only because the Task Difficulty table is based on the ideal of a "normal" person, a "trained" person, and so on. It's humanocentric.

Most characters probably are willing to use one or two levels of Effort on a task, and they might have an appropriate skill or asset to decrease the difficulty by a step. That means that a difficulty 4 task will often be treated as difficulty 2 or even 1, and those are easy rolls to make. Don't hesitate, then, to pull out higher-level difficulties. The PCs can rise to the challenge, especially if they are experienced.

THE IMPOSSIBLE DIFFICULTIES

Difficulties 7, 8, 9, and 10 are all technically impossible. Their target numbers are 21, 24, 27, and 30, and you can't roll those numbers on a d20 no matter how many times you try.

TASK DIFFICULTY

TASK DIFFICULTY	DESCRIPTION	TARGET NO.	GUIDANCE
0	Routine	0	Anyone can do this basically every time.
1	Simple	3	Most people can do this most of the time.
2	Standard	6	Typical task requiring focus, but most people can usually do this.
3	Demanding	9	Requires full attention; most people have a 50/50 chance to succeed.
4	Difficult	12	Trained people have a 50/50 chance to succeed.
5	Challenging	15	Even trained people often fail.
6	Intimidating	18	Normal people almost never succeed.
7	Formidable	21	Impossible without skills or great effort.
8	Heroic	24	A task worthy of tales told for years afterward.
9	Immortal	27	A task worthy of legends that last lifetimes.
10	Impossible	30	A task that normal humans couldn't consider (but one that doesn't break the laws of physics).

Consider, however, all the ways that a character can reduce difficulty. If someone spends a little Effort or has some skill or help, it brings difficulty 7 (target number 21) into the range of possibility—difficulty 6 (target number 18). Now consider that she has specialization, uses a lot of Effort, and has help. That might bring the difficulty down to 1 or even 0 (reducing it by two steps from training, three or four steps from Effort, and one step from the asset of assistance). That practically impossible task just became routine.

A fourth-tier character can and will do this—not every time, due to the cost, but perhaps once per game session. You have to be ready for that. A well-prepared, motivated sixth-tier character can do that even with a difficulty 10 task. Again, she won't do it often (even with an Edge of 6, she'd have to spend 7 points from her Pool, and that's assuming she's specialized and has two levels of asset), but it can happen if she's really prepared for the task (being specialized and maxed out in asset opportunities reduces the difficulty by four more steps). That's why sixth-tier characters are at the top of their field, so to speak.

FALSE PRECISION

One way to look at difficulty is that each step of difficulty is worth 3 on the die. That is to say, increase the difficulty by one step, and the target number rises by 3. Decrease the difficulty by one step, and the target number is lowered by 3. Those kinds of changes are big, meaty chunks. Difficulty, as a game mechanic, is not terribly precise. It's measured in large portions. You never have a target number of 13 or 14, for example—it's always 3, 6, 9, 12, 15, and so on. (Technically, this is not true. If a character adds 1 to his roll for some reason, it changes a target number of 15 to 14. But this is not worth much discussion.)

Imprecision is good in this case. It would be false precision to say that one lock has a target number of 14 and another has a target number of 15. What false precision means in this context is that it would be a delusion to think we can be that exact. Can you really say that one lock is 5% easier to pick than another? And more important, even if you could, is the difference worth noting? It's better to interact with the world in larger, more meaningful chunks than to try to parse things so carefully. If we tried to rate everything on a scale of 1 to 30 (using target numbers and not difficulty), we'd start to get lost in the proverbial weeds coming up with a meaningful distinction between something rated as an 8 and something rating as a 9 on that scale.

CONSISTENCY

Far more important than that level of precision is consistency. If the PCs need to activate a device that opens a portal to another recursion, and the GM rules that it is a difficulty 6 task to get the antimatter rods spinning at the proper rates to achieve a specific harmonic frequency, then it needs to be a difficulty 6 task when they come back the next day to do it again (or there needs to be an understandable reason why it's not). The same is true for simpler tasks like walking across a narrow ledge or jumping up onto a platform. Consistency is key. The reason is that players need to be able to make

informed decisions. If they remember how hard it was to open that portal yesterday, but it's inexplicably harder to open it today, they'll get frustrated because they tried to apply their experience to their decision-making process, and it failed them. If there's no way to make an informed decision, then all decisions are arbitrary.

Think about it in terms of real life. You need to cross the street, but a car is approaching. You've crossed the street thousands of times before, so you can look at the car and pretty easily judge whether you can cross safely or whether you have to wait for it to pass first. If the real world had no consistency, you couldn't make that decision. Every time you stepped into the street, you might get hit by a car. You'd never cross the street.

Players need that kind of consistency, too. So when you assign a difficulty to a task, note that number and try to keep it consistent the next time the PCs try the same task. "Same" is the key word. Deciphering one code isn't necessarily like deciphering another. Climbing one wall isn't the same as climbing another. You'll make mistakes while doing this, so just accept that fact now. Excuse any mistakes with quick explanations about "a quirk of fate" or something along the lines of a surprisingly strong wind that wasn't blowing the last time.

MISTAKES

Sometimes the PCs will break down a door, and you'll realize that you rated it too low. Or the PCs will try to paddle an inflatable raft down a fast-moving river, and you (and probably they) will quickly discover that the difficulty you gave the task was ridiculously high. Don't fret.

That door was already weakened by an earthquake, a structural flaw, or the fact that other explorers pounded on it all day a while back. That river was actually moving far faster than the PCs thought at first, or their raft was faulty.

The point is, mistakes are easy to cover up. And sometimes, you can even tell your players it was just a mistake. They might even help provide an explanation if you do. It's not the end of the world.

More important, most of the time, no one will even know. Should have rated a task as difficulty 3 and instead you said it was 4? Oh well. Unless the player rolls a 9, 10, or 11—which would have succeeded for difficulty 3 but not difficulty 4—it won't matter. And even if he does roll one of those numbers, who cares? Maybe the rain was really coming down that day, and it increased the difficulty by a step.

The thing to take away is this: don't let fear of making a mistake keep you from freely and quickly assessing the difficulty of a task and moving on with the game. Don't agonize over it. Give it a difficulty, call for a roll, and keep the game moving. Hesitating over a rating will be far more detrimental to the game than giving something the wrong rating.

ROUTINE ACTIONS

Don't hesitate to make actions routine. Don't call for die rolls when they're not really needed. Sometimes GMs fall into the trap illustrated by this dialog:

GM: What do you do?
Player: I _________.
GM: Okay, give me a roll.

That's not a good instinct—at least, not for The Strange. Players should roll when it's interesting or exciting. Otherwise, they should just do what they do. If the PCs tie a rope around something and use it to climb down into a pit, you could ask for tying rolls, climbing rolls, and so on, but why? Just to see if they roll terribly? So the rope can come undone at the wrong time, or a character's hand can slip? Most of the time, that makes players feel inadequate and isn't a lot of fun. A rope coming undone in the middle of an exciting chase scene or a battle can be a great complication (and that's what GM intrusions are for). A rope coming undone in the middle of a simple "getting from point A to point B" scene only slows down gameplay. The real fun—the real story—is down in the pit. So get the PCs down there.

There are a million exceptions to this guideline, of course. If creatures are throwing poisoned darts at the PCs while they climb, that might make things more interesting and require a roll. If the pit is filled with acid and the PCs must climb halfway down, pull a lever, and come back up, that's a situation where you should set difficulty and perhaps have a roll. If a PC is near death, carrying a fragile item of great importance, or something similar, then climbing down the rope is tense, and a roll might add to the excitement. The important difference is that these kinds of complications have real consequences.

On the flip side, don't be afraid to use GM intrusion on routine actions if it makes things more interesting. Breaking into the UN to address the delegates only to fall prey to an allergy attack or some other character-related malady? That could have huge ramifications for the character and the story.

OTHER WAYS TO JUDGE DIFFICULTY

Rating things on a scale of 1 to 10 is something that most people are very familiar with. You can also look at it as rating an object or creature on a similar scale, if that's easier. In other words, if you don't know how hard it would be to climb a particular cliff face, think of it as a creature the PCs have to fight. What level would the creature be? You could look in the Creatures chapter and say, "I think this wall should be about as difficult to deal with as a sirrush. A sirrush is level 5, so the task of climbing the wall will be difficulty 5." That's a weird way to do it, perhaps, but it's fairly straightforward. And if you're the kind of GM who deals in terms of "How tough will this fight be?" then maybe rating tasks as NPCs to fight isn't so strange after all. It's just another way to relate to them. The important thing is that they're on the same scale. Similarly, if the PCs have to tackle a knowledge task—say, trying to determine if they know where a caravan is headed based on its tracks—you could rate the task in terms of an object. If you're used to rating doors or other objects that the PCs have broken through recently, the knowledge task is just a different kind of barrier to bust through.

Chapter 16: Creatures, page 256

Sirrush, page 290

Everything in The Strange—characters, creatures, objects, tasks, and so on—has a level. It might be called a tier or a difficulty instead of a level, but ultimately it's a numerical rating system used to compare things. Although you have to be careful about drawing too many correlations—a first-tier character isn't easily compared to a difficulty 1 wall or a level 1 animal—the principle is the same. Everything can be rated and roughly compared to everything else in the world. (It works best to take PCs out of this equation. For example, you shouldn't try to compare a PC's tier to a wall's level. Character tiers are mentioned here only for completeness.)

Last, if your mind leans toward statistics, you can look at difficulty as a percentage chance. Every number on the d20 is a 5% increment. For example, you have a 5% chance of rolling a 1. You have a 10% chance of rolling a 1 or a 2. Thus, if you need to roll a 12 or higher, you have a 45% chance of success. (A d20 has nine numbers that are 12 or higher: 12, 13, 14, 15, 16, 17, 18, 19, and 20. And 9 × 5 equals 45.)

GM intrusion, page 121

For some people, it's easier to think in terms of a percentage chance. A GM might think, "She has about a 30% chance to know that fact about Ardeyn's geography." Each number on a d20 is a 5% increment, and it takes six increments to equal 30%, so there are six numbers that mean the PC succeeds: 15, 16, 17, 18, 19, and 20. Thus, since she has to roll 15 or higher, that means the target number is 15. (And that means the task is level 5, but if you've already determined the target number, you likely don't care about the level.)

ADVANTAGES OF THE SYSTEM

1. The GM makes measured adjustments in large, uniform steps. That makes things faster than if players had to do arithmetic using a range of all numbers from 1 to 20.
2. You calculate a target number only once no matter how many times the PCs attempt the action. If you establish that the target number is 12, it's 12 every time a PC tries that action. (On the other hand, if you had to add numbers to your die roll, you'd have to do it for every attempt.) Consider this fact in light of combat. Once a player knows that she needs to roll a 12 or higher to hit her foe, combat moves very quickly.
3. If a PC can reduce the difficulty of an action to 0, no roll is needed. This means that an Olympic gymnast doesn't roll a die to walk across a balance beam, but the average person does. The task is initially rated the same for both, but the difficulty is reduced for the gymnast. There's no chance of failure.
4. This is how everything in the game works, whether it's climbing a wall, sweet-talking a guard, or fighting a bioengineered horror.
5. Perhaps most important, the system gives GMs the freedom to focus entirely on the flow of the game. The GM doesn't use dice to determine what happens (unless he wants to)—the players do. There aren't a lot of different rules for different actions, so there is little to remember and very little to reference. The difficulty can be used as a narrative tool, with the challenges always meeting the expected logic of the game. All the GM's mental space can be devoted to guiding the story.

GM Intrusion Options: *An NPC ally disavows the PC who is caught spying. The PC is incorrectly singled out as a pickpocket in a public area. The security routine of the guards doesn't match the intelligence the PC was given. The PC's disguise slips. A woman named Zelda appears, claiming to be the PC's long-lost lover, sister, creditor, or brother (having undergone radical surgery in the last case).*

GM INTRUSION

GM intrusion is the main mechanic that the GM uses to inject drama and additional excitement into the game. It's also a handy tool for resolving issues that affect the PCs but do not involve them. GM intrusion is a way to facilitate what goes on in the world outside the characters. Can the enemy qephilim track the PCs' movements through the complex? Will the fraying rope hold?

Since the players roll all the dice, GM intrusion is used to determine if and when something happens. For example, if the PCs are fighting September Project agents, and the GM knows that more agents are nearby, the GM doesn't need to roll dice to determine if the other agents hear the scuffle and intervene (unless he wants to). He just decides when it would be best for the story—which is probably when it would be worst for the characters. In a way, GM intrusion replaces the GM's die rolling.

The mechanic is also one of the main ways that GMs award experience points to the PCs. This means that the GM uses experience points as a narrative tool. Whenever it seems appropriate, he can introduce complications into the game that affect a specific player, but when he does so, he gives that player 1 XP. The player can refuse the intrusion, but doing so costs her 1 XP. So by refusing an intrusion, the player does not get the experience point that the GM is offering, and she loses one that she already has. (This kind of refusal is likely to happen very rarely in your game, if ever. And, obviously, a player can't refuse an intrusion if she has no XP to spend.)

Here's how a GM intrusion might work in play. Say the PCs find a hidden console with some buttons. They learn the right order in which to press the buttons, and a trapdoor in the floor opens. As the GM, you don't ask the players specifically where their characters are standing. Instead, you give a player 1 XP and say, "Unfortunately, you're standing directly over the trapdoor." If he wanted, the player could refuse the XP, spend one of his own, and say, "I leap aside to safety." Most likely, though, he'll make the defense roll that you call for and let it play out.

There are two ways for the GM to handle this kind of intrusion. You could say, "You're standing in the wrong place, so make a roll." (It's a Speed defense roll, of course.) Alternatively, you could say, "You're standing in the wrong place. The floor opens under your feet, and you fall down into the darkness." In the first example, the PC has a chance to save himself. In the second example, he doesn't. Both are viable options. The distinction is based on any number of factors, including the situation, the characters involved, and the needs of the story. This might seem arbitrary or even capricious, but you're the master of

Remember that anytime you give a player 1 XP for a GM intrusion, you're actually giving him 2; one to keep and one to give to another player.

what the intrusion can and can't do. RPG mechanics need consistency so players can make intelligent decisions based on how they understand the world to work. But they'll never base their decisions on GM intrusions. They don't know when intrusions will happen or what form they will take. GM intrusions are the unpredictable and strange twists of fate that affect a person's life every day.

When player modifications (such as skill, Effort, and so on) determine that success is automatic, the GM can use GM intrusion to negate the automatic success. The player must roll for the action at its original difficulty level or target number 20, whichever is lower.

PLAYER-AWARDED EXPERIENCE POINTS

Players who gain 1 XP as the result of GM intrusion also get 1 XP to award to another player for whatever reason they wish—maybe the other player had a good idea, told a funny joke, lent a helping hand, or whatever seems appropriate. This means that whenever the GM uses GM intrusion, he's actually giving out 2 XP. The ability to award XP to your friends is empowering and interactive. It helps the players regulate the flow of XP so that no one is left out. It rewards good play that pleases the group as a whole, ensuring that everyone contributes to everyone else's enjoyment. It shouldn't just be the GM who decides which players have done well. Some groups will want to decide the criteria for player-awarded points ahead of time. Some will just want to play it by ear.

Variant: Alternatively, the group could combine the player-awarded points and vote at the end of a session to decide who gets how many XP. This might be the most egalitarian way to do it, but it's probably not as fun or empowering to the individual players.

USING GM INTRUSIONS AS A NARRATIVE TOOL

A GM can use this narrative tool to steer things. That doesn't mean railroad the players or direct the action of the game with a heavy hand. GM intrusion doesn't enable you to say, "You're all captured, so here's your 1 XP." Instead, the GM can direct things more subtly—gently, almost imperceptibly influencing events rather than forcing them. GM intrusion represents things going wrong. The bad guys planning well. Fortune not favoring the PCs.

Consider this scenario: the GM plants an interesting adventure seed in a small Ardeyn village, but the PCs don't stay there long enough to find it. Just outside the village, the PCs run afoul of a vicious viper that bites one of them. The GM uses intrusion to say that the poison from the snake will make the character debilitated unless he gets a large dose of a very specific antitoxin, which the group doesn't have. Of course, they aren't required to go back to the village where the GM's interesting adventure can start, but it's likely that they will, looking for the antitoxin.

Some players might find intrusion heavy-handed, but the XP softens the blow. And remember, they can refuse these narrative nudges. Intrusion is not meant to be a railroading tool—just a bit of a rudder. Not an inescapable track, but a nudge here and there.

What's more, the GM doesn't need to have a deliberate goal in mind. The complication he introduces could simply make things more

GM Intrusion Options: *A letter from the IRS arrives—the PC is being audited. A knock at the door heralds the appearance of a group of FBI agents who want the PC in connection to something she did during her misspent youth. A PC's weapon is damaged, knocked away, swallowed, or broken. A PC intent on fleeing the scene runs into backup summoned by enemies. The PC, having just suffered damage from a fall, an explosion, or another source, must make a Speed defense roll to toss away her grenade cypher before it prematurely explodes.*

interesting. He might not know where it will take the story, just that it will make the story better.

This is wonderfully empowering to the GM—not in a "Ha ha, now I'll trounce the PCs" way, but in an "I can control the narrative a little bit, steering it more toward the story I want to create rather than relying on the dice" sort of way. Consider that old classic plot development in which the PCs get captured and must escape from the bad guys. In heroic fiction, this is such a staple that it would almost seem strange if it didn't happen. But in many roleplaying games, it's a nearly impossible turn of events—the PCs usually have too many ways to get out of the bad guys' clutches even before they're captured. The dice have to be wildly against them. It virtually never happens. With GM intrusion, it could happen (again, in the context of the larger encounter, not as a single intrusion that results in the entire group of PCs being captured with little explanation or chance to react).

Sark, page 288

For example, let's say the PCs are surrounded by sark. One character is badly injured—debilitated—and the rest are hurt. Some of the sark produce a large weighted net. Rather than asking for a lot of rolls and figuring the mechanics for escape, the GM uses intrusion and says that the net goes over the PCs who are still on their feet. The rest of the sark point spears menacingly. This is a pretty strong cue to the players that surrender is a good (and possibly the only) option. Some players won't take the hint, however, so another use of intrusion might allow the sark to hit one of the trapped PCs on the head and render him unconscious while his friends struggle in the net. If the players still don't surrender, it's probably best to play out the rest of the encounter without more GM intrusions—using more would be heavy-handed by anyone's measure—although it's perfectly reasonable to rule that a character rendered debilitated is knocked unconscious, since the sark are trying to take the PCs alive.

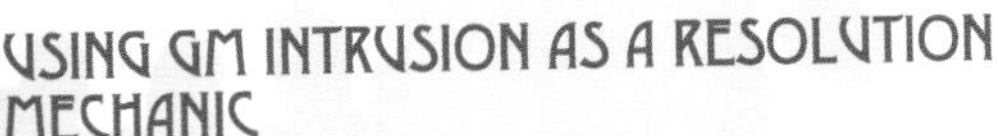

USING GM INTRUSION AS A RESOLUTION MECHANIC

This mechanic offers a way for the GM to determine how things happen in the game without leaving it all to random chance. Bad guys trying to smash down the door to the room where the PCs are holed up? The GM could roll a bunch of dice, compare the NPCs' stats to the door's stats, and so on, or he could wait until the most interesting time, have the bad guys break in, and award an experience point to the PC who tried his best to bar the door. The latter way is The Strange way. Intrusion is a task resolution tool for the GM. In other words, he doesn't base things on stats but on narrative choice. (Frankly, a lot of great GMs over the years—even in the very early days of the hobby—have run their games this way. Sometimes they rolled dice or pretended to roll dice, but they were really manipulating things.) This method frees the GM from worrying about mechanics and looking up stats and allows him to focus on the story.

This isn't cheating—it's the rules of the game. This rule simply replaces traditional dice rolling with good GMing, logic, and intelligent storytelling. When a PC is climbing a burning rope, and everyone knows that it will break at some point, the game has a mechanism to ensure that it breaks at just the right time.

Variant: If you want more randomness in your game, or if you want your game to seem like more of a simulation, assign a flat percentage chance for whatever you're trying to resolve. For example, each round, the bad guys have a 20% chance to break down the door—or, if you want the risk to escalate, a cumulative 20% chance to break down the door. By not using GM intrusion, this method robs the PCs of a few XP, but when they see you rolling dice, it might help with their immersion. Alternatively, you can pretend to roll dice but really use GM intrusion, though this method seriously robs the characters of XP.

There's a better way. Announce your intrusion, but say that there's only a chance it will happen (state the percentage chance), and then roll the dice in plain view of everyone. If the intrusion occurs, award the XP as normal. This is likely the best of both worlds. However, it takes the narrative power out of your hands and gives it to the dice. Perhaps this method is best used only occasionally. If nothing else, it injects some variety and certainly some drama.

USING (AND NOT ABUSING) GM INTRUSION

Too much of a good thing will make the game seem utterly unpredictable—even capricious. The ideal is to use about four GM intrusions per game session, depending on the length of the session, or about one intrusion per hour of game play. This is in addition to any intrusions that are triggered by players rolling 1s.

INTRUSION THROUGH PLAYER ROLLS

When a PC rolls a 1, handle the GM intrusion the same way that you'd handle an intrusion you initiated. The intrusion could mean the PC fumbles or botches whatever she was trying to do, but it could mean something else. Consider these alternatives:

- In combat, the PC's foe is not as hurt as she thought. Give the foe 5 extra health.
- In combat, the PC drops her guard and the foe gets a free attack.
- In combat, reinforcements for the PC's foes show up.
- In combat (or any stressful situation), an ally decides to flee.
- In combat (or any stressful situation), an ally doesn't like the PCs as much as they thought. He steals from them or betrays them.
- Out of combat, the PC's backpack falls open. The sole of his shoe tears open.
- Out of combat, it begins to rain heavily.
- Out of combat, a surprise foe appears and it turns into a combat.
- In an interaction, the GM introduces a surprising motive for the NPC. For example, the PCs are trying to bribe an official for information, and the NPC reveals that what he really wants isn't money but for someone to rescue his kidnapped son.

GM INTRUSION THAT AFFECTS THE GROUP

The core of the idea behind GM intrusion is that the player being adversely affected gains an experience point. But what if the intrusion affects the whole group equally? What if the GM uses it to have an unstable device overload and explode, harming all the characters? In this case, if no PC is involved more than the others (for example, no single PC was frantically attempting to repair the device), the GM should give 1 XP to each character but not give any of them an extra XP to hand out to someone else.

However, this kind of group intrusion should be an exception, not the rule. GM intrusions are much more effective if they are more personal.

EXAMPLE GM INTRUSIONS

It's not a good idea to use the same events as GM intrusions over and over ("Dave dropped his shotgun *again*?"). Below are a number of different intrusions you can use.

BAD LUCK

Through no fault of the characters, something happens that is bad or at least complicating. For example:

- The floorboard beneath the PC gives way.
- The boat lists to starboard at just the wrong moment.
- A gust of wind blows the papers out of the character's hand.
- The buckle of the PC's backpack snaps at an inopportune time.
- The NPC that the characters need to speak with is home sick today.
- A device malfunctions and gives the user a jolt.

AN UNKNOWN COMPLICATION EMERGES

The situation was more complex (and therefore more interesting) than the PCs knew—perhaps even more than the GM knew, at least at the start. For example:

- A poisonous snake darts out from the tall grass and attacks.
- The box that the plans are stored in is trapped with a poison needle.
- The NPC that the characters need to befriend doesn't speak their language.
- The NPC that the characters were going to bribe is allergic to the bottle of alcohol they offer him.
- The PCs find the old book they need, but the pages are so brittle that if they open it, it might crumble.

AN IMPENDING COMPLICATION EMERGES

GMs can use this type of intrusion as a resolution mechanic to determine NPC success or failure.

Rather than rolling dice to see how long it takes an NPC to rewire a damaged force field generator, it happens at a time of the GM's choosing—ideally, when it would be most interesting. For example:

- The villain's henchmen finally get through the locked door.
- The ropes of the old rope bridge finally snap.
- The city guards show up.
- The unstable ceiling collapses.
- The NPC who holds a dagger to a character's throat and says "Don't move" cuts the PC when he does, in fact, move, putting him immediately at debilitated on the damage track.

GM Intrusion Options (Group): *PCs engaged in a car chase or other activity outdoors are struck by a vehicle driven by an unrelated NPC. The airplane the PCs are flying on loses an engine. The roof the PCs are taking shelter under is lifted away by an explosion, a collapse, or a giant creature. The PCs use an object from a recursion as the basis for their translation, but the object is from a different recursion than they thought, so they don't end up where they expected.*

OPPONENT LUCK OR SKILL

The PCs aren't the only ones with surprising tricks up their sleeves. For example:

- The PC's opponent uses a lightning-fast maneuver to dodge all attacks.
- The PC's opponent sees an opening and makes an additional, immediate attack.
- The NPC commander rallies her troops and they all deal 2 additional points of damage for a round.
- The PC's opponent uses a cypher or similar device that produces just the right effect for the situation.
- A bit of the wall collapses in the middle of the fight, preventing the characters from chasing the fleeing NPC.

GM intrusions are not a way for an adversarial GM to screw over PCs or players, they are not a means of punishing players, and they are not the means to make PCs constantly fumble and look like idiots. Don't fall into that trap. Your players will soon begin to distrust you.

FUMBLES

Although you might not want every player roll of 1 to be a fumble, sometimes it could be just that. Alternatively, the GM could simply declare that a fumble has occurred. In either case, consider the following examples:

- In combat, the PC drops his weapon.
- In combat, the PC misses and strikes the wall, breaking or damaging his weapon.
- In combat, the NPC hits the PC harder than usual, inflicting 2 additional points of damage.
- In combat, the PC hits an ally by accident and inflicts regular damage.
- Out of combat, the PC drops or mishandles an important object or piece of equipment.
- In an interaction, the PC inadvertently (or even unknowingly) says something offensive.

PARTIAL SUCCESS

GM intrusion doesn't have to mean that a PC has failed. For example:

The PC disables the bomb before it goes off, but if someone doesn't remain and hold the detonator, it will explode.

The PC creates the antidote, but it will turn the imbiber's flesh blue for the next few weeks.

The PC jumps across the pit, but in so doing knocks stones on the edge loose, making the jump harder for her friend right behind her.

THE REST OF THE RULES

It's worth repeating: the rules exist to be used as tools to shape the game, the story, and the experience. When you tell a player that the bestial giant at the top of the cliff throws heavy stones down on her character and she gets hurt, the rules give you a way to explain just how hurt.

One way to look at it is this: the GM is the sensory input for the player. The player can't know anything about what's going on in the fictional reality of the game unless the GM tells her. The rules, then, are one way to convey information to the players in a manner that is meaningful to everyone sitting at the table. The GM could say, "You're quite hurt," but the rules clarify how hurt she is. The GM could say, "You can hurl that spear pretty far," but the rules provide a definition of "pretty far" that helps keep things consistent, moderately realistic, and understandable so the GM doesn't have to repeat things over and over.

The rules do more than that, of course. They determine success or failure for PCs and NPCs. They help define what resources characters have to interact with the world (although the best resource is the players' ingenuity, and that isn't defined by the rules).

ADJUDICATING

A lot of working within the rules is what people sometimes call "adjudicating." Adjudicating is basically the difference between a computer game and a game run by an actual, living human being. All a computer can do (as of yet) is follow the rules. But a human can use his sense of logic (we'll discuss that in detail in the next section) to determine whether the rules make sense for a given situation, and he can do it on a case-by-case basis. Because there's a human GM using logic, the rules for how to play The Strange take up only a small part of this hefty book. If the rules had to cover every imaginable situation, well, this would be a very different book.

Needler, page 91

For example, imagine that the PCs encounter a Ruk assassin who tries to kill them with a needler loaded with poisoned needles. One of the PCs is heavily armored, so she takes no damage from the needles—not even close. That sort of sounds like the needles just bounced off her armor. Should the poison on a needle that can't penetrate a character's armor affect that character? Probably not. But that's not an actual rule. Well, why not make it a rule? Because then suddenly anyone wearing a leather jacket can't be affected by poison needles. Should that be the case? No, because the thick leather doesn't protect every area on the PC's body. It's more complex than that. Could you devise a rule to cover both situations? Probably, but why bother? The GM can make a decision based on the situation. (She can also use GM intrusion and say that a needle hit where the armor didn't offer protection—GM intrusion really does solve a lot of these issues.)

Likewise, sometimes a character who falls off a high ledge should be stunned and lose his next turn. That isn't the rule, but it makes sense—sometimes. And the key word is sometimes. Because sometimes the situation or the context means you don't want that to happen, so you adjudicate.

A character falling from a 100-foot (30 m) ledge might take 10 points of damage. That's a lot, but a fresh character with a decent amount of Might can take that and keep going. Sometimes that's okay, but sometimes it stretches our suspension of disbelief. If a player reads the rules on how much damage is dealt by falling, she might even have her character jump off a high cliff deliberately, knowing that she can take it. So you adjudicate that she doesn't just lose her next turn, but the fall also knocks her down a step on the damage track. That's harsh, and the player will really feel it. But she should, and it will keep her from exploiting what might seem like a hole in the rules in a way that no real person would (and no one in a story would).

Remember, it's your job to use the rules to simulate the world, even if the world is a fictional place with all kinds of strangeness. You're not a slave to the rules—it's the other way around. If you come across a hole in the rules or something that doesn't make sense, don't shrug your shoulders and say, "Well, that's what the rules say (or don't say)." Fix it.

When talking about rules, sometimes people will toss around words like "game balance" or refer to rules as "broken." These concepts belong in games where players build characters using extensive rules and make a lot of choices and then pit those characters against specific challenges to see how they fare. In such a game, a challenge rated or designed poorly, or a character option that grants too much or too little power, can throw everything completely out of whack. Advancing and improving characters is the point of that kind of game, and the way that characters "win" is by

overcoming challenges (often, by fighting).

Because The Strange is not a game about matching PC builds against specific challenges, nor is it a game about advancing characters (at least not solely, and in any event, characters do not advance due to fights or overcoming challenges), these concepts really don't apply. If something seems broken, change it. If a PC ability is too powerful, make it less so. Either do it as a part of the story, or—perhaps even better—just be up front with the players. "Hey, guys, this new psychic power of Ray's is just too good. It's making every fight a pushover, and that's not fun. So I'm going to tone down its effect. Sound okay?" An honest discussion with the players is often the best way to handle just about any problem that crops up in a game. And if a player can't handle that kind of interaction, maybe you don't want him at your table anyway.

LOGIC

Running a game requires a lot of logic rather than a careful reading of the rules. For example, some things give characters a resistance to fire (almost always expressed as Armor). But there is no special rule for "fire damage" as opposed to "slicing damage" or "lightning damage." Instead, you use logic to determine whether the damage inflicted counts as fire. In these situations, there are only two times when your answer is wrong.

While GMs always have notes with them that they put together before the game session, it's smart to have a lot of blank paper to scribble notes on during the game. You'll invariably have to make stuff up as you go, and you might want to be able to remember what you did for later. Sometimes it will be a rules issue (remembering that it was a difficulty 4 jump to get across the pit, so that it will be consistent when they come back that way again), and sometimes it will just be an NPC's name or some detail about him.

The first is when the answer breaks the players' suspension of disbelief. For example, something that makes a PC fire resistant should probably provide some protection against a heat-based weapon. If it doesn't, your answer will spoil the moment for the group.

The second wrong answer is when you're inconsistent. If you allow the fireproof armor a PC wears to give him some protection against lava one time but not the next, that's a problem—not only because it breaks the suspension of disbelief but also because it gives the players nothing to base their decisions on. Without predictable consistency, they can't make intelligent decisions.

The Strange rules are written with the assumption that the GM does not need to fall back on rules for everything, either for her own sake or as a defense against the players. "There's no rule that says you can't wear two kinds of armor, so that means I can wear two leather jackets and get double protection, right?" Of course not. That makes no sense. The GM's logic rules the day here.

You shouldn't need pedantic rules to defend against the players. You and the players should work together to create a logical, consistent, and believable world and story. Players who try to use the lack of pedantry in the rules to gain unrealistic and illogical advantages for their characters should revisit the basic concept of The Strange.

Further, the rules don't say things like, "The GM decides if the NPC knows the answer to the question, or if he will answer, or how he will answer." Of course that's the kind of thing you decide—that's your role. The rules don't state that you decide if something is logical and appropriate to the story or setting any more than they state that the player decides what actions his character will take. That's just the way the game works.

Does this put more pressure on the GM? Yes and no. It means that you need to make more judgment calls—more of the adjudication described above—which can be challenging if you're new at it. But being an arbiter of what seems appropriate and makes sense is something that we all do, all day long. Look at it this way: when you're watching a television show or a movie, at some point you might say, "That seems wrong," or "That seems unrealistic." There's no difference between doing that and using logic as a GM.

In the long run, relying on logic frees the GM. No longer saddled with hundreds (or thousands) of individual rules, compatibility issues, loopholes, and the like, you are free to move ahead with the story being told by the group. You can focus more on the narrative elements of the game than on the mechanical ones. To look at it a different way, in other games GMs sometimes spend a lot of time preparing, which is almost always rules-related stuff: creating NPC stat blocks, memorizing rules subsystems that will come into play, carefully balancing encounters, and so on. A GM running The Strange does very little of that. Prepping for the game means figuring out cool storylines, weird new devices or foes, and the best way to convey the atmosphere. The mechanical elements can be handled during the game, using logic at the table.

DICE ROLLING

Using the rules involves rolling dice. If the dice don't mean anything, then everything is predetermined, and it's no longer a game by any definition—just a story being told. So the dice need to matter. But that means that sometimes a PC will fail when she would succeed if it were a story, and vice versa. That's not a flaw; it's a feature. It's what makes roleplaying games so exciting. When we're watching an action movie, we know that in the third act the hero will defeat the villain at just the right moment. But in an RPG, maybe not. It's not so predictable. That's one of the things that makes them so special.

On the other hand, things like GM intrusions sometimes trump the die rolls to help the story move along in a direction that is (hopefully) best for the game. How do you manage it all?

As you describe the action or as the PCs move about the world, the vast majority of things that happen shouldn't involve dice. Walking around, buying things in a store, chatting with NPCs, crossing a wilderness, looking for an ancient ruin—these are not actions that normally require die rolls. However, it's easy to think of exceptions where rolls might be needed. How do you decide? There are two rules of thumb.

First, don't ask for a roll unless it seems like there should be a chance of failure and a chance of success. If a PC wants to fire his gun and hit the moon, there's no need to roll, because there's no chance for success. Likewise, if he wants to shoot that same gun at a large building from 10 feet (3 m) away, there's no chance for failure. You and logic run the game, not the dice.

Second, if a creature (PC or NPC) or object is affected in a harmful way—or, in the case of a creature, in a way that he doesn't want to be affected, harmful or not—you need to involve a die roll. Whether the action is slashing with a blade, using deception to trick someone, intrusively reading an NPC's mind, breaking down a door, or applying poison, something is being harmed or affected in a way that it doesn't want to be, so a die roll is needed.

Thus, someone using a power to become invisible likely doesn't require a roll. It just works. There's really no chance of failure (unless the power comes from a faulty device or some other extraneous force is at work), and it doesn't directly affect anyone or anything other than the character becoming invisible. However, using a device to shape the emotions of another creature would require a die roll.

Of course, sometimes a character can use Effort to reduce the difficulty so there's no need to make a roll. But you, as the GM, can also waive the need for a roll. Consider a character who throws an incendiary grenade into a bunch of level 1 rats. Each has only 3 health, and the PC needs to roll only 3 or higher to affect each one, but there are twenty-four rats. You can simply say, "With a powerful explosion of heat, you incinerate the swarm of rodents, leaving little behind but scorch marks and the smell of burned hair." This keeps things moving and prevents the game from coming to a dead stop while the player makes two dozen rolls. Frankly, most first-tier characters will find level 1 creatures merely a nuisance, so no drama is ruined when the character takes them all out. Move on to another, greater challenge.

When you waive the need for a die roll, what you're effectively doing is making the action routine, so no roll is needed. In the case of the grenade-tossing character, you're reducing the difficulty by one step due to circumstances: the rats just aren't that tough. That's not breaking the rules—that's *using* the rules. That's the way the game is meant to be played.

As an aside, this doesn't mean that the swarm of rats is a bad encounter. It would be bad in a game where it takes an hour and a half to resolve a fight that was no real challenge. But in The Strange? Even if a character doesn't have a grenade, an encounter like that can be resolved in five minutes. Not every encounter needs to be life-or-death to be interesting. But we'll talk about designing encounters (and the related issue of pacing) in the next chapter.

TYING ACTIONS TO STATS

Although the decision is open to your discretion, when a PC takes an action, it should be fairly obvious which stat is tied to that action. Physical actions that involve brute force or endurance use Might, as do those that draw upon the physical essence of the character. Physical actions that involve quickness, coordination, or agility use Speed. Actions that involve intelligence, education, insight, willpower, or charm use Intellect—this includes most psychic abilities, magic spells, and so on.

In rare instances, you could allow a PC to use a different stat for a task. For example, a character might try to break down a door by examining it closely for flaws and thus use Intellect rather than Might. This kind of change is a good thing because it encourages player creativity. Just don't let it be abused by an exuberant or too-clever player. It's well within your purview to decide that the door has no flaws, or to rule that the character's attempt will take half an hour rather than one round. In

GMs can encourage smart players to be ready with their actions, and to know enough about how actions work so that you don't have to ask if they're using Effort, or even tell them that they need to make a roll. In a perfect world, when it's Miranda's turn and you ask what she's doing, she says, "I'm going to try to swing my sword to hit the umber wolf. I'm going to use a level of Effort, and I rolled a 14." That way, you can just take that information and immediately tell her if she succeeded or not. This keeps play moving at a wonderfully brisk pace, and doesn't let game-mechanics talk bog things down.

other words, using a stat that is not the obvious choice should be the exception, not the rule.

THE FLOW OF INFORMATION

You are the eyes and ears of the players. They can't know anything about the world unless you tell them. Make sure that the information you provide is both precise and concise. (We'll discuss good description in the next chapter.) Be evocative, but not to the point that the players lose details in the language you use. Be open to answering their questions about the world around them.

Remember, most of the time, powers, abilities, devices, and so forth are written from the point of view of the PC. But only players make die rolls. So, for example, if the circumstances call for an NPC to make a defense roll, that means a PC should make an attack roll instead.

Sometimes it's easy: a PC looks over the top of the hill, and you tell her what she sees. Other times things are hidden, or there's a chance that she misses something important—secret panels, cloaked assassins, creatures with natural camouflage, details of significance in a crowded marketplace, and so on. In these cases, perhaps a roll is involved. But it's odd to ask players to roll when they haven't taken any actions. It's within the bounds of the rules, but it can be jarring. There are different ways to handle the situation: you can call for a roll, compare levels, or use an intrusion.

GM Calls for Rolls: This is the most straightforward approach. It's always the best choice if a PC's action is to search, listen, or otherwise keep an eye out. If a PC is on watch while her comrades rest, call for an Intellect roll immediately and use the result if anything happens during the entire time she is guarding.

But what if the PC isn't actively looking? Let's say a pickpocket moves up behind her to lift her wallet, so you ask the player to make an Intellect roll with a difficulty equal to the pickpocket's level. (Arguably, she could make a Speed-based roll to see if she is quick enough to catch a glimpse—it's up to you.) Some PCs are skilled in perceiving, and that would come into play here. Success means that you tell the PC what she sees, and failure means that she notices nothing. However, the player knows that she had to make a roll, so she knows that something was up. One way to keep players on their toes is to call for rolls when there is nothing to notice.

GM Compares Levels: You can take the player out of the equation (so as not to alert her suspicions) by comparing the PC's tier to the difficulty of the perceiving task. Ties go to the PC. You can still figure in skills and assets as bonuses to the PC's tier. So a third-tier character trained in perceiving will spot the level 4 sark stalking up behind him. This method is particularly good for determining simple results, such as whether the PC hears a river in the distance. That kind of thing isn't worth a roll, but for some reason, you might not want to give out the information automatically. This method also rewards a perceptive character, who will hear the noise before anyone else. Don't forget to increase the difficulty for distance in such a situation.

Sark, page 288

GM Intrudes: Rarely, you can keep things to yourself and spring the knowledge of what happened as a GM intrusion. If the PC discovers that her pocket is now empty of her wallet, that's certainly a complication. Sometimes the "discovery" itself is a complication—for example, the PC notices a mugging going on in the alley as she walks by.

In addition, the GM is the source of knowledge about the part of the PCs' lives that doesn't take place in a game session. If a character used to be in the military and needs to know the name of her old unit commander, you need to give it to the player (or, better yet, let her come up with the name).

FAILURE TO NOTICE

Consider PCs missing a sensory detail very carefully. If there's a cool secret chamber in the ancient complex or an important clue under the desk in the office, maybe a perceptive PC should just find it (no roll required), particularly if she said she was looking. To do otherwise might mean submitting to the tyranny of the dice. Just because the PC rolled a 2, should the adventure come to a dead stop?

Well, in the first place, don't design a scenario that can come to a dead stop if the PCs botch one roll. There should always be multiple paths to success. In the second, consider your other options. Maybe the PCs will learn about the secret chamber later and they'll have to backtrack to find it. If the characters don't find the clue under the table, an NPC might—and then lord it over them with a show of superiority.

If all else fails, as noted above, sometimes discovery is a complication, and you can simply foist it upon a PC through GM intrusion. In such a case, however, you might want to include a challenge. For example, the PC finds the secret door accidentally by leaning against the hidden control pad, which lets out the sark guarding the chamber before the characters are ready for them.

On the other hand, perhaps in such a situation, the PCs didn't "earn" the discovery—if there was no roll, then no Effort was expended and no risks were taken. That's not good. Maybe the PCs just miss out this time. Maybe they should learn to be more observant. In other words, the answer depends on the situation. Don't hesitate to vary things. It keeps the players guessing.

GRADUATED SUCCESS

Sometimes, a GM will break away from the traditional model that governs task resolution and allow for a graduated success. With this method, she sets a difficulty as usual, but if the player succeeds at a difficulty at least one step higher, his success is better than normal. Likewise, if his roll indicates that he would have succeeded at one step (or more) lower, he might have a partial success.

For example, a PC is tracking wolves across a farm in South Dakota. Given the terrain and the weather, the GM decides that the difficulty is 4, so the target number is 12. The player rolls a 10. This isn't enough to accomplish the task that the PC set out to do, but since he would have succeeded if the difficulty had been 3, the GM decides that he still learns that something had come down the path recently—he just isn't certain if it was wolves or some other animal. The reason is that if the PC had simply been looking for tracks of any kind, the GM would have set a difficulty of 3.

Similarly, if the player had rolled a 17—a success at least one step higher—the GM would have said that not only did he find wolf tracks, but there were five of them, and their tracks show that one of them was injured. In other words, the player would have received more information than he asked for.

In a situation where there are more results than simply success or failure, the GM can convey these results based on multiple difficulties. A player can state an action, and a GM can come up with not one difficulty but two, three, or more. For example, if the PCs try to persuade a clerk to give them information, the GM can predetermine that he gives them one minor bit of information if they succeed at a task with a difficulty of 2, a fair bit of information if they succeed at a task with a difficulty of 3, and everything he knows on the topic if they succeed at a task with a difficulty of 4. The players don't make three different rolls. They make one roll with a scaled, graduated success.

As a rule of thumb, reverse-engineer the situation. If the player rolls considerably higher or lower than the target number (more than 3 away), consider what a success at the difficulty he did overcome would have gained him. If creating a makeshift electronic key to open an electronic door has a target number of 18, what does the PC create if the player rolls 16? Perhaps the answer is nothing, but perhaps it is a makeshift key that works intermittently.

This system is rarely (if ever) used in combat or situations where something either works or doesn't. But when crafting an object, interacting with an NPC, or gaining information, it can be very useful. Of course, the GM is never required to use this model of task resolution—sometimes success or failure is all you need to know. Usually, graduated success involves going only one step higher or lower than the original difficulty, but the GM can be as flexible about that as she wishes.

Last, sometimes a GM can offer a "consolation prize" for trying. Say a PC fears that a door has been rigged with a trap. He searches it but fails the roll. The GM might still reveal something about the door. "You don't find anything special, but you do note that the door appears quite sturdy and is locked." It's the kind of information the GM might give automatically (think of it as a difficulty of 0), but it softens the blow of failure. Some information is better than none, and it makes sense that the PC will learn at least something if he studies an object for a few minutes.

It's true the GM's job requires preparation and planning. But don't let that discourage you from trying it. If you use an adventure that's been prepared ahead of time, such as The Curious Case of Tom Mallard on page 386 of this corebook, you'll discover that a lot of the heavy lifting has already been done.

DEALING WITH CHARACTER ABILITIES

A lot of people might think that The Strange is a class-and-level game because it has things that are enough like classes (types) and levels (tiers) that it's easy to see the misconception. And that's fine.

But here's the real secret: it's not tiers, types, or any of that stuff that is the key to really understanding the system.

It's the cyphers.

In fact, the game system behind both The Strange and Numenera is called the Cypher System. The cyphers are the key to making the game work differently than other games. The Strange isn't about playing for years before a character is allowed to teleport, lay waste to a dozen enemies at once, or create a mechanical servant to do his bidding. He can do it right out of the gate if he has the right cypher.

This system works because both the GM and the player have a say over what cyphers a character has. It's not limiting—it's freeing.

The easiest way to design a good game is to limit—and strictly define—PC power. Characters of such-and-such a level (or whatever) can do this kind of thing but not that kind of thing. The GM knows that the characters aren't going to ruin everything because they can see into the past or create a nuclear explosion.

But that's not the only way to design a good game. What if you—the GM—decide that while it would not be so great if the PCs could see into the past (which would ruin the mystery of your scenario), it would be okay if they could blow up half the city? The Cypher System allows you to permit anything you feel is appropriate or interesting.

To put it another way (and to continue the ever-more-absurd examples), PCs who can solve every mystery and blow up every city probably end up making the game a pushover (and thus dull), but PCs who can solve one mystery or blow up one city won't ruin the campaign. Cyphers allow the characters to do amazing, cool, and fun things—just not reliably or consistently. Thus, although they potentially have access to great power from time to time, they have to use it wisely.

As the GM, it's important to remember the differences among a character ability gained through type or focus, an ability or advantage gained through an artifact, and an ability gained through a cypher. The first two kinds of abilities will shape the way you expect the characters to behave, but the cyphers won't. If a PC has the Works the System focus, she's going to be messing around with mechanical systems all the time—it's what she does—so it shouldn't catch you off guard. In a way, you should "prepare" for it. That word is in quotes because it doesn't mean that you nullify it. Don't put in a bunch of machines that are impossible to hack. That's no fun. Hacking is what she does, and if you take that away, she doesn't get to do anything. (Foiling her power every once in a while is fine because it might add to the challenge, but it should be the exception, not the rule.) By "preparing" for her ability, don't expect an electronic security system to keep her out. Be ready when she slips inside the installation, and be ready to tell her what she finds.

Works the System, page 83

But with cyphers, no preparation is necessary. First of all, most of them don't throw a wrench into anything—they just help the character deal with a situation in a faster way, giving her some healing, a temporary boost, or a one-use offensive power. Second, the PCs never end up with a cypher that you didn't give them, so you can have as much say over their cyphers as you want. And third (and perhaps most important), when a PC pulls out a grenade cypher and blows up the lead cycle in a motorcycle club's "cavalcade," completely changing the situation, that's part of the fun. You'll have to figure out on the fly what happens next, and so will the players. That's not ruining things—that's what is supposed to happen. Players surprising the GM is part of the game. Cyphers just make those surprises more frequent, and in ways as interesting as you're willing to allow.

We'll look at designing encounters later, but for now, remember this point: no single encounter is so important that you ever have to worry about the players "ruining" it. You hear those kinds of complaints all the time. "Her telepathic power totally ruined that interaction," or "The players came up with a great ambush and killed the main villain in one round, ruining the final encounter."

No. No, no, no. See the forest instead of the trees. Don't think about the game in terms of encounters. Think about it in terms of the adventure or the campaign. If a PC used a potent cypher to easily kill a powerful and important opponent, remember these three things:

1. She doesn't have that cypher anymore.
2. There will be more bad guys.
3. Combat's not the point of the game—it's merely an obstacle. If the players discover a way to overcome an obstacle more quickly than you expected, there's nothing wrong with that. They're not cheating, and the game's not broken. Just keep the story going. What happens next? What are the implications of what just happened?

SKILLS AND OTHER ABILITIES

Sometimes, the rules speak directly to character creativity. For example, players can make up their own skills. It's possible to have a skill called "tightrope walking" that grants a character a better chance to walk across a tightrope, and another skill called "balance" that gives a character a better chance to walk across a tightrope and perform other balance actions as well. This might seem unequal at first, but the point is to let players create

precisely the characters they want. Should you let a character create a skill called "doing things" that makes him better at everything? Of course not. The GM is the final arbiter not only of logic but also of the spirit of the rules, and having one or two single skills that cover every contingency is clearly not in the spirit.

It's important that players play the character they want. This concept is supported not only with the open-ended skill system but also with the ability to get an experience point advance to tailor a character further. Likewise, the GM should be open to allowing a player to make small modifications to refine her character. In many cases, particularly ones that don't involve stat Pools, Armor, damage inflicted, or the costs of Effort or actions (like revisions or twists), the answer from the GM should probably be, "Sure, why not?" If a PC ends up being really good at a particular skill— better than she "should" be—what's the harm? If Thomas the vector can swim incredibly well, how does that hurt the game in terms of the play experience or the story that develops? It doesn't. If Victoria the spinner can pick practically any mundane lock she finds, why is that a bad thing? In fact, it's probably good for the game—there's likely something interesting on the other sides of those doors.

In a way, this is no different than adjudicating a not-so-straightforward solution to a challenge. Sometimes you have to say "No, that's not possible." But sometimes, if it makes sense, open yourself up to the possibility.

HANDLING NPCs

Nonplayer characters are people and creatures that live in the world alongside the PCs. They are just as much a part of the world as the PCs and should be portrayed as realistically as PCs. NPCs are the main way to breathe life into the world, tell the stories the world has to tell, and portray the kind of game you want to run. Memorable NPCs can make or break a campaign.

NPCs shouldn't be "cannon fodder" because no one thinks of themselves that way. Real people value their lives. They shouldn't be idiots, easily fooled into doing things or acting in ways that no person ever would, simply because a die roll suggests it (unless they're not very bright or something more powerful—like mind control—is at work).

Think about real people that you know or characters from books, television, and movies. Base your NPCs' personalities on them. Make them as widely varying, as interesting, and as deep as those people.

Remember, too, that there are minor characters and major ones, just like in a book. The Ardeyn Borderlands bandits who waylay the PCs are in the spotlight for only a few minutes at most and don't need a lot of development, but a major adversary or ally might get a lot of attention from the players and therefore deserves a lot from you. As with so many things related to being a good GM, consistency and believability are the keys to developing a good NPC.

NPC GAME STATS

NPCs should be easy to create. Most can simply be pegged at a level from 1 to 10 and you're done. Working on how to describe or portray them will take longer than working up their game stats.

Sometimes, though, you'll want to elaborate on the NPC's capabilities and tailor them to the concept. A level 4 NPC who is an electrical engineer might be level 5 or 6 in engineering-related tasks, such as repairing electrical devices. But don't simply make the NPC level 5 or 6 overall because then she'd also be better at combat, interactions, climbing, jumping, and everything else, and that doesn't fit your concept.

When naming NPCs, consider their recursion of origin. Earth names can be based on current Earth names, anywhere in the world.

Names in Ardeyn should recall fantasy tropes, ancient Sumerian, or both (such as Urun of the Blade or Anazarbus of the White Eye).

In Ruk, names follow the form of X-y, such as Kun-murim, Warad-arad, and Sin-susil.

Use the NPCs in Chapter 17: Nonplayer Characters as good starting points or as examples for what you can do. But you're not limited by them. In fact, you're not limited in any way. The most important thing to remember about NPCs in The Strange is that they do not follow the same rules as PCs. They don't have descriptors, types, or foci. They don't have tiers or any of the same stats. They don't even roll dice.

NPCs work precisely as you (and the setting and story) need them to. If an NPC is the greatest swordsman in the land, you can give him obvious advantages with a sword in attack and defense, but you can go outside the box as well, allowing him to attack more than once per turn, attempt to disarm foes with a flick of his blade, and so on.

There are no hard-and-fast rules for creating an NPC who can be matched perfectly against the PCs in combat—it's not that kind of game, and that's not the purpose of NPCs. Instead, use the game's simple mechanics to portray the NPCs in the world and in your narrative so that they make sense and can do what you want them to do (and cannot do what you don't want them to do).

Like the player characters, NPCs often carry and use cyphers. Thus, any NPC could have virtually any capability at his disposal as a one-shot power. In theory, NPCs can heal themselves, create force fields, teleport, turn back time, hurt a foe with a sonic blast, or do anything else. An NPC might also use magic, possess mutant powers, or have biotech implants, depending on the recursion. You can lay out these cyphers and abilities when preparing for the game, or you can just go with the idea that certain NPCs can produce amazing and surprising effects and make them up as you go along—with some caveats.

If all NPCs can do whatever they want, whenever they want, that won't instill much believability in the players or give you much credibility as a GM. So keep the following things in mind.

Keep to the Level: NPCs should generally keep to their level parameters. Sure, you can give a tough NPC more health than his level might indicate, and the aforementioned great swordsman might attack and defend with his blade at higher than his normal level, but these are minor exceptions.

Explain Things However You Want: If you keep to the level parameters generally, you can express them in all sorts of interesting ways. For example, a level 5 NPC usually inflicts 5 points of damage. But that damage might come from waves of magical force that he can produce thanks to an ancient curse that affects his family.

Wild Cards: You might give some NPCs—wizards, cobblers with many strange devices, and the like—a wild card ability that allows them to do interesting things like levitate, use telekinesis, construct objects of pure force, and so forth. You don't have to nail down these powers ahead of time. These rare NPCs can just do weird things. As long as you keep them reasonable most of the time, no one will bat an eye. (If every important foe has a force field, that will seem repetitious, dull, and unfair to the PCs.)

Use GM Intrusions: Since a PC can produce all kinds of interesting, useful, and surprising effects thanks to cyphers, you can occasionally replicate this for an NPC by using GM intrusion to give him precisely the ability needed in the current situation. If the NPC has been poisoned, he pulls out a vial of antivenom. If a villain is cornered by the PCs, she activates a device on her belt that lets her phase down through the floor. If the foe is at the extreme edge of health, he injects himself with a temporary adrenaline boost that restores 15 points of health immediately.

NPCs AND DEATH

As explained in chapter 17, NPCs have a health score rather than three stat Pools. When an NPC reaches 0 health, he is down. Whether that means dead, unconscious, or incapacitated depends on the circumstances as dictated by you and the players. Much of this can be based on logic. If the NPC is cut in half with a

ENCOURAGING PLAYER CREATIVITY

The Strange is a game that places more importance on creativity than on understanding the rules. The players should succeed not because they've chosen all the "right" options when creating their characters but because they come up with the best ideas when facing challenges. This means that for every challenge, there should be a straightforward solution (destroy the lightning-emitting turret to get into the tower) and a not-so-straightforward one (sneak up to the tower, find the power conduit to the turret, and sever it). It's not your responsibility as the GM to come up with both. The players will come up with the not-so-straightforward solutions. You just have to be willing to go with their ideas.

This doesn't mean you have to let them succeed if they try something weird. On the contrary, the not-so-straightforward solution might end up being as hard as or harder than the straightforward one. But you have to be ready to adjudicate the idea no matter what. It's tempting to say that there's no way to find or sever the power conduit and the PCs have to destroy the turret the old-fashioned way (a combat encounter). In some situations, that might be appropriate—perhaps the conduit is simply not accessible to the PCs on the outside of the tower. But a GM has to be willing to say that sometimes it is possible and to adjudicate the details on the fly. If you don't, and you shut down the players' outside-the-box ideas, they will learn that the only thing to do is charge into the fray every time. That the obvious solution is the only possible solution. Eventually, this will make for boring play because things will seem repetitive and too tightly structured.

The best solution is not to develop preconceived notions of how the PCs might deal with the encounters in an adventure. If they're going to break into a clone factory in Ruk, you can note that the factory has a few guards, a bio-sensing alert system around the perimeter, and a lightning-emitting turret on the top. But you don't know if the PCs will fight the guards, bribe them, or sneak past them. You don't know how they're going to deal with the alert system and the turret. That's not the kind of thing you need to think about ahead of time, but you have to be ready when it comes up at the table. You should prepare for the most obvious situations—for example, predetermine the level of the turret and how much damage it does. But when a player states that his action is to look around for spots where the turret cannot strike because a wall blocks it or the angle prevents it, that's when you take a second to consider and (particularly if he rolls well on an Intellect action) maybe say, "Yes, as a matter of fact, there is a spot," even if no such thing had occurred to you before that moment.

chainsaw, he's probably dead. If he's mentally assaulted with a telepathic attack, he might be insane instead. If he's hit over the head with a club, well, that's your call.

It depends on the intentions of those who are fighting the NPC, too. PCs who want to knock out a foe rather than kill him can simply state that as their intention and describe their actions differently— using the flat of the blade, so to speak.

INTERACTIONS

Let's say the PCs want to learn more about a missing man, so they talk to his best friend. You and the players roleplay the conversation. The players are friendly and helpful and ask their questions with respect. Do you call for an Intellect roll (using the friend's level to determine the difficulty) to see if he will talk to them, or do you simply decide that he reacts to them well and gives them the information?

As another example, an old woman has watched over the entrance to an ancient ruin for years. She considers it a duty given to her by the gods and has never told anyone the secrets she knows. The PCs come along with some training in interactions, roll dice, and expect the woman to spill her guts. Does she tell them everything?

The answer to both questions is: it depends. In either situation, you're justified in ignoring the dice and mechanics and simply handling things through table conversation. That's what makes interaction encounters so interesting and so distinctive from, say, combat. You can't put aside the dice and act out the fight between the PCs and a dark energy pharaoh, but you can roleplay a conversation. In such cases, you can portray the NPCs precisely as you want, in ways that seem fitting to their personalities, without worrying about die rolls. The best friend

Dark energy pharaoh, page 264

probably wants to help the PCs find his missing comrade. The old woman would never give her secrets to a band of smooth talkers that shows up on her doorstep one day. You can also ensure that the players get the information you want them to get—and don't get the information you don't want them to get.

On the other hand, sometimes using game mechanics is a better option. For example, a person who isn't particularly eloquent might want to play a character who's a smooth talker. You wouldn't require a player who's never fired a gun in real life to prove that he's a marksman to win a fight in the game, so you should not force the player of a charming character to be, well, charming. The game mechanics can simulate those qualities.

And sometimes, you can use both approaches. You can let the conversation with the NPC play out around the table, and then call for rolls—not to determine whether the PCs succeed or fail at the interaction but to get an idea of the degree of success. For example, if the characters have a good cover story for why the guards at the gate should let them pass, the roll might determine not whether the guards say yes (you can use logic for that) but whether the guards accompany the PCs beyond the gate. In a way, the die roll shapes an NPC's reaction. It's not an on/off switch but a general degree of the overall trust that the PCs earn.

When an NPC joins the group, consider how long you want that situation to hold. If the PCs seem to enjoy their interactions with that NPC, maybe she should stick around for a while. On the other hand, if the PCs frequently forget that she is even around, or if the load of running that NPC becomes too much for you with other GM duties to attend to, you can come up with an excuse as to why she must leave or arrange for her to come to a bad end during exploration or combat.

NPC ALLIES

Because the players usually roll all the dice, NPCs who are not opponents raise unique issues in The Strange. If a character gains an NPC ally who accompanies the group, how are the ally's actions resolved?

Most of the time, the GM should decide what makes the most sense in the context of the situation and the NPC. If the characters climb up a steep slope and must make rolls to ascend, the NPC doesn't make a roll. Instead, the GM quickly considers whether he could climb it and goes from there. A fit, able ally should simply climb the slope. A feeble or overweight NPC will need assistance. In other words, the NPC doesn't face the challenge (that's what the PCs do)—he remains a part of the unfolding story. The old man the PCs must escort through dangerous mountains needs help climbing because that's part of the story of the adventure. His able-bodied son who also travels with the group does not need help because that wouldn't make much sense.

If the entire group is caught in a landslide later in that same adventure, the GM can do one of two things in regard to the NPCs. Either decide what happens to them as seems most logical or fitting (perhaps using GM intrusion, since what befalls the NPCs also affects the PCs), or have the players roll on behalf of the NPCs and treat them just like the player characters in every way possible.

CREATURES

Whenever possible, creatures should be handled like other NPCs. They don't follow the same rules as the PCs. If anything, they have greater latitude in doing things that don't fit the normal mold. A many-armed beast should be able to attack multiple foes. A charging rhino ought to be able to move a considerable distance and attack as part of a single action.

Consider creature size very carefully. For those that are quick and hard to hit, increase the difficulty to attack them by one step. Large, strong creatures should be easier to hit, so decrease the difficulty to attack them by one step. However, you should freely give the stagger ability to anything twice as large as a human. This means that if the creature strikes a foe, the target must make an immediate Might defense roll or lose its next turn.

A creature's level is a general indicator of its toughness, combining aspects of power, defense, intelligence, speed, and more into one rating. In theory, a small creature with amazing powers or extremely deadly venom could be high level, and a huge beast that isn't very bright and isn't much of a fighter could be low level. But these examples go against type. Generally, smaller creatures have less health and are less terrifying in combat than larger ones.

The Strange has no system for building creatures. There is no rule that says a creature with a certain ability should be a given level, and there is no rule dictating how many abilities a creature of a given level should have. But keep the spirit of the system in mind. Lower-level creatures are less dangerous. A level 1 creature could be poisonous, but its venom should inflict a few points of damage at most. The venom of a level 6 creature, however, might knock a PC down a step on the damage track or put him into a coma if he fails a Might defense roll. A low-level creature might be able to fly, phase through objects, or teleport because these abilities make it more interesting but not necessarily more dangerous. The value of such abilities depends on the creature that uses them. In other words, a phasing rodent is not overly dangerous, but a phasing battle juggernaut is terrifying. Basic elements such as health, damage, and offensive or defensive powers (such as poison, paralysis, disintegration, immunity to attacks, and so on) need to be tied directly to level—higher-level creatures get better abilities and more of them.

GAMEPLAY OPTIONS

In an attempt to keep the game relatively simple, the rules in chapter 8 are designed to be streamlined, straightforward, and easy to use. However, some might desire a bit more complexity, especially as the game goes on, in order to remain engaged and challenged. If you want more robust rules or more options to tailor the game, use some or all of the optional rules in this section.

TRADING DAMAGE FOR EFFECT

You can decrease the amount of damage you inflict in combat in exchange for a special effect that is usually attained only on a roll of 19 or 20. To determine the amount of damage you must sacrifice from a single attack, consult the following table, and add the amount for the desired effect to the foe's level. For example, if you want to impair a level 5 monster, you'd have to sacrifice 12 points of damage from an attack (7 plus 5). The player can wait to determine if he hits before deciding whether to trade damage for an effect.

Damage Reduction	Effect
1	Hinder/distract
2	Specific body part
3	Knock back
3	Move past
3	Strike held object
4	Knock down
7	Disarm
7	Impair
8	Stun

Hinder/Distract: For one round, the difficulty of the opponent's actions is modified by one step to his detriment.

Specific Body Part: The attacker strikes a specific spot on the defender's body. The GM decides what special effect, if any, results. For example, hitting a creature's tentacle that is wrapped around your ally might make it easier for the ally to escape. Hitting a foe in the eye might blind it for one round. Hitting a creature in its one vulnerable spot might ignore Armor.

Knock Back: The foe is knocked or forced back a few feet. Most of the time, this effect doesn't matter much, but if the fight takes place on a ledge or next to a pit of lava, the effect can be significant.

Move Past: The character can make a short move at the end of the attack. This effect is useful to get past a foe guarding a door, for example.

Strike Held Object: Instead of striking the foe, you strike what the foe is holding. To determine results, refer to the rules for attacking objects.

Knock Down: The foe is knocked prone. It can get up on its turn if it wishes.

Disarm: The opponent drops one object that it is holding.

Impair: For the rest of the combat, the difficulty of all tasks attempted by the foe is modified by one step to its detriment.

Stun: The opponent loses its next turn.

LASTING DAMAGE

For a more realistic simulation of damage, the GM can use an intrusion to indicate that damage suffered by a player character is "lasting." Most of the time, this damage is described as being a concussion, a broken bone, a torn ligament, or severe muscle or tissue damage. This damage does not heal normally, so the points lost cannot be regained by using restoration rolls. Instead, the points return at a rate of 1 point per day of complete rest (or 1 point per three days of regular activity). Until the points are restored, the damage has a secondary effect.

Using lasting damage is particularly appropriate in cases where it would be an obvious consequence, such as when a character falls a long distance. It is also appropriate for characters who are already impaired or debilitated.

PERMANENT DAMAGE

Similar to lasting damage, permanent damage is a special situation adjudicated by the GM. Permanent damage never heals normally, although certain spells or technology found in recursions that operate under the law of Magic or Mad Science, respectively, might be able to repair damage or replace lost body parts. This kind of damage should be used sparingly and only in special situations.

LASTING OR PERMANENT DAMAGE AS DEATH REPLACEMENT

The GM can use lasting or permanent damage as a substitute for death. In other words, if a PC reaches 0 in all of her stat Pools, she would normally be dead, but instead you could say that she is knocked unconscious and wakes up with some kind of lasting or permanent damage.

ALTERNATIVES TO POINTS OF DAMAGE

Sometimes, a GM might want to portray the dangers of the Strange in ways other than points of damage. For example, a particularly nasty disease or wound might give a character a weakness or inability.

Inability, page 45

Weakness: Weakness is, essentially, the opposite of Edge. If you have a weakness of 1 in Intellect, all Intellect actions that require you to spend points cost 1 additional point from your Pool.

Inability: Damage can also inflict inabilities. As explained in Chapter 5: Character Descriptor, inabilities are like "negative skills." Instead of being one step better at that kind of task, you're one step worse.

MODIFYING ABILITIES

Sometimes, a player can use a special ability in a way that goes beyond its normal bounds. Such changes can be done on the fly. In some cases, it simply costs more points to use the ability in a new way. In other cases, more challenges are involved.

For any Intellect ability with a specific range, you can increase the range by using more mental energy. If you spend 1 additional Intellect point, you can change the range by one step—from short to long, or from long to 500 feet (152 m). You can't increase a range beyond 500 feet. Any Intellect ability that has a duration (anything more than a single action in a single round) usually lasts one minute, ten minutes, or one hour. By spending 1 additional point of Intellect, you can increase the duration by one step, so an ability that lasts one minute can be made to last ten minutes. Durations cannot be increased more than one step.

A player can make a special roll to modify the range, area, or other aspects of an ability. The roll is always modified by the stat it's normally based on.

The GM sets the difficulty for the roll based on the degree of modification. As with any roll, the player can use Effort, skill, and assets to reduce the difficulty.

LASTING DAMAGE TABLE

Damage Type	Description	Other Effect
Might	Broken arm	Useless arm
Might	Muscle damage	Difficulty of all physical tasks is increased by one step
Might	Tissue damage	Difficulty of all tasks is increased by two steps
Speed	Torn ligament	Move at half speed; short move is no more than 25 feet (8 m); long move is no more than 50 feet (15 m)
Speed	Broken leg	Cannot move without assistance
Intellect	Concussion	Difficulty of all Intellect actions is increased by one step

PERMANENT DAMAGE TABLE

Damage Type	Description	Other Effect
Might	Severed hand or arm	Self-explanatory
Speed	Permanent limp	Move at half speed; short move is no more than 25 feet (8 m), long move is no more than 50 feet (15 m)
Speed	Severed leg	Cannot move without assistance
Intellect	Missing eye	Difficulty of most or all physical actions is increased by one step
Intellect	Brain damage	Difficulty of all Intellect actions is increased by one step
Intellect	Blindness	Character acts as if always in complete darkness
Intellect	Deafness	Character cannot hear

Generally, the difficulty falls into one of three categories:

Impossible (modifying an ability to accomplish an effect that has nothing to do with its description or intent)

Formidable (modifying an ability to do something similar to the description or intent, but changing its nature)

Difficult (modifying an ability to do something within the spirit and general idea of the ability)

For example, say a paradox knows the Levitate Creature revision and wants to modify its use in the middle of an encounter. If he wanted to use it to blast someone with fire, that's an impossible task (difficulty 10) because fire has nothing to do with the ability.

If he wanted to use it offensively within the general description of the ability, he might try to make a foe fly up and hit its head on the ceiling. However, turning an ability that is only potentially offensive into an attack changes its nature somewhat, making the task difficult (difficulty 4), but not unreasonable.

CHOOSING TO ROLL

Sometimes, if a player spends points on an action (for example, to apply Effort or to activate an ability), she might want to toss a die even if there is no chance for failure because a roll of 20 reduces the number of points that need to be spent.

In addition, in some situations, particularly in combat, a roll of 17 or higher indicates more damage or a special effect.

In these cases, players are allowed to roll not to determine success but to determine whether they achieve an above-and-beyond success. However, there is risk involved because if they roll a 1, that results in a GM intrusion. It does not necessarily mean failure, although that's an obvious GM intrusion to use.

ACTING WHILE UNDER ATTACK

When a character is engaged in melee combat, doing anything other than fighting makes him more vulnerable. This is true for PCs and NPCs. If a character engaged in melee takes an action other than fighting, each of his opponents can make an immediate extra attack. The only exception to this rule is moving. If the character's only action is to move, he is assumed to be moving slowly and carefully out of the fight, safely withdrawing from combat.

For example, Katherine Manners has her back to a tomb door while fighting two demons. If she tries to open the door, she is taking an action other than fighting, and both demons get to make an attack against her.

MODIFYING THE RANGE OF WEAPONS

If a character with a ranged weapon wants to attack a foe outside the weapon's range, he can do so, but the difficulty of the attack is increased by two steps.

Generally, the increase in range does not extend infinitely. A character using a weapon that has a short range can only try to hit a target that is a long distance away. A character using a weapon that has a long range can try to hit a target up to 200 feet (61 m) away with a difficulty modification of two steps, a target up to 500 feet (152 m) away with a difficulty modification of four steps, and a target up to 1,000 feet (300 m) away with a difficulty modification of six steps. Weapons with ranges that start out greater than long range must be adjudicated by the GM.

Attacks with hard limits, such as the blast radius of an explosive, can't be modified.

OPTIONAL MAJOR EFFECT

When a player's roll would grant him a major effect, instead of taking the effect, he can choose to roll a d6 and add the result to the initial roll. This option makes it possible to succeed at tasks with target numbers greater than 20 without decreasing the difficulty.

Katherine Manners, page 149

Paradox, page 30
Levitate Creature, page 32
Revision, page 30

CHARACTER CUSTOMIZATION OPTIONS

Characters for The Strange are easy to create, but some players will want to customize them more than the system initially allows. They can use the following rules to slightly (or significantly) customize their characters precisely as they wish. As always, the GM is the final arbiter of which optional rules are available in the game.

Inability, page 45

CUSTOMIZING CHARACTER TYPES

The following aspects of the three character types can be modified at character creation as suggested. Other abilities should not be changed. No character should ever give up or trade away her Translation ability.

Stat Pools: Each character type has a starting stat Pool value. A player can exchange points between her Pools on a one-for-one basis, so, for example, she can trade 2 points of Might for 2 points of Speed. However, no starting stat Pool should be higher than 20.

Edge: A player can start with an Edge of 1 in whichever stat he wishes. Because vectors start with an Edge of 1 in both Might and Speed, using this optional rule allows a vector to have an Edge of 1 in any two stats (not just Might and Speed).

Cypher Use: If a starting character sacrifices one starting skill, he can use one more cypher than is listed. Alternatively, if a character gives up one cypher, he gains an additional skill of his choosing. Either way, no more than one cypher should be changed.

Nonvariable Abilities: Each type has static, unchanging abilities at the first tier that don't involve any of the above aspects or any player choice. For a first-tier spinner, that ability is Practiced With Light and Medium Weapons. For paradoxes, it is Practiced With Light Weapons. For vectors, they are Defensive and Practiced With All Weapons. Any one of these abilities can be sacrificed to gain training in one skill of the player's choice.

Spinner, page 38
Practiced With Light and Medium Weapons, page 39

Paradox, page 30
Practiced With Light Weapons, page 32

Vector, page 25
Defensive, page 26
Practiced With All Weapons, page 26

CUSTOMIZING DESCRIPTORS

Under the normal rules, each descriptor is based on some modification of the following: Some descriptors offer +4 to one stat Pool and either two narrow skills or one broad skill. Other descriptors offer +2 to one stat Pool and either three narrow skills or one narrow skill and one broad skill.

A broad skill covers many areas (such as all interactions). A narrow skill covers fewer actions (such as deceptive interactions). Combat-related skills, such as defense or initiative, are considered broad skills.

Regardless, you can add an additional skill if it is balanced by an inability. You can add other nonskill abilities by eyeballing them and trying to equate them to the value of a skill, if possible. If the descriptor seems lacking, add a few hundred dollars of additional equipment to balance things out.

With this general information, you can customize a descriptor, but keep in mind that a heavily customized descriptor isn't a descriptor if it no longer says one thing about a character. It's better to use this information to create a new descriptor that fits exactly how the player wants to portray the character.

CUSTOMIZING FOCI

At any tier, a player can select one of the following abilities in place of the ability granted by the tier. Many of these replacement abilities, particularly at the higher tiers, involve bodily modification with devices or something similar.

Tier 1

Self-Improvement: You gain 6 new points to divide among your stat Pools however you wish. Enabler.

Bringing the Pain: You deal 1 additional point of damage with every attack you make. Enabler.

More Training: You gain an additional skill of your choice (not combat or defense) in which you are not already trained. Enabler.

Tier 2

Lower-Tier Ability: Choose any Tier 1 ability, above.

Offensive Combat Training: Choose one type of attack in which you are not already trained: light bashing, light bladed, light ranged, medium bashing, medium bladed, medium ranged, heavy bashing, heavy bladed, or heavy ranged. You are trained in attacks using that type of weapon. Enabler.

Defensive Combat Training: Choose one type of defense task in which you are not already trained: Might, Speed, or Intellect. You are trained in defense tasks of that type. Enabler.

Tier 3

Lower-Tier Ability: Choose any Tier 1 or 2 ability, above.

Nanotech Health: Thanks to an injection

of artificial antibodies and immune defense nanobots into your bloodstream, you are now immune to diseases, viruses, and mutations of any kind.

Hardy: You have +1 to Armor.

Tier 4

Lower-Tier Ability: Choose any Tier 1, 2, or 3 ability, above.

Resistance: You are immune to poisons, toxins, or any kind of particulate threat. You are not immune to viruses, bacteria, or radiation.

Tier 5

Lower-Tier Ability: Choose any Tier 1, 2, 3, or 4 ability, above.

Adaptive: You are immune to radiation, diseases, and gases. You are resistant to temperature changes (within reason)

Crushing Damage (5 Might points): You inflict 6 additional points of damage in melee.

Keen Eye (5 Speed points): You inflict 6 additional points of damage with ranged attacks.

Tier 6

Lower-Tier Ability: Choose any Tier 1, 2, 3, 4, or 5 ability, above.

Two Attacks (6 Speed points): On your turn, when you would normally make an attack, you make two attacks, either against the same foe or against two different foes.

DRAWBACKS AND PENALTIES

In addition to other customization options, a player can choose to take a variety of drawbacks or penalties to gain further advantages.

Weakness: As noted earlier, weakness is, essentially, the opposite of Edge. If you have a weakness of 1 in Speed, all Speed actions that require you to spend points cost 1 additional point from your Pool. At any time, a player can choose to give a character a weakness and in exchange gain +1 to his Edge in one of the other two stats. So a PC can take a weakness of 1 in Speed to gain +1 to his Might Edge.

Normally, you can have a weakness only in a stat in which you have an Edge of 0. Further, you can't have more than one weakness, and you can't have a weakness greater than 1, unless the additional weakness comes from another source (such as a disease or disability arising from actions or conditions in the game).

Inabilities: Inabilities are like "negative skills." They make one type of task harder by increasing the difficulty by one step. If a character chooses to take an inability, he gains a skill of his choosing. Normally, a character can have only one inability unless the additional inability comes from another source (such as a descriptor or from a disease or disability arising from actions or conditions in the game).

OPTIONAL XP RULES

Usually, players earn experience points by making discoveries or through GM awards. As an alternative to that system, players can suggest that other players earn XP. The GM calls for nominations at the end of an adventure, and the players discuss who did what, who came up with the best ideas, who handled a particular situation well, and so forth. Every character still receives XP, but the players decide who gets how much.

Another option is for a GM to offer XP to the group between sessions and let them split it up however they feel is fair. This method can be used with XP earned for discovery or through GM awards.

Last, the group can decide that experience points earned in different ways are spent differently. One method is to declare that XP earned through GM intrusion is available only for immediate, short-term, and long-term uses, while XP awarded between sessions is used for advancing in tiers.

The advantage to this option is that all characters advance through the six tiers at about the same rate—an important issue for some players. Of course, a good GM can achieve this result on his own by carefully handing out rewards, and many groups will discover while playing that equal advancement isn't an important issue in The Strange, but people should get to play the game they want to play.

GETTING AN XP ADVANCE

By introducing a story complication based on her character's background, a player can start the game with a significant amount of XP (and can spend them immediately if desired, even to advance in tiers). The GM has final approval over this option, and it should be used only in groups that don't insist on all characters having precisely the same power levels.

This story-based concept allows a player to create exactly the character she wants at the outset at the cost of building in a narrative complication for herself.

For example, a player might want to start the game with a sidekick or a defensive field projector somehow brought from a recursion with higher levels of technology. Under the normal rules, these options aren't available to a beginning player, but she could find or build them given time (and perhaps after spending XP). With the optional rule, the character gets an advance XP amount that can be used to "buy" the companion or device, but in exchange, she has an inability with all NPC interactions.

As another example, let's say a player doesn't want to start by playing a new, young vector—she wants to play someone who is older and more experienced. Although The Strange does not assume that all starting characters are fresh young recruits, the player's vision doesn't quite sound like a first-tier vector. So she comes up with a significant drawback, such as a severe addiction to a costly drug, in exchange for an advance of XP that allows her to start at the second tier, with all the benefits of a second-tier character.

These story complications are worth an advance of 4 to 6 XP:

- People find the character extremely unlikable. No matter what he does or says, intelligent creatures and even animals find him unpleasant. Any attempt to interact with creatures is done so as if they were one step higher than normal. Further, the GM should make a default assumption that the baseline with which people treat the character is distaste and contempt.
- The character has a bum leg. It acts up every now and again (at least once per adventure, usually once per session), and when it does, the difficulty of all of her Speed tasks is increased by one step.
- The character has an inability with a significant task, such as attacks, defense, movement, or something of that nature. As a result, the difficulty of such tasks is increased by one step for him.
- The character has an occasionally debilitating condition (bad back, alcoholism, eating issues, and so on). This problem should result in a significant penalty once per session.
- The character is wanted by the law and must keep a low profile. This drawback is something that can cause story-based issues rather than mechanical ones, but it can make life difficult for him at times.
- The character has a defenseless relative or friend who is often at risk. Again, this is not a mechanical issue, but rather one that will affect how the character is played. At times, he will have to stop what he is doing to help the person out of a jam. At other times, the person's life might actually be at risk, compelling the PC to action.
- The character must perform a regular action to retain his abilities. For example, each morning, he must "commune" with an ultrapowerful, artificially intelligent "god" who grants his powers. If this communion is disturbed or prevented, or if the transmission connection is broken or blocked, the PC does not have access to his powers that day.
- The character must have a specific item to use his abilities. For example, he needs a power cell, a focusing crystal, or another object that can be destroyed, lost, or stolen. Perhaps, like a power cell, it needs to be replaced or recharged from time to time.

These story complications are worth an advance of 12 to 20 XP:

- The character is wanted by the law and is actively pursued by multiple NPCs. This isn't just a matter of laying low when she is in town. Instead, NPCs will show up at the worst possible times and attempt to abduct or kill her.
- A condition that the character has causes the difficulty of all tasks involving combat or NPC interaction to increase by one step.
- The character has a truly debilitating condition, such as blindness, deafness, being crippled, severe drug addiction, and so on).
- The character has a defenseless relative or friend who, for some vital reason, must accompany her at least 75% of the time. She will spend a great many actions protecting this person instead of doing what she would rather be doing.
- The character's abilities rely on a rare drug. Without a regular dose of this substance, she is virtually powerless.
- The character was experimented on as a young child, which gave her powers and abilities. To gain new abilities, she must find the original experimenter and replicate the process. This is a major mission and could result in a long delay of character advancement (effectively giving her a boost in power at the beginning but no boosts for a long time afterward).

CHAPTER 20

BUILDING A STORY

TEACHING THE RULES

It's not really your job to teach the players the rules, yet it often falls upon the game master (GM) to do just that. Before beginning a game, encourage players to read Chapter 2: How to Play The Strange to get an overview of the game. It won't take them long.

You'll probably also want to give them an overview of the setting. Focus primarily on the kinds of characters a player can create and what they might do in the game. Once players understand who they are and what they'll do, the rest of the setting is just details they can discover as they go along.

The key to teaching someone the game is to start with the idea of the dice rolls and how they use the same mechanic no matter what a character tries to do. Then explain using Effort, which involves an introduction to the three stat Pools. After that, a player is ready to start making a character. Taking a new player through the character-creation process gets him ready to play. Don't overload him with a lot of details beyond that. All of those can be picked up as needed in the course of play.

THE FIRST FEW SESSIONS

With any game, GMs should consider running it a little differently the first few times, and The Strange is no exception. There are a few things a GM can expect with a table full of new players. First of all, they won't get the terminology and the jargon right—they'll use the terminology and jargon of the last game they played. And that's fine. But the GM should try to get it right because the players will follow her lead, and after a session or two, they'll start getting it right too. If the GM always calls things by the wrong name, the players will, too. However, don't just spout jargon. Each time you use a new term for the first time, such as "damage track," "GM intrusion," or even "difficulty," explain what it means. Make sure everyone's on the same page, even with the basic stuff.

The players won't know what's easy and what's hard. Part of good play in The Strange is knowing when to use Effort and when to conserve, but beginning players will have no frame of reference. In this case, the best way to give them solid ground on which to stand is to be fairly transparent. Tell them the target number for each task before they attempt an action. Guide them through the process. Remind them that they can use Effort if need be, although they probably won't forget. On the contrary, beginning players tend to use Effort on every roll. You can almost count on it. This means you can expect beginning characters to do very well in whatever they set out to do, but they'll have to rest more often because they'll deplete their stat Pools more quickly.

THE FIRST FEW TRANSLATIONS

The first few times the player characters translate, they could become a bit overwhelmed, given the scope of possible change. You have some easy ways to deal with this potential issue, all of which have to do with starting players in the shallow end of the pool rather than dumping them straight into the deep end.

One way is to have your players begin play with characters who are already cognizant of the Strange and how things work, perhaps as agents of the Estate. Even if you do so, or when you specifically want to begin play with characters naive to the Strange, following the tips below can make those first few translations exciting rather than confusing.

Don't Translate During the First Few Sessions: The easiest way to keep players from struggling with the concept of their characters is to run a game where they don't translate for the first session or two. Instead, let the players

Difficulty, page 98

Target number, page 10

Effort, page 17
Stat Pool, page 16

For additional assistance in character creation, see the Character Creation Walkthrough and The Strange *Character Sheets, starting on page 412.*

Translation, page 125

The Estate, page 148

Damage track, page 108
GM intrusion, page 121

enjoy their characters and their first foci on Earth (or whatever recursion you started play on) for a while. Doing so will increase player confidence as their understanding of their characters and of the rules grows. After the players have had a few sessions to "walk in the shoes" of their characters, they'll feel more grounded. When they finally do translate, the players can choose to retain the personalities, looks, descriptors, and types of the characters that they're already comfortable playing, even if their foci and equipment change.

Acclimation period, page 134

The Characters' New Look and Focus: Instead of having naive characters choose their new look and focus the first time they translate to a new recursion, you could do so instead. Appearance is easy—have your players look exactly like they appear on Earth, except with new equipment determined by their focus. You can also choose the PCs' new focus for them, or recommend that they drag their focus to the new recursion (if it's draggable). The next time the PCs visit that recursion, they can choose a different look and focus if they want.

Draggable, page 52

No Encounters During Acclimation: It's tempting for the GM to throw an encounter at players while they are still acclimating from a translation, but for the first few translations, think carefully about doing that, and perhaps avoid it. The acclimation period isn't just for the characters, but also for the players as they get used to the new lay of the land and potentially the new abilities they may have, as well as the lack of a few abilities they had on Earth or a previous recursion.

Don't Overwhelm a Player With New Recursion Knowledge: When the PCs first translate to a new recursion, the translation itself gives them some context about the recursion they're entering, above and beyond any specific knowledge and abilities they might gain from new foci. That knowledge is provided in bullet points at the top of each recursion listing under the header What A Recursor Knows About [this recursion]. Even though the bullet points are supposed to provide recursors with a high-level summary of the recursion, all the bullet points could end up being a little much. Here's a way you can soften that learning curve—give all PCs the first bullet point (the one that describes what law the recursion operates under), and then give each of them one of the other bullet points, which you prepare ahead of time as a note you can easily pass to each player. Then, the PCs can get a better picture of what's going on in the recursion by questioning each other about the bullet point information and the recursion-specific focus information.

RUNNING STRANGE COMBATS

Combats in The Strange should be *about* something. There should be something interesting at stake. "Trying not to die" is an interesting stake, but it's not the only one. Combat can be fun and hopefully exciting in its own right, but it's not necessarily the focus. In other words, fighting through a long combat isn't the point, and finding a way to win a combat quickly through creative thought isn't cheating. In fact, it should be encouraged. Defeating the "big boss monster" easily should not be a letdown; it should be the result of smart, creative play. And adventures shouldn't always have a climax involving a "big boss monster," anyway. The exciting end to the story could involve surviving a massive landslide, finding a way to shut down a dangerous machine, or convincing a tyrannical commander to let the hostages go.

The Strange is about discovery. Can you have discovery through combat? Sure. Say the PCs are exploring the Strange itself and encounter a bizarre life form. The creature attacks, but during the fight, it telepathically says things like "Curious" and "Creature unknown" and "Protect the sanctum." It's telepathically talking to someone else, but the PCs "overhear." Although the combat is fairly standard, the PCs have discovered a new creature, and they know it's something that's never encountered a human before. There are more of them, somewhere, and there's a kind of sanctum. It's not just a fight. The PCs have learned something.

In a more standard setup, the combat is the obstacle that the PCs must overcome to reach the discovery, which again reinforces the idea that there is no right or wrong way to overcome the obstacle. Sneak past the foes or convince them to let the PCs pass—both are entirely valid.

Mechanically, combat in The Strange doesn't play out as it does in many games where damage whittles down a character's hit points or health score. This kind of slow attrition is less likely to happen in The Strange because the PCs will try to avoid getting hit. For example, many players will spend points from their Speed Pool to add Effort to their defense rolls to ensure that they don't get hit (and thus don't lose points from their Might Pool). Characters also have numerous abilities to add to their Speed defense rolls or reduce the difficulty of a Speed defense task. Last, and perhaps most significant, the most frequent use of experience points for rerolls will probably be defensive in nature. Players just don't like their characters to get hit.

There are two important aspects to this. The first is that it's the players' choice. They're in control of which points they lose and how many, so it feels different, even though the effect is largely the same—a slow loss of points over time. The second aspect is that, narratively, you don't have to explain and describe lots of minor wounds and scratches that eventually amount to something. In The Strange combats, when PCs are struck, it's likely significant. Plus, so many creatures and foes have effects that paralyze, infect, poison, stun, and so on that the damage is not necessarily the interesting or significant part of what they do to the PCs. That's why there are creatures whose attacks can move a PC down the damage track a step or two. It's not so much about the points of damage but the consequences of being hit at all.

Encourage the players to describe their actions, not the mechanics involved. The game is more fun if a player says things like, "I leap up on the table and swing my sword down upon the creature," instead of "I use my jump skill to get up on the table to get a one-step advantage on my attack roll."

CRAFTING STORIES

Your biggest job as the GM is to provide the impetus for stories in the game. The stories themselves arise out of gameplay, but they are started and guided by you. You provide the seed of the story and present the events as they unfold because of what the PCs and NPCs do.

Crafting a good story is a topic that could fill a book of this size. Interested GMs should read books or articles aimed at fiction writers (many of which are available on the Internet) that provide advice on plot. For that matter, similar sources about characterization can help in the creation of NPCs, as well. For now, remember these few key concepts:

- Learn what motivates the players at your table. Exploration? Combat? Puzzle-solving? Interacting with NPCs? Cater to these desires.
- Learn what motivates the PCs that they run. What are the characters' goals? What do they seek? Wealth? Curiosity? Power? Protecting others? Use these things to start your stories.
- Create stories that involve the PCs as directly as possible. If something bad is affecting

people, have it affect the PCs or their loved ones too. Rather than enticing them to strive to save a random farmer, get them to save a character's brother or best friend.
- Weave multiple stories together. Have the PCs learn about the beginning of one while they're still embroiled in another.
- Vary your stories. Follow a combat-heavy exploration of an ancient ruin with an intrigue-filled adventure that takes place in a large city that involves a lot of interaction. Create one story that is a long quest but then follow it up with another that wraps up in a single game session.
- Vary the encounters within a story. Even in the middle of a series of battles, there's always room for some exploration or interaction (and it breaks things up).
- Not every story needs to be about saving the world. Sometimes the smaller stories about helping just one person can be the most interesting.
- Base your stories on real human emotion. NPC villains can be driven by greed or power, but also by love, longing, curiosity, or even misguided altruism. Don't make your players just interact with the events—make them react to the emotions behind them. Villains should inspire actual hate and anger. The loss of a valued ally should inspire actual sadness and loss.
- Remember that the players are your co-storytellers, and that the PCs are the main characters of the story, so their decisions should have direct impact on what happens.
- Twists and unexpected events are wonderful and should be used often, but sometimes the biggest twist is to have things go exactly the way the players think it will.
- Don't get bogged down justifying, rationalizing, or explaining every detail. It's okay if the players don't understand everything.
- Stories that involve a lot of events the PCs are unaware of will end up making little sense to the players, and should probably be avoided.
- Occasionally, create stories that are sequels to your previous stories. The decisions that the players made in the past affect things in the present. Villains return for another try at reaching their goal, or perhaps just for revenge.

PACING

The key to running a great game as opposed to an adequate one is often the simple matter of pacing. Well, pacing is simple to describe, but it's not so simple to understand or implement. It comes with practice and a sort of developed intuition.

Pacing can mean many things. Let's briefly break them down.

PACING WITHIN AN ENCOUNTER

Keep things moving. Don't let the action get bogged down by indecisive players, arguments about the rules, or irrelevant minutiae. Don't let the middle of an encounter get sidetracked by something that reminds a player (or worse, you) of a gaming story, a movie, or a funny thing on the Internet. There's time for all of that later, probably after the game session is over.

Don't let the end of the encounter drag out. When it's clear how things are going to turn out, and people might start to get bored, wrap it up. If the PCs were fighting two dozen venom troopers and only three are left, there's nothing wrong with saying that those last three run away or surrender or that the PCs handily dispatch them. Wrap things up and move along.

Venom trooper, page 300

PACING WITHIN A GAME SESSION

Have many different encounters in a session—some long, some short, some complex, some straightforward. One of the trickiest aspects of game session pacing is deciding what to play out and what to skip. For example, the PCs want to buy new gear with the money they were paid for a job in Ardeyn. You could describe the town's market and roleplay each interaction with various merchants. You could even call for occasional rolls to see if the characters get good deals or not. Alternatively, you could say, "Okay, you guys buy whatever you want," and then move on. There are good cases to be made for both approaches, depending on the context. Maybe one of the PCs contracted a disease on the last mission and doesn't realize it until he is interacting with people in the market. Maybe a thief in the market attempts to steal from the PCs, or they notice a thief stealing from a merchant. Maybe the players like interacting with NPCs and enjoy your portrayal of minor characters. All of these are good reasons to play out a shopping encounter. But if there's no compelling reason, just advance through it.

Ardeyn, page 160

Sometimes, you should do this even if one player wants to play out every moment of his character's life and describe everything in

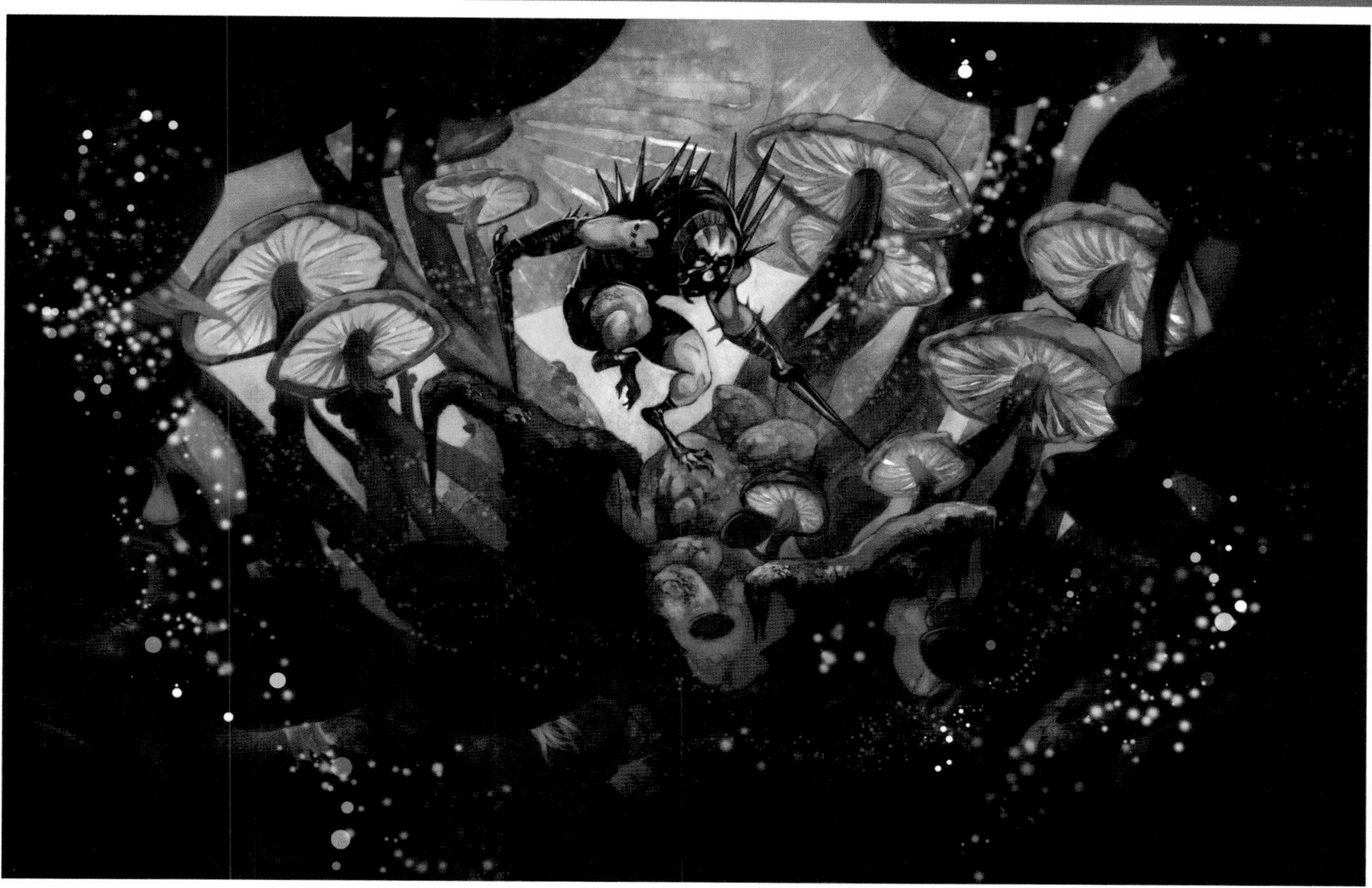

excruciating detail. Although you want everyone to be happy, you're in charge of pacing. If you must err, make the players struggle to keep up, rather than letting them be bored and wondering when you're going to get on with it. Thus, if there's no compelling reason against it, don't hesitate to advance time, even in large chunks. If the PCs finish a big scenario and some downtime makes sense, there's nothing wrong with announcing, "So, three weeks later, you hear that . . ." and starting in on the next storyline (as long as the players are content with it). Books and movies do this kind of thing all the time. *Skip the boring bits.*

In addition, feel free to intrude on player discussions for the purpose of moving things along. Sometimes players spin their wheels or plan and plan their next move, never accomplishing anything. You can intrude by throwing an encounter or a surprise their way ("An agent of OSR sends a message asking for your help"), or you can simply say, "Let's move things along, guys."

Keep a clock handy so you can see how much time is left in the session. *Never lose track of time.* You want to end a session at a good point—a place where everyone can catch their breath, at a good cliffhanger, or as everything in a story wraps up so you can start anew next time. These are all fine stopping points, but you want to control which one you use. Next session, you'll have to start things up again, recap past events, and get everyone back into the swing of things.

Try to ensure that at the end of any session, the players can look back on what they did and feel like they accomplished something.

PACING WITHIN A STORY

This aspect of pacing goes back to researching how fiction writers handle story creation, and it's a huge subject, but consider the standard three-act structure as a good starting point. In act one, the problem is introduced. In act two, things get worse (or a new complication is introduced). In act three, things are resolved. There are many other ways to do it, but remember that the action needs to ebb and flow. You need downtime between the moments of action, horror, or high drama.

PACING WITHIN A CAMPAIGN

Mix short scenarios in with longer ones. Weave the plotlines together so that as one story ends, the PCs still have things to do. But don't be afraid of downtime. Let the characters have a week, a month, or longer here or there to live their normal lives before throwing them once again into the heart of danger. If a campaign takes a year of play time in the real world, you don't want it to take place in only three weeks of game time. That never feels right.

DESCRIPTION

Chapter 19: Using the Rules recommends using description that is both precise and concise. Precision comes from avoiding relative terms like "big" or "small" or emotional words like "terrifying" because these words mean different things to different people. This doesn't mean you have to specify the exact height of every structure the PCs find. But rather than describing a building as "a tall tower," consider saying "a tower at least five times the height of the trees around it."

Being concise is important, too. Go on too long with descriptions, and the players' minds will drift. Sometimes, what works best are short, declarative, evocative descriptions with pauses in between for player comments or questions.

DESCRIBING THE ACTION

Great roleplaying game sessions often involve immersion. Immersion comes from a sense of being truly caught up in the action and the fictional world. Just as when you read a great book or watch a well-made movie, playing an RPG can get you caught up in your own imagination. And best of all, you're sharing your imaginative escape with everyone else at the table. For immersion to work, you have to give great descriptions.

Ardeyn, page 160
Ruk, page 190

Combat in The Strange, for example, is very simple and open-ended rather than precise, giving you lots of room to describe how characters move, how they attack, and how they avoid attacks. A successful Speed defense roll might mean dodging, blocking with a weapon, or ducking behind a pillar. A character who is struck in combat for 3 points of damage might have dodged the weapon attack but fallen backward off an apartment balcony.

The players should describe their actions, too. Encourage them to be creative in what they do and how they perform a task, whether it involves the way they attack, what they do to give themselves the best chance to make a difficult leap over a pit, or how they slip into a noble's study to steal the map they need.

Don't take any of this as a requirement. Long descriptions can be tedious as easily as they can be interesting. Sometimes the best way to serve the pacing of a combat encounter is to state whether an attack hit and how much damage is dealt and keep things moving. Vivid description is great, but it's not a valid excuse for you or a player to drag things out and destroy the pacing.

DESCRIBING RECURSIONS

It's easy enough to describe locations on Earth—we all live here. In fact, it's wonderful to use that to your advantage as much as possible. Utilize places that you have actually been to really give a lot of detail. Use locations that the players are familiar with to add immediacy, or describe a new place using a familiar place: "It's just like the nearby shopping mall, except that it has a second story" or "From the outside, the mansion looks a lot like the old library down the street."

Recursions, however, should be weirder and less familiar. It's tempting to use shorthand descriptions. "The castle looks like Dracula's castle in the movie," for example. Even if that's true, it doesn't convey the otherness of the place. If anything, it just puts the location in the realm of the familiar. But a recursion is an entirely different world. It should always feel alien and strange—not quite right.

Even Ardeyn and Ruk, our most detailed recursions, should be weird and different. In Ardeyn, remember, *magic really works*. That might not seem like such a big deal to roleplaying gamers, but just think what it would be like to go there for real and see sorcerers, minotaurs, dragons—and creatures and places even less familiar than that.

And Ruk? Ruk is literally an alien craft built inconceivably far in the past to travel through a data network outside our own universe.

One way to bring recursions to life is to take a little time to describe what the characters see, hear, feel, and smell. Ardeyn likely seems almost impossibly verdant and alive, utterly untouched by pollution or even Earthlike realities of weather. It's a place imagined, not born of reality. Ruk is ancient and derelict. Even the colors are somewhat off. Ruk probably smells like a cross between an old chemical factory, a rendering plant, and a rainforest.

It's important to note that recursions aren't parallel universes. After translating to a recursion, a character should always be immediately aware that he's someplace strange and unfamiliar. Even those recursions that "mimic" real Earth locations very likely do so with a unique sort of atmosphere. Innsmouth doesn't feel like any old New England coastal town. The Thunder Plains doesn't at any time feel like the real Great Plains.

PREPARING FOR THE GAME SESSION

The Strange doesn't require you to spend hours carefully designing stats for NPCs (unless you want to). There aren't a lot of rules to memorize. It's not worth writing out elaborate descriptions of each encounter because if you allow things to proceed organically, many planned encounters might not be used. The rules of The Strange allow you to come up with a lot of the details as you go along, since you don't have to reference loads of books and stats during the game session.

To prepare for a session, you need to create only three things: a list of names, a brief outline, and a list of ideas.

1. A list of names. No matter how much you prepare, you'll end up creating some NPCs on the fly, so have a list of names to use when this happens. Leave room to write a quick note next to each name you use in case that NPC shows up in the game again.

2. A brief outline. The outline is an idea of where you think the story could go. Of course, the key word is *think*. You can't know for certain—the actions of the PCs will take things in unexpected directions. In truth, "outline" is probably not the right word. Think in terms of places the PCs might go, people or creatures they might interact with, and events that might occur. For example, let's say that the PCs are in a small town on Earth. You plan to start the session by having them hear about a local man named Rob Horner who disappeared mysteriously because he accidentally activated a cypher that took him to another recursion (Ruk). Your notes might say:

- Rob disappeared outside the auto parts store where he worked. North of town.
- Rob lived in a small, run-down house. Wife: Becky, and two kids. Becky: distraught and prone to drink.
- Auto parts store: Six employees. Boss: Michael Finney.
- Witness: Sarah is very religious. Sarah saw Rob disappear right in front of her. Doesn't want to talk to anyone about it because she's scared it might be a sign of the end times (level 4). Knows Rob recently won a strange object in a poker game from a guy named Todd Rorvick—looked like two silver coins joined at the edges.
- Local toughs (who don't like strangers in town) attempt to start a fight with the PCs (level 3).
- Todd Rorvick: Recluse with the spark who doesn't want to talk about it, but has translated to Ruk and back before (level 5). Willing to trade information for information, however, since he's very curious about anything having to do with the Strange.

And so on.

Obviously, that's just the beginning, but you've covered a lot of the contingencies, assuming the PCs investigate Rob's disappearance at all. Some of that material might not get used. The PCs might not go to his house—only to the store and then to Todd. Maybe they won't go to Todd at all, but the PCs will recognize the item as a translation cypher (a Strange lore task). Or maybe the PCs will come up with a wholly unexpected path of investigation.

3. A list of ideas. Just like with the list of names, jot down a bunch of random ideas. These are things you can throw into the game at a moment's notice. They might be flavor, cool visuals, or important side plots. For example, your list might include:

- Insane Rukian woman with tentacle grafts
- Encounter on a collapsing bridge
- Someone tries to poison the PCs' food
- Man with violet eyes and an impossibly deep voice
- Injured dog that will befriend the PCs if they help it.

These are all ideas that you can sprinkle into the game when appropriate. You haven't tied them to a specific encounter, so you can insert them whenever you want.

HANDLING PLAYERS

Part of being a GM is "handling" players. This means a lot of things. For example, it's partially

Innsmouth, page 253

Thunder Plains, page 246

your job to make sure that everyone has a good time. You need to ensure that all the players get to do the kinds of things they like to do in games, and that no one is left out. If one player really likes combat and another enjoys NPC interaction, provide some of both. Before you can do that, you need to find out what the players want in the first place, so talk to them and learn their expectations.

Another big part of handling players is coping with disruptive players. Disruptive players can be the death of a game. They can hog all the attention, tell other players what to do, or challenge your rulings at every turn. A lot of GMs are tempted to deal with such players during the game by punishing them or giving them negative feedback. For example, they have the character get attacked more often, lose experience points, or suffer similar consequences. Resist this temptation. Instead, speak with the player person to person (not GM to player) outside of the game and explain that his behavior is causing problems. Be clear, direct, and firm, but also be friendly.

The bottom line, however, is don't play games with jerks. One disruptive, rude, or offensive player can ruin the whole group's fun.

A different problem player is one who just doesn't get the narrative focus of The Strange. These kinds of players tend to see all games as competitive enterprises, and they might try to "win" The Strange by exploiting what they see as holes in the rules to create and play an unbeatable character. Although part of many people's RPG experience is the fun of playing a powerful character, it shouldn't be the ultimate goal in The Strange because such a player will get frustrated and bored.

For example, a player might try to use the Energy Protection revision to protect against kinetic energy and then claim that he is immune to all attacks. He'll see this as a hole that he was smart enough to exploit, and he'll hold up the rules and say, "Show me where I'm wrong!"

When a player does that, point him here: "You're wrong."

On the other hand, some players absolutely will get it. They'll understand that it's the spirit of the rules, not the letter, that's important. They'll get that the story being told is key. Rather than poring over the description of a power and trying to twist the words to an unintended meaning, they'll use their intelligence and creativity to figure out the best way to use the power to portray a character who fits the setting and is fun to play.

Sometimes, even the term "adventure" gets just as messy as "encounter." Deciding where one adventure begins and another ends can be—and perhaps should be— difficult. "Adventure" is a useful term for published products, but for your own use, you might want to toss the concept out and just let one story or event flow into another naturally.

People who try to exploit the *rules* don't understand The Strange, but people who exploit the *situations* do. If a player is smart and creative enough to turn the tables on his foes in an unexpected way by using what's around him, allow it (if it makes sense). If the PCs find a pool of caustic fluid and lure their foes into it rather than fighting them in a straightforward manner, that's not cheating—that's awesome.

Be certain you don't accidentally penalize players for not doing the obvious or straightforward thing. Be generous with people who take nonstandard actions or who do something realistic (such as using their action to take stock of the situation rather than attack—grant them a step bonus). Don't make "attack" always the right choice. It's a creative game, so allow the players to be creative.

MATURE THEMES

Sometimes, it's appropriate to involve mature themes in The Strange games. Sex, extreme violence, and other topics certainly fit into the setting. But the members in the group are going to have to decide for themselves if it fits into their game. You should also prepare your stories with your specific players in mind. If one or more are very young, or have issues with certain topics, avoid things that would be inappropriate. Also be aware that some topics, like overt sexuality, rape, and graphic violence are the kinds of things that might disturb players even when you aren't expecting it. It's always best to know for certain before allowing these topics into your game.

Think of it like the movie rating system. If you can tell the story that you want to tell in a G or PG (or even PG-13) way, you're likely fine. If events unfold that are going to give your game an R rating or higher, it's best to talk with your players ahead of time. It's not a matter of good or bad, it's a matter of appropriateness for the "audience" and giving people a heads up ahead of time—just like movie ratings.

DESIGNING ENCOUNTERS

Encounters are to a game session what scenes are to a movie or a book. They're a way to break up the session, and the adventure at large, into smaller, more manageable chunks.

Sometimes it's difficult to know where one encounter ends and another begins. For that reason, "encounter" is not always a useful or meaningful game term. It's only useful for you when you think about the scenes of your adventure. When the PCs go talk to the agents of the Estate, that's one encounter. After they do so, hopefully getting the information they need, they translate to Ardeyn, which might be an encounter itself. Once in Ardeyn, they head off into the wilderness where they have to cross a deep chasm—another encounter. When a giant appears and attacks, that's another encounter, and so on.

Thus, not everything that happens is an encounter. Heading off into the wilderness, for example, probably involved gathering supplies, deciding on a route, and so on, but it isn't really an "encounter." An encounter is when you, the GM, are going to provide a lot of detail. You and the players are going to interact a lot in an encounter. You might decide to subdivide everyone's actions into rounds to help keep track of who's doing what, when.

COMPLEX ENCOUNTERS

Encounters aren't just about combat. As mentioned above, talking to NPCs is an encounter. Dealing with a physical obstacle is an encounter. Figuring out how to use an alien machine is an encounter. The best encounters—the really memorable ones, in fact—are going to involve multiple things happening at once. A fight on a boat racing down the rapids, for example, is an interesting encounter. An encounter where a couple of PCs must disable a giant bomb while the others fend off attacking inklings is interesting too.

Sometimes, then, an encounter can be intentionally designed with that goal. At least occasionally, you should take an idea you have for an encounter and then add in something else that will make it even more interesting, exciting, or challenging. In The Strange, the possibilities are endless. Perhaps gravity functions differently than expected. There's a weird fungus giving off spores that alter perception. The encounter takes place inside a sentient machine that must be reasoned with and appeased while everything else is going on. And that's just for starters. Use the strangeness of the setting to your advantage to make things crazy and fun. Design encounters that are like nothing that the players have ever experienced.

But sometimes these kinds of encounters with multiple levels of action or weird complications just arise out of the game itself. The PCs have to leap onto a moving platform to get down into the high-tech factory's interior conduit system, which is interesting, but the defense robots that they ran from earlier suddenly show up while they're doing so, having finally caught up with them. You didn't plan for that ahead of time; it just happened because that's the way things went. Which is great.

Lastly, GM intrusions can bring about these kinds of encounters on the fly. The PCs have to close an inapposite gate beneath a vampire's castle before a planetovore uses it to enter the recursion. With a GM intrusion that occurs to you at the last moment, you reveal that the exhalations of the planetovore's minions guarding the gate are filling the atmosphere with hallucinogenic gas that makes the encounter even more difficult and bizarre.

Inkling, page 273
GM intrusion, page 121

Inapposite gate, page 135
Planetovore, page 8

BALANCING ENCOUNTERS

In The Strange, there is no concept of a "balanced encounter." There is no system for matching creatures of a particular level or tasks of a particular difficulty to characters of a particular tier. To some people, that might seem like a bad thing. But as mentioned earlier, matching character builds to exacting challenges is not a part of this game. It's about story. So whatever you want to happen next in the story is a fine encounter as long as it's fun. You're not denying PCs XP if you make things too easy or too difficult, because that's not how XP are earned. If things are too difficult for the PCs, they'll have to flee, come up with a new strategy, or try something else entirely. The only thing you have to do to maintain "balance" is set difficulty within that encounter accurately and consistently.

In a game like The Strange, if everyone's having fun, the game is balanced. Two things will unbalance the game in this context.

One or more PCs are far more interesting than the others. That's "more interesting," not "more powerful." If one character can do all kinds of cool things but can't kill inklings as efficiently as another does, that player still might have a whole lot of fun.

The challenges the PCs face are routinely too easy or too difficult. The first issue should be handled by the character creation rules. If there's a problem, it might be that poor choices were made or a player isn't taking full advantage of her options. If someone really doesn't enjoy playing her character, allow her to alter the character or—perhaps better—create a new one.

The second issue is trickier. As previously stated, there is no formula that states that N number of level X NPCs is a good match for Tier Y characters. However, when the game has four or five beginning characters, the following guidelines are generally true.

- Level 1 foes will be nothing but a nuisance, even in sizable numbers (twelve to sixteen).
- Level 2 opponents will also not be a challenge unless in numbers of twelve or more.
- Level 3 opponents will be an interesting challenge in numbers of four to eight.
- Level 4 opponents will be an interesting challenge in numbers of two or three.
- A single level 5 opponent might be an interesting challenge.
- A single level 6 opponent will be a serious challenge.
- A single level 7 or 8 opponent will likely win in a fight.
- A single level 9 or 10 opponent will win in a fight without breaking a sweat.

Damage track, page 108

But be forewarned, and this can't be stressed enough—it depends on the situation at hand. If the PCs are already worn down from prior encounters, or if they have the right cyphers, any of the expectations listed above can change. That's why there is no system for balancing encounters. Just keep in mind that beginning characters are pretty hardy and probably have interesting resources, so you aren't likely to wipe out the group by accident. Character death is unlikely unless the PCs have already been through a number of other encounters and are worn down.

RESOLVING ENCOUNTERS

Don't plan for how an encounter will end. Let the game play determine that. This ensures that players have the proper level of input. You decide, for example, that if the PCs go into the tower, there is a gang of mutants inside that will attack. You can't, however, decide how that encounter will end. Maybe the PCs will be victorious. Maybe they won't. Maybe they'll flee, or maybe they'll bargain for their lives.

If you try to decide such things ahead of time, that's called railroading the game, and it puts the players in the role of observer rather than actor. Even if you try to plan out the results of an encounter ahead of time but then let the game play dictate them, you still might end up planning a lot on outcomes that don't happen. In other words, if you base a whole plotline on the PCs fleeing out of the tower with the mutants, but instead they drive the mutants out instead, all your plans are wasted.

Plan for various possible outcomes, but don't predetermine them. Think of your story as having many possible plotlines, not just one.

CHALLENGING CHARACTERS

If the game has a balance problem, it's more likely due to players finding things too easy rather than too hard. If things are too hard, they should run away and find something else to do (or you should lighten up a bit). But if the characters in the group need a greater challenge, try one or more of the following options.

Damage Track: Sometimes a few points of damage aren't enough to scare a player, but a weapon or effect that immediately moves him one step down the damage track will terrify him. No matter how big a character's stat Pools are, no matter how much Armor he has, there are only three such steps to death.

Ongoing Damage: Poisons that inflict even a small amount of damage (1 or 2 points) every round until an antidote is found can be extremely deadly. Or consider this: one of the reasons that napalm is so terrible is that it clings to surfaces, including flesh. Imagine a weapon or effect that inflicts 5 points of fire damage every round and persists for eight rounds unless the characters can figure out a way to douse it.

Effects Other Than Damage: Attacks can blind, stun, grapple, paralyze, infect, hobble, or otherwise hinder a character without dealing any points of damage at all.

Effects That Harm Equipment: A PC's gear is often the source of his abilities. Destroying or nullifying cyphers or artifacts damages him just as surely as breaking his leg would—it limits a player's options, which really hurts.

Enemies Working in Concert: Although a group effectively acting as one is a special ability of some creatures (such as inklings), you could apply it to any creature you like. As a general rule, for every four creatures working together, treat them as one creature with a level equal to the highest of them plus 1, with a minimum of a +2 damage bonus. So a level 4 bandit who has three level 3 allies could team up and attack one foe as a level 5 NPC. That means their attack deals more damage and is harder to defend against. It also means less die rolling, so the combat moves along faster.

Beef up the Foes: You're in charge of the NPC stats. If they need more Armor, more health, or higher levels to be a challenge, simply make it so. It's easy and straightforward to give an NPC a "boost package" of four things:

- +10 health
- +1 to Armor
- +3 points of damage
- Attacks and defends as one level higher

That should do the trick, but if necessary, give the boost package to the same NPC again.

Beef up the Obstacles: Include more exotic materials in doors and other barriers, which increase their difficulty by one to three steps. Make physical challenges more difficult—the surfaces that need to be climbed are slippery, the waters that need to be swum are roiling, and other actions are hampered by strong winds. Don't beef up obstacles in this way too often, but remember that circumstances such as weather are your tools for adjusting the difficulty of any action.

HIGHER-TIER CHARACTERS

Although characters start out quite capable, by the time they reach the fifth or sixth tier, they will be truly legendary. Both you and the players might find reaching the upper tiers more rewarding and satisfying if the journey unfolds more gradually, so you can slow down this progress if desired. To do this, starting at third or fourth tier, you can specify how the players can spend the experience points they earn. Requiring that some XP (as much as half) must be spent on immediate, short-term, or long-term advantages—rather than on character advancement—will slow down the progression through the upper tiers. But it won't take anything away from the play experience because spending XP on those advantages is fun and rewarding, too.

CHARACTER DEATH

Challenging characters is important. If there is no threat of failure—or at least the perceived threat of failure—it's hard for them to feel compelled into the story. And very often, the ultimate failure a PC might face is death. The Strange is a dangerous place. But death is serious because it means the player can no longer play his character.

If a character dies, the easiest and most straightforward response is to have the player create a new character. Ideally, he will make a beginning character (which is the easiest to create), but if the other characters are third tier or higher, it will be more satisfying to let the player create his new character at an advanced tier.

However, keep in mind that a lower-tier character can operate effectively in the company of higher-tier characters. The differences are not so striking. If a player brings a new beginning character into a group of advanced characters, be particularly generous with XP to help the new character catch up to the others a bit. Regardless, arrange the circumstances of the story so that you can bring in the new character in a logical fashion and as quickly as possible.

Not Quite Dead: There is an alternative for a player who really, really wants to keep playing the same character. Allow the PC to teeter on the brink of death but survive, saved by his companions (or through sheer luck). Such a character might recover but have serious injuries that result in a weakness, an inability, or another drawback. The point is not to penalize the PC (although barely escaping death should have some repercussions) but to change the character in a memorable way.

"I didn't enjoy killing my team. But they'd been infected with the Second Seed virus. If they'd come back to Earth through the inapposite gate, who knows what might've happened? Still, their deaths are on my hands, and I live with the guilt every day." ~Sergeant Wallace, OSR recursor

GM

ARTHUR

AN EXAMPLE OF PLAY

Sometimes the best way to understand a game is to see it played. This section provides the next best thing: a script depicting a group playing through an encounter in The Strange.

GAME MASTER: You know the woman who stole the ancient tablet works at a small appliance shop in the city, and your informant gave you the address after you bribed him. You finally find the address around dusk. By the time you get out of your car, you can see that the door into the little shop has a "closed" sign on it. It's locked.

ARTHUR (playing a paradox named Kingston): Is it a busy street?

GM: No, it's quiet.

GWEN (playing a spinner named Reina): Let's see if we can break in.

LANCE (playing a vector named Locke): I don't know if that's a good idea.

ARTHUR: Is there a way to jimmy the lock or pick it? I don't want to smash a window or anything if we don't have to. Gwen, can you use your Hack the Impossible ability to open the lock?

GWEN: I think that's mostly for computer system and electronics. This is just a regular lock, right?

GM: If there's a more complex security system, you're not aware of it.

ARTHUR: Just him saying that makes me a bit nervous. Now I'm worried there might be alarms or a security camera or something.

GWEN: If we see something like that, I can take care of it.

ARTHUR: I search more carefully for signs like that.

LANCE: I just keep a watch out on the street.

GM: Okay, both of you should make rolls. It's an Intellect task in both cases.

ARTHUR: I'm going to apply a level of Effort. I have an Edge of 1 in Intellect, so it costs me 2 points from my Pool.

The GM knows there's no complex security system here, but she muses for half a second as if pretending to figure out a target number.

GM: Roll.

ARTHUR: Rolled a 7.

GM: You don't find anything.

LANCE: Well, I don't have an Edge in Intellect, so I'm not going to use Effort for this. I roll a 13.

The GM also spends a heartbeat pretending to consider this, but again, she knows there's nothing to see on the street.

GM: You think it's still clear.

GWEN: I'm going to try to pick the lock. I don't have that skill, though.

GM: As you fish around in your bag to find something to try to pick the lock, you notice through the window in the door that a light has come on inside—in the back.

GWEN: Oh!

ARTHUR: Lance, I thought you were keeping a watch!

LANCE: On the street, not in the store.

GWEN: I'm going to knock on the door then.

ARTHUR: Are you sure you should?

GWEN: I'm better with people than with locks.

GM: After you knock on the door a few times, you see more lights come on inside. An older man sort of shuffles up to the door. He has thick glasses and a balding head. "We're closed!" he shouts.

GWEN: I say loudly, "I just need to talk to you for a moment, sir." You two try to look nonthreatening.

LANCE: I smile broadly.

ARTHUR: Whatever.

GWEN: "I'm sorry to bother you. I won't take but a minute of your time."

GM: He seems hesitant. Particularly since there's three of you.

GWEN: I was going to wait until he opened the door, but I guess this is the time to use my Fast Talk ability. It costs 1 Intellect point, but I also have an Edge of 1 in Intellect, so it costs me nothing. I want to tell him it's okay to open the door.

GM: You need to make a roll.

The old man is level 2, so Gwen needs to roll a 6 or higher.

GWEN: I roll 11.

GM: The old man looks at you, and then just shrugs and opens the door. "Whattaya need, miss?"

GWEN: "Thank you, sir. We're looking for a woman named Faye who we believe works here?"

The GM knows that she could have Gwen roll again for this interaction—the Fast Talk was just to get the door open—but Gwen is being polite and her character, Reina, is trained in pleasant social interactions. So the GM decides to give her some information without a roll. In game terms—although the GM might not take the time to fully spell this out—she's giving Reina an asset for being polite. That, coupled with Reina's training, reduces the difficulty 2 task by two steps, making it a routine task.

GM: "Oh, yes, Faye works here. Sweet lady. Didn't show up for work today, though."

ARTHUR: "Aha! That's what we figured."

GM: The old man scowls at Kingston. "What's all this about?"

GWEN: Let me do the talking! "Faye has something of ours. We were supposed to pick it up from her."

The GM knows this is a lie, and now the old man is suspicious. That's going to increase the difficulty by one step to 3.

GM: That's an Intellect-based task.

GWEN: I'm going to use Effort.

LANCE: I'm going to help. I'm an Appealing vector, so I have training in this.

GM: Okay, well, with Gwen's Effort and skill, and Lance's help, that reduces the difficulty to 0, so there's no roll needed. Nice work. The man says, "Well, I can show you where she sits. She does our books in the back. Maybe she left it there. Funny she didn't say anything to me about it, though."

LANCE

GWEN

GM

ARTHUR

GWEN: "We really appreciate this." We follow him in.

ARTHUR: I'm still going to keep an eye out for a security camera or anything like that.

GM: The old man takes you through the little store and into the back. It's kind of a shabby little office with some file cabinets, a coffee machine, a box of stale-looking donuts, and a couple of desks. He motions to one of them. "That's where Faye sits." The desk is pretty tidy.

ARTHUR: We search it.

LANCE: Actually, I'm going to focus my attention on the old man. I ask him his name and make general chit-chat.

GWEN: We both will. We want to keep his attention while Kingston searches.

GM: Okay, the two of you completely distract him. You find out his name is Charlie. Arthur, you find some ledgers, office supplies, and that kind of thing—nothing surprising. There's an old computer on the desk, powered off.

ARTHUR: I'm no good with computers. Gwen's character's Hack the Impossible ability would come in handy right now. I look around for a handbag or anything like that.

GM: There's a bag next to the desk.

ARTHUR: I open it.

GM: You see a strange stone tablet hastily wrapped in bubble wrap.

ARTHUR: That's it! I grab the whole bag. "Well, here it is! Just like Faye said."

GM: Before anyone can react, there's a noise from the front of the store. Two women and a man come in. They're all well-dressed. The dark-haired woman says, "We're here for the tablet."

LANCE: Who are these guys?

GWEN: It's the September Project! They're looking for the tablet too, remember?

GM: The old man looks frightened and confused.

LANCE: I put myself between the old man and these intruders. In fact, I put myself in front of everyone.

GM: Okay. After that, you're all going to have to roll initiative.

These agents of the September Project are all level 4 NPCs. That means that the target number to beat them in initiative (and just about anything else) is 12. It also means that they have 12 health and if they hit in combat, they will do 4 points of damage.

LANCE: I roll a 17.

GWEN: You know what? I really want to go first. I apply a level of Effort, which will cost me 2 points from my Speed Pool since I have an Edge of 1 in that. I roll a 10.

ARTHUR: Oh no. I roll a 1.

GM: Arthur, I'm guessing you were probably going for your weapon on your turn?

ARTHUR: Yes.

GM: In your haste to do so, you drop the bag on the floor. There's a loud thunk that draws everyone's attention.

GWEN: Oh no!

ARTHUR: I check to see if the tablet's all right.

GM: You can do that on your turn. Meanwhile, it's clear that the agents all know exactly where the tablet is as they looked at the bag when they heard the thunk. Lance, what do you do?

LANCE: They haven't made any hostile moves yet, and it seems wrong to attack first. I'll wait, but if any of them tries anything besides talking, I'll punch them.

GM: Okay. Gwen, your Effort paid off. You go before they do.

GWEN: Great. I use Fast Talk again. This time, I say to the dark-haired woman, "We don't know what you're talking about. You should just let us go home." I roll a 14.

The GM decides that since the agents heard the stone tablet hit the ground, they think Gwen is obviously lying. She's using a special ability, but the difficulty is 5 with an increase of one step.

GM: The woman's pretty clearly not buying it. In fact, she draws a gun and levels it at Arthur. "Back away from the bag."

LANCE: That sounds like my cue. I attack.

GM: Okay.

LANCE: I have the No Need for Weapons ability as well as the Brawler ability. I roll a 20!

GM: Do you want to deal 4 extra points of damage, or get a special effect?

LANCE: Well, I'm already inflicting 5 points. The extra damage would be nice, but I think I'll take the special effect and knock the gun out of her hand. I'd like it to go flying as far away as possible.

GM: Your blow almost knocks her off her feet. Her pistol sails away and slides across the floor beneath a shelf of goods. You foil her action entirely. The other woman also draws a handgun, however, and fires it at you, at point blank range. Make a Speed defense roll for Locke.

LANCE: I roll a 7.

GM: The bullet grazes your left arm, drawing blood and inflicting 4 points of damage. The old man, Charlie, shouts, "Don't shoot! Don't shoot! Take the money!"

GWEN: Poor guy has no idea what's going on.

GM: The male agent grabs the bag on the floor.

ARTHUR: No!

GM: It's your turn, Arthur.

ARTHUR: I grab the bag away from this guy.

GM: That's going to require an attack roll, and—if you succeed—a Might-based task to pull it out of his hands.

ARTHUR: I roll a 15 to grab it.

GM: Okay. You've got your hands on the bag as well. Now let's see if you can pull it away from the agent.

ARTHUR: I'm going to use Effort, so that's 3 points from my Might Pool. I roll an 11.

GM: You have the bag.

ARTHUR: Do I have time to glance down at the tablet quickly?

GM: Sure. You can see that a piece did break off, but it's mostly intact.

LANCE

GWEN

GM

ARTHUR

ARTHUR: Let's hope it's still okay.

GM: Lance, it's your turn.

LANCE: I attack the woman who just shot me. I roll a 10.

GM: She blocks your punch with her forearm and takes a step back. Gwen?

GWEN: I tell Charlie to hide behind the desk and then I'm going to leap to attack the woman with the gun. I don't have a weapon, so I'll just grab the first thing I can get my hands on from one of the desks.

The GM thinks for a moment and then slides a pair of XP cards toward Gwen. Gwen knows this means GM intrusion.

GM: The old man panics and tries to run out of the room entirely, but in doing so, he gets right in your way, Gwen. What do you do?

GWEN: I don't want to do anything to risk harming him. What are my options?

GM: You can do whatever you like, but if you still want to attack, you'll have to get around Charlie. That will be a Speed-based task.

GWEN: Can I change my action entirely? Use a twist?

GM: Yes, but the old man is still right in your way. He's going to make things harder, most likely.

GWEN: I'll just try to grab a weapon but not attack with it.

GM: You can grab a coffee pot half full of cold coffee. It's a light weapon.

GWEN: Good enough. I'll give my additional XP to Lance for disarming the first woman.

GM: Speaking of whom, she says, "Get that bag!" Then, since the old man is mainly in her way as well, she just grabs him and tosses him against the wall.

GWEN: I hate her.

GM: The other woman fires her gun again. Lance, make another Speed defense roll.

LANCE: This time I use Effort. My Speed Edge of 1 makes that 2 points from my Pool. I roll a 15.

GM: You duck out of the way of her second shot. The man tries to grab the bag back from you, Arthur. Make a Speed defense roll.

ARTHUR: I roll a 13.

GM: You keep it out of his reach. What do you do?

ARTHUR: Time to pull out the big guns. I use my Exception revision on this guy. I roll a 19! I'll take the extra damage, so that's 7 points.

GM: He yells out in pain as there is a strange flash of light around him for a moment. He seems quite hurt. Lance?

LANCE: I attack the woman who keeps shooting. I kick her and roll a 14. If that's a hit, I inflict 5 points.

GM: You kick her and she slams against the wall. She's hurt, but she's still got her weapon trained on you.

GWEN: I smash her in the face with a coffee pot. I roll a 10.

GM: It's a light weapon, so that reduces the difficulty by a step. You strike her for 2 points of damage. The pot doesn't shatter. She uses her pistol as a melee weapon and lashes back at you, Gwen.

LANCE: I want to intervene and block that blow.

GM: Well, you're right next to her, so if you want, you can take the blow. You're automatically hit for 5 points of damage.

LANCE: Ow!

GWEN: Chivalry isn't always necessary.

LANCE: Yes, it is.

ARTHUR: If you two are done flirting?

GM: Both the man and the disarmed woman try to grab the bag with the tablet from Kingston. In these close quarters, I'm going to say that at this point, working together, they get their hands on it. The only thing in question is whether Kingston can keep his grip with both of them tugging on it.

ARTHUR: I'm going to use Effort to hang onto it. But my Pool is dwindling fast. I roll a 16.

GM: You hang onto it, but it's really hard.

ARTHUR: I need a free hand to use my revisions, and I want to keep both on the bag, so instead, I'll use my Good Advice ability and try to give Lance a hand with his next attack.

LANCE: Thanks! On my action, I'll attack the woman one more time.

GWEN: No, attack one of the people with the bag. I'll take care of her.

LANCE: Well, uh . . . okay. It's kind of against my nature, but I'll leave Gwen's side and attack the dude pulling on the bag. I'll use Effort to add to damage. I roll a 10, but Arthur's advice is giving me training in this task, right?

GM: Right, so you deck him. Effort adds 3 points to your normal damage of 5, which knocks him to the floor, out cold.

The level 4 NPC agent with 12 health had taken 7 points already. Suffering 8 more points, then, takes him down. Since Lance is punching, the GM rules that the guy is just knocked out.

GM: Gwen?

GWEN: I swing the coffee pot again at the pistol woman. I roll a 4, so that's probably a miss.

GM: It is. She ducks. However, she sees the guy on the ground and rubs her jaw where she got hit already. She bolts for the front door. The other woman curses and follows her, clearly not willing to be left here alone. Do you want to try to stop them?

ARTHUR: Let's let them go. We have what we need. With this tablet, we can translate to the secret tower in Ardeyn.

LANCE: Fine by me. I'll give them quarter. Besides, I could use a moment to catch my breath and make a recovery roll.

GWEN: I help the old man.

As the PCs recover from the fight, the GM determines what the September Project agents will do. They'll likely call for backup and return, guns blazing. Of course, if the characters don't wait to translate, they'll be long gone by then. Instead, they'll be in Ardeyn with new bodies, new gear, and new foci. But the September Project has the means to cause them trouble in that recursion as well...

LANCE

GWEN

CHAPTER 21

RUNNING A STRANGE GAME

The Strange offers a setting like no other. It is, in many ways, multiple settings linked together. A campaign can be science fiction one session, fantasy the next, and superheroes in the third. When players translate during gameplay, there's even the opportunity to span two or more of those settings in a single session.

INTRODUCING PLAYER CHARACTERS TO THE STRANGE

The standard campaign for The Strange assumes that the PCs begin play on Earth with some knowledge of the dark energy network of the Strange. The benefit to this approach is that it avoids heaping the responsibility of *all* the revelation on the GM's shoulders via all the NPCs under the GM's control as the game begins. It also eases the tension on the PCs to continually pretend to be utterly amazed, when most of the players already know full well that the concepts of the game include translation into alternate worlds. For instance, gameplay is eased if all the characters already know something about the dark energy network and recursions, because play isn't constantly interrupted by characters asking themselves, "Now, *why* would *I*, having just learned about all this crazy stuff, jump through that portal? Wouldn't I just call the CIA or Homeland Security?" and similar questions.

If having all the characters know about the Strange is too much for you, try a mix: some, but not all, of the player characters begin the game knowing about the Strange and recursions. That way, the characters in the know can reveal information to the characters who are "off the street" and don't have all the facts.

Of course, you should do what you want. But to accomplish the goals described above, we suggest that you use one of the following in-the-know character scenarios to begin a game in the Strange for most (or all) of the player characters. Then, along with those characters in the know, you might still start one or more characters with no prior knowledge of the Strange, possibly by using one of the naive character suggestions.

PCS IN AN ORGANIZATION

Characters that begin "in the know" are likely members of the Estate or the Quiet Cabal. To accomplish their goals, these organizations employ agents to explore recursions, defend the Earth, and create conditions that foster safety. The PCs were likely invited to join due to being quickened, which makes them a rare and valuable asset.

In exchange for the organization's direction, guidance, and resources, the PC pledges to uphold the organization's charter (which varies in specifics between the Quiet Cabal and the Estate, but generally has to do with protecting the Earth from dangers of the Strange).

The guidance and resources provided by the organization vary depending on the campaign, the mission, and the PC's relationship to the organization. Either way, the PCs were recruited for the abilities they possess, which have the potential to outshine other organization members who aren't quickened. Ultimately, this means that instead of relying on the organization to do their job for them, characters should get in the habit of taking charge and accomplishing things on their own initiative.

IN THE KNOW CHARACTERS	NAIVE CHARACTERS
Estate Operative	Off the Street
Quiet Cabal Agent	Six Weeks Later
Ardeyn Native	Character Player

ESTATE OPERATIVE

A character can begin play as an associate or operative of the Estate. The exact relationship of the PC to the organization depends on the character's background, but at least one of the PCs should begin as a full-fledged operative.

Operatives have a wide (though probably not deep) knowledge of the nature of the Strange, recursions, and the difference between quickened and nonquickened people (PCs are always quickened). They may have even translated to Ardeyn or Ruk a few times prior to the first game.

Associates are closer to recruits, but they have probably encountered certain aspects of the Strange already, especially their own peculiar abilities. They probably also know that the world isn't as mundane as most people believe.

First Mission: Play begins when characters are assigned their first Estate mission by a field supervisor, usually in a branch office or other covert location. Typically, the mission involves several other associates and/or operatives (the rest of the PCs in the group). This mission is meant to be for training. As such, it's straightforward, possibly along the lines of a simple research trip, an investigation of a location that's seen recent Strange action, or something similar.

You can design a mission of your own or run The Curious Case of Tom Mallard, the adventure in chapter 22 of this corebook. The first part of the adventure has been designed with this scenario in mind.

What's Next: If the PCs finish the first mission successfully, an associate may be promoted to operative, other characters picked up along the way may be invited to become associates, and PCs that were already operatives may receive a commendation.

QUIET CABAL AGENT

Unlike the Estate, which is headquartered on Earth, the Quiet Cabal is based in Ruk, with several sanctums scattered around Earth. One

Many more details regarding the Estate are presented in chapter 11 (page 148) including some history, a roster, and other elements of the organization.

The Curious Case of Tom Mallard, page 386

Quickened, page 22

Ardeyn, page 160
Ruk, page 190

is either a full-fledged agent of the Quiet Cabal or not associated with the organization at all. Although different agents can have different jobs, all are expected to do the work of the Cabal in whatever capacity is necessary.

A PC Quiet Cabal agent could be an Earth native and work out of a sanctum, or a Ruk native who has translated to Earth to work out of that same sanctum. Either way, the PC begins with a broad knowledge of the Strange in general and a deep knowledge of the recursion of Ruk. On the other hand, a Ruk native is likely still somewhat naive when it comes to many specific details of living on Earth.

Sanctum, page 153

The Quiet Cabal, page 153

First Mission: The Cabal assumes that its agents do not need handholding, though the value of teamwork is well understood when team members are available. A PC's first in-game mission isn't likely to be a training run; instead, it's a dangerous situation that needs handling, fast. The mission might be to kill a dragon that's come through an inapposite gate, put down a faction of the Karum discovered to be operating out of a warehouse, or infiltrate a location in Ruk where terrorists are keeping hostages.

The Karum, page 200

You can design a mission of your own or run The Curious Case of Tom Mallard, the adventure in chapter 22 of this book. Though the introductory text presents the first half of the mission as a training mission, the whole adventure is perfectly viable for all characters and could be presented as such.

What's Next: Being an agent of the Quiet Cabal means the PC has a room of her own in the sanctum, access to whatever weaponry or research material is available, and full run of the facilities. Accomplishing a mission means the PC continues that access. In chapter 11, you'll find descriptions of a typical sanctum on Earth and the activities of the Quiet Cabal.

ARDEYN NATIVE

In this case, the PC originated in Ardeyn instead of on Earth. At some point, she discovered the truth about Earth, other recursions, and the Strange. Of course, all natives of Ardeyn know something of the Chaosphere, which surrounds the world and is visible from most places in it. However, this PC has special knowledge over the average Ardeyn native, equivalent to Estate operatives and Quiet Cabal agents, vouchsafed to her from another Ardeyn source. It might have come from the writings of a soulshorn, from the lips of the Oracle, from the patronage of a qephilim master, or perhaps as an inheritance in the form of a magic artifact with sentience and purpose.

First Adventure: If you want a PC from Ardeyn to join other PCs on Earth, the first mission of an Ardeyn native might be a solo one. This could be the exploration of a ransacked Estate outpost with a working translation gate, the delivery of a warning to someone on Earth regarding actions of the Betrayer or his agents, fleeing from a kray infestation, or a similar situation that lets the PC from Ardeyn rendezvous with PCs who begin on Earth.

What's Next: Ardeyn natives are often motivated by the same thing that entices typical fantasy adventurers to risk their lives: loot. In the course of any adventure of The Strange, loot in the form of crowns, better equipment, cyphers, and artifacts should almost always be forthcoming.

OFF THE STREET

Despite the popularity of origin stories, we recommend that you do not begin play with all the players naive to the Strange unless you have time to do a little extra planning and preparation. That said, having just one or two players who are "off the street" join characters who know more about the situation can be quite satisfying. That way, the burden of explaining background naturally falls to the knowledgeable characters as a normal part of roleplaying, allowing the GM to concentrate on the main adventure.

For many off-the-street characters, the first adventure may be their first brush with new powers unlocked by their type, with concepts of alternate worlds called recursions, and with the idea that magic may actually work in the right recursion. That said, when a naive character first finds a cypher or attempts to try one of his abilities, the GM should encourage the PC so it doesn't feel out of character for him to try something new.

For example, if the PC finds a cypher, tell the character something like, "The object seems familiar to a part of you that you've only glimpsed in dreams prior to now. You know this object has a special property that you can call on if you try." If an off-the-street character is dealing with a dangerous situation, remind her that it's fine to use her type-granted powers, even if she's never done so before. For instance, you might say, "The threat kindles new knowledge in you. You don't know why or how, but you know that if you try, you might shatter the pistol in the gunman's hand."

First Close Encounter: Like the first mission described for an Estate member, the off-the-street character's first mission should be straightforward. Ideally, a naive character joins a character in the know, or the knowledgeable character rescues this character, after which the naive character has to take responsibility for his own safety by becoming part of the team.

What's Next: The main reward for off-the-street characters is probably that they survive, thanks to their abilities and/or the efforts of the rest of the group. A nonquickened person in the same situation probably would have died.

In all likelihood, a naive character will lose a portion of his naiveté by the end of the first adventure and join a group of recursors or a larger organization. However, it's likely that many revelations are yet in store for this character.

SIX WEEKS LATER

This option is a hybrid between a naive character and a character in the know. Begin a particular campaign as an origin story, and start with the guidance provided for characters who are off the street. After the introductory session or sessions, advance the campaign by six weeks (or a similar amount of time). Explain to the PCs that during that time they learned more about recursions and their abilities, and they gained broad strokes of knowledge about the setting (such as a member of the Estate or the Quiet Cabal would know).

First Mission and What's Next: Presumably, the characters' introductory mission occurred during the six-week time advancement. For the follow-up mission, you can jump back into regular campaign mode and create an adventure of your own or use the one in chapter 22 of this book.

CHARACTER PLAYER

For a potentially funky twist on the option of beginning play with an off-the-street character, your players may like the idea of playing themselves. Everything that's true of an off-the-street character is true of a player character

Soulshorn, page 291
Oracle, page 170

Betrayer, page 178
Kray, page 276

It's a good idea to have the first scenario include opportunities for an off-the-street character to put her relatively mundane skills—computer use or talking to people as opposed to fighting or using special powers—to good use.

Characters who begin the game off the street probably don't start with cyphers but instead acquire them in the course of the first adventure.

Starting Cyphers

Cyphers and In-the-Know Characters: A quickened PC can generally identify a cypher merely by handling it, but he would need to make a Strange knowledge roll to identify its exact effect. Nonquickened NPCs and creatures are not sensitive to cyphers. If characters begin play as part of an organization, such as the Estate or the Quiet Cabal, or if they are adventurers in Ardeyn, the organization or guild they belong to is the source of their starting cyphers.

Cyphers and Naive Characters: Quickened naive characters may get a funny feeling when they handle a cypher, but until they gain a little context or experiment with newfound cyphers, they can't really identify the items with the facility of in-the-know characters.

Naive characters should not begin the game with cyphers. Instead, finding some should be part of their awakening to the reality of the Strange. That said, a naive character might have a cypher and not know it. Maybe a favorite smartwatch, a brooch from the thrift store that sparkles so nicely, or an odd device found at the electronics shop is actually a cypher, and the character just didn't realize it before.

playing his or her real-life self.

Creating a character meant to be the player isn't so much different than creating any other character. What's important to remember is that the character created doesn't have to exactly mimic the player; it only has to evoke what the player is like, and how the player roleplays will provide all the rest.

Follow the character creation rules provided at the beginning of the corebook, but tell the player to choose a descriptor, type, and Earth focus most akin to what she does as her hobby, her profession, or a combination of both if possible.

First Encounter With Something Strange: If the players are playing themselves, the first encounter with something odd might be straightforward from the point of view of an experienced player, but terrifying from the point of view of a normal person. For instance, a creature of Ardeyn found in a closet, a Ruk creature at the front door, or a Strange artifact delivered while everyone is sitting around the table playing a game might be a great way to get things going. After that, channel them into the adventure in chapter 22 as if they were off the street.

Making the Strange the Strange

Running games set in the worlds of The Strange is unlike running most other roleplaying games. While The Strange covers many different kinds of genres, this isn't *just* a game about mashing genres together. Although it can be fantasy one session and science fiction the next, it's more about tying those two things together. Why do the characters have to go to the fantasy realm and the science fiction realm? What thread connects them? How will the characters themselves change in light of the transition and their new surroundings? That's what The Strange is all about.

Most adventures should have a component of multiple worlds. Traveling to and from various recursions is worked into the basic abilities of even a beginning character. Some of this travel is prompted by the actions of NPCs. Agents from Ruk are coming to Earth. Nefarious people from Earth are mucking around in Ardeyn. A dangerous terrorist from Earth is hiding in Sherlock's London. A power-crazed sorcerer from Ardeyn is trying to establish her own kingdom in Oz. A maniac from Ruk is trying to awaken the spark in creatures in Innsmouth. And so on.

Some of the travel, however, is prompted by the PCs themselves. They learn that an artifact in Ruk holds the secret to solving a problem in Ardeyn, and they attempt to find it. They realize that to get more applicable information about the creatures of a seemingly new recursion, they need to return to Earth and search the Estate's files. To fight a dragon in Ardeyn, they find a way to bring a rocket-propelled grenade from Earth. They want to create a recursion of their own and must venture out into the Strange itself.

What it comes down to is this: *What do PCs do in this game?* They travel from recursion to recursion, exploring and defending, and eventually creating a recursion of their own.

Explore. Defend. Create. This is the mantra of The Strange.

It's fine to have adventures that take place wholly in one recursion. Perhaps simply finding and exploring a new recursion is itself the adventure. Or maybe the PCs just want to

explore a dungeon in Ardeyn, or track down and confront a long-term enemy in Ruk. That's okay. But even then, it's always about forward motion. The PCs *go to* Ardeyn to find the Staff of Killanis, which can raise the dead. The PCs *go to* Ruk to infiltrate the Church of the Embodiment, to unmask Reg-ulla, who has been posing as an apostle in disguise.

TRANSLATING VERSUS GOING THROUGH A GATE

Characters have many ways to get from recursion to recursion. From the GM's point of view, the important thing is the information that is conveyed to the players when it happens.

When PCs translate or use a translation gate, they become a part of the new world they enter—they integrate into its context. That means that they don't show up knowing nothing. All of the recursions in Part 4: The Setting have a few key points that every recursor knows upon translating there. In most cases, the players have to choose new foci, and they need to base those choices on something.

That's the advantage of being quickened and being able to translate. You don't go in unprepared. You have some clue as to what's going on. In a way, you start out as a part of things rather than as a complete outsider.

Going through an inapposite gate, however, can be a completely disorienting experience. No information is provided. The characters won't even know what recursion they are in. They don't translate and neither does their equipment. Their abilities and gear might be all wrong for their new location.

THE SPARK

The spark could be described many ways, but the easiest way to define it is "free will." Everyone on Earth has the spark. Even if they don't always live examined lives, they all have the potential to do so. But in recursions, a smaller percentage of natives have the spark, which means even in worlds created by fictional leakage, there will always be those with the spark who question their surroundings, work against the imparted fictional scenario, and ask why. How and why the spark develops in some recursion natives and not others isn't fully understood, though it seems that the larger the recursion, the larger the number of natives who eventually develop the spark. External disruption (through PC interaction in some cases) could also cause NPCs to gain the spark, though that's the exception, not the rule.

How does the spark start? Can it start on its own, or does it require outside influence? Is it a blessing or a curse? That's up to you and the players to discover and explore.

NPCS WITH THE SPARK AND WITHOUT

Many recursions are populated with sapient creatures who don't possess the spark. One could make a good case that NPCs without the spark aren't actually sapient, but more akin to avatars that game players on Earth encounter inside video games. At first, an NPC without the spark might seem completely normal, but given enough observation, his behavior probably seems extremely routine-oriented, almost robotic. Over time, he just does the same things over and over, unless the PCs interact with him in some fashion.

Once they interact with an NPC without the spark, that NPC's normal routine is probably disrupted, and the NPC may show evidence of personal initiative as it reacts. But given enough time after the interaction, the NPC returns to its original routine.

On the other hand, NPCs with the spark have more free will. Even so, they are creatures of their environment. Despite possibly seeming a bit confused or dissatisfied, and perhaps wondering if there's more to life, most won't ever find out, unless the PCs show them the wider world. Then, an NPC with the spark reacts as a fully free-willed individual, according to his personality. One NPC might be struck with wonder and beg to accompany the PCs when they leave, while another might find it too much to handle, and react negatively.

NPCs who are vital to a recursion's identity, whether they have the spark or not, are entangled in the recursion's nature, and they might be more like forces of nature than individuals. If they die, they might reappear later, or show up in an alternate recursion.

NATURE OF RECURSIONS

Many of the recursions seeded around Earth are a result of fictional leakage. Such recursions often conform to a specific theme or nature. For instance, Innsmouth's nature is toward run-down, abandoned structures where terrible things lurk in the shadows. If one were to build a shiny new casino in a place like that, it probably wouldn't stay shiny and new for long.

Church of the Embodiment, page 197

Translation, page 125
Translation gate, page 134

Inapposite gate, page 135

Innsmouth, page 253

Likewise, because the Red Queen is so vital to a recursion like Wonderland, she would be hard to permanently kill. Unless the PCs go to extraordinary lengths (such as stealing her head, burning her body, and keeping watch against Wonderland thieves looking for the remains), it's unlikely that she'd stay dead.

Wonderland, page 253

COMMINGLED AND DUPLICATE RECURSIONS

Many recursions are commingled versions of all the various fictions that have been written, said, or shown in film about them. For example in the recursion hosting the Great Detective, Sherlock Holmes might look like an amalgam of all the actors who've portrayed the character. Alternatively, on some days he might look like one actor, and on other days more like another. Some days, he might look exactly as he did in the very first illustration ever made of him.

Sometimes fiction pieces detailing the same topic are too divergent to form a single commingled recursion, creating more than one recursion. Such recursions are not exact duplicates but have similar features and, possibly, similar NPCs with different agendas. As a result, there could be more than one Wicked Witch, more than one Red Queen, or more than one Sherlock Holmes, if it suits the GM's campaign. Maybe rival Red Queens vie for control over the Qinod Singularity in Ruk, or a later Sherlock hunts an earlier version, thinking that the earlier one is the real adversary he's sought for so long. Perhaps OSR maintains a highly valued base in Oz, then discovers there's another Oz recursion, and the two are about to merge. OSR might send PCs on a mission into the newly discovered Oz to accomplish something so divergent that the two do not commingle into a single recursion.

Qinod Singularity, page 208

OSR, page 157

Similarly, a popular science fiction brand where space travel is common doesn't seed a recursion into the Strange that's light years across, but might seed several different recursions, each one reflecting a particularly important setting of the science-fiction story that created them.

EXPLORING THE STRANGE

Heading out into the Strange itself can be a terrifying experience. Who knows what you'll find? Should you venture out from Ardeyn, equipped with magic, or from Ruk, geared up with biotechnology? It's dangerous and always bewildering out there, no matter how experienced you are. It is the ultimate wilderness, and it should always be presented that way. Adventures in the Strange should never seem trivial, easy, or straightforward. Every time the PCs go into the Strange, prepare to play with their heads a bit. They should experience a new sight, a bizarre creature or entity, or something that should not be there at all. Even if you don't want to make it an actual "encounter," consider the following experiences:

- A vision of a loved one in a completely inappropriate context
- The sight of a color not in the normal visible spectrum
- A smattering of utterly alien speech
- A whiff of an entirely heretofore unexperienced odor
- A bizarre, ghostly creature that the characters cannot interact with in any way
- A bit of a song that they've never heard before gets stuck in their head.
- A memory of their past comes to mind, but it's something that never happened.
- A piece of their clothing or equipment is changed in color, texture, or composition.
- A new goatee graces the face of one or more PCs.
- A character forgets the name of someone important and close to her.

If you want to have an actual encounter, consider something inexplicable, such as the following:

- An alien being wants to barter with the PCs, but they have no straightforward way to communicate or even fully understand what it wants to trade.
- Shadowy duplicates of the PCs from the past appear and attack, fading away when "slain."
- The PCs get lost and stand on the shore of a heretofore undiscovered, tiny little recursion.
- The PCs get lost for an inordinate amount of time, and even though they survive the alienation, they've somehow been gone for *months.*
- Creatures that should never be in the Strange come along. There's a chance they are not hostile—a very small chance.

A STRANGE ADVENTURE OUTLINE

This sample outline illustrates the idea of how an adventure can involve a number of different recursions. This is not an introductory scenario for characters "off the street" but for those who are already a part of the larger setting.

1. The PCs are on Earth. Through their connections, they learn that Citadel Hazurrium is under attack by warriors wielding powerful new weapons. Hazurrium is holding out for now but will likely fall soon.

2. The PCs translate to Ardeyn and travel to Citadel Hazurrium, where they find legions of sark wielding sophisticated projectile weapons. These weapons are clearly assault rifles from Earth. They can choose to help fend off the latest attack. (If they do not, many in Hazurrium will die in the fight.)

3. If the PCs wish, they can investigate the existence of these weapons. It is very difficult to transmit standard inorganic matter into a recursion, so they know there is an open inapposite gate somewhere allowing this to happen. When they discover the gate, they can try to close it on the Ardeyn side or translate back to Earth and close it there.
3a. On the Ardeyn side, the sorcerers who maintain the gate have a legion of undead souls holding the conduit open in a deep dungeon. Putting these spirits to rest will be difficult and likely involves an open assault.
3b. On the Earth side, they find a private security firm called Black Falcon guarding the gate in a hastily built secret structure in Yellowstone National Park. They can try an open assault here as well, but clever PCs will realize that a far simpler tactic involves sneaking in and destroying the massive, portable power generator.

4. If the PCs ask questions about who is behind the creation of this matter gate, as well as why and how it was created, they have more work ahead of them. In Ardeyn, it seems obvious that this is part of the plan of the Betrayer, which likely leads the PCs to believe that the September Project from Earth are involved. However, investigations on Earth into that lead result in nothing of interest.

5. If the PCs go back to Ardeyn, they learn of a woman named Vallia Deshavin who serves the Betrayer. She claims to be an Ardeyn native. If they track her down in the city of Telenbar and confront her, they discover that she is a powerful master of the soulblade and has a number of smoldering mage bodyguards known as fire sorcerers. The PCs, however, might discover that she is not the Ardeyn native she claims to be. She is, in fact, a bioengineered spy from Ruk, working for an organization within the Karum that seeks to undermine power structures in Ardeyn (with the ultimate goal of one day causing the collapse of the entire recursion). Searching Vallia's secret lair within one of the city's labyrinthine libraries, the PCs can find information on the location of a cell of the Karum back on Earth. Perhaps more important, they find the plans to create another inapposite gate, this time leading directly from Ruk. It looks like the PCs have even more work ahead of them!

CREATING NEW RECURSIONS

Part 4 of this book offers a wide variety of recursions for PCs to discover and explore. But part of the fun of The Strange is creating your own recursions. While The Strange is limited by issues like copyright, you are not. We can't provide you with a recursion based on a movie that just came out, but nothing is stopping you from using the setting from that film in your own campaign. That's not cheating—that's what The Strange is all about. With the concept of fictional leakage, the worlds of fiction are a part of the setting. Creating recursions from whole cloth is cool, but you're not being lazy by using the work of your favorite author. That's what you're supposed to do.

Here are a few ideas to get you thinking:

- The setting of your favorite novel, movie, or television series
- A campaign world from another roleplaying game (published or of your creation)
- A synthesis of a genre or a literary style (noir films, for example, in an urban landscape all in black and white)
- A world centered around a single character from history or fiction, twisted so that everything focuses on them
- A world based in real-world myths, fables, or tall tales

You can get as crazy with recursions as you want, or at least as far as you think your players will find it fun. A recursion based on cartoons? Yes. Puppets? Sure. A collectible card game? Why not?

It's worth noting again that recursions aren't parallel Earths or alternate histories. They can

Citadel Hazurrium, page 166

Sark, page 288

Vallia Deshavin: level 5

Betrayer, page 178

Soulblade: One of a set of level 8 artifact broadswords. It provides an asset when attacking a living foe and deals 4 additional points of damage whenever the wielder strikes with the sword and applies a level of Effort (but draws upon his Intellect Pool to do so). Depletion: —

seem that way, but they aren't really bound by many of the rules that such places need to "make sense." And no recursion is as large as Earth. Ardeyn is an example of a very large recursion.

In fact, a recursion can be very small. It might just be a single room, a single castle, a single street of a single town, and so on—whatever's appropriate. The recursion is no larger than its concept. A recursion based around Dracula's castle includes the castle, the nearby village, and some scary woodlands around it. But nothing more.

This means that all the wonderful advice out there about "world-building" doesn't really apply. Each recursion (with perhaps Ruk as a possible exception) starts as a concept. Not a place, but an *idea* of a place. Its reality doesn't extend beyond that single concept. A recursion that is nothing but a sprawling, frightening orphanage is nothing more than that. The people there might on some level think that there's a world outside the orphanage, but there isn't, and thus they never venture into the outside world and can't be convinced to go there. What do the children and the staff eat? Food might just show up in the cupboard every morning. Or perhaps food is irrelevant there. In a recursion so small, the idea of nutrition and so on probably isn't a part of the context.

The people of a recursion might not age. They might just do the same things over and over, like characters stuck in television reruns. They do whatever is appropriate for the recursion.

In the end, remember that The Strange is about exploration and discovery. As soon as a place starts to become familiar, it will hold less mystery and less interest for players. Either keep the campaign moving to new places, or change things in the familiar ones. The PCs should always be looking at the world around them with wonder as well as less-than-complete certainty.

A PARTING NOTE

Above all else, The Strange is about wonder. It's about discovering new things. It's about ideas. In a good session of The Strange, someone says "Wow!" (That someone might be you, the GM.) In a great session, someone's mind is blown. Keep things moving. Keep things fresh. Always be presenting the players with new, amazing concepts, even if they're small ones. Secrets, hidden locations, plot twists, weird encounters, whole new worlds never before discovered—these are the things that make The Strange a fun game to play.

Part 7: Adventures

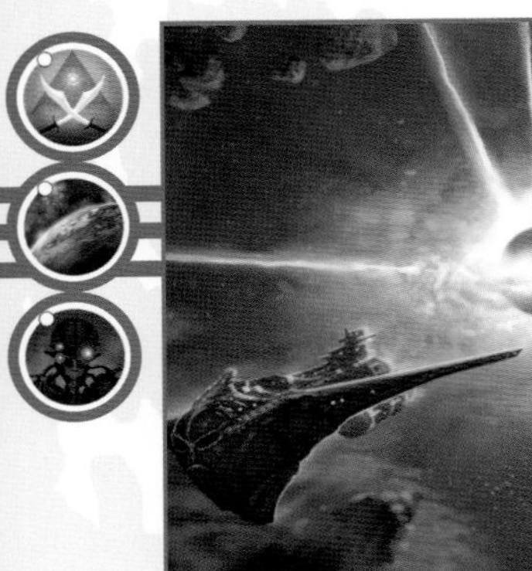

CHAPTER 22

THE CURIOUS CASE OF TOM MALLARD

Recursions, page 134
Quickened, page 22

The Curious Case of Tom Mallard is an adventure for characters who know something about recursions and quickened abilities, and who might already possess an association with the Estate (or a similar organization). That said, the adventure is designed to provide players with their first real taste of adventuring in The Strange. Although this adventure assumes the characters are in the know about the Chaosphere, it can be used for starting characters of any sort, including naive characters.

Naive vs. in-the-know characters, page 22

Recursion key, page 130
Ardeyn, page 160

BACKGROUND

The Estate monitors the active recursion miners it knows about, including one Tom Mallard. To date, Mr. Mallard hasn't done anything especially dangerous, which is why he remains on the Estate's "watch" list instead of graduating to the "lock up" list—or the "eliminate with prejudice" list.

Lambsblood Tap, page 391

At first glance, Mallard doesn't seem in any way connected with the city of Shalmarn in the recursion of Ardeyn, but he is. A few years ago, Shalmarn was invaded by sark. Thanks to the efforts of a passing sortie of Free Battalion mercenaries and doughty city residents, the sark were vanquished. In the aftermath, the inhabitants learned the sark were led by a human named Tokmal the Master, who got away. Apparently the Master wanted something in the qephilim ruins under the city, and Shalmarn was in the way.

Shalmarn, page 169
Sark, page 288
Free Battalion, page 284

Tokmal the Master, page 398

What the Estate doesn't realize is that Tom Mallard and Tokmal the Master are one and the same. The Estate believes they've got Mallard's number, but right under their noses, Mallard has been planning another raid on Shalmarn and the ruins beneath. He learned his lesson the hard way last time, so his next attempt will be a covert intrusion, using the tools of the Estate against them. Mallard/the Master believes that the ruins hold something called the Last Gospel of Lotan, which he wants for himself.

The Estate, page 148
OSR, page 157

SYNOPSIS

If the PCs begin the game as operatives of the Estate, their first mission is to shadow the recursion miner Tom Mallard for a month, making sure he continues in his presumably inconsequential ways. But the PCs discover that Mallard is nowhere to be found, and that his home is something of an enigma. They also learn that a recursion key to Ardeyn is hidden in a secret room in Mallard's basement. The man isn't as inconsequential as everyone assumed.

The recursion key provides access to Ardeyn, specifically to the back room of an establishment called the Lambsblood Tap in the city of Shalmarn. Coincidentally(?), the Lambsblood also happens to be the watchpost of another undercover Estate operative.

If the PCs want to find out what Mallard is up to, they'll have to follows clues into the ruins beneath Shalmarn. The trail leads through some interesting and dangerous areas, and finally to the Chamber of the Gospel. Instead of the man they expect, they find Tokmal the Master, who is in the process of procuring the object as the PCs arrive. If the PCs can stop him, the threat is ended for now. If they can't, he escapes to Ruk, with something in his possession that could spell Earth's eventual destruction.

GETTING THE PCs INVOLVED

You can use any of the following hooks to get the PCs to Shalmarn and the ruins beneath.

Mission: Most of the PCs are operatives fresh to the Estate (or possibly to the Office of

Strategic Recursion, the Quiet Cabal on Earth, or some other mission-giving organization); one or two PCs could be more senior members assigned to assist trial associates. To prove their mettle, the PCs are assigned their first real mission: take a shift monitoring Tom Mallard, a recursion miner. Nothing is likely to happen, but the Estate knows that anyone with the ability to travel between recursions could be a potential danger to Earth.

The PCs are briefed by Lead Operative Katherine Manners in an Estate briefing room. She provides the following information in connection with Mallard:

- The receiver for an electronic bug installed in Mallard's house several years ago
- A Seattle address (see Tom Mallard's House)
- A picture (a short man with brown hair)
- A list of known associates (no one, essentially)
- His method of recursion travel (Mallard is quickened)
- A psychological profile (Mallard is pedantic and annoying, but mostly harmless)
- The recursions he is known to translate to (primarily Ardeyn, usually to shop in the markets of Hazurrium looking for cyphers, but he has also visited Crow Hollow)

If Mallard is believed to have translated, Manners says, the PC operatives are to enter the house and, using clues available, check him out covertly. If Mallard is doing little more than retrieving various souvenirs from the recursions he visits, it's not the end of the world. But if he is somehow drawing planetovore interest in Earth (through overuse of inapposite gates, for instance), the world *could* end. The PCs would, of course, want to step in before that. But don't worry, Manners reassures them—that's unlikely to happen.

Thrust Into the Strange: PCs with quickened powers but no prior recursion experience are awakened to their abilities unexpectedly. This occurs when Ramis (a secret agent of the Estate who is based in Ardeyn) calls for help with a malfunctioning portal sphere. Instead of escaping back to Earth to warn the Estate, she creates a translation gate between the Lambsblood Tap tavern and a location where the PCs are present on Earth in such a way that they can't avoid noticing it. Maybe anyone who goes into the kitchen doesn't come back, or maybe the floor disappears, and anyone standing on it falls through into Ardeyn, translating as they do. If this scenario is used, Ramis isn't the double agent she's portrayed as in this adventure. Instead, she is bound and gagged in the pantry, and a shapechanger in the Master's employ poses as her.

Exploration: For PCs who begin in Ardeyn, the ruins of Shalmarn are well known for luring adventurers into their depths. Unlike many other ruins, those under Shalmarn are well preserved, and treasures and dangers of ancient days can be found therein. Ramis, the barkeep of the local watering hole preferred by the PCs, invites them to the Lambsblood Tap for a "send-off shindig." Ramis sets an ambush to kill the PCs to keep the ruins clear of intruders while the Master goes for the gospel.

TOM MALLARD'S HOUSE

The Seattle address of Tom's house is in a quiet neighborhood. The house is a green two-story structure with an attached garage. Signs and stickers on the window prominently advertise that the house is protected by ADC SECURITY. From the exterior, the house seems in good repair. Every two weeks, a landscaping service stops by to clean up the small yard.

Visual surveillance doesn't reveal anything out of the ordinary at first. All the blinds in the house are closed, but every night lamps are switched on as it gets dark outside, then are switched off again as it gets late. (If the PCs pay attention, it soon becomes clear that the lamps go on and off again in the same sequence and at the same time each day.)

Audio surveillance using the receiver provided by Manners reveals normal sounds of a single person living alone: radio alarm in the morning, shower, and breakfast, followed by the sounds of a day filled with typing on a computer keyboard.

What's Really Going On: No matter how long the PCs monitor the house, Mallard is never seen to leave, because he's not really there. Knowing he was a target of Estate surveillance, Mallard created a lifestyle to put them at ease, including a home retrofitted with smart appliances, such as lights that go on and off automatically. A similar appliance keeps the electronic bug happy with a partly randomized mix of sounds that simulate someone living alone. In fact, Mallard left recently by translating to Ardeyn through a gate hidden in the basement.

The Quiet Cabal, page 194

Katherine Manners, page 149

The agents previously assigned to monitor Mallard have already moved on to a new, more dangerous mission in a recursion called Cataclyst, and they are out of touch.

Planetovore, page 8

Ramis, page 392

Portal sphere, page 135

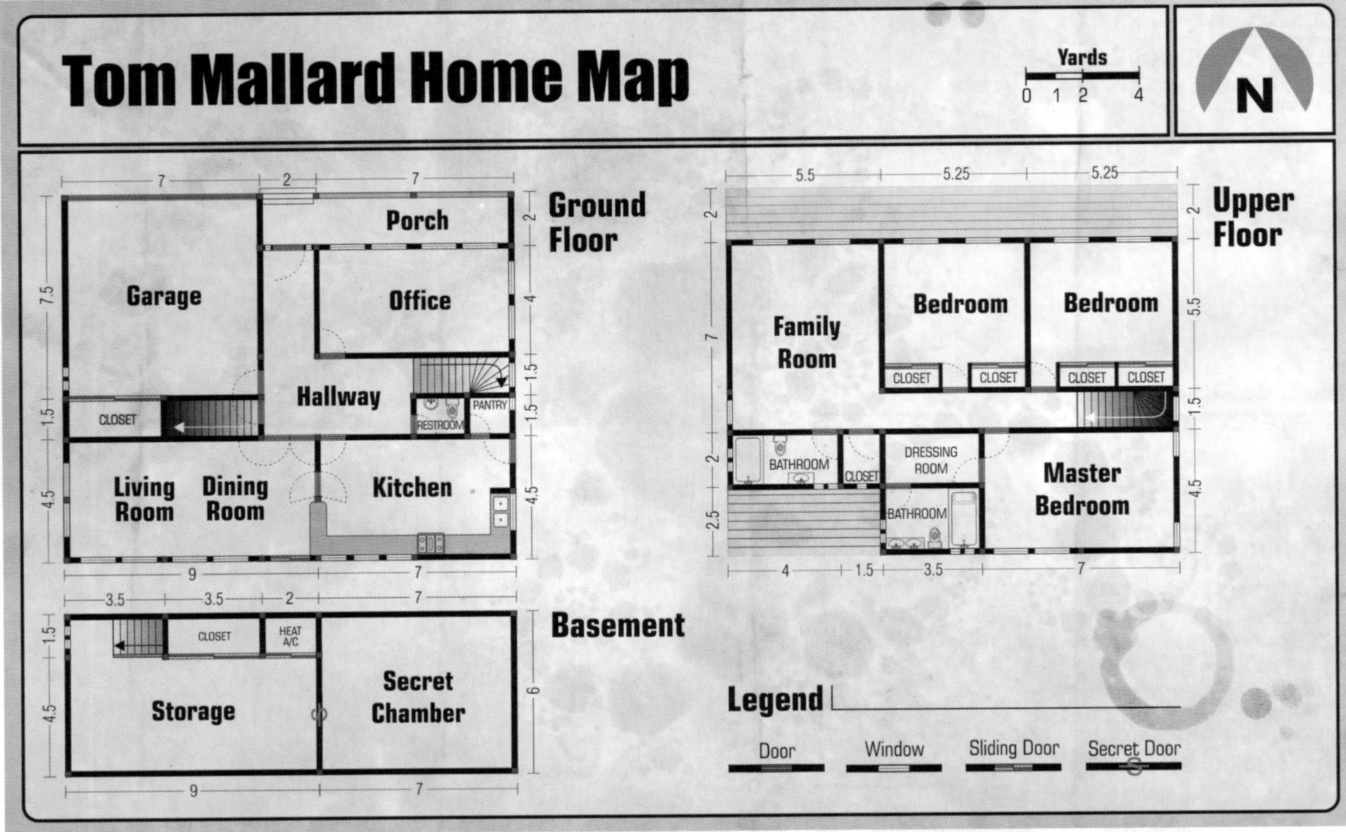

Analeptic, page 313
Curative, page 315
Meditation aid, page 322
Matter translation ray, page 321

Mallard House Security: The locks on the front and back doors of Mallard's house are level 5. Of course, a rock through the window would provide instant access. But any entry that doesn't first involve deactivating a particular door or window security sensor (a difficulty 5 Intellect-based task for each) trips a silent alarm, and ADC security personnel are dispatched. Hacking into the house's Wi-Fi (called "Twispavia") and deactivating the entire security system at one go is a difficulty 6 Intellect-based hacking task. A failed attempt at this latter task is as good as tripping the alarm.

Inkling, page 273

Security guard, page 303

If security is dispatched, a car pulls up in about ten minutes with three level 3 security guards. The ADC security guards are ex-military mercenaries itching to confront "criminals," but that doesn't mean they couldn't be fooled or otherwise put off without a gunfight.

Inklings typically can't travel to Earth under their own power. However, some powerful cyphers can provide them with safe passage. Those who deal in this dangerous endeavor know to keep such cyphers sealed in lead chests for their own safety and the safety of anyone else around them.

GROUND FLOOR

GARAGE

Mostly used for storage, the garage is filled with boxes of junk, old clothes, broken lawn equipment, a motor scooter, and so on. A locked tool chest (level 5 lock, no security) contains three cyphers (an analeptic, a curative, and a meditation aid) plus a smaller chest made of lead that has been bolted completely shut. If the lead chest is broken open (a difficulty 5 Might-based task), PCs will discover it contains an additional cypher: a matter translation ray. This ray has an additional secret quality beyond what's described in the Strange Cyphers chapter. If the cypher is used, in addition to triggering its effect, a level 4 inkling seeps from the cypher like smoke and attacks whoever triggered the cypher (or, failing that, whoever's nearest).

LIVING ROOM

This chamber holds a comfortable couch, a couple of chairs, a TV with cable, and bookshelves that cover the walls. Books are randomly organized without much care regarding topic, though fiction seems particularly well represented. A search through the shelves reveals the following "tome" of note: *A Player's Guide to Ardeyn, Land of the Curse* is a thick booklet apparently produced for a computer game (a computer game that never made it to market). The creatures, threats, and land described within, for all its brevity, are remarkably similar to that of the recursion of Ardeyn. Anyone who spends five minutes referring to it gains an asset for tasks related to Ardeyn lore; it lasts for one hour.

KITCHEN

Regular kitchen appliances are here, including a fairly expensive espresso maker. The fridge doesn't contain anything particularly likely to spoil. On the other hand, the quantity and variety of hot sauces, chili sauces, and habanero pastes is notable. One bit of oddness: a couple of items in the freezer, wrapped in white butcher's paper, are abnormally large. If unwrapped, they contain slabs of flesh that seem like they might've been cut from the tentacle of a huge octopus.

OFFICE

The office features an expansive desk, a broadband Internet connection, filing cabinets, and an elaborate birdcage with a posed stuffed parrot.

A Wi-Fi router under the desk automates the lights around the house, and operates an Ethernet-connected tablet computer duct taped to the Estate's electronic bug. The tablet reproduces the sounds of Mallard's daily routine for anyone listening. Messing with this setup is another way that PCs could accidentally trigger the silent alarm that draws ADC security.

The filing cabinets contain several notable folders amid normal stuff like mortgage loans and contracts for prepaid services.

Ramis of Ardeyn: One filing-cabinet file is a dossier on "Ramis of Ardeyn," complete with a hand-inked likeness on parchment of a woman in heavy leather robes, notes on Ramis's ownership of something called the Lambsblood Tap in a city called Shalmarn, and a timeline of Ramis's occasional travel between Shalmarn and a known Estate safehouse in Hazurrium. The travel implicates Ramis as an undercover Estate operative.

If the PCs go through Estate channels, they can confirm that Ramis is indeed an agent in good standing who keeps tabs on the Shalmarn area. She's based at the "Lambsblood," which is also referred to in the Estate as the "Shalmarn Watchpost." Ramis is a cover identity, but no alternative names are provided.

Like all embedded agents, Ramis keeps in contact with headquarters back on Earth by using a quickened courier who makes his way to the Lambsblood every month or so. A courier last got a message from her just a month earlier, and all was well.

Gospels of Lotan: Another folder is labeled "Gospels of Lotan." According to parchment scraps in this folder, the gospels are "real" artifacts in Ardeyn, though mostly lost. According to the file, the quantum code responsible for Ardeyn's anomalous creation might actually be imprinted in any one of the gospels, of which seventeen are believed to exist. One of those gospels almost certainly lies in the qephilim ruins beneath Shalmarn. A message written on a sticky note adds, "Soon, the Master will have what he seeks."

Master's Lair: A final folder is labeled "Master's Lair." This file is fragmentary, but it suggests that Tom Mallard frequently visits someone called the Master in a secret lair in Ardeyn. One loose piece of parchment contains a painted likeness of the Master sitting on some kind of throne.

UPPER FLOOR

MASTER BEDROOM

This spartan room features a king-size bed, a couple of nightstands, and an attached master bathroom and walk-in closet.

One of the nightstand drawers holds a medium-caliber handgun with a clip of 9mm ammo. Another drawer holds two cyphers: a level 4 curative and a level 5 cell-disrupting grenade.

A piece of art on the wall is an artistic rendition of a fractalscape obviously inspired by mathematical chaos theory. The piece is titled "Resonance Island in the Strange." The art is signed by "the Master."

The walk-in closet has a few articles of clothing, including a leather trench coat and a lot of shoes in a huge rack. A key ring is tucked away in the pocket of the coat; it holds four unlabeled keys. One key fits the front door, one fits the garage, the third fits the wardrobe in the basement storage room, and the fourth opens the concealed door to a secret chamber in the basement.

Mallard's house is set up like a standard "dungeon crawl" despite its contemporary aspects. So if the PCs tell you they explore the house and then wait for you to tell them what they find, break it down by asking, "How do you get in?" and "The door's locked, so what do you do?" and so on, until they get the idea.

Mallard's Wi-Fi network is called Twispavia and the password is kronus1; there are nine other Wi-Fi networks in the same neighborhood.

Curative, page 315
Cell-disrupting grenade, page 318

PCs who take a few minutes to look through the boxes and shelves for anything that might serve as a weapon find a long crowbar, a baseball bat, and a rusty machete (all medium weapons).

"Mummy": level 4; health 12; Armor 3; one melee attack for 5 points of damage

If the PCs investigate, they might discover that the mummy was a burglar named Davis Katz, wanted in connection to a string of petty larceny charges in the Seattle area, who disappeared several years ago.

Enduring shield, page 317

OTHER BEDROOMS AND FAMILY ROOM

These rooms are mostly empty, except for a few household items (vacuum cleaner, ironing board, folding chairs, and so on). The family room looks like it once held a painter's studio, but nothing remains except splashed paint, paint supplies, and a few bare canvasses.

BASEMENT

BASEMENT STAIRS

The basement stairs, made of polished wood, are trapped.

Trapped Stairs (level 5): The trap on the stairs is an ingenious mechanism that flattens the steps, sending everyone standing on them on an unexpected slide into a fake wall section at the bottom of the stairs. The fake wall is on compressible springs. Bodies striking the fake wall push it back, to reveal noncompressible 6-inch spikes. Up to three people on the stairs can be simultaneously affected when the stairs flatten. Those who fail a Speed or Might defense roll are subject to 3 points of ambient damage from the impact, and 6 points of damage from the piercing spikes.

If anyone thinks to look for the trap beforehand, perceiving it is a difficulty 5 Intellect-based task. Once found, it's easy to locate the deactivation switches at the top and bottom of the stairs.

STORAGE

At first glance, this basement room is full of holiday decorations, boxes of old clothing, a variety of partially broken chairs and other small furnishings, and shelves of pickled vegetables of every sort. A large wardrobe stands against one wall.

Wardrobe: If the wardrobe is unlocked (either with the key or with a successful difficulty 5 Intellect-based roll), a humanoid form wrapped in stained white cloth lurches out. The "mummy" attacks anyone present with the speed and ferocity of something far more lively than a mummy.

The mummy is actually a burglar Mallard caught a few years ago. After subjecting the man to torments in Ardeyn, Mallard returned him here, wrapped him in preservative cloth, and set him as a guardian. He's still alive, but he is now a mental zombie with no memory of a former existence. On the other hand, his strength and resistance to pain are radically improved.

If the PCs decide to help the man, returning him to normal requires medical and psychological intervention by professionals. With enough care (a few weeks, at minimum), he could return to society, but with no memory of the intervening years he spent in Mallard's thrall.

A bedraggled coat also hangs in the wardrobe. In one pocket is a cypher: a level 6 enduring shield.

False Wall: The false wall opposite the wardrobe conceals a door to a secret chamber. Due to some water leakage from outside, discovering its false nature is only a difficulty 3 Intellect-based task for anyone who thinks to look. Once discovered, a section of the wall slides away to reveal a locked iron door. The lock opens with one of the keys from the trench coat in the master bedroom, or on a successful difficulty 5 Intellect-based roll. Attempting to pick the lock unleashes the "mummy" from its wardrobe if it hasn't already been dealt with.

SECRET CHAMBER

The secret chamber is barren. It contains several sets of manacles

set into the cement of the walls and a piece of art set in a large wooden frame. By marks on the walls, it's clear that at least two other large pieces of art once graced the room, but they're gone now.

The remaining piece of art is similar to the one in the master bedroom, and it shows a fractal landscape signed by "the Master." It's larger than the one in the bedroom and lacks a title. A quickened character who studies the painting and succeeds at a difficulty 3 Intellect-based roll will recognize that it is actually a recursion key.

The recursion key leads to Shalmarn, a location in Ardeyn, though even if the character succeeds on her roll to recognize the key, she probably doesn't know that, and she certainly won't know where in Ardeyn the key leads. If the recursion key is used for a translation attempt (Ardeyn is level 3), everyone participating in a successful translation appears in Ardeyn, in the city of Shalmarn, in the back room of an establishment called the Lambsblood Tap.

SHALMARN, ARDEYN

PCs who use the recursion key in Tom Mallard's basement can translate to the city of Shalmarn in the recursion of Ardeyn (specifically, to the pantry of the Lambsblood Tap). Give the PCs some time to come to grips with translating if it's the first time that they've done so; make sure nothing immediately threatens them upon their arrival. The PCs may have new foci, new equipment, a new look, and new information about Ardeyn suddenly floating about their brain (such as one or more of the bullet points in What a Recursor Knows About Ardeyn on page 160).

If the PCs leave the Lambsblood, they can explore Shalmarn as they wish, or if they feel time is pressing, they can head directly down into the qephilim ruins in pursuit of Tom Mallard.

LAMBSBLOOD TAP

Besides the other features described for the city of Shalmarn, the city also hosts the Lambsblood Tap. The Lambsblood is a trading post, tavern, and public house. Its proprietor is a woman named Ramis, who is much beloved by the patrons, despite coming to Shalmarn only in the last few years.

In addition to a large common room where food and drink is served, the Lambsblood has a kitchen, a large pantry (which is where the PCs appear after translating), and an upper floor with rooms available for let.

REPORTING BACK

If the PCs are operatives of a larger organization, they're free to report back to their superiors at any time if doing so doesn't endanger the mission. PCs can also use the facilities and request additional equipment if the situation at hand seems to warrant it. What PCs usually can't do is acquire the direct aid of additional NPC operatives. Quickened operatives don't grow on trees, and the PCs were selected precisely because of their abilities and, hopefully, their initiative in dealing with situations.

Recursion key, page 130
Shalmarn, page 169
Translation, page 125

If the PCs seem uncertain what to do with the recursion key, it's a fine time to suggest they check in with the Estate (or have the Estate check in with them). The Estate is likely to express alarm at this recent discovery and urge the PCs to take quick—but careful—action.

LAMBSBLOOD PANTRY

This windowless chamber contains floor-to-ceiling shelves and racks on which all manner of foodstuffs, platters, and utensils are stored. Foodstuffs come in the form of smoked haunches from a variety of different animals, burlap bags filled with various grains, and barrels sloshing with ale. It also contains a wide-open spot in the center, perfect for accommodating arriving recursors. What it doesn't have is a translation gate leading back to Tom Mallard's house.

The only obvious door (unlocked) leads to the Lambsblood kitchen. The sounds of someone banging about with pots is audible from the opposite side.

LAMBSBLOOD KITCHEN

A qephilim named Zurk works in the kitchen. Zurk is mute, a bit deaf, and heavily scarred from past fighting. He eyes anyone who walks out of the pantry, but he doesn't react other than to shrug and go back to his cooking. His indifference (and inability to communicate) is why Ramis employs him.

The kitchen has two exits: one to the pantry and the other to the common room.

Zurk: level 4, level 5 for all tasks related to cooking and brewing

LAMBSBLOOD COMMON ROOM

This large area contains enough tables to seat thirty or more patrons at a time, plus a bar. At any given time, the common room contains only a handful of patrons (five level 2 patrons and two level 4 patrons) who are variously caught up in Shalmarn gossip and spirits.

Ramis is usually found in the common room.

RAMIS, LAMBSBLOOD PROPRIETOR 5 (15)

Description: A woman in leather robes who always carries an ale flagon, often filled

Motive: Secret double agent working against the Estate's interests

Health: 15

Damage Inflicted: 5 points

Armor: 1

Movement: Short

Modifications: Resists mental effects as level 6, deceives as level 6.

Combat: Ramis carries an artifact called the flagon of plenty. In addition to serving as a bottomless tankard of ale, it can be induced to spray a jet of ale with such incredible force that it inflicts 5 points of damage to a target within short range. Those struck must also make a Might defense roll or lose their next turn, having been thrown back by the yeasty jet. The flagon of plenty has a depletion roll of 1 in 1d20.

Ramis can also levitate 20 feet (6 m) per round, turn invisible for one minute via a distortion field, and gain +1 to Armor for ten minutes by using a force field.

Ramis has two cyphers: a level 4 intelligence enhancement and a level 3 lift.

Intelligence enhancement, page 320

Lift, page 321

Interaction: Ramis seems the soul of sincerity in all her interactions, without many "tells" when she's lying. When she ultimately betrays the PCs, she seems truly sorry about it.

Use: The Lambsblood Tap proprietor is a center of Shalmarn gossip and local knowledge, and she probably knows a little bit about everything around town.

Loot: Ramis has 10 crowns, the two cyphers described under Combat (unless she uses them), the flagon of plenty, a variety of tools, and other normal gear.

RAMIS, ESTATE OPERATIVE?

If the PCs found Ramis's file in Tom Mallard's office, they may already know she's an Estate operative, and they may proceed as if they have an ally. For her part, Ramis is eager to prove that assumption true. She will aid the PCs any way she can, including helping them trail Mallard into the ruins (see below).

But the truth is that Ramis and Mallard have been secretly working together for months. Ramis is a double agent, and if she sees PCs show up from her pantry, she knows that the Estate is on to Mallard. What she doesn't know is whether her own status has come into question, so she tries to assess what the PCs know and, if possible, fool them into believing that she remains a loyal Estate operative who is just as mystified and concerned as to why Mallard has a recursion key to her pantry. Later, once they trust her, she'll betray their confidence when it hurts them the most.

Nammu Mountains, page 168

Age of Myth, page 162

If Ramis is attacked in the Lambsblood, the assembled patrons come to her defense.

In her guise as an Estate operative, Ramis provides the following in the course of questioning and conversation, as it comes up.

- I know Tom Mallard; he's a recursion miner. He's very interested in the qephilim ruins beneath Shalmarn. (Truth.)
- Mallard visits the Lambsblood Tap from time to time. (Truth.)
- Mallard never let on that he knew I was an undercover Estate operative. (False.)
- I can show you the entrance to the ruins that Mallard probably uses. Let me know when you're ready and I can close up here. (Truth.)
- The Master? He's a local bogeyman ever since he appeared several years ago with a small army of sark. The locals say he tried to get into the qephilim ruins beneath Shalmarn and overrun the city with sark in the process. I wasn't around then. (Truth.)
- I have no idea what Mallard and the Master have in common. Maybe Mallard was forced to serve the Master or is working with him. (False.)

RAMIS'S INEVITABLE BETRAYAL

Though Ramis is casual in her manner, she insists on showing the PCs to the ruin entrance, and once there, accompanying them even farther to "give them the edge they need to succeed." That said, Ramis may even initially give the PCs a bit of help if her fate and their own become tied together in a particular area. However, if she sees a chance to take out some of the characters in one go (such as remaining in the rear if the PCs decide to investigate the sacred ash in room 3, or pushing someone off a catwalk in room 5), she takes the opportunity.

QEPHILIM RUINS

Abandoned qephilim ruins and mines are scattered throughout the Nammu Mountains. The city of Shalmarn is built over one of those ruins, and indeed, many of Shalmarn's buildings are converted remnants of structures first built during the Age of Myth. Several

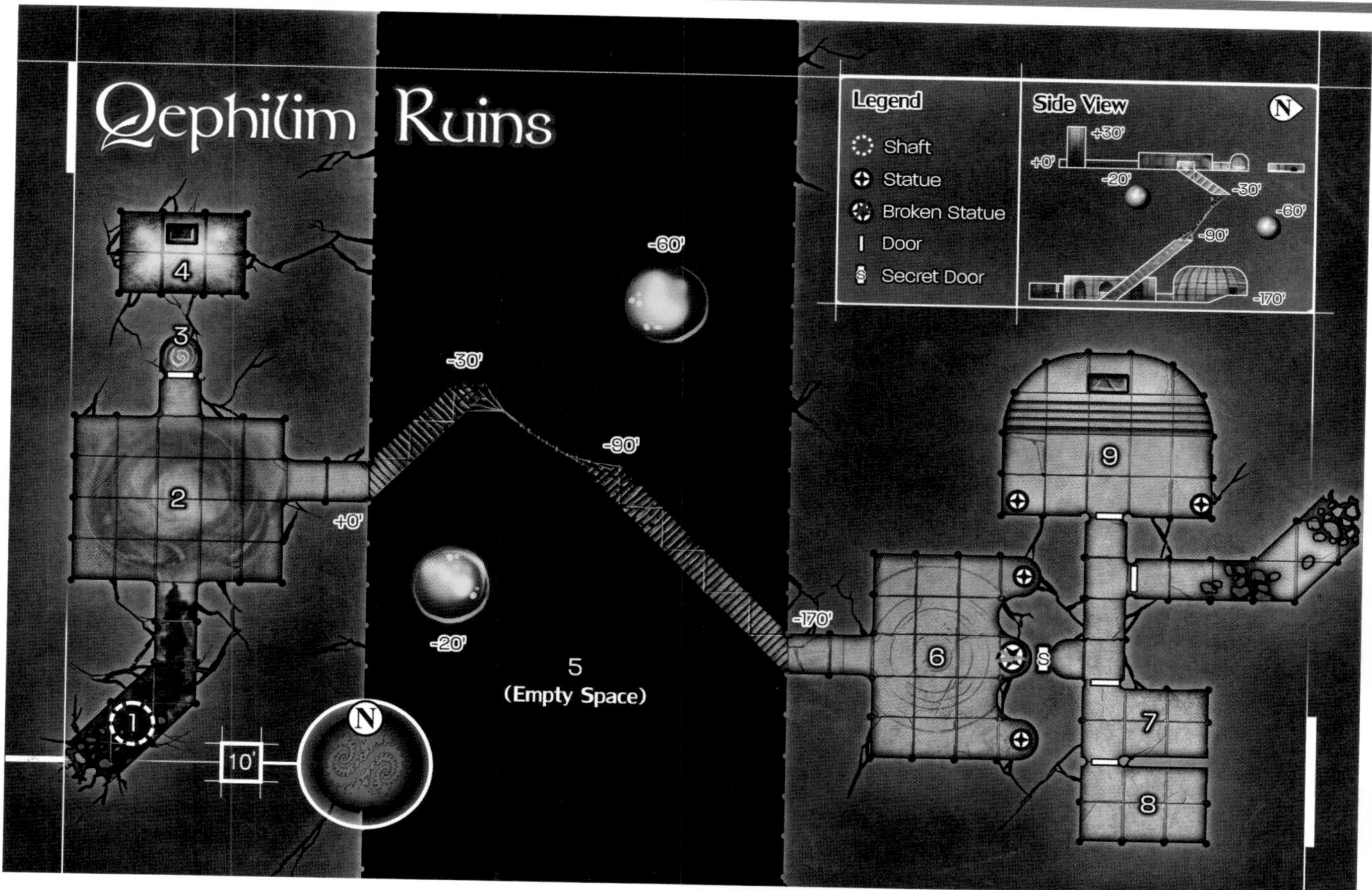

entrances into deeper, buried ruins open in and around Shalmarn, but most lead to closed-off areas that have been previously looted of ancient relics by adventurers.

A ruin entrance near the city's center is called the Winged Arch. Most everyone in Shalmarn knows the Winged Arch leads to a much more expansive area of subterranean tunnels that have yet to be mapped or looted, thanks to unspeakable creatures that guard the way. The Winged Arch is also the entrance that the Master and his sark tried to command years before.

Unless noted otherwise, the ruins in this area are composed of silvery metal and crystal (a level 6 substance).

Asking About the Winged Arch or the Master: If the PCs ask around Shalmarn about the arch, specifically inquiring if anyone noticed it being accessed recently, a couple of residents note that adventurers sometimes try their luck with the arch, as they do through other entrances around Shalmarn. Those who do rarely return. Upon further investigation, the PCs can talk to a beggar named Callon, who sets up in the area. Callon saw a large group of adventurers recently enter through the Winged Arch. He noticed them not because of the hoods they all wore, hiding their features, but because of how they smelled of blood, shit, and rot. One growled like an animal when it realized the group was under observation, which is the point at which Callon fled.

1. WINGED ARCH RUIN ENTRANCE

The Winged Arch is the best way into the ruins beneath the city where the Master has ventured.

Read aloud: *The arch appears to be part of a larger structure that curves up out of the ground before plunging back. Various segments of silvery metal and stone blocks compose the structure. The material shudders ever so slightly if touched, and it seems as warm as human flesh. A litter of tiny crude dolls—winged qephilim in form—are deposited around the arch's exterior. The arch leads back into an enclosed area that contains a hole in the ground. The odor of cinnamon and the sea emerges from the darkness.*

Although Callon didn't realize it, the creatures he saw and smelled were sark. When the PCs encounter sark during the course of their adventure in the ruins (or elsewhere later in Ardeyn), consider foreshadowing that encounter with an odor like the one the beggar described.

The hole is 10 feet (3 m) in diameter. It drops 30 feet (9 m) into a corridor adrift with several feet (0.5 m) of sediment. Residents say they deposit the tiny qephilim dolls—winged like the ancient qephilim were said to be—as offerings to keep whatever lies beneath quiescent.

The southern end of the corridor is blocked with debris from a past cave-in.

2. HYDRA IN THE MISTS

Read aloud: *A haze the color of blood fills this chamber, making it difficult to see more than a few feet in any direction. The haze smells of cinnamon, sea salt, and, beneath that, something more dank.*

The red haze hides the room's contents, which includes a hydra dozing in the far corner of the chamber. A glass vessel set only a few feet into the chamber is barely visible to someone remaining in the haze-free corridor who succeeds on a difficulty 3 Intellect-based roll. The vessel is called the Breath of Oblivion, and it has a head shaped like that of a dragon (or maybe a vicious crow).

Hydra, page 272

Breath of Oblivion: This delicate, 3-foot-high (1 m) glass art piece originally hails from Crow Hollow. Set by the Master to bypass the hydra, the gas released by the Breath has a soporific effect to anyone exposed to it. Because the hydra has several breathing heads, it proved particularly susceptible. As long as the Breath of Oblivion is in place, any living creature in area 2 must succeed on a difficulty 5 Might defense roll each round or fall asleep. Sleeping creatures can be awakened with vigorous slapping or rougher treatment, but they could fall victim to the gas again as long as they remain in the area. Moving the Breath or smashing it ends the gas production, and the mist in the chamber begins to clear. A couple of rounds later, it is possible to see all the way across the chamber, and all creatures affected by the gas wake up.

Crow Hollow, page 242

One of the hydra heads can unleash a conflagration of sinfire, burning up to three targets within short range once a minute. This burst inflicts 5 points of Intellect damage (and thus ignores Armor).

Hydra: The hydra likely begins this encounter as a victim of the Breath of Oblivion. If it's awakened, it's hungry and angry at being put to sleep. Two of its heads are sark, recently added thanks to the Master's intrusion into the ruins. The PCs have to be clever to talk their way out of an extended conflict with the hydra, especially since the sark heads continue to argue for attacking them. If the PCs successfully negotiate with the hydra, it sends them east toward room 5. If they fail, it sends them toward room 3 (and attacks them when they return).

3. SACRED ASH

The door to room 3 is of stone set on heavy silver metal hinges. A thin layer of sediment on the floor shows that the door has been recently opened. (The Master sent a sark to investigate before turning east himself.)

Read aloud: *White silt, ash, or sand completely covers the floor of this chamber. Ripples like those you might see on a pool's surface are frozen into the white substance.*

Prodding the ashlike material with a pole or other long implement from outside has no effect other than smearing the ripple designs. Characters sensitive to sorcery might sense the presence of magic (a level 3 Intellect task) and perhaps even realize that the magic is related to instantaneous travel (a level 5 Intellect task). Anything or anyone who completely enters the room disappears and then reappears in room 4. (A rope tied to something or someone outside the room will prevent this from happening.)

4. DEATH'S TEST

This chamber is usually inaccessible except for those who enter by way of room 3. Those who are transported here from room 3 appear in darkness, unless they can see in the dark or have a light.

Read aloud: *This stone chamber has no exits. A thick layer of fine white sand or ash covers the floor. The ceiling is only 6 feet (2 m) overhead. A pristine white human skull sits on an eroded altar. The body of a sark, unmarked but as still as death, lies at the altar's foot.*

What was once a ceremonial rite of passage for qephilim pledged to the Incarnation of Death during the Age of Myth is a far more serious and deadly matter in the modern age for those who lack context.

If the skull is touched or picked up, its eyes light up, and it says (in the Maker's Tongue), "Do you choose Death?"

The skull isn't sentient and doesn't respond

or react to anything that is not an answer to the question it posed.

Characters who answer the skull in the affirmative are instantaneously transported to the surface near area 1, the Winged Arch. For one day, the first character who answered the skull in the affirmative gains +3 to Armor against damage dealt by rot, necrosis, or similar death magic.

Characters who answer in the negative must succeed on a Might defense roll or descend one step on the damage track and suffer 2 points of ambient damage as their bodies shrivel from a surge of death magic. A character who answered in the negative can continue to try her luck with the skull, though she may want to consider changing her answer.

If the skull is smashed, the skull of the dead sark bursts from the body and settles in place on the altar. If *this* skull is smashed, a new one won't form until another corpse enters the chamber. Until that happens, there is no way to release anyone who remains in the ceremonial chamber.

The sark's corpse has a pouch that contains 10 crowns and a flashburst cypher (level 4).

5. EMPTY AIR

Read aloud: *The corridor opens into a truly vast subterranean cavity. It's difficult to judge how big, because it's dark as far as your eyes can pierce to the left and right, and above and below. A free-hanging stair pokes out into the cavity from the corridor's exit, descending about 30 feet before ending with jagged shards—an indication of a past cataclysm. A second broken stair segment is visible farther down. A rope ladder connects the two ends of the shattered stair. A spectral light clings to the intact stair segments, which reflects off a couple of free-floating silver spheres hanging in the void nearby. One figure stands at the top of the rope ladder, and three figures stand at the bottom.*

The figures on the upper and lower stairs are sark, left by the Master to guard the rope ladder in case he wants to return physically. The sark have medium bows and pepper PCs if they attempt to advance.

A PC who rolls a natural 1 when making a Speed defense roll against attacks while on the stairs nearly falls off, dangling over the darkness by her fingertips. A PC who rolls a 1 on a defense roll while descending the rope ladder is knocked off and falls into the void (but see the silver spheres).

Rope Ladder: This single strand of rope is knotted every couple of feet, and it connects the upper broken stair terminus with the lower. It is spiked into the bridge at both ends, and it stretches 30 feet (9 m) vertically and about 20 feet (6 m) laterally. Ascending or descending is a routine task under ideal conditions but is a difficulty 3 Speed- or Might-based task during combat. On a failed roll that isn't a 1, a PC becomes entangled in an awkward hanging position, requiring someone else to help free him. On a 1, he falls.

GM Intrusion: *If Ramis hasn't already betrayed the PCs, she does so now. She attempts to push them over the edge. If a PC is already dangling from the edge for some other reason, she stamps on his fingers.*

Silver Spheres: If someone falls into the void, a silver sphere farther down flares as bright as a star as it moves to position itself to stop the fall. The victim falls about 60 feet (18 m) on average before being brought up short by a sphere. While he is saved from a much longer fall, he takes 6 points of ambient damage from the impact. He must also devise his own way of getting back to where he started; maybe a friend will lower a rope.

The silver spheres are actually captive, somnolent stars of the kind that surround Ardeyn. A relief carving of a winged qephilim can be made out on the surface of a sphere by a PC who has fallen onto one. If a PC addresses the figure and asks for further aid, the sphere may rise and deposit the character at the level where he started.

Flashburst, page 317

Vast Cavity: The qephilim ruins beneath Shalmarn are far too extensive to detail here. Someone who chooses to descend the cavity discovers new broken (and sometimes whole) stair segments connecting deeper levels across the cavity sides. These levels are mostly dark and empty, but persistent explorers who choose not to follow the obvious path of the Master might have one of the following encounters.

- A chamber contains a statue of a larger-than-life qephilim holding a spear animated by a mad spirit. The spear launches itself at intruders (long movement), inflicting 8 points of damage. The spear is level 2 (level 3 for Speed defense due to size) with 1 point of Armor and 12 health.
- A domed chamber contains a pool of green, mildly acidic fluid (it inflicts 3 points of acid damage to flesh per round of contact). A corpse lying 10 feet (3 m) below the surface is mostly bones, but it clutches an Ardeyn artifact.

- A trapped room: A PC must succeed on a difficulty 4 Intellect-based task or her psyche is exchanged with that of a spirit trapped in one of the hundreds of urns lining the shelves in the room. The psyche tries to pass itself off as the PC, but given that it's a psychopath from an earlier age, it likely runs into difficulties.

Retrying a task, page 102

Ardeyn artifact, page 186

6. THREE STATUES

Read aloud: *The stone floor of this chamber is covered in carved concentric rings. Three alcoves along the east wall each hold a statue, though the one in the center is shattered, and its pieces lie scattered on the floor.*

A PC with a strong sense of magic might be able to sense the spell of preservation that protects the wooden barrels (and their contents) from decay as long as they remain in this chamber.

A secret door restricts access farther east (detecting it is a difficulty 3 Intellect-based task of perception). Anyone who tries to open it from this side while the center statue remains shattered suffers a surge of death magic that inflicts 5 points of damage, and the door doesn't open. Reassembling the statue is the best way to get through the door from here. From the east, opening the secret door is as easy as pushing on it, and doing so doesn't trigger a surge of death magic.

The two intact statues are qephilim. The one to the north wears the armor of a warrior with inscriptions pledging him to the Incarnation of Death. The statue to the south bears similar inscriptions but appears more like a sorcerer.

If the central statue is pieced together, it's revealed to be an impressive armored female human figure. She wears a helm with the likeness of a skull.

Reassembling the statue properly is a level 3 Intellect task that takes about twenty minutes. (Those who fail the first time may retry, and normal rules apply.) Once done, the statue's seams and cracks melt away. The statue animates briefly, bowing to those who rebuilt it, then opens the secret door. (It opened the door to the Master, who thanked it by having his sark batter it to pieces, sealing off the route to anyone who might be following.)

7. MYTHICAL VINTAGE

The lack of dust and sediment in this portion of the ruins makes it difficult to determine if the door to this chamber was recently opened. Opening it requires a successful difficulty 2 Might roll.

Read aloud: *Wooden barrels rest on their sides, filling the east end of this stone chamber.*

The barrels are filled with wine, and the wine does indeed retain its freshness. A sample reveals a bouquet like spring blooms that gives way to a blend of lavender, cherry, and peace. The first time a PC drinks an amount equal to at least one glass, she feels unstoppable. The imbiber can immediately make a free recovery roll that doesn't count against her recovery rolls per day. Drinking additional wine confers no benefit (and could result in drunkenness).

8. QUESTIONABLE VINTAGE

The stone door to this chamber has a level 5 lock and is trapped with a level 5 poison needle. Opening the door, once unlocked, requires a successful difficulty 2 Might roll.

Read aloud: *The room beyond the stone door appears similar to the previous chamber, in that it serves as a storage chamber. Instead of barrels, hundreds of smaller casks are stored here. Many of the casks and ewers are smashed and broken, empty of whatever they once contained. But dozens more are still intact.*

Inquisitive characters who investigate the containers find most of them empty; however, a few contain residue and a shred of magical energy. The chamber contains a few dozen undamaged casks. Whenever one is opened, roll a d20 to determine its properties.

01–05	Cask explodes in immediate radius, inflicting 5 points of fire and shrapnel damage
06–08	Cask contains minty-smelling liquid; level 5 poison if consumed
09–14	Cask contains strawberry-smelling liquid; no effect if consumed
15–17	Cask contains odorless liquid; imbiber gains +1 to Might, Speed, or Intellect Edge for one hour
18–20	Cask contains coffee-smelling liquid; imbiber gains +2 to Might, Speed, or Intellect Edge for one hour

9. GOSPEL OF LOTAN

The stone door to this area is closed, but it shows signs of having been recently forced (and the sounds of activity are audible on the opposite side). The door is inscribed with the following warning:

DO NOT ENTER. NO HIGHLY ESTEEMED DEED IS COMMEMORATED HERE. NOTHING VALUED IS HERE. WHAT IS HERE IS DANGEROUS AND REPULSIVE. THIS MESSAGE IS A WARNING ABOUT DANGER. THE DANGER IS TO YOUR BODY, YOUR MIND, AND YOUR SOUL. DO NOT ENTER.

Read aloud: *This chamber is brilliantly lit by a globe of fire that hangs unsupported near the ceiling. Two statues of qephilim stand in the two southern corners of the chamber. Opposite the door, on the far wall, an altar of black stone squats on a dais. A scroll case of dimly glowing red iron lies on the altar. In a place of prominence in front of the altar, a human man is in the midst of a ritual. Four sark stand in the room, watching the ritual unfold.*

The man conducting the ritual is Tokmal the Master (also known as Tom Mallard). If the PCs enter the room, he pauses in his ritual to talk to them (motioning his sark to stay calm, at least for the moment).

The truth is that the Master is finished with the main part of the ritual. He was only practicing variations on the final few stanzas, hoping to figure out some way to extend the ritual's nullification effect to the qephilim guardian golems. He also hopes the ritual will allow him to remove the Gospel of Lotan from the altar safely. Normally, removing it would strike everyone in the chamber with a level 10 death curse.

TALKING WITH THE MASTER

If the PCs haven't pieced together the basics of what's going on, they can discover what's really happening via a couple of different routes.

One way is by rescuing an operative that the Master took captive (an undercover operative who'd also been trailing Mallard—perhaps the Estate conveniently "forgot" to mention her, or perhaps she was acting on her own initiative). Once the Master is defeated or flees, the PCs find Operative Karol Blethers trussed up behind the altar. She fills the PCs in on what she discovered.

The other route is the more classic approach to which so many narcissists fall victim: the Master sneeringly fills the characters in on his true identity, how he kept the Estate in the dark for years as to his actual agenda, and what he's really up to: extracting one of the guarded Gospels of Lotan. Previously, he wasn't able to take it, even though he'd discovered its location, because he didn't know the proper ritual for safely removing it from the altar in this chamber. Someone who just picks it up would be struck down with a death curse.

Besides the underlying quantum code, the Gospel of Lotan can provide nearly anything the user tries to call up, though each use releases one or more demons of Lotan. If the Gospel of Lotan is destroyed, it reforms somewhere else in Ardeyn, though not under the guard of an ancient qephilim "security system."

Why does the Master want a Gospel of Lotan? Because he believes he can extract the quantum code responsible for Ardeyn's anomalous creation. That code would be incredibly valuable to certain factions in Ruk. He already has a few potential buyers lined up. He says that representatives from the Karum seem prepared to pay the most. (He's not interested in hearing about how that could be dangerous for Earth.)

If the PCs seem inclined to continue speaking, the Master suggests that he'd be willing to split some fraction of the fee he makes for selling the Gospel of Lotan, if the PCs agree to help him. Ritual or no, he says, the moment the scroll leaves the altar, the two golems in the chamber will animate and kill any thieves present, and then trail those who get away.

FIGHTING THE MASTER

If the PCs oppose him, the Master fights back. He orders his sark into the fray and joins in himself. A fight in the chamber also rouses the animate golems, even if the Gospel remains undisturbed. They animate and are somewhat indiscriminate, but they focus first on those who most clearly seem like thieves.

Sark, page 288

Golem, page 270

If the Master begins to suspect he'll lose the fight, he grabs the Gospel of Lotan from the altar. When he does, all golems not already focused on him change their focus to him. In the following round, the Master plucks a portal sphere from his belt pouch, dashes it to the ground, and steps through. Before the portal sphere closes behind him, the PCs see a vision of the recursion of Ruk.

Animate Golems: The golems indiscriminately target PCs, sark, or the Master, unless they see clear evidence that the PCs are not the thieves (in which case they restrict themselves to attacking the sark and the Master). If the Master is defeated and the scroll is placed back on the altar (or if it was never disturbed), the golems return to their positions. If the Master escapes by using his portal sphere, the golems freeze in place for several minutes before charging from the area as if on a new mission.

TOKMAL THE MASTER 5 (15)

Description: A self-important man with real power. The image on page 390 is a portrait the Master commissioned of himself in Hazurrium, and it is a fair likeness.
Motive: Power and influence
Health: 20
Damage Inflicted: 5 points
Armor: 1
Movement: Short
Combat: The Master can target up to two foes in short range at once, causing electricity to arc and snap between them, dealing 5 points to each target. Alternatively, he can target one foe within long range and deal 4 points of damage that also stuns a target not native to the current recursion for one round.
He also has three cyphers, all level 3 (a curative, a meditation aid, and an Intellect booster), not to mention a portal sphere for a fast escape.

Curative, page 315
Meditation aid, page 322
Intellect booster, page 320
Portal sphere, page 135

Interaction: The Master is self-important and vain, but he is no fool. He's willing to negotiate, but only as long as he gets his own way.
Use: If the PCs don't stop the Master in this adventure, he could become a recurring thorn in their side, whether as the Master, as Tom Mallard on Earth, or as other people in other recursions.
Loot: The cyphers described under Combat (unless he uses them), an artifact that grants +1 to Armor for an hour per day (depletion roll 1–3 in d20), and a variety of tools.

ENDING THE ADVENTURE

At the end of the adventure, the PCs should report back to the Estate, and specifically to Manners.

If the PCs stopped the Master from taking the Gospel of Lotan into Ruk, the Estate is extraordinarily happy with them. Each character receives a commendation and perhaps some other special dispensation. The Estate treats the PCs as its hottest new acquisitions—until given reason to believe otherwise.

If the PCs failed, Manners isn't happy about it, but she lets the characters off the hook a bit by noting that if not for them, no one would've realized what Tom Mallard was up to. The Estate is disappointed but offers the PCs a new mission elsewhere. They are advised to put the Master behind them. Other agents will pursue the case for now.

In this latter case, the question is whether the PCs saw enough of Ruk through the portal sphere to try to follow the Master by using the translation rules for having a likeness of the destination recursion. If you want the PCs to pursue the Master, then they did. If you'd rather move on to something else, then they probably did not.

DESCRIBING RUK

When the PCs see a vision of Ruk through the portal, the GM should describe the place without naming the recursion, since the PCs aren't likely to know what they're seeing. If you are planning to send them to Ruk at a later date, you might choose to describe a place they will eventually go, for a greater sense of worldbuilding and storyline.

This can also tie into any future missions regarding the Master (see Ending the Adventure, above).

CHAPTER 23

ADVENTURE IDEAS

These adventure "seeds" provide the GM with additional ideas for getting PCs involved in the mystery and action of The Strange. While not entire adventures unto themselves, they are designed to jumpstart the creativity of the GM and showcase what's possible in a campaign in The Strange.

SINGULARITY PART TWO

Some members of an Estate recursion field team were found dead on the edges of Newk in the recursion of Cataclyst. Just one more bad luck story, right? Wrong. The field team was monitoring a roach infestation that is rumored to include kray. If kray are somehow invading the recursion, then the defenses Earth normally enjoys against planetovores might be slipping.

Getting the PCs Involved: If the PCs are working for the Estate, they're assigned the mission of locating the rest of the missing field team. If the PCs are freelance, they're looking for an artifact from Cataclyst called a gravity maul, reputed to be just as effective in Ardeyn as in Cataclyst (perhaps they need it to open a sealed vault in an ancient qephilim ruin).

Complicating Factor: The PCs find or are provided a guide by the name of Indira Suresh. The guide has the credentials of an operative in good standing with the Estate but is actually a double agent whose first loyalty lies with the Office of Strategic Recursion (OSR).

"Boss" Fight: A swarm of Cataclyst roaches under the command of a mutant Cataclyst roach/kray drone hybrid; one of its roach servitors wields the gravity maul. If not stopped, the hybrid kray/roach will use its special quality to begin encroaching on other recursions, and eventually Earth.

SECOND SEED

The Office of Strategic Recursion (OSR) sent a field team into a series of recursions that had hosted zombie apocalypses. Classified as Zed Omegas, such recursions operate under the law of Mad Science or Magic (zombies don't normally arise under Standard Physics). However, the field team returned with a unique cocktail of virus samples that retained residual activity on Earth. That worked out about as well as might be expected.

Getting the PCs Involved: One of OSR's large research installations is called Castle One. Castle One is located in a mile-wide recursion of its own, but it's been sealed off (all connecting translation and inapposite gates were destroyed) because of a "zed outbreak" inside. Hundreds of living people

Newk, page 239
Cataclyst, page 238
Kray, page 276
Gravity maul, page 242
OSR, page 157

(one quickened) are also still inside, and they need saving.

Complicating Factor: A couple of the OSR guards sent along to help the PCs were treated with the "Second Seed" formula, and they convert to zombies just when the characters can least afford it.

"Boss" Fight: A zombie swarm in the facility's core, led by a level 6 zombie with the spark, is trying to open a gate back to Earth. Can the PCs stop it in time?

Zombie: level 3, Speed defense as level 2; health 12. If an attack would reduce the zombie's health to 0, it does so only if the number rolled by the attack was an even number; otherwise, the zombie's health is reduced to 1 instead.

WEAPONS DEALER

Zelda Goswmi, a recursion miner native to Earth, discovered an artifact in the Strange itself she dubbed the "frequency nullifier." The nullifier works on Earth under the law of Standard Physics, and Zelda claims that someone could reverse-engineer it to create a weapon more devastating than a nuke. She's made contact with the Karum, offering them a chance to buy it. Given how the Karum want to see the Earth destroyed, they're likely to say yes.

Getting the PCs Involved: The arms deal is going down under the cover of a masquerade gala held by the rich computer investor Alex Terra in New York City, USA. Several other national and international investment celebrities will also be attending. The PCs' mission, should they choose to accept it, is to unmask either Zelda or the Karum agent in the crowd and spoil the deal. If possible, they should also recover the frequency nullifier.

Complicating Factor: Other Ruk faction agents are also present, vying for the nullifier. Though they don't want the Karum to get it, they also don't want the PCs to spoil their opportunity to put it in "proper" hands (namely, their own).

"Boss" Fight: The Karum agent is Alex Terra himself. If unmasked, he grabs the nullifier and flees through a translation gate to his sanctum in Ruk.

Recursion miner, page 156

Frequency nullifier (Standard Physics): *Deals 20 points of damage to an object the user can see within direct line of sight, no matter how far that sight line extends. Depletion: 1–4 in 1d20.*

The frequency nullifier is one of those rare artifacts that is able to translate.

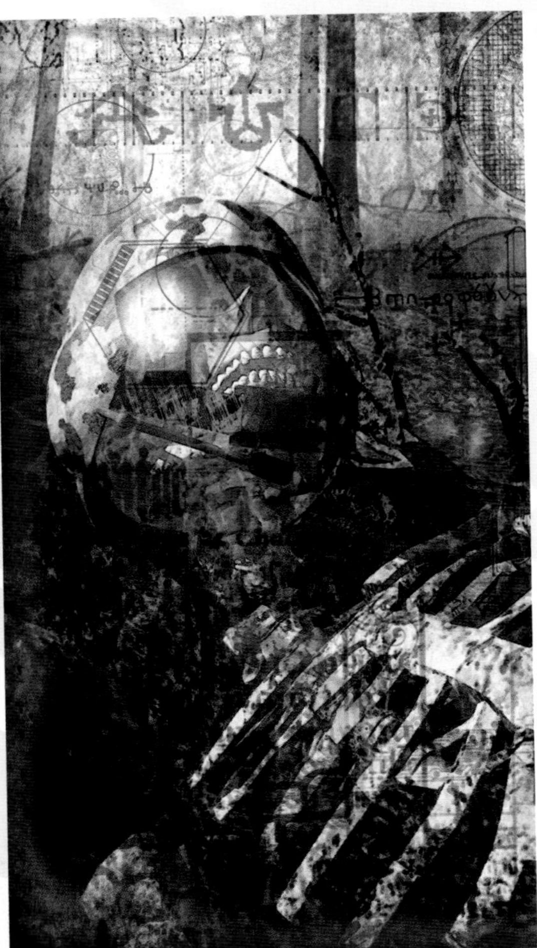

DRIVERLESS

With great fanfare, a newly formed car company called Lancer Motors leapfrogged Google, GM, Toyota, and other entities working on driverless cars by releasing their Model D.I. "dashtop box" (D.I. standing for driving intelligence). Thousands of the units have been sold, and as advertised, the cars they're installed on drive themselves with simple voice operation by the passengers. The only problem is that in cities where D.I. dashtop boxes have been installed, the rate of accidents involved pedestrians and cars has gone up sharply.

Getting the PCs Involved: One of the PCs (this works best with a paradox but could be anyone with a strong knowledge of the Strange) is almost run down in the street by a car without a driver. The PC gets the distinct feeling that something of the Strange was influencing the car. If the characters investigate, they discover the roving fleets of D.I. cars are running down every quickened individual they can sense, and apparently the vehicles can sense quickened people for miles.

Complicating Factor: The D.I. dashtop boxes are the translated forms of captive sacrosancts (natives of the Graveyard of the Machine God recursion) forced into a new form on Earth and enslaved to the will of Lancer Motors programming.

"Boss" Fight: Lancer Motors is a corporation front for the controlling intelligence of the "quickened quell," an evil level 6 tick-tock automaton of Oz named Tom Sawhand.

Part 8: Back Matter

APPENDIX A: RESOURCES

While writing The Strange, we were influenced by countless things, only a few of which we've managed to capture here. Our research of the science underlying The Strange was mainly done via online sources, but anyone interested in delving into dark energy, inflation, and the question of whether humans are alone in the universe will find a lot of great print material sure to get their mind spinning.

Besides the inspiration that the biggest questions stumping science can provide, fiction in all its many forms—novels, TV shows, movies, comic books—all have had a part to play in shaping The Strange. While these sources each contributed a seed or two to the corebook, we mostly just wanted to share them with you so you can be inspired in the same way. You never know how a particular story, scene, or character reaction is going to strike you. But when it does and you find yourself thinking, "Wow, that's awesome," then you've probably just found something worthy of your own game of The Strange.

FICTION

2001: A Space Odyssey, Arthur C. Clarke
2010: Odyssey Two, Arthur C. Clarke
The Authority (comic book series), Warren Ellis and Bryan Hitch
The Chronicles of Amber series, Roger Zelazny
City at the End of Time, Greg Bear
The Eternal Champion series, Michael Moorcock
Daemon, Daniel Suarez
Dust, Elizabeth Bear
The Incredible Umbrella, Marvin Kaye
The Long Earth, Terry Pratchett and Stephen Baxter
Manifold trilogy, Stephen Baxter
The Martian: A Novel, Andy Weir
Neptune's Brood, Charles Stross
The Number of the Beast, Robert Heinlein
Peter Grant series, Ben Aaronovitch
Songs of Earth and Power, Greg Bear
Soon I Will Be Invincible, Austin Grossman
Surface Detail, Iain M. Banks
Three Parts Dead, Max Gladstone
Well World series, Jack L. Chalker
World of Tiers series, Philip Jose Farmer

NONFICTION

The 4 Percent Universe: Dark Matter, Dark Energy, and the Race to Discover the Rest of Reality, Richard Panek
Big Picture Science podcast
From Eternity to Here: The Quest for the Ultimate Theory of Time, Sean Carroll
The Inflationary Universe, Alan Guth
Planetary Radio podcast
Science Friday podcast
This Week in Science podcast
Wikipedia

MOVIES & TV

2001: A Space Odyssey
2010: The Year We Make Contact
Chuck (series)
Cosmos (series)
Eureka (series)
Fringe (series)
Inception
The Killing (series)
The Matrix
Pleasantville
Sherlock (series)
Supernatural (series)
The Thirteenth Floor
Tron: Legacy

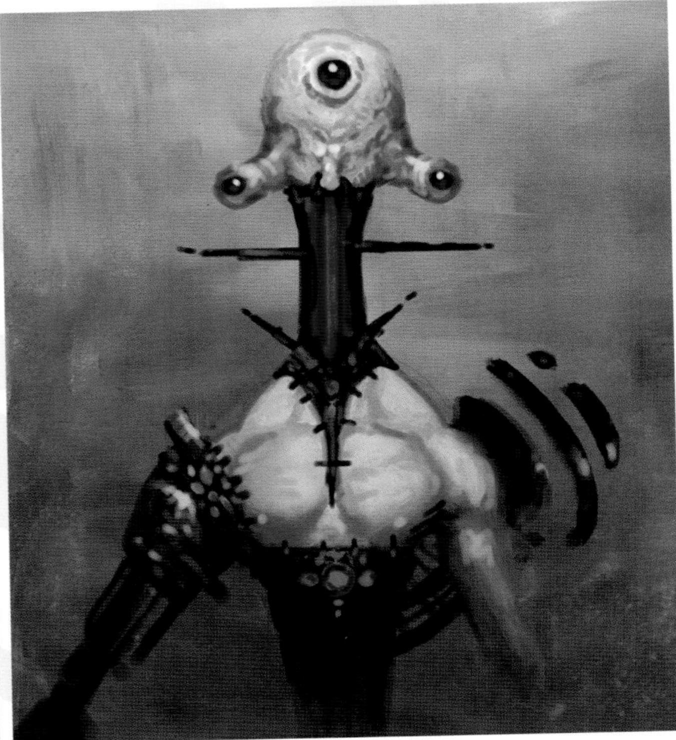

APPENDIX B: KICKSTARTER BACKERS

STRANGE EBOOK LOVER

~~PsyCow~~
1* Racing
A.P. Graham
A.P. van der Meer
Aaron "Jalinth" Davis
Aaron A. Virag
Aaron Alberg
Aaron Renfroe
Adam Nemo
Adam Rajski
Adam Shive
Adam the Strange
Admiral Willikins Wesleydale-Arboreal Tweed the Third
Adrian Bigland
Adrian Hughson
Aireona Raschke
Al Gonzalez
Alain "Thepp" Neuvens
Alan Spadoni
Alan Z. Eisinger
Aleix Grau Pons
Alex Bergquist
Alex Kent
Alex Koza
Alex Manduley
Alex Robin
Alex von Hochtritt
Alex Wreschnig
Alexander Opoku-Agyemang
Alexander Y. Hawson
Amiel Kievit
Amitai G
Ana-Rae Harris
Andreas "Beini" Beinhauer
Andreas Kolyvas
Andreas Monitzer
Andres Aguirre S
Andrew "Ranneko" Delaney
Andrew Betts
Andrew Cain
Andrew Cawdell
Andrew Connolly
Andrew Doucet
Andrew Duryea
Andrew Girdwood
Andrew Guastella
Andrew Hackard
Andrew J. Luther
Andrew Jenkins
Andrew Lazar
Andrew M Cady
Andrew Montgomery-Hurrell
Andrew Otto Linke
Andrew Topperwien
Andrew, Stacy, and Griffin Davis
Andries du Fay
Andy Gibson
Andy Goldman
Andy Rennard
Antoine Pempie
Arikail D'Marco
Artur Ganszyniec
Ashley "Arlyansor" McKay
Baradaelin
Bas Smeets
Bastien Daugas
Bekir Cihangir Buyukataman
Ben Archer
Ben Keeler
Ben Kidd
Ben P. Balestra
Benedict Hall
Benjamin and Christina Hernandez
Benjamin Reynolds
Benoit Devost
Bertil Jonell
Billie Abbitt
Black Light
Blake Bagwell
Brad Osborne
Bradley Russo
Brakus Blue
Brandon "Xar" McKee
Brant Clabaugh
Brendan Meghani
Brian M. Creswick
Brian "Chainsaw" Campbell
Brian Horstmann
Brian Petersen
Brian Zuber
Brice Chidester
Brice Coolen
Brooks G. Banks
Bruce Gray
Bruce Paris
Bruno Freitas
Bruno Patatas
Bryan Lee Davidson-Tirca
Bryan Whitlock
burningcrow
Butch2k
C. Paul Counts
C. S. Ferguson
CainSF
Caleb Shelley
Carl A Pabst Jr
Carl L Gilchrist
Casey Stutes
Casper Kvan Clausen
Catherine Evans-Gist
Cédric Jeanneret
Chad Bartlett
Chad Brown
Chad Stevens
Chadwick Shinabargar
Charles 'Dreamstreamer' Alston
Charles Moore
Charlie Reece
Chase Henderson
Chris
Chris 'The Silicoid' Preston
Chris Brashier
Chris Dolunt
Chris Edwards
Chris Gottbrath
Chris Heilman
Chris Michael Jahn
Chris Miles
Chris Shannon
Chris Sleep
Chris Thompson
Chris Turner
Chris Wachal
Christian Lambert
Christian Meyer
Christopher Anderson
Christopher Popp
Christopher Rogers
Christopher William Gilbert
Clay Karwan
Clay Pelon
Coboney
Cody Black
Colin "Mephit James" Wilson
Colin Campbell
Colin Fredericks
Colin Sng
Conrad Murkitt
Corey Pierno
Cormac Ó Foghlú
Craig Hackl
Craig Wright
CS Williams
Curt Meyer
Curtis Shephard
Damon Richard
Dan Alexander
Dan Maloy
Dan Martland
Dan Nicholson
dan0001
Daniel Abigail
Daniel Ley
Daniel McSorley
Daniel Pogoda
daniel singhal
Daniel Stack
Daniel Strange
Darrell Ottery
Dave Thompson
Dave Weinstein
David 'Zirnike' Gibeau
David "Tsu" Reichgeld
David Bagdan
David Berkompas
David Chart
David Dalton
David Dawson
David Dorward
David E Choate
David Lundy
David M-G
David McFall
David Nielsen
David Orna-Ornstein
David R Cooper Jr.
David R. Murrell
David Windrim
DelDotB
Derek Letterson
Derek Weister
Derick Larson
Devin Redd
DocChronos
Donald Wheeler
Doug "Dhomal" Raas
Doug Nordwall
Drew Astolfi
Duane P. Musiol
Duncan White
Dustin Rector
e. carletti
Earl Weaver
Edgar Black the Cyborg
Edward Durant
Edward Gray
Elias-John Fernandez-Aubert
Emily Leathers
Epheros Aldor
Eric C. Magnuson
Eric M Jackson
Eric Moffitt
Eric Pickney
Erick Allen
Erik Ingersen
Erik Olsen
Ernesto "Montalve" Ramirez
Eugenio Ruggiero
Ezra Harrington
Fabio Sgambuzzi
Felix Laurie von Massenbach
Flash, Mercury, and Blade
Francis Richardson
Francisco Di Lorenzo
Frank aka PurpleTentacle
Frank L Emanuel
Frank Niemeyer
Frank Reding
FrictionX42
G. Hartman
Gabriel Brouillard
Gaël Le Mignot
Galen Pejeau
Gareth Lewis
Garin Hiebert
Garry Jenkins
Gary M Stetler-Williams
Gavin Kenny
George Chatzipetros
George Kapp
Gerald L Rose Jr
Gian Holland
Glazius
Glen "Zenfar" Martin
Glen Green
Gökhan Akdeniz
Graeme Lewis
Greg Conant
Greg Morrow
Greg Mount
Greg Patchett
Gregory 'Jadedpaladin' Bowes
Gry Haram
Guillaume Tremblay
Gunnar Bangsmoen
Gunnar Högberg
Guzman Vilanova
H. M. 'Dain' Lybarger
Hamish Laws
Hans "Infernalistgamer" Watts
Hans Christoffer Sandnes
Haran Sened
Heath Rezabek
Heather White
His Strangeness Count Count
Hudds Magruder
Ian Foster
Ian Kitley
Ian M Kirby
Ian Whitehead
Ilya Konovalov
Imfarias
Iskaltyr the Sly
Izak Tait
J-P Spore
Jack Bross
Jacob Dylan Riddle
Jacob Haronga
Jacob Kopczynski
Jacob N. Hudson
James Byrne
James Husum
James Kreutz
James Ramirez
James Vannier
James Worley
Jamie 'Reech' Walker
Jamie Heywood
Jamie Wells
Jamie Wheeler
Jan Mäkinen
Janet L. Oblinger
Janne Luukkonen
Janning Cunis
Jared Buckley
Jared Groth
Jared Kinkade
Jason F. Broadley
Jason Levine
Jason Martinez
Jason Morgan
Jason R.
Jason Sunday
Jason Tack
Jason Van Ess
Jason Wayne Keesey
Jay Kint
Jay Peters
Jayna Pavlin
Jean-philippe Bardot
Jeff Hitchcock
Jeff Jones
Jeff Narucki
Jeff R. Hildebrand
Jeff Segal
Jeff Shepherd
Jeff Stoner
Jeff Terrill
Jeff Xilon
Jeffrey Allan Boman
Jeffrey Chen
Jeffrey E. Niebres
Jeffry Rinkel
Jenny Graham-Jones
Jeremiah Brougher
Jeremiah Patrick
Jeremie Gravel
Jeremy Ackerman-Yost
Jeremy Griffin
Jeremy Marshall
Jesse Reynolds
Jessica Hammer
Jim Clunie
Jim Stutz
Jimbo Staggins
João Carrera
Joe DaSilva
Joe Dunham
Joe Fusion
Joe Kirby
Joe Slucher
Joe Stroup
Joerg Sterner
John 'imjedi' Long
John "Millionwordman" Dodd
John "Oz" Oswald
John Buczek
John D
John D. Barr
John Davies
John Patrick Miner
John R. Trapasso
John Speck
John T. Overath
John Thompson
John Thontos Rutkowski
John Ward
Johnathan L Munroe
Jon Michaels
Jon Swanson
Jon Wright
Jonas "TheSpaceMan" Pettersson
Jonathan 'Weasel' Dibblee
Jonathan Agens
Jonathan Cliffen
Jonathan G. Tinsley
Jonathan Korman
Jonathan Metzger
Jonathan Ruffin
Jonathan Shaver
Jonathan Spengler
Jordan Fong
Jordan Springer
Jordi Rabionet
Joseph Cortese
Joseph Geary
Josh "JP" Parrish
Josh Lowry
Josh S. Ziegler
Josh Solomon
Josh the dwarf Flint
Joshua Cameron
Joshua Edwards
Joshua Lenon
JP Lee
Juan Adolfo Lucha Garcia

Juan Diego Pucurull
Juan Pablo de Betolaza
Judd M. Goswick
Jude Vais
Jürgen Hubert
Justin Delaney
Justin Dorsey
Justin McDaniel
Kari Lehtikari
Karl A. Rodriguez
Karl Larsson
Karl Lommerse
Kary "Realm Master K" Williams
Kash Tan Kah Shin
Katie and Marc Davignon
Kenneth Hite
Kesipyc
Kevin C Jenkins (Keovar)
Kevin C. Carpenter
Kevin M Sullivan
Kevin McLean
Kevin Mueller
Kielo Blomqvist
Kieron Gilbert
Kiith
Kim L. Fenwick
Kiraen
Kitty Milar
Kris, Elizabeth, Lina and Jennifer Herzog
Kristopher Volter
Kurtis Franks
Kyle D. Jones
Kyle Ryan
Lachlan Bakker
Laura Schmidt
Laurent Labrot
Laurent Tastet
Lawrence Huang
Lee Barklam
Leigh George Kade
Leo Lee
Liyana Von Zuiden
lobachevsky
Lobo
lobo pampeano
Loren 'Shadolrds' Foster
Lowell Brandt Stouder II
Luke Day
Luke Moran
M. Alexander Jurkat
M. Scott Veach
MakorDal
Malcolm E. Fisher
Manuel Quick
Manuel Siebert
Marc Senecal
Marcel Pockrandt
Marco "_Journeyman_" Bignami
Marcus Ilgner
Marcus Luft
Mark Chu-Carroll
Mark Cockerham
Mark Galpin
Mark Hanna
Mark Mealman
Mark Sweetman
Markus Pfeil
Markus Raab
Markus Wagner
Marsell
Martin Chesnay
Mason Zedaker
Massimo Spiga
Matt Banning
Matt Kovich
Matt Park
Matt Sceadu
Matthew "Haxar" Shaw
Matthew and Teresa Neves-Craft
Matthew Gross
Matthew Houghton
Matthew Johnston
Matthew R May-Day
Matthew Rees
Matthew Smitheram
Matthew Tucker, Geekmaster
Matthew York
Matthias Nagy
Matti Rintala
Mattia Norando
Maurizio Mancino
Max Kaehn
Max Woerner Chase
Maximilian Gottwein
Michael Beck
Michael D. Blanchard
Michael Eringsmark
Michael Feldhusen
Michael Friedrich Knaus
Michael Hill
Michael Langford
Michael Macaulay
Michael Oney
Michael Schmitz
Michael Sutch
Michael Van Altena
Mikael Assarsson
Mike "Black Wolf" Browne
Mike Bowie
Mike Carlson
MIKE DAVEY
Mike Montgomery
Mike Parkinson
Mike Welham
Mike Zwick
Mindy Chua (:
Mitchell M. Evans
Morten N A
MP
N. B. Perley
Nathan Revere
Nathan Turner
Neil Coles
Neil T. Hetzel
Nicholas "Technomancer" Roberts
Nicholas Alexander Tan
Nicholas Peterson
Nicholas R. Cawley
Nicholas Zakhar
Nick & Kyle Vertodoulos
Nick Bate
Nicole Vaicunas
Nigel Garrett
Niklas Nymann Westensee
Nikolaj Kaare Nørskov
Nikolas Stelmashenko
Nobilis Reed
Nofar Spalter
Ogasnor
Olin Petty
Oliver Baillie
Oscar Ulloa
Otmar Rausch
Ovidnine
Owen Meldrim Moore
Pablo Hernández Hellín
Pablo Palacios
Patrice Mermoud
Patrick Harnack
Paul "Fragarach" Hodges
Paul Beyard
Paul Brincat
Paul D. Kroll
Paul Hayes
Paul Hazen
Paul S. Kim
Paul Sheppard
Pedro García
Pedro R. Martínez Pérez
Pete Griffith
Pete Newell
Peter "PJDanger" Dean
Peter Andersson
Peter Klevvall
Peter R Brooks
Petit Manchot
Petr "de Canzaparca" Asalkhanov
Phil Nicholls
Philip Adler
Philippe Niederkorn
Phillip Bailey
Philo Pharynx
Pinto Town
Qali Va'Shen
R. Austin Hager
R. Stephens Summerlin
Raf Bressel
Random - the dog.
Ray Slakinski
Raymond M. S. Quignon
"Reseru" Sansone
Ria Hawk
Richard 'Vidiian' Greene
Richard "Ritter" Carroll
Richard "Zashier" Hletko
Richard A. Oliver
Richard Avirett
Richard Fannon
Richard Keen, Jr.
Richard Lord
Richard Malena
Rick Wheeler
Rob Donoghue
Rob Downing
Rob Johns
Rob van Vlimmeren
Rob Winkler
Robb Thomas
Robert Biskup
Robert C
Robert G. Male
Robert McClanahan
Robert Peacock
Robert Stehwien
Robin Hampton
Rohit Sodhia
Roman Kalik
Ron Searcy
Ronald Corn
Ronny "RoninRa" Anderssen
Ross Chow
Roxane Tourigny
Ryan Hart
Ryan Mathes
Ryan Quinn
Ryan S. Dancey
S. R. Dreamholde
S. Scott Mullins
Sami Kemper
Scott 'Blade' Hamilton
Scott "Gunstar" Berger
Scott Boehmer
Scott Butler
Scott Fitzgerald Gray
Sean Beattie
Sean K.I.W. Steele
Sean McLaughlin
Sean Richmond
Sean Sherman
Sebastian Gebski
Sebastian Hans Wilhelm Hamke
Seth Hartley
Shadrick Paris
Shane Cubis
Shane Mclean
Sharang Biswas & Clio Davis
Shaun Tabone
Shawn Lamb
Shawn Riley-Rau
Shawna Rothgeb-Bird
Sigurbjörn L. Þrastarson
Silvio Herrera Gea
Simon
Single Helix Studios
SJ Renton
some vaguely creepy dude
Steen Hefsgaard Jacobsen
Stefan Kiczko
Stefan Mars
Stefan Sautter
Steph Turmer
Stephan Szabo
Stephan Zacharias
Stephanie Bryant
Stephen Egolf
Stephen Esdale
Stephen Fotta
Stephen Wilcoxon
Sterling Hershey
Steve Acheson
Steve Leventhal
Steven A. Torres-Roman
Steven Conforti
Steven D Warble
Steven Helberg
Steven Moore
Steven Owens
Steven T. Myers
Sumeet Jain
Sven Bott
Tealus
Ted Atkinson
Ted Ludemann
Teo Wan Liang
Terrence Rideau
the Encaffeinated ONE
The Veterans of a Thousand Midnights
Theo
Theodore T. Posuniak, II
thewyvernslayer
Thomas Gassner
Thomas M. Smith
Thomas Maund
Thomas P. Kurilla
Thorizan d'Peregrin
Tim Harron
Tim Soholt
Timothy T Cheng
Todd "webRat" Rafferty
Todd Christopher
Todd Wilkes
Tom Ladegard
Tomá Denemark
Tony McDowell
Tony Mynttinen
Tophe LaGarde
Tor Iver Wilhelmsen
Trey Mercer
Trip Space-Parasite
Tripleyew
Tristan Zimmerman
Troy Baker
Troy Larson
Ultra Bithalver
Umberto Lenzi
Vlad Zsariski
Vojtech Pribyl
Werewolf
Wesley Williams
Whitney Lee
Will
William D. Seurer
William Guyaux
William Hensley
WOoDY GamesMaster
Wyldstar
Yann Krehl

BASIC STRANGER

a_ferret
Aaron "KaBLaQ" Farrington
Aaron Benjamin Carter
Aaron Blair Teixeira
Aaron Buttery
Adam Felder
Adam Waggenspack
Adam Wise Francis
Adam Y.
Adem Sawyer
Adrian Zollinger
Adriano Varoli Piazza
Agustín Van Rompaey
AL Lajeunesse
Alan Larkin
Aleksander Lie
Aleksi Airaksinen
Alessandro "Seghetto" Milani
Alex Chobot
Alexander Dempsey
Alexander Turner
Alonso O. Rubio
Amauris Morel
Amy Mundt
Andrea Baruzzi - Imola - Italy
Andrea E Phillips
Andrea Gaulke
Andrea Gillespie
Andrew D. Devenney
Andrew Lloyd
Andrew Lohmann
Andrew Morris
Andrew Reid
Andrija Popovic
Andy "awmyhr" MyHR
Andy Rau
Annette
anterobot
Anthony Della Rocco
Anthony Jones
Antoine Aka Illyan
Antoine V.
Araswen
Artur "SySCR" Jeziorski
Ashran Firebrand
Axel GOTTELAND
Amorphous
"Bajorque" aka Anne-Sylvie Betsch
Barrett W Nuzum
Bart Hennigan
Beachfox
Becky Weisgerber
Belegdel
Ben Ferguson
Ben Novack
Ben Quant
Benjamin A. Hoyt
Benjamin Loy
Benjamin McCann
Betsy J
Big Game Reviews
Bill Bridges
Bill G Tinnin-Timm
Black Bunny
Bob Johnson
Bob Munsil
Brad Gunnels
Brad Jones
Brad Larson
Brandon "Drake" Reed
Brandon Eymann
brazil808
Brennan Dawson
Brett Abbott
Brett Hennock
Brett Weidman
Brian Adam & Kai Laurent Ellis
Brian Benincasa
Brian C. Vander Veen
Brian Carpenter
Brian DiTullio
Brian Everett
Brian Oma Thomas
Brit Garrett
Bruce Powell
Bruce Turner
Bryan Reed
BXS
C Cosper
Callum Shaw
Calvin D. Jim
Calvin Grimm
Cameron Haggett
Cameron Harris
Cameron Paine
Carey Williams
Carl Malota
Casey A.P.D. Karch
Cassio Yamamura
Chad Myles
Chaos
Charles "I make children cry" Tippett

Charles Chapman
Charles Meyer
Charlie Smith
Charlie Vick, Adapting to the Strange
Chevaliers
Chip Morris
Chris Bremer
Chris Burnside
Chris C Cerami
Chris Camburn
Chris Conway
Chris Dulsky
Chris Farrell
Chris Fenton
Chris Gwinn
Chris McLean
Chris W. Harvey
Chris William Mobberley
Chris Wolfe (Wolfman1911)
Christian Denton
Christian Rothe
Christian Seiler
Christophe Hertigers
Christophe Saura
Christopher Avery
Christopher C Gray
Christopher E. Gerber
Christopher Hill
Christopher J. Williams
Christopher Lockey
Christopher M. Sniezak
Christopher Naylor
Chuck Childers
Chuck Mock
Cj. Young
Clint Elliot "Pippin" Malcolm
Clinton Macgowan
Cody Swatek
Colen McAlister
Colin Buckler
Corwyn Crawford And Brianna Wyn
Craig Brierley
Craig J. Parent
Craig Mead
Craig Steinhoff
Crash Collison
Cronuz Awesome
Cullen "Towelman" Gilchrist
Curtis Tom
Cynthia Kira Cooper
D. Jon Mattson
Damon Dougherty
Dan Dubinsky
Dan Forinton
Dan L Pierson
Dan Stewart
Dancing Golem
Daniel G. Dimitroff
Daniel Helman
Daniel Kassiday
Daniel Singer
Daniel Yauger
Darrell S. Lusardi
Darren Miguez
Darryl Park
Darryl R. Farr
Dave Blewer
Dave Chalker
Dave Gross
Dave Teske
David Ackerman
David Adwokat
David Amburgey
David Annandale
David Bates
David Birchall
David Glennie
David Gutierrez Arribas
David H. Lake
David Harold
David Hinojosa
David Hoffman
David Hughart
David Hughes
David J. Zimmerman
David Joy
David LaMacchia
David M Jacobs
David McCown
David Meese
David Myers
David Neumann
David Noonan
David Paul
David R. Hill
David Tejera Expósito
David Terhune
David Wiley Holton
Dean Lucius
DeAnna Ferguson
Dennis D. Rude
Dennis Pejcha
Derek and Ashley Torgerson
Derek Curtis-Tilton
Derek Garrison
Derek Groothuis
Derek Guder
Devin La Salle
Dirk Koch
Dirtybacon
DJ Blackford
Dom "by the tentacles" Toghill
Don Kamillo
Doug Patriarche
Doug Pippy
Dougal
Dr. Dustin Spencer DNP
Dr. Mandark
Dr. Mike Capps
Drew (Andrew) South
Drew Wendorf
Duley Crabbe
Dwayne Schueller
Dyami Chiasson
Ed Sagritalo
Edgar G.
Edouard Contesse
Eeshwar Rajagopalan
Elijah Elefson
Ely Dane
Epic RPG Blog
Eric & Stephanie Franklin
Eric Baker
Eric Rossing
Eric Schroeder
Erik Emrys Carl
Erik Hymel
Erik Parker
Erik Stant
Erika Eby
Etienne Gagné
Eugene Sax
Evan Braaten
Evan D. Myers
Evan Dorman
Evan W.J. Parson
Everitt Long
Fabrice Mangin
Fatma Alici
Felipe Brumatti Sentelhas
Felipe Leal Sabino
Fletcher
Forest Pavel
Francis Egerton
François Labrecque
Frank Armenante
Frank C. Carr
Frédéric Méthot
Gabe Usry
Gabriel L. Helman
Gareth B. Johnson sirgarethskeep
Garrett Pauls
Gemma Charles
Geoffrey T. Nelson
George Leandro Luna Bonfim
Geza Letso
Giacomo Lodi
Giampaolo Agosta
Goliath Typho
Gordon Guy
Gordon Hage
Gothhog
Graham Pierson
Graham Spearing
Graham Wills
Greg Childress
Greg Higgins
Greg Medhurst
Grendel MacCaine
Grey Growl
Gustavo "Tanaka" La Fontaine
Hal Greenberg
Hanover Fiste
Hectaimon
Henk Birkholz
Henry Wong
Hollis McCray
Holly Cook
Hrvoje Ruhek
Hugh Ashman
IAMCRAWFORD
Ian D Ward
Ian Grey
Ian M Jordan
Ian Newborn
Ian Spaulding
Ignatius Montenegro
Imanol Bautista Trancón
INCyr
J. Quincy Sperber
J. Stuart Pate
J.B. Scott
Jack Norris
Jacob Kessler
James Alan Gardner
James Allen
James Becker
James Bridges
James Bryant
James C. Ross
James Cruise
James Doherty
James F Tillman
James Powell
James Weibel
Japegrape
Jarick Cammarato
Jason Bradley
Jason Coleman (BinaryAgent)
Jason Cortese
jason e. bean
Jason Gilmore
Jason Lescalleet
Jason M. Baker
Jason M. Stewart
Jason Marks
Jason Mavor
Jason Nell
Jason Ramboz
Jason Riek
Jason Smith
Jason, Kristin, and Peter Childs
Javier Díaz Suso
Javier Viruete
Jay Earle
Jay Warner
Jazzman Lewis
Jean-Baptiste Vlassoff
Jeb Woodard
Jeff D. Hershberger
Jeff Healy
Jeff Heaney
Jeff Iverson
Jeff Lindsay
Jeff Zitomer
Jeffery Hines
Jeffery Szudzik
JEFFREY A. JONES
Jeffrey B. Miller
Jeffrey Edgington
Jeffrey Gates
Jeffrey Hosmer
JEFFREY J CRAIG
Jeffrey Palmer
Jeffrey Weiskopff
Jen W
Jere Manninen
Jeremy Land
Jeremy Puckett
Jesse Paul Thacker
Jesus A. Rodriguez
Jhereth Jax
Jim Groves
Jim Johnson
Jim Long
Jim Moss
Jim Reader
Joe Frankovitch
Joe Larson
Joel Flank
Joerg M. Mosthaf
Joey Ruina
John "Goon" Williams
John "johnkzin" Rudd
John "Vezketh" Swinkels
John Beattie
John Bellando
John Brewer
John Kingdon
John Kirkland
John Kovalic
John M. Portley
John Paul Ashenfelter
John Pierce
John Pingo
John R. Troy
John Roberts
John Singleton
John Spey
John T Coleman
John T. Lafin
John WS Marvin
John-Matthew DeFoggi
Jon Blackwell
Jon J Stoltenberg
Jon Moore
Jon Scott Edwards
Jonas Karlsson
Jonathan Eskritt
Jonathan Killstring
Jonathan Leopold
Jonathon Dyer
Joos Ketelslegers
Jordan Cwang
Jorge Carrero Roig
José 'Hoser' Fitchett
José The Weird Porfírio
Jose Toledo Fuster
Joseph "Eponymous" Kogin
Joseph A. Russell
Joseph Choe
Joseph Henrich
Joseph McRoberts
Joseph Thater
Josh and Lindsey Ricard
Josh Arnold
Josh Demaree - THE ESTABLiSHED FACTS Podcast
Josh Meunier
Josh Murray
Joshua James Gervais
Joshua Kale
Joshua O'Connor-Rose
Joshua P. Smith
Joshua Pender
Joshua Sears-Gamache
Joshua Tanase
Joshua Taylor Smith
JP Sugarbroad
Julian C. Steen
justchris
Justin Cabuster Edwards
Justin Dunmyre
Justin Thomason
K. Stuckmeyer
k'Bob42
KAHMAL THE SHAMAN
Karel van Breda
Karen S. Conlin
Karl Charles
Karl Grette
Karl Thiebolt
Katie and Fil Rhinehart
Kazekami
Keith E. Clendenen
Keith Hamm
Keith I. Duncan
Keith Nelson
Keith Shaw
Ken Burruss
Ken Richardson
Kevin "Psyches" Plante-Germain
Kevin & Kaylee Rank
Kevin E. Mowery
Kevin Hislop
Kevin Ohannessian
Kevin Shilling
Kevin Stout
Kilian Klebes
Kim Nohr
Kirt Andrew Dankmyer
Kjetil Kverndokken
Krister Looveer
Kristina Tracer
Kristopher T Zachman
Kyle Jackson
Kyle MacKay
Kyle Takamoto
Lars J Hiim
Lateef Livers
Laura Thompson
Lauren Anne Perpetua Marino
Lenurd the Joke Gnome
Leo Campos
Lex Starwalker
Lin Wyeth
Lisandro Gaertner
Lissa Guillet
Lloyd "OmegaSol" Stang
Lorcan Murphy
Lord Darth Travis Bartholomew Winston Gary Woodall IX, Esq.
Lou Bajuk-Yorgan
Luca Beltrami
Luke C Niedner
Luke Greene
M. Christopher Freeman
M.R. Gorgone
Malik Amoura
Marc Noordzij
marc watson
Marion Nalepa
Mark "Dojo" Brown
Mark Argent
Mark Craddock
Mark Fielding
Mark Llewellyn James
Mark Perneta
Mark Sherman
Mark Teppo
Mark W. Bruce
Mark Woodside
Martin Cumming
Martin Hills
Martin Wagner
Mary Kay Johnston
Mathew Reuther
Matt Bridgeman-Rivett
Matt Burns
Matt Popke
Matt Shursen
Matthew 'RebelliousUno' Robertson
Matthew "Quady" Bohme
Matthew "Vinco" Taylor
Matthew Bongers
Matthew Broome
Matthew Markland
Matthew Nielsen
Matthew Swinburne
Matthew Trent
Mattia Davolio
Mauricio "MSex" Moura
Max Kadmus

MaxMahem
Mendel Schmiedekamp
Meric and Jennifer Moir
Mia & Dan Eng-Kohn
Michael "CodexofRome" Bay
Michael "The Mad Hatter" Pye
Michael & Danielle Beekman
Michael Babich
Michael Bjørn Bahne Christensen
Michael Chorney
Michael D Hoteck
Michael De Rosa
Michael Dempsey
Michael J. Dulock
Michael Mockus
Michael Norman
Michael O'Reilly
Michael Ostrokol
Michael Penny
Michael Prettiman
Michael R. Smith
Michael R. Underwood
Michael Richards
Michael Thomas & John Kusters
Michael W. Mattei
Michel Cayer
Mike "Blue" Kanarek
Mike "Sly Flourish" Shea
Mike Coleman
Mike Loftus
Miko
Miles Matton
minitrue
MIR
Morgan Hay
mundanename
Murph.
Mykel Alvis
Nathan Graham
Nathan Lax
Nathan Trail
Neal Kaplan
Nicholas Guttenberg
Nick "Firavin" Bell
Nick Barone
Nick Keyuravong
Nick Mulherin
Nick Pawps Salony
Nick Schweitzer
Nicolas Lathoumetie
Ninjar
Noah Klosinski
Nohwear
Norbert Baer
Oh Seung Han (Wishsong)
Oliver Peltier
Omaq Bek
Oren Geshuri
Owen 'Sanguinist' Thompson
Parus Paron "Par" Donner
Pascal "Plageman" Pflugfelder
Pascal M. Daniel
Patrick Henry Downs
Patrick Joynt
Patrick Kraft
Patrick Pautler
Patrick Tubach
Paul 'the Bastard' Douglas
Paul "Tankmodeler" Roberts
Paul C
Paul G. Harris
Paul Havens
Paul Kohler
Paulo Rafael Guariglia Escanhoela
Pedro Dani Calvo Romeo
Pete Hurley
Petteri Sulonen
Phil Lucas
Philipp Hinderer
Philippe Debar
Phillip Sacramento
Pierre "Kergonan" Feunteun
Piers Beckley
Piotr Kraciuk
PrometheusUB
Quinn Halligan
R Little
Randall Dederick
Randy Nichols
Randy White
Raymond Finch
Real Atomsk
Ren Decena
Reto M. Kiefer
Rev. Dr. Jackson Keddell
Reverance Pavane
RFP
Ricardo "Sardonis" Penteado
Rich Chamberlain
Richard A M Green
Richard Dufault
Richard E Flanagan
Richard Hirsch
Richard W. Rohlin
Rick "Brelach" White
Rick Caldwell
Rick Harrelson
RJ Howe
Rob Eisenberg
Rob Heinsoo
Rob Lowry
Robert "Ayslyn" Van Natter
Robert "Barasawa" Rosenthal
Robert "Mystical Seeker" Kupcek
Robert Austin O'Neal
Robert D. Grier
Robert Freeborn
Robert Gilson
Robert J. Schwalb
Robert James
Robert L. Flowers Jr.
Robert Morris
Robert Murray
Robert Poulin
Robert Rees
Robert S. Aldrich II
Robert van Wijk
Robert Verboom
Roberto "Sunglar" Micheri
Roberto Quintans
Rod & Anne Shelton
Rod Meek
Ron Lipke
Rory J. Murphy
Ross Bundy
Roy Grantham
Roy Killington
Russell Brown
Russell Ventimeglia
Ruth Hyatt
Ryan Clark Thames
Ryan Gigliotti
Ryan Hinson
Ryan Nelson-Rury
Ryan Percival
S. Viswanathan
Sage Brush
Sam Conway
Sam Hillaire
Sam Parker
Sameer Yalamanchi
Samir El Aouar
Sandu Bogi Nasse
Sara and her strange cat Toast
Scott Alvarado
Scott C. Bourgeois
Scott C. Nolan
Scott Gable
Scott Geisler
Scott Paeth
Scott Smith
Scott Tooker
Scott Vandehey
Sean 'Ariamaki' Riedinger
Sean Brady
Sean Gibb
Sean M Smith
Sean M. Hope
Sean McClure
Sean McNeil
Sean O'Dell
Selene O'Rourke
Sephie Lunawind
Seth Newell
Seth Silvernail
Seth Thomson
sev
Shane "The Pain" Emmons
Shane Kennedy
Shane Runkle
Shaun D. Burton
Shawn Schultz
Simon "Smescrater" Carter
Simon `Flatliner' Jones
Simon Berg
Simon D. McAleney
Simon Ward
Skwiziks
Spellforger
Spencer Davis
Stan!
Stefan Miller
Stefan Scott Huddleston
Stephanie Wagner
Stephen Abel
Stephen Adkins
Stephen Childs
Stephen R. Brandon
Steve "Leidus" Gilman
Steve Arensberg
Steve Benton
Steve Elliott
Steve Holder
Steve Mumford
Steve Salem
Steven Danielson
Steven Gurr
Steven K. Watkins
Stijn Hoop
Stuart Hodge
Stuart Smith
Sune Gamby
SUNSHINE corp.
Susan Davis
Sven Howard
Svend Andersen
Sylvain "Sly" Pronovost
T. E. Hendrix
T. H. M. Gellar-Goad
T. Rob Brown
tavernbman
Ted Childers
Terrell Scoggins
Thiago Goncalves
Thibaut Gaillard
Thomas Colard
Thomas Darlington
Thomas Fleming
Thomas Krømke
Thomas R. Smith
Thomas Siemens
Tiago Marinho
Tim Bogosh
Tim Czarnecki
Tim Partridge
Tim Thomas
Tim Vandenberghe
Timo Liimatta
Timothy Albert Rascher
Timothy E.M. Morris
Tom Deprez "zifnabbe"
Tom Lommel
Tom McCarthy
Torbjörn Johnson
Traveler Farlander
Travis Boettcher
Travis Middleton
Tristan Knight
Tristen S. Gardner
Trond "Antitakt" Birkeland
Troy Ellis
Troy Pichelman
Turbiales (Román Moreno Urdiales)
Tyler Dalious
Tyler J. Duckworth
Tyson Mueller
Van Butler
Vesku N. Fyador
Viktor Haag
Vincent "le Saint" Langlois
Vincent "Sabbak" Zimmermann
W Ryan Carden
Wade Jones
Walter Manbeck
Walter Wattenburger III
Waning Gibbous Games
Warren Sistrom
Wayne Reid
"Weird Dave" Olson
Weston Clowney
Whitt.
William 'Mycroft' Curtis
William & Sheila
William G Adams
William Gordon
William J. (B.J.) Altman
William Jared Walker
William Ogden
William Thorpe
Wizbang The Mighty
Wolrum
Worldlinemine
wraith808
Xeantho-Mas of Dhuth
Zabuni
Zach Brown
Zalzator

STRANGE SIGNATURES

Alberto Bermudo Delgado
Alexander "Xan" Kashev
Amauri antunes pereira junior
Andrew Laliberte
Benjamin L. Liew
Bennett Nason
Bradford Chatterjee
Carlos A. Steffens
Chris Flipse
Chris W Mercer
Christopher Lefevre
Christopher WJ Rueber
Dan Harms
David Edward Watt
David Gori
Denis Gagnon
Dominic McDiarmid
Gordon Duke
Ignacio Blasco López
James T Edwards
Jamie Varni
Jason Templeton
Jesse R. Davis
Joe Rapoza
Jonna Hind
Kristofer Castro
Lester Ward
M Goldrich
Marco Veltri
Marni Erwin
Matthew "Thrantor" Allen
Matthew Wallace
Miguel Luis "Dindo" N. Moreno IV
Mitchell "Haematite" Christov
Nathaniel Rosenberg
Nicholas Edwards
Niels Adair
Paul Foster
Pirata Poldo
Rafael Loureiro
Ric Wagner
Robert Fisher
S. Adam Surber
Samuli "Hertzila" Hannuksela
Signorini Matteo
Tim Smith
Tracy Landrum
Wolfgang Knebel
Zaid Crouch

TWO GAMES TOGETHER

A. Leslie
Alaina Orwitz
Alistair Rigg
Andrew Elliott
Barry Snyder
Benjamin "The Merchant of the Strange" Schwarze
Benjamin Tolputt
Bert Shaw
Blake Thomas
Bradley Reddell
Brent Erdman
brian peters
Cesar Cesarotti
Christopher Leth
Christopher Malone
Clayton "Wise Kobold" Rennie
Clem Powell
Craig Bishell
Dan McCormack
Dante Warborn
David W. Morrow
David Wood
Donald Derrick
Eric Bontz
Evan Hicks
Francis Kavanagh
Gastón Keller (aka Gurtaj)
Greg Linklater
Greg Stockton
Griffin D. Morgan
gumboots_smithy
Helen June Crumpholt
Ian Cox
Ian Keeley
Ivo de Mooij
Jäger Hein
Jake "Yachabus" Scheirer
jenofdoom
Jens Thorup Jensen
Jerry "RWL" Bocci
Jesse Thomas Alford
Jim Burakiewicz
Jim F.
Joe Schillizzi
Joel Tone
John A. Judd
John Perrine
Jon "Stillbjorn" Jurisich
Jon Wegner
Jonathan Flavius Richards
Joseph B. Connors Jr.
Josh Daniels
Joshua Ross-Daly
Kara Baker
Kazuyuki Kitajima
Ken Anderson
Kevin Wine
Kyle Burckhard
Lee and Mel Guille
Leonardo Carvalho da Paixão
Marcos Cavalheiro Pereira
Matt Rock
Matthew Orwig
Michael Falinski
Millet
Mitchell Frazer
Nate Koehler
Nate Taylor
Nicholas D. Dragisic
Nikita Burachenko
Oliver Rathbone
Paul Andrews
Paul Whitfield
Pellanor
Randall Wald
Raven O'Fiernan
Robert C. Kim
Ron Sparks
Ryan Junk
Sam Hing
Samuel "DMSamuel" Dillon
Sergey Saltykov
Simen Pettersen
SK Lim

Stephen Johnston
Stephen R. Shulusky
Steve McGarrity
Steven Joncas
Tad Rudnicki
Ted Conti, Jr.
Teppo Pennanen
The great and powerful Bunny
Thomas Neville
Tiffany Korta
Tim C Kryselmire
Tim Deschene
Todd Terwilliger
Tony Fiorentino
Vaughan Sanders
Wackomus
Will Rencenberger
William Fellows
William Roger Wakeman
William W. Lynt III
Xavid
Yann Lachance Cantarella

STRANGE SPECIAL SIGNATURES
Aaron DeChant
Aaron Wong
Bryan Allen Hickok
Craig "Zeejin" Walmsley
Daniel Casey O'Donovan
Dave 'Wintergreen' Harrison
Drew Pessarchick
Eric Toczek
Jay Watson
Joe Yun
Leslie S. Sedlak
Mr Bunraku
Nicole Mezzasalma
Ramien
Shenzoar
Todd Beaubien
Violaytor Melvin

STRANGE BOOKS
Allan Mills
Andrew Beasley
Andrew Wilson
Ben McFarland
Ben shultz
Benjamin Mishler
Braden Dougherty
Breanna Magallones
Cédric Steffen
Chris and Carol Ellison
Christopher Martin
Craig T.
Dan Bond
Daniel Andrlik
Daniel B. Nissman
DAv
David J. Clark
David Lewis
David Mandeville
David Morgan
Deana Lancaster
Duncan Eshelman
Dylan J Robinson
Edward Chavers
Eric Josue
Eric T Walchak DO
Erik Cooper
Gary E. Weller
Geoff Skinner
Geoffrey Sears
George Richardson III
Hans Cummings
J. Patrick Walker
James A. Velez
James Klingler
James Vogel
Jason "Tyrian" Emery
Jeff Rosenberg
Jeff Schultz
Jesse Nash
John Michael Hess
Josh Hamilton
Joshua Wayne Davis
Karl Okerholm
Keith Baker
Ken Ditto
Kristian Robben
Leo Byrne Jenicek, Knight of M.A.R.S.H.A.L.
Lorien Radmer
Marco Andre Mezzasalma
Matt Riek
Matthew James Mulherin
Mattizo
Michael Lane
Michael Ray McLaughlin
Murray K. Dahm
Orin Holland
Owen Clarke
Paco Garcia Jaen
Patrick Halverson
Patryk 'Ruemere' Adamski
Phil McGregor
Phillip Millman
Ralf van der Enden
Randy, Char, Iaine & Aydan MacKay
Richard Tamalavitch II
Robert Biddle
Ron Robinson
Ryan Moore
Scott Krok
Shan Lewis
Shawn "theDINGbat" R.
Steve Howes
Steve Lord
Steven Samorodin
Sylvain Sylvaniel Bouvier
Terry Mealy
Tom Lynch
Tone Berg
Tracy J. Gosell
Troy "Wrongtown" Hall
Vladimir Dzundza
William Lockwood

STRANGE PLAYTESTER
Adam Ness
Benjamin Liepis
Christian Taylor
Craig Edwards
David Futterrer
David Hatfield
David Walker
Etienne Moreau
Ian Jenkinson
Jason Blalock
Jeffrey Zimmer
John Gregory
John Rogers
Kat Richardson
M Grancey
Matt Hufstetler
Michael Waters
Nancy Feldman
Richard J. Gresham II
Ronald Pyatt
Scott Lindsay
Stuart Greenwell
Sungam Siirf
Tim Broach
Wajanai Snidvongs

A STRANGE FAMILY
Ben Mandall
Mishy Stellar

STRANGE PRINT BOOK LOVER
Aaron D. Fleming
Aaron R Corff
Aaron Reimer
Adam R. Easterday
Alex Meadows
Allen Thornton
Amber Thiesen
Andrea Steiner
Andrew & Monica Marlowe
Andrew James David Taylor
ANIMAfelis
Arthur C. Adams
Ben "pmumble" Harrison
Ben Madden
Ben Wilson
Bertrand BRY
Bradford Cone
Brian Nielsen
Carlos Sari
Chanti
Charles L. Allen
Chris Fong
Chris McLaren
Chris Mortika
Chris Sylvis
Chris Von Wahlde
Christopher Baar
Clément Jauvion
cOgnaut
Craig McGeachie
Dan Luxenberg
Dane Winton
Daniel Evans
Daniel Randlett
Darcy Town
Darius "Wayward son" Sayers
Darred Surin
Darren J. Stengel
Dave Thomas
David Cadoret
David Jackson
David M. Higgins
David Nix
David Poppel
David Wilson Brown
Dean Mathison
Dustin Headen
Ed Kowalczewski
Ellerain
Emilie Nouveau
Eoin Burke
Eric Fickenscher
Eric Nielsen
Eric Stankiewicz
Eric White
Erik T. Johnson
Ethan P Wellman
Fabio Passamonti
Felipe "failWizard" Jeges
Felipe de Amorim
Filthy Monkey
Fizzikx
Frazer Porritt
Fredrik 'Dremacon' Oskarsson
Gerald V.
Grandy Peace
Greg Krywusha
HeySteve
Ian Burba
Ian Stewart
J. Colin Madden
Jack Carabas
Jack Nils
James Bell
James MacGeorge
Jan Egil "Jedidiah Curzon" Bjune
Jared Lightle
Jason Carpenter
Jason D. Alexander
Jason G. Rak
Jason Jordaan
Jason Liswood
Jason MacGillivray
Jason Wicke
Jay Goodfader
JC Cohen
Jennifer Dery
Jeremy "Kelrizian" Kofoot
Jeremy Greene
Jeremy Zombied00d Patterson
Jim Murray
John B. McCarthy
John Esslinger
John Simutis
Jon Messenger
Jon W. Huss III
Jonathan Elder
Jorien Saelens & Nils Smeuninx
Joseph Carroll
Joseph DeSimone
Joseph Noll
Joseph Ross Goforth
Karl J. Smith
Ken "Professor" Thronberry
Kenny Loh Kern Siang
Kevin J. Lee
Kevin Lai
Kevin Scully
khatre
Kiera Kathleen O'Brien
Kristopher Ramsey
Kyle Harder
Kyle Olson
Lachlan Jones
LATERRADE Morgan
Leroy 'Falstep' Lee
Leslie A. Wilson
LordNightwinter
Louise and David Michael Sugar
Lucas Toddy
Luke Stowell
Luke Strotz
Mac Dara Mac Donnacha
Malijhurn Ahnkiicahn
Marcus Arena
Mark Cogan
Mark Hirschman
Mark Miller
Mark S
Martin Kratochvíl
Martin Severin
Marty Chodorek
Matthew Bull
Matthias Weeks
Michael & Jennifer Stacy
Michael J. Chernicoff
Michael Wood
Mike Maughmer
Mike Ott
Mitchell Young
Mock
Morten Jørgensen
Morten Strårup, son of Aage, son of Holger.
Nate Robinson
Nathan Mitchell
Nathaniel Clay
Neal Edwards
Neil Crampin
Nick Kerr
Nick Watkins
Nicki Holighaus
Noah Cantor
Ocean Druen
Patrick Deja
Paul Gerecht
Paul S. Boudreaux
Peter Hoogeveen
Petter Wäss
Preston Poland
Richard Mundy
Richard Nichols
Rick Neal
Robert Flinchum
Robert Hahn
Robert Loper
Ross A. Isaacs
Rune Wandall-Holm
Ryan Ashe
Ryan Houlette
Sam Stoute
Sandie Wilkinson
Sean Blakey
Shane Blake
Simon Threasher
Solaniis Rex
Stephan Pipenhagen
Stephen Joseph Ellis
Steve Jakab
Taliesin Hoyle
Ted Lee
Till H.
Tim Cooke aka Thoth
Timothy Gibbons Jr.
Timothy R. Vojta
Torah Cottrill
Trampas Johnson
Troy J Kidder
Troy Kiefer
Will Trufant
William Healy
William Lewis
William Scotland
Willie Davis
Zack Bowman

STRANGE LOVER OF ALL BOOKS
Alex Gagnon
Alexander W. Corrin
Alexis Plasse-Ferland
Alia Felton
Andre Braghini
Andreas Turriff
Andreas Walters
Andrew "Druid523" Seguel
Andrew J. Yeckel
Andrew Maizels
Andrew Taylor
Annabeth Leong
Anthony Nijssen
Ashley Veigel
Benton Wilson
Boyd Stephenson
Brad D. Kane
Brage Alexander Helleland
Branden Fonovic
Brent Cerrato
Brian and Amanda Cook
Brian Grant Kearns
Brian Griffith
Brian K. Eason
Brian Onstot
Brian W. Habenicht
Callum Prior
Cam Doell
Carlos Caro
Carlos Ovalle
Cary "Frang" Sandvig
Charles Manser
Charles St-Laurent
Chia-Hao Chang
Chris Volcheck
Christian Barrett
Christopher @chaupt Haupt
Christopher Anthony
Christopher Mangum
Colin Pyle
Colton McBryer
Connor Shanks-Lumgair
Dan Derby
Dan Quattrone
Dan Rogart
dan sinclair
Darin Kerr
DarkFlite
Darren Hubbard
Dave "Mefisto" Laithwaite
David Bigg
David Lucardie
David M. Johnson
David Stephenson
David Stoll
Dexter Macleod
Dr Adrian Melchiori
Ed "Buxley" Hall
Eli Todd
Eric "ogehn" Brenders
Eric Coates
Eric G
Eric Tillemans
Erik Olsen
Fabio Mano
Felix Shafir

Fredric Åkerman
Gareth Hodges
Geno
Geoffrey Ford
Gerald J Smith
Gerry Green
Gilles Tremblay
Gjorbjond
Glen R. Taylor
Glenn Berry
Greg Principato
Gregory Morris
Guy M. Caley
Guy Thompson
H. Ravlin
Håkon Gaut
Hugo Mardolcar
Ian McFarlin
j. diaz
Jack Gulick
James Crouch
James Dawsey
James W. Wood
Jarrod Holst
Jason Lund
Jeffrey A. Robbins
Jen & Andy Fritz
Jennifer Gubernath
John "Johenius" Richter
John Cmar
Jonathan Mickelson
Jordan Cunningham
Josh 'Tallknight' Higgins
Joshua Wolfe
Jyri Tasala
Kerion D'Arcangeli
Kevin Nicholas
Kevin Reynolds
Kier Duros
Krellic
Kyle Watt
Lari Kukkonen
Lars Holgaard
Lee Perry
Lukas Daniel Klausner
Lykos Vlk
Manuel Dennis III
Marcel Beaudoin
Marcus Schiess
Mark Engelbert
Mark Evan Jones
Mark Greco
Mark Magagna
Mark ten Brink
Martin A McDowell
Martin Breuss
Matei-Eugen Vasile
Mathias Gehl
Matt "Catapult" Wang
Matthew Sercely
Matthew Whiteacre
Matthias Uschold
Maurice Schekkerman
Michael Baker
Michael Finigan
Michael Mair
Mike Therrien
Mike Tidman
Morte Oakley
Nathan Barnes
Nathan Reed
Nathan Wiltse
NICHOLAS A BARNETT
Nicholas A. DeLateur
Nicholas Kruger
Patrick Plouffe
Paul A. H. Stone
Paul Chiaverotti
Paul Golds
Paul Heinze Jr
Paul Maloney
Paul Venner
Paul Weimer
Pete Apple
Peter Aronson
Peter Engebos
Peter Petrovich
Phil Binkowski
Rhel ná DecVandé
Rich Woods (Shadizar)
Richard Harrison
Richard Libera
Robert Djordjevich
Robert H. Mitchell Jr.
Robert N. Emerson
Robin Stirzaker
Russell Mettendorf
Scott "Agent" Coulson
Scott Thede
Shawn Campbell
Shawn TJ Miller
Simon English
Stefan Radermacher
Steve Dulson
T.R. Fullhart
Thierry De Gagne
Thomas Faßnacht
Tiana & Victor Serrano
Tim Callahan
Timothy A. Hochman
Travis Bryant
Trentin C Bergeron
Trevor W. Schadt
Tristan Smith
Troels Pedersen
Victor Kardeby
W. T. Piggott
Wallace Thomas Clark IV
William I Johnson
William Ke
William R. Edgington
Zach Murray

PITCH ROOM ACCESS

Adam Doochin
Akimotos
C. Joshua Villines
Christopher Rothwell
Jeremy Kear
Joshua "Kazzamo" Scott
Julias R. Shaw
Matthew "Random_Interrupt" Keevil
Nate Miller
Paul J. Banyai
Philippe Daigneault
Raymond Rivera
Rich Howard
Rick Blair
Sam Roberts

MCG SUPERFAN

42!
Adam Del Conte
aleksandar stossitch
Alex Draconis
Alexander Childress
Anselmi Stefano
Anthony Thomas Martin
Aric Wieder
Barry L Tebon
Ben B. Bainton
Brett Granger
Bryce Jones
Carly Robertson
Chris Wiemer
Christopher MZ Sauro
Christopher Roy & Eric Wells
Craig Johnston (flash_cxxi)
Daniel Berryhill
David Lai
David Rubenach
De Cesco Giuliano
Eric Lai
Francesco Di Maria
Gabriel Sharrow
Guilherme Nepomuceno
GuiOhm
Gustavo Torrents Schmidt
J.P. "Hex" Enbom
James A. Walls
James Current
Jean-Christophe Cubertafon
Jeremy Morton
Joe Mitchell
Joel "Bunny" Bodnar
John & Kimberly Poole
John A W Phillips
Juan Sebastian Caicedo
Julian A. Blasi
Justin Alexander
Justin Trapani
Lilian W. Thévenet
LORD AMON
Lorenz "Silversteel" Aschaber
Marc Massé
Markus Plate
Martin Legg
Matthew Arbo
Matthew D Shaver
Matthew Hayes
Matthew K. Gray
Max Cameron
MICHAEL ADAM BRACE
Michael Beard
Mike Rudziensky
Morgan Heinemann
Nathan Gillispie
Nick Goede
P.J. Smith
Perry Gabriele Jones
Phil Laco
pumchu
Raphael Reitzig
retnuH Kelly
Robert Winchester
Ronaldo Mascarenhas
Sam"urai" Demosthenes Ellis
Scott C Giesbrecht
Shawn Kehoe
Stina & Emil
Tim Barth
Tyson Neumann
Victor Lockwood
Wesley N. Goodwin

EARLY BIRD STRANGE SUPERFAN

Aaron J. Schrader
Alexander Wilkins
Andrew 'Whitenoise' Rogers
Andrew Hurley
Andrew Parran
Anestis Kozakis
Austin McDonald
Bradley Colver
Brandon Ording
Bruno Pereira
Charles Parker
Chris Collins
Chris Piazzo
Christian A. Nord
Christian Thériault
Christopher Paul Smith
Christopher Tavares
Conan Brasher
Cory Rewcastle
Daniel Petersen
Danny Jensen
Dawid Wojcieszynski
Emiliano Marchetti
Eric Lopez
Eric M. Anderson
Ethan Zimmerman
George N.
Grant kinsley
Greg Schoenberg
Günther Kronenberg
Helder Lavigne
James D Pacheco
James ME Patterson
Jeff Scifert
Jered Heeschen
Jesse Goble
Jon Harrison
Kaminiwa
Karsten Alexander Kopplin
Katherine Gohring
Keith Preston
Kyle "Fiddy" Pinches
Leander Van Reeth
Lee DeBoer
M. Sean Molley
Magus
Mario Vandaele
Mark Solino
Mark W. H. Lambe
Martin Blake
Mathew Schelsky
Matt Leitzen
Mike Bell
Mike Swiernik
Neal Dalton
Neal Tanner
Nicholas W. Peddicord
Norm Walsh
Olga Kurchenko-Luciano Fernandez
Oliver Kasteleiner
Olna Jenn Smith
Patty Stadnicki
R Zemlicka
Reverend Jones
Robert Biskin
Ryan Blackstock
Ryan M Ford
Scott Kehl
Scott McKinley
Sean Anderson
Sean Gore
Sean K King
Shannon Maclean
Shawn P
Stéphan Coquelet
Steven William Cosky Jr.
Tara Imbery
Victoria Klemm
William James Cuffe
Y. K. Lee
Zach Shepherd

STRANGE SUPERFAN

Adam Chunn
Adrian Scully
Adric Clifton
Andrew Shebanow
Brian M Bentley
Bryan Hilburn
Chad Drummond
Charles Myers
Chris de Putron
Dean Thomas
Dustin D Rippetoe
Eric Jensen
Frédéri Volk Kommissar Friedrich POCHARD
Henry R Moore III
J.R. & Leann Knight
Jared Wadsworth
Jeremy "opsirus" Roberts
John " Voidwalker" Horton
John D. Prins
John Dwyer
Jonathan Borzilleri
Jorge A. Torres
Joshua Archer
Julie Bidault des Chaumes
Keavin Hill II
Keith E. Hartman
Kessa
Kevin Schantz
Marc Plourde
Matthew Bates
Matthew Wasiak
Mike Bryant
Paul A. Nemeth
Paul Anderson
Paul Ryan Kuykendall
PK
Richard Rutten
Robert Fensterman
Scott E. Robinson
Seana McGuinness
Terrence van Ettinger
The Fat Man of Ruk
Thomas Bockert
Tim Rudolph
Timothy J. Watkins
Travis Carpenter
Urdlen

STRANGE CONTRIBUTOR

ALEXIS G DÍAZ, Trotamundos Virtual
Antonio Jesús Rodríguez Fuentes
Bret Holien
Brett Bozeman
Kevin Allen
Lawrence Sica
W. Dove and Sarah Boyett

STRANGE CONVENTION GAMER

Nitza Ramirez-Blackstock
Shale Blackstock

STRANGE ONLINE GAMER

Anand Krishna
Michael Tillman Curtis Peters

ULTIMATE SUPERFAN

Andrew MacLennan
Andy Walker
Belinda Kelly
Brad Warren
Brian Allred
Chad Patterson
Chris Iverach-Brereton
Christian Sciple
Christopher Brind
Darcy "Danger" Ross
Darren Hoglund
David Bresson
Dr. Donald A. Turner
Emmanuel BODIN
Fenric Cayne
Gary Riley
George Panopoulos
James McKendrew
James Z. Candalino
Jason "Hierax" Verbitsky
Jason Sterrett
Joseph W. Edge
Kean P Stuart
Kevin Lawrence
KRD
Lars Lauridsen
Laurent Corgnet
Lee Sims
Lee Wendel
Luca Geretti
Martin L Goodson
Matthew Davison
Matthew Dimalanta
Michael Dake
Nicholas J Thompson
Nicolas Barbezat
Paul Nasrat
Peter Korcz
Philip Minchin & Hang Tran
Ray M.
Robert Seitz
Thorbjørn Snorre Kaiser
Travis Bliss
Vic Smith
Walt Larson
William Dovan
Yann Abaziou

HAND-TOOLED TOME ULTIMATE SUPERFAN

Andrew Brereton
Andrew Cotgreave
Brian J. Hickey
Federico Franceschi
James a.k.a. uber

A STRANGE DINNER

Pal'Drem Shon'Ai

GLOSSARY

Adventure: A single portion of a campaign with a beginning and an end.

All Song, the: A biological data network that "sings" through every cell of every engineered tissue in Ruk. The All Song stores information and allows communication over vast distances. Some believe it has a kind of consciousness of its own.

Artifact: Major device with powers beyond the norm that typically can be used more than once to produce the same result.

Campaign: A series of sessions strung together with an overarching story (or linked stories) with the same characters.

Chaosphere: See Strange, the.

Character: Anything that can take actions in the game. Includes PCs and human NPCs, as well as creatures, aliens, mutants, automatons, and animate plants.

Character Descriptor: Defines your character.

Character Focus: What your character does best.

Character Type: The core of your character, similar to a class. The three types are vector, paradox, and spinner.

Creature: Anything that can take actions in the game.

Cypher: A self-contained snippet of "god code" taken from the Strange that creates a one-time effect within a limited area, usually an effect that can break a recursion's rules or a prime world's natural laws. A cypher reliably translates between recursions and even up to Earth.

Cypher System: The game system of The Strange.

Damage Track: A system for tracking a PC's health. It has four states: hale, impaired, debilitated, and dead.

Dark Energy: Roughly 70% of the universe is made of dark energy. It permeates the cosmos and is accelerating the expansion of the universe at an ever-increasing rate. It's what scientists who are not quickened or who otherwise remain oblivious to the truth call the Strange.

Difficulty: How easy or hard any given task is, as determined by the GM (on a scale of 1 to 10).

Edge: A stat that reduces the cost of using points from your Pool.

Effort: A stat that can be applied to lower the difficulty of a task.

Estate, the: An organization on Earth that is cognizant of the Strange and its recursions, with ties to Ardeyn.

Experience Points (XP): Awarded during gameplay for discoveries and GM intrusions. Can be used for a variety of things, including purchasing character benefits.

Game Master (GM): The player who doesn't run a character, but instead guides the flow of the story (and runs all the NPCs).

GM Intrusion: A game mechanic that allows the GM to slightly alter events in the game for the betterment of the story.

Intellect: This stat determines how smart, knowledgeable, and likable your character is.

Maker, the: A godlike entity who created Ardeyn as a prison for the evil god Lotan. Carter Morrison, creator of the Ardeyn video game, was entangled for a time with the Maker, though both Maker and Carter "Strange" are apparently dead.

Might: A stat that defines how strong and durable your character is.

Moves: An ability that is specific to vectors.

Nonplayer Character (NPC): A character run by the GM. Think of NPCs as the minor characters in the story, or the villains or opponents.

Paradox: A character type in The Strange that breaks the rules of reality, whether using science, the power of the mind, spells, or something else entirely.

Party: A group of player characters (and perhaps some NPC allies).

Planetovore: Voracious entity of the Strange that seeks out prime worlds in the universe of normal matter to convert to its own needs (displacing or killing any life on those worlds in the process).

Player: The players who run characters in the game.

Player Character (PC): A character run by a player rather than the GM. Think of them as the main characters in the story.

Qephilim: A mortal race in Ardeyn descended from angelic beings who originally served one of the seven Incarnations of the Maker, but who are now free agents.

Quickened: A unique connection to the Strange that gives PCs a portion of their type abilities.

Quiet Cabal, the: An organization on Earth whose members are cognizant of the Strange and its recursions, with ties to Ruk.

Recovery Roll: A d6 roll that allows you to regain points in one or more of your Pools.

Recursion: A self-contained universe within the Strange, no matter how large or small, that has its own unique set of laws that govern the reality within it.

Recursion Miner: A derogatory term that some groups (including the Estate) apply to recursors, especially recursors who translate cyphers up to Earth.

Recursor: Someone who leaves Earth to explore recursions and the Strange.

Revision: An ability that is specific to paradoxes.

Seeding a Recursion: The process by which a brand new recursion is created in the Strange. Methods vary, but PCs who attempt this usually work together as a group.

Session: A single play experience, usually lasting a few hours.

Shoals of Earth: The area of the Strange that is near Earth, and which has been identified as having unique properties not found elsewhere.

Spark, the: The touch of consciousness and self-awareness that can (but does not always) occur in beings native to a recursion. The spark tends to spread virally once it occurs.

Speed: A stat that describes how fast and physically coordinated your character is.

Spinner: A character type in The Strange that spins tales, spins lies, or spins a version of the truth that makes others see things in a whole new way.

Stat Pool: The most basic measurement of your Might, Intellect, and Speed stats.

Stats: The defining characteristics of a player character, divided into Might, Intellect, and Speed.

Strange, the: An alien data network composed of what Earth scientists have dubbed "dark energy" that lies just outside what we know. Also known as the Chaosphere.

Stranger: A creature from the Strange (or, perhaps more often, from a recursion) that comes to Earth.

Target Number: The number you're attempting to get on a roll, based on the difficulty of the task. The target number is always three times the task's difficulty.

Tier: A measurement of a character's power, toughness, and ability.

Translation: The process of moving between Earth and a recursion, or between recursions. Recursors usually say that they translate "up" to Earth if coming from a recursion or the Strange, or translate "down" to a recursion if coming from Earth.

True Code, the: The original genetic sequence of the Ruk native race, now lost. Ruk scientists constantly look for fragments of the True Code.

Twist: An ability that is specific to spinners.

Vector: A character type in The Strange that uses persistent force to accomplish goals and overcome problems.

INDEX

INDEX

CHARACTER CREATION WALKTHROUGH

Follow these steps to create your character for The Strange.

GET PREPARED

If you're using the character sheets in the back of this book, make a two-sided photocopy of the main character sheet (pages 414 and 415) to create your character in her homeworld (which is most likely Earth).

Along the top of the sheet, you'll see a place to write your character's name, descriptor, type, focus, and starting world or recursion. Beneath that, you'll see a place for all of your character's stats, skills, abilities, and equipment. On the back of the sheet, you'll see a place for your character's background, portrait, notes, and advancement tracking.

CHOOSE YOUR CHARACTER DESCRIPTOR, TYPE, AND FOCUS

Starting at the top of the sheet, record your character's name, descriptor, type, and focus to complete the sentence.

For this example, let's say I am an Appealing vector who Conducts Weird Science on Earth.

FILL IN YOUR STAT POOLS, AS DETERMINED BY YOUR TYPE

First, take a detailed look at your type, because that's where you'll get your Pool starting values. Fill in those values under Might, Speed, and Intellect Pool.

For my vector, my starting values are Might 10, Speed 10, and Intellect 8, plus 6 additional points to spread between the Pools. I'm going to add 3 points to Might, 1 to Speed, and 2 to Intellect, for totals of: Might 13, Speed 11, and Intellect 10.

Your descriptor might also add to your Pools. Feel free to check your descriptor now to see if it gives you additional points, and, if so, add them to the appropriate starting Pool.

My descriptor of Appealing gives me +2 to my Intellect Pool. This increases my starting stat Pool numbers to Might 13, Speed 11, and Intellect 12.

FILL IN YOUR EDGE STATS, AS DETERMINED BY YOUR TYPE

My vector has a Might Edge of 1, a Speed Edge of 1, and an Intellect Edge of 0.

WRITE IN ADDITIONAL STATS AND ABILITIES, AS DETERMINED BY YOUR TYPE

Note any Effort, skills, and cypher limits, as well as any special abilities provided by your type. These include moves, revisions, and twists. Be sure to write down the cost (if any) of any special abilities and to note whether you are trained (T) or specialized (S) in a skill.

My vector has an Effort of 1 and a cypher limit of 2.

Under Skills, I'll note that I'm trained in Speed defense when not wearing armor. I am also trained in two skills of my choice. I'll choose jumping and running. All of these will be listed as skills under Speed, and I'll mark the T to show that I'm trained (not specialized) in them.

Under Special Abilities, I'll note that I am Practiced With All Weapons. All of the PCs can also translate as a special ability. As a vector, I am most effective at easing a translation.

As a vector, I can also choose two moves, so I'll take Bash and Fleet of Foot.

WRITE IN ADDITIONAL STATS AND ABILITIES, AS DETERMINED BY YOUR DESCRIPTOR & FOCUS

If you haven't already added any additional points from your descriptor and focus to your starting Pools, do so now. Add any additional skills or equipment from your descriptor and focus as well.

Appealing means that I am trained in pleasant social interactions and resisting persuasion or seduction; I'll list these as trained skills under Intellect.

I'll also add that my focus, Conducts Weird Science, means that I am trained in one area of scientific knowledge of my choice. I'll add chemistry to my skills list under Intellect.

Most foci also give you a special ability. Feel free to look at your focus now and add any special abilities.

My focus, Conducts Weird Science, gives me a special ability called Lab Analysis.

CHOOSE YOUR POSSESSIONS, AS DETERMINED BY YOUR TYPE

The possessions that you start the game with are dictated by your type and include weapons, armor, packs, and other gear. If you wear armor, or if you have a special ability that grants you Armor, note the total amount of Armor in the space provided.

Check to see if your descriptor gives you additional possessions, such as equipment or extra money.

My focus allows me to start the game with street clothes, a science field kit, light tools, a pen knife, a smartphone, and $2,000.

LIST YOUR ATTACKS

Attacks are based on your chosen weapons and your moves, revisions, or twists.

My focus doesn't include a weapon, so I will ask my GM if I can spend some of my money to purchase a medium handgun for $700.00. Then I can list that weapon as doing 4 points of damage.

ADD YOUR STARTING CYPHERS

Your GM will provide you with starting cyphers, if any.

INCLUDE YOUR BACKGROUND

The aspects of your character can help define your background. Your type gives you some general information about your experience in the world and society, your descriptor gives you an initial link to the first adventure, and your focus gives you a connection to the other PCs. You can list these on the back of your character sheet.

For my link to the first adventure (descriptor), I'll say that I got involved by pure happenstance. For my connection to another PC (focus), I'll talk to one of the other players, and we'll work it out that he asked me to design a gun that could shoot through walls.

DURING PLAY, NOTE DAMAGE TRACK, RECOVERY ROLLS, AND XP

During gameplay, keep track of how many recovery rolls you've used each day and where you are on the damage track. (If you're hale or dead, you won't need to mark anything; otherwise, it's important to make a note of your status on the damage track.) The 1D6+ box is for recording the amount that you add to your recovery rolls; this number is usually your current tier, but it can be altered by various modifiers.

Additionally, note what tier you are and how many experience points you currently have.

Last, there is space on the back to mark off your advancement progress, which allows you to track how you spend XP to advance to the next tier.

KEEP GOOD NOTES

The notes section is designated for events and experiences that happen to your character once the game begins.

ADDING A NEW RECURSION

When your character is ready to go to a new recursion, print out the recursion sheet (page 416). You'll see that if you fold it along the FOLD HERE line and wrap it horizontally over the main character sheet, it fits perfectly over the parts of the character sheet that could change when you go to a new recursion.

When you switch recursions, your clothing, belongings, and focus are likely to change (unless you're using a draggable focus). Thus, you'll want to add any new stats and equipment that you gain from your focus. Your cyphers will carry over to the new recursion, but you'll want to make a note about their new appearance after you translate. You can also add a new portrait to the back side, if your character's appearance changes (some foci, such as Embraces Qephilim Ancestry, provide you with a new appearance, or you can work out a new look with your GM).

When I translate to Ardeyn, I choose a new focus. Thus, I change from an Appealing vector who Conducts Weird Science to an Appealing vector who Embraces Qephilim Ancestry. Now I look like a qephilim, and I trade my Earth focus equipment, abilities, and skills for ones that work with my new focus in Ardeyn.

THE STRANGE
TIER
EFFORT
XP
NAME
IS A
DESCRIPTOR
TYPE
WHO
RECURSION SHEET HERE
FOCUS
ON
RECURSION
• MIGHT •
• SPEED •
• INTELLECT •
POOL
CURRENT
EDGE
• SKILLS •
T
S
• ATTACKS •
MOD
DAM
• SPECIAL ABILITIES •
• EQUIPMENT •
ARMOR
MONEY
• CYPHERS •
LIMIT
• RECOVERY ROLLS •
1 ACTION
10 MINS
1D6+
1 HOUR
10 HOURS
• DAMAGE TRACK •
IMPAIRED
+1 EFFORT PER LEVEL
IGNORE MINOR & MAJOR EFFECT RESULTS ON ROLLS
COMBAT ROLL OF 17-20 ONLY DEALS +1 DAMAGE
DEBILITATED
CAN ONLY MOVE AN IMMEDIATE DISTANCE
IF SPEED POOL IS ZERO YOU CANNOT MOVE.

THE STRANGE

CONSTRUCTING YOUR CHARACTER

USE THE PRIMARY SHEET TO DESCRIBE YOUR CHARACTER ON YOUR STARTING RECURSION

USE A FOLDED RECURSION SHEET FOR EACH ADDITIONAL RECURSION IN YOUR GAME

THE INFORMATION ON A RECURSION SHEET MAY CHANGE FROM ONE RECURSION TO ANOTHER

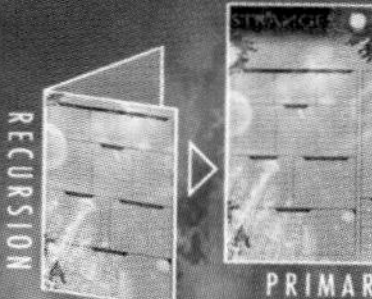

•ADVANCEMENT•

(You must have four of these to advance in Tier. Cost = 4XP each.)

☐ INCREASE CAPABILITIES	☐ MOVE TOWARDS PERFECTION	☐ EXTRA EFFORT	☐ SKILL TRAINING	☐ OTHER
+4 points into stat Pools	+1 point to the Edge of your choice	+1 point into Effort	Train in a skill or Specialize in a pre-existing skill	Refer to The Strange corebook

↓ RECURSION SHEET HERE ↓

•BACKGROUND•

•PORTRAIT•

•NOTES•

↓ RECURSION SHEET HERE ↓

↓ RECURSION SHEET HERE ↓

FOCUS
ON
RECURSION
PORTRAIT
NOTES
MIGHT
SPEED
INTELLECT
POOL
CURRENT
EDGE
FOLD HERE
SKILLS
T
S
ATTACKS
MOD
DAM
SPECIAL ABILITIES
EQUIPMENT
ARMOR
MONEY

SHOALS OF EARTH

EARTH AND A SELECTION OF ITS RECURSIONS

DISTANCES ARE RELATIVE